Why Do You Need this New Edition?

If you're wondering why you should buy this new edition of *American Government*, here are 11 good reasons!

1. New **learning objectives** appear at the start of each chapter in the "What Should I Know About . . ." boxes to prime you for the material you are about to read and to help you navigate the chapters more efficiently. These objectives also appear in the body of the chapters and inform the structure of the "What Should I Have Learned?" summary sections and accompanying online exercises in MyPoliSciLab.

2. New **"Test Yourself" quizzes** at the end of each chapter provide you with avenues to check your understanding and reinforce each chapter's learning objectives. Each quiz consists of ten questions: one multiple choice question (with five answer choices) for each objective, with the remaining short answer and essay questions focused on critical thinking.

3. All **photo, figure, and table titles appear as questions,** to encourage you to think critically about every visual element.

4. Revised **Analyzing Visuals features** include targeted critical thinking questions that encourage you to progressively engage in deeper understanding and analysis. These features take you beyond answering solely the "what" of the visual and help you to better focus on the "why."

5. Streamlined **Join the Debate boxes** prompt you to develop your own well-thought-out arguments "for" and "against" each position. New topics in this edition include debates over the federal government's involvement in healthcare, student loans, the election of Supreme Court justices, former members of Congress as lobbyists, and partisan bias in the news media.

6. Expanded **Thinking Globally** features include a more substantial overview of key comparative topics, including visuals where relevant, followed by critical thinking questions that ask you to examine some of the most commonly held assumptions about how American government does or should function.

7. New news article excerpts in all of the **Politics Now** boxes help guide you through an in-depth examination of contemporary issues.

8. Complete coverage of **the outcome of the 2010 congressional elections** and the makeup of the 112th Congress is included, as well as a discussion of major recent shifts in congressional rules and roles in budgeting, lawmaking, and oversight.

9. The **political behavior chapters have been extensively revised and edited** to reflect the most current and pertinent issues and to help you focus on the most important themes and topics.

10. The **policy chapters have been dramatically revised to take a case study approach** and to reflect the interactions among branches in domestic, economic, and foreign policy.

11. Annotations to *Federalist Papers Nos. 10, 51,* and *78* in the Appendix guide you through an analysis of these seminal documents to enhance your understanding of their significance.

PEARSON

TIMELINE: Selected Events in American Government and Politics

1773 **The Boston Tea Party—** Public protest in Boston Harbor is held in reaction to what the colonists believe to be oppressive taxes on tea and other goods.

1801 **John Marshall Becomes Chief Justice—** The Marshall Court increases the Supreme Court's role, formalizes the opinion-writing process, and expands the power of the Court over the states.

1607 **Jamestown Colony—**The first English settlement in the new world is established in present-day Virginia.

1789 **First Congress Meets—** One of the most important tasks of the first Congress is to pass a Bill of Rights to appease Anti-Federalists.

1823 **Monroe Doctrine—**This document attempts to limit European colonization of the Western Hemisphere.

1620 **Massachusetts Bay Colony—**The English Pilgrims sail to the new world on the Mayflower and establish a settlement in Plymouth.

1787 **Constitution Written—**The Framers craft the first federal system, where national and state governments share power and both are ultimately responsible to the people.

1803 *Marbury* v. *Madison—*The Supreme Court asserts that judicial review can be implied from the Constitution's supremacy clause.

1776 **The Declaration of Independence—** Twelve of thirteen colonies vote for independence.

1832 **First Presidential Nomination Convention—** The Democratic Party holds its first presidential nomination convention, re-nominating President Andrew Jackson.

1796 **First Presidential Campaign—**After President George Washington decides to end his tenure in office, the nation experiences a spirited campaign between Federalist John Adams and Democratic-Republican Thomas Jefferson.

1860 The Civil War—President Abraham Lincoln takes a number of legally questionable actions during the Civil War. He claims these actions are justified by the inherent powers of the presidency.

1893 Joseph Pulitzer Launches *New York World*—Known for its sensationalism and progressive crusades, Pulitzer's approach is nicknamed "yellow journalism."

1872 Tammany Hall Gains Power—Tammany Hall, one of the best known party machines, enforces voters' party loyalty by providing jobs and services in exchange for votes.

1916 National Woman's Party Founded—The organization's goal is to achieve woman suffrage, a goal it meets with the ratification of the Nineteenth Amendment in 1920.

1870 Creation of the Department of Justice—Although there was an attorney general, the Department of Justice did not attain Cabinet status until after the Civil War.

1909 NAACP Created—The nation's preeminent African American civil rights group is created out of the earlier Niagara Movement.

1887 Dawes Act—This Act divides Indian reservation land and gives it to individuals.

1929 League of United Latin American Citizens Formed—Several service organizations unite, creating LULAC, the largest Hispanic service organization in the country.

1890 Sherman Anti-Trust Act—This Act allows government to deal with the growing number of monopolies forming in American business.

ELECTORAL COLLEGE VOTES IN THE 2008 ELECTION

A political map showing the number of electoral votes per state on a standard map

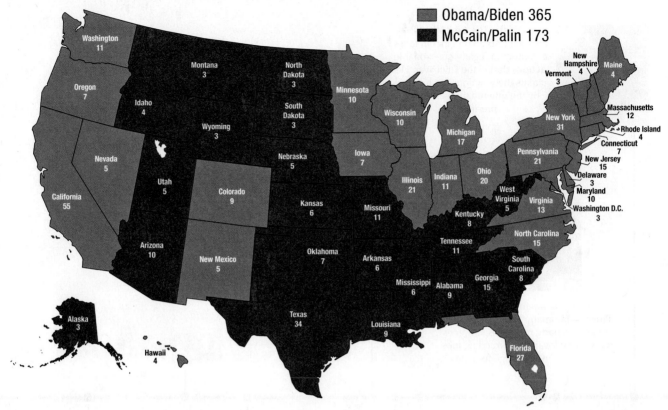

A political map with states drawn in proportion to the number of electoral votes

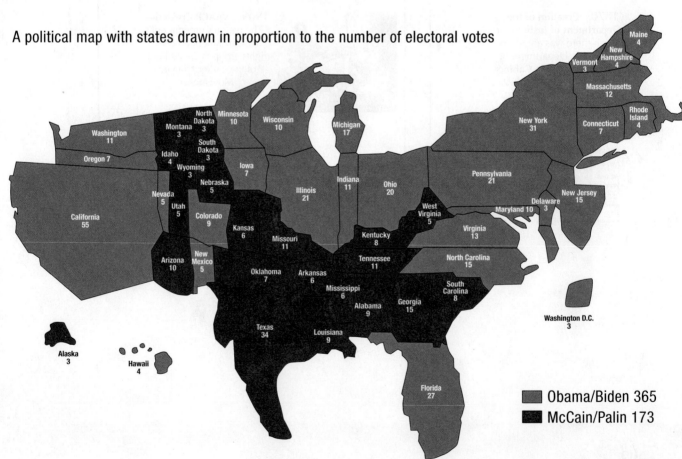

Essentials of
American
Government
ROOTS AND REFORM

2011 Edition

Karen O'Connor

Jonathan N. Helfat
Distinguished Professor of Political Science
American University

Larry J. Sabato

University Professor
and Robert Kent Gooch Professor of Politics
University of Virginia

Alixandra B. Yanus

Assistant Professor of Political Science
High Point University

Longman
Boston   Columbus   Indianapolis   New York   San Francisco   Upper Saddle River
Amsterdam   Cape Town   Dubai   London   Madrid   Milan   Munich   Paris   Montreal   Toronto
Delhi   Mexico City   São Paulo   Sydney   Hong Kong   Seoul   Singapore   Taipei   Tokyo

Executive Editor: Reid Hester
Editorial Assistant: Elizabeth Alimena
Director of Development: Meg Botteon
Development Editor: Lisa Sussman
Associate Development Editor: Donna Garnier
Marketing Manager: Lindsey Prudhomme
Production Manager: Eric Jorgensen
Project Coordination, Text Design, and Electronic Page Makeup:
    Electronic Publishing Services Inc., NYC

Senior Cover Design Manager/Cover Designer: Nancy Danahy
Cover Image: © Corbis/SuperStock
Photo Researcher: Julie Tesser
Senior Manufacturing Buyer: Roy L. Pickering, Jr.
Printer and Binder: RR Donnelley & Sons Company
Cover Printer: Lehigh–Phoenix Color Corp.

For permission to use copyrighted material, grateful acknowledgment is made to the copyright holders acknowledged throughout the book, which are hereby made part of this copyright page.

Chapter opening image credits: p. 2, MPI/Getty Images; p. 3, AP/Wide World Photos; p. 24, Joseph Sohm/Visions of America/Corbis; p. 25, Bob Daemmrich/PhotoEdit, Inc.; p. 80, Lewis W Hine/Getty Images; p. 81, Matt Nager/Bloomberg via Getty Images/Getty Images; p. 104, The Advertising Archives; p. 105, Kevin Clark/The Washington Post via Pictopia.com; p. 134, Flip Schulke/Corbis; p. 135, Chip Somodevilla/Getty Images; p. 166, AP/Wide World Photos; p. 167, AP/Wide World Photos; p. 198, George Eastman House/Getty Images; p. 199, Dennis Brack; p. 222, Popperfoto/Getty Images; p. 223, Official White House Photo by Pete Souza; p. 244, Photograph by Abdon Daoud Ackad, Collection of the Supreme Court of the United States; p. 245, Larry Downing/Reuters/Landov; p. 276, W. Eugene Smith/Time Life Pictures/Getty Images; p. 277, Jeff Haynes/Reuters/Landov; p. 308, MPI/Getty Images; p. 309, AP/Wide World Photos; p. 340, Bettmann/Corbis; p. 341, AP/Wide World Photos; p. 374, Bettmann/ Corbis; p. 375, AP/Wide World Photos; p. 404, Paul Schutzer/Time Life Pictures/Getty Images; p. 405, AP/Wide World Photos

Library of Congress Cataloging-in-Publication Data
O'Connor, Karen, 1952-
    Essentials of American government : roots and reform / Karen O'Connor, Larry J. Sabato, Alixandra B. Yanus.—2011 ed.
        p. cm.
    Includes bibliographical references and index.
    ISBN 978-0-205-82576-9
    1. United States—Politics and government.   I. Sabato, Larry.   II. Yanus, Alixandra B.   III. Title.

JK276.O36 2011
320.473—dc22

                                                                            2010045729

1 2 3 4 5 6 7 8 9 10—DOW— 13 12 11 10

Longman
is an imprint of

www.pearsonhighered.com

ISBN-13: 978-0-205-82576-9
ISBN-10: 0-205-82576-1

To Meghan,
who grew up with this book

Karen O'Connor

To my Government 101 students
over the years, who all know that
"politics is a good thing"

Larry J. Sabato

To my family:
You have never loved government,
but have always loved me.

Alixandra B. Yanus

Brief Contents

PART 1   Foundations of Government

CHAPTER 1   The Political Landscape   2

Detailed Contents

How to Clean a Gun and Keep Your Head...

PART 2 Institutions of Government

CHAPTER 6   Congress   166

CHAPTER 7   The Presidency   198

CHAPTER 8   The Executive Branch and the Federal Bureaucracy   222

CHAPTER 9   The Judiciary   244

PART 3   Political Behavior

CHAPTER 10   Public Opinion and The News Media   276

CHAPTER 12   Campaigns, Elections, and Voting   340

PART 4   Public Policy

CHAPTER 13   Social and Economic Policy   374

Appendices

ANALYZING VISUALS

Analyzing Visuals

Join the Debate

The Living Constitution

The Living Constitution

Politics Now

Thinking Globally

Timeline

We believe that one cannot fully understand the actions, issues, and policy decisions facing the U.S. government, its constituent states, or "the people" unless we examine their evolution over time. Consequently, the title of this book is *American Government: Roots and Reform*. In its pages, we try to examine how the United States is governed today by looking not just at present structures and behavior but also at the *Framers' intentions and how they have been implemented and adapted over the years*. For example, we believe that it is critical to an understanding of the role of political parties in the United States to understand the Framers' fears of factionalism, how parties evolved, and when and why party realignments occurred.

To understand all levels of American government, students must appreciate its constitutional underpinnings. Our text includes a full, *annotated* Constitution of the United States after chapter 2 and a boxed feature, The Living Constitution, in each chapter. These aids are to help to ensure that students understand and appreciate the role of the Constitution in American government and their everyday lives.

In addition to the constitutional and historical origins of American government, we explore issues that the Framers could never have envisioned, and how the basic institutions of government have changed in responding to these new demands. For instance, no one more than two centuries ago could have foreseen election campaigns in an age when nearly all American homes contain television sets, and the Internet allows instant access to information from across the nation and around the globe. Moreover, citizen demands and expectations routinely force government reforms, making an understanding of the dynamics of change essential for introductory students.

Our overriding concern is that students understand their government as it exists today, so that they may become better citizens and make better choices. Thus, this new edition, like the others before it, is carefully updated to include new events and offer opportunities for class discussion of key events that often divide the electorate. We believe that by providing students with information about government, and by explaining why it is important and why their participation counts, students will come to see that politics can be, and most often is, a good thing.

What's New to This Edition?

This edition has been substantially revised throughout to capture the historic events of the last two years and reflect the latest scholarship. In addition to updating the data in all tables and figures, where relevant and available, below are just some of the specifics on what's new to each chapter.

- **Chapter 1 (The Political Landscape)** revisions give greater consideration to who "We the People" are and to how this notion has shaped American government, providing a stronger framework and context for the rest of the book. This chapter opens with a new vignette on the first colonists, includes a new Living Constitution box on the Preamble, a new Timeline dealing with colonial settlement of the New World, a new Thinking Globally box addressing democracies around the world, and a new Politics Now box that asks, "What Happens to the American Dream in a Recession?"
- **Chapter 2 (The Constitution)** includes a new Analyzing Visuals on the Declaration of Independence, a new Thinking Globally box dealing with constitutions around the world, and a new Politics Now focusing on how state and local governments are reinterpreting the U.S. Constitution.

- **Chapter 3 (Federalism)** begins with a new opening vignette dealing with Arizona's controversial immigration law, a new Analyzing Visuals on the American Recovery and Reinvestment Act, a new Toward Reform section that deals with balancing national and state powers, and a new Politics Now on the role of the federal government during the BP oil spill.

- **Chapter 4 (Civil Liberties)** includes key civil liberties cases from the U.S. Supreme Court's 2009–2010 term, a new Analyzing Visuals on trying suspected terrorists, and a new Politics Now box on the Supreme Court's ruling that suspects must assert a right to silence.

- **Chapter 5 (Civil Rights)** features a new Join the Debate on the use of American Indian mascots. The chapter also includes a new Politics Now box on the Arizona immigration law.

- **Chapter 6 (Congress)** includes complete coverage of the outcome of the 2010 congressional elections and the makeup of the 112th Congress, as well as a discussion of major recent shifts in congressional rules and roles in budgeting, lawmaking, and oversight. The chapter opens with a new vignette on the 2010 Patient Protection and Affordable Care Act. It also includes a new Timeline on the congressional budget process, a new Join the Debate feature that considers the role of partisanship in democracy, and a new Politics Now box on congressional caucuses.

- **Chapter 7 (The Presidency)** considers the impact of President Barack Obama's first two years in office. The chapter also features a new Thinking Globally box on presidential term limits, a new Timeline on the development of presidential power, and a new Politics Now box focusing on the Obama administration.

- **Chapter 8 (The Executive Branch and the Federal Bureaucracy)** opens with a new vignette on the failed airline bomb plot by a Nigerian national on Christmas Day in 2009. It also includes a new Thinking Globally box on bureaucracy around the world. In addition, the chapter features a new Timeline on the growth of the Cabinet, a new Join the Debate that asks if the federal bureaucracy should help fund higher education, and a new Politics Now on the role of regulation.

- **Chapter 9 (The Judiciary)** features updates on the Supreme Court's 2009–2010 term in addition to information on the nominations and confirmations of Justices Sonia Sotomayor and Elena Kagan. Also included are a new Thinking Globally box on advisory opinions, a new Join the Debate on electing judges, and a new Politics Now box focusing on Kagan's nomination.

- **Chapter 10 (Public Opinion and the News Media)** revisions focus on making students good consumers of polling information and enabling students to understand how public opinion influences politics. In addition, the chapter features extensive coverage of current news media trends including the impact of social networking sites, the increased use of experts, and citizen journalists. Also included are a new Analyzing Visuals on public opinion on the Iraq War, and a new Politics Now on robo-polling.

- **Chapter 11 (Political Parties and Interest Groups)** has been significantly streamlined. It begins with a new vignette comparing the Boston Tea Party of 1773 with the contemporary tea party movement. The chapter also features a new Politics Now on corporate lobbying.

- **Chapter 12 (Campaigns, Elections, and Voting)** has been heavily updated to account for the 2010 congressional elections. The chapter also features revised and updated information on assembling a campaign staff and raising money in campaigns, a new Analyzing Visuals on the Daisy Ad, a new Politics Now box on campaign volunteers, a new Timeline on recent developments in voting technology, and a new Living Constitution on the Electoral College.

■ **Chapter 13 (Social and Economic Policy)** has been dramatically revised to take a case study approach. In addition to a new opening vignette on the factors that led to the recent economic crisis and recession, the chapter includes case studies on health, income security, and fiscal policies. The chapter also features a new Living Constitution on policy making, a new Timeline on federal involvement in health care, a new Analyzing Visuals on the Supplemental Nutritional Assistance Program, a new Join the Debate on the role of economic stimulus funds, and a new Politics Now on the Federal Reserve.

■ **Chapter 14 (Foreign and Defense Policy)** features extensive updates and revisions. The chapter opens with a new vignette on President Barack Obama's approach to foreign policy and includes case studies on contemporary challenges in foreign and defense policy, such as trade, immigration and border security, terrorism, and nuclear weapons. A new Toward Reform section deals with the rethinking of American power. In addition, the chapter features a new Timeline on the development of U.S. foreign policy, a new Thinking Globally box on the European Union, a new Living Constitution on the powers of Congress in foreign policy, a new Join the Debate on opening American borders, and a new Politics Now on the firing of General Stanley McChrystal.

Historical Perspective

Every chapter uses history to serve three purposes: first, to show how institutions and processes have evolved to their present states; second, to provide some of the color that makes information memorable; and, third, to provide students with a more thorough appreciation of the fact that that our government was born amid burning issues of representation and power, issues that continue to smolder today. A richer historical texture helps to explain the present.

Roots of and **Toward Reform** sections highlight the text's emphasis on the importance of the history of American government, as well as the dynamic cycle of reassessment and reform that allows the United States to continue to evolve. Every chapter begins with a "Roots of" section that gives a historical overview of the topic at hand, and ends with a "Toward Reform" section devoted to a particularly contentious aspect of the topic being discussed.

ROOTS OF the Federal System

★ 3.1 ... Trace the roots of the federal system and the Constitution's allocation of governmental powers.

As discussed in **chapter 2**, the United States was the first country to adopt a **federal system** of government (although the word "federal" never appears in the U.S. Constitution). This system of government, where the national government and state governments share power and derive all authority from the people, was designed to remedy many of the problems experienced under the Articles of Confederation.

TOWARD REFORM: Attempts to Balance National and State Power

★ 3.6 ... Assess the challenges in balancing national and state powers and the consequences for policy making.

As we have seen throughout this chapter, attempting to find equilibrium between the powers and responsibilities of national and state governments is one of the greatest difficulties of a federal system. The roles and relative strengths of the national and

Illustrated Timelines in every chapter provide students with a clear and visual understanding of the development of key topics in American government. All timelines include images that cue students to the appropriate subject matter discussion in the text.

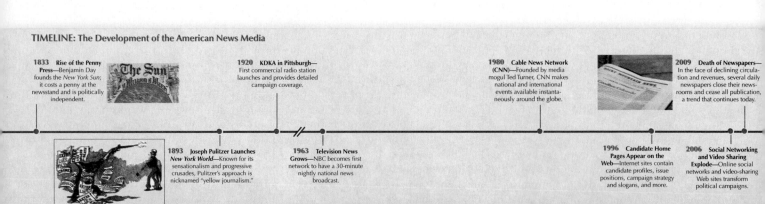

TIMELINE: The Development of the American News Media

1833 Rise of the Penny Press—Benjamin Day founds the *New York Sun*; it costs a penny at the newsstand and is politically independent.

1920 KDKA in Pittsburgh— First commercial radio station launches and provides detailed campaign coverage.

1980 Cable News Network (CNN)—Founded by media mogul Ted Turner, CNN makes national and international events available instantaneously around the globe.

2009 Death of Newspapers— In the face of declining circulation and revenues, several daily newspapers close their newsrooms and cease all publication, a trend that continues today.

1893 Joseph Pulitzer Launches *New York World*—Known for its sensationalism and progressive crusades, Pulitzer's approach is nicknamed "yellow journalism."

1963 Television News Grows—NBC becomes first network to have a 30-minute nightly national news broadcast.

1996 Candidate Home Pages Appear on the Web—Internet sites contain candidate profiles, issue positions, campaign strategy and slogans, and more.

2006 Social Networking and Video Sharing Explode—Online social networks and video-sharing Web sites transform political campaigns.

The Living Constitution

The Living Constitution reflects the authors' emphasis on the origins of America's democratic system. To further support the text's emphasis on the constitutional underpinnings of government and politics, this boxed feature appears in every chapter. Each feature examines the chapter's topic in light of what the Constitution says or does not say about it.

The Living Constitution

No Person except a natural born Citizen, or a Citizen of the United States, at the time of the Adoption of this Constitution, shall be eligible to the Office of President; neither shall any Person be eligible to that Office who shall not have attained to the Age of thirty five Years, and been fourteen Years a Resident within the United States.

—ARTICLE II, SECTION 1, CLAUSE 4

This provision of Article II is referred to as the presidential eligibility clause. It requires that the president be a natural-born citizen, at least thirty-five years old, and a resident of the United States for at least fourteen years. The Framers believed that each of these requirements was necessary to have a reasoned, respected chief executive who was loyal to the United States and familiar with its internal politics. In the 1700s, for example, it was not uncommon for a diplomat to spend years outside the country; without air travel and instantaneous communication, it was easy to become detached from politics at home.

the time of McCain's birth in 1936, those born in the Panama Canal Zone were considered U.S. nationals, but not citizens; this status was retroactively altered by legislation passed a year after his birth, in 1937. The concern surrounding his eligibility was so great that the Senate passed an official resolution declaring him to be eligible for the presidency.

Senator Obama, on the other hand, was born in Hawaii to an American mother and a Kenyan father. Some critics claimed that his citizenship was governed by his father's British lineage (Kenya was a colony of Great Britain at the time of Obama's

---

POLITICS NOW

| WORLD | NATION | LOCAL | POLITICS | OPINION | HEALTH & SCIENCE | ARTS | SPORTS | LEISURE |

Through Oil-Fouled Water, Big Government Looks Better and Better

May 4, 2010
Washington Post
www.washingtonpost.com

By Dana Milbank

. . . About 10:30 Monday morni[ng] ... government, posted a blog item o[n] ... [in the] Gulf of Mexico. "I strongly believe ...

About an hour later came word ... Mississippi—all three governed by ... government conservatives—want [the expense,] of course) more National Guard tr[oops] ...

Critical Thinking Questions

1. Should state or federal governments be responsible for cleaning up from natural disasters such as the oil spill? Explain your answer.

Politics Now boxes provide in-depth examinations of contemporary issues, showcasing the book's currency and serving as a counterbalance to the text's thorough treatment of America's origins and history. Excerpts from news articles are accompanied by critical thinking questions that allow students to analyze current political issues for themselves.

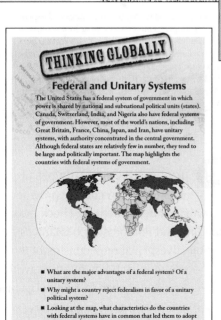

THINKING GLOBALLY

Federal and Unitary Systems

The United States has a federal system of government in which power is shared by national and subnational political units (states). Canada, Switzerland, India, and Nigeria also have federal systems of government. However, most of the world's nations, including Great Britain, France, China, Japan, and Iran, have unitary systems, with authority concentrated in the central government. Although federal states are relatively few in number, they tend to be large and politically important. The map highlights the countries with federal systems of government.

- What are the major advantages of a federal system? Of a unitary system?
- Why might a country reject federalism in favor of a unitary political system?
- Looking at the map, what characteristics do the countries with federal systems have in common that led them to adopt federal systems?

Thinking Globally features underscore the commonalities and differences between the United States and other nations to provide students with a comparative perspective on a range of issues. Thinking Globally features occur once in each chapter and consist of an overview of a key comparative topic followed by critical thinking questions.

Putting It into Action

The new and revised pedagogical features help students actively engage with the material, focus on key concepts, and become stronger political participants.

What Should I Know About . . .

After reading this chapter, you should be able to:

★ **1.1** Trace the origins of American government, p. 4.

★ **1.2** Show how European political thought provided the theoretical foundations of American government, p. 7.

★ **1.3** Describe American p[...] the basic tenets of A[...]

★ **1.4** Explain the functions [...] p. 13.

★ **1.5** Analyze the changing [...] American public, p. 1[...]

★ **1.6** Assess the role of po[...]

- First, we discuss *the roots of American government* by revealing who "We the People" really were.
- Second, we examine *the theoretical foundations of American government.*
- Third, we delve into *American political culture and the basic tenets of American democracy.*
- Fourth, we explore *the functions of American government.*
- Fifth, we analyze *the chang[...]*
- Sixth, we consider the role [...]
- Finally, we discuss reforms [...]

What Should I Know? and **What Should I Have Learned?** sections now include learning objectives that allow students to preview and review the key topics and concepts explored in each chapter. Every chapter begins with a set of "What Should I Know?" learning objectives tied to the sections within the chapter. These objectives, as well as a bulleted list of section descriptions that follows the opening vignette, preview the key content of the chapter and help to focus student attention on the overall chapter structure. A "What Should I Have Learned?" section at the end of every chapter revisits each of the "What Should I Know?" learning objectives and answers it with a succinct summary paragraph.

ROOTS OF American Government: We the People

★ **1.1 . . .** Trace the origins of American government.

The Preamble to the U.S. Constitution begins with the phrase "We the People." But, who are "the People"? In this section, we begin to explore that question by looking at the earliest inhabitants of the Americas, their initial and continued interactions with European colonists, and how Americans continually built on the experiences of the past to create a new future. (To learn more about how the meaning of the Preamble has evolved, see The Liv[...] [...])

What Should I Have LEARNED?

Now that you have read this chapter, you should be able to:

★ **1.1** Trace the origins of American government, p. 4.

American government is rooted in the cultures and experiences of early European colonists as well as interactions with the indigenous populations of the New World. The first colonists sought wealth. Later pilgrims came seeking religious freedom. The colonies set up systems of government that differed widely in terms of form, role, and function. As they developed, they sought more independence from the British monarchy.

Test Yourself: The Political Landscape

★ **1.1** Trace the origins of American government, p. 4.

Which of the following settlements was not founded for religious reasons?
A. Pennsylvania
B. Portsmouth
C. New Amsterdam
D. Massachusetts Bay Colony
E. Boston

★ **1.2** Show how European political thought provided the theoretical foundations of American government, p. 7.

The Declaration of Independence was most directly influenced by the ideas of which political philosopher?
A. John Locke.
B. Thomas Hobbes.
C. Isaac Newton.
D. Puritans.
E. Jean-Jacques Rousseau.

NEW! Test Yourself Quizzes at the end of each chapter provide students with avenues to actively check their understanding and reinforce each chapter's learning objectives. Each quiz consists of ten questions: one multiple choice question (with five answer choices) for each learning objective, with the remaining being essay questions focused on critical thinking.

Join the DEBATE | Should U.S. Supreme Court Justices Be Elected?

Article II of the Constitution grants the president of the United States authority to make judicial appointments to federal courts with the advice and consent of the Senate. Thus, judges serving on federal courts, including the U.S. Supreme Court, are not elected by the people. But, at the state level, it is common for judges to be elected rather than appointed. Seven states (Alabama, Illinois, Louisiana, New York, Pennsylvania, Texas, and West Virginia) elect judges in partisan elections, while twenty-nine others provide for other forms of election (nonpartisan ballots or gubernatorial appointment with confirmation or retention through popular election).

To develop an ARGUMENT FOR the election of U.S. Supreme Court justices, think about how:

■ **The decisions of the U.S. Supreme Court impact public policy.** Should public policy be made by a group of nine individuals who are not directly elected by the people? How might electing judges help judicial decisions reflect the times?

To develop an ARGUMENT AGAINST the election of U.S. Supreme Court justices, think about how:

■ **The U.S. Supreme Court provides stability to the entire court system.** What would happen to the principle of *stare decisis* if Supreme Court justices were regularly voted out of office? What role would legal precedent play in such a system?

Join the Debate boxes explore provocative, student-oriented topics and encourage students to develop their own well-thought-out arguments "for" and "against" each position. Each box begins with a topic overview, includes opposing points of view, and provides critical thinking questions that guide students in the development of arguments related to the issue. New topics in this edition include debates over the federal government's involvement in funding higher education, the election of Supreme Court justices, the use of American Indian names and mascots for sports teams, and the assimilation of immigrants.

The Constitution of the United States of America, carefully annotated to make it accessible to students, is placed between **chapters 2** and **3**, providing students with a careful walkthrough of this seminal document.

The Constitution of the United States of America

We the People of the United States, in Order to form a more perfect Union, establish Justice, insure domestic Tranquility, provide for the common defence, promote the general Welfare, and secure the Blessings of Liberty to ourselves and our Posterity, do ordain and establish this Constitution for the United States of America.

• The preamble to the U.S. Constitution is little more than a declaration of intent; it carries no legal weight. Instead, it describes what the people of the United States can expect from their government. •

ARTICLE I
Section 1.

All legislative Powers herein granted shall be vested in a Congress of the United States, which shall consist of a Senate and House of Representatives.

• Article I is the longest and most detailed of any of the articles, sections, or amendments that make up the U.S. Constitution. By *enumerating* the powers of Congress, the Framers attached limits to the enormous authority they had vested in the legislative branch. At the same time, they ensured that the legislative branch would maintain control over certain vital areas of public policy and that it would be protected from attacks by the executive and judicial branches. In addition, by clearly vesting Congress with certain powers (e.g., the power to regulate interstate commerce), Article I established limits for the exercise of state power in what were now national affairs.

Despite the great care the Framers took to limit the exercise of congressional authority to those powers

proper clause) in broad fashion. Rarely has the Court challenged the legislative power vested in Congress to engage in numerous areas of public policy that some constitutional scholars (and politicians and voters) believe are the province of the states. •

Section 2.

The House of Representatives shall be composed of Members chosen every second Year by the People of the several States, and the Electors in each State shall have the Qualifications requisite for Electors of the most numerous Branch of the State Legislature.

No person shall be a Representative who shall not have attained to the Age of twenty five Years, and been seven Years a Citizen of the United States, and who shall not, when elected, be an Inhabitant of that State in which he shall be chosen.

• The qualifications clause, which sets out the age and residency requirements for individuals who wish to run for the House of Representatives, became the centerpiece of a national debate that emerged during the late 1980s and early 1990s over term limits for members of Congress. In *U.S. Term Limits v. Thornton* (1995), the Supreme Court ruled that no state government could enact legislation to restrict a qualified individual's right to run for Congress. Instead, any modification to the qualifications clause would have to come through a constitutional amendment. •

Representatives and direct Taxes shall be apportioned among the several States which may be included within this Union, according to their respective Numbers which shall be determined by adding to the whole Number of free Persons

Analyzing Visuals

Visual literacy—the ability to analyze, interpret, synthesize, and apply visual information—is essential in today's world. We receive information from the written and spoken word, but knowledge also comes in visual forms. We are used to thinking about reading written texts critically, but we do not always think about "reading" visuals in this way. We should, because images and informational graphics can tell us a lot if we read and consider them carefully. In order to emphasize these skills, the Analyzing Visuals feature in each chapter prompts students to think about the images and informational graphics they will encounter throughout this text, as well as those they see every day in the newspaper, in magazines, on the Web, on television, and in books. Critical thinking questions assist students in learning how to analyze visuals.

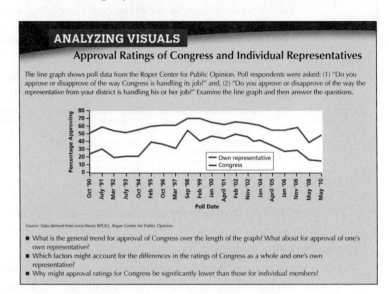

ANALYZING VISUALS

Approval Ratings of Congress and Individual Representatives

The line graph shows poll data from the Roper Center for Public Opinion. Poll respondents were asked: (1) "Do you approve or disapprove of the way Congress is handling its job?" and, (2) "Do you approve or disapprove of the way the representative from your district is handling his or her job?" Examine the line graph and then answer the questions.

Source: Data derived from Lexis-Nexis RPOLL, Roper Center for Public Opinion.

- What is the general trend for approval of Congress over the length of the graph? What about for approval of one's own representative?
- Which factors might account for the differences in the ratings of Congress as a whole and one's own representative?
- Why might approval ratings for Congress be significantly lower than those for individual members?

Tables

Tables consist of textual information and/or numerical data arranged in tabular form, in columns and rows. Tables are frequently used when exact information is required and when orderly arrangement is necessary to locate and, in many cases, to compare the information. All tables in this edition include questions that encourage critical thinking.

Students are encouraged to ask the following kinds of analytical questions about the tables:

How does a president affect the federal judiciary?

President	Appointed to Supreme Court	Appointed to Courts of Appeals[a]	Appointed to District Courts[b]	Total Appointed	Total Number of Judgeships[c]	Percentage of Judgeships Filled by President
Carter (1977–1981)	0	56	203	259	657	39
Reagan (1981–1989)	3	83	290	376	740	50
Bush (1989–1993)	2	42	148	192	825	22
Clinton (1993–2001)	2	66	305	373	841	44
G. W. Bush (2001–2009)	2	61	261	324	866	37
Obama (2009–)[d]	2	11	30	43	866	5

[a]Does not include the U. S. Court of Appeals for the Federal Circuit.
[b]Includes district courts in the territories.
[c]Total judgeships authorized in president's last year in office.
[d]Barack Obama data through September 20, 2010.
Source: "Imprints on the Bench," *CQ Weekly Report* (January 19, 2001): 173. Reprinted by permission of Copyright Clearance Center on behalf of Congressional Quarterly, Inc. Updated by authors.

- What is the purpose of the table? What information does it show?
- What information is provided in the column headings (provided in the top row)? How are the rows labeled?
- Is there a time period indicated, such as January to June 2010? Or, are the data as of a specific date, such as June 30, 2010?
- If the table shows numerical data, what do these data represent? In what units? Dollars a special interest lobby provides to a political party? Estimated life expectancy in years?
- What is the source of the information presented in the table?

Charts and Graphs

Charts and graphs depict numerical data in visual forms. Examples that students will encounter throughout this text are line graphs, pie charts, and bar graphs. Line graphs show a progression, usually over time (as in how the U.S. population has grown over time). Pie charts (such as ones showing population demographics) demonstrate how a whole (total American population) is divided into its parts (different racial and ethnic groups). Bar graphs compare values across categories, showing how proportions are related to each other (as in the numbers of women and minorities in Congress). Bar graphs can present data either horizontally or vertically. All charts and graphs in this edition are based on questions that encourage critical thinking.

Students will learn to ask the following kinds of questions about visual information:

- What is the purpose of the chart or graph? What information does it provide? Or, what is being measured?
- Is there a time period shown, such as January to June 2009? Or, are the data as of a specific date, such as June 30, 2009? Are the data shown at multiple intervals over a fixed period, or at one particular point in time?
- What do the units represent? Dollars a candidate spends on a campaign? Number of voters versus number of nonvoters in Texas? If there are two or more sets of figures, what are the relationships among them?
- What is the source? Is it government information? Private polling information? A newspaper? A private organization? A corporation? An individual?
- Is the type of chart or graph appropriate for the information that is provided? For example, a line graph assumes a smooth progression from one data point to the next. Is that assumption valid for the data shown?
- Is there distortion in the visual representation of the information? Are the intervals equal? Does the area shown distort the actual amount or the proportion?

How does the racial and ethnic composition of America today differ from that of 1967?

Source: U.S. Census Bureau, *2010 Statistical Abstract of the United States.*

1967

2008

How has the U.S. population grown over time?

Since around 1890, when large numbers of immigrants began arriving in America, the United States has seen a sharp increase in population. The major reasons for this increase are new births and increased longevity, although immigration is also a contributing factor.

Source: U.S. Census Bureau Population Projections, www.census.gov.

How many women and minorities serve in Congress?

Source: Data compiled by the authors.

How is voting power apportioned in the Electoral College?

This map visually represents the respective electoral weights of the fifty states in the 2008 presidential election. For each state, the projected gain or loss of Electoral College votes based on the 2010 Census is indicated in parentheses.

Source: synapse.princeton.edu/~sam/ev_projection_current_map.jpg and www.edssurvey.com/images/File/NR_Appor07wTables.pdf.

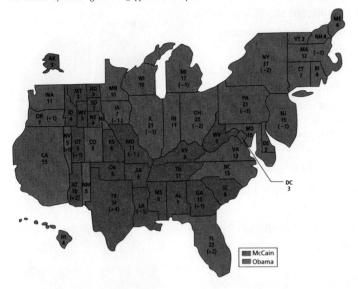

Maps

Maps—of the United States, of particular regions, or of the world—are frequently used in political analysis to illustrate demographic, social, economic, and political issues and trends. All maps in this edition include questions to encourage critical thinking.

Students learn to consider the following issues when analyzing maps:

- Is there a title that identifies the purpose or subject of the map?
- What does the map key/legend show? What are the factors that the map is analyzing?
- What is the region being shown?
- What source is given for the map?
- Maps usually depict a specific point in time. What is the point in time being shown on the map?

News Photographs

Photos can have a dramatic—and often immediate—impact on politics and government. Visual images usually evoke a stronger emotional response from people than do written descriptions. For this reason, individuals and organizations have learned to use photographs as a means to document events, make arguments, offer evidence, and even in some cases to manipulate the viewer into having a particular response.

Students are encouraged to consider the following about photographs:

- When was the photograph taken?
- What is the subject of the photograph?
- Why was the photo taken? What appears to be the purpose of the photograph?

- Is it spontaneous or posed? Did the subject know he or she was being photographed?
- Who was responsible for the photo? (An individual, agency, or organization?) Can you discern the photographer's attitude toward the subject?
- Is there a caption? If so, what kind of information does it provide? Does it identify the subject of the photo? Does it provide an interpretation of the subject?

Political Cartoons

Some of the most interesting commentary on American politics takes place in the form of political cartoons. The cartoonist's goal is to comment on and/or criticize political figures, policies, or events. The cartoonist uses several techniques to accomplish this goal, including exaggeration, irony, and juxtaposition. For example, the cartoonist may point out how the results of governmental policies are the opposite of their intended effects (irony). In other cartoons, two people, ideas, or events that don't belong together may be joined to make a point (juxtaposition). Knowledge of current events is helpful in interpreting political cartoons.

Students learn to appreciate the nuances of political humor and satire by asking the following kinds of questions:

- What labels appear on objects or people in the cartoon? Cartoonists will often label some of the elements. For example, a building with columns might be labeled "U.S. Supreme Court."
- What does the caption or title contribute to the meaning or impact of the cartoon?
- Can any of the people shown be identified? Presidents, well-known members of Congress, and world leaders are often shown with specific characteristics that help to identify them.

- Can the event being depicted be identified? Historical events, such as the American Revolution, or contemporary events, such as the 2010 congressional elections, are often the subject matter for cartoons.
- What are the elements of the cartoon? Objects often represent ideas or events. For example, a donkey is often used to depict the Democratic Party.
- How are the characters interacting? What do the speech bubbles contribute to the cartoon?
- What is the overall message of the cartoon? Can you determine what the cartoonist's position is on the subject?

Resources in Print and Online

Name of Supplement	Print	Online	Available to	Description
MyClassPrep		✔	Instructor	This new resource provides a rich database of figures, photos, videos, simulations, activities, and much more that instructors can use to create their own lecture presentation. For more information visit www.mypoliscilab.com
Instructor's Manual 0205077021		✔	Instructor	Offers chapter overviews, lecture outlines, teaching ideas, discussion topics, and research activities. All resources hyperlinked for ease of navigation.
Test Bank 0205023800		✔	Instructor	Contains over 100 questions per chapter in multiple-choice, true-false, short answer, and essay format. Questions are tied to text Learning Objectives and have been reviewed for accuracy and effectiveness. Created by the authors.
MyTest 0205076785		✔	Instructor	All questions from the Test Bank can be accessed in this flexible, online test generating software.
Study Guide 0205076726	✔		Student	Contains learning objectives, chapter summaries, key terms, and practice tests.
PowerPoint Presentation 0205077048		✔	Instructor	Slides include a lecture outline of the text, graphics from the book, and quick check questions for immediate feedback on student comprehension. Created by the authors.
Transparencies 0205109950		✔	Instructor	These slides contain all maps, figures, and tables found in the text.
PearsonPearson Political Science Video Program	✔		Instructor	Qualified adopters can peruse our list of videos for the American government classroom. Contact your local Pearson representative for more details.
Classroom Response System (CRS) 0205082289		✔	Instructor	A set of lecture questions, organized by American government topics, for use with "clickers" to garner student opinion and assess comprehension.
American Government Study Site		✔	Instructor/ Student	Online package of practice tests, flashcards and more organized by major course topics. Visit www.pearsonamericangovernment.com
You Decide! Current Debates in American Politics, 2011 Edition 020511489X	✔		Student	This debate-style reader by John Rourke of the University of Connecticut examines provocative issues in American politics today by presenting contrasting views of key political topics.
Voices of Dissent: Critical Readings in American Politics, Eighth Edition 0205697976	✔		Student	This collection of critical essays assembled by William Grover of St. Michaels College and Joseph Peschek of Hamline University goes beyond the debate between mainstream liberalism and conservatism to fundamentally challenge the status quo.
Diversity in Contemporary Government 0205550363	✔		Student	Edited by David Dulio of Oakland University, Erin E. O'Brien of University of Massachusetts—Boston, and John Klemanski of Oakland University, this reader examines the significant role that demographic diversity plays in our political outcomes and policy processes, using both academic and popular sources.
Writing in Political Science, Fourth Edition 0205617360	✔		Student	This guide, written by Diane Schmidt of California State University—Chico, takes students through all aspects of writing in political science step-by-step.
Choices: An American Government Database Reader		✔	Student	This customizable reader allows instructors to choose from a database of over 300 readings to create a reader that exactly matches their course needs. For more information go to www.pearsoncustom.com/database/choices.html.
Ten Things That Every American Government Student Should Read 020528969X	✔		Student	Edited by Karen O'Connor of American University. We asked American government instructors across the country to vote for the ten things beyond the text that they believe every student should read and put them in this brief and useful reader. Available at no additional charge when packaged with the text.
American Government: Readings and Cases, Eighteenth Edition 0205697984	✔		Student	Edited by Peter Woll of Brandeis University, this longtime best-selling reader provides a strong, balanced blend of classic readings and cases that illustrate and amplify important concepts in American government, alongside extremely current selections drawn from today's issues and literature. Available at a discount when ordered packaged with this text.
Penguin-Longman Value Bundles	✔		Student	Longman offers 25 Penguin Putnam titles at more than a 60 percent discount when packaged with any Longman text. Go to www.pearsonhighered.com/penguin for more information.
Longman State Politics Series	✔		Student	These primers on state and local government and political issues are available at no extra cost when shrink-wrapped with the text. Available for Texas, California, and Georgia.

*Visit the Instructor Resource Center to download supplements at www.pearsonhighered.com/educator

Improve Results With

Acknowledgments

Karen O'Connor thanks the thousands of students in her American Government courses at Emory and American Universities who, over the years, have pushed her to learn more about American government and to have fun in the process. She especially thanks Jonathan and Robin Helfat for their support and Natalie N. Greene, whose help updating the Texas chapters was invaluable. Her former students, too, have contributed in various ways to this project, especially John R. Hermann, Sue Davis, and Laura van Assendelft.

For the last five editions of the book, Alixandra B. Yanus of High Point University has offered invaluable assistance, unflagging support, and friendship. Her fresh perspectives on politics and ideas about things of interest to students, as well as her keen eye for the typo, her research abilities, and her unbelievably hard work, have made this a much better book. For the last two editions of the book, Jon L. Weakley, a graduate student at American University who had the foresight (or the stupidity) to first offer to help during the 2006 election update, provided necessary reinforcement and enthusiasm. Jon's copyediting skills, love of the electoral process, and unlimited patience have significantly improved this text, end of chapter questions, and the Test Bank.

Larry J. Sabato would like to acknowledge the 15,000 students from his University of Virginia Introduction to American Politics classes over 33 years and the many student interns at the UVA Center for Politics who have offered valuable suggestions and an abundance of thoughtful feedback. A massive textbook project like this one needs the very best assistance an author can find, and this author was lucky enough to find some marvelously talented people. Alixandra B. Yanus, assistant professor of political science at High Point University, worked endless hours researching the new edition and weaving together beautifully constructed sections on recent American politics. Her attention to detail and editor's eye have refined the behavior chapters and improved the overall text. As always, the staff of the University of Virginia Center for Politics and a team of extraordinary interns contributed in many important ways toward the successful completion of this volume, especially his chief of staff Ken Stroupe, Joseph Figueroa, and Isaac Wood. Their commitment to excellence is also obvious in their work for the Center's Crystal Ball website (www.centerforpolitics.org/crystalball)—a very useful resource in completing this volume.

Alixandra B. Yanus thanks Karen O'Connor and Larry Sabato for the opportunity to work on this textbook. Karen, especially, has been both mentor and "mom." She also thanks her colleagues at High Point University, Mark Setzler and Martin Kifer, who have relentlessly supported her work, both on the book and in the classroom. Adam Chamberlain at Coastal Carolina University, Ellen Gutman at the University of North Carolina at Chapel Hill, and Nicholas Pyeatt at Penn State—Altoona have also provided important advice on matters small (political science) and large (life).

She also acknowledges the hard work of Jon L. Weakley, a graduate student at American University, who answered 2 a.m. emails, researched minute details, and provided a steady support system on good days and bad.

Most especially, she is grateful, as always, to her parents, Karen and Mark Yanus, for the assistance, encouragement, and guidance they have provided throughout her life. She also appreciates the patience and devotion of Daniel P. Tappen, who watches the Mets when she has to work, and takes her to Phillies games when she doesn't.

Particular thanks go to Dennis L. Dresang at the University of Wisconsin–Madison, who has once again brought a keen eye and insightful analysis to the State and Local Government chapter; Noah Zerbe of Humboldt State University, who revised and wrote new Join the Debate features in the book; Christopher Simon at the University of Utah, who contributed to the revisions of the Domestic Policy and

Economic Policy chapters; and Glenn Hastedt of James Madison University, who provided great assistance in tackling the rapidly shifting landscape of Foreign and Defense Policy for this edition and also revised the Thinking Globally features. Our continued thanks go to Steven Koven at the University of Louisville, Daniel S. Papp of the University System of Georgia, and Kiki Caruson of the University of South Florida whose earlier work on the policy chapters continues to serve as such a strong foundation. We also thank Brian Bearry of the University of Texas at Dallas for his past help with many of the Join the Debate features.

In the now many years we have been writing and rewriting this book, we have been blessed to have been helped by many people at Longman. Former political science editor, Eric Stano, was a fantastic editor as well as fun to work and play with. Our new editor, Reid Hester, is probably still in a state of shock having joined the project close to the election when everything gets frenetic. So far, he seems unflappable, and we thank him for that. Our development editor, Lisa Sussman, has met a tremendous challenge head-on; she has been a stern taskmaster, attentive editor, and invaluable sounding board. Our marketing manager, Lindsey Prudhomme, has done a terrific job. We would also like to acknowledge the tireless efforts of the Pearson Education sales force. In the end, we hope that all of these talented people see how much their work and support have helped us to write a better book.

Many of our peers reviewed past editions of the book and earned our gratitude in the process. We list a number who reviewed recent editions here:

Danny Adkison, *Oklahoma State University*
Weston H. Agor, *University of Texas at El Paso*
Victor Aikhionbare, *Salt Lake Community College*
James Anderson, *Texas A&M University*
William Arp, *Southern University, Baton Rouge*
Judith Baer, *Texas A&M University*
Vanessa Baird, *University of Colorado, Boulder*
Ruth Bamberger, *Drury College*
Christine Barbour, *Indiana University*
Ken Baxter, *San Joaquin Delta College*
Brian Bearry, *University of Texas at Dallas*
Jon Bond, *Texas A&M University*
Stephen A. Borrelli, *University of Alabama*
Ann Bowman, *University of South Carolina*
Robert C. Bradley, *Illinois State University*
Holly Brasher, *University of Alabama, Birmingham*
Michelle Brophy-Baermann, *University of Wisconsin*
Gary Brown, *Montgomery College*
John Francis Burke, *University of Houston–Downtown*
Kevin Buterbaugh, *Northwest Missouri State University*
Mark Byrnes, *Middle Tennessee State University*
Greg Caldeira, *Ohio State University*
John H. Calhoun, *Palm Beach Atlantic University*
David E. Camacho, *Northern Arizona University*
Alan R. Carter, *Schenectady County Community College*
Carl D. Cavalli, *North Georgia College and State University*
Steve Chan, *University of Colorado*
Richard Christofferson Sr., *University of Wisconsin–Stevens Point*
David Cingranelli, *SUNY Binghamton*
Clarke E. Cochran, *Texas Tech University*
Paul W. Cook, *Cy-Fair College*

Tracy Cook, *Central Texas College*
Kevin Corder, *Western Michigan University*
Anne N. Costain, *University of Colorado*
Cary Covington, *University of Iowa*
Lorrie Clemo, *SUNY Oswego*
Stephen C. Craig, *University of Florida*
Lane Crothers, *Illinois State University*
Abraham L. Davis, *Morehouse College*
Robert DiClerico, *West Virginia University*
Brian Dille, *Odessa College*
John Dinan, *Wake Forest University*
John Domino, *Sam Houston State University*
Keith L. Dougherty, *University of Georgia*
David E. Dupree, *Victor Valley College*
Craig F. Emmert, *Texas Tech University*
Walle Engedayehu, *Prairie View A&M University*
Alan S. Engel, *Miami University*
Timothy Fackler, *University of Nevada, Las Vegas*
Frank B. Feigert, *University of North Texas*
Terri S. Fine, *University of Central Florida*
Evelyn Fink, *University of Nebraska*
Scott R. Furlong, *University of Wisconsin–Green Bay*
James D. Gleason, *Victoria College*
Dana K. Glencross, *Oklahoma City Community College*
Sheldon Goldman, *University of Massachusetts, Amherst*
Doris Graber, *University of Illinois at Chicago*
Jeffrey D. Green, *University of Montana*
Roger W. Green, *University of North Dakota*
James Michael Greig, *University of North Texas*
Charles Hadley, *University of New Orleans*
Mel Hailey, *Abilene Christian University*
William K. Hall, *Bradley University*

Robert L. Hardgrave Jr., *University of Texas at Austin*
Chip Hauss, *George Mason University/University of Reading*
Stacia L. Haynie, *Louisiana State University*
John R. Hermann, *Trinity University*
Marjorie Hershey, *Indiana University*
Justin Holmes, *University of Minnesota*
Steven Alan Holmes, *Bakersfield College*
Jerry Hopkins, *East Texas Baptist University*
Tim Howard, *North Harris College*
John C. Hughes, *Oklahoma City Community College*
Jon Hurwitz, *SUNY Buffalo*
Thomas Hyde, *Pfeiffer University*
Joseph Ignagni, *University of Texas at Arlington*
Willoughby Jarrell, *Kennesaw State College*
Susan M. Johnson, *University of Wisconsin–Whitewater*
Dennis Judd, *University of Missouri–St. Louis*
Ngozi Kamalu, *Fayetteville State University*
Carol J. Kamper, *Rochester Community College*
David Kennedy, *Montgomery College*
Kenneth Kennedy, *College of San Mateo*
Donald F. Kettl, *University of Wisconsin–Madison*
Quentin Kidd, *Christopher Newport University*
John Kincaid, *Lafayette College*
Karen M. King, *Bowling Green State University*
Alec Kirby, *University of Wisconsin–Stout*
Aaron Knight, *Houston Community College*
John F. Kozlowicz, *University of Wisconsin–Whitewater*
Jonathan E. Kranz, *John Jay College of Criminal Justice*
John C. Kuzenski, *The Citadel*
Mark Landis, *Hofstra University*
Sue Lee, *North Lake College*
Ted Lewis, *Collin County Community College*
Matt Lindstrom, *St. John's University*
Robert Locander, *North Harris College*
Brad Lockerbie, *University of Georgia*
Susan MacFarland, *Gainesville College*
Cecilia Manrique, *University of Wisconsin–La Crosse*
Larry Martinez, *California State University–Long Beach*
Lynn Mather, *SUNY Buffalo*
Laurel A. Mayer, *Sinclair Community College*
Steve Mazurana, *University of Northern Colorado*
Clifton McCleskey, *University of Virginia*
Percival Robert McDonogh, *Catholic University*
James L. McDowell, *Indiana State University*
Carl E. Meacham, *SUNY Oneonta*
Stephen S. Meinhold, *University of North Carolina–Wilmington*
John Mercurio, *San Diego State University*
Mark C. Miller, *Clark University*
Billy Monroe, *University of Texas at Dallas*
Dana Morales, *Montgomery College*
Kenneth F. Mott, *Gettysburg College*
Katarina Moyon, *Winthrop University*

Joseph Nogee, *University of Houston*
John O'Callaghan, *Suffolk University*
Bruce Oppenheimer, *Vanderbilt University*
Richard Pacelle, *Georgia Southern University*
Marian Lief Palley, *University of Delaware*
David R. Penna, *Gallaudet University*
Ron Pettus, *St. Charles Community College*
Richard M. Pious, *Columbia University*
David H. Provost, *California State University–Fresno*
Lawrence J. Redlinger, *University of Texas at Dallas*
James A. Rhodes, *Luther College*
Leroy N. Rieselbach, *Indiana University*
David Robertson, *Public Policy Research Centers, University of Missouri–St. Louis*
David Robinson, *University of Houston–Downtown*
Norman Rodriguez, *John Wood Community College*
David W. Rohde, *Duke University*
Frank Rourke, *Johns Hopkins University*
Thomas Rowan, *Chicago State University*
Donald Roy, *Ferris State University*
Ronald Rubin, *City University of New York, Borough of Manhattan Community College*
Bruce L. Sanders, *MacComb Community College*
Denise Scheberle, *University of Wisconsin–Green Bay*
Gaye Lynn Scott, *Austin Community College*
Kathleen Sedille, *College of DuPage*
Martin P. Sellers, *Campbell University*
Daniel M. Shea, *Allegheny College*
John N. Short, *University of Arkansas–Monticello*
Michael Eric Siegel, *American University*
Mark Silverstein, *Boston University*
James R. Simmons, *University of Wisconsin–Oshkosh*
Andrea Simpson, *University of Richmond*
Philip M. Simpson, *Cameron University*
Elliott E. Slotnick, *Ohio State University*
Michael W. Sonnleitner, *Portland Community College*
Frank J. Sorauf, *University of Minnesota*
David Sprick, *University of Missouri, Kansas City*
Gerald Stanglin, *Cedar Valley College*
Robert Sullivan, *Dallas Baptist University*
C. S. Tai, *University of Arkansas–Pine Bluff*
Leena Thacker-Kumer, *University of Houston–Downtown*
Richard J. Timpone, *Ohio State University*
Ron Velten, *Grayson County College*
Albert C. Waite, *Central Texas College*
Brian Walsh, *University of Maryland*
Shirley Anne Warshaw, *Gettysburg College*
Matt Wetstein, *San Joaquin Delta College*
Richard Whaley, *Marian College*
Rich Whisonant, *York Technical College*
Harold Wingfield, *Kennesaw State University*
Martin Wiseman, *Mississippi State University*
Kevan Yenerall, *Bridgewater College*

Finally, we'd also like to thank our peers who reviewed and aided in the development of the current edition:

Janet Adamski, *University of Mary Hardin Baylor*

R. Bruce Anderson, *Baker University*

Cindy Boyles, *University of Virginia*

Lynn Brink, *North Lake College*

Brian Calfano, *Missouri State University*

Brian Cravens, *Blinn College–Schulenburg*

JoAnn DiGeorgio-Lutz, *Texas A&M University–Commerce*

John Domino, *Sam Houston State University*

Cecil Dorsey, *San Jacinto College–South*

Amy Gossett, *Lincoln University*

Jeffrey Herndon, *Texas A&M University–Commerce*

John Hitt, *North Lake College*

Lisa Huffstetler, *University of Memphis*

Ahad Hayaud-Din, *Brookhaven College*

Jean-Gabriel Jolivet, *Southwestern College*

Lisa Langenbach, *Middle Tennessee State University*

Julie Lantrip, *Tarrant County College*

David Larkin, *Paris Junior College*

Robert Locander, *Lone Star College–North Harris*

John Maynor, *Middle Tennessee State University*

Tim Meinke, *Lynchburg College*

Stephen Nicholson, *University of California, Merced*

Ted Ritter, *University of Richmond*

Ted Williams, *Kennedy-King College*

Laura Wood, *Tarrant County College Northwest*

1 The Political Landscape

In December 1606, three ships—the *Susan Constant*, the *Godspeed*, and the *Discovery*—set sail from Blackwall, England, to America. On these ships were 104 men and boys seeking their fortunes, for it had been reputed that the New World offered tremendous riches. However, this sorry mix of laborers lacked the skills necessary to sustain a colony in the harsh terrain they were to encounter.

The colonists were financed by the London Company, a joint stock company created to attract much-needed capital to aid in the British colonization of the New World. Joint stock companies allowed potential investors to purchase shares of stock in companies anticipating large payoffs for their investments several years down the road. Enthusiasm for this new business model led thousands of English citizens to invest in the London Company. The

company was issued the first Virginia Charter in April 1606, allowing it to settle a region extending from present-day Cape Fear, North Carolina, to Long Island Sound, New York. The settlers were under the direction of Sir Thomas Smith, reputed to be one of London's wealthiest financiers, giving further credibility to the venture.

Although Smith directed the expedition, he chose to remain in England when the ships set sail for the New World. The colonists settled in a swampy area 30 miles from the mouth of the James River, creating Jamestown, Virginia—the first permanent settlement in America in 1607. Immediately, conditions were dismal. Insufficient numbers of settlers opted to pursue agricultural ventures, and people began to starve. Settlers died from hunger, Indian attacks, lack of proper supplies, and disease.

The United States is a nation of immigrants. At left is an artist's rendition of the first permanent English settlement in the New World, Jamestown, in what is today Virginia. At right, American immigrants take an oath of citizenship in 2010. Today, the people who make up the American body politic are far more diverse than those who settled Virginia or any of the other thirteen original colonies.

One of the major problems with the settlement was a lack of strong leadership. This improved with the election of Captain John Smith as the colony's third president. Smith instituted improvements forcing all colonists to work and attempting to negotiate food trade with local Indians. These efforts were successful for a short time, but even these eventually failed, and the harsh winter of 1609–1610 was deemed "The Starving Time." The situation became so dire that a few settlers resorted to cannibalism.

Although the introduction of tobacco as a cash crop in 1612 improved the economic conditions of the settlement, living conditions remained grim. One resident called the area "an unhealthy place, a nest of Rogues, whores, desolate, and rooking persons; a place of intolerable labour, bad usage, and a hard Diet."[1] While eventually conditions improved, it is important to remember the sacrifices of early colonists and the trials other waves of immigrants have faced to be part of the American dream.

What Should I Know About . . .

After reading this chapter, you should be able to:

★ **1.1** Trace the origins of American government, p. 4.

★ **1.2** Show how European political thought provided the theoretical foundations of American government, p. 7.

★ **1.3** Describe American political culture, and identify the basic tenets of American democracy, p. 10.

★ **1.4** Explain the functions of American government, p. 12.

★ **1.5** Analyze the changing characteristics of the American public, p. 13.

★ **1.6** Assess the role of political ideology in shaping American politics, p. 17.

★ **1.7** Characterize changes in Americans' attitudes toward and expectations of government, p. 19.

I n this text, we explore the American political system through a historical lens. This perspective allows us to analyze the ways that the ideas and actions of a host of different Americans—from Indians, to colonists, to the Framers of the Constitution and beyond—have affected how our government works. Much has changed since the days of the Jamestown Colony, and the people who live in America today are very different from those early settlers. Their experiences and values, however, continue to influence politics. This chapter explores the political process, placing people at its center.

- First, we discuss *the roots of American government* by revealing who *"We the People"* really were.

- Second, we examine *the theoretical foundations of American government.*

- Third, we delve into *American political culture and the basic tenets of American democracy.*

- Fourth, we explore *the functions of American government.*

- Fifth, we analyze *the changing American public.*

- Sixth, we consider the role of *political ideology* in American politics.

- Finally, we discuss *reforms* as a result of *people and politics.*

ROOTS OF American Government: We the People

★ **1.1** . . . Trace the origins of American government.

The Preamble to the U.S. Constitution begins with the phrase "We the People." But, who are "the People"? In this section, we begin to explore that question by looking at the earliest inhabitants of the Americas, their initial and continued interactions with European colonists, and how Americans continually built on the experiences of the past to create a new future. (To learn more about how the meaning of the Preamble has evolved, see The Living Constitution: Preamble.)

The Earliest Inhabitants of the Americas

By the time the first colonists arrived in what is now known as the United States, indigenous peoples had been living in the area for more than 30,000 years. Most historians and archaeologists believe that these peoples migrated from present-day Russia through the Bering Strait into North America and then dispersed throughout the American continents.

The indigenous peoples were not a homogeneous group; their cultures, customs, and values varied widely, as did their political systems. The number of these indigenous peoples is impossible to know for certain. Estimates, however, have ranged as high as 100 million people, a number that quickly diminished as colonists brought with them to the New World a range of diseases to which the indigenous peoples had not been exposed. In addition, warfare with the European settlers as well as within tribes not only killed many American Indians but also disrupted previously established

The Living Constitution

We the People of the United States, in Order to form a more perfect Union, establish Justice, insure domestic Tranquility, provide for the common defence, promote the general Welfare, and secure the Blessings of Liberty to ourselves and our Posterity, do ordain and establish this Constitution for the United States of America.

—PREAMBLE

The Preamble to the United States Constitution is little more than a declaration of intent; it carries no legal weight. But, its language has steered the American government, politics, institutions, and people for over 200 years. While the language of the Preamble has not changed since the Constitution was written, its meaning in practice has evolved significantly; this is what we mean by a living constitution. For example, the phrases "We the People" and "ourselves" included a much smaller group of citizens in 1787 than they do today. Voting was largely limited to property-owning white males. Indians, slaves, and women could not vote. Today, through the expansion of the right to vote, the phrase "the People" encompasses men and women of all races, ethnic origins, and social and economic statuses. This has changed the demands that Americans place on government, as well as expectations about the role of government in people's lives.

Many citizens today question how well the U.S. government can deliver on the goals set out in the Preamble. Few Americans classify the union as "perfect," and many feel excluded from "Justice" and the "Blessings of Liberty." Even our leaders do not believe that our domestic situation is particularly tranquil, as evidenced by the continuing debates about the best means to protect America. Still, in appraising how well government functions, it is imperative to look at not only the roots of the political system, but also how it has been reformed over time through amendment, legislation, common usage, and changing social mores.

CRITICAL THINKING QUESTIONS

1. How do you think the Framers would respond to the broad interpretation of the Preamble's intent embraced by many modern political leaders?
2. What are some specific examples of demands placed on government by the American people?
3. How have ideas such as promoting "the general Welfare" evolved over time? How has this affected the role and power of American government?

ways of life. The European settlers also displaced Indians, repeatedly pushing them westward as they created settlements and later, colonies.

The First Colonists

Colonists came to North America for a variety of reasons. Many wealthy Englishmen and other Europeans came seeking to enhance their fortunes. With them came a host of laborers who hoped to find their own opportunities for riches. In fact, commerce was the most common initial reason for settlement in North America.

In addition to the English commercial settlements in Virginia, in 1609 the Dutch settled along the Hudson and lower Delaware Rivers, calling the area New Netherlands. Both Fort Orange, in what is now Albany, New York, and

New Amsterdam, New York City's Manhattan Island, were populated not by colonists but by salaried employees. Among those who flocked to New Amsterdam (renamed New York in 1664) were settlers from Finland, Germany, and Sweden. The varied immigrants also included free blacks. This ethnic and racial mix created its own system of cultural inclusiveness that continues to make New York City and its citizenry unique today.

A RELIGIOUS TRADITION TAKES ROOT   During what is referred to as the Enlightenment period of the 1600s, philosophers and scientists such as Isaac Newton (1642–1727) began to argue that the world could be improved through the use of human reason, science, and religious toleration. These intellectual and religious developments encouraged people to seek alternatives to absolute monarchies and to ponder the divine right of kings and the role of the church in their lives.

Among those who rejected the role of the Church of England were a group of radical Protestants known as Puritans. These people had been persecuted for their religious beliefs by the English monarchy. They decided that better opportunities for religious freedom might lie in the New World.

In 1620, a group of these Protestants, known as the Pilgrims, left Europe aboard the *Mayflower*. Although they were destined for Virginia, they found themselves off course and instead landed in Plymouth, in what is now Massachusetts. These new settlers differed from those in Virginia and New York, who saw their settlements as commercial ventures. The Pilgrims came instead as families bound together by a common belief in the powerful role of religion in their lives.

Soon, challenges arose to the ideas at the core of these strict Puritanical values. In 1631, Roger Williams arrived in Boston, Massachusetts. He preached extreme separation from the Church of England and even questioned the right of Europeans to settle on Indian lands. He believed that the Puritans went too far when they punished settlers who deviated from their strict code of morality, arguing that it was God, not people, who should punish individuals for their moral dalliances. These "heretical views" prompted local magistrates to banish him from the colony. Williams then helped to establish Providence, a village in present-day Rhode Island.

A later challenge to the Puritans' religious beliefs came from midwife Anne Hutchinson. She began to share her views that churches as they had been established in Massachusetts had lost touch with the Holy Spirit. Many of her followers were women, and her progressive views on the importance of religious tolerance, as well as on the equality and rights of women, led to her expulsion from Massachusetts. She and her followers eventually settled in Portsmouth, Rhode Island, which became a beacon for those seeking religious toleration. (To learn more about colonial settlement, see Figure 1.1.)

Figure 1.1 *What did colonial settlement look like before 1700?*

RELIGIOUS TOLERANCE GROWS   Later colonies established in the New World were created with religious tolerance in mind. In 1632, King Charles I granted a well-known English Catholic's son a charter to establish a Catholic colony in the New World. This area eventually became known as Maryland, after Mary the mother of Jesus.

In 1681, King Charles II bestowed upon William Penn a charter giving him sole ownership of a vast area of land just north of Maryland. The king called the land Pennsylvania, or Penn's Woods. Penn, a Quaker, eventually also purchased the land that is present-day Delaware. In this area, Penn launched what he called "the holy experiment," attracting other persecuted Europeans, including German Mennonites and Lutherans and French Huguenots.

Becoming Americans

Common to all of these colonies was the immediately apparent need for some type of governance and a divine God. Ultimately, the beginnings of **government,** the formal vehicle through which policies are made and affairs of state are conducted, began to emerge. The structures created in each colony varied greatly, from initial chaos to far more inclusive and stable types of local and colonial self-governance. The Virginia House of Burgesses, created in 1619, was the first representative assembly in North America. In this body, twenty-two elected officials were chosen to make the laws for all of the colonists. In contrast, in the Massachusetts Bay Colony, all church members were permitted the right to participate in what were called town meetings. This more direct form of government enabled a broader base of participation and allowed the colonists to keep their religious and cultural values at the center of their governing process.

Eventually, the power of self-government as well as a growing spirit of independence resulted in tension with British rule. Though there were differences among the colonists about the proper form, role, and function of government, there was widespread agreement that the king of England was out of touch and unresponsive to the colonists' needs (see **chapter 2**).

government
The formal vehicle through which policies are made and affairs of state are conducted.

The Theoretical Foundations of American Government

★ **1.2 . . . Show how European political thought provided the theoretical foundations of American government.**

The current American political system is the result of philosophy, religious tradition, trial and error, and even luck. To begin our examination of why we have the type of government we have today, we will look at the theories of government that influenced the Framers who drafted the Constitution and created the United States of America.

Social Contract Theory

Even before the Pilgrims arrived in the New World, they saw the necessity for a **social contract,** an agreement among the people signifying their consent to be governed. While at sea, they wrote a document called the **Mayflower Compact,** which enumerated the scope of their government and its expectations of citizens. This document was based on a social contract theory of government. Two English theorists of the seventeenth century, Thomas Hobbes (1588–1679) and John Locke (1632–1704), built on conventional notions about the role of government and the relationship of the government to the people in proposing a **social contract theory** of government. They argued that all individuals were free and equal by natural right. This freedom, in turn, required that all people give their consent to be governed.

In Hobbes's *Leviathan,* (1651), he argued pessimistically that humanity's natural state was one of war. Government, Hobbes theorized, particularly a monarchy, was necessary to restrain humanity's bestial tendencies because life without government was but a "state of nature." Without written, enforceable rules, people would live like animals— foraging for food, stealing, and killing when necessary. To escape the horrors of the natural state and to protect their lives, Hobbes argued, people must give up certain rights to government. Without government, Hobbes warned, life would be "solitary, poor, nasty, brutish, and short"—a constant struggle to survive against the evil of others.[2] For these reasons, governments had to intrude on people's rights and liberties significantly to better control society and to provide the necessary safeguards for property.

Hobbes argued strongly for a single ruler, no matter how evil, to guarantee the rights of the weak against the strong. Leviathan, a biblical sea monster, was his characterization

social contract
An agreement between the people and their government signifying their consent to be governed.

Mayflower Compact
Document written by the Pilgrims while at sea enumerating the scope of their government and its expectations of citizens.

social contract theory
The belief that people are free and equal by natural right, and that this in turn requires that all people give their consent to be governed; espoused by Thomas Hobbes and John Locke and influential in the writing of the Declaration of Independence.

TIMELINE: Colonial Settlement in the New World

1607 **Jamestown Colony**—The first English settlement in the New World is established in present-day Virginia.

1609–1610 **Starving Time**—Settlers in Jamestown struggle to survive the harsh winter; some resort to cannibalism.

1620 **Massachusetts Bay Colony**—The English Pilgrims sail to the New World on the *Mayflower* and establish a settlement in Plymouth.

1609 **New Netherlands**—The Dutch establish a commercial settlement in present-day New York.

of an all-powerful government. Strict adherence to the laws, however all-encompassing or intrusive on liberty, was a small price to pay for living in a civilized society.

In contrast to Hobbes, John Locke, like many other political philosophers of the era, took the basic survival of humanity for granted. Locke argued that a government's major responsibility was the preservation of private property, an idea that ultimately found its way into the U.S. Constitution. In two of his works—*Second Treatise of Civil Government* (1689) and *Essay Concerning Human Understanding* (1690)—Locke not only denied the divine right of kings to govern but argued that individuals were born equal and with natural rights that no king had the power to void. Under Locke's conception of social contract theory, the consent of the people is the only true basis of any sovereign's right to rule. According to Locke, people form governments largely to preserve "the right of making laws with penalties . . . for the regulating and preserving of property, and of employing the force of the community in the execution of such laws . . . all this only for the public good."[3] If governments act improperly, they break their contract with the people and therefore no longer enjoy the consent of the governed. Because he believed that true justice comes from the law, Locke argued that the branch of government that makes laws—as opposed to the one that enforces or interprets laws—should be the most powerful.

Locke believed that having a chief executive to administer laws was important, but that he should necessarily be limited by law or by the social contract with the governed. Locke's writings influenced many American colonists, especially Thomas Jefferson, whose original draft of the Declaration of Independence noted the rights to "life, liberty, and property" as key reasons to separate from England.[4]

Two French political philosophers also had a significant impact on the theoretical foundations of American government. In 1749, Charles-Louis, the Second Baron of Montesquieu, published *Spirit of the Laws,* in which he adopted Hobbes's and Locke's concepts of the social contract. He offered that the best form of government is one that fits best with the "peculiar character of its people."[5] His most critical contribution

1636 Providence— Roger Williams and others banished from Massachusetts Bay Colony establish a settlement in present-day Rhode Island.

1682 Pennsylvania— King Charles II grants a charter to William Penn, a Quaker who establishes an ethnically and religiously diverse settlement.

1632 Maryland— King Charles I grants a charter to establish a Catholic haven in the New World.

1637 Portsmouth— Anne Hutchinson and others persecuted in Massachusetts Bay Colony establish a settlement in present-day Rhode Island.

was his theory of liberty, which held that governmental power was best when divided into distinct branches that provided a system to check power with power.

Jean Jacques Rousseau's *Social Contract*, written in 1762, went far beyond Locke and Hobbes, arguing that feeling, not reason, is what draws people to life in a community. He contended that property rights, the freedoms of speech and religion, and other basic rights come from society, not a state of nature. He believed that society based on a true social contract would provide absolute equality and freedom for individuals.

Devising a National Government in the American Colonies

The American colonists rejected a system with a strong ruler, such as the British monarchy, when they declared their independence. The colonists also were fearful of replicating the landed and titled system of the British aristocracy. They viewed the formation of a republican form of government as far more in keeping with their values.

The Framers wanted to create a political system that involved placing the people at the center of power. Due to the vast size of the new nation, **direct democracy** was unworkable. As more and more settlers came to the New World, many town meetings were replaced by a system of **indirect democracy,** in which people vote for representatives who work on their behalf.

Many citizens were uncomfortable with the term democracy because it conjured up Hobbesian fears of the people and mob rule. Instead, they preferred the term republic, government rooted in the consent of the governed in which citizens elect leaders to represent their political interests. Today, representative democracies are more commonly called republics, and the words democracy and republic often are used interchangeably. Yet, in the United States, we still pledge allegiance to our "republic," not a democracy.

direct democracy

A system of government in which members of the polity meet to discuss all policy decisions and then agree to abide by majority rule.

indirect democracy

A system of government that gives citizens the opportunity to vote for representatives who work on their behalf.

republic

A government rooted in the consent of the governed; a representative or indirect democracy.

monarchy

A form of government in which power is vested in hereditary kings and queens who govern in the interests of all.

totalitarianism

A form of government in which power resides in a leader who rules according to self-interest and without regard for individual rights and liberties.

oligarchy

A form of government in which the right to participate is conditioned on the possession of wealth, social status, military position, or achievement.

democracy

A system of government that gives power to the people, whether directly or through elected representatives.

political culture

Commonly shared attitudes, beliefs, and core values about how government should operate.

Table 1.1 *What were Aristotle's classifications of government?*

Rule By	In Whose Interest?	
	Public	Self
One	Monarchy	Tyranny
The Few	Aristocracy	Oligarchy
The Many	Polity	Democracy

Source: Aristotle, *Politics* 3, 7.

Types of Government: The People Choose

Early Greek theorists such as Plato and Aristotle tried to categorize governments by who participates, who governs, and how much authority those who govern enjoy. As revealed in Table 1.1, a **monarchy,** the form of government in England from which the colonists fled, is defined by the rule of one hereditary king or queen in the interest of all of his or her subjects. The Framers also rejected adopting an aristocracy, which is defined as government by the few in the service of the many.

The least appealing of Aristotle's classifications of government is **totalitarianism,** a form of government that he considered rule by "tyranny." Tyrants rule their countries to benefit themselves. In tyrannical or totalitarian systems, the leader exercises unlimited power, and individuals have no personal rights or liberties. Generally, these systems tend to be ruled in the name of a particular religion or orthodoxy, an ideology, or a personality cult organized around a supreme leader.

Another unappealing form of government, an **oligarchy,** occurs when a few people rule in their own interest. In an oligarchy, participation in government is conditioned on the possession of wealth, social status, military position, or achievement.

Aristotle called rule of the many for the benefit of all citizens a "polity" and referred to rule of the many to benefit themselves as a "democracy." The term **democracy** is derived from the Greek words *demos* (the people) and *kratia* (power or authority) and may be used to refer to any system of government that gives power to the people, either directly, or indirectly through elected representatives.

THINKING GLOBALLY

Democracies Worldwide

The United States was part of a first wave of democratization that took place worldwide from 1787 to 1926. A second wave followed from 1943 to 1962 and included West Germany, Japan, and India. A third wave from 1974 to 1991 brought democracy to Eastern Europe, Latin America, and Africa. Freedom House presents an annual count of the number of electoral democracies in existence, and this table shows some of its findings:

Year	Number of Electoral Democracies	Percentage of Countries That Are Electoral Democracies
1989	69	41%
1993	108	57%
2000	120	63%
2009	119	62%

- What might explain the large increase in the number of electoral democracies between 1989 and 1993?

- Why might it be harder to create a democracy today than it was during the first wave of democratization?

- Does it matter how many democracies exist in the world? Is it better for American democracy if the majority of governments are democracies?

American Political Culture and the Basic Tenets of American Democracy

★ 1.3 . . . Describe American political culture, and identify the basic tenets of American democracy.

The representative democratic system devised by the Framers to govern the United States is based on a number of underlying concepts and distinguishing characteristics that sometimes conflict with one another. Taken together, these ideas lie at the core of American political culture. More specifically, **political culture** can be defined as commonly shared attitudes, beliefs, and core values about how government should operate. American political culture emphasizes the values of liberty and equality; popular consent, majority rule, and popular sovereignty; individualism; and religious faith and freedom.

Liberty and Equality

Liberty and equality are the most important characteristics of the American republican form of government. The Constitution itself was written to ensure life and liberty. Over the years, however, our concepts of **personal liberty** have changed and evolved from freedom *from* to freedom *to*. The Framers intended Americans to be free from governmental infringements on freedom of religion and speech, from unreasonable searches and seizure, and so on (see **chapter 4**). The addition of the Fourteenth Amendment to the Constitution and its emphasis on due process and on equal protection of the laws as well as the subsequent passage of laws guaranteeing civil rights and liberties, however, expanded Americans' concept of liberty to include demands for freedom to work or go to school without discrimination. Another key characteristic of our democracy is **political equality,** the principle that all citizens are the same in the eyes of the law. Notions of political equality have changed dramatically from the founding time. The U.S. Constitution once treated slaves as equal to only three-fifths of a white man for purposes of assessing state population. No one then could have imagined that in 2008, Barack Obama would be elected president by large margins.

personal liberty
A key characteristic of U.S. democracy. Initially meaning freedom *from* governmental interference, today it includes demands for freedom *to* engage in a variety of practices without governmental interference or discrimination.

political equality
The principle that all citizens are the same in the eyes of the law.

Popular Consent, Majority Rule, and Popular Sovereignty

Popular consent, the principle that governments must draw their powers from the consent of the governed, is another distinguishing characteristic of American democracy. Derived from John Locke's social contract theory, the notion of popular consent was central to the Declaration of Independence. Today, a citizen's willingness to vote represents his or her consent to be governed and is thus an essential premise of democracy.

Majority rule, another core political value, means that officials will be elected and policies will be made into law only if the majority (normally 50 percent of the total votes cast plus one) of citizens in any political unit support such changes. This principle holds for both voters and their elected representatives. Yet, the American system also stresses the need to preserve minority rights, as evidenced by myriad protections of individual rights and liberties found in the Bill of Rights.

Popular sovereignty, or the notion that the ultimate authority in society rests with the people, has its basis in **natural law,** a doctrine that society should be governed by certain ethical principles that are a part of nature and, as such, can be understood by reason. Ultimately, political authority rests with the people, who can create, abolish, or alter their governments. The idea that all governments derive their power from the people is found in the Declaration of Independence and the U.S. Constitution, but the term popular sovereignty did not come into wide use until pre–Civil War debates over slavery. At that time, supporters of popular sovereignty argued that the citizens of new states seeking admission to the union should be able to decide whether or not their states would allow slavery within their borders.

popular consent
The principle that governments must draw their powers from the consent of the governed.

majority rule
The central premise of democracy in which only policies that collectively garner the support of a majority of voters will be made into law.

popular sovereignty
The notion that the ultimate authority in society rests with the people.

natural law
A doctrine that society should be governed by certain ethical principles that are part of nature and, as such, can be understood by reason.

Individualism

Although many core political tenets concern protecting the rights of others, tremendous value is placed on the individual in American democracy, an idea highly valued by the Puritans. This emphasis on individualism makes Americans quite different from citizens of other democracies such as Canada, which practices a group approach to governance. Group-focused societies reject the American emphasis on individuals and try to improve the lives of their citizens by making services and rights available on a group or universal basis. In contrast, in the U.S. system, all individuals are deemed rational and fair and endowed, as Thomas Jefferson proclaimed in the Declaration of Independence, "with certain unalienable rights." Those rights are ones social contact theorists believed were beyond the scope of governmental intervention except in extreme instances.

Religious Faith and Religious Freedom

Religious conflicts in Europe brought many settlers to the New World. Men, women, and their families settled large sections of the East Coast seeking an opportunity to practice their religious faith. However, that faith did not always imply religious tolerance. The clashes that occurred within settlements, as well as within colonies, led the Framers to agree universally that the new nation had to be founded on notions of religious freedom. Religious tolerance, however, has often proved to be more of an ideal than a reality. For example, as the nation wages war in Iraq and Afghanistan and attempts to export democracy, large numbers of Americans consider Islam "a religion that encourages violence" and do not view Islam as having much in common with their own religion.[6]

Functions of American Government

★ **1.4 . . . Explain the functions of American government.**

In attempting "to form a more perfect Union," the Framers, through the Constitution, set out several key functions of American government, as well as governmental guarantees to the people, that have continuing relevance today. As discussed in this section, several of the Framers' ideas centered on their belief that the major function of government was creating mechanisms to allow individuals to solve conflicts in an orderly and peaceful manner. Moreover, it is important to note that each of these principles has faced challenges over time, restricting or expanding the underlying notion of a "more perfect Union."

Establishing Justice

One of the first things expected from any government is the creation of a system of laws that allows individuals to abide by a common set of principles. Societies adhering to the rule of law allow for the rational dispensing of justice by acknowledged legal authorities. Thus, the Constitution authorized Congress to create a federal judicial system to dispense justice. The Bill of Rights also entitles people to a trial by jury, to be informed of the charges against them, and to be tried in a courtroom presided over by an impartial judge. (To learn more about these liberties, see **chapter 4**.)

Insuring Domestic Tranquility

As we will discuss throughout this text, the role of governments in insuring domestic tranquility is a subject of much debate and has been so since the time of Hobbes and Locke. In times of crisis, such as the terrorist attacks of September 11, 2001, the federal government, as well as state and local governments, took extraordinary measures to contain the threat of terrorism from abroad as well as within the United States. Local governments also have police forces, the states have national guards, and the federal government can always call up troops to quell any threats to order.

Providing for the Common Defense

The Framers recognized that one of the major purposes of government is to provide for the defense of its citizens against threats of foreign aggression. Thus, the Constitution calls for the president to be the commander in chief of the armed forces, and Congress is given the authority to raise an army. The defense budget continues to be a considerable and often controversial proportion of all federal outlays.

Promoting the General Welfare

When the Framers added "promoting the general Welfare" to their list of key government functions, they never envisioned how the involvement of the government at all levels would expand so tremendously. In fact, promoting the general welfare was more of an ideal than a mandate for the new national government. Over time, however, our notions of what governments should do have expanded along with the number and size of governments. As we discuss throughout this text, however, there is no universal agreement on the scope of what governments should do.

Securing the Blessings of Liberty

Americans enjoy a wide range of liberties and freedoms and feel free to prosper. They are free to criticize the government and to petition it when they disagree with its policies or have a grievance. This is perhaps the best way to "secure the Blessings of Liberty."

Taken together, these principal functions of government and the guarantees they provide to citizens permeate our lives. Whether it is your ability to obtain a low-interest student loan, buy a formerly prescription-only drug such as Claritin or Plan B over the counter, or be licensed to drive a car at a particular age, government plays a major role. And, without government-sponsored research, we would not have cell phones, the Internet, four-wheel-drive vehicles, or even Velcro.

The Changing American Public

★ 1.5 . . . Analyze the changing characteristics of the American public.

One year after the U.S. Constitution was ratified, fewer than 4 million people lived in the thirteen states. Most were united by a single language and a shared Protestant-Christian heritage, and those who voted were white male property owners. The Constitution mandated that each of the sixty-five members of the original House of Representatives should represent 30,000 people.

As the nation grew westward, hundreds of thousands of new immigrants came to America, often in waves, fleeing war or famine or simply in search of a better life. Although the geographic size of the United States has remained stable since the addition of Alaska and Hawaii as states in 1959, in 2010 there were more than 309 million Americans, and a single member of the House of Representatives from Montana represented more than 974,000 people. (To learn more about population growth, see Figure 1.2.)

Racial and Ethnic Composition

The American population has been altered constantly by the arrival of immigrants from various regions—Western Europeans fleeing religious persecution in the 1600s to early 1700s, slaves brought in chains from Africa in the late 1700s, Chinese laborers arriving to work on the railroads following the Gold Rush in 1848, Irish Catholics escaping the potato famine in the 1850s, Northern and Eastern Europeans from the 1880s to 1910s, and most recently, South and Southeast Asians, Cubans, and Mexicans, among others.

Figure 1.2 *How has the U.S. population grown over time?*
Since around 1890, when large numbers of immigrants began arriving in America, the United States has seen a sharp increase in population. The major reasons for this increase are new births and increased lifespans, although immigration is also a contributing factor.
Source: U.S. Census Bureau Population Projections, www.census.gov.

Figure 1.3 *How does the racial and ethnic composition of America today differ from that of 1967?*

Source: U.S. Census Bureau, *2010 Statistical Abstract of the United States.*

1967

2008

- White, Non-Hispanic
- Hispanic
- Black
- Asian and Pacific Islander
- All other

Immigration to the United States peaked in the first decade of the 1900s, when nearly 9 million people, many of them from Eastern Europe, entered the country. The United States did not see another major wave of immigration until the late 1980s, when nearly 2 million immigrants were admitted in one year.

Immigration has led to significant changes in American racial and ethnic composition. As revealed in Figure 1.3, the racial and ethnic balance in America has changed dramatically since 1967, with the proportion of Hispanics growing at the quickest rate and taking over as the second most common racial or ethnic group in the United States.* More importantly, what the figure does not show is that 40 percent of Americans under age twenty-five are members of a minority group, a fact that will have a significant impact not only on the demographics of the American polity but also on how America "looks." (To learn more about the debate about immigrant assimilation, see Join the Debate: Should Immigrants Be Assimilated into American Political Culture?)

Aging

Just as the racial and ethnic composition of the American population is changing, so too is the average age. "For decades, the U.S. was described as a nation of the young because the number of persons under the age of twenty greatly outnumber[ed] those sixty-five and older," but this is no longer the case.[7] Because of changes in patterns of fertility, life expectancy, and immigration, the nation's age profile has changed drastically.

---

* In this text, we have made the decision to refer to those of Spanish, Latin American, Mexican, Cuban, and Puerto Rican descent as Hispanic instead of Latino/a. Although this label is not accepted universally by the community it describes, Hispanic is the term used by the U.S. government when reporting federal data. In addition, a 2008 survey sponsored by the Pew Charitable Trusts found that 36 percent of those who responded preferred the term Hispanic, 21 percent preferred the term Latino, and the remainder had no preference. See www.pewhispanic.org.

Join the DEBATE | Should Immigrants Be Assimilated into American Political Culture?

One of the greatest strengths of the United States historically has been its ability to absorb and assimilate, or integrate into the social body, the diverse people who enter its borders. Indeed, the United States has long been described as a "melting pot" that collectively embraces immigrants and blends them into the one shared American culture based on the principles of equality, individual rights, and government by consent. However, according to authors such as Samuel Huntington, a new wave of immigrants coming from Mexico and Latin America is less likely to assimilate into American political culture.[a] This has resulted in the creation of linguistic and cultural enclaves, or communities within the United States (areas of Los Angeles or Miami, for example), in which there is no need for those who live there to learn the language, history, and political values of America.

Some observers worry that the failure of America to assimilate this new wave of immigrants may foster a type of dual national or cultural allegiance that could weaken ties to American core values and undermine the distinctive features of American political culture. This trend raises serious questions. Are American core ideals so exceptional that only people who share those values should be members of the political community? What are the implications for American politics of assimilation or lack of assimilation by immigrants?

To develop an ARGUMENT FOR the assimilation of immigrants into American political culture, think about how:

- **Assimilation provides the foundation for a common identity, which is necessary to create a political community.** In what ways would competing sources of identity weaken individuals' attachments to one another and their government? How does having a stronger political community facilitate more egalitarian policy making?
- **Previous generations of immigrants successfully assimilated into American political culture.** What do the experiences of early Irish, Polish, German, Japanese, and Chinese immigrants to America show us about the benefits of assimilation? How did these immigrants overcome language and cultural barriers to become Americans?
- **The United States has been called a melting pot of immigrants.** How has the assimilation of immigrants historically strengthened and transformed American political culture? How did successive waves of immigrants move the United States toward the realization of the ideals espoused in the Declaration of Independence?

To develop an ARGUMENT AGAINST the assimilation of immigrants into American political culture, think about how:

- **Principles such as personal liberty and individualism are central to American political culture.** In what ways are decisions about what language to speak, what cultural traditions and customs to practice, and what values to hold fundamentally individual decisions that should not be subject to governmental dictates? Why does it matter if citizens speak a different language if they share the same fundamental values as other Americans?
- **The major public policy challenges facing the United States have little to do with the assimilation (or lack of assimilation) of immigrants.** Would the assimilation of immigrants fundamentally change debates over the wars in Iraq and Afghanistan, or the state of the U.S. budget? How might forced assimilation actually complicate policymaking?
- **Multiculturalism has benefits for society.** By emphasizing the need for assimilation rather than embracing diversity, do we deprive ourselves of the benefits of a multicultural society? Should American values and identity evolve with the times?

---

[a] See, for example, Samuel Huntington, *Who Are We? The Challenges to America's National Identity* (New York: Simon and Schuster, 2004).

When the United States was founded, the average life expectancy was thirty-five years; by 2010, it was eighty-one years for women and seventy-six years for men.

An aging population places a host of costly demands on the government. In 2008, the first of the Baby Boomers (the 76.8 million people who were born between 1946 and 1964) reached age sixty-two and qualified for Social Security; in 2011, they will reach sixty-five and qualify for Medicare.[8] An aging America also poses a great financial burden on working Americans, whose proportion of the population is rapidly declining.

These dramatic changes could potentially pit younger people against older people and result in dramatic cuts in benefits to the elderly and increased taxes for younger workers. Moreover, the elderly often vote against programs favored by younger voters, such as money for new schools and other items that they no longer view as important. At the same time, younger voters are less likely to support some things important to seniors, such as Medicare and prescription drug reform.

Religious Beliefs

As we have discussed throughout this chapter, many of the first settlers came to America to pursue their religious beliefs free from governmental intervention. Though these early immigrants were members of a number of different churches, all identified with the Christian religion. Moreover, they viewed the Indians' belief systems, which included multiple gods, to be savage and unholy. Their Christian values permeated American social and political systems.

While many people still view the United States as a Christian nation, a great number of religious groups—including Jews, Buddhists, Hindus, and Muslims—have established roots in the country. With this growth have come different political and social demands. For example, evangelical Christians regularly demand that school boards adopt textbooks with particular viewpoints. In 2010, the Texas Board of Education required that textbooks use the term "capitalism" instead of "free enterprise system," question the Framers' concept of a purely secular government, and present conservative beliefs in a much more positive light.

Regional Growth and Expansion

Regional sectionalism emerged almost immediately in the United States. Settlers from the Virginia colony southward were largely focused on commerce. Those seeking various forms of religious freedom populated many of the settlements to the North. That search for political freedom also came with puritanical values so that New England evolved differently from the South in many aspects of culture.

One of the most long-standing and dramatic regional differences in the United States continues to be that between the South and the North. During the Constitutional Convention, most Southerners staunchly advocated a weak national government. The Civil War was later fought in part because of basic differences in philosophy toward government as well as toward slavery, which many Northerners opposed. As we know from the results of modern political polling, the South has continued to lag behind the rest of the nation in support for civil rights while continuing to favor return of power to the states at the expense of the national government.

The West, too, has always appeared different from the rest of the United States. Populated first by those seeking free land and then by many chasing dreams of gold, the American West has often been seen as "wild." Its population today is a study in contrasts. Some people have moved there to avoid city life and have an anti-government bias. Other Westerners are very interested in issues such as water rights and seek governmental solutions to their problems.

Significant differences in attitudes are also seen in rural versus urban areas. Those who live in rural areas are much more conservative than those who live in large cities.[9] One need only look at a map of the vote distribution in the 2008 presidential election to see stark differences in candidate appeal. Barack Obama carried almost every large city in America; John McCain carried 53 percent of the rural and small-town voters as well as most of America's heartland.[10] Republicans won the South, the West, and much of the Midwest; Democrats carried the Northeast and West Coast.

Family and Family Size

In the past, familial gender roles were clearly defined. Women did housework and men worked in the fields. Large families were imperative; children were a source of cheap farm labor. Industrialization and knowledge of birth control methods, however, began to put a dent in the size of American families by the early 1900s. No longer needing children to work for the survival of the household, couples began to limit the sizes of their families.

By 1949, 49 percent of those polled thought that four or more children was the "ideal" family size; in 2007, only 9 percent favored large families, and 56 percent responded that no children to two children was "best."[11] In 1940, nine out of ten households were traditional family households. By 2008, just 69.9 percent of children under eighteen lived with both parents. In fact, over 25 percent of children under eighteen lived with just one of their parents; the majority of those children lived with their mother. Moreover, by 2008, over 27 percent of all households consisted of a single person, a trend that is in part illustrative of the aging American population and declining marriage rate.

Political Ideology

⭐ **1.6 ... Assess the role of political ideology in shaping American politics.**

Political ideologies are sets or systems of beliefs that shape the thinking of individuals and how they view the world, especially in regard to issues of "race, nationality, the role and function of government, the relations between men and women, human responsibility for the natural environment, and many other matters."[12] They have been recognized increasingly as a potent political force. Isaiah Berlin, a noted historian and philosopher, noted that two factors above all others shaped human history in the twentieth century: "one is science and technology; the other is ideological battles—totalitarian tyrannies of both right and left and the explosions of nationalism, racism, and religious bigotry that the most perceptive social thinkers of the nineteenth century failed to predict."[13]

Political scientists note that ideologies perform four key functions:

1. *Explanation.* Ideologies can provide us with reasons for why social and political conditions are the way they are, especially in time of crisis.
2. *Evaluation.* Ideologies can provide the standards for evaluating social conditions and political institutions and events.
3. *Orientation.* Much like a compass, ideologies provide individuals with an orientation toward issues and a position within the world.
4. *Political Program.* Ideologies help people to make political choices and guide their political actions.

Finding a Political Ideology

The four functions of ideology discussed above clearly have real-world implications. Religious, philosophical, and cultural beliefs can become cohesive ideologies that create natural groups within society and lead to political conflict. In America, one most often hears about conservative, liberal, and moderate political ideologies. (To learn more about the distribution of ideologies in the United States, see Figure 1.4.)

CONSERVATIVES **Conservatives** tend to believe that a government is best when it governs least. They want less government, especially in terms of regulation of the economy. Conservatives favor local and state action over federal intervention, and they emphasize fiscal responsibility. Conservatives are also likely to believe that

political ideology
The coherent set of values and beliefs about the purpose and scope of government held by groups and individuals.

conservative
One who believes that a government is best that governs least and that big government should not infringe on individual, personal, and economic rights.

Figure 1.4 *What are Americans' political ideologies?*

Source: Roper Center at the University of Connecticut, *Public Opinion Online*, Roper iPoll.

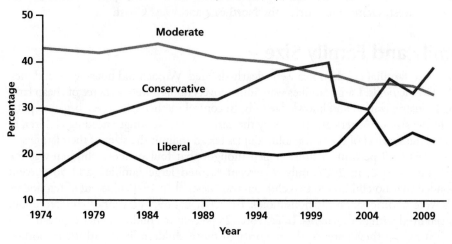

domestic problems such as homelessness, poverty, and discrimination are better dealt with by the private sector than by the government.

Since the 1970s, a growing number of **social conservative** voters (many with religious ties, such as the evangelical or Religious Right) increasingly have affected politics and policies in the United States. Social conservatives believe that moral decay must be stemmed and that traditional moral teachings should be supported and furthered by the government. Social conservatives support government intervention to regulate sexual and social behavior and have mounted effective efforts to restrict abortion and ban same-sex marriage. While a majority of social conservatives are evangelical Protestants and Roman Catholics, some Jews and many Muslims are also social conservatives. Others are not affiliated with a traditional religion.

LIBERALS   A **liberal** is one who seeks to change the political, economic, and social status quo to foster the development of equality and the well-being of individuals.[14] The meaning of the word liberal has changed over time, but in the modern United States, liberals generally value equality over other aspects of shared political culture. They are supportive of well-funded government social welfare programs that seek to protect individuals from economic disadvantages or to correct past injustices, and they generally oppose government efforts to regulate private behavior or infringe on civil rights and liberties.

MODERATES   In general, a **moderate** is one who takes a relatively centrist view on most political issues. Aristotle actually favored moderate politics, believing that domination in the center was better than any extremes, whether dealing with issues of wealth, poverty, or the role of government.

Problems with Ideological Labels

In a perfect world, liberals would be liberal and conservatives would be conservative. Studies reveal, however, that many people who call themselves conservative actually take fairly liberal positions on many policy issues. In fact, anywhere from 20 percent to 60 percent of people will take a traditionally conservative position on one issue and a traditionally liberal position on another.[15]

Many also view themselves as **libertarians.** Political scientists generally do not measure for this choice. Libertarians believe in limited government and decry governmental interference with personal liberties.

---

social conservative

One who believes that traditional moral teachings should be supported and furthered by the government.

liberal

One who favors governmental involvement in the economy and in the provision of social services and who takes an activist role in protecting the rights of women, the elderly, minorities, and the environment.

moderate

A person who takes a relatively centrist or middle-of-the-road view on most political issues.

libertarian

One who believes in limited government and no governmental interference in personal liberties.

What Happens to the American Dream in a Recession?

By Katharine Q. Seelye

May 7, 2009
New York Times
www.nytimes.com

. . . Although the nation has plunged into its deepest recession since the Great Depression, 72 percent of Americans in this nationwide survey said they believed it is possible to start out poor in the United States, work hard and become rich — a classic definition of the American dream.

And yet only 44 percent said they had actually achieved the American dream, although 31 percent said they expect to attain it within their lifetime. Only 20 percent have given up on ever reaching it. Those 44 percent might not sound like much, but it is an increase over the 32 percent who said they had achieved the American dream four years ago, when the economy was in much better shape.

Compared with four years ago, fewer people now say they are better off than their parents were at their age or that their children will be better off than they are.

So even though their economic outlook is worse, more people are saying they have either achieved the dream or expect to do so.

What gives?

We asked Barry Glassner, who is a professor of sociology at the University of Southern California and studies contemporary culture and beliefs.

"You want to hold on to your dream even more when times are hard," he said. "And if you want to hold on to it, then you better define it differently."

In other words, people are shifting their definition of the American dream. And the poll—conducted on April 1 to 5 with 998 adults, with a margin of sampling error of plus or minus 3 percentage points—indicated just that.

The Times and CBS News asked this same open-ended question four years ago and again last month: "What does the phrase 'The American dream' mean to you?"

Four years ago, 19 percent of those surveyed supplied answers that related to financial security and a steady job, and 20 percent gave answers that related to freedom and opportunity.

Now, fewer people are pegging their dream to material success and more are pegging it to abstract values. Those citing financial security dropped to 11 percent, and those citing freedom and opportunity expanded to 27 percent. . . .

Critical Thinking Questions

1. What does the American dream mean to you?
2. Do you agree that the American dream is more important during a recession? Why or why not?
3. How does achieving the American dream affect the demands citizens place on government?

TOWARD REFORM: People and Politics

★ **1.7 . . . Characterize changes in Americans' attitudes toward and expectations of government.**

As the American population has changed over time, so has the American political process. **Politics** is the study of who gets what, when, and how—the process by which policy decisions get made. This process is deeply affected by the evolving nature of the American citizenry. Competing demands often lead to political struggles, which create winners and losers within the system. A loser today, however, may be a winner tomorrow in the ever changing world of politics. The political ideologies of those in control of Congress, the executive, and state houses also have a huge impact on who gets what, when, and how.

Nevertheless, American political culture continues to bind together citizens. Many Americans also share the common goal of achieving the **American dream**—an American ideal of a happy and successful life, which often includes wealth, a house, a better life for one's children, and for some, the ability to grow up to be president. (To learn more about the American Dream, see Politics Now: What Happens to the American Dream in a Recession?)

politics
The study of who gets what, when, and how—or how policy decisions are made.

American dream
An American ideal of a happy, successful life, which often includes wealth, a house, a better life for one's children, and for some, the ability to grow up to be president.

ANALYZING VISUALS

Faith in Institutions

This line graph shows the percentages of Americans declaring they had a "great deal" of confidence in American institutions. Examine the graph and answer the questions.

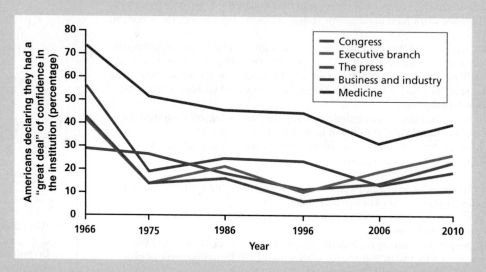

- Which institution received the highest overall ratings from 1966 to 2010? The lowest overall ratings?
- Congress, the executive branch, and business and industry all experienced a significant drop in ratings in 1975. What political events may have contributed to Americans' lack of faith in these institutions at that time?
- Why do you think faith in institutions has declined over time?

Source: *Newsweek* (January 8, 1996): 32; *Public Perspective* 8 (February/March 1994): 4; Lexis-Nexis RPOLL; *Washington Post* (June 13, 2006): A2; www.pollingreport.com.

Redefining Our Expectations

In roughly the first 150 years of our nation's history, the federal government had few responsibilities, and citizens had few expectations of it beyond national defense, printing money, and collecting tariffs and taxes. The state governments were generally far more powerful than the federal government in matters affecting the everyday lives of Americans.

As the nation and its economy grew in size and complexity, the federal government took on more responsibilities, such as regulating some businesses, providing poverty relief, and inspecting food. With these new responsibilities come greater demands on government.

Today, many Americans lack faith in the country's institutions. And, a 2010 poll revealed that nearly six in ten Americans think the country is headed in the wrong direction.[16] These concerns make it even easier for citizens to blame the government for all kinds of woes—personal as well as societal—or to fail to credit governments for the things they do well. Many Americans, for example, enjoy a remarkably high standard of living, and much of it is due to governmental programs and protections. (To learn more about Americans' confidence in institutions, see Analyzing Visuals: Faith in Institutions.)

Even in the short time between when you get up in the morning and when you leave for classes or work, the government—or its rulings or regulations—pervades your life. National or state governments, for example, set the standards for whether you wake up on Eastern, Central, Mountain, or Pacific Time. The national government regulates the airwaves and licenses the radio and television broadcasts you might listen to as you eat and get dressed. States, too, regulate and tax telecommunications. Whether the water you use as you brush your teeth contains fluoride is a state or local governmental issue. The federal Food and Drug Administration inspects your breakfast meat and sets standards for the advertising on your cereal box, orange juice carton, and other food packaging.

The current frustration and dissatisfaction with politics and government may be just another phase, as the changing American body politic seeks to redefine its ideas about and expectations of government and how it can be reformed. This process is likely to define politics well into the future, but the individualistic nature of the American system will have long-lasting consequences on how that redefinition can be accomplished. Many Americans, for example, say they want less government, but as they get older, they don't want less Social Security. They want lower taxes and better roads, but they don't want to pay road tolls.

In this text, we present you with the tools that you need to understand how our political system has evolved and to prepare you to understand the changes that are yet to come. If you approach the study of American government and politics with an open mind, it should help you become a better citizen. We hope that you learn to ask questions, to understand how various issues have come to be important, and to see why a particular law was enacted, how it was implemented, and if it is in need of reform. We further hope that, with such understanding, you will learn not to accept at face value everything you see on the television news, hear on the radio, or read in the newspaper and on the Internet, especially in the blogosphere. Work to understand your government, and use your vote and other forms of participation to help ensure that your government works for you.

What Should I Have LEARNED?

Now that you have read this chapter, you should be able to:

⭐ **1.1 Trace the origins of American government, p. 4.**

American government is rooted in the cultures and experiences of early European colonists as well as interactions with the indigenous populations of the New World. The first colonists sought wealth. Later pilgrims came seeking religious freedom. The colonies set up systems of government that differed widely in terms of form, role, and function. As they developed, they sought more independence from the British monarchy.

⭐ **1.2 Show how European political thought provided the theoretical foundations of American government, p. 7.**

The ideas of social contract theorists John Locke, Charles-Louis, the Second Baron of Montesquieu, Thomas Hobbes, and Jean-Jacques Rousseau have had continuing implications for our ideas of the proper role of government in our indirect democracy. They held the belief that people are free and equal by natural right and therefore must give their consent to be governed.

⭐ **1.3 Describe American political culture, and identify the basic tenets of American democracy, p. 10.**

Political culture is a group's commonly shared attitudes, beliefs, and core values about how government should operate. Key tenets of Americans' shared political culture are liberty and equality; popular consent, majority rule and popular sovereignty; individualism; and religious freedom.

⭐ **1.4 Explain the functions of American government, p. 12.**

The functions of American government include establishing justice, insuring domestic tranquility, providing for the common defense, promoting the general welfare, and securing the blessings of liberty.

⭐ **1.5 Analyze the changing characteristics of the American public, p. 13.**

Several characteristics of the American electorate can help us understand how the system continues to evolve and change. Among these are changes in size and population, racial and ethnic composition, age, religious beliefs, regional growth and expansion, and family and family size.

⭐ **1.6 Assess the role of political ideology in shaping American politics, p. 17.**

Ideologies, the belief systems that shape the thinking of individuals and how they view the world, affect people's ideas about government. The major categories of political ideology in America are conservative, liberal, and moderate.

⭐ **1.7 Characterize changes in Americans' attitudes toward and expectations of government, p. 19.**

Shifts in population have created controversy in the American electorate throughout America's history. Americans have high and often unrealistic expectations of government, yet often fail to appreciate how much their government actually does for them. Americans' failing trust in institutions also explains some of the apathy among the American electorate.

Test Yourself: The Political Landscape

⭐ **1.1 Trace the origins of American government, p. 4.**

Which of the following settlements was not founded for religious reasons?
A. Pennsylvania
B. Portsmouth
C. New Amsterdam
D. Massachusetts Bay Colony
E. Boston

⭐ **1.2 Show how European political thought provided the theoretical foundations of American government, p. 7.**

The Declaration of Independence was most directly influenced by the ideas of which political philosopher?
A. John Locke.
B. Thomas Hobbes.
C. Isaac Newton.
D. Puritans.
E. Jean-Jacques Rousseau.

⭐ **1.3 Describe American political culture, and identify the basic tenets of American democracy, p. 10.**

Natural law forms the basis for which of the following principles?
A. Majority rule
B. Political equality
C. Popular sovereignty
D. Indirect democracy
E. Civil law

⭐ **1.4 Explain the functions of American government, p. 12.**

Which of the following is not a function of American government, as outlined in the Preamble of the U.S. Constitution?
A. Providing for the common defense
B. Promoting the general welfare
C. Securing the blessings of privacy
D. Establishing justice
E. Insuring domestic tranquility

⭐ **1.5 Analyze the changing characteristics of the American public, p. 13.**

Which of the following statements best describes recent population trends in the United States?
A. The size of the U.S. population has leveled out in the past twenty years.
B. African Americans have consistently comprised the second largest minority group.
C. Couples favor having more children than in the mid-twentieth century.
D. The average age in the United States has increased in recent years.
E. Nearly 40 percent of American children today live with only one parent.

⭐ **1.6 Assess the role of political ideology in shaping American politics, p. 17.**

Since 1974, most Americans have identified themselves as
A. conservative.
B. liberal.
C. libertarian.
D. moderate.
E. socialist.

⭐ **1.7 Characterize changes in Americans' attitudes toward and expectations of government, p. 19.**

The ideal of being able to live a happy and successful life in the United States is often called
A. the American expectation.
B. the American dream.
C. a constitutional right.
D. the American Creed.
E. impossible to reach.

Essay Questions

1. Describe the differences between John Locke's and Thomas Hobbes's views on the ideal form of government.
2. What are the implications of the changing demographics of the U.S. population?
3. Why do Americans hold unrealistically high expectations of government and its ability to institute reform?

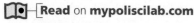 **Exercises**

Apply what you learned in this chapter on MyPoliSciLab.

Read on **mypoliscilab.com**

   eText: Chapter 1

✔**Study** and **Review** on **mypoliscilab.com**

   Pre-Test
   Post-Test
   Chapter Exam
   Flashcards

👁**Watch** on **mypoliscilab.com**

   Video: Facebook Privacy Concerns
   Video: The President Addresses School Children
   Video: Mexico Border Security
   Video: The Bailout Hearings
   Video: Vaccines: Mandatory Protection
   Video: Who is in the Middle Class?
   Video: America's Aging Population

⊕┤**Explore** on **mypoliscilab.com**

Simulation: What Are American Civic Values?
Comparative: Comparing Political Landscapes
Timeline: Major Technological Innovations That
Have Changed the Political Landscape
Visual Literacy: Using the Census to Understand
Who Americans Are
Visual Literacy: Who Are Liberals and Conservatives?
What's the Difference?

Key Terms

American dream, p. 19
conservative, p. 17
democracy, p. 10
direct democracy, p. 9
government, p. 7
indirect democracy, p. 9
liberal, p. 18
libertarian, p. 18
majority rule, p. 11

Mayflower Compact, p. 7
moderate, p. 18
monarchy, p. 10
natural law, p. 11
oligarchy, p. 10
personal liberty, p. 11
political culture, p. 10
political equality, p. 11
political ideology, p. 17

politics, p. 19
popular consent, p. 11
popular sovereignty, p. 11
republic, p. 9
social conservative, p. 18
social contract, p. 7
social contract theory, p. 7
totalitarianism, p. 10

To Learn More on the Political Landscape

In the Library

Almond, Gabriel A., and Sidney Verba. *Civic Culture: Political Attitudes and Democracy in Five Nations,* new ed. Ann Arbor: UMI Research Press, 1990.

Ball, Terence, and Richard Dagger. *Political Ideologies and the Democratic Ideal,* 8th ed. New York: Longman, 2010.

Cullen, Jim. *The American Dream: A Short History of an Idea that Shaped a Nation.* New York: Oxford University Press, 2004.

Dahl, Robert A. *Polyarchy: Participation and Opposition.* New Haven, CT: Yale University Press, 1972.

Fiorina, Morris P., Samuel J. Abrams, and Jeremy C. Pope. *Culture War? The Myth of a Polarized America,* 3rd ed. New York: Longman, 2010.

Fournier, Ron, Douglas B. Sosnick, and Matthew J. Dowd. *Applebee's America: How Successful Political, Business, and Religious Leaders Connect with the New American Community.* New York: Simon and Schuster, 2007.

Jamieson, Kathleen Hall. *Everything You Think You Know About Politics...and Why You're Wrong.* New York: Basic Books, 2000.

Hobbes, Thomas. *Leviathan.* Ed. Richard Tuck. New York: Cambridge University Press, 1996.

Hochschild, Jennifer L. *Facing Up to the American Dream: Race, Class, and the Soul of the Nation.* Princeton, NJ: Princeton University Press, 1996.

Locke, John. *Two Treatises of Government.* Ed. Peter Lasleti. New York: Cambridge University Press, 1988.

Nye, Joseph S., Jr. *The Paradox of American Power: Why the World's Superpower Can't Go It Alone.* New York: Oxford University Press, 2002.

Putnam, Robert D. *Bowling Alone: Collapse and Revival of the American Community.* New York: Simon and Schuster, 2001.

Rosenfeld, Michael J. *The Age of Independence: Interracial Unions, Same Sex Unions, and the Changing American Family.* Cambridge, MA: Harvard University Press, 2009.

Skocpol, Theda, and Morris P. Fiorina, eds. *Civic Engagement in American Democracy.* Washington, DC: Brookings Institution Press, 1999.

Verba, Sidney, Kay Schlozman, and Henry Brady. *Voice and Equality: Civic Volunteerism in American Politics,* 2nd ed. Cambridge, MA: Harvard University Press, 2002.

On the Web

To learn more about your political ideology, go to the Political Compass at **www.politicalcompass.org.**

To learn about the policy positions and attitudes of American conservatives, go to the American Conservative Union at **www.conservative.org.**

To learn more about the policy positions and attitudes of American liberals, go to the Liberal Oasis at **www.liberaloasis.com.**

To learn more about shifts in the American population, go to the U.S. Census Bureau at **www.census.gov.**

2 The Constitution

At age eighteen, all American citizens are eligible to vote in state and national elections. This has not always been the case. It took an amendment to the U.S. Constitution—one of only seventeen that have been added since the Bill of Rights was ratified in 1791—to guarantee the vote to those under twenty-one years of age.

In 1942, during World War II, Representative Jennings Randolph (D–WV) proposed a constitutional amendment that would lower the voting age to eighteen, believing that since young men were old enough to be drafted to fight and die for their country, they also should be allowed to vote. He continued to reintroduce his proposal during every session of Congress, and in 1954, President Dwight D. Eisenhower endorsed the idea in his State of the Union Address. Presidents Lyndon B. Johnson and Richard M. Nixon—men who had also called upon the nation's young men to fight on foreign shores—echoed his appeal.[1]

During the 1960s, the campaign to lower the voting age took on a new sense of urgency as hundreds of thousands of young men were drafted to fight in Vietnam, and thousands of men and women were killed in action. "Old Enough to Fight, Old Enough to Vote," was one popular slogan of the day. By 1970, four states–the U.S. Constitution allows states to set the eligibility requirements for their voters— had lowered their voting ages to eighteen. Later that year, Congress passed legislation lowering the voting age in national, state, and local elections to eighteen.

The state of Oregon, however, challenged the constitutionality of the law in court, arguing that Congress had not been given the authority to establish a uniform voting age in state and local government elections by the Constitution. The U.S. Supreme Court agreed.[2] The decision from the sharply divided Court meant that those under age twenty-one could vote in national elections but that the states were free to prohibit them from voting in state and local elections. The decision presented the states with a logistical nightmare. States setting

When the U.S. Constitution was written in 1787, only white property owning males were allowed to vote. Today, suffrage has been broadly expanded to include African Americans, women, and people age eighteen and over, shown on the right.

the voting age at twenty-one would be forced to keep two sets of registration books: one for voters twenty-one and over, and one for voters under twenty-one.

Jennings Randolph, by then a senator from West Virginia, reintroduced his proposed amendment to lower the national voting age to eighteen.[3] Within three months of the Supreme Court's decision, Congress sent the proposed Twenty-Sixth Amendment to the states for their ratification. The required three-fourths of the states approved the amendment within three months—making its adoption on June 30, 1971 the quickest in the history of the constitutional amending process.

While young people traditionally have not exercised their Twenty-Sixth Amendment rights in large numbers, there seems to be some indication that voter turnout among those 18 to 24 is on the rise. Record numbers of young voters went to the polls in the 2008 presidential election; many credited discussions on Facebook and other social networking sites for

their political interest and activism. The votes of young people also played an important role in electing Barack Obama. In 2010, however, some commentators attributed Democratic losses to low voter turnout among young people. Only 11 percent of those who voted were under age twenty-nine.

What Should I Know About . . .
After reading this chapter, you should be able to

★ **2.1** Trace the historical developments that led to the colonists' break with Great Britain and the emergence of the new American nation, p. 26.

★ **2.2** Identify the key components of the Articles of Confederation and the reasons why it failed, p. 31.

★ **2.3** Outline the issues and compromises that were central to the writing of the U.S. Constitution, p. 33.

★ **2.4** Analyze the underlying principles of the U.S. Constitution, p. 37.

★ **2.5** Explain the conflicts that characterized the drive for ratification of the U.S. Constitution, p. 42.

★ **2.6** Distinguish between the methods for proposing and ratifying amendments to the U.S. Constitution, p. 45.

The U.S. Constitution was never intended to be easy to change. The process by which it could be changed or amended was made time consuming and difficult. Over the years, thousands of amendments—including those to prohibit child labor, provide equal rights for women, grant statehood to the District of Columbia, balance the federal budget, and ban flag burning—have been debated or sent to the states for their approval, only to die slow deaths. Only twenty-seven amendments have successfully made their way into the Constitution. What the Framers wrote in Philadelphia has continued to work, in spite of increasing demands on and dissatisfaction with our national government. Although Americans often clamor for reform, perhaps they are happier with the system of government created by the Framers than they realize.

The ideas that went into the making of the Constitution and the ways that it has evolved to address the problems of a growing and changing nation are at the core of our discussion in this chapter.

- First, we will examine *the roots of the new American nation* and the circumstances surrounding the adoption of the Declaration of Independence and the colonists' break with Great Britain.

- Second, we will discuss *the first attempt at American government* created by *the Articles of Confederation.*

- Third, we will examine the circumstances surrounding *writing the U.S. Constitution* in Philadelphia.

- Fourth, we will review the results of the Framers' efforts: *the U.S. Constitution.*

- Fifth, we will present *the drive for ratification of the U.S. Constitution.*

- Finally, we will address *methods of amending the U.S. Constitution.*

ROOTS OF the New American Nation

2.1 ... Trace the historical developments that led to the colonists' break with Great Britain and the emergence of the new American nation.

Starting in the early seventeenth century, colonists came to the New World for a variety of reasons. Often, as detailed in **chapter 1**, it was to escape religious persecution. Others came seeking a new start on a continent where land was plentiful. The independence and diversity of the settlers in the New World made the question of how best to rule the new colonies a tricky one. More than merely an ocean separated Great Britain from the colonies; the colonists were independent people, and it soon became clear that the crown could not govern its subjects in the colonies with the same close rein used at home. King James I thus allowed some local participation in decision making through arrangements such as the first elected colonial assembly, the Virginia House of Burgesses, formed in 1619, and the elected General Court that governed the Massachusetts Bay Colony after 1629. Almost all of the colonists agreed that the king ruled by divine right, but British monarchs allowed the colonists significant liberties in terms of self-government, religious practices, and economic organization. For 140 years, this system worked fairly well.[4]

By the early 1760s, however, a century and a half of physical separation, development of colonial industry, and the relative self-governance of the colonies led to weakening ties with—and loyalties to—the crown. By this time, each of the thirteen colonies had drafted its own written constitution, which provided the fundamental rules or laws for each colony. Moreover, many of the most oppressive British traditions—feudalism, a rigid class system, and the absolute authority of the king—were absent in the New World. Land was abundant. The guild and craft systems that severely limited entry into many skilled professions in Great Britain did not exist in the colonies. Although religion was central to the lives of most colonists, there was no single state church.

Trade and Taxation

Mercantilism, an economic theory designed to increase a nation's wealth through the development of commercial industry and a favorable balance of trade, justified Britain's maintenance of strict import/export controls on the colonies. After 1650, for example, the British Parliament passed a series of navigation acts to prevent its chief rival, Holland, from trading with the British colonies. From 1650 until well into the 1700s, Britain tried to regulate colonial imports and exports, believing that it was critical to export more goods than it imported as a way of increasing the gold and silver in its treasury. These policies, however, were difficult to enforce and were widely ignored by the colonists, who saw little self-benefit in them. Thus, for years, an unwritten agreement existed. The colonists relinquished to the crown and the British Parliament the authority to regulate trade and conduct international affairs, but they retained the right to levy their own taxes.

This fragile agreement was soon put to the test. The French and Indian War, fought from 1756 to 1763 on the western frontier of the colonies and in Canada, was part of a global war initiated by the British, then the greatest power in the world. This American phase of what was called the Seven Years War was fought between Britain and France with Indian allies. In North America, its immediate cause was the rival claims of those two European nations for the lands between the Allegheny Mountains and the Mississippi River. The Treaty of Paris, signed in 1763, not only signaled the end of this war but also greatly increased the size of land claimed by Great Britain in North America. France ceded to Great Britain the control of all lands east of the Mississippi River. The colonists expected that with the Indian problems on the western frontier now under control, westward expansion could begin in earnest. In 1763, however, they were shocked when the crown decreed that the colonists were not to expand their settlements west of the Allegheny Mountains. Parliament believed that expansion into Indian territory would lead to new expenditures for the defense of the settlers, draining the British treasury.

To raise money to pay for the war as well as the expenses of administering the colonies, Parliament enacted the Sugar Act in 1764. This act placed taxes on sugar, wine, coffee, and other products commonly exported to the colonies. A postwar colonial depression heightened resentment of the tax. Major protest, however, failed to materialize until imposition of the Stamp Act by the British Parliament in 1765. This law required that all paper items, from playing cards to books, bought and sold in the colonies carry a stamp mandated by the crown. The tax itself was not offensive to the colonists. However, they feared this act would establish a precedent for the British Parliament not only to regulate commerce in the colonies, but also to raise revenues from the colonists without the approval of the colonial governments. Around the colonies, the political cry "no taxation without representation" became prominent.

Colonists were outraged. Men throughout the colonies organized the Sons of Liberty, under the leadership of Samuel Adams and Patrick Henry. Women formed the Daughters of Liberty. Protests against the Stamp Act were violent and loud. Riots, often led by the Sons of Liberty, broke out. They were especially violent in Boston, where the colonial governor's home was burned by an angry mob, and British stamp agents charged with collecting the tax were threatened. A boycott of goods needing the stamps as well as British imports also was organized.

mercantilism
An economic theory designed to increase a nation's wealth through the development of commercial industry and a favorable balance of trade.

TIMELINE: Key Events Leading to American Independence

1763 Treaty of Paris—The treaty ends the French and Indian War—France cedes its claims to any lands east of the Mississippi River.

1767 Townshend Acts—These acts passed by the British Parliament impose duties on a host of colonial imports, including the colonists' favorite drink, tea.

1765 Stamp Act Congress—Meeting convenes in New York City at the urging of Samuel Adams.

1770 Boston Massacre—British troops open fire on a mob, killing five colonists.

Who was Samuel Adams? Today, Samuel Adams (1722–1803), cousin of President John Adams, is well known for the beer that bears his name. His original claim to fame was as an early leader against the British and loyalist oppressors, although he did bankrupt his family's brewery business.

First Steps Toward Independence

In 1765, at the urging of Samuel Adams, nine of the thirteen colonies sent representatives to a meeting in New York City, where a detailed list of crown violations of the colonists' fundamental rights was drafted. Known as the **Stamp Act Congress,** this gathering was the first official meeting of the colonies and the first step toward creating a unified nation. Attendees defined what they thought to be the proper relationship between colonial governments and the British Parliament; they ardently believed Parliament had no authority to tax them without colonial representation in that body yet still remained loyal to the king. In contrast, the British believed that direct representation of the colonists was impractical and that members of Parliament represented the best interests of all the British, including the colonists.

The Stamp Act Congress and its petitions to the crown did little to stop the onslaught of taxing measures. Parliament did, however, repeal the Stamp Act and revise the Sugar Act in 1766, largely because of the uproar made by British merchants who were losing large sums of money as a result of the boycotts. Rather than appeasing the colonists, however, these actions emboldened them to increase their resistance. In 1767, Parliament enacted the Townshend Acts, which imposed duties on all kinds of colonial imports, including tea. Responses from the Sons and Daughters of Liberty were immediate. Another boycott was announced, and almost all colonists gave up their favorite drink in a united show of resistance to the tax and British authority.[5] Tensions continued to run high, especially after

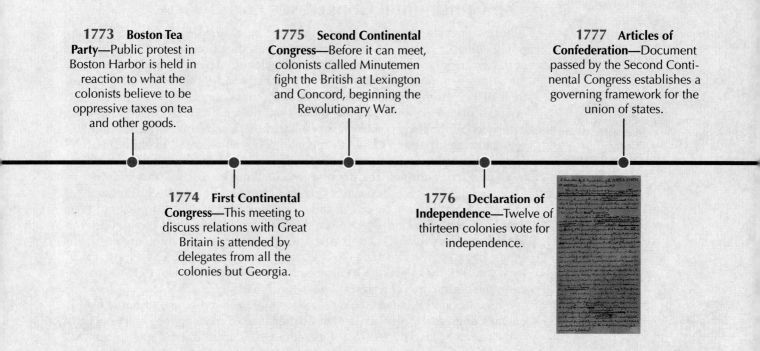

1773 Boston Tea Party—Public protest in Boston Harbor is held in reaction to what the colonists believe to be oppressive taxes on tea and other goods.

1775 Second Continental Congress—Before it can meet, colonists called Minutemen fight the British at Lexington and Concord, beginning the Revolutionary War.

1777 Articles of Confederation—Document passed by the Second Continental Congress establishes a governing framework for the union of states.

1774 First Continental Congress—This meeting to discuss relations with Great Britain is attended by delegates from all the colonies but Georgia.

1776 Declaration of Independence—Twelve of thirteen colonies vote for independence.

the British sent 4,000 troops to Boston. On March 5, 1770, British troops opened fire on an unruly mob that included disgruntled dock workers, whose jobs had been taken by British soldiers, and members of the Sons of Liberty, who were taunting the soldiers and throwing objects at British sentries stationed in front of the Boston Customs House. Five colonists were killed in what became known as the Boston Massacre. Following this confrontation, all duties except those on tea were lifted. The tea tax, however, continued to be a symbolic irritant.

In 1773, despite dissent in England over the treatment of the colonies, Parliament passed the Tea Act, granting a monopoly to the financially strapped East India Company to sell the tea imported from Britain. The company was allowed to funnel business to American merchants loyal to the crown, thereby undercutting colonial merchants, who could sell only tea imported from other nations. The effect was to drive down the price of tea and to hurt colonial merchants.

When the next shipment of tea arrived in Boston from Great Britain, the colonists responded by throwing the Boston Tea Party. Similar tea parties were held in other colonies. When the news of these actions reached King George III, he flew into a rage against the actions of his disloyal subjects. "The die is now cast," the king told his prime minister. "The colonies must either submit or triumph."

King George III's first act of retaliation was to persuade Parliament to pass the Coercive Acts of 1774. Known in the colonies as the Intolerable Acts, they contained a key provision calling for a total blockade of Boston Harbor cutting off Bostonians' access to many food stuffs, until restitution was made for the tea. Another provision gave royal governors the authority to house British soldiers in the homes of local Boston citizens, allowing Britain to send an additional 4,000 soldiers to patrol Boston.

Stamp Act Congress
Meeting of representatives of nine of the thirteen colonies held in New York City in 1765, during which representatives drafted a document to send to the king listing how their rights had been violated.

Committees of Correspondence
Organizations in each of the American colonies created to keep colonists abreast of developments with the British; served as powerful molders of public opinion against the British.

First Continental Congress
Meeting held in Philadelphia from September 5 to October 26, 1774, in which fifty-six delegates (from every colony except Georgia) adopted a resolution in opposition to the Coercive Acts.

The Continental Congresses

The British could never have guessed how the cumulative impact of these actions would unite the colonists. **Committees of Correspondence**—organizations in each of the American colonies created to keep the colonists abreast of developments with the British—spread the word, and food and money were sent to the people of Boston from all over the thirteen colonies. The tax itself was no longer the key issue; now the extent of British authority over the colonies was the far more important question. At the request of the colonial assemblies of Massachusetts and Virginia, all but Georgia's colonial assembly agreed to select a group of delegates to attend a continental congress authorized to communicate with the king on behalf of the now-united colonies.

The **First Continental Congress** met in Philadelphia from September 5 to October 26, 1774. It was made up of fifty-six delegates. The colonists had yet to think of breaking with Great Britain; at this point, they simply wanted to iron out their differences with the king. By October, they had agreed on a series of resolutions to oppose the Coercive Acts and to establish a formal organization to boycott British goods. The Congress also drafted a Declaration of Rights and Resolves, which called for colonial rights of petition and assembly, trial by peers, freedom from a standing army, and the selection of representative councils to levy taxes.

King George III refused to yield, tensions continued to rise, and a **Second Continental Congress** was deemed necessary. Before it could meet, fighting broke out early in the morning of April 19, 1775, at Lexington and Concord, Massachusetts, with what Ralph Waldo Emerson called "the shot heard round the world." Eight colonial soldiers, called Minutemen, were killed, and 16,000 British troops besieged Boston.

When the Second Continental Congress convened in Philadelphia on May 10, 1775, delegates were united by their increased hostility to Great Britain. In a final attempt to avert conflict, the Second Continental Congress adopted the Olive Branch Petition on July 5, 1775, asking the king to end hostilities. King George III rejected the petition and sent an additional 20,000 troops to quell the rebellion.

Second Continental Congress
Meeting that convened in Philadelphia on May 10, 1775, at which it was decided that an army should be raised and George Washington of Virginia was named commander in chief.

Declaration of Independence
Document drafted by Thomas Jefferson in 1776 that proclaimed the right of the American colonies to separate from Great Britain.

The Declaration of Independence

In January 1776, Thomas Paine, with the support and encouragement of Benjamin Franklin, issued (at first anonymously) *Common Sense*, a pamphlet forcefully arguing for independence from Great Britain. *Common Sense* galvanized the American public against reconciliation with Great Britain. On May 15, 1776, Virginia became the first colony to call for independence, instructing one of its delegates to the Second Continental Congress to introduce a resolution to that effect. On June 7, 1776, Richard Henry Lee of Virginia rose to move "that these United Colonies are, and of right ought to be, free and independent States, and that all connection between them and the State of Great Britain is, and ought to be, dissolved." His three-part resolution—which called for independence, the formation of foreign alliances, and preparation of a plan of confederation—triggered hot debate among the delegates. A proclamation of independence from Great Britain was treason, a crime punishable by death. Although six of the thirteen colonies had already instructed their delegates to vote for independence, the Second Continental Congress was suspended to allow its delegates to return home to their respective colonial legislatures for final instructions. Independence was not a move to be taken lightly.

Committees were set up to consider each point of Richard Henry Lee's proposal. A committee of five was selected to begin work on the **Declaration of Independence.** The Congress selected Benjamin Franklin of Pennsylvania, John Adams of Massachusetts, Robert Livingston of New York, and Roger Sherman of Connecticut as members of the committee. Adams lobbied hard for the addition of Thomas Jefferson, a Southerner, to add balance. He was also impressed with Jefferson's writings, which revealed a "peculiar felicity of expression." Thus, Jefferson of Virginia was selected as chair.

On July 2, 1776, twelve of the thirteen colonies (with New York abstaining) voted for independence. Two days later, the Second Continental Congress voted to adopt the Declaration of Independence largely penned by Thomas Jefferson. On July 9, 1776, the Declaration, now with the approval of New York, was read aloud in Philadelphia.[6]

In simple but eloquent language, Jefferson set out the reasons for the colonies' separation from Great Britain. Most of his stirring rhetoric drew heavily on the works of seventeenth- and eighteenth-century political philosophers, particularly the English philosopher John Locke (see **chapter 1**), who argued that governments exist based on the consent of the governed.

Thus, in stirring language, the Declaration of Independence proclaims:

> We hold these truths to be self-evident, that all men are created equal, that they are endowed by their Creator with certain unalienable Rights, that among these are Life, Liberty and the pursuit of Happiness.

Jefferson and others in attendance at the Second Continental Congress wanted to have a document that would stand for all time, justifying their break with Great Britain and clarifying their notions of the proper form of government. So, Jefferson continued:

> That to secure these rights, Governments are instituted among Men, deriving their just powers from the consent of the governed. That whenever any Form of Government becomes destructive of these ends, it is the Right of the People to alter or abolish it, and to institute new Government, laying its foundation on such Principles and organizing its Powers in such form, as to them shall seem most likely to effect their Safety and Happiness.

After this stirring preamble, the Declaration enumerates the wrongs that the colonists suffered under British rule. After the declaration was signed and transmitted to the King, the Revolutionary War waged on, and the Continental Congress attempted to fashion a new government. (To learn more about a modern take on the Declaration of Independence, see Analyzing Visuals: We Hold These Truths to Be Self-Evident. . . .)

Where did the ideas of the Declaration of Independence come from? Thomas Jefferson's draft (below) drew heavily from the ideas of social contract theorist John Locke.

Photo courtesy: The Granger Collection, New York

The First Attempt at Government: The Articles of Confederation

★ **2.2** . . . Identify the key components of the Articles of Confederation and the reasons why it failed.

The British had no written constitution. The delegates to the Second Continental Congress were attempting to codify arrangements that had never before been put into legal terminology. To make things more complicated, the delegates had to arrive at these decisions in a wartime atmosphere. Nevertheless, in late 1777, the

ANALYZING VISUALS

We Hold These Truths to Be Self-Evident . . .

This political cartoon was published in March 2009, shortly after President Barack Obama signed the American Recovery and Reinvestment Act, otherwise known as the "stimulus" bill. Look at the cartoon and consider the questions.

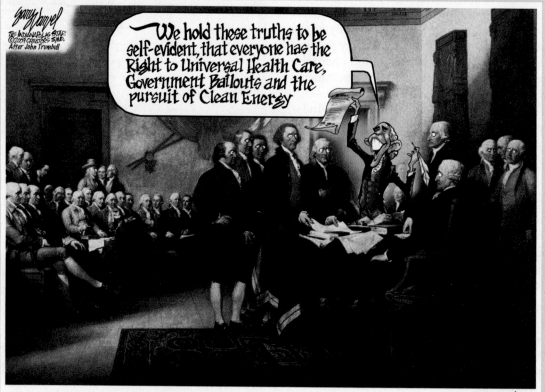

garyvarvel.com

Photo courtesy: By permission of Gary Varvel and Creators Syndicate, Inc.

- What meeting is referenced in this cartoon?
- What point is the cartoonist trying to communicate?
- How do the political leanings of the cartoonist reveal themselves?

Articles of Confederation

The compact among the thirteen original colonies that created a loose league of friendship, with the national government drawing its powers from the states.

Articles of Confederation, creating a loose "league of friendship" between the thirteen sovereign or independent colonies, were passed by the Congress and presented to the states for their ratification.

The Articles were finally ratified by all thirteen states in March 1781. Unlike Great Britain's unitary system of government, wherein all of the powers of the government reside in the national government, the national government in a confederation derives all of its powers directly from the states. Thus, the national government in a confederacy is weaker than the sum of its parts, and the states often consider themselves independent nation-states linked together only for limited purposes such as national defense. So, the Articles of Confederation proposed the following:

- A national government with a Congress empowered to make peace, coin money, appoint officers for an army, control the post office, and negotiate with Indian tribes.
- Each state's retention of its independence and sovereignty, or ultimate authority, to govern within its territories.

- One vote in the Continental Congress for each state, regardless of size.
- The vote of nine states to pass any measure (a unanimous vote for any amendment).
- The selection and payment of delegates to the Congress by their respective state legislatures.

Problems Under the Articles of Confederation

In 1784, just one year after the Revolutionary Army was disbanded, governing the new nation under the Articles of Confederation proved unworkable.[7] Congress rarely could assemble the required quorum of nine states to conduct business. Even when it did meet, there was little agreement among the states on any policies. To raise revenue to pay off war debts and run the government, various land, poll, and liquor taxes were proposed. But, since Congress had no specific power to tax, all these proposals were rejected. At one point, Congress was even driven out of Philadelphia (then the capital of the new national government) by its own unpaid army.

Although the national government could coin money, it had no resources to back up the value of its currency. Continental dollars were worth little, and trade between states became chaotic as some states began to coin their own money. Another weakness was that the Articles of Confederation did not allow Congress to regulate commerce among the states or with foreign nations. As a result, individual states attempted to enter into agreements with other countries, and foreign nations were suspicious of trade agreements made with the Congress of the Confederation.

The Articles of Confederation, moreover, had no provision for an executive branch or a judicial system to handle the growing number of economic conflicts and boundary disputes among the individual states. Several states claimed the same lands to the west, and Pennsylvania and Virginia went to war with each other.

The Articles' greatest weakness, however, was the lack of a strong central government. Although states had operated independently before the war, during the war they acceded to the national government's authority to wage armed conflict. Once the war was over, however, each state resumed its sovereign status and was unwilling to give up rights, such as the power to tax, to an untested national government. Consequently, the government was unable to force the states to abide by the provisions of the second Treaty of Paris, signed in 1783.

The crumbling economy was made worse by a series of bad harvests that failed to produce cash crops, thus making it difficult for farmers to get out of debt quickly. George Washington and Alexander Hamilton, both interested in the questions of trade and frontier expansion, soon saw the need for a stronger national government with the authority to act to solve some of these problems.

The Miracle at Philadelphia: Writing the U.S. Constitution

★ 2.3 ... Outline the issues and compromises that were central to the writing of the U.S. Constitution.

On February 21, 1787, in the throes of economic turmoil and with domestic tranquility gone haywire, the Congress passed an official resolution. It called for a Constitutional Convention in Philadelphia for "the sole and express purpose of revising the Articles of Confederation."

What happened during Shays's Rebellion? With Daniel Shays in the lead, a group of farmers who had served in the Continental Army marched on the courthouse in Springfield, Massachusetts, to stop the state court from foreclosing on the veterans' farms.

Photo courtesy: Bettmann/Corbis

However, many delegates that gathered in sweltering Philadelphia on May 25, 1787, were prepared to take potentially treasonous steps to preserve the union. For example, on the first day the convention was in session, Edmund Randolph and James Madison of Virginia proposed fifteen resolutions creating an entirely new government (later known as the Virginia Plan). Their enthusiasm, however, was not universal. Many delegates, including William Paterson of New Jersey, considered these resolutions to be in violation of the convention's charter, and proposed the New Jersey Plan, which took greater steps to preserve the Articles. These proposals met heated debate on the convention's floor.

The Characteristics and Motives of the Framers

The fifty-five delegates who attended the Constitutional Convention labored long and hard that hot summer. Owing to the high stakes of their action, all of the convention's work was conducted behind closed doors. George Washington of Virginia, who was unanimously elected the convention's presiding officer, cautioned delegates not to reveal details of the convention even to their family members.

All of the delegates to the Constitutional Convention were men; hence, they often are referred to as the "Founding Fathers." In this text, we generally refer to them as the Framers, because their work provided the framework for the new United States government. Most of them were quite young; many were in their twenties and thirties, and only one—Franklin at eighty-one—was quite old. Seventeen owned slaves.

constitution

A document establishing the structure, functions, and limitations of a government.

The Framers brought with them a vast amount of political, educational, legal, and business experience. It is clear that they were an exceptional lot who ultimately produced a brilliant **constitution,** or document establishing the structure, functions, and limitations of a government.

However, debate about the Framers' motives filled the air during the ratification struggle and has provided grist for the mill of historians and political scientists over the years. In his *Economic Interpretation of the Constitution of the United States* (1913), Charles A. Beard argued that the 1780s were a critical period not for the nation as a whole, but rather for business owners who feared that a weak, decentralized government could harm their economic interests.[8] Beard argued that the merchants wanted a strong national government to promote industry and trade, to protect private property, and to ensure payment of the public debt—much of which was owed to them.

By the 1950s, this view had fallen into disfavor when other historians were unable to find direct links between wealth and the Framers' motives for establishing the Constitution. Others faulted Beard's failure to consider the impact of religion and individual views about government.[9] In the 1960s, however, another group of historians began to argue that social and economic factors were, in fact, important motives for supporting the Constitution. In *The Anti-Federalists* (1961), Jackson Turner Main posited that while the Constitution's supporters might not have been the united group of creditors suggested by Beard, they were wealthier, came from higher social strata, and had greater concern for maintaining the prevailing social order than the general public.[10] In 1969, Gordon S. Wood's *The Creation of the American Republic* resurrected this debate. Wood deemphasized economics to argue that major social divisions explained different groups' support for (or opposition to) the new Constitution. He concluded that the Framers were representative of a class that favored order and stability over some of the more radical ideas that had inspired the American Revolutionary War and the break with Britain.[11]

The Virginia and New Jersey Plans

Virginia Plan

The first general plan for the Constitution offered in Philadelphia. Its key points were a bicameral legislature, and an executive and a judiciary chosen by the national legislature.

The **Virginia Plan,** proposed by Edmund Randolph and written by James Madison, called for a national system based heavily on the European nation-state model, wherein the national government derives its powers from the people and not from the member states.

Its key features included:

- Creation of a powerful central government with three branches—the legislative, executive, and judicial.
- A two-house legislature with one house elected directly by the people, the other chosen from among persons nominated by the state legislatures.
- A legislature with the power to select the executive and the judiciary.

In general, smaller states such as New Jersey and Connecticut felt comfortable with the arrangements under the Articles of Confederation. These states offered another model of government, the **New Jersey Plan.** Its key features included:

- Strengthening the Articles, not replacing them.
- Creating a one-house legislature with one vote for each state and with representatives chosen by state legislatures.
- Giving Congress the power to raise revenue from duties on imports and from postal service fees.
- Creating a Supreme Court with members appointed for life by the executive officers.

New Jersey Plan
A framework for the Constitution proposed by a group of small states. Its key points were a one-house legislature with one vote for each state, a Congress with the ability to raise revenue, and a Supreme Court with members appointed for life.

Constitutional Compromises

The final Constitution was shaped by a series of compromises. Two of these were particularly important. Below, we discuss the Great Compromise, which concerned the form of the new government, and the Three-Fifths Compromise, which dealt with representation.

THE GREAT COMPROMISE   The most serious disagreement between the Virginia and New Jersey plans concerned state representation in Congress. When a deadlock loomed, Connecticut offered its own compromise. Representation in the lower house would be determined by population, and each state would have an equal vote in the upper house. Again, there was a stalemate.

A committee to work out an agreement soon reported back what became known as the **Great Compromise.** Taking ideas from both the Virginia and New Jersey plans, it recommended:

Great Compromise
The final decision of the Constitutional Convention to create a two-house legislature with the lower house elected by the people and with powers divided between the two houses. It also made national law supreme.

- A two-house, or bicameral, legislature.
- In one house of the legislature (later called the House of Representatives), there would be fifty-six representatives—one representative for every 30,000 inhabitants. Representatives would be elected directly by the people.
- That house would have the power to originate all bills for raising and spending money.
- In the second house of the legislature (later called the Senate), each state would have an equal vote, and representatives would be selected by the state legislatures.
- In dividing power between the national and state governments, national power would be supreme.[12]

The Great Compromise ultimately met with the approval of all states in attendance. The smaller states were pleased because they got equal representation in the Senate; the larger states were satisfied with the proportional representation in the House of Representatives. The small states then would dominate the Senate while the large states, such as Virginia and Pennsylvania, would control the House. But, because both houses had to pass any legislation, neither body could dominate the other.

THE ISSUE OF SLAVERY The Great Compromise dealt with one major concern of the Framers—how best to treat the differences in large and small states—but other problems stemming largely from regional differences remained. Slavery, which formed the basis of much of the southern states' cotton economy, was one of the thorniest issues to address. To reach an agreement on the Constitution, the Framers had to craft a compromise that balanced southern commercial interests with comparable northern concerns. Eventually the Framers agreed that Northerners would support continuing the slave trade for twenty more years, as well as a twenty-year ban on taxing exports to protect the cotton trade, while Southerners consented to a provision requiring only a majority vote on navigation laws, and the national government was given the authority to regulate foreign commerce. It was also agreed that the Senate would have the power to ratify treaties by a two-thirds majority, which assuaged the fears of southern states, who made up more than one-third of the nation.

THE THREE-FIFTHS COMPROMISE One major conflict had yet to be resolved: how to determine state population for purposes of representation in the House of Representatives. Slaves could not vote, but the southern states wanted them included for purposes of determining population. After considerable dissension, it was decided that population for purposes of representation and the apportionment of direct taxes would be calculated by adding the "whole Number of Free Persons" to "three-fifths of all other Persons." "All other Persons" was the delegates' euphemistic way of referring to slaves. Known as the **Three-Fifths Compromise,** this highly political deal assured that the South would hold 47 percent of the House—enough to prevent attacks on slavery but not so much as to foster the spread of slavery northward.

Unfinished Business: The Executive Branch

The Framers next turned to fashioning an executive branch. While they agreed on the idea of a one-person executive, they could not settle on the length of the term of office, nor on how the chief executive should be selected. The delegates feared putting too much power, including selection of a president, into the hands of the lower classes. At the same time, representatives from the smaller states feared that the selection of the chief executive by the legislature would put additional power into the hands of the large states.

Amid these fears, the Committee on Unfinished Portions, whose sole responsibility was to iron out problems and disagreements concerning the office of chief executive, conducted its work. The committee recommended that the presidential term of office be fixed at four years instead of seven, as had earlier been proposed. The committee also made it possible for a president to serve more than one term.

The Framers also created the Electoral College as a mechanism for selecting the chief executive of the new nation. The Electoral College system gave individual states a key role, because each state would select electors equal to the number of representatives it had in the House and Senate. It was a vague compromise that removed election of the president and vice president from both the Congress and the people and put it in the hands of electors whose method of selection would be left to the states.

In drafting the new Constitution, the Framers also were careful to include a provision for removal of the chief executive. The House of Representatives was given the sole responsibility of investigating and charging a president or vice president with "Treason, Bribery, or other high Crimes and Misdemeanors." A majority vote then would result in issuing articles of impeachment against the president or vice president. In turn, the Senate was given sole responsibility to try the president or vice president on the charges issued by the House. A two-thirds vote of the Senate was required to convict and remove the president or the vice president from office.

Three-Fifths Compromise
Agreement reached at the Constitutional Convention stipulating that each slave was to be counted as three-fifths of a person for purposes of determining population for representation in the U.S. House of Representatives.

The U.S. Constitution

⭐ **2.4** . . . Analyze the underlying principles of the U.S. Constitution.

The U.S. Constitution's opening line, "We the People," ended, at least for the time being, the question of from where the government derived its power: it came directly from the people. The Constitution next explained the need for the new outline of government: "in Order to form a more perfect Union" indirectly acknowledged the weaknesses of the Articles of Confederation in governing a growing nation. Next, the optimistic goals of the Framers for the new nation were set out: to "establish Justice, insure domestic Tranquility, provide for the common defence, promote the general Welfare, and secure the Blessings of Liberty to ourselves and our Posterity;" followed by the formal creation of a new government: "do ordain and establish this Constitution for the United States of America." The Constitution was approved by the delegates from all twelve states in attendance on September 17, 1787.

The Basic Principles of the Constitution

The proposed structure of the new national government owed much to the writings of the French philosopher Montesquieu (1689–1755), who advocated distinct functions for each branch of government, called **separation of powers,** with a system of **checks and balances** between each branch. The Constitution's concern with the distribution of power between states and the national government also reveals the heavy influence of political philosophers, as well as the colonists' experience under the Articles of Confederation.[13]

FEDERALISM   The question before and during the convention was how much power states would give up to the national government. Given the nation's experiences under the Articles of Confederation, the Framers believed that a strong national government was necessary for the new nation's survival. However, they were reluctant to create a powerful government after the model of Great Britain, the country from which they had just won their independence. Its unitary system was not even considered by the colonists. Instead, they employed a system (now known as the **federal system**) that divides the power of government between a strong national government and the individual states, with national power being supreme.

SEPARATION OF POWERS   Separation of powers is simply a way of parceling out power among the three branches of government. Its three key features are:

1. Three distinct branches of government: the legislative, the executive, and the judicial.
2. Three separately staffed branches of government to exercise these functions.
3. Constitutional equality and independence of each branch.

As illustrated in Figure 2.1, the Framers were careful to create a system in which law-making, law-enforcing, and law-interpreting functions were assigned to independent branches of government. Only the legislature has the authority to make laws; the chief executive enforces laws; and the judiciary interprets them. Moreover, initially, members of the House of Representatives, members of the Senate, the president, and members of the federal courts were selected by and were therefore responsible to different constituencies.

The Framers could not have foreseen the intermingling of governmental functions that has since evolved. Locke, in fact, cautioned against giving a legislature the ability to delegate its powers. In Article I of the Constitution, the legislative power is vested in the Congress. But, the president is also given legislative power via his ability

separation of powers
A way of dividing the power of government among the legislative, executive, and judicial branches, each staffed separately, with equality and independence of each branch ensured by the Constitution.

checks and balances
A constitutionally mandated structure that gives each of the three branches of government some degree of oversight and control over the actions of the others.

federal system
System of government where the national government and state governments share power and derive all authority from the people.

Figure 2.1 *What are the separation of powers and checks and balances under the U.S. Constitution?*

Legislative Checks on the Executive
Impeach the president
Reject legislation or funding the president wants
Refuse to confirm nominees or approve treaties*
Override the president's veto by a two-thirds vote

LEGISLATIVE BRANCH POWERS
Pass all federal laws
Pass the federal budget
Declare war
Approve treaties and
  presidential appointments
Establish lower federal courts
  and the number of judges

Executive Checks on the Legislative
Veto legislation
Call Congress into special session
Implement (or fail to implement) laws
passed by Congress

EXECUTIVE BRANCH POWERS
Enforce federal laws and court orders
Propose legislation to Congress
Make foreign treaties
Nominate officers of the United
  States government and federal
  judges
Serve as commander in chief of the
  armed forces
Pardon people convicted in federal
  courts or grant reprieves

Judicial Checks on the Legislative
Rule federal and state laws
unconstitutional

Judicial Checks on the Executive
Declare executive branch
actions unconstitutional
Chief justice presides over
impeachment trial

JUDICIAL BRANCH POWERS
Interpret federal laws and U.S.
  Constitution
Review the decisions of lower state
  and federal courts

Legislative Checks on the Judicial
Change the number and
jurisdiction of federal courts
Impeach federal judges
Propose constitutional amendments to
override judicial decisions

Executive Checks on the Judicial
Appoint federal judges
Refuse to implement decisions

*This power belongs to the Senate only.

to veto legislation, although his veto can be overridden by a two-thirds vote in Congress. Judicial interpretation also helps to clarify the language or implementation of legislation enacted through this process.

CHECKS AND BALANCES   The separation of powers among the three branches of the national government is not complete. According to Montesquieu and the Framers, the powers of each branch (as well as the two houses of the national legislature and between the states and the national government) could be used to check the powers of the other two branches of government. The power of each branch of government is checked, or limited, and balanced because the legislative, executive, and judicial branches share some authority, and no branch has exclusive domain over any single activity. The creation of this system allowed the Framers to minimize the threat of tyranny from any one branch. Thus, for almost every power granted to one branch, an equal control was established in the other two branches.

The Articles of the Constitution

The document finally signed by the Framers condensed numerous resolutions into a Preamble and seven separate articles remedying many of the deficiencies within the Articles of Confederation. (To learn more about the differences between the Articles n this.

Table 2.1 *How do the Articles of Confederation and the U.S. Constitution compare to one another?*

	Articles of Confederation	Constitution
Formal name of the nation	The United States of America	Not specified, but referred to in the Preamble as "the United States of America"
Legislature	Unicameral, called Congress	Bicameral, called Congress, divided into the House of Representatives and the Senate
Members of Congress	Between two and seven members per state	Two senators per state, representatives apportioned according to population of each state
Voting in Congress	One vote per state	One vote per representative or senator
Appointment of members	All appointed by state legislatures, in the manner each legislature directed	Representatives elected by popular vote; senators appointed by state legislatures
Term of legislative office	One year	Two years for representatives, six for senators
Term limit for legislative office	No more than three out of every six years	None
When Congress is not in session	A Committee of States had the full powers of Congress	The president of the United States can call for Congress to assemble
Chair of legislature	President of Congress	Speaker of the House of Representatives; U.S. vice president is president of the Senate
Executive	None	President
National judiciary	Maritime judiciary established—other courts left to states	Supreme Court established, as well as other courts Congress deems necessary
Adjudicator of disputes between states	Congress	U.S. Supreme Court
New states	Admitted upon agreement of nine states (special exemption provided for Canada)	Admitted upon agreement of majority of Congress
Amendment	When agreed upon by all states	When agreed upon by three-fourths of the states
Navy	Congress authorized to build a navy; states authorized to equip warships to counter piracy	Congress authorized to build a navy; states not allowed to keep ships of war
Army	Congress to decide on size of force and to requisition troops from each state according to population	Congress authorized to raise and support armies
Power to coin money	United States and the states	United States only
Taxes	Apportioned by Congress, collected by the states	Laid and collected by Congress
Ratification	Unanimous consent required	Consent of nine states required

of Confederation and the Constitution, see Table 2.1.) The first three articles established the three branches of government, defined their internal operations, and clarified their relationships with one another. The four remaining articles define the relationships among the states, declare national law to be supreme, and set out methods of amending the Constitution.

ARTICLE I: THE LEGISLATIVE BRANCH Article I vests all legislative powers in the Congress and establishes a bicameral legislature, consisting of the Senate and the House of Representatives. It also sets out the qualifications for holding office in each house, the terms of office, the methods of selection of representatives and senators, and the system of apportionment among the states to determine membership in the House of Representatives.

One of the most important sections of Article I is section 8. It carefully lists the powers the Framers wished the new Congress to possess. These specified or **enumerated powers** contain many key provisions that had been denied to the Continental Congress under the Articles of Confederation.

After careful enumeration of seventeen powers of Congress in Article I, section 8, a final, general clause authorizing Congress to "make all Laws which shall be necessary and proper for carrying into Execution the foregoing Powers" was added to

enumerated powers
Seventeen specific powers granted to Congress under Article I, section 8, of the Constitution.

necessary and proper clause
The final paragraph of Article I, section 8, of the Constitution, which gives Congress the authority to pass all laws "necessary and proper" to carry out the enumerated powers specified in the Constitution; also called the elastic clause.

implied powers
Powers derived from the enumerated powers and the necessary and proper clause. These powers are not stated specifically but are considered to be reasonably implied through the exercise of delegated powers.

Article I. Often referred to as the elastic clause, the **necessary and proper clause** has been a source of tremendous congressional activity never anticipated by the Framers, including the passage of laws that regulate the environment, welfare programs, education, and communication. The necessary and proper clause is the basis for the **implied powers** that Congress uses to execute its other powers.

ARTICLE II: THE EXECUTIVE BRANCH   Article II vests the executive power, that is, the authority to execute the laws of the nation, in a president of the United States. Section 1 sets the president's term of office at four years and explains the Electoral College. It also states the qualifications for office and describes a mechanism to replace the president in case of death, disability, or removal from office.

The powers and duties of the president are set out in section 3. Among the most important of these are the president's role as commander in chief of the armed forces, the authority to make treaties with the consent of the Senate, and the authority to "appoint Ambassadors, other public Ministers and Consuls, the Judges of the supreme Court, and all other Officers of the United States." Other sections of Article II instruct the president to report directly to Congress "from time to time," in what has come to be known as the State of the Union Address, and to "take Care that the Laws be faithfully executed." Section 4 provides the mechanism for removal of the president, vice president, and other officers of the United States.

Article II also limits the presidency to natural-born citizens. A new amendment would be needed to change that qualification. (To learn more about the natural-born citizen clause, see Join the Debate: Should the Equal Opportunity to Govern Amendment Be Passed?)

ARTICLE III: THE JUDICIAL BRANCH   Article III establishes a Supreme Court and defines its jurisdiction. During the Philadelphia meeting, the small and large states differed significantly as to the desirability of an independent judiciary and on the role of state courts in the national court system. The smaller states feared that a strong unelected judiciary would trample on their liberties. In compromise, Congress was permitted, but not required, to establish lower national courts. Thus, state courts and the national court system would exist side by side with distinct areas of authority. Federal courts were given authority to decide cases arising under federal law. The U.S. Supreme Court was also given the power to settle disputes between states, or between a state and the national government.

Although some delegates to the convention urged that the president be allowed to remove federal judges, ultimately judges were given appointments for life, presuming "good behavior." And, like the president's, their salaries cannot be lowered while they hold office. This provision was adopted to ensure that the legislature did not attempt to punish the Supreme Court or any other judges for unpopular decisions.

full faith and credit clause
Section of Article IV of the Constitution that ensures judicial decrees and contracts made in one state will be binding and enforceable in any other state.

supremacy clause
Portion of Article VI of the U.S. Constitution mandating that national law is supreme to (that is, supersedes) all other laws passed by the states or by any other subdivision of government.

ARTICLES IV THROUGH VII   The remainder of the articles in the Constitution attempted to anticipate problems that might occur in the operation of the new national government as well as its relations to the states. Article IV begins with what is called the **full faith and credit clause,** which mandates that states honor the laws and judicial proceedings of the other states. Article IV also includes the mechanisms for admitting new states to the union.

Article V (discussed in greater detail on p. 64) specifies how amendments can be added to the Constitution. The Bill of Rights, which added ten amendments to the Constitution in 1791, was one of the first items of business when the First Congress met in 1789.

Article VI contains the supremacy clause, which asserts the basic primacy of the Constitution and national law over state laws and constitutions. The **supremacy clause** provides that the "Constitution, and the laws of the United States" as well as all treaties

Join the DEBATE | Should the Equal Opportunity to Govern Amendment Be Passed?

Article II, section 1, clause 5, of the U.S. Constitution declares: "No person except a natural-born citizen, or a citizen of the United States at the time of the Adoption of this Constitution, shall be eligible to the Office of President." In drafting this restriction, the Framers expressed concern that, as Chief Justice John Jay argued, the duty of commander in chief was too important to be given to a foreign-born person—the potential conflict of interest, danger, and appearance of impropriety in matters of war and foreign policy should not be left to chance.

However, even though the requirement that the president be a "natural-born" citizen is constitutionally mandated, the term "natural-born" has never been defined. Currently, naturalized citizens (those who were citizens of a foreign country but became U.S. citizens and pledged allegiance to this country) are not allowed to serve as president.

A constitutional amendment proposed by Senator Orrin Hatch (R–UT) in 2004 would have stricken the natural-born citizen clause from the Constitution. The amendment took into account the Framers' fear of foreign intervention and of divided loyalty by placing a lengthy citizenship requirement—twenty years—before naturalized citizens would become eligible to run for presidential office. Although the amendment was not passed by Congress, the proposal could be made again. Should the Equal Opportunity to Govern Amendment be passed?

To develop an ARGUMENT FOR passage of the Equal Opportunity to Govern Amendment, think about how:

- **The United States is a nation of immigrants.** Would opening the presidency to naturalized citizens expand the talent pool of presidential nominees, thus increasing the quality and choice of presidential candidates for the American people?
- **Naturalized citizens have all of the other rights and freedoms accorded to natural-born citizens.** Does the restriction on naturalized citizens being elected president deny them equality of opportunity? If the Constitution allows foreign-born citizens to attain other political offices, why should naturalized citizens be denied the presidency?
- **The Constitution has been amended to address other areas of discrimination, including expanding the franchise to women and African Americans.** Is the Equal Opportunity to Govern Amendment another example of the evolution of popular opinion and political values since the Constitution's ratification?

To develop an ARGUMENT AGAINST passage of the Equal Opportunity to Govern Amendment, think about how:

- **Concerns over the potential undue influence of foreign governments are longstanding.** How did the revolutionary experience influence the Framers' views of the danger of foreign influence in U.S. politics? Were the Framers correct in assuming foreign governments would attempt to manipulate American politics? In what ways would foreign-born citizens be more likely to suffer from conflicted and divided loyalties than natural-born citizens?
- **There is a fundamental difference between being born in the United States and being a naturalized citizen of the United States.** How do Chief Justice John Jay's concerns reflect this difference? Do restrictions on who can serve as president provide institutional safeguards against presidential corruption?
- **Only twenty-seven amendments have passed since the adoption of the U.S. Constitution.** Is the proposed amendment a worthwhile endeavor, with so many other pressing issues facing the country? Should the constitutional amendment process be reserved for areas of more immediate public concern?

are to be the supreme law of the land. All national and state officers and judges are bound by national law and take oaths to support the federal Constitution above any state law or constitution. Because of the supremacy clause, any legitimate exercise of national power supersedes any state laws or action, in a process that is called preemption, further discussed in **chapter 3**. Without the supremacy clause and the federal courts' ability to invoke it, the national government would have little actual enforceable power; thus, many commentators call the supremacy clause the linchpin of the entire federal system.

Article VI also specifies that no religious test shall be required for holding any office. This mandate is strengthened by the separation of church and state guarantee that was quickly added to the Constitution when the First Amendment was ratified.

The seventh and final article of the Constitution concerns the procedures for ratification of the new Constitution: nine of the thirteen states would have to agree to, or ratify, its new provisions before it would become the supreme law of the land.

The Drive for Ratification of the U.S. Constitution

⭐ 2.5 . . . Explain the conflicts that characterized the drive for ratification of the U.S. Constitution.

The Congress of the Confederation immediately accepted the work of the convention and forwarded the proposed Constitution to the states for their vote. It was by no means certain, however, that the new Constitution would be adopted. From the fall of 1787 to the summer of 1788, the proposed Constitution was debated hotly around the nation.

Federalists Versus Anti-Federalists

Federalists
Those who favored a stronger national government and supported the proposed U.S. Constitution; later became the first U.S. political party.

Anti-Federalists
Those who favored strong state governments and a weak national government; opposed the ratification of the U.S. Constitution.

Almost as soon as the ink was dry on the last signature to the Constitution, those who favored the new strong national government chose to call themselves **Federalists.** They were well aware that many people still generally opposed the notion of a strong national government. They did not want to risk being labeled nationalists, so they tried to get the upper hand in the debate by nicknaming their opponents **Anti-Federalists.** As noted in Table 2.2, Anti-Federalists argued that they simply wanted to protect state governments from the tyranny of a too powerful national government.[14]

Table 2.2 *What were the differences between the Federalists and the Anti-Federalists?*

	Federalists	Anti-Federalists
Who were they?	Property owners, landed rich, merchants of Northeast and Middle Atlantic states	Small farmers, shopkeepers, laborers
Political philosophy	Elitist; saw themselves and those of their class as most fit to govern (others were to be governed)	Believed in the decency of "the common man" and in participatory democracy; viewed elites as corrupt; sought greater protection of individual rights
Type of government favored	Powerful central government; two-house legislature; upper house (six-year term) further removed from the people, whom they distrusted	Wanted stronger state governments (closer to the people) at the expense of the powers of the national government; sought smaller electoral districts, frequent elections, referendum and recall, and a large unicameral legislature to provide for greater class and occupational representation
Alliances	Pro-British, anti-French	Anti-British, pro-French

Federalists and Anti-Federalists participated in the mass meetings that were held in state legislatures to discuss the pros and cons of the new plan. Tempers ran high at these meetings, and fervent debates were published in newspapers, which played a powerful role in the adoption process.

The Federalist Papers

Between October 1787 and May 1788, eighty-five essays written under the pen name of "Publius" (Latin for "the people") routinely appeared in newspapers in New York, a state where ratification was in doubt. Most were written by Alexander Hamilton and James Madison. Hamilton, a young, fiery New Yorker born in the British West Indies, wrote fifty-one; Madison, a Virginian who later served as the fourth president, wrote twenty-six; jointly they penned another three. John Jay, also of New York, and later the first chief justice of the United States, wrote five of the pieces. These eighty-five essays became known as *The Federalist Papers*, and are perhaps the best explanations of the Framers' intentions as they drafted the new Constitution.

Forced on the defensive, the Anti-Federalists responded to *The Federalist Papers* with their own series of letters written under the pen names "Brutus" and "Cato," two ancient Romans famous for their intolerance of tyranny. These letters (actually essays) undertook a line-by-line critique of the Constitution.

Anti-Federalists argued that a strong central government would render the states powerless.[15] They stressed the strengths the government had been granted under the Articles of Confederation, and argued that the Articles, not the proposed Constitution, created a true federal system. Moreover, they argued that the strong national government would tax heavily, that the U.S. Supreme Court would overwhelm the states by invalidating state laws, and that the president eventually would have too much power as commander in chief of a large and powerful army.[16]

In particular, the Anti-Federalists feared the power of the national government to run roughshod over the liberties of the people. They proposed that the taxing power of Congress be limited, that the executive be curbed by a council, that the military consist of state militias rather than a national force, and that the jurisdiction of the Supreme Court be limited to prevent it from reviewing and potentially overturning the decisions of state courts. But, their most effective argument concerned the absence of a bill of rights in the Constitution. James Madison answered these criticisms in *Federalist Nos. 10* and *51*. (The texts of these two essays, along with *Federalist No. 78*, are printed in Appendix II.) In *Federalist No. 10*, Madison pointed out that the voters would not always succeed in electing "enlightened statesmen" as their representatives. The greatest threat to individual liberties would therefore come from factions within the government, who might place narrow interests above broader national interests and the rights of citizens. While recognizing that no form of government could protect the country from unscrupulous politicians, Madison argued that the organization of the new government would minimize the effects of political factions. The great advantage of a federal system, Madison maintained, was that it created the "happy combination" of a national government too large to be controlled by any single faction, and several state governments that would be smaller and more responsive to local needs. Moreover, he

Why were The Federalist Papers *written? The Federalist Papers* highlighted the reasons for the structure of the new government and its benefits. As seen on the cover page, the papers had the approval of those at the Constitutional Convention.

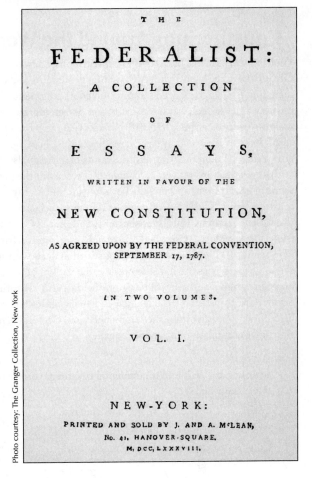

Photo courtesy: The Granger Collection, New York

THE

FEDERALIST:

A COLLECTION

OF

ESSAYS,

WRITTEN IN FAVOUR OF THE

NEW CONSTITUTION,

AS AGREED UPON BY THE FEDERAL CONVENTION, SEPTEMBER 17, 1787.

IN TWO VOLUMES.

VOL. I.

NEW-YORK:

PRINTED AND SOLD BY J. AND A. McLEAN, No. 41, HANOVER-SQUARE. M, DCC, LXXXVIII.

The Federalist Papers
A series of eighty-five political essays written by Alexander Hamilton, James Madison, and John Jay in support of ratification of the U.S. Constitution.

argued in *Federalist No. 51* that the proposed federal government's separation of powers would prohibit any one branch from either dominating the national government or violating the rights of citizens.

Constitutions Around the World

While most countries have written constitutions, a few do not. Great Britain relies on a variety of written documents and laws, including the Magna Carta, treaties, and court judgments, but it has no single, formal, written constitution. Israel, too, has no formal constitution, although its officials are trying to write one. Instead, Israel is governed by basic laws that outline how the government should function and the rights of individuals.

All constitutions reflect philosophical ideas about the proper scope of government and include both routine and highly sensitive topics. The U.S. Constitution contains seven articles and twenty-one sections. This is far shorter than France's Constitution (ninety-two articles), China's (138 articles), and South Africa's (243 sections). The South African Constitution deals with such symbolic matters as the flag, the presidential oath of office, and how the national anthem will be determined. It also identifies South Africa's eleven official languages, bans racial and sexual discrimination, and establishes an independent electoral commission and a commission for gender equality.

- Is it better to have a very detailed constitution or one that lays out only basic and fundamental rules of government?

- What might be some benefits and drawbacks to having an unwritten constitution versus a written one?

- Should newly independent countries use the U.S. Constitution as a model? Why or why not?

Ratifying the Constitution

Debate continued in the thirteen states as votes were taken from December 1787 to June 1788, in accordance with the ratifying process laid out in Article VII of the proposed Constitution. Three states acted quickly to ratify the new Constitution. Two small states, Delaware and New Jersey, voted to ratify before the large states could rethink the notion of equal representation of the states in the Senate. Pennsylvania, where Federalists were well organized, was also one of the first three states to ratify. Massachusetts assented to the new government but tempered its support by calling for an immediate addition of amendments, including one protecting personal rights. New Hampshire became the crucial ninth state to ratify on June 21, 1788. This action completed the ratification process outlined in Article VII of the Constitution and marked the beginning of a new nation. But, New York and Virginia, which at that time accounted for more than 40 percent of the new nation's population, had not yet ratified the Constitution. Thus, the practical future of the new nation remained in doubt.

Hamilton in New York and Madison in Virginia worked feverishly to convince delegates to their state conventions to vote for the new government. In New York, sentiment against the Constitution ran high. In Albany, fighting resulting in injuries and death broke out over ratification. When news of Virginia's acceptance of the Constitution reached the New York convention, Hamilton finally was able to convince a majority of those present to follow suit by a narrow margin of three votes. Both states also recommended the addition of a series of structural amendments and a bill of rights.

The Bill of Rights

Bill of Rights

The first ten amendments to the U.S. Constitution, which largely guarantee specific rights and liberties.

Once the Constitution was ratified, elections were held. When Congress convened, it immediately sent a set of amendments to the states for their ratification. An amendment authorizing the enlargement of the House of Representatives and another to prevent members of the House from raising their own salaries failed to garner favorable votes in the necessary three-fourths of the states. The remaining ten amendments, known as the **Bill of Rights,** were ratified by 1791 in accordance with the procedures set out in the Constitution. Sought by Anti-Federalists as a protection for individual liberties, they offered numerous specific limitations on the national government's ability to interfere with a wide variety of personal liberties, some of which were already guaranteed by many state constitutions. (To learn more about the Bill of Rights, see Table 2.3.)

Table 2.3 *What rights are included in the Bill of Rights?*

First Amendment	Freedom of religion, speech, press, and assembly
Second Amendment	The right to bear arms
Third Amendment	Prohibition against quartering of troops in private homes
Fourth Amendment	Prohibition against unreasonable searches and seizures
Fifth Amendment	Rights guaranteed to the accused: requirement for grand jury indictment; protections against double jeopardy, self-incrimination; due process
Sixth Amendment	Right to speedy and public trial before an impartial jury, to cross-examine witness, and to have counsel
Seventh Amendment	Right to a trial by jury in civil suits
Eighth Amendment	Prohibition against excessive bail, fines, and cruel and unusual punishment
Ninth Amendment	Rights listed in the Constitution are not exclusive
Tenth Amendment	States or people reserve those powers not denied to them by the Constitution or delegated to the national government

TOWARD REFORM: Methods of Amending the U.S. Constitution

⭐ **2.6 . . . Distinguish between the methods for proposing and ratifying amendments to the U.S. Constitution.**

The Framers did not want to fashion a government that could be too influenced by the whims of the people. Therefore, they made the formal amendment process a slow one to ensure that the Constitution was not impulsively amended. In keeping with this intent, only seventeen amendments have been added since the addition of the Bill of Rights. However, informal amendments, prompted by judicial interpretation and cultural and social change, have had a tremendous impact on the Constitution.

Formal Methods of Amending the Constitution

Article V of the Constitution creates a two-stage amendment process: proposal and ratification. The Constitution specifies two ways to accomplish each stage. As illustrated in Figure 2.2, amendments to the Constitution can be proposed by: (1) a vote of two-thirds of the members in both houses of Congress; or, (2) a vote of two-thirds of the state legislatures specifically requesting Congress to call a national convention to propose amendments. (To learn more about the amendment process, see The Living Constitution: Article V.)

Figure 2.2 *How can the U.S. Constitution be amended?*

Methods of Proposal		Methods of Ratification
By two-thirds vote in both houses of Congress	*Usual method* →	By legislatures in three-fourths of the states
Or		Or
By national constitutional convention called by Congress at the request of two-thirds of the state legislatures. (This method never has been used to propose an amendment.)	*Used once (21st Amendment)* →	By conventions in three-fourths of the states

The Living Constitution

The Congress, whenever two thirds of both houses shall deem it necessary, shall propose amendments to this Constitution, or, on the application of the legislatures of two thirds of the several states, shall call a convention for proposing amendments, which, in either case, shall be valid to all intents and purposes, as part of this Constitution, when ratified by the legislatures of three fourths of the several states, or by conventions in three fourths thereof, as the one or the other mode of ratification may be proposed by the Congress.

—ARTICLE V

With this article, the Framers acknowledged the potential need to change or amend the Constitution. This article provides for two methods to propose amendments: by a two-thirds vote of both houses of Congress or by a two-thirds vote of the state legislatures. It also specifies two alternative methods of ratification of proposed amendments: by a three-quarters vote of the state legislatures, or by a similar vote in specially called state ratifying conventions.

During the Constitutional Convention in Philadelphia, the Framers were divided as to how frequently or how easily the Constitution was to be amended. The original suggestion was to allow the document to be amended "when soever it shall seem necessary." Some delegates wanted to entrust this authority to the state legislatures; however, others feared that it would give states too much power. James Madison alleviated these fears by suggesting that both Congress and the states have a role in the process.

In the late 1960s and early 1970s, leaders of the new women's rights movement sought passage of the Equal Rights Amendment (ERA). Their efforts were rewarded when the ERA was approved in the House and Senate by overwhelming majorities in 1972 and then sent out to the states for their approval. In spite of tremendous lobbying, a strong anti-ERA movement emerged and the amendment failed to gain approval in three-quarters of the state legislatures.

The failed battles for the ERA as well as other amendments, including one to prohibit child labor and another to grant statehood to the District of Columbia, underscore how difficult it is to amend the Constitution. Thus, unlike the constitutions of individual states or many other nations, the U.S. Constitution rarely has been amended. Still, the ERA has been proposed in every session of Congress since 1923.

CRITICAL THINKING QUESTIONS

1. What would it take to get an equal rights amendment added to the U.S. Constitution?
2. Does your state already have an equal rights amendment? What does it guarantee?
3. Are the rights of women best protected by state or federal statute, or should they be protected by constitutional amendment?

The second method has never been used. Historically, it has served as a fairly effective threat, forcing Congress to consider amendments that might otherwise never have been debated.

The ratification process is fairly straightforward. When Congress votes to propose an amendment, the Constitution specifies that the ratification process must occur in one of two ways: (1) a favorable vote in three-fourths of the state legislatures;

or, (2) a favorable vote in specially called ratifying conventions in three-fourths of the states.

The Constitution itself was ratified by the favorable vote of nine states in specially called ratifying conventions. The Framers feared that the power of special interests in state legislatures would prevent a positive vote on the new Constitution. Since ratification of the Constitution, however, only one ratifying convention has been called. The Eighteenth Amendment, which outlawed the sale of alcoholic beverages nationwide, was ratified by the first method—a vote in state legislatures. Millions of people broke the law, others died from drinking homemade liquor, and still others made their fortunes selling bootleg or illegal liquor. After a decade of these problems, Congress decided to act. An additional amendment—the Twenty-First—was proposed to repeal the Eighteenth Amendment. It was sent to the states for ratification, but with a call for ratifying conventions, not a vote in the state legislatures.[17] Members of Congress correctly predicted that the move to repeal the Eighteenth Amendment would encounter opposition in the state houses, which were largely controlled by conservative rural legislators.

The intensity of efforts to amend the Constitution has varied considerably, depending on the nature of the change proposed. Whereas the Twenty-First Amendment took only ten months to ratify, an equal rights amendment

Why are constitutional amendments repealed? For all its moral support from groups such as the Women's Christian Temperance Union (WCTU), whose members invaded bars to protest the sale of alcoholic beverages, the Eighteenth (Prohibition) Amendment was a disaster. Among its side effects was the rise of powerful crime organizations responsible for illegal sales of alcoholic beverages. Once proposed, it took only ten months to ratify the Twenty-First Amendment, which repealed the Prohibition Amendment.

Photo courtesy: U.S. Department of Interior. National Park Service. Edison National Historical Site

(ERA) was introduced in every session of Congress from 1923 until 1972, when Congress finally voted favorably for it. Even then, years of lobbying by women's groups were insufficient to garner necessary state support. By 1982, the congressionally mandated date for ratification, only thirty-five states—three short of the number required—had voted favorably on the amendment.[18]

Informal Methods of Amending the Constitution

The formal amendment process is not the only way that the Constitution has been changed over time. Judicial interpretation and cultural and social change also have had a major impact on the way the Constitution has evolved.

JUDICIAL INTERPRETATION   As early as 1803, the Supreme Court declared in *Marbury* v. *Madison* that the federal courts had the power to nullify acts of the nation's government when they were found to be in conflict with the Constitution.[19] Over the years, this check on the other branches of government and on the states has increased the authority of the Court and significantly altered the meaning of various provisions of the Constitution, a fact that prompted President Woodrow Wilson to call the Supreme Court "a constitutional convention in continuous session." (To learn more about the Supreme Court's role in interpreting the Constitution see **chapters 4, 5,** and **9.**)

Today, some analysts argue that the original intent of the Framers, as evidenced in *The Federalist Papers,* as well as in private notes taken by James Madison at the

POLITICS NOW

Constitution, States' Rights Energizing Local Politics

May 30, 2010
The Citizen of Laconia
www.citizen.com

By Adam D. Krauss

. . . Earlier this month, the conference room at St. Mary's Church was packed for the first official meeting of the Dover 912 Project and a presentation on the dismantling of the American republic by city resident Greg Vatistas. The 30-year-old self-employed contractor rejoiced that so many people came out to "talk liberty." He said it was a sign of the times.

The 912 Project, brainchild of conservative commentator Glenn Beck, has spawned local groups dedicated to restoring what they see as the nation's founding ideals.

"Everyone wants to do their part, but it's hard to focus everybody," Vatistas said. "We can't leave this for anybody else. . . . We have to do the heavy lifting . . . we have to read the original texts."

A couple weeks earlier, on May 6, the Rochester 912 Project hosted a debate between Republican U.S. Senate candidates that almost exclusively focused on the Constitution. After the debate, Jim Bender's campaign spread a couple dozen pocket-sized copies of the Constitution on a table. Rochester businessman Gary Dworkin picked up a copy. He said he wanted to freshen his understanding of what "everybody was coming back to . . . as a core base of their beliefs."

. . . The emergence of the Tea Party and 912 groups, and their focus on the Constitution, complicates things for candidates and campaigns, Spiliotes said. "They have to make a decision about how far they're willing to go down that path and what it holds for them for political value."

. . . During the presentation, Vatistas drew two diagrams on a blackboard depicting the difference between a simple and compound republic. Today the nation operates under a simple republic, where voters elect U.S. senators, as promised by the adoption of the 17th Amendment in 1913. Before that the nation was a compound republic, he said, with the power to elect senators resting with state legislatures.

Before the change, Vatistas said, each state had an "enforcer of the 10th Amendment" whose loyalty to their home state meant they would serve as a protector of local sovereignty. Before the 17th Amendment, he said, senators brought the country each state's ideals and was in a position to resist changes opposed at home.

Several people left the talk charged to take some sort of action. They said they felt they no longer had a choice.

"We were like sleeping giants," said Dover City Councilor Catherine Cheney. "People had a faith that this could not be eroded. People had a certain faith in the government, so we stayed at home . . . now we're realizing our lives as we know them could be very different unless we say this is our life, this is who we are, and the documents and the history backs that up." . . .

Critical Thinking Questions

1. How was the Constitution shaped by the Framers' values and experiences?
2. Should all American citizens have to be familiar with the Constitution and other founding texts?
3. Are there groups in your town that hold studies of the Constitution?

Constitutional Convention, should govern judicial interpretation of the Constitution.[20] Others argue that the Framers knew that a changing society needed an elastic, flexible document that could adapt to the ages.[21] In all likelihood, the vagueness of the document was purposeful. Those in attendance in Philadelphia recognized that they could not agree on everything and that it was wiser to leave interpretation to future generations.

SOCIAL AND CULTURAL CHANGE Even the most far-sighted of those in attendance at the Constitutional Convention could not have anticipated the vast changes that have occurred in the United States. For example, although many people were uncomfortable with the Three-Fifths Compromise and others hoped for the abolition of slavery, none could have imagined that an African American would one day become president of the United States.

Social change has also caused changes in the way institutions of government act. As problems such as the Great Depression appeared national in scope, Congress took on more and more power at the expense of the states. In fact, Yale law professor Bruce Ackerman argues that extraordinary times call for extraordinary measures such as the New Deal that, in effect, amend the Constitution. Thus, congressional passage (and the Supreme Court's eventual acceptance) of sweeping New Deal legislation that altered the balance of power between the national government and the states truly changed the Constitution without benefit of amendment.[22] Still, in spite of massive changes such as these, the Constitution survives, changed and ever changing after more than 200 years. (To learn more about how certain groups are using the Constitution to make a case for states' rights, see Politics Now: Constitution, States' Rights Energizing Local Politics.)

What Should I Have LEARNED?

Now that you have read this chapter, you should be able to:

⭐ **2.1 Trace the historical developments that led to the colonists' break with Great Britain and the emergence of the new American nation, p. 26.**

Settlers came to the New World for a variety of reasons, but most of these early inhabitants remained loyal to Great Britain and considered themselves subjects of the king. Over the years, as new generations of Americans were born on colonial soil, those ties weakened. A series of taxes levied by the British crown ultimately led colonists to convene the Second Continental Congress and to declare their independence.

⭐ **2.2 Identify the key components of the Articles of Confederation and the reasons why it failed, p. 31.**

The Articles of Confederation (1781) created a loose league of friendship between the new national government and the states. Numerous weaknesses in the new government quickly became apparent. Among the major flaws were Congress's inability to tax or regulate commerce, the absence of an executive to administer the government, the lack of a strong central government, and no judiciary.

⭐ **2.3 Outline the issues and compromises that were central to the writing of the U.S. Constitution, p. 33.**

When the weaknesses under the Articles of Confederation became apparent, the states called for a meeting to reform them. The Constitutional Convention (1787) threw out the Articles of Confederation and fashioned a new, more workable form of government. The U.S. Constitution was the result of a series of compromises, including those over representation, issues involving large and small states, slavery, and how to determine population. Compromises were

also made about how members of each branch of government were to be selected. The Electoral College was created to give states a key role in the selection of the president.

⭐ **2.4 Analyze the underlying principles of the U.S. Constitution, p. 37.**

The proposed U.S. Constitution created a federal system that drew heavily on Montesquieu's ideas about separation of powers. These ideas concerned a way of parceling out power among the three branches of government. A system of checks and balances also prevented any one branch from having too much power.

⭐ **2.5 Explain the conflicts that characterized the drive for ratification of the U.S. Constitution, p. 42.**

The drive for ratification became a fierce fight between Federalists and Anti-Federalists. Federalists lobbied for the strong national government created by the Constitution; Anti-Federalists favored greater state power.

⭐ **2.6 Distinguish between the methods for proposing and ratifying amendments to the U.S. Constitution, p. 45.**

The Framers did not want the government to be too swayed by the whims of the people. Therefore, they designed a deliberate two-stage, formal amendment process that required approval on the federal and state levels; this process has rarely been used. However, informal amendments, prompted by judicial interpretation and by cultural and social change, have had a tremendous impact on the Constitution.

Test Yourself: The Constitution

⭐ **2.1 Trace the historical developments that led to the colonists' break with Great Britain and the emergence of the new American nation, p. 26.**

The purpose of the First Continental Congress in 1774 was to
A. Devise a plan to secede from Great Britain.
B. Protest the British taxes on tea.
C. Bring the colonies together to keep abreast of the developments with the British.
D. Formally oppose the Coercive Acts.
E. Adopt the Olive Branch Petition.

⭐ **2.2 Identify the key components of the Articles of Confederation and the reasons why it failed, p. 31.**

Why did the Articles of Confederation create a national system of government whose power was derived from the states?
A. The disagreements in the Continental Congress necessitated a compromise between those who wanted a strong national government and those who supported strong state governments.
B. The Articles simply formalized the system of government proposed by the Declaration of Independence.
C. The Framers sought to create a system similar to other democracies in the world.
D. It was a reaction to Great Britain's unitary system of government.
E. The states wanted a system wherein they would be loosely dependent on a national government.

⭐ **2.3 Outline the issues and compromises that were central to the writing of the U.S. Constitution, p. 33.**

During the formation of the United States, smaller states such as New Jersey and Connecticut supported a model of government that included all of the following features EXCEPT
A. a legislature with the power to select the executive.
B. a one-house legislature with one vote for each state.
C. congressional powers to raise revenue from duties on imports and from postal services.
D. revision—not replacement—of the Articles of Confederation.
E. creation of a Supreme Court with members appointed for life by executive officers.

⭐ **2.4 Analyze the underlying principles of the U.S. Constitution, p. 37.**

With which aspect of government does Article III of the U.S. Constitution deal?
A. The supremacy of the Constitution
B. The executive branch of government
C. Proper procedures for adding states to the union
D. The legislative branch of government
E. The judicial branch of government

⭐ **2.5 Explain the conflicts that characterized the drive for ratification of the U.S. Constitution, p. 42.**

Which of the following was one of the views of the Anti-Federalists?
A. The most elite groups of society are the most fit to govern.
B. A strong government could strip powers away from the states.
C. Separation of powers would prevent any one group from dominating the national government.
D. There can be a happy combination between a strong national government and state governments responsive to local needs.
E. The U.S. Constitution, in its original form, provided sufficient protections of the citizens.

⭐ **2.6 Distinguish between the methods for proposing and ratifying amendments to the U.S. Constitution, p. 45.**

In what ways has the U.S. Constitution NOT been amended?
A. Ratification by legislatures in three-fourths of the states
B. Judicial interpretation
C. Social and cultural change
D. Ratification by conventions called in one-fourth of the states
E. Proposal by two-thirds vote in both houses of Congress

Essay Questions

1. What were some of the weaknesses of the Articles of Confederation, and how did the U.S. Constitution correct those weaknesses?
2. Why was the Bill of Rights added to the U.S. Constitution?
3. How is power checked and balanced in the national government?
4. In what way was ratification of the Twenty-First Amendment different from ratification of the others, and what accounts for this difference?

myp⊙liscilab Exercises

Apply what you learned in this chapter on MyPoliSciLab.

📖—Read on **mypoliscilab.com**

eText: Chapter 2

✓—Study and Review on **mypoliscilab.com**

Pre-Test
Post-Test
Chapter Exam
Flashcards

👁—Watch on **mypoliscilab.com**

Video: Animal Sacrifice and Free Exercise
Video: Polygamy and the U.S. Constitution
Video: Animal Sacrifice and Free Exercise
Video: Polygamy and the U.S. Constitution

⊕—Explore on **mypoliscilab.com**

Simulation: You Are James Madison
Simulation: You Are Proposing a Constitutional Amendment
Comparative: Comparing Constitutions
Timeline: The History of Constitutional Amendments
Visual Literacy: The American System of Checks and Balances

Key Terms

Anti-Federalists, p. 42
Articles of Confederation, p. 32
Bill of Rights, p. 44
checks and balances, p. 37
Committees of Correspondence, p. 30
constitution, p. 34
Declaration of Independence, p. 30
enumerated powers, p. 39
federal system, p. 37

The Federalist Papers, p. 43
Federalists, p. 42
First Continental Congress, p. 30
full faith and credit clause, p. 40
Great Compromise, p. 35
implied powers, p. 40
mercantilism, p. 27
necessary and proper clause, p. 40

New Jersey Plan, p. 35
Second Continental Congress, p. 30
separation of powers, p. 37
Stamp Act Congress, p. 29
supremacy clause, p. 40
Three-Fifths Compromise, p. 36
Virginia Plan, p. 34

To Learn More on the Constitution

In the Library

Ackerman, Bruce. *The Failure of the Founding Fathers: Jefferson, Marshall, and the Rise of Presidential Democracy,* new ed. Cambridge, MA: Belknap Press, 2007.

Beard, Charles A. *An Economic Interpretation of the Constitution of the United States,* reissue ed. Mineola, NY: Dover, 2004.

Beeman, Richard. *Plain, Honest Men: The Making of the American Constitution.* New York: Random House, 2009.

Bowen, Catherine Drinker. *Miracle at Philadelphia.* Boston: Little, Brown, 1986.

Breyer, Stephen. *Active Liberty: Interpreting Our Democratic Constitution.* New York: Vintage, 2007.

Brinkley, Alan, Nelson W. Polsby, and Kathleen M. Sullivan. *New Federalist Papers: Essays in Defense of the Constitution.* New York: Norton, 1997.

Dahl, Robert A. *How Democratic is the American Constitution?* 2nd ed. New Haven, CT: Yale University Press, 2004.

Hamilton, Alexander, James Madison, and John Jay. *The Federalist Papers.* New York: Bantam Books, 1989 (first published in 1788).

Ketcham, Ralph, ed. *The Anti-Federalist Papers and the Constitutional Convention Debates.* New York: Signet Classics, 2003.

Main, Jackson Turner. *The Anti-Federalists: Critics of the Constitution, 1781–1788.* Chapel Hill: University of North Carolina Press, 2004.

Sabato, Larry J. *A More Perfect Constitution.* New York: Walker, 2008.

Stewart, David O. *The Summer of 1787: The Men Who Invented the Constitution.* New York: Simon and Schuster, 2007.

Storing, Herbert J. *What the Anti-Federalists Were For.* Chicago: University of Chicago Press, 1981.

Tushnet, Mark. *Taking the Constitution Away from the Courts.* Princeton, NJ: Princeton University Press, 2002.

Wood, Gordon S. *The Creation of the American Republic, 1776–1787,* reissue ed. Chapel Hill: University of North Carolina Press, 1998.

On the Web

To learn more about the founding of the United States, the Articles of Confederation, and the writing and ratification of the Constitution, go to the educational resources site of the House of Representatives at **www.house.gov/house/Educate.shtml.**

To learn more about the Declaration of Independence, the Constitution, the Bill of Rights, and the Framers, go to the National Archives site at **www.archives.gov/exhibits/charters/charters.html.**

To learn more about the eighteenth-century documents related to the national founding and the Revolutionary War, go to the Avalon Project at Yale Law School at **www.yale.edu/lawweb/avalon/18th.htm.**

To learn more about *The Federalist Papers,* go to the Library of Congress at **thomas.loc.gov.**

The Constitution of the United States of America

We the People of the United States, in Order to form a more perfect Union, establish Justice, insure domestic Tranquility, provide for the common defence, promote the general Welfare, and secure the Blessings of Liberty to ourselves and our Posterity, do ordain and establish this Constitution for the United States of America.

• The preamble to the U.S. Constitution is little more than a declaration of intent; it carries no legal weight. Instead, it describes what the people of the United States can expect from their government. •

ARTICLE I
Section 1.

All legislative Powers herein granted shall be vested in a Congress of the United States, which shall consist of a Senate and House of Representatives.

• Article I is the longest and most detailed of any of the articles, sections, or amendments that make up the U.S. Constitution. By *enumerating* the powers of Congress, the Framers attached limits to the enormous authority they had vested in the legislative branch. At the same time, they ensured that the legislative branch would maintain control over certain vital areas of public policy and that it would be protected from attacks by the executive and judicial branches. In addition, by clearly vesting Congress with certain powers (e.g., the power to regulate interstate commerce), Article I established limits for the exercise of state power in what were now national affairs.

Despite the great care the Framers took to limit the exercise of congressional authority to those powers enumerated in Article I, the power of Congress has grown tremendously since the nation's founding. Under Chief Justice John Marshall (1801–1835), the U.S. Supreme Court interpreted the Constitution to favor the power of the national government over the states and to permit Congress to exercise both its *enumerated powers* (e.g., the power to regulate interstate commerce) and *implied powers* (e.g., as indicated in the necessary and

proper clause) in broad fashion. Rarely has the Court challenged the legislative power vested in Congress to engage in numerous areas of public policy that some constitutional scholars (and politicians and voters) believe are the province of the states. •

Section 2.

The House of Representatives shall be composed of Members chosen every second Year by the People of the several States, and the Electors in each State shall have the Qualifications requisite for Electors of the most numerous Branch of the State Legislature.

No person shall be a Representative who shall not have attained to the Age of twenty five Years, and been seven Years a Citizen of the United States, and who shall not, when elected, be an Inhabitant of that State in which he shall be chosen.

• The qualifications clause, which sets out the age and residency requirements for individuals who wish to run for the House of Representatives, became the centerpiece of a national debate that emerged during the late 1980s and early 1990s over term limits for members of Congress. In *U.S. Term Limits* v. *Thornton* (1995), the Supreme Court ruled that no state government could enact legislation to restrict a qualified individual's right to run for Congress. Instead, any modification to the qualifications clause would have to come through a constitutional amendment. •

Representatives and direct Taxes shall be apportioned among the several States which may be included within this Union, according to their respective Numbers which shall be determined by adding to the whole Number of free Persons, including those bound to Service for a Term of Years, and excluding Indians not taxed, three fifths of all other Persons. The actual Enumeration shall be made within three Years after the first Meeting of the Congress of the United States, and within every subsequent Term ten Years, in such Manner as they shall by Law direct. The Number of Representatives shall not exceed one for every thirty Thousand, but each State shall have at Least one Representative; and until such enumerations shall be made, the State of New Hampshire shall be entitled to chuse three, Massachusetts eight, Rhode-Island and Providence Plantations one, Connecticut five, New-York six, New Jersey four, Pennsylvania eight, Delaware one, Maryland six, Virginia ten, North Carolina five, South Carolina five, and Georgia three.

• Under the Articles of Confederation, "direct" taxes (such as taxes on property) were apportioned based on land value, not population. This encouraged states to diminish the value of their land to reduce their tax burden. Prior to the Constitutional Convention of 1787, several prominent delegates proposed changing the method for direct taxation from land value to the population of each state. A major sticking point among the delegates on this issue was how to count slaves for taxation purposes. Southern states wanted to diminish the value of slaves for tax purposes, while counting slaves as "whole persons" for purposes of representation in the House of Representatives, but northern states rejected this proposal. Ultimately, the delegates settled on the Three-Fifths Compromise, which treated each slave as three-fifths of a person for tax and representation purposes.

At the beginning, the Three-Fifths Compromise enhanced southern power in the House. Over time, however, the population of the South remained relatively stagnant, while the North's population grew, and so the South saw its power in the House diminish. By the 1830s, the South held just over 30 percent of House seats, which gave it enough power to thwart northern initiatives on slavery questions and territorial issues, but not enough power to defeat the growing power of the North to control commercial and economic policy. This standoff between the North and South led to such events as South Carolina Senator John C. Calhoun's doctrine of nullification and secession, which argued that a state could nullify any federal law not consistent with regional or state interests. By the 1850s, the Three-Fifths Compromise had made the South dependent on expanding the number of slaveholding territories eligible for admission to the union and a judicial system sympathetic to slaveholding interests. The Three-Fifths Compromise was repealed by section 2 of the Fourteenth Amendment (see page 72). •

When vacancies happen in the Representation from any State, the Executive Authority thereof shall issue Writs of Election to fill such Vacancies.

• This clause permits the governor of a state to call an election to replace any member of the House of Representatives who is unable to complete a term of office due to death, resignation, or removal from the House. In some cases, a governor will appoint a successor to fill out a term; in other cases, the governor will call a special election. This decision depends on both partisan interests and state laws. •

The House of Representatives shall chuse their speaker and other Officers; and shall have the sole Power of Impeachment.

• Clause 5 establishes the only constitutional officer of the House of Representatives—the Speaker. The members of the House create the remaining offices (party leaders and whips, for example).

The House also has the sole power of impeachment against members of the executive and judicial branches. The House, like the Senate, is responsible for disciplining its own members. In *Nixon* v. *U.S.* (1993), the Supreme Court ruled that government officials who are the subject of impeachment proceedings may not challenge them in court; the sole power given to the House over impeachment precludes judicial intervention. •

Section 3.

The Senate of the United States shall be composed of two Senators from each State chosen by the Legislature thereof, for six Years; and each Senator shall have one Vote.

• This clause establishing the election of senators by state legislatures was repealed by the Seventeenth Amendment (see page 73). •

Immediately after they shall be assembled in Consequence of the first Election, they shall be divided as equally as may be into three Classes. The Seats of the Senators of the first Class shall be vacated at the Expiration of the second year, of the second Class at the Expiration of the fourth Year, and of the third Class at the Expiration of the sixth Year, so that one third may be chosen every second Year and if Vacancies happen by Resignation, or otherwise, during the Recess of the Legislature of any State, the Executive thereof may make temporary Appointments until the next Meeting of the Legislature, which shall then fill such Vacancies.

• To assure continuity in government, all senators do not run for reelection at one time. Instead, they are grouped into three sets of senators who run for reelection on a staggered basis. Thus, one-third of the senators are up for reelection in 2012, the next third in 2014, and another third in 2016.

The Seventeenth Amendment also modified the vacancy clause. No longer do state legislators choose senators' replacements; vacancies in the Senate are handled the same way as vacancies for representatives—through appointment or special election. •

No Person shall be a Senator who shall not have attained to the Age of thirty Years, and been nine Years a Citizen of the United States, and who shall not, when elected, be an Inhabitant of that State for which he shall be chosen.

• Clause 3 lays out the requirements to serve as a member of the Senate. •

The Vice President of the United States shall be President of the Senate, but shall have no Vote, unless they be equally divided.

• Clause 4 gives the vice president the authority to vote to break a tie in the Senate. This is the only constitutional duty the Constitution specifies for the vice president. As president of the Senate, the vice president also presides over procedural matters of that body, although this is not a responsibility that vice presidents shoulder. •

The Senate shall chuse their other Officers, and also a President pro tempore, in the Absence of the Vice President, or when he shall exercise the Office of President of the United States.

• Clause 5 creates the position of *president pro tempore* (the president of the time), the only Senate office established by the Constitution to handle the duties of the vice president set out in section 3, clause 4. •

The Senate shall have the sole Power to try all Impeachments. When sitting for that Purpose, they shall be on Oath or Affirmation. When the President of the United States is tried, the Chief Justice shall preside: And no Person shall be convicted without the Concurrence of two thirds of the Members present.

Judgment in Cases of Impeachment shall not extend further than to removal from Office, and disqualification to hold and enjoy any Office of honor, Trust or Profit under the United States; but the Party convicted shall nevertheless be liable and subject to Indictment, Trial, Judgment and Punishment, according to law.

• Just as the House of Representatives has the sole power to bring impeachment proceedings against executive and judicial branch officials, the Senate has the sole power to try all impeachments. Unless the president faces trial in the Senate, the vice president serves as the presiding officer. In 1998, President Bill Clinton was tried on two articles of impeachment (four were brought against him in the House) and found not guilty on each count. Chief Justice William H. Rehnquist presided over President Clinton's impeachment trial.

A conviction results in the removal of an official from office. It does not prohibit subsequent civil or criminal action against that individual. Nor does it prohibit an impeached and convicted official from returning to federal office. In 1989, Alcee Hastings, a trial judge with ten years experience on the U.S. District Court for the Southern District of Florida, was convicted on impeachment charges and removed from office. In 1992, he ran successfully for the 23rd District seat of the U.S. House of Representatives, where he continues to serve as of this writing. •

Section 4.

The Times, Places and Manner of holding Elections for Senators and Representatives, shall be prescribed in each State by the Legislature thereof; but the Congress may at any time by Law make or alter such Regulations, except as to the Places of chusing Senators.

• Section 4 authorizes the states to establish the rules governing elections for members of Congress. Congress, however, has exercised its law-making power in this area when it has believed that improvements to the electoral process were necessary (e.g., the Voting Rights Act of 1965). •

The Congress shall assemble at least once in every Year, and such Meeting shall be on the first Monday in December, unless they shall by Law appoint a different Day.

• This clause is no longer relevant; innovations in air conditioning and travel made it possible for Congress to become a professionalized legislature that meets for long stretches of time. •

Section 5.

Each House shall be the Judge of the Elections, Returns and Qualifications of its own Members, and a Majority of each shall constitute a Quorum to do business; but a smaller Number may adjourn from day to day, and may be authorized to compel the Attendance of absent Members, in such Manner, and under such Penalties as each House may provide.

• This clause authorizes Congress to judge the internal elections of its members, requires a quorum for either chamber to conduct official business, to compel the attendance of its members, and to punish them for failing to adhere to the rules of their respective chambers. •

Each House may determine the Rules of its Proceedings, punish its Members for disorderly

Behaviour, and with the Concurrence of two thirds, expel a Member.

• Clause 2 gives power to the House and Senate to establish the rules and decorum for each chamber. Expulsion from either the House or the Senate does not preclude a member from running for congressional office again or serving in any other official capacity. In *Powell* v. *McCormack* (1969), the Supreme Court ruled that the House's authority to expel a member was limited to those already in office. •

Each House shall keep a Journal of its Proceedings, and from time to time publish the same, excepting such Parts as may in their judgment require Secrecy; and the Yeas and Nays of the Members of either House on any question shall, at the Desire of one fifth of those present, be entered on the Journal.

• The *Congressional Record* is the official journal of Congress. Justice Joseph Story, in his much praised scholarly treatment of the U.S. Constitution, *Commentaries on the Constitution* (1833), said the purpose of this clause was "to insure publicity to the proceedings of the legislature, and a correspondent responsibility of the members to their respective constituents." Recorded votes (and yea-or-nay voice votes, if agreed to by one-fifth of the House or Senate), speeches, and other public business are contained in the *Congressional Record*. •

Neither House, during the Session of Congress, shall, without the Consent of the other, adjourn for more than three days, nor to any other Place than that in which the two Houses shall be sitting.

Section 6.

The Senators and Representatives shall receive a Compensation for their Services, to be ascertained by Law, and paid out of the Treasury of the United States. They shall in all Cases, except Treason, Felony and Breach of the Peace, be privileged from Arrest during their Attendance at the Session of their respective Houses, and in going to and returning from the same; and for any Speech or Debate in either House, they shall not be questioned in any other Place.

• From the nation's founding until 1967, Congress determined the salaries of its members. Then, Congress passed legislation giving the president the responsibility to recommend salary levels for members of Congress, since the president already had the responsibility to recommend pay levels for other federal officials. The Twenty-Seventh Amendment, ratified in 1992, currently

governs the procedures for compensation of members of Congress.

Clause 1 also protects the right of senators and representatives from criminal prosecution for any "Speech or Debate" made in Congress. This protection stemmed from lessons drawn from the persistent conflicts between the House of Commons and the Tudor and Stuart monarchies in Great Britain, who used their power to bring civil and criminal actions against legislators whose opinions were deemed seditious or dangerous. The Supreme Court held, however, in *Gravel* v. *U.S.* (1972), that the speech or debate clause does not immunize senators or representatives from criminal inquiry, if their activities in the Senate or House are the result of alleged or proven illegal action.

The privilege from arrest clause has little application in contemporary America. The clause applies only to arrests in civil suits, which were fairly common when the Constitution was ratified. The Court has interpreted the phrase "except Treason, Felony or Breach of the Peace" to make members eligible for arrest for crimes that would fall into that category, for example a serious traffic offense, such as drunk or reckless driving, on the way to or from legislative business. •

No Senator or Representative shall, during the Time for which he was elected, be appointed to any civil Office under the Authority of the United States, which shall have been created, or the Emoluments whereof shall have been encreased during such time; and no Person holding any Office under the United States, shall be a Member of either House during his Continuance in Office.

• Clause 2 prohibits any senator or representative from holding a simultaneous office in the legislative or executive branches. This is one of the least controversial provisions of the Constitution. The general purpose of this clause is to prevent one branch of government from having an undue influence on another by creating dual incentives. It is also another safeguard in the separation of powers. •

Section 7.

All Bills for raising Revenue shall originate in the House of Representatives; but the Senate may propose or concur with Amendments as on other Bills.

• The power to raise revenue found in clause 1 is unique to the House of Representatives. In *Federalist No. 58*, James Madison argued that vesting such authority in the House was a key feature of the separation of powers. No bill either raising or lowering taxes may originate in the Senate. Legislation that creates incidental revenue may begin in the Senate, as long as the legislation does not involve taxation. •

Every Bill which shall have passed the House of Representatives and the Senate, shall, before it become a Law, be presented to the President of the United States; If he approve he shall sign it, but if not he shall return it, with his Objections to that House in which it shall have originated, who shall enter the Objections at large on their Journal, and proceed to reconsider it. If after such Reconsideration two thirds of that House shall agree to pass the Bill, it shall be sent, together with the Objections, to the other House, by which it shall likewise be reconsidered, and if approved by two thirds of that House, it shall become a Law. But in all such Cases the Votes of both Houses shall be determined by Yeas and Nays, and the Names of the Persons voting for and against the Bill shall be entered on the Journal of each House respectively. If any Bill shall not be returned by the President within ten Days (Sundays excepted) after it shall have been presented to him, the Same shall be a Law, in like Manner as if he had signed it, unless the Congress by their Adjournment prevent its Return, in which Case it shall not be a Law.

• This clause establishes several key features of presidential-congressional relations. For a bill to become law, it must be passed by the House and Senate, and it must be signed by the president.

The Supreme Court has ruled that the veto regulations outlined in this clause serve two purposes. First, by giving the president ten days to consider a bill for approval, clause 2 provides the president with ample time to consider legislation and protects him from having to approve legislation in the wake of congressional adjournment. But clause 2 also provides Congress with a countervailing power to override a presidential veto, a procedure that requires a two-thirds vote in each chamber. •

Every Order, Resolution, or Vote to which the Concurrence of the Senate and House of Representatives may be necessary (except on a question of Adjournment) shall be presented to the President of the United States; and before the Same shall take Effect, shall be approved by him, or being disapproved by him, shall be repassed by two thirds of the Senate and House of Representatives, according to the Rules and Limitations prescribed in the Case of a Bill.

• Clause 3 covers the presentation of resolutions, not actual legislation. For any resolution to have the force of law, it must be presented to the president for approval. Should the president veto the resolution, Congress may override this veto in the same manner expressed in section 7, clause 2. Resolutions that do not have the force of law do not require presidential approval. Preliminary votes taken on constitutional amendments and other legislative matters covered by clause 3 do not require presentation to the president.

This clause has been the subject of two major Supreme Court decisions dealing with the separation of powers. In *INS* v. *Chadha* (1983), the Court ruled that the House-only legislative veto, a practice begun during the 1930s to give Congress control over power delegated to a rapidly expanding executive branch, violated both the bicameralism principles of Article I, section 1, and the presentment clause of section 7, clause 3. At the time, the ruling struck down about 200 legislative vetoes that had been included in various pieces of congressional legislation. In *Clinton* v. *City of New York* (1998), the Court ruled that the line-item veto passed by Congress to give the president the power to veto specific provisions of legislation rather than an entire bill violated the presentment clause of Article I, section 7, clause 3. The Court claimed that the line-item veto permitted the president to "repeal certain laws," a power that belonged to Congress and not the president. •

Section 8.

The Congress shall have Power To lay and collect Taxes, Duties, Imposts and Excises, to pay the Debts and provide for the common Defence and general Welfare of the United States; but all Duties, Imposts and Excises shall be uniform throughout the United States;

To borrow Money on the credit of the United States;

To regulate Commerce with foreign Nations, and among the several States, and with the Indian Tribes;

To establish a uniform Rule of Naturalization, and uniform Laws on the subject of Bankruptcies throughout the United States;

To coin Money, regulate the Value thereof, and of foreign Coin, and fix the Standard of Weights and Measures;

To provide for the Punishment of counterfeiting the Securities and current Coin of the United States;

To establish Post Offices and post Roads;

To promote the Progress of Science and useful Arts, by securing for limited Times to Authors and Inventors exclusive Right to their respective Writings and Discoveries;

To constitute Tribunals inferior to the supreme Court;

To define and punish Piracies and Felonies committed on the high Seas, and Offences against the Law of Nations;

To declare War, grant Letters of Marque and Reprisal, and make rules concerning Captures on Land and Water;

To raise and support Armies, but no Appropriation of Money to that Use shall be for a longer Term than two Years;

To provide and maintain a Navy;

To make Rules for the Government and Regulation of the land and naval Forces;

To provide for calling forth the Militia to execute the Laws of the Union, suppress Insurrections and repel Invasions;

To provide for organizing, arming, and disciplining, the Militia, and for governing such Part of them as may be employed in the Service of the United States, reserving to the States respectively, the Appointment of the Officers, and the Authority of training the Militia according to the discipline prescribed by Congress;

• Article I, section 8, is, in many ways, the engine of congressional power. It contains all of the enumerated powers of Congress. First, clause 1 gives Congress the power to tax and spend, a power the Supreme Court has interpreted as "exhaustive" and "reaching every subject." Second, in giving Congress the power to provide for the common defense and general welfare, it encourages Congress to spend public funds on federal programs. Third, section 8 gives Congress complete authority in numerous areas of policy that affect Americans at home and abroad. These powers include the power to regulate interstate commerce (which Congress has relied on to establish federal civil rights law), to make war (a power that Congress, since the end of World War II in 1945, has increasingly deferred to the president), and to establish the federal judicial system. •

To exercise exclusive Legislation in all Cases whatsoever, over such District (not exceeding ten Miles square) as may, by Cession of particular States, and the Acceptance of Congress, become the Seat of the Government of the United States, and to exercise like Authority over all Places purchased by the Consent of the Legislature of the State in which the Same shall be for the Erection of Forts, Magazines, Arsenals, dock-Yards, and other needful Buildings;

• Clause 17 establishes the seat of the federal government—first New York City, now Washington, D.C. The clause also makes Congress the legislative body of the nation's capital, a power that extends to other federal bodies, such as forts, military bases, and other places where federal buildings are located. •

—And To make all Laws which shall be necessary and proper for carrying into Execution the foregoing Powers, and all other Powers vested by this Constitution in the Government of the United States, or in any Department or Officer thereof.

• Better known as the necessary and proper clause, Article I, section 8, clause 18 is the basis for the implied powers of Congress. It was one of the most contested points between Federalists and Anti-Federalists during the ratification debates over the Constitution. Anti-Federalists feared that the language was too broad and would give Congress limitless power over state and local matters.

In *McCulloch* v. *Maryland* (1819), Chief Justice John Marshall offered what constitutional scholars believe remains the definitive interpretation of the necessary and proper clause, which was that Article 1, section 8, specifically gives Congress the authority to pass all laws "necessary and proper" to carry out the enumerated powers specified in the Constitution. While *McCulloch* cemented the power of Congress in the federal system, the expansive definition by the Court is also testament to the flexible nature of the Constitution, and why so few amendments have been added to the original document. •

Section 9.

The Migration or Importation of such Persons as any of the States now existing shall think proper to admit, shall not be prohibited by the Congress prior to the Year one thousand eight hundred and eight, but a Tax or duty may be imposed on such Importation, not exceeding ten dollars for each Person.

• Like the other provisions of the Constitution that refer to slavery, such as the Three-Fifths Compromise, section 9 creates policy governing the institution of slavery without ever mentioning the word. The importation clause was a compromise between slave traders, who wanted to continue the practice, and opponents of slavery, who needed southern support to ratify the Constitution. In 1808, Congress passed legislation banning the importation of slaves; until then, Congress used its power to tax slaves brought to the United States. •

The Privilege of the Writ of *Habeas Corpus* shall not be suspended, unless when in Cases of Rebellion or Invasion the public Safety may require it.

• Clause 2 is the only place where the writ of *habeas corpus*—the "Great Writ," as it was known to the Framers—is mentioned in the Constitution, and only the federal government is bound by clause 2. A writ is a court order in which a judge requires authorities to prove that a prisoner is being held lawfully and that allows the prisoner to be freed if the judge is not persuaded by the government's case. *Habeas corpus* rights imply that prisoners have a right to know what charges are being made against them. The writ may only be suspended in times of crisis and rebellion, and then it is Congress that has the power, not the president. In *Boumediene* v. *Bush* (2008), the Supreme Court ruled unconstitutional the provision of the Military Commissions Act of 2006 stripping the federal courts of their jurisdiction to hear *habeas corpus* petitions from detainees at a U.S. military prison at Guantanamo Bay, Cuba. •

No Bill of Attainder or *ex post facto* Law shall be passed.

• A bill of attainder is a law declaring an act illegal without a judicial trial. The fundamental purpose of the ban on bills of attainder is to prevent trial by legislature and other arbitrary punishments. An *ex post facto* law is a law that is passed "after the fact," thereby making previously legal activity illegal and subject to current penalty. Thus, if a law is passed prohibiting texting while driving, no citizens can be punished for having texted while driving if they did it before the law was passed. A similar restriction on the states is found in Article I, section 10, clause 1. •

No Capitation, or other direct, Tax shall be laid, unless in Proportion to the Census or Enumeration herein before directed to be taken.

• This clause, which originally prohibited Congress from levying an income tax, was modified by the Sixteenth Amendment, passed in 1913 (see page 73). •

No Tax or Duty shall be laid on Articles exported from any State.

• Clause 5 prohibits Congress from levying a tax on any good or article exported from a state to a foreign country or to another state. Many southern states feared that northern members of Congress would attempt to weaken the South's slave-based economy by taxing exports. This clause prohibited such action. Congress may prohibit the shipment of certain items from one state to another and to other countries. •

No Preference shall be given by any Regulation of Commerce or Revenue to the Ports of one State over those of another: nor shall Vessels bound to, or from, one State, be obliged to enter, clear, or pay Duties in another.

• Congress is prohibited from making laws regulating trade that favor one state over another. Clause 6 also prohibits Congress from establishing preferences for certain ports or trade centers over others, although it may, under its power to regulate interstate commerce, pass laws that incidentally benefit certain states or maritime outlets. •

No money shall be drawn from the Treasury, but in Consequence of Appropriations made by Law; and a regular Statement and Account of the Receipts and Expenditures of all public Money shall be published from time to time.

• Clause 7 serves two fundamental purposes. First, the clause prohibits any governmental body receiving federal funds from spending those funds without the approval of Congress. Once Congress has determined that federal funds are to be spent in a certain way, the executive branch may not exercise any discretion over that decision. Second, by restricting executive control of spending power, the clause firmly reinforces congressional authority over revenue and spending, a key feature of the separation of powers. •

No Title of Nobility shall be granted by the United States: And no Person holding any Office of Profit or Trust under them, shall, without the Consent of the Congress, accept of any present, Emolument, Office, or Title, of any kind whatever, from any King, Prince, or foreign State.

• To reinforce the commitment to representative democracy, the Framers prohibited a title of nobility from being conferred on any public official. This clause also prohibits any government official from accepting compensation, gifts, or similar benefits from any foreign government for services rendered without the consent of Congress. •

Section 10.

No state shall enter into any Treaty, Alliance, or Confederation; grant Letters of Marque and Reprisal; coin Money; emit Bills of Credit; make any Thing but gold and silver Coin a Tender in Payment of Debts; pass any Bill of Attainder, *ex post facto* Law, or Law impairing the Obligation of Contracts, or grant any Title of Nobility.

• This clause denies several powers to the states that were once permissible under the Articles of Confederation, and it emphasizes the Framers' commitment under the Constitution to a strong national government. During the Civil War, the Union relied on this clause in support of its view that the Confederate states had no legal existence but instead were merely "states in rebellion" against the United States.

The restrictions on states passing either bills of attainder or *ex post facto* laws have come into play at various points in American history. During Reconstruction, several states enacted legislation prohibiting any individual who aided the Confederacy from entering certain professions or enjoying other benefits available to citizens who remained loyal to the Union. The Supreme Court struck down these laws on the grounds that they violated this clause.

The provision prohibiting states from passing any law "impairing the Obligation of Contracts," better known as the contract clause, has been the subject of considerable litigation before the Supreme Court. The contract clause was intended to bar the states from interfering in private contracts between consensual parties and was considered an important limit on the power of states. Early on, the Court considered many laws that restricted the terms set out in private contracts as unconstitutional. But as the United States became a more industrial society, and as citizen demands grew for government regulation of the economy, the environment, and social welfare benefits, the Court softened its position on the contract clause to permit states to make laws that served a reasonable public interest. A key case involving the contract clause is *Home Building and Loan Association v. Blaisdell* (1934). In *Blaisdell*, the Court ruled that a Depression-era law passed by the Minnesota legislature forgiving mortgage payments by homeowners to banks did not violate the contract clause. In *Energy Reserves Group v. Kansas Power & Light* (1983), the Court ruled that the contract clause does not prohibit the state from "impairing" contracts if a regulation is intended to address a "broad and general social or economic problem." •

No State shall, without the Consent of the Congress, lay any Imposts or Duties on Imports or Exports, except what may be absolutely necessary for executing its inspection Laws: and the net Produce of all Duties and Imposts, laid by any State on Imports or Exports, shall be for the Use of the Treasury of the United States, and all such Laws shall be subject to the Revision and Controul of the Congress.

• No state may tax goods leaving or entering a state, although it may charge reasonable fees for inspections considered necessary to the public interest. The restriction on import and export taxes applies only to those goods entering from or leaving for a foreign country. •

No State shall, without the Consent of Congress, lay any Duty of Tonnage, keep Troops, or Ships of War in time of Peace, enter into any Agreement or Compact with another State, or with a foreign Power, or engage in War, unless actually invaded, or in such imminent Danger as will not admit of delay.

• Clause 3 cements the power of Congress to control acts of war and make treaties with foreign countries. The Framers wanted to correct any perception that states were free to act independently of the national government on negotiated matters with foreign countries. They also wanted to ensure that any state that entered into a compact with another state—something this clause does not prohibit—must receive permission from Congress. More than 200 interstate compacts exist today. The Drivers License Compact, for example, was signed by all fifty states to facilitate nationwide recognition of licenses issued in respective states. •

ARTICLE II
Section 1.

The executive Power shall be vested in a President of the United States of America. He shall hold his Office during the Term of four Years, and, together with the Vice President, chosen for the same Term, be elected as follows.

• In *Federalist No. 70*, Alexander Hamilton argued for an "energetic executive" branch headed by a single, elected president not necessarily beholden to the majority party in Congress. Hamilton believed that a nationally elected president would not be bound by the narrow, parochial interests that drove legislative law-making. The president would possess both the veto power over Congress and a platform from which to articulate a national vision in both domestic and foreign affairs.

Hamilton believed that the constitutional boundaries placed on executive power through the separation of powers and the fact that the president was accountable to a national electorate constrained any possibility that the office would come to resemble the monarchies of Europe. However, most presidential scholars agree that the modern presidency has grown in power precisely because of the general nature of the enabling powers of Article II. •

Each State shall appoint, in such Manner as the Legislature thereof may direct, a Number of Electors, equal to the whole Number of Senators and Representatives to which the State may be entitled in the Congress; but no Senator or Representative, or Person holding an Office of Trust of Profit under the United States, shall be appointed an Elector.

• Clause 2 established the Electoral College and set the number of electors from each state at the total of senators and representatives serving in Congress from each state. •

The Electors shall meet in their respective States, and vote by Ballot for two Persons, of whom one at least shall not be an Inhabitant of the same State with themselves. And they shall make a List of all the Persons voted for, and, of the Number of Votes for each; which List they shall sign and certify, and transmit sealed to the Seat of the Government of the United States, directed to the President of the Senate. The President of the Senate shall, in the Presence of the Senate and House of Representatives, open all the Certificates, and the Votes shall then be counted. The Person having the greatest Number of Votes shall be the President, if such Number be a Majority of the whole Number of Electors appointed; and if there be more than one who have such Majority, and have an equal Number of Votes, then the House of Representatives shall immediately chuse by Ballot one of them for President; and if no Person have a Majority, then from the five highest on the List the said House shall in like Manner chuse the President. But in chusing the President, the Votes shall be taken by States, the Representation from each State having one Vote; A quorum for this Purpose shall consist of a Member or Members from two thirds of the States, and a Majority of all the States shall be necessary to a Choice. In every Case, after the Choice of the President, the Person having the greatest Number of Votes of the Electors shall be the Vice President. But if there should remain two or more who have equal Votes, the Senate shall chuse from them by Ballot the Vice President.

• This provision of section 1 describes the rules for calling the Electoral College to vote for president and vice president. Originally, the electors did not vote separately for president and vice president. After the 1800 election, which saw Thomas Jefferson and Aaron Burr receive the identical number of electoral votes even though it was clear that Jefferson was the presidential candidate and Burr the vice presidential candidate, the nation ratified the Twelfth Amendment (see page 70).

The Twelfth Amendment did not resolve what many constitutional scholars today believe are the inadequacies of the Electoral College system. In 1824, the presidential election ended in a four-way tie, and the House of Representatives elected second-place finisher John Quincy Adams president. In 1876, Benjamin Harrison lost the popular vote but won the presidency after recounts awarded him an Electoral College majority. But perhaps the most controversial election of all came in 2000 when George W. Bush, who lost the popular contest to Al Gore by approximately 500,000 votes, was named the presidential victor after a six-week

court battle over the vote count in Florida. After the Supreme Court ruled against a recount of the Florida popular vote, Bush was awarded Florida's electoral votes and thus won the election. Outraged Democrats pledged to mount a case for Electoral College reform, but nothing happened. •

The Congress may determine the Time of chusing the Electors, and the Day on which they shall give their Votes; which Day shall be the same throughout the United States.

No Person except a natural born Citizen, or a Citizen of the United States, at the time of the Adoption of this Constitution, shall be eligible to the Office of President; neither shall any Person be eligible to that Office who shall not have attained to the Age of thirty five Years, and been fourteen Years a Resident within the United States.

• This provision of Article II is referred to as the presidential eligibility clause. In addition to setting out the age and resident requirements of presidential aspirants, this clause defines who may *not* run for president—any foreign-born individual, even one who has obtained U.S. citizenship. For example, California Governor Arnold Schwarzenegger, who was born in Austria but has lived in the United States his entire adult life, may not run for president. •

In Case of the Removal of the President from Office, or of his Death, Resignation, or Inability to discharge the Powers and Duties of the said Office, the Same shall devolve on the Vice President, and the Congress may by Law provide for the Case of Removal, Death, Resignation or Inability, both of the President and Vice President, declaring what Officer shall then act as President, and such Officer shall act accordingly, until the Disability be removed, or a President shall be elected.

• This presidential succession clause has been modified by the Twenty-Fifth Amendment (see page 77). •

The President shall, at stated Times, receive for his Services, a Compensation, which shall neither be increased nor diminished during the Period for which he shall have been elected, and he shall not receive within that Period any other Emolument from the United States, or any of them.

• Presidential compensation, like compensation for members of Congress, may not be increased for the current occupant of the office. The president is not eligible for any other public compensation during time in office. However, the president may continue to receive income such as interest on investments or book royalties. •

Before he enter on the Execution of his Office, he shall take the following Oath or Affirmation:— "I do solemnly swear (or affirm) that I will faithfully execute the Office of President of the United States, and will to the best of my Ability, preserve, protect and defend the Constitution of the United States."

• Since George Washington's inauguration in 1789, each president has added the phrase "so help me God" to the end of the presidential oath. Although Abraham Lincoln cited the oath to justify his suspension of the writ of *habeas corpus* during the Civil War, no other president has relied on the oath to justify action that stretched the boundaries of executive power. Presidents taking extraordinary action either at home or abroad have relied on either the commander in chief clause of section 2, clause 1, or the provision of section 3 authorizing the president to see that the laws of the United States are "faithfully executed." •

Section 2.

The President shall be Commander in Chief of the Army and Navy of the United States, and of the Militia of the several States, when called into the actual Service of the United States; he may require the Opinion, in writing, of the principal Officer in each of the executive Departments, upon any Subject relating to the Duties of their respective Offices, and he shall have Power to grant Reprieves and Pardons for Offences against the United States, except in Cases of Impeachment.

• Section 2, clause 1, establishes the president as commander in chief of the U.S. Army and Navy. In modern times, that authority has extended to the Air Force, the Marines, and all other branches of the armed forces operating under the command of the United States, including state militias, reserve units, and national guards. Article I provides that Congress, and not the president, has the power to declare war. But, since World War II, no American president has received or requested a declaration of war to commit the armed forces to military conflicts, including those clearly acknowledged as large-scale war (Korea, Vietnam, the 1991 Persian Gulf War, Afghanistan, and the Iraq War). For these conflicts, the president received congressional *authorization* to use force, but not an Article I declaration.

Although the Supreme Court has ruled that the president has *inherent* power—that is, power to carry out the essential functions of his office in times of crisis, war, or emergencies that are not *expressly* spelled out under Article II—it has not concluded that such power is unlimited. In *Youngstown Sheet & Tube* v. *Sawyer*

(1952), the Court ruled that President Harry S Truman did not have the power to seize control of the nation's steel mills to continue the production of munitions and other war supplies without congressional authorization. More recently, the Court ruled in *Hamdan* v. *Rumsfeld* (2006) that President George W. Bush exceeded his authority when he established military commissions that had not been approved by Congress to try detainees and other "enemy combatants" captured in the War on Terror. To address the Court's concerns, Congress passed the Military Commissions Act, which authorized trial by military commissions.

Clause 1 also implicitly creates the Cabinet by authorizing the president to request the opinion "in writing" of the principal officers of the executive branch. The power to create Cabinet-level offices resides with Congress, not the president.

Presidential power to pardon is broad and limited only in cases of impeachment. Perhaps the most controversial pardon in American political history was President Gerald R. Ford's decision to pardon former President Richard M. Nixon, who resigned his office on August 8, 1974, after news reports and congressional inquiries strongly implicated him in the Watergate scandal. A real possibility existed that President Nixon could be tried on criminal charges as the result of his alleged activities during the Watergate scandal. •

He shall have Power, by and with the Advice and Consent of the Senate, to make Treaties, provided two thirds of the Senators present concur; and he shall nominate, and by and with the Advice and Consent of the Senate, shall appoint Ambassadors, other public Ministers and Consuls, Judges of the supreme Court, and all other Officers of the United States, whose Appointments are not herein otherwise provided for, and which shall be established by Law: but the Congress may by Law vest the Appointment of such inferior Officers, as they think proper, in the President alone, in the Courts of Law, or in the Heads of Departments.

The President shall have Power to fill up all Vacancies that may happen during the Recess of the Senate, by granting Commissions which shall expire at the End of their next Session.

• Clause 2 describes several powers the president may exercise in conjunction with the advice and consent of the Senate. These powers include the power, upon the approval of two-thirds of the Senate, to make treaties with foreign countries. But, the Constitution is silent on the question of whether a president (or Congress) may terminate a treaty by refusing to honor it or simply repealing it outright.

When President Jimmy Carter terminated a 1955 treaty with China over the objection of Congress, several members sought a judicial resolution; the Court, however, dismissed the case on a technicality and offered no resolution on the matter.

The president does not require a two-thirds majority for approval of appointments to the federal judiciary, foreign ambassadorships, Cabinet-level positions, high-ranking positions in non-Cabinet agencies, and high-level military offices. But, the fact that the Senate must approve presidential appointments in these areas provides Congress with an important check on presidential power to shape the contours of the executive branch. •

Section 3.

He shall from time to time give to the Congress Information of the State of the Union, and recommend to their Consideration such Measures as he shall judge necessary and expedient; he may, on extraordinary Occasions, convene both Houses, or either of them, and in Case of Disagreement between them, with Respect to the Time of Adjournment, he may adjourn them to such Time as he shall think proper; he shall receive Ambassadors and other public Ministers; he shall take Care that the Laws be faithfully executed, and shall Commission all the Officers of the United States.

• The president is required to deliver a State of the Union message to Congress each year. Today, the State of the Union Address is a major media event, although it is less an assessment of the nation's health and happiness and more a presidential wish-list for policy initiatives and the touting of partisan accomplishments.

The final provision of section 3 authorizing the president to faithfully execute the laws of the United States has proven controversial over the years. Presidents have cited this broad language to justify such far-reaching action as the suspension of the writ of *habeas corpus* and the doctrine of executive privilege, which permits the executive branch to withhold sensitive information from the public or the other branches of government for national security reasons. The Court has been of two minds about the doctrine of executive privilege. On the one hand, the Court has said in such cases as *New York Times* v. *U.S.* (1971) and *U.S.* v. *Nixon* (1974) that the president has the power to withhold information to protect vital secrets and the nation's security. On the other hand, the Court has said, in ruling against the assertion of executive privilege in these two cases, that only an exceptional and demonstrated case can justify allowing the president to withhold information. •

Section 4.

The President, Vice President and all civil Officers of the United States, shall be removed from Office on Impeachment for, and Conviction of, Treason, Bribery, or other High Crimes and Misdemeanors.

• Presidential impeachment, like impeachment of the other described offices in section 4, is the responsibility of the House of Representatives. There is no judicial definition as to what constitutes a high crime or misdemeanor, and only the House and Senate are given responsibility over the impeachment process. No federal official subject to impeachment may challenge the action in federal court. Only two presidents, Andrew Johnson in 1868 and Bill Clinton in 1998, have ever been impeached. Neither president was convicted by the Senate of the charges brought against them. •

ARTICLE III
Section 1.

The judicial Power of the United States, shall be vested in one supreme Court, and in such inferior Courts as the Congress may from time to time ordain and establish. The Judges, both of the supreme and inferior Courts, shall hold their Offices during good Behaviour, and shall, at stated Times, receive for their Services, a Compensation, which shall not be diminished during their Continuance in Office.

• Article III is the briefest of the institutional articles; the Framers viewed the courts as a necessity in design, but less important in practice. In *Federalist No. 78*, for example, Alexander Hamilton referred to the courts as the "least dangerous branch." Article III thus establishes only one federal court, the Supreme Court, and leaves to Congress the power to establish "inferior" courts as it deems necessary. •

Section 2.

The judicial Power shall extend to all Cases, in Law and Equity, arising under this Constitution, the Laws of the United States, and Treaties made, or which shall be made, under their Authority;—to all Cases affecting Ambassadors, other public Ministers and Consuls;—to all Cases of admiralty and maritime Jurisdiction;—to Controversies to which the United States shall be a Party;—to Controversies between two or more States;—between a State and Citizens of another State;—between Citizens of different States;—between Citizens of the same State claiming

Lands under Grants of different States,—and between a State, or the Citizens thereof, and foreign States, Citizens or Subjects.

In all Cases affecting Ambassadors, other public Ministers and Consuls, and those in which a State shall be Party, the supreme Court shall have original Jurisdiction. In all the other Cases before mentioned, the supreme Court shall have appellate Jurisdiction, both as to Law and Fact, with such Exceptions, and under such Regulations as the Congress shall make.

The Trial of all Crimes, except in Cases of Impeachment, shall be by Jury; and such Trial shall be held in the State where the said Crimes shall have been committed; but when not committed within any State, the Trial shall be at such Place or Places as the Congress may by Law have directed.

• Section 2 establishes the types of cases the Court may hear. It also clearly lays out the original and appellate jurisdiction of the Court. By extending the judicial power to all "Cases, in Law and Equity, arising under the Constitution, [and] the laws of the United States," section 2 authorizes the Court to both decide matters of law and, if necessary, mandate a remedy appropriate to the degree of a constitutional violation. For example, in *Swann* v. *Charlotte-Mecklenburg Board of Education* (1971), the Court ruled that a lower court, having found that a school system had failed to meet desegregation requirements, had the power to order busing and other remedies to the constitutional violations it found in *Brown* v. *Board of Education* (1954).

Federal judicial power no longer extends to cases involving lawsuits between a state and citizens of another state. This provision was superceded by the Eleventh Amendment.

Section 2 also includes the exceptions and regulations clause, which allows Congress to enact a law altering the appellate jurisdiction of the Court if it sees fit. This clause has been used by congressional opponents of some of the Court's more controversial and generally liberal decisions. Some opponents of the Court's decisions legalizing abortion, authorizing school busing, and upholding affirmative action have attempted to curb the power of federal courts to rule in such areas by stripping them of jurisdiction in such cases. To date, no president has ever signed such legislation. •

Section 3.

Treason against the United States, shall consist only in levying War against them, or in adhering to their Enemies, giving them Aid and Comfort. No Person shall be convicted of Treason unless on the Testimony of two Witnesses to the same overt Act, or on Confession in open Court.

The Congress shall have Power to declare the Punishment of Treason, but no Attainder of Treason shall work Corruption of Blood, or Forfeiture except during the Life of the Person attainted.

• Article III defines the only crime mentioned by the Constitution: treason. •

ARTICLE IV
Section 1.

Full Faith and Credit shall be given in each State to the public Acts, Records, and judicial Proceedings of every other State. And the Congress may by general Laws prescribe the Manner in which such Acts, Records and Proceedings shall be proved, and the Effect thereof.

• The full faith and credit clause rests on principles borrowed from international law that require one country to recognize contracts made in another country absent a compelling public policy reason to the contrary. Here, this principle, referred to in the law as comity, applies to the relationship between the states. For example, a driver's license issued in Ohio is good in Montana. The full and faith credit clause also requires a state to recognize public acts and court proceedings of another state. Advocates of same-sex marriage have suggested that a marriage performed in one state must be recognized in another state, as is the case with heterosexual marriage. A constitutional challenge to the clause may well center on the "public policy exception," which says that a state, in the event of a conflict, is not required to substitute the public policy of another state for its own. •

Section 2.

The Citizens of each State shall be entitled to all Privileges and Immunities of Citizens in the several States.

A Person charged in any State with Treason, Felony, or other Crime, who shall flee from Justice, and be found in another State, shall on Demand of the executive Authority of the State from which he fled, be delivered up, to be removed to the State having Jurisdiction of the Crime.

• The extradition clause requires that the governor of one state deliver a fugitive from justice to the state from which that fugitive fled. Congress passed the Fugitive Act of 1793 to give definition to this provision, but the federal government has no authority to compel state authorities to extradite a fugitive from one state to another. A state may, however, sue another state in federal court to force the return of a fugitive. •

No Person held to Service or Labour in one State under the Laws thereof, escaping into another, shall, in Consequence of any Law or Regulation therein, be discharged from such Service or Labour, but shall be delivered up on Claim of the Party to whom such Service or Labour may be due.

• The fugitive slave clause, which required any state, including those outside the slave-holding states of the South, to return escaped slaves to their owners, was repealed in 1865 by the Thirteenth Amendment. Prior to 1865, Congress passed laws in 1793 and 1850 to enforce the clause, leaving states without power to make concurrent laws on the subject, ensuring that the southern states would always have the Constitution on their side to protect slavery. •

Section 3.

New States may be admitted by the Congress into this Union; but no new State shall be formed or erected within the Jurisdiction of any other State; nor any State be formed by the Junction of two or more States, or Parts of States, without the Consent of the Legislatures of the States concerned as well as of the Congress.

The Congress shall have Power to dispose of and make all needful Rules and Regulations respecting the Territory or other Property belonging to the United States; and nothing in this Constitution shall be so construed as to Prejudice any Claims of the United States, or of any particular State.

Section 4.

The United States shall guarantee to every State in this Union a Republican Form of Government, and shall protect each of them against Invasion; and on Application of the Legislature, or of the Executive (when the Legislature cannot be convened) against domestic Violence.

• Nowhere in the Constitution is a "republican form of government" defined or explained. And, the Court ruled in *Luther* v. *Borden* (1849) that responsibility for the meaning of a republican government for the states is a "political question" not subject to judicial review. •

ARTICLE V

The Congress, whenever two thirds of both Houses shall deem it necessary, shall propose Amendments to this Constitution, or, on the Application of the Legislatures of two thirds of the several States, shall call a Convention for proposing Amendments, which, in either Case, shall be valid to all Intents and Purposes, as Part of this Constitution, when ratified by the Legislatures of three fourths of the several States, or by Conventions in three fourths thereof, as the one or the other Mode of Ratification may be proposed by the Congress; Provided that no Amendment which may be made prior to the Year One thousand eight hundred and eight shall in any Manner affect the first and fourth Clauses in the Ninth Section of the first Article; and that no State, without its Consent, shall be deprived of its equal Suffrage in the Senate.

• Article V was crucial to the ratification of the Constitution. Federalists wanted to ensure that any additions or modifications to the nation's charter would require the approval of more than a simple majority of citizens. This is why any amendment coming out of Congress requires two-thirds of the House and Senate for approval. The same is true for the rule requiring three-fourths of the states to ratify an amendment (either through conventions or state legislative action). Anti-Federalists were soothed by the prospect of an amending process that did not require the unanimous approval of the states; unanimous approval was one of the major shortcomings of the Articles of Confederation.

Only twenty-seven amendments since 1789 have been added to the Constitution, the first fifteen of which were added by 1870. Since 1933, when the nation repealed Prohibition by passing the Twenty-First Amendment, the Constitution has been amended only six times. In the modern constitutional era, efforts to amend the Constitution generally have centered on unhappiness with Supreme Court decisions (on school prayer, flag burning, school busing, abortion rights) or state court rulings with national implications (such as same-sex marriage) rather than any structural defect in the original Constitution. To date, none of these efforts have been successful. •

ARTICLE VI

All Debts contracted and Engagements entered into, before the Adoption of this Constitution, shall be as valid against the United States under this Constitution, as under the Confederation.

• Article VI made the national government responsible for all debts incurred by the Revolutionary War. This ensured that manufacturing and banking interests would be repaid for the losses they sustained during the conflict. But, the most important provisions of Article VI by far are contained in its second and third clauses. •

This Constitution, and the Laws of the United States which shall be made in Pursuance thereof; and all Treaties made, or which shall be made, under the Authority of the United States, shall be the supreme Law of the Land; and the Judges in every State shall be bound thereby, any Thing in the Constitution or Laws of any State to the Contrary notwithstanding.

• Clause 2 makes "this Constitution" and all laws made under its authority the "supreme Law of the Land," creating what constitutional scholars call the supremacy clause. The Supreme Court has invoked the supremacy clause on several occasions to rebut challenges mounted by states to its decisions or acts of Congress. Among the more notable decisions by the Supreme Court that have cited the supremacy clause is *Cooper* v. *Aaron* (1958). In *Cooper*, the U.S. Supreme Court rejected the argument of Governor Orval Faubus of Arkansas claiming that local schools were not obligated to follow the *Brown* v. *Board of Education* (1954) ruling. The Court said that *Brown* was the law of the land and, as such, all school boards were required to comply with its requirement to desegregate their schools. •

The Senators and Representatives before mentioned, and the Members of the several State Legislatures, and all executive and judicial Officers, both of the United States and of the several States, shall be bound by Oath or Affirmation, to support this Constitution; but no religious Test shall ever be required as a Qualification to any Office or public Trust under the United States.

• Although most Americans rightly point to the First Amendment as the baseline for the guarantee for religious freedom, clause 3 of Article VI contains an important contribution to this principle—the ban on religious tests or qualifications to hold public office. Holders of all public offices were required to affirm their allegiance to the Constitution and the laws of the United States, but they could not be required to profess a belief in God or meet any other religious qualification. •

ARTICLE VII

The Ratification of the Conventions of nine States, shall be sufficient for the Establishment of this Constitution between the States so ratifying the Same.

• Debates over whether or not to ratify the Constitution continued in the thirteen states as votes were taken from December 1787 to June 1788. Delaware, New Jersey, and Pennsylvania were the first three states to ratify the Constitution. New Hampshire became the crucial ninth state to ratify on June 21, 1788. •

Done in Convention by the Unanimous Consent of the States present the Seventeenth Day of September in the Year of our Lord one thousand seven hundred and Eighty seven and of the Independence of the United States of America the Twelfth. IN WITNESS whereof We have hereunto subscribed our Names,

G. WASHINGTON,
Presid't. and deputy from Virginia

Attest
WILLIAM JACKSON,
Secretary

DELAWARE
George Read
Gunning Bedford, Jr.
John Dickinson
Richard Basset
Jacob Broom

MASSACHUSETTS BAY
Nathaniel Gorham
Rufus King

CONNECTICUT
William Samuel Johnson
Roger Sherman

NEW YORK
Alexander Hamilton

NEW JERSEY
William Livingston
David Brearley
William Paterson
Jonathan Dayton

PENNSYLVANIA
Benjamin Franklin
Thomas Mifflin
Robert Morris
George Clymer
Thomas FitzSimons
Jared Ingersoll
James Wilson
Gouverneur Morris

NEW HAMPSHIRE
John Langdon
Nicholas Gilman

MARYLAND
James McHenry
Daniel of St. Thomas
  Jenifer
Daniel Carroll

VIRGINIA
John Blair
James Madison, Jr.

NORTH CAROLINA
William Blount
Richard Dobbs Spaight
Hugh Williamson

SOUTH CAROLINA
John Rutledge
Charles Cotesworth
  Pinckney
Charles Pinckney
Pierce Butler

GEORGIA
William Few
Abraham Baldwin

Articles in addition to, and amendment of the Constitution of the United States of America, proposed by Congress and ratified by the Legislatures of the several states, pursuant to the Fifth Article of the original Constitution.

(The first ten amendments were passed by Congress on September 25, 1789, and were ratified on December 15, 1791.)

AMENDMENT I

Congress shall make no law respecting an establishment of religion, or prohibiting the free exercise thereof; or abridging the freedom of speech, or of the press; or the right of the people peaceably to assemble, and to petition the Government for a redress of grievances.

• For many Americans, the First Amendment represents the core of what the Bill of Rights stands for: limits on government power to restrict or compel religious beliefs, the right to hold political opinions and express them, a free press, the right to assemble peaceably, and the right to petition, through protest or the ballot, the government for a redress of political grievances. But it is also important to remember that the First Amendment, like most of the Bill of Rights, did not apply to state governments until the U.S. Supreme Court applied their substantive guarantees through the Fourteenth Amendment, a process that did not begin until 1925 in *Gitlow* v. *New York*.

Until then, state and local governments often failed to honor the rights and liberties that Congress, and by extension the national government, had to honor. For example, southern states, prior to the Civil War, outlawed pro-abolition literature; numerous states continued to collect taxes on behalf of state-sponsored churches and religious education; newspapers often were forbidden from publishing exposés on industry or political leaders because such speech was considered seditious and thus subject to prior restraint; and public protests on behalf of unpopular causes were often banned by state breach of peace laws.

The Supreme Court has recognized other important rights implied by the enumerated guarantees of the First Amendment. These include the right to association, even when such association might come in the form of clubs or organizations that discriminate on the basis of race, sex, or religion, and the right to personal privacy, which the Supreme Court held in *Griswold* v. *Connecticut* (1965) was based in part on the right of married couples to make decisions about contraception, a decision protected by one's personal religious and political beliefs. •

AMENDMENT II

A well regulated Militia, being necessary to the security of a free State, the right of the people to keep and bear Arms, shall not be infringed.

• Few issues in American politics generate as much emotional heat as the extent to which Americans have a right to keep and bear arms. Supporters of broad gun ownership rights, such as the National Rifle Association, argue that the Second Amendment protects an almost absolute individual right to own just about any small arm that can be manufactured, whether for reasons of sport or self-defense. Proponents of gun control, such as the Brady Campaign to Prevent Gun Violence, argue that the amendment creates no such individual right, but refers instead to the Framers' belief—now outdated—that citizen militias had the right to form to protect themselves against other states and, if need be, the national government. Under this view, Congress and the states are free to regulate gun ownership and use as they see fit, provided that the national and state governments are within their constitutional orbit of power to do so.

In 1939, the Supreme Court, for the first time, offered an interpretation of the Second Amendment. There, a unanimous Court upheld a federal law requiring the registration of sawed-off shotguns purchased for personal use. The justices also rejected the argument that the Second Amendment established an individual right to keep and bear arms; the Court did, however, leave open the question by holding that not all weapons were intended for militia use only. The Court revisited the question in *McDonald* v. *Chicago* (2010), holding that the second Amendment was incorporated, and a Chicago ban on handguns and regulations on rifles and shotguns, were unconstitutional. •

AMENDMENT III

No Soldier shall, in time of peace be quartered in any house, without the consent of the Owner, nor in time of war, but in a manner to be prescribed by law.

• Among the complaints directed at King George III in the Declaration of Independence was the colonial-era practice of quartering or housing large numbers of troops in private homes. The Third Amendment was intended to protect individuals and their property from the abuse common to the practice of quartering soldiers. •

AMENDMENT IV

The right of the people to be secure in their persons, houses, papers, and effects, against unreasonable searches and seizures, shall not be violated, and no warrants shall issue, but upon probable cause, supported by Oath or affirmation, and particularly describing the place to be searched, and the persons or things to be seized.

• Although the Fourth Amendment is often discussed in tandem with the Fifth, Sixth, and Eighth Amendments—the other major provisions of the Bill of Rights outlining the criminal due process guarantees of citizens—it shares a similar undercurrent that motivated the adoption of the Third Amendment: to eliminate the practice of British officers from using the general writ of assistance to enter private homes, conduct searches, and seize personal property.

The twin pillars of the Fourth Amendment, the probable cause and warrant requirements, did not apply to state and local law enforcement practices until well after the ratification of the Fourteenth Amendment. Until *Wolf* v. *Colorado* (1949), when the Court ruled that the Fourteenth Amendment made the Fourth Amendment binding on the states, evidence seized in violation of the probable cause or warrant requirements could be used against a criminal suspect in state court. The Court's best-known decision on the Fourth Amendment, *Mapp* v. *Ohio* (1961), established the exclusionary rule, which prohibits police from using illegally seized evidence at trial, and marked the high-water point in the rights afforded to criminal suspects challenging an unlawful search. Since the late 1970s, the Court has steadily added exceptions to the Fourth Amendment to permit law enforcement officers to engage in warrantless searches and seizures, provided that such practices meet a threshold of reasonableness. •

AMENDMENT V

No person shall be held to answer for a capital, or otherwise infamous crime, unless on a presentment or indictment of a Grand Jury, except in cases arising in the land or naval forces, or in the Militia, when in actual service in time of War or public danger; nor shall any person be subject for the same offence to be twice put in jeopardy of life or limb; nor shall be compelled in any criminal case to be a witness against himself, nor be deprived of life, liberty, or property, without due process of law; nor shall private property be taken for public use, without just compensation.

• The Fifth Amendment, along with the Sixth Amendment, is the legacy of the ruthless and secretive tactics that figured prominently in the colonial-era system of British justice. By requiring that no person could be held for a "capital, or otherwise infamous"

crime except upon indictment by a grand jury, the Fifth Amendment took an important step toward making the criminal indictment process a public function. Also, by guaranteeing that no person could be compelled to testify against himself or herself in a criminal proceeding, the Fifth Amendment highlighted the adversarial nature of the American criminal justice system, a feature that is distinct from its British counterpart. "Pleading the Fifth" is permissible in any criminal, civil, administrative, judicial, or investigatory context. *Miranda* v. *Arizona* (1966), one of the most famous rulings of the Supreme Court, established a right to silence that combined the ban against self-incrimination of the Fifth Amendment with the Sixth Amendment's guarantee of the assistance of counsel. The right to silence, unlike the ban against self-incrimination, extends to any aspect of an interrogation.

The Fifth Amendment also forbids double jeopardy, which prohibits the prosecution of a crime against the same person in the same jurisdiction twice, and prevents the government from taking life, liberty, or property without due process of law. This phrase was reproduced in the Fourteenth Amendment, placing an identical set of constraints on the states. Some constitutional scholars also consider the due process clause of the Fifth Amendment to embrace an equal protection provision when applied to federal cases.

The final provision of the Fifth Amendment prohibits the government from taking private property for public use without just compensation. Litigation on the takings clause, as some scholars refer to this provision, has generally centered on two major questions. The first is what constitutes a taking, either by the government's decision to seize private property or by regulating it to the point where its value is greatly diminished. The second question centers on what the appropriate level of compensation is for owners who have successfully established a taking.

The Supreme Court has taken an expansive definition of what it means to "take" private land for "public use." In *Kelo* v. *New London* (2004), the Court ruled that government could take private property and then sell it to private developers so long as that property was slated for economic development that would benefit the surrounding community. This marked the first time the Court had authorized a taking for something other than public use by governmental authorities. •

AMENDMENT VI

In all criminal prosecutions, the accused shall enjoy the right to a speedy and public trial, by an impartial jury of the State and district wherein the crime shall have been committed, which district shall have been previously ascertained by law, and to be informed of the nature and cause of the accusation; to be confronted with the witnesses against him; to have compulsory process for obtaining witnesses in his favor, and to have the assistance of counsel for his defence.

• The centerpiece of the constitutional guarantees afforded to individuals facing criminal prosecution, the Sixth Amendment, sets out eight specific rights (more than any other provision of the Bill of Rights). As with the Fifth Amendment, the core features of the Sixth Amendment build on the unfortunate legacy of the repressive practices of colonial-era Britain. The very first provision mandates that individuals subject to criminal prosecution receive "a speedy and public trial." A defendant must also be informed of the cause and nature of the accusation made against him or her. The common theme underlying these sections of the Sixth Amendment is that any citizen threatened with the deprivation of liberty is entitled to have the case made against him or her in public, establishing, in principle, the American criminal justice system as one that is open and public.

Since the vast majority of criminal prosecutions in the United States are undertaken by state and local authorities, the parchment promises of the Sixth Amendment did not extend to most Americans until the Supreme Court began incorporating the guarantees of the Bill of Rights to the states through the Fourteenth Amendment. Perhaps the best-known case involving the Sixth Amendment is *Gideon* v. *Wainwright* (1963), which held that all persons accused of a serious crime are entitled to an attorney, even if they cannot afford one, a rule that was soon extended to cover misdemeanors as well.

The speedy and public trial clauses only require that criminal trials take place in public within a reasonable amount of time after the period of indictment, and that juries in such cases are to be unbiased. Americans also often cite the Sixth Amendment as entitling them to a trial by a "jury of one's peers." This is true to the extent individuals are entitled to a trial in the jurisdiction where the crime is alleged to have been committed. It does not mean, however, that they are entitled to a trial by persons of a similar age or background, for example. •

AMENDMENT VII

In Suits at common law, where the value in controversy shall exceed twenty dollars, the right of trial by jury shall be preserved, and no fact tried by a jury, shall be otherwise re-examined in any Court of the United States, than according to the rules of the common law.

• One feature of the British courts that the Framers sought to preserve in the American civil law system was the distinction between courts of common law and courts of equity. Common law courts heard cases involving strict legal rules, while equity courts based their decisions on principles of fairness and totality of circumstances. Common law courts featured juries that were authorized to return verdicts entitling plaintiffs to financial compensation, whereas equity courts relied on judges to make determinations about appropriate relief for successful parties. Relief in equity courts consisted of injunctions, cease-and-desist orders, and so on. The Seventh Amendment carried over this British feature into the Constitution.

In 1938, Congress amended the Federal Rules of Civil Procedure to combine the function of civil common law and equity courts. In cases involving both legal and equitable claims, a federal judge must first decide the issue of law before moving to the equitable relief, or remedy, component of the trial. Judges are permitted to instruct juries on matters of law and fact, and may emphasize certain facts or legal issues in their instructions to the jury. But, the jury alone decides guilt or innocence. In some extraordinary cases, a judge may overturn the verdict of a jury. This happens only when a judge believes the jury has completely disregarded the facts and evidence before it in reaching a verdict.

Congress has also changed the $20 threshold for the right to a trial by jury. The amount is now $75,000. Finally, the Seventh Amendment has never been incorporated to the states through the Fourteenth Amendment. •

AMENDMENT VIII

Excessive bail shall not be required, nor excessive fines imposed, nor cruel and unusual punishments inflicted.

• The origin of the excessive bail clause stems from the reforms to the British system instituted by the 1689 English Bill of Rights. Having had limited success in preventing law enforcement officials from detaining suspects by imposing outrageous bail requirements, Britain amended previous laws to say that "excessive bail ought not to be required." Much like the British model, the Eighth Amendment does not state what an "excessive bail" is or the particular criminal offense that warrants a high bail amount. The Supreme Court has offered two fundamental rules on the excessive bail clause. First, a judge has the discretion to decide if a criminal offense is sufficiently serious to justify high bail. Second, a judge has the power, under *U.S.* v. *Salerno* (1987), to deny a criminal defendant bail as a "preventative measure." In both such cases, a judge's action must be considered proportionate to the nature of the criminal offense for which an individual stands accused.

Like the excessive bail clause, the excessive fines clause is rooted in the English Bill of Rights. The clause applies only to criminal proceedings, not civil litigation. For example, a tobacco company cannot appeal what it believes is an excessive jury award under this clause. An indigent criminal defendant, however, can challenge a fine levied in connection with a criminal conviction.

The most controversial section of the Eighth Amendment is the clause forbidding cruel and unusual punishments. The absence of such a guarantee from the Constitution was a major impetus for the adoption of the Bill of Rights. While most historians agree that the Framers wanted to prohibit barbaric forms of punishment, including torture, as well as arbitrary and disproportionate penalties, there is little consensus on what specific punishments met this definition. By the late 1800s, the Supreme Court had ruled that such punishments as public burning, disembowelment, and drawing and quartering crossed the Eighth Amendment barrier. In *Weems* v. *U.S.* (1910), the Court went the additional step of concluding that any punishment considered "excessive" would violate the cruel and unusual punishment clause. And, in *Solem* v. *Helm* (1983), the Court developed a "proportionality" standard that required punishments, even simple incarceration, to bear a rational relationship to the offense.

Although the Court has never ruled that the death penalty violates the Eighth Amendment, it has developed certain rules and exceptions governing the application of the death penalty. In 1976, the Court ruled in *Coker* v. *Georgia* (1977) that the death penalty could not be applied to a crime that did not involve a killing or attempted killing. Since 2002, the Court has ruled that mentally retarded persons (*Atkins* v. *Virginia*, [2002]) and individuals who commit capital crimes while still juveniles (*Roper* v. *Simmons*, [2005]) cannot be eligible for the death penalty. But, it has also ruled that racial disparities in the application of the death penalty do not violate the Eighth Amendment. More recently, in *Baze* v. *Rees* (2008), the Court rejected an argument that intravenous executions using a "lethal injection" crossed a pain threshold making them unconstitutional. •

AMENDMENT IX

The enumeration in the Constitution, of certain rights, shall not be construed to deny or disparage others retained by the people.

• A major point of contention between the Federalists and Anti-Federalists was the need for a Bill of Rights. In *Federalist No. 84*, Alexander Hamilton argued that a bill of rights was unnecessary, as there was no need to place limits on the power of government to do things that it was not authorized by the Constitution to do. Hamilton also argued that it would be impossible to list all the rights "retained by the people." Protecting some rights but not others would suggest that Americans had surrendered certain rights to their government when, in Hamilton's view, the Constitution did nothing of the sort.

Other Federalists agreed with Hamilton's point but feared that the work of the constitutional convention would be undone without a Bill of Rights. Thus, they insisted that the document include language such as that used in the Ninth Amendment, which stipulates that the enumeration of certain rights and liberties in the Constitution should not be understood to deny others that exist as a condition of citizenship in a free society.

The Supreme Court has never offered a clear and definitive interpretation of the Ninth Amendment, primarily because it has been wary of giving such general language any substantive definition. The amendment has been cited in such decisions as *Griswold* v. *Connecticut* (1965) and *Richmond Newspapers* v. *Virginia* (1980) along with other constitutional amendments to bolster the case on behalf of an asserted constitutional right. The difficulty in constructing a specific meaning for the Ninth Amendment can be illustrated by the fact that both supporters and opponents of legal abortion have cited it to defend the feasibility of their respective positions. •

AMENDMENT X

The powers not delegated to the United States by the Constitution, nor prohibited by it to the States, are reserved to the States respectively, or to the people.

• The Tenth Amendment generated little controversy during the ratification process over the Bill of Rights. As the Supreme Court later ruled in *U.S.* v. *Darby Lumber Co.* (1941), the Tenth Amendment states a truism about the relationship between the boundaries of national and state power—that the states retain those powers not specifically set out in the Constitution as belonging to the national government.

The earliest political and constitutional developments involving the Tenth Amendment tilted the balance of power firmly in favor of national power. Alexander Hamilton's vision for a national bank to consolidate the nation's currency and trading position was realized in *McCulloch v. Maryland* (1819), in which the Court held that Article I granted Congress broad power to make all laws "necessary and proper" to the exercise of its legislative power. By no means, however, did *McCulloch* settle the argument over the power reserved to the states. Led by Chief Justice Roger B. Taney, the Court handed down several decisions in the three decades leading up to the Civil War that offered substantial protection to the southern states on the matters closest to their hearts: slavery and economic sovereignty. From the period after the Civil War until the New Deal, the Court continued to shield states from congressional legislation designed to regulate the economy and to promote social and political reform. However, when the Court threw its support behind the New Deal, Congress received a blank constitutional check to engage in the regulatory action that featured an unprecedented level of federal intervention in economic and social matters once the purview of the states, one that would last almost sixty years.

Beginning in *New York v. U.S.* (1992), however, the Court, in striking down a key provision of a federal environmental law, began to revisit the New Deal assumptions that underlay its modern interpretation of the Tenth Amendment. A few years later, in *U.S.* v. *Lopez* (1995), it invalidated a federal gun control law on the grounds that Congress lacked authority under the commerce clause to regulate gun possession. And, in *U.S.* v. *Printz* (1997), the Tenth Amendment was cited to strike down an important section of the Brady Bill, a federal law that required states to conduct background checks on prospective gun buyers. These decisions make clear that the constitutional status of the states as actors in the federal system has dramatically strengthened. •

AMENDMENT XI
(Ratified on February 7, 1795)

The Judicial power of the United States shall not be construed to extend to any suit in law or equity, commenced or prosecuted against one of the United States by Citizens of another State, or by Citizens or Subjects of any Foreign State.

• The Eleventh Amendment was prompted by one of the earliest notable decisions of the Supreme Court, *Chisolm v. Georgia* (1793). In *Chisholm*, the Court held that Article III and the enforcement provision of the Judiciary Act of 1789 permitted a citizen of one state to bring suit against another state in federal court. Almost immediately after *Chisholm*, the Eleventh Amendment was introduced and promptly ratified, as the states saw this decision as a threat to their sovereignty under the new Constitution. The amendment was passed in less

than a year, which, by the standards of the era, was remarkably fast.

The Eleventh Amendment nullified the result in *Chisholm* but did not completely bar a citizen from bringing suit against a state in federal court. Citizens may bring lawsuits against state officials in federal court if they can satisfy the requirement that their rights under federal constitutional or statutory law have been violated.

The Eleventh Amendment has not been extensively litigated in modern times, but the extent to which states are immune under federal law from citizen lawsuits has reemerged as an important constitutional question. For example, the Court has said in several cases that the doctrine of sovereign immunity prevents citizens from suing state agencies under the Americans with Disabilities Act of 1990. But, as recently as 2003, the Court, in *Nevada Department of Human Resources v. Hibbs*, ruled that the Family and Medical Leave Act of 1993 did not protect state government agencies against lawsuits brought by former state employees. States are also free to waive their immunity and consent to a lawsuit. •

AMENDMENT XII
(Ratified on June 15, 1804)

The Electors shall meet in their respective states, and vote by ballot for President and Vice-President, one of whom, at least, shall not be an inhabitant of the same state with themselves; they shall name in their ballots the person voted for as President, and in distinct ballots the person voted for as Vice-President, and they shall make distinct lists of all persons voted for as President, and of all persons voted for as Vice-President, and of the number of votes for each, which lists they shall sign and certify, and transmit sealed to the seat of the government of the United States, directed to the President of the Senate;

The President of the Senate shall, in the presence of the Senate and House of Representatives, open all the certificates and the votes shall then be counted;

The person having the greatest number of votes for President, shall be the President, if such number be a majority of the whole number of Electors appointed; and if no person have such majority; then from the persons having the highest numbers not exceeding three on the list of those voted for as President, the House of Representatives shall choose immediately, by ballot, the President. But in choosing the President, the votes shall be taken by states, the representation from each state having one vote; a quorum for this purpose shall consist of a member or members from two-thirds of the states, and a majority of all the states shall be necessary to a choice. And if the House of Representatives shall not choose a President whenever the right of choice shall devolve upon them, before the fourth day of March next following, then the Vice-President shall act as President, as in the case of the death or other constitutional disability of the President.

The person having the greatest number of votes as Vice-President, shall be the Vice-President, if such number be a majority of the whole number of Electors appointed, and if no person have a majority, then from the two highest numbers on the list, the Senate shall choose the Vice-President; a quorum for the purpose shall consist of two-thirds of the whole number of Senators, and a majority of the whole number shall be necessary to a choice. But no person constitutionally ineligible to the office of President shall be eligible to that of Vice-President of the United States.

• The Twelfth Amendment was added to the Constitution after the 1800 presidential election was thrown into the House of Representatives. Thomas Jefferson and Aaron Burr, running on the Democratic-Republican Party ticket, each received seventy-three electoral votes for president, even though everyone knew that Jefferson was the presidential candidate and Burr the vice presidential candidate. This was possible because Article II, section 1, did not require electors to vote for president and vice president separately. The Twelfth Amendment remedied this deficiency.

Whether it intended to or not, the Twelfth Amendment took a major step toward institutionalizing the party system in the United States by requiring electors to make their presidential and vice presidential choices separately. The development of a party system was inevitable but nonetheless disappointing to the architects of the original constitutional vision. •

AMENDMENT XIII
(Ratified on December 6, 1865)
Section 1.

Neither slavery nor involuntary servitude, except as a punishment for crime whereof the party shall have been duly convicted, shall exist within the United States, or any place subject to their jurisdiction.

Section 2.

Congress shall have power to enforce this article by appropriate legislation.

• The Thirteenth, Fourteenth, and Fifteenth Amendments are known collectively as the Civil War Amendments.

In anticipation of a Union victory, the Thirteenth Amendment was passed by Congress and sent to the states for ratification before the end of the Civil War. The amendment not only formally abolished slavery and involuntary servitude but also served as the constitutional foundation for the nation's first major civil rights legislation, the Civil Rights Act of 1866. This law extended numerous rights to African Americans previously held in servitude as well as those having "free" status during the Civil War, including the right to purchase, rent, and sell personal property, to bring suit in federal court, to enter into contracts, and to receive the full and equal benefit of all laws "enjoyed by white citizens." The Thirteenth Amendment also overturned *Dred Scott v. Sandford* (1857), which held that slaves were not people entitled to constitutional rights, but property subject to the civil law binding them to their masters.

In modern times, the Court has ruled that the Thirteenth Amendment prohibits any action that recognizes a "badge" or "condition" of slavery, such as housing discrimination and certain forms of employment discrimination. The Department of Justice also has used the Thirteenth Amendment to file lawsuits against manufacturing sweatshops and other criminal enterprises in which persons are forced to work without compensation. •

AMENDMENT XIV
(Ratified on July 9, 1868)
Section 1.

All persons born or naturalized in the United States, and subject to the jurisdiction thereof, are citizens of the United States and of the State wherein they reside. No State shall make or enforce any law which shall abridge the privileges or immunities of citizens of the United States; nor shall any State deprive any person of life, liberty, or property, without due process of law; nor deny to any person within its jurisdiction the equal protection of the laws.

• Many constitutional scholars believe the Fourteenth Amendment is the most important addition to the Constitution since the Bill of Rights was ratified in 1791. This amendment guarantees equal protection and due process of the law to all U.S. citizens, a term that is clarified in Section 1. This section also eliminated the distinction between the rights and liberties of Americans as citizens of their respective states and as citizens of the United States. Although this incorporation was the subject of much debate in post-Reconstruction politics, the selective incorporation of the Bill of Rights to the states made this a reality during the twentieth century.

In interpreting cases brought under the equal protection clause, the Supreme Court applies three standards of review. The Court decided early on that certain freedoms were so fundamental that a heavy burden would be placed on any government that sought to restrict those rights. Thus, the Court uses a heightened standard of review known as strict scrutiny to determine the constitutional validity of challenged practices based on fundamental freedoms and other suspect classifications, including race, alienage, and national origin. The Court uses an intermediate standard of review for claims based on gender and a minimum rationality standard for claims based on age, wealth, mental retardation, or sexual orientation.

The Court has also interpreted the "liberty" provision of the due process clause to protect the right to abortion (*Roe* v. *Wade* [1973]) with limits (*Gonzales* v. *Carhart* [2007]), to permit consensual sex between persons regardless of sexual orientation (*Lawrence* v. *Texas* [2003]), to prohibit states from criminalizing the use of birth control and other matters related to reproductive and sexual privacy (*Griswold* v. *Connecticut* [1965]; *Eisenstadt* v. *Baird* [1972]). •

Section 2.

Representatives shall be apportioned among the several States according to their respective numbers, counting the whole number of persons in each State, excluding Indians not taxed. But when the right to vote at any election for the choice of electors for President and Vice President of the United States, Representatives in Congress, the Executive and Judicial officers of a State, or the members of the Legislature thereof, is denied to any of the male inhabitants of such State, being twenty-one years of age, and citizens of the United States, or in any way abridged, except for participation in rebellion, or other crime, the basis of representation therein shall be reduced in the proportion which the number of such male citizens shall bear to the whole number of male citizens twenty-one years of age in such State.

• Section 2 established two major changes to the Constitution. First, by stating that representatives from each state would be apportioned based on the number of "whole" persons in each state, section 2 modified the Three-Fifths Compromise of Article 1, section 2, clause 3, of the original Constitution. Note, however, that section 2 still called for the exclusion of Indians "not

taxed" from the apportionment criteria. Second, section 2, for the first time anywhere in the Constitution, mentions that only "male" inhabitants of the states age twenty-one or older would be counted toward representation in the House of Representatives and eligible to vote. •

Section 3.

No person shall be a Senator or Representative in Congress, or elector of President and Vice President, or hold any office, civil or military, under the United States, or under any State, who, having previously taken an oath, as a member of Congress, or as an officer of the United States, or as a member of any State legislature, or as an executive or judicial officer of any State, to support the Constitution of the United States, shall have engaged in insurrection or rebellion against the same, or given aid or comfort to the enemies thereof. But Congress may by a vote of two-thirds of each House, remove such disability.

• Section 3 eliminated the eligibility of former Confederates for public office to serve as an elector for president or vice president. This measure also allowed African Americans to run for and hold office in the South, which they were doing by 1870, the same year the Fifteenth Amendment was ratified.

In December 1868, five months after the ratification of the Fourteenth Amendment, President Andrew Johnson declared universal amnesty for all former Confederates. Republican president Ulysses S. Grant, who defeated Johnson in 1868, further signed the Amnesty Act of 1872, pardoning all but a few hundred remaining Confederate sympathizers. Decisions such as these began the gradual undoing of civil rights for African Americans in the South. •

Section 4.

The validity of the public debt of the United States, authorized by law, including debts incurred for payment of pensions and bounties for services in suppressing insurrection or rebellion, shall not be questioned. But neither the United States nor any State shall assume or pay any debt or obligation incurred in aid of insurrection or rebellion against the United States, or any claim for the loss or emancipation of any slave, but all such debts, obligations and claims shall be held illegal and void.

• Section 4 repudiated the South's desire to have Congress forgive the Confederacy's war debts. It also rejected any claim that former slaveholders had to be compensated for the loss of their slaves. •

Section 5.

The Congress shall have power to enforce, by appropriate legislation, the provisions of this article.

• By giving Congress the power to enforce the provisions of the Fourteenth Amendment, section 5 reiterated the post–Civil War emphasis on national citizenship and the limit on state power to deny individuals their constitutional rights. Section 5 also extended congressional law-making power beyond those areas outlined in Article I. But, the Court has taken a mixed view of the scope of congressional power to enforce the Fourteenth Amendment. In *Katzenbach v. Morgan* (1966), for example, the Supreme Court held that Congress could enact laws establishing rights beyond what the Court said the Constitution required, as long as such laws were designed to establish a remedial constitutional right or protect citizens from a potential constitutional violation. In other cases, such as *Boerne v. Flores* (1997) and *U.S. v. Morrison* (2000), the Court ruled that Congress may not intrude upon the authority of the judicial branch to define the meaning of the Constitution or intrude on the power of the states to make laws within their own domain. •

AMENDMENT XV
(Ratified on February 3, 1870)
Section 1.

The right of citizens of the United States to vote shall not be denied or abridged by the United States or by any State on account of race, color, or previous condition of servitude.

Section 2.

The Congress shall have power to enforce this article by appropriate legislation.

• The Fifteenth Amendment was the most controversial of the Civil War Amendments, both for what it did and did not do. Although the adoption of the Thirteenth and Fourteenth Amendments made clear that blacks could not be returned to their pre–Civil War slavery, enthusiasm for a constitutional right of African American suffrage, even among the northern states, was another matter. On the one hand, the extension of voting rights to African Americans was the most dramatic outcome of the Civil War. The former Confederate states had to ratify the Fifteenth Amendment as a condition for readmission into the Union. On the other hand, the rejection of proposed language forbidding discrimination on the basis of property ownership, education, or religious belief gave states the power to regulate the vote as they wished. And, with the collapse of Reconstruction after the 1876 election, southern states implemented laws created by this opening with full force, successfully crippling African American voter registration for generations to come in the region where most African Americans lived. Full enfranchisement for African Americans would not arrive until the passage of the Voting Rights Act of 1965, almost one hundred years after the ratification of the Fifteenth Amendment.

The Fifteenth Amendment also divided women's rights organizations that had campaigned on behalf of abolition and African American enfranchisement. Feminists such as Elizabeth Cady Stanton and Susan B. Anthony were furious over the exclusion of women from the Fifteenth Amendment and opposed its ratification, while others, such as Lucy Stone, were willing to support African American voting rights at the expense of woman suffrage, leaving that battle for another day. The Supreme Court sided with those who opposed female enfranchisement, ruling in *Minor v. Happersett* (1875) that the Fourteenth Amendment did not recognize among the privileges and immunities of American citizenship a constitutional right to vote. •

AMENDMENT XVI
(Ratified on February 3, 1913)

The Congress shall have power to lay and collect taxes on incomes, from whatever source derived, without apportionment among the several States, and without regard to any census or enumeration.

• The Sixteenth Amendment, which allows for the collection of a federal income tax, was a response to the Supreme Court's sharply divided ruling in *Pollock v. Farmers' Loan & Trust Co.* (1895), which struck down the Income Tax Act of 1894 as unconstitutional. The Court, by a 5–4 margin, held that the law violated Article I, section 9, which prevented Congress from enacting a direct tax (on individuals) unless in proportion to the U.S. Census. •

AMENDMENT XVII
(Ratified on April 8, 1913)

The Senate of the United States shall be composed of two Senators from each State, elected by the people thereof, for six years; and each Senator shall have one vote. The electors in each State shall have the qualifications requisite for electors of the most numerous branch of the State legislatures.

When vacancies happen in the representation of any State in the Senate, the executive authority of such State shall issue writs of election to fill such vacancies: Provided, That the legislature of any State may empower the executive thereof to make temporary appointments until the people fill the vacancies by election as the legislature may direct.

This amendment shall not be so construed as to affect the election or term of any Senator chosen before it becomes valid as part of the Constitution.

• The Seventeenth Amendment repealed the language in Article I, section 3, of the original Constitution, which called for the election of U.S. senators by state legislatures. This method was the preferred method of the Framers, who believed that having state legislatures elect senators would strengthen the relationship between the states and the national government, and also contribute to the stability of Congress by removing popular electoral pressure from the upper chamber.

Dissatisfaction set in with this method during the period leading up to the Civil War. Indiana, for example, deeply divided between Union supporters in the northern part of the state and Confederate sympathizers in the southern part, could not agree on the selection of senators and was without representation for two years. After the Civil War, numerous Senate elections were tainted by corruption, and many more resulted in ties that prevented seating senators in a timely fashion. In 1899, Delaware's election was so mired in controversy that it did not have representation in the Senate for four years.

The ratification of the Seventeenth Amendment was the result of almost two decades of persistent efforts at reform. Although many powerful legislators entrenched in the Senate resisted such change, the tide of reform, aided by journalists and scholars sympathetic to the cause, proved too powerful to withstand. •

AMENDMENT XVIII
(Ratified on January 16, 1919)
Section 1.

After one year from the ratification of this article the manufacture, sale, or transportation of intoxicating liquors within, the importation thereof into, or the exportation thereof from the United States and all territory subject to the jurisdiction thereof for beverage purposes is hereby prohibited.

Section 2.

The Congress and the several States shall have concurrent power to enforce this article by appropriate legislation.

Section 3.

This article shall be inoperative unless it shall have been ratified as an amendment to the Constitution by the legislatures of the several States, as provided in the Constitution, within seven years from the date of the submission hereof to the States by the Congress.

• The Eighteenth Amendment was the result of a crusade against the consumption of alcoholic beverages that began during the early nineteenth century. A combination of Christian organizations and women's groups, who believed alcohol contributed greatly to domestic violence and poverty, campaigned to abolish the manufacture, sale, and use of alcoholic beverages in the United States.

Founded in 1874 and 250,000 strong by 1911, the Women's Christian Temperance Union and the Anti-Saloon League, founded in 1913, pressed the case for Prohibition. Among the arguments offered by supporters of Prohibition were that the cereal grains used in the manufacture of beer and liquor diverted valuable resources from food supplies and that the malaise of drunkenness sapped the strength of manufacturing production at home and the conduct of America's soldiers in World War I. Underneath the formal case for Prohibition was a considerable anti-immigrant sentiment, as many Prohibitionists considered the waves of Italian, Irish, Polish, and German immigrants unduly dependent on alcohol.

In 1919, Congress passed the Eighteenth Amendment over President Woodrow Wilson's veto. That same year, Congress passed the Volstead Act, which implemented Prohibition and authorized law enforcement to target illegal shipments of alcohol into the United States (mostly from Canada, which, ironically, also mandated Prohibition in most of its provinces during this time) as well as alcoholic beverages illegally manufactured in the United States. Evidence remains inconclusive over just how successful the Eighteenth Amendment was in reducing alcohol consumption in the United States. More certain was the billion-dollar windfall that Prohibition created for organized crime, as well as small-time smugglers and bootleggers. •

AMENDMENT XIX
(Ratified on August 18, 1920)

The right of citizens of the United States to vote shall not be denied or abridged by the United States or by any State on account of sex.

Congress shall have power to enforce this article by appropriate legislation.

• The two major women's rights organizations of the nineteenth century most active in the battle for female enfranchisement were the National Woman Suffrage Association (NWSA) and the American Woman Suffrage Association (AWSA). NWSA campaigned for a constitutional amendment modeled on the Fifteenth Amendment, which had secured African American voting rights, while AWSA preferred to pursue women's voting rights through state-level legislative initiatives. In 1890, the two organizations combined to form the National American Woman Suffrage Association. By 1919, NAWSA, the newer, more radical National Woman's Party, and other activists had secured congressional passage of the Nineteenth Amendment by a broad margin. It was ratified by the states just over a year later. •

AMENDMENT XX
(Ratified on February 6, 1933)
Section 1.

The terms of the President and Vice President shall end at noon on the 20th day of January, and the terms of Senators and Representatives at noon on the 3d day of January, of the years in which such terms would have ended if this article had not been ratified; and the terms of their successors shall then begin.

Section 2.

The Congress shall assemble at least once in every year, and such meeting shall begin at noon on the 3d day of January, unless they shall by law appoint a different day.

Section 3.

If, at the time fixed for the beginning of the term of the President, the President elect shall have died, the Vice President elect shall become President. If a President shall not have been chosen before the time fixed for the beginning of his term, or if the President elect shall have failed to qualify, then the Vice President elect shall act as President until a President shall have qualified; and the Congress may by law provide for the case wherein neither a President elect nor a Vice President elect shall have qualified, declaring who shall then act as President, or the manner in which one who is to act shall be selected, and such person shall act accordingly until a President or Vice President shall have qualified.

Section 4.

The Congress may by law provide for the case of the death of any of the persons from whom the House of Representatives may choose a President whenever the rights of choice shall have devolved upon them, and for the case of the death of any of the persons from whom the Senate may choose a Vice President whenever the right of choice shall have devolved upon them.

Section 5.

Sections 1 and 2 shall take effect on the 15th day of October following the ratification of this article.

Section 6.

This article shall be inoperative unless it shall have been ratified as an amendment to the Constitution by the legislatures of three-fourths of the several States within seven years from the date of its submission.

• The Twentieth Amendment is often called the lame duck amendment because its fundamental purpose was to shorten the time between the November elections and the starting date of the new presidential term and/or commencement of the new congressional session. The amendment modified section 1 of the Twelfth Amendment by moving the beginning of the annual legislative session from March 4 to January 3. This change meant that the newly elected Congress would decide any presidential election thrown into the House of Representatives. It also eliminated the possibility that the nation would have to endure two additional months without a chief executive.

The Twentieth Amendment also modified Article I of the Constitution by placing a fixed time—noon—to begin the congressional session. •

AMENDMENT XXI
(Ratified on December 5, 1933)
Section 1.

The eighteenth article of amendment to the Constitution of the United States is hereby repealed.

Section 2.

The transportation or importation into any State, Territory, or possession of the United States for delivery or use therein of intoxicating liquors, in violation of the laws thereof, is hereby prohibited.

Section 3.

This article shall be inoperative unless it shall have been ratified as an amendment to the Constitution by conventions in the several States, as provided in the Constitution, within seven years from the date of the submission hereof to the States by the Congress.

- The Twenty-First Amendment repealed the Eighteenth Amendment mandating Prohibition, which was the first and last time that a constitutional amendment has been repealed. The Twenty-First Amendment is also the only amendment to the Constitution approved by state ratifying conventions rather than a popular vote.

By the late 1920s, Americans had tired of Prohibition, and the arrival of the Great Depression in 1929 did nothing to lift their spirits. Few public officials, aware of the extensive criminal enterprises that had grown up around Prohibition, attempted to defend Prohibition as a success. Indeed, Franklin D. Roosevelt, in his initial bid for the presidency in 1932, made the repeal of Prohibition a campaign promise. In January 1933, Congress amended the Volstead Act to permit the sale of alcoholic beverages with an alcohol content of 3.2 percent.

The ratification of the Twenty-First Amendment in December returned absolute control of the regulation of alcohol to the states. States are now free to regulate alcohol as they see fit. They may, for example, limit the quantity and type of alcohol sold to consumers, or ban alcohol sales completely. The Supreme Court, in *South Carolina* v. *Dole* (1984), ruled that Congress may require the states to set a certain age for the consumption of alcohol in return for participation in a federal program without violating the Twenty-First Amendment. In 2005, however, in *Granholm* v. *Heald*, the Court ruled that states could not ban out-of-state wineries from shipping directly to consumers, citing the Twenty-First Amendment. •

AMENDMENT XXII
(Ratified on February 27, 1951)
Section 1.

No person shall be elected to the office of the President more than twice, and no person who has held the office of President, or acted as President, for more than two years of a term to which some other person was elected President shall be elected to the office of the President more than once. But this Article shall not apply to any person holding the office of President when this Article was proposed by the Congress, and shall not prevent any person who may be holding the office of President, or acting as President, during the term within which this Article becomes operative from

holding the office of President or acting as President during the remainder of such term.

Section 2.

This article shall be inoperative unless it shall have been ratified as an amendment to the Constitution by the legislatures of three-fourths of the several States within seven years from the date of its submission to the States by the Congress.

- Thomas Jefferson, who served as the third president of the United States, was the first person of public stature to suggest a constitutional provision limiting presidential terms. "If some termination to the services of the chief Magistrate be not fixed by the Constitution," said Jefferson, "or supplied by practice, his office, nominally four years, will in fact become for life." Until Ulysses S. Grant's unsuccessful attempt to secure his party's nomination to a third term, no president had attempted to extend the two-term limit that had operated in principle. Theodore Roosevelt, having ascended to the presidency after the assassination of William McKinley in 1901, was elected to his second term in 1904. He then sat out a term but ran against Woodrow Wilson in the 1912 election and lost.

The first president to serve more than two terms was Franklin D. Roosevelt, and it was his success that inspired the enactment of the Twenty-Second Amendment. In 1946, Republicans took control of Congress for the first time in sixteen years. A year later, in one of the most party-line votes in the history of the amending process, Congress approved the Twenty-Second Amendment. Every Republican member of the House and Senate who voted on the amendment voted for it. The remaining votes came almost exclusively from southern Democrats, whose relationship with Roosevelt was never more than a marriage of convenience. Ironically, some Republicans began to call for the repeal of the Twenty-Second Amendment toward the end of popular Republican Dwight D. Eisenhower's second term in 1956. A similar movement emerged in the late 1980s toward the end of Republican Ronald Reagan's second term. The American public at large, however, has shown little enthusiasm for repealing the Twenty-Second Amendment. •

AMENDMENT XXIII
(Ratified on March 29, 1961)
Section 1.

The District constituting the seat of Government of the United States shall appoint in such manner as the Congress may direct:

A number of electors of President and Vice President equal to the whole number of Senators and

Representatives in Congress to which the District would be entitled if it were a State, but in no event more than the least populous State; they shall be in addition to those appointed by the States, but they shall be considered, for the purposes of the election of President and Vice President, to be electors appointed by a State; and they shall meet in the District and perform such duties as provided by the twelfth article of amendment.

Section 2.

The Congress shall have power to enforce this article by appropriate legislation.

• Article II, section 2, of the Constitution limits participation in presidential elections to citizens who reside in the states. The Twenty-Third Amendment extended this provision to include residents of the District of Columbia. Since the District was envisioned as the seat of the national government with a transient population, the Constitution afforded no right of representation to its residents in Congress. By the time the Twenty-Third Amendment was ratified, the District had a greater population than twelve states.

In 1978, Congress introduced a constitutional amendment to give the District of Columbia representation in the House and Senate. By 1985, the ratification period for the amendment expired without the necessary three-fourths approval from the states. This issue continues to come up in Congress, but it has not won support—largely for political reasons. •

AMENDMENT XXIV
(Ratified on January 23, 1964)
Section 1.

The right of citizens of the United States to vote in any primary or other election for President or Vice President, for electors for President or Vice President, or for Senator or Representative in Congress, shall not be denied or abridged by the United States or any State by reason of failure to pay any poll tax or other tax.

Section 2.

The Congress shall have power to enforce this article by appropriate legislation.

• The Twenty-Fourth Amendment continued the work of the Fifteenth Amendment. By abolishing the poll tax, essentially a fee to vote, the amendment eliminated one of the most popular tools used by voting registrars to prevent most African Americans and other minorities from taking part in the electoral process.

Congress had begun to debate a constitutional amendment to abolish the poll tax as far back as 1939, but it took the momentum of the civil rights movement to move this process forward. Shortly after the ratification of the Twenty-Fourth Amendment, Congress enacted the Civil Rights Act of 1964, the most sweeping and effective federal civil rights law to date. By the time of ratification of the Twenty-Fourth Amendment, only five states had poll taxes on their books. Spurred on by the spirit of the times, Congress enacted the Voting Rights Act of 1965, which enforced the poll tax ban of the Twenty-Fourth Amendment and also abolished literacy tests, property qualifications, and other obstacles to voter registration. In 1966, in *Harper* v. *Board of Elections*, the Supreme Court rejected a constitutional challenge to the historic voting rights law. •

AMENDMENT XXV
(Ratified on February 10, 1967)
Section 1.

In case of the removal of the President from office or of his death or resignation, the Vice President shall become President.

Section 2.

Whenever there is a vacancy in the office of the Vice President, the President shall nominate a Vice President who shall take office upon confirmation by a majority vote of both Houses of Congress.

Section 3.

Whenever the President transmits to the President pro tempore of the Senate and the Speaker of the House of Representatives his written declaration that he is unable to discharge the powers and duties of his office, and until he transmits to them a written declaration to the contrary, such powers and duties shall be discharged by the Vice President as Acting President.

Section 4.

Whenever the Vice President and a majority of either the principal officers of the executive departments or of such other body as Congress may by law provide, transmit to the President pro tempore of the Senate and the Speaker of the House of Representatives their written declaration that the President is unable to discharge the powers and duties of his office, the Vice President shall immediately assume the powers and duties of the office as Acting President.

Thereafter, when the President transmits to the President pro tempore of the Senate and the Speaker of the House of Representatives his written declaration that no inability exists, he shall resume the powers and duties of his office unless the Vice President and a majority of either the principal officers of the executive department or of such other body as Congress may by law provide, transmit within four days to the President pro tempore of the Senate and the Speaker of the House of Representatives their written declaration that the President is unable to discharge the powers and duties of his office. Thereupon Congress shall decide the issue, assembling within forty-eight hours for that purpose if not in session. If the Congress, within twenty-one days after receipt of the latter written declaration, or, if Congress is not in session, within twenty-one days after Congress is required to assemble, determines by two-thirds vote of both Houses that the President is unable to discharge the powers and duties of his office, the Vice President shall continue to discharge the same as Acting President; otherwise, the President shall resume the powers and duties of his office.

• Several tragedies to the men who occupied the offices of president and vice president and the lack of constitutional clarity about the path of succession in event of presidential and vice presidential disability spurred enactment of the Twenty-Fifth Amendment.

Whether the vice president was merely an acting president or assumed the permanent powers of the office for the remainder of the term upon the death of a president was answered in 1841 when John Tyler became president upon the death of William Henry Harrison, who died only a month after his inauguration. Seven more presidents died in office before the enactment of the Twenty-Fifth Amendment, and in each case the vice president assumed the presidency without controversy.

This amendment also addressed the method of vice presidential succession. The vice presidency often went unfilled for months at a time as the result of constitutional ambiguity. Since the enactment of the amendment, there have been two occasions when the president appointed a vice president, and both took place during the second term of President Richard M. Nixon. For the first time in U.S. history, a presidential term was served out by two men, President Gerald R. Ford and Vice President Nelson A. Rockefeller, who had been not been elected to the positions.

The Twenty-Fifth Amendment also settled the path of succession in the event of presidential disability. This provision of the amendment was prompted by the memories of James Garfield lying in a coma for eighty days after being struck by an assassin's bullet and Woodrow Wilson's bedridden state for the last eighteen months of his term after a stroke. The first president to invoke the disability provision of the Twenty-Fifth Amendment was Ronald Reagan, who made Vice President George Bush acting president for eight hours while he underwent surgery. George W. Bush also twice transferred the powers of his office to Vice President Dick Cheney, both times while he was undergoing a colonoscopy.

The provision authorizing the vice president, in consultation with Congress and members of the Cabinet, to declare the president disabled has never been invoked. •

AMENDMENT XXVI
(Ratified on July 1, 1971)
Section 1.

The right of citizens of the United States, who are eighteen years of age or older, to vote shall not be denied or abridged by the United States or by any State on account of age.

Section 2.

The Congress shall have power to enforce this article by appropriate legislation.

• The Twenty-Sixth Amendment was a direct response to the unpopularity of the Vietnam War and was spurred by calls to lower the voting age to eighteen so that draft-eligible men could voice their opinion on the war through the ballot box. In 1970, Congress had amended the Voting Rights Act of 1965 to lower the voting age to eighteen in all national, state, and local elections. Many states resisted compliance, claiming that Congress, while having the power to establish the voting age in national elections, had no such authority in state and local elections. In *Oregon* v. *Mitchell* (1970), the Supreme Court agreed. Congress responded by drafting the Twenty-Sixth Amendment, and the states ratified it quickly and without controversy. •

AMENDMENT XXVII
(Ratified on May 7, 1992)

No law, varying the compensation for the services of the Senators and Representatives, shall take effect until an election of Representatives shall have intervened.

• The Twenty-Seventh Amendment originally was introduced in 1789 during the 1st Congress as one of the original twelve amendments to the Constitution. Only six of the necessary eleven (of thirteen) states had ratified the amendment by 1791. As more states came into the union, the prospect of the amendment's passage only dwindled. No additional state ratified the amendment until 1873, when Ohio approved its addition to the Constitution.

In the early 1980s, a University of Texas student discovered the amendment and launched an intensive effort to bring it to the public's attention for ratification. The amendment's core purpose, preventing members of Congress from raising their salaries during the terms in which they served, meshed well with another grassroots movement that began during this time, the campaign to impose term limits on members of the House and Senate. Nothing in the nation's constitutional or statutory law prohibited the resurrection of the Twenty-Seventh Amendment for voter approval. In 1939, the Supreme Court had ruled in *Coleman* v. *Miller* that amendments could remain indefinitely before the public unless Congress had set a specific time limit on the ratification process. By 1992, the amendment had received the necessary three-fourths approval of the states, making it the last successful effort to amend the Constitution. The Twenty-Seventh Amendment has not, however, barred Congress from increasing its compensation through annual cost-of-living adjustments. •

3

Federalism

On April 24, 2010, Arizona Governor Jan Brewer signed into law the nation's toughest immigration regulations. Aimed at identifying and deporting illegal immigrants, these regulations go so far as to authorize local police officers to stop and question anyone they think may be an illegal immigrant. Those detained must produce evidence of citizenship or legal residency.

A large proportion of the immigrant population in the state of Arizona—and the population the bill is most intended to target—is of Mexican descent. Even before the bill was officially enacted, the Mexican American Legal Defense and Education Fund vocally expressed concerns that the law would create "a spiral of pervasive fear, community distrust, increased crime and costly litigation, with nationwide repercussions."[1]

Another surprisingly vocal critic of the bill was President Barack Obama. Presidents, as the head of the national government, do not usually comment on state legislation; such an intervention compromises the federal system we hold dear. However, President Obama noted that the bill's provisions undermined "basic notions of fairness that we cherish as Americans, as well as the trust between police and our communities that is so crucial to keeping us safe."[2] He urged Congress to act quickly on the immigration issue, perhaps in the hopes that a federal law might preempt the Arizona law.

Supporters of the Arizona bill, however, charge that the state government was fully within its rights to enact the legislation. The Constitution grants the national government supreme authority over foreign affairs, presumably including immigration. But, the reserved powers of the Tenth Amendment also enable states to take action when the national government has not.

Illegal immigration is a serious problem that lawmakers in Washington, D.C. have long avoided. In fact, Arizona lawmakers are not

Immigration has long been a difficult issue for state and national governments. At left, a customs official processes a family of German immigrants at Ellis Island in 1905. At right, a border patrol agent searches an undocumented immigrant at the U.S.–Mexico border.

alone in filling the void of federal legislation. Since 2007, 48 states have enacted more than 200 laws dealing with immigration.[3]

Moreover, supporters of the Arizona law argue, the state government is actually better equipped than the national government to handle the modern immigration problem because politicians and law enforcement officers in Arizona have more practical experience than most lawmakers in Washington, D.C. This enables state legislators to craft a solution that best serves their needs. It also enables states to act as "laboratories of democracy" and test solutions to political problems that may later be adopted by the national government.

Since the day it was enacted, the law has been the subject of federal litigation questioning its legality. In July 2010, a federal district court judge issued an injunction to stop the enforcement of many of the most controversial provisions of the law. Among these were the requirements that allowed police officers to

verify citizens' immigration status while stopping them for other offenses. Governor Brewer has vowed to appeal the court's decision, continuing to fuel a lively debate about state and federal power that is likely to end up in the U.S. Supreme Court.

What Should I Know About . . .

After reading this chapter, you should be able to

★ **3.1** Trace the roots of the federal system and the Constitution's allocation of governmental powers, p. 82.

★ **3.2** Determine the impact of the Marshall Court on federalism, p. 87.

★ **3.3** Describe the emergence and decline of dual federalism, p. 89.

★ **3.4** Explain how cooperative federalism led to the growth of the national government, p. 92.

★ **3.5** Identify new trends in federalism, p. 94.

★ **3.6** Assess the challenges in balancing national and state powers and the consequences for policy making, p. 97.

Figure 3.1 *How many governments are there in the United States?*

Source: U.S. Census Bureau, www.census.gov/govs/cog/GovOrgTab033ss.html

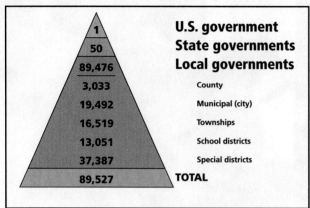

1	**U.S. government**
50	**State governments**
89,476	**Local governments**
3,033	County
19,492	Municipal (city)
16,519	Townships
13,051	School districts
37,387	Special districts
89,527	**TOTAL**

From its very beginning, the challenge for the United States of America was to preserve the traditional independence and rights of the states while establishing an effective national government. The Framers, fearing tyranny, divided powers between the state and the national governments. At each level, moreover, powers were divided among the executive, legislative, and judicial branches. The people are the ultimate source of power for the national and state governments.

Today, the Constitution ultimately binds more than 89,000 different governments at the national, state, and local levels. (To learn more about governments in the United States, see Figure 3.1.) The Constitution lays out the duties, obligations, and powers of each of these units. Throughout history, however, this relationship has been reshaped continually by crises, historical evolution, public expectations, and judicial interpretation. All of these forces have had tremendous influence on who makes policy decisions and how these decisions get made.

To understand the current relationship between the states and the federal government and to better grasp some of the issues that arise from this constantly changing relationship, in this chapter, we will examine the following topics:

- First, we will look at *the roots of the federal system* created by the Framers.

- Second, we will explore the relationship between *federalism and the Marshall Court.*

- Third, we will examine the development of *dual federalism, the Taney Court, slavery, and the Civil War.*

- Fourth, we will analyze *cooperative federalism and the growth of the national government.*

- Fifth, we will discuss *new trends in federalism.*

- Finally, we will examine *attempts to balance national and state power.*

ROOTS OF the Federal System

⭐ **3.1 . . . Trace the roots of the federal system and the Constitution's allocation of governmental powers.**

federal system

System of government where the national government and state governments share power and derive all authority from the people.

unitary system

System of government where the local and regional governments derive all authority from a strong national government.

As discussed in **chapter 2**, the United States was the first country to adopt a **federal system** of government (although the word "federal" never appears in the U.S. Constitution). This system of government, where the national government and state governments share power and derive all authority from the people, was designed to remedy many of the problems experienced under the Articles of Confederation.

The new system of government also had to be different from the **unitary system** found in Great Britain, where the local and regional governments derived all their power from a strong national government. (To learn more about these forms of government, see Figure 3.2.) Having been under the rule of English kings, whom they considered

Figure 3.2 *What is the source of governmental authority?*

tyrants, the Framers feared centralizing power in one government or institution. Therefore, they made both the state and the federal government accountable to the people at large. While the governments shared some powers, such as the ability to tax, each government was supreme in some spheres, as described in the following section.

National Powers Under the Constitution

Chief among the exclusive powers of the national government are the authorities to coin money, conduct foreign relations, provide for an army and navy, and declare war. All of these powers set out in Article I, section 8, of the Constitution are called enumerated powers. Article I, section 8, also contains the necessary and proper clause (also called the elastic clause), which gives Congress the authority to enact any laws "necessary and proper" for carrying out any of its enumerated powers. These powers derived from enumerated powers and the necessary and proper clause are known as implied powers.

The federal government's right to collect duties and excises was also clearly set out in the Constitution. The Framers wanted to avoid the financial problems that the national government experienced under the Articles of Confederation. If the new national government was to be strong, its power to raise revenue had to be unquestionable. Allowing the new national government to collect tariffs, or taxes on imported goods, was one way to assert this power. And, giving the national government

Federal and Unitary Systems

The United States has a federal system of government in which power is shared by national and subnational political units (states). Canada, Switzerland, India, and Nigeria also have federal systems of government. However, most of the world's nations, including Great Britain, France, China, Japan, and Iran, have unitary systems, with authority concentrated in the central government. Although federal states are relatively few in number, they tend to be large and politically important. The map highlights the countries with federal systems of government.

- What are the major advantages of a federal system? Of a unitary system?

- Why might a country reject federalism in favor of a unitary political system?

- Looking at the map, what characteristics do the countries with federal systems have in common that led them to adopt federal systems?

the exclusive power to do so eliminated the excise wars between states that had occurred under the Articles.

Article VI of the federal Constitution underscores the notion that the national government is to be supreme in situations of conflict between state and national law. It declares that the U.S. Constitution, the laws of the United States, and its treaties, are to be "the supreme Law of the Land; and the Judges in every State shall be bound thereby." In spite of this explicit language, the meaning of what is called the supremacy clause has been subject to continuous judicial interpretation.

State Powers Under the Constitution

Because states had all the power at the time the Constitution was written, the Framers felt no need, as they did for the new national government, to list and restate the powers of the states. Article I, however, allows states to set the "Times, Places, and Manner, for holding elections for senators and representatives." Article II requires that each state appoint electors to vote for president. And, Article IV provides each state a "Republican Form of Government," meaning one that represents the citizens of the state.

It was not until the **Tenth Amendment,** the final part of the Bill of Rights, that the states' powers were described in greater detail: "The powers not delegated to the United States by the Constitution, nor prohibited by it to the States, are reserved to the States respectively, or to the people." These powers, often called the states' **reserved** or **police powers,** include the ability to legislate for the public health, safety, and morals of their citizens. Today, the states' rights to legislate under their police powers are used as the rationale for many states' restrictions on abortion. Police powers are also the basis for state criminal laws, including varied laws concerning the death penalty.

Tenth Amendment
The final part of the Bill of Rights that defines the basic principle of American federalism in stating that the powers not delegated to the national government are reserved to the states or to the people.

reserved (or police) powers
Powers reserved to the states by the Tenth Amendment that lie at the foundation of a state's right to legislate for the public health and welfare of its citizens.

concurrent powers
Powers shared by the national and state governments.

Concurrent Powers Under the Constitution

As revealed in Figure 3.3, national and state powers overlap. The area where the systems overlap represents **concurrent powers**—powers shared by the national and state governments. States already had the power to tax; the Constitution extended this power to the national government as well. Other important concurrent powers include the rights to borrow money, establish courts, charter banks, and spend money for the general welfare.

Powers Denied Under the Constitution

Some powers are explicitly denied to the national government or the states under Article I of the Constitution. Congress, for example, is barred from favoring one state over another in regulating commerce, and it cannot lay duties on items exported from any state. The national government is also prohibited from granting

Figure 3.3 *How is governmental power distributed in the federal system?*

NATIONAL POWERS (ENUMERATED POWERS)	CONCURRENT POWERS	STATE POWERS (RESERVED POWERS)
Collect duties, imposts, and excises Regulate commerce with foreign nations, among the states, and with Indian tribes Establish rules of naturalization Coin money Establish a post office Declare and conduct war Provide for an army and a navy Make laws necessary and proper toy carry out Article I powers	Tax Borrow money Establish courts Make and enforce laws Charter banks and corporations Spend money for the general welfare	Set times, places, and manner of elections and appoint electors Ratify amendments to the U.S. Constitution Take measures for public health, safety, and morals Exert powers the Constitution does not delegate to the national government or prohibit the states from using Establish local governments Regulate commerce within a state

titles of nobility and employees of the government may not accept salaries or gifts from foreign heads of state.

State governments (as well as the national government) are denied the authority to take arbitrary actions affecting constitutional rights and liberties. Neither national nor state governments may pass a **bill of attainder,** a law declaring an act illegal without a judicial trial. The Constitution also bars the national and state governments from passing *ex post facto* **laws,** laws that make an act punishable as a crime even if the action was legal at the time it was committed.

Interstate Relations Under the Constitution

In addition to delineating the relationship of the states with the national government, the Constitution provides a mechanism for resolving interstate disputes and facilitating relations among states. To avoid any sense of favoritism, it provides that disputes between states be settled directly by the U.S. Supreme Court under its original jurisdiction as mandated by Article III of the Constitution. (To learn more about the Supreme Court, see **chapter 9**.) Moreover, Article IV requires that each state give "Full Faith and Credit . . . to the public Acts, Records, and judicial Proceedings of every other State." The **full faith and credit clause** ensures that judicial decrees and contracts made in one state will be binding and enforceable in another, thereby facilitating trade and other commercial relationships. Full faith and credit cases continue to make their way through the judicial system. For example, a state's refusal to honor same-sex marriage contracts poses interesting constitutional questions. (To learn more about the full faith and credit clause, see The Living Constitution: Article IV, Section 1.)

Article IV also contains the **privileges and immunities clause,** guaranteeing that the citizens of each state are afforded the same rights as citizens of all other states. In addition, Article IV contains the **extradition clause,** which requires states to extradite, or return, criminals to states where they have been convicted or are to stand trial.

bill of attainder
A law declaring an act illegal without a judicial trial.

ex post facto **law**
Law that makes an act punishable as a crime even if the action was legal at the time it was committed.

full faith and credit clause
Section of Article IV of the Constitution that ensures judicial decrees and contracts made in one state will be binding and enforceable in any other state.

privileges and immunities clause
Part of Article IV of the Constitution guaranteeing that the citizens of each state are afforded the same rights as citizens of all other states.

extradition clause
Part of Article IV of the Constitution that requires states to extradite, or return, criminals to states where they have been convicted or are to stand trial.

The Living Constitution

Full Faith and Credit shall be given in each State to the public Acts, Records, and judicial Proceedings of every other State.

—ARTICLE IV, SECTION 1

The full faith and credit clause of Article IV of the Constitution rests on principles borrowed from international law that require one country to recognize contracts made in another country absent a compelling public policy reason to the contrary. In the United States, this principle applies to the relationship between the states.

The full faith and credit clause requires a state to recognize public acts and court proceedings of another state. In 1997, the Supreme Court ruled that the full faith and credit clause mandates that state courts always honor the judgments of other state courts, even if to do so is against state public policy or existing state laws. Failure to do so would allow a single state to "rule the world," said Supreme Court Justice Ruth Bader Ginsburg during oral argument.[a]

For the most part, interpretation of the full faith and credit clause has not been controversial. That is likely to change, however, as advocates of same-sex marriage have suggested that marriages of same-sex couples performed and legally sanctioned in one state must be recognized in another state, as is the case with heterosexual marriages.

In the mid 1990s, the possible legalization of marriage between same-sex couples threw numerous state legislatures and the U.S. Congress into a virtual frenzy. Twenty-five states passed laws in 1996 and 1997 to bar legal recognition of same-sex marriages. The U.S. Congress also got into the act by passing what is called the Defense of Marriage Act (DOMA), which President Bill Clinton signed into law in 1996. It was designed to undercut possible state recognition of same-sex marriages. This federal law permits states to disregard same-sex marriages even if they are legal in other states. The constitutionality of this law, however is questionable. The U.S. Constitution does not formally give Congress legislative authority to create exceptions to the full faith and credit clause. As a result, some observers believe that such an exception would require a constitutional amendment. With the legalization of same-sex marriages in several states and the District of Columbia, years of litigation are likely to ensue.

CRITICAL THINKING QUESTIONS

1. How could a same-sex couple married in one state be granted a divorce in a state that does not recognize same-sex marriage?
2. Should states or the federal government be allowed to create public policy exceptions to the full faith and credit clause?
3. Is a federal law such as DOMA consistent with the wishes of the Framers, who left regulation of marriage largely to the states?

---

[a]Oral argument by Thomas in *Baker v. General Motors Corporation*, 522 U.S. 222 (1998), noted in Linda Greenhouse, "Court Weighs Whether One State Must Obey Another's Courts," *New York Times* (October 16, 1997): A25.

interstate compacts

Contracts between states that carry the force of law; generally now used as a tool to address multistate policy concerns.

To facilitate relations among states, Article I, section 10, clause 3, of the U.S. Constitution sets the legal foundation for interstate cooperation in the form of **interstate compacts,** contracts between states that carry the force of law. More than 200 interstate compacts exist today. While some deal with rudimentary items such as state boundaries, others help states carry out their policy objectives and administrative functions. Although several bistate compacts still exist, other compacts have as many as fifty signatories.[4] The Drivers License Compact, for example, was signed by all fifty states to facilitate nationwide recognition of licenses issued in the respective states.

Local Governments Under the Constitution

The Constitution gives local governments, including counties, municipalities, townships, and school districts, no independent standing. Thus, their authority is not granted directly by the people but through state governments, which establish, or charter, administrative subdivisions to execute the duties of the state government on a smaller scale.

Federalism and the Marshall Court

★ **3.2** . . . Determine the impact of the Marshall Court on federalism.

The nature of federalism, including its allocation of power between the national government and the states, has changed dramatically over the past two hundred years. Much of this change is due to the rulings of the U.S. Supreme Court, which has played a major role in defining the nature of the federal system because the distribution of power between the national and state governments is not clearly delineated in the Constitution. Few Supreme Courts have had a greater impact on the federal–state relationship than the one headed by Chief Justice John Marshall (1801–1835). In a series of decisions, he and his associates carved out an important role for the Court in defining the balance of power between the national government and the states. Three rulings in the early 1800s, *McCulloch* v. *Maryland* (1819), *Gibbons* v. *Ogden* (1824), and *Barron* v. *Baltimore* (1833), were particularly important.

McCulloch v. *Maryland* (1819)

McCulloch v. *Maryland* **(1819)** was the first major Supreme Court decision to define the relationship between the national and state governments. In 1816, Congress chartered the Second Bank of the United States. (The charter of the First Bank had been allowed to expire.) In 1818, the Maryland state legislature levied a tax requiring all banks not chartered by Maryland (that is, the Second Bank of the United States) to: (1) buy stamped paper from the state on which their bank notes were to be issued; (2) pay the state $15,000 a year, or, (3) go out of business. James McCulloch, the head cashier of the Baltimore branch of the Bank of the United States, refused to pay the tax, and Maryland brought suit against him. After losing in a Maryland state court, McCulloch appealed the decision to the U.S. Supreme Court by order of the U.S. secretary of the treasury. In a unanimous opinion, the Court answered the two central questions that had been presented to it: Did Congress have the authority to charter a bank? And, if it did, could a state tax it?

Chief Justice John Marshall's answer to the first question—whether Congress had the right to establish a bank or another type of corporation—continues to stand as the classic exposition of the doctrine of implied powers and as a reaffirmation of the authority of a strong national government. Although the word "bank" cannot be found in the Constitution, the Constitution enumerates powers that give Congress the authority to levy and collect taxes, issue a currency, and borrow funds. From these enumerated powers, Marshall found, it was reasonable to imply that Congress had the power to charter a bank, which could be considered "necessary and proper" to the exercise of its aforementioned enumerated powers.

Marshall next addressed the question of whether a federal bank could be taxed by any state government. To Marshall, this was not a difficult question. The national government was dependent on the people, not the states, for its powers. In addition, Marshall noted, the Constitution specifically calls for the national law to be supreme.[5]

McCulloch v. *Maryland* (1819)

The Supreme Court upheld the power of the national government and denied the right of a state to tax the federal bank using the Constitution's supremacy clause. The Court's broad interpretation of the necessary and proper clause paved the way for later rulings upholding expansive federal powers.

TIMELINE: The Evolution of Federalism

1787 U.S. Constitution—The Framers craft the first federal system, where national and state governments share power and both are ultimately responsible to the people.

1861 Civil War—War and Reconstruction necessitate greater involvement by the federal government in policy areas traditionally reserved for the states.

1933 Cooperative Federalism—Period that began with the New Deal in which the responsibilities of national, state, and local governments became intertwined; marble cake federalism.

1800s Dual Federalism—Belief articulated by the Taney Court that having separate and equally powerful national and state governments is the best arrangement; layer cake federalism.

1913 Sixteenth and Seventeenth Amendments—These two amendments enhance the power of the national government at the expense of the states and pave the way for future changes.

The Court's decision in *McCulloch* has far-reaching consequences even today. The necessary and proper clause is used to justify federal action in many areas, including social welfare problems. Furthermore, had Marshall allowed the state of Maryland to tax the federal bank, it is possible that states could have attempted to tax all federal agencies located within their boundaries, a costly proposition that could have driven the federal government into insurmountable debt.[6]

Gibbons v. *Ogden* (1824)

Gibbons v. Ogden (1824)
The Supreme Court upheld broad congressional power to regulate interstate commerce. The Court's broad interpretation of the Constitution's commerce clause paved the way for later rulings upholding expansive federal powers.

Shortly after *McCulloch*, the Marshall Court had another opportunity to rule in favor of a broad interpretation of the scope of national power. ***Gibbons* v. *Ogden* (1824)** involved a dispute that arose after the New York state legislature granted to Robert Fulton the exclusive right to operate steamboats on the Hudson River.[7] Simultaneously, Congress licensed a ship to sail on the same waters. By the time the case reached the Supreme Court, it was complicated both factually and procedurally. Suffice it to say that both New York and New Jersey wanted to control shipping on the lower Hudson River. But, *Gibbons* actually addressed one simple, very important question: what was the scope of Congress's authority under the commerce clause? The states argued that "commerce," as mentioned in Article I, should be interpreted narrowly to include only direct dealings in products. In *Gibbons*, however, the Supreme Court ruled that Congress's power to regulate interstate commerce included the power to regulate commercial activity as well, and that the commerce power had no limits except those specifically found in the Constitution. Thus, New York had no constitutional authority to grant a monopoly to a single steamboat operator, an action that interfered with interstate commerce.[8]

1964 Great Society—
President Lyndon B. Johnson's program to combat poverty and discrimination; hallmark is the use of specific categorical grants to state and local governments.

1994 Devolution Revolution—Republicans, led by then House Minority Whip Newt Gingrich, introduced a "Contract with America," in which they pledged to continue to scale back the federal government.

1980 New Federalism—President Ronald Reagan proposed a new federal–state relationship in which administrative powers would be returned to the state governments; hallmark is the use of broad block grants.

2010 Progressive Federalism—Under progressive federalism, the national government gives state officials significant leeway on setting policy in areas traditionally reserved for the states, such as environmental protection and transportation.

Barron v. *Baltimore* (1833)

In 1833, in one of Chief Justice Marshall's last major cases on the federal–state relationship, in *Barron* v. *Baltimore,* the Court addressed the issue of whether the due process clause of the Fifth Amendment applied to actions of the states.[9] John Barron, a Baltimore businessman, ran a successful docking business off the city's wharf. As the city entered into a period of extensive building and road construction, dirt was deposited into Barron's wharf. In addition, sand and silt drifted to his section of the wharf making it unusable as a place for ships to harbor. Barron then sued the city and state for damages, arguing that the city took his lands "without just compensation" as guaranteed by the Fifth Amendment of the U.S. Constitution. The Marshall Court ruled that Barron had no federal claim because enumerated rights contained in the Bill of Rights were not a limit on states. In fact, states were free to add to those rights or ignore them all together.[10]

Barron v. *Baltimore* (1833)
The Supreme Court ruled that the due process clause of the Fifth Amendment did not apply to the actions of states. This decision limited the Bill of Rights to the actions of Congress alone.

Dual Federalism: The Taney Court, Slavery, and the Civil War

★ **3.3 . . . Describe the emergence and decline of dual federalism.**

In the early to mid-1800s, the nation was growing at such a rapid pace that the political clout of big business was declining. Changes in many state constitutions extended the right to vote from those who owned property to others, including the poor, farmers, and workers. This expansion of the electorate brought with it a decline in influence for pro-business voters, who tended to view the economy through a nationalist lens.

Chief Justice Roger B. Taney (1835–1863), who succeeded John Marshall in 1835, saw the Court as above these pressures and as an arbiter of those competing state and nationalist views.

In a series of cases involving the scope of Congress's power under the commerce clause, the Taney Court began to articulate further the notions of concurrent power and **dual federalism.** Dual federalism posits that having separate and equally powerful state and national governments is the best constitutional arrangement and one envisioned by the Framers. Adherents of this theory typically believe that the national government should not exceed its constitutionally enumerated powers, and as stated in the Tenth Amendment, all other powers are, and should be, reserved to the states or to the people.

dual federalism
The belief that having separate and equally powerful levels of government is the best arrangement.

The *Dred Scott* Decision

During the Taney Court era, the role of the Supreme Court as the arbiter of competing national and state interests became troublesome when the justices were called upon to deal with the controversial issue of slavery. In cases such as **Dred Scott v. Sandford (1857),** the Court tried to manage the slavery issue by resolving questions of ownership, the status of fugitive slaves, and slavery in the new territories.[11] These cases generally were settled in favor of slavery and states' rights within the framework of dual federalism.

Dred Scott, for example, was born into slavery around 1795. In 1833, he was sold by his original owners to a family in Missouri. Later he tried to buy his freedom. His ability to take this action was questioned, so abolitionists gave money to support a test case seeking Scott's freedom. They believed his earlier residence with a family living in free states and the Wisconsin Territory, which prohibited slavery, made Scott a free man even though he now lived in a slave state, Missouri. In 1857 after many delays, the U.S. Supreme Court ruled 7–2 that Scott was not a citizen of the United States. "Slaves," said the Court, "were never thought of or spoken of except as property." Thus, the Court found that Congress lacked the authority to ban slavery in the territories. In so doing, this decision narrowed the scope of national power, while it enhanced that of the states. Eventually, however, no form of federalism could accommodate the existence of slavery.

Dred Scott v. *Sandford* (1857)
The Supreme Court concluded that the U.S. Congress lacked the constitutional authority to bar slavery in the territories. This decision narrowed the scope of national power, while it enhanced that of the states.

Nullification

As early as 1798, Congress approved the very unpopular Alien and Sedition Acts, which were passed by the Federalist Congress to prevent criticism of the national government. Thomas Jefferson, James Madison, and others who opposed the acts suggested that the states had the right to nullify, or declare void, any federal law that in the opinion of the states violated the Constitution.

The question of **nullification** came up again in 1828 when the national government enacted a tariff act, most commonly referred to as the "Tariff of Abominations," that raised duties on raw materials, iron, hemp, and flax and reduced protections against imported woolen goods. John C. Calhoun, who served as vice president from 1825 to 1832 under President Andrew Jackson, broke with Jackson over the tariff bill because it badly affected his home state of South Carolina. Not only did South Carolinians have to pay more for raw materials because of the tariff bill, it was also becoming more and more difficult for them to sell their dwindling crops abroad for a profit. Calhoun thus formulated a theory to justify South Carolina's refusal to abide by the federal tariff law.

Calhoun theorized that the federal government was but the agent of the states (the people and the individual state governments) and that the Constitution was

nullification
The purported right of a state to declare void a federal law.

simply a compact that provided instructions about how the agent was to act. Thus, according to Calhoun, the U.S. Supreme Court was not legally competent to pass judgment on the constitutional validity of acts of Congress. Like Congress, the Court was only a branch of a government created by and answerable to the states. Calhoun posited that if the people of any individual state did not like an act of Congress, they could hold a convention to nullify that act of Congress. In the state contesting the act, the law would have no force until three-fourths of all of the states ratified an amendment expressly giving Congress that power. Then, if the nullifying state still did not wish to be bound by the new provision, it could secede, or withdraw from the union. In their fight to keep slavery, which began in the 1850s, the southern states relied heavily on Calhoun's theories to justify their secession from the union, which ultimately led to the Civil War.

The Transformation of Dual Federalism

The Civil War forever changed the nature of federalism, as the concept of dual federalism and its emphasis on the role of the states was destroyed along with the Confederacy. After 1861, there was a slow but erratic increase in the role of the national government. The states and the national government began to work together on a variety of projects, including railroad construction, banking, canal building, and ports.[12]

The Supreme Court assisted in this gradual transition to increased federal power, recognizing the need for national control over new technological developments such as the telegraph.[13] And, beginning in the 1880s, the Court allowed Congress to regulate many aspects of economic relationships such as the outlawing of monopolies, a type of regulation or power formerly thought to be in the exclusive realm of the states. By the 1890s, passage of laws such as the Interstate Commerce Act and the Sherman Anti-Trust Act allowed Congress to establish itself as the supreme player in a growing national economy.

But, the Supreme Court did not consistently enlarge the scope of national power in the pre-New Deal period. In 1895, for example, the United States filed suit against four sugar refiners, alleging that the sale of those four companies would give their buyer control of 98 percent of the U.S. sugar-refining business. The Supreme Court ruled that congressional efforts to control monopolies (through passage of the Sherman Anti-Trust Act) did not give Congress the authority to prevent the sale of these sugar-refining businesses, because manufacturing was not commerce. Therefore, the companies and their actions were found to be beyond the scope of Congress's authority to regulate.[14]

Later that same year, the U.S. Supreme Court found a congressional effort to tax personal incomes unconstitutional, although an earlier Court had found a similar tax levied during the Civil War constitutional.[15] Thus, Congress and the state legislatures were moved to ratify the **Sixteenth Amendment.** The Sixteenth Amendment gave Congress the power to levy and collect taxes on incomes without apportioning them among the states. If money is power, the income tax and the revenues it generated greatly enhanced the power of the federal government and its ability to enter policy areas where it formerly had few funds to spend.

The **Seventeenth Amendment,** ratified in 1913, similarly enhanced the power of the national government at the expense of the states. This amendment terminated the state legislatures' election of senators and put their election in the hands of the people. With senators no longer directly accountable to the state legislatures, states lost their principal protectors in Congress. Coupled with the Sixteenth Amendment, this amendment paved the way for more drastic changes in the relationship between national and state governments in the United States.

Sixteenth Amendment
Amendment to the U.S. Constitution that authorized Congress to enact a national income tax.

Seventeenth Amendment
Amendment to the U.S. Constitution that made senators directly elected by the people, removing their selection from state legislatures.

Cooperative Federalism: The Growth of National Government

⭐ **3.4** . . . Explain how cooperative federalism led to the growth of the national government.

The era of dual federalism came to an end in the 1930s. While the ratification of the Sixteenth and Seventeenth Amendments set the stage for expanded national government, the catalyst for dual federalism's demise was a series of economic events that ended in the cataclysm of the Great Depression:

- Throughout the 1920s, bank failures were common.
- In 1921, the nation experienced a severe slump in agricultural prices.
- In 1926, the construction industry went into decline.
- In the summer of 1929, inventories of consumer goods and automobiles were at an all-time high.
- On October 29, 1929, stock prices, which had risen steadily since 1926, crashed, taking with them the entire national economy.

Despite the severity of these indicators, Presidents Calvin Coolidge and Herbert Hoover took little action, believing that the national depression was an amalgamation of state economic crises that should be dealt with by state and local governments. However, by 1933, the situation could no longer be ignored.

The New Deal

New Deal
The name given to the program of "Relief, Recovery, Reform" begun by President Franklin D. Roosevelt in 1933 to bring the United States out of the Great Depression.

Rampant unemployment (historians estimate it was as high as 40 to 50 percent) was the hallmark of the Great Depression. In 1933, to combat severe problems facing the nation, newly elected President Franklin D. Roosevelt (FDR) proposed a variety of innovative programs, collectively called the **"New Deal,"** and ushered in a new era in American politics. FDR used the full power of the office of the president as well as his highly effective communication skills to sell the American public and Congress on a new level of government intervention intended to stabilize the economy and reduce suffering. Most politicians during the New Deal period (1933–1939) agreed that to find national solutions to the depression, which was affecting the citizens of every state in the union, the national government would have to exercise tremendous authority.

In the first few weeks of the legislative session after FDR's inauguration, Congress passed a series of acts creating new federal agencies and programs proposed by the president. These new agencies, often known by their initials, created what many termed an alphabetocracy. Among the more significant programs were the Federal Housing Administration (FHA), which provided federal financing for new home construction; the Civilian Conservation Corps (CCC), a work relief program for farmers and homeowners; the Agricultural Adjustment Administration (AAA) and the National Recovery Administration (NRA), which imposed restrictions on production in agriculture and many industries while also providing subsidies to farmers.

New Deal programs forced all levels of government to work cooperatively with one another. Indeed, local governments—mainly in big cities—became a third partner in the federal system as FDR relied on big-city

How did the New Deal change federalism? The New Deal included a variety of public works programs such as the Works Progress Administration (WPA). These new programs were symbolic of increasing federal–state interactions and the end of dual federalism.

Photo courtesy: The Granger Collection, New York

Democratic political machines to turn out voters to support his programs. Cities were embraced as equal partners in an intergovernmental system for the first time and became players in the national political arena because many members of Congress wanted to bypass state legislatures, where urban interests usually were underrepresented.

New Deal programs also enlarged the scope of the national government. Those who feared this unprecedented use of national power quickly challenged the constitutionality of the programs in court. And, at least initially, the U.S. Supreme Court often agreed with them. Through the mid-1930s, the Court continued to rule that certain aspects of New Deal programs went beyond the authority of Congress to regulate commerce. The Court's laissez-faire, or hands-off, attitude toward the economy was reflected in a series of decisions ruling various aspects of New Deal programs unconstitutional.

FDR and the Congress were livid. FDR's frustration with the Court prompted him to suggest what ultimately was nicknamed his "Court-packing plan." Knowing that he could do little to change the minds of those already on the Court, FDR suggested enlarging its size from nine to thirteen justices. This would have given him the opportunity to pack the Court with a majority of justices predisposed toward the constitutional validity of the New Deal.

Even though Roosevelt was popular, the Court-packing plan was not.[16] Congress and the public were outraged that he even suggested tampering with an institution of government. Nevertheless, the Court appeared to respond to this threat. In 1937, it reversed its series of anti-New Deal decisions, concluding that Congress (and therefore the national government) had the authority to legislate in any area so long as what was regulated affected commerce in any way. The Court also upheld the constitutionality of the bulk of the massive New Deal relief programs, including the National Labor Relations Act of 1935, which authorized collective bargaining between unions and employees;[17] the Fair Labor Standards Act of 1938, which prohibited the interstate shipment of goods made by employees earning less than the federally mandated minimum wage;[18] and the Agricultural Adjustment Act of 1938, which provided crop subsidies to farmers.[19] Congress then used this newly recognized power to legislate in a wide array of areas, including maximum hour and minimum wage laws and regulation of child labor.

The Changing Nature of Federalism: From Layer Cake to Marble Cake

Before the Depression and the New Deal, most political scientists likened the federal system to a layer cake: in most policy areas, each level or layer of government—national, state, and local—had clearly defined powers and responsibilities. After the New Deal, however, government looked more like a marble cake:

> Wherever you slice through it you reveal an inseparable mixture of differently colored ingredients. . . . Vertical and diagonal lines almost obliterate the horizontal ones, and in some places there are unexpected whirls and an imperceptible merging of colors, so that it is difficult to tell where one ends and the other begins.[20]

The metaphor of marble cake federalism refers to what political scientists call **cooperative federalism,** a term that describes the intertwined relationship among the national, state, and local governments that began with the New Deal. States began to take a secondary, albeit important, cooperative role in the scheme of governance, as did many cities. This shift in power from the states to the national government is exemplified by the New Deal and other social welfare programs such as President Lyndon B. Johnson's Great Society.

cooperative federalism
The intertwined relationship between the national, state, and local governments that began with the New Deal.

Federal Grants and National Efforts to Influence the States

President Franklin D. Roosevelt's New Deal programs increased the flow of federal dollars to the states for a variety of public works programs, including building and road construction. In the boom times of World War II, even more new federal programs were introduced. By the 1950s and 1960s, federal grant-in-aid programs were well entrenched. They often defined federal–state relationships and made the national government a major player in domestic policy. Until the 1960s, however, most federal grant programs were constructed in cooperation with the states and were designed to assist the states in the furtherance of their traditional responsibilities to protect the health, welfare, and safety of their citizens.

Most of these programs were **categorical grants,** ones for which Congress appropriates funds for specific purposes. Categorical grants allocate federal dollars by a precise formula and are subject to detailed conditions imposed by the national government, often on a matching basis; that is, states must contribute money to match federal funds, although the national government may pay as much as 90 percent of the total.

In 1964, the Democratic administration of President Lyndon B. Johnson (LBJ) launched its "Great Society" program, which included what LBJ called a "War on Poverty." The Great Society program was a broad attempt to combat poverty and discrimination. In a frenzy of activity in Washington not seen since the New Deal, federal funds were channeled to states, to local governments, and even directly to citizen action groups in an effort to alleviate social ills that the states had been unable or unwilling to remedy. Money was allocated for urban renewal, education, and poverty programs, including Head Start and job training. The move to fund local groups directly was made by the most liberal members of Congress to bypass not only conservative state legislatures, but also conservative mayors and councils in cities such as Chicago, who were perceived as disinclined to help their poor, often African American, constituencies. Thus, these programs often pitted governors and mayors against community activists, who became key players in the distribution of federal dollars.

These new grants altered the fragile federal–state balance of power that had been at the core of many older federal grant programs. During the Johnson administration, the national government began to use federal grants as a way to further national (and not state) needs. Grants based on what states wanted or believed they needed began to decline, while grants based on what the national government wanted states to do to foster national goals increased dramatically. From pollution to economic development and law enforcement, creating a federal grant seemed like the perfect solution to every problem.[21]

Not all federal programs mandating state or local action came with federal money, however. And, while presidents during the 1970s voiced their opposition to big government, their efforts to rein it in were largely unsuccessful.

categorical grant
Grant that allocates federal funds to states for a specific purpose.

New Trends in Federalism

⭐ 3.5 . . . Identify new trends in federalism.

In 1980, former California Republican Governor Ronald Reagan was elected president, pledging to advance what he called **New Federalism** and a return of power to the states. Presidents and Congresses since Reagan have struggled with the balance of federal–state power. The Supreme Court has often been called upon to be an umpire in this relationship.

New Federalism
Federal–state relationship proposed by Reagan administration during the 1980s; hallmark is returning administrative powers to the state governments.

The Reagan Revolution

The Reagan Revolution had at its heart strong views about the role of states in the federal system. While many Democrats and liberal interest groups argued that federal grants were an effective way to raise the level of services provided to the poor, many Republicans, including Reagan, attacked them as imposing national priorities on the states. Thus, in the early 1980s, for the first time in thirty years, federal aid to state and local governments declined.[22] Reagan also persuaded Congress to consolidate many categorical grants into far fewer, less restrictive **block grants**—large amounts of money given to states with only general spending guidelines. Many of these went to education and health care. These programs were popular with governors, who urged the consolidation of even more programs into block grants. Calls to reform the welfare system, particularly to allow the states more latitude in an effort to get back to the notion of states as laboratories of democracy, seemed popular with citizens and governments alike. (To learn more about the notion of states as laboratories of democracy, see Join the Debate: Should States Be Given Greater Freedom to Experiment with Public Policy?).

block grant
A large grant given to a state by the federal government with only general spending guidelines.

The Devolution Revolution

In 1994, Republican candidates for the House of Representatives joined together in their support for the Contract with America, a campaign document proposed by then House Minority Whip Newt Gingrich (R–GA). In it, Republican candidates pledged to force a national debate on the role of the national government in regard to the states. A top priority was scaling back the federal government, an effort that some commentators called the devolution revolution.

Running under a clear set of priorities contained in the Contract, Republican candidates took back the House of Representatives for the first time in more than forty years. A majority of the legislative proposals based on the Contract passed the House of Representatives during the first one hundred days of the 104th Congress. However, very few of the Contract's proposals, including acts requiring a balanced budget, tax reforms, and term limits, passed the Senate to become law.

On some issues, however, the Republicans were able to achieve their goals. For example, before 1995, **unfunded mandates,** national laws that direct state or local governments to comply with federal rules or regulations (such as clean air or water standards) but contain no federal funding to defray the cost of meeting these requirements, absorbed nearly 30 percent of some local budgets. Republicans in Congress, loyal to the concerns of these governments, secured passage of the Unfunded Mandates Reform Act of 1995. This act prevented Congress from passing costly federal programs without debate on how to fund them and addressed a primary concern for state governments.

unfunded mandates
National laws that direct state or local governments to comply with federal rules or regulations (such as clean air or water standards) but contain little or no federal funding to defray the cost of meeting these requirements.

Another important act passed by the Republican-controlled Congress and signed into law by President Bill Clinton in 1996 was legislation that replaced the existing federal welfare program with a program known as Temporary Assistance for Needy Families (TANF). TANF returned much of the administrative power for welfare programs to the states and became a hallmark of the devolution revolution.

Federalism under the Bush Administration

On the campaign trail in 2000, then Texas Governor George W. Bush, the Republican candidate for president, made it clear that he would follow in the tradition of former President Ronald Reagan in moving to return power to the states. Yet, no one could have foreseen the circumstances that would surround much of Bush's

What was the devolution revolution? Here, then House Minority Whip Newt Gingrich (R–GA) promotes the tenets of the Contract with America in 1994. A top priority of the program was to scale back the scope and size of the federal government. Though some of the Contract's proposals became law, most of its goals remained unfulfilled.

Photo courtesy: AP/Wide World Photos

Join the DEBATE | Should States be Given Greater Freedom to Experiment with Public Policy?

In 1932, Supreme Court Justice Louis Brandeis wrote that states should be "laboratories of democracy." Denying states' ability to fulfill this role, he argued, "may be fraught with serious consequences to the nation. It is one of the happy incidents of the federal system that a single courageous state may, if its citizens choose, serve as a laboratory; and try novel social and economic experiments without risk to the rest of the country."[a]

Indeed, the federal government has learned a great deal from the experiments of the states. The No Child Left Behind Act, for example, was modeled after standards and choice-based education programs enacted by the states of Texas and Florida in the 1990s. The recent federal healthcare reform bill was, at least in part, inspired by efforts in states such as Hawaii and Massachusetts to provide insurance to all citizens. Several states also provided prescription drug benefits or discount programs for senior citizens before the federal government enacted Medicare Part D.

But, some commentators note that allowing states such broad authority to experiment with public policy leads to a patchwork of standards that pose costly compliance issues. They may also lead citizens to go "shopping" for a state that has particular public policies, increasing the burden on these state governments and encouraging other states to ignore pressing policy problems. Should these potential side effects limit states' ability to experiment with public policy? Should the federal government become more involved in a wider range of public policy programs? Or, should states have broad latitude to experiment with public policy, particularly in issue areas traditionally reserved to the states under the Tenth Amendment?

To develop an ARGUMENT FOR giving states greater freedom to experiment with public policymaking, think about how:

- **State governments are more familiar than the federal government with the unique needs of their citizens.** How might the needs of citizens in Mississippi or Alabama differ from the needs of citizens in New York or Connecticut? What geographic, political, and demographic factors contribute to these differences?
- **Fifty states can develop and test a greater diversity of solutions to public policy problems than one national government.** How might the national government learn from states' successes and failures in policymaking? What benefits might this policy learning have for the national government?
- **The federal government may not act decisively enough to address pressing state policy needs.** How does the recent debate over the Arizona immigration law demonstrate the ways states fill policy voids left by the national government? In what other areas have states addressed their own needs in the face of national inaction? How does such action help to set the national agenda?

To develop an ARGUMENT AGAINST giving states greater freedom to experiment with public policymaking, think about how:

- **The federal government has greater financial resources than the state governments and, as a result, is more able to solve policy problems.** Why can the federal government raise and spend more money than state governments? Why might funding be necessary to public policy implementation?
- **Having unified national standards is sometimes necessary.** How might having fifty different policies in an area such as environmental protection or healthcare be inefficient and costly? In what other issue areas might a unified national policy be necessary?
- **Inconsistent state standards can pose more problems than they solve.** How does the recent debate over gay marriage illustrate the problems that may result from a patchwork of state standards? In what other policy areas might citizens and the government face similar problems?

[a] *New State Ice Co. v. Liebmann*, 285 U.S. 262 (1932).

presidency. A struggling economy, terrorist attacks on the World Trade Center and the Pentagon, the invasion of Afghanistan, and the costly war in Iraq, as well as the rising costs of entitlement programs, produced state and federal budget deficits that would have been unimaginable only a few years before.

The No Child Left Behind Act, which imposed a host of federal requirements on everything from class size to accountability testing,[23] was also viewed by many as an unprecedented **preemption** of state and local powers. Allowing the national government to override state or local actions in certain areas is not new. The growth of preemption statutes began in 1965 during the Johnson administration. However, until recently, preemption statutes generally were supported by Democrats in Congress and the White House, not Republicans. The Bush administration's support of this law reflected a new era in preemption.

Judicial Federalism

The role of the Supreme Court of the United States in determining the parameters of federalism cannot be underestimated. Neither can the role of the executive branch in advocating certain positions before the Court. Although in the 1930s Congress passed sweeping New Deal legislation, it was not until the Supreme Court finally reversed itself and found those programs constitutional that any real change occurred in the federal–state relationship. From the New Deal until the 1980s, the Supreme Court's impact on the federal system generally was to expand the national government's authority at the expense of the states.

Beginning in the late 1980s, however, the Court's willingness to allow Congress to regulate in a variety of areas waned. Once Ronald Reagan was elected president, he attempted to appoint new justices committed to the notion of states' rights and to rolling back federal intervention in matters that many Republicans believed were state responsibilities.

According to one observer, the Court's federalism decisions during the late 1980s and the 1990s were "a reexamination of the country's most basic constitutional arrangements."[24] The Court's decisions largely agreed with Reagan's states' rights view and limited powers of Congress. For example, in *U.S.* v. *Lopez* (1995), which involved the conviction of a student charged with carrying a concealed handgun onto school property, a five-person majority of the Court ruled that Congress lacked constitutional authority under the commerce clause to regulate guns within 1,000 feet of a school.[25] The majority concluded that local gun control laws, even those involving schools, were a state, not a federal, matter. Similarly, in 2000, the Court ruled that Congress had exceeded its powers again under the commerce clause in enacting some provisions of the Violence Against Women Act.[26]

This victory for state power, however, may be short lived. The Supreme Court's decisions in federalism cases under Chief Justice John G. Roberts Jr. appear much more mixed. Instead of considering the kind of highly visible cases taken up by the Rehnquist Court, observers are still looking for indications of a new direction. The extent to which the Roberts Court will ultimately throw its support to national or to state authority in our federal system remains to be seen, but the Court is clearly in a strong position to arbitrate the contentious balance of power in the American republic.

TOWARD REFORM: Attempts to Balance National and State Power

★ 3.6 . . . Assess the challenges in balancing national and state powers and the consequences for policy making.

As we have seen throughout this chapter, attempting to find equilibrium between the powers and responsibilities of national and state governments is one of the greatest difficulties of a federal system. The roles and relative strengths of the national and

preemption
A concept that allows the national government to override state or local actions in certain areas.

POLITICS NOW

Through Oil-Fouled Water, Big Government Looks Better and Better

May 4, 2010
Washington Post
www.washingtonpost.com

By Dana Milbank

. . . About 10:30 Monday morning, Sen. David Vitter (R-La.), an ardent foe of big government, posted a blog item on his campaign Web site about the huge oil spill in the Gulf of Mexico. "I strongly believe BP is spread too thin," he wrote. . . .

About an hour later came word from the Pentagon that Alabama, Florida and Mississippi—all three governed by men who once considered themselves limited-government conservatives—want the federal government to mobilize (at taxpayer expense, of course) more National Guard troops to aid in the cleanup.

That followed an earlier request by the small-government governor of Louisiana, Bobby Jindal (R), who issued a statement saying he had called the Obama administration "to outline the state's needs" and to ask "for additional resources." Said Jindal: "These resources are critical."

About the time that Alabama, Florida and Mississippi were asking for more federal help, three small-government Republican senators, Richard Shelby and Jeff Sessions of Alabama and George LeMieux of Florida, were flying over the gulf on a U.S. government aircraft with small-government Republican Rep. Jeff Miller (Fla.).

"We're here to send the message that we're going to do everything we can from a federal level to mitigate this," Sessions said after the flight, "to protect the people and make sure when people are damaged that they're made whole." . . .

It may have taken an ecological disaster, but the gulf-state conservatives' newfound respect for the powers and purse of the federal government is a timely reminder for them. As conservatives in Washington complain about excessive federal spending, the ones who would suffer the most from spending cuts are their own constituents.

An analysis of data from the nonpartisan Tax Foundation by Washington Post database specialist Dan Keating found that people in states that voted Republican were by far the biggest beneficiaries of federal spending. In states that voted strongly Republican, people received an average of $1.50 back from the federal government for every dollar they paid in federal taxes. In moderately Republican states, the amount was $1.19. In moderately Democratic states, people received on average of 99 cents in federal funds for each dollar they paid in taxes. In strongly Democratic states, people got back just 86 cents on the tax dollar. . . .

Critical Thinking Questions

1. Should state or federal governments be responsible for cleaning up from natural disasters such as the oil spill? Explain your answer.
2. Should members of Congress compromise their views on federalism to assure their constituents are taken care of? Why or why not?
3. What factors might help to explain the variation in the amount of money states receive from the federal government?

state governments in the United States have changed over time and continue to evolve today. Here, we explore the current status of this relationship, and examine its consequences for policy making. (To learn more about how a crisis can impact people's views on the relationship between the states and the federal government, see Politics Now: Through Oil-Fouled Water, Big Government Looks Better and Better.)

The Price of Federalism

In 1995, political scientist Paul E. Peterson published his seminal exploration of the balance between state and national powers, *The Price of Federalism*.[27] In this book, Peterson considered how governments should best divide policy-making responsibility in two broad issue areas: redistributive and developmental policies. Redistributive policies are ones where the government collects money (usually through taxation) from one group of citizens to finance a service, such as health care or welfare, for another group of citizens. In contrast, developmental policies are those that are designed to strengthen a

ANALYZING VISUALS

Greenhouse Gas Emission Standards

In 2002, the state of California passed a law aimed at reducing greenhouse gas emissions from automobiles by 30 percent before 2016. This law went far beyond the national standards for greenhouse gas emissions established by the Environmental Protection Agency. California applied for a waiver from the federal government to be allowed to increase its standards. Once this waiver was approved by the Obama administration in 2009, other states were permitted to follow California's lead and adopt similar, more stringent standards. Examine the map below, which shows states that have adopted California's emission standards, and then answer the questions.

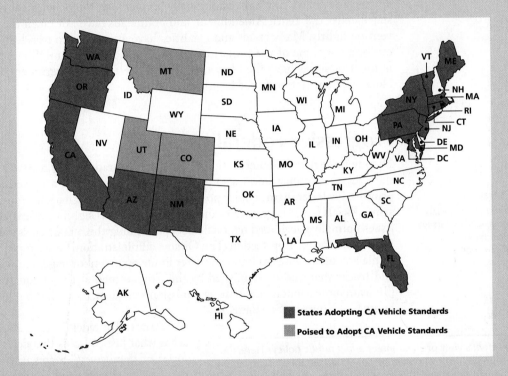

States Adopting CA Vehicle Standards
Poised to Adopt CA Vehicle Standards

- What geographic patterns do you observe among the states that have adopted stricter standards? Among states that have not?
- What does this map tell you about how states may learn from the policies adopted by other states?
- Should states be able to set standards stricter than those provided by the federal government in the area of environmental policy? In other policy areas?

Source: Pew Center on Global Climate Change, "Vehicle Greenhouse Gas Emissions Standards." www.pewclimate.org/what_s_being_done/in_the_states/vehicle_ghg_standard.cfm.

government's economic standing, such as building roads and other infrastructure. The national government's greater financial resources and ability to assure a uniform standard, Peterson argued, made it better suited to handle redistributive programs. In contrast, developmental programs would be best left to state governments, which are closer to the people and better able to assess and address regional needs.

The problem with this arrangement—and the price of American federalism—is that, historically, the division of labor has not followed this pattern. The national government, and particularly members of Congress, have had reelection incentives to create and fund developmental programs (often in the form of "pork") that have a direct impact on constituents. As a result, administration of redistributive policies was often left to the states, perhaps with federal financial assistance.

In more recent years, however, the federal government, while not totally abandoning developmental projects, has begun to take greater responsibility for redistributive policies. One such example is the enactment of the Patient Protection and Affordable Care Act of 2010, which establishes a system to assure that nearly all Americans have access to health insurance. This legislation represents a huge step by the national government into the area of redistributive policy. Consistent with Peterson's theory, analysts at the Congressional Budget Office expect that the health care legislation, once fully implemented, will be more financially efficient than the existing system and that citizens will save trillions of dollars.[28]

States, however, are less happy about these steps toward policy efficiency. Both education and health care have traditionally been among the policy areas reserved to the states under the Tenth Amendment, and politicians have not taken the federal intervention lightly. Many states and localities have attempted to pass legislation opting out of all or some of the provisions of No Child Left Behind. Similarly, a growing number of states have filed lawsuits against the federal government attempting to block implementation of the health care bill.

Progressive Federalism

Despite these national interventions in policy areas traditionally reserved for the states, the Obama administration also appears to be receptive to a movement known as **progressive federalism.** Under progressive federalism, the national government gives state officials (such as governors and attorneys general) significant leeway in acting on issues normally considered national in scope. Among these issue areas are the environment and consumer protection. The Obama administration, for example, allowed California and other states to impose stricter limits on greenhouse gas emissions from cars and trucks than those established by the Environmental Protection Agency (EPA). (To learn more about greenhouse gas emission standards, see Analyzing Visuals: Greenhouse Gas Emission Standards.)

progressive federalism
Movement that gives state officials significant leeway in acting on issues normally considered national in scope, such as the environment and consumer protection.

Progressive federalism encourages states to act as what Justice Louis Brandeis called "laboratories of democracy." States can, in effect, test new and innovative solutions to policy problems that, if successful, may later be adopted by the federal government. In addition, this approach to federalism is a pragmatic one. It allows policy makers to achieve their policy goals gradually—in this case, more stringent emission standards—without having to work with the U.S. Congress, where such policies may not be well received.

But, not everyone views progressive federalism positively. Critics, including the U.S. Chamber of Commerce, have called progressive federalism "free-for-all federalism." They charge that the emission standards, in particular, will lead to a costly "patchwork of laws impacting a troubled [automotive] industry."[29] Complying with a variety of state standards, they note, is more costly than meeting one national standard. It is also more expensive to monitor and lobby the legislatures of each of the fifty states than it is to address only the EPA.

How does a president's view of government affect public policy? Here, the cartoonist uses satire to illustrate contrasting views on the roles of the federal government. Although overstated, this comparison between Presidents Ronald Reagan and Barack Obama shows how their views of federalism are reflected in their policy agendas.

Then

Now

What Should I Have LEARNED?

Now that you have read this chapter, you should be able to:

⭐ **3.1 Trace the roots of the federal system and the Constitution's allocation of governmental powers, p. 82.**

The national government has both enumerated and implied powers under the Constitution. An additional group of concurrent powers are shared by national and state governments. Other powers are reserved to the states or the people or expressly denied to both governments, although the national government is ultimately declared supreme. The Constitution also lays the groundwork for the Supreme Court to be the arbiter in disagreements between states.

⭐ **3.2 Determine the impact of the Marshall Court on federalism, p. 87.**

Early on, the Supreme Court under the leadership of John Marshall played a key role in defining the relationship and powers of the national government through its broad interpretations of the supremacy and commerce clauses.

⭐ **3.3 Describe the emergence and decline of dual federalism, p. 89.**

For many years, dual federalism, as articulated by the Taney Court, tended to limit the national government's authority in areas such as slavery and civil rights, and it was the norm in relations between the national and state governments. The Civil War, however, forever charged the nature of federalism when the nation was reunited, and a departure from this view became evident with the ratification of the Sixteenth and Seventeenth Amendments in 1913.

⭐ **3.4 Explain how cooperative federalism led to the growth of the national government, p.92.**

The notion of a limited federal government met its demise in the wake of the Great Depression. Franklin D. Roosevelt's New Deal ushered in an era of cooperative federalism, in which the power of the national government increased and states and local governments took a secondary, albeit important role in governance. This growth in the size and role of the federal government escalated during Lyndon B. Johnson's administration and into the 1970s. Federal grants became popular solutions for a host of state and local problems.

⭐ **3.5 Identify new trends in federalism, p. 94.**

After becoming president in 1981, Ronald Reagan tried to shrink the size and powers of the federal government through New Federalism. This trend continued through the 1990s and included the Contract with America. Initially, George W. Bush's administration seemed committed to this devolution, but the September 11, 2001, terrorist attacks led to substantial growth in the size of the federal government. The Roberts Court has set an ambiguous course in determining the direction and role of the federal government.

⭐ **3.6 Assess the challenges in balancing national and state powers and the consequences for policy making, p. 97.**

The roles and relative strengths of the national and state governments have changed over time. Political scientists argue that the national government is best suited for redistributive policy and the states for developmental policy. Recent changes in progressive federalism have embraced these roles.

Test Yourself: Federalism

⭐ **3.1 Trace the roots of the federal system and the Constitution's allocation of governmental powers, p. 82.**

The idea that powers not delegated to the national government are reserved to the states is outlined in which amendment to the U.S. Constitution?
- A. Sixth
- B. Eighth
- C. Ninth
- D. Tenth
- E. Fourth

⭐ **3.2 Determine the impact of the Marshall Court on federalism, p. 87.**

The Supreme Court ruled in *Gibbons* v. *Ogden* (1824) that Congress has expansive powers to regulate
- A. taxation.
- B. banks.
- C. interstate commerce.
- D. slavery.
- E. intrastate compacts.

★ **3.3 Describe the emergence and decline of dual federalism, p. 89.**

After the Civil War, the federal government
A. decreased in power.
B. took a passive role in regulating technological developments.
C. erratically increased its power.
D. was able to prevent the sale of sugar-refining businesses.
E. quickly enlarged the scope of its powers to unprecedented levels.

★ **3.4 Explain how cooperative federalism led to the growth of the national government, p. 92.**

Which of the following describes the federal system soon after the changes instituted during the New Deal?
A. Cooperative federalism
B. Dual federalism
C. Layer-cake federalism
D. Laissez-faire federalism
E. New Federalism

★ **3.5 Identify new trends in federalism, p. 94.**

In 1995, Republicans gained control of the House of Representatives largely as a result of what?
A. The public desire to increase the role of federal government.

B. President Clinton's policy agenda during the first months of his presidency.
C. Corruption on the part of House Democrats.
D. The need to replace New Federalism.
E. Republican Newt Gingrich's Contract with America.

★ **3.6 Assess the challenges in balancing national and state powers and the consequences for policy making, p. 97.**

Political scientists argue that the national government is best suited to make policy in which of the following areas?
A. Renewable energy
B. Transportation
C. Health care
D. Building infrastructure
E. Family law

Essay Questions

1. What are the implied powers of the federal government and where are they found in the Constitution?
2. How do the Alien and Sedition Acts illustrate the nullification doctrine?
3. In what ways did the Sixteenth and Seventeenth Amendments enhance the power of the national government?
4. How has federalism evolved from the New Deal to what it has become today?

---

mypoliscilab Exercises

Apply what you learned in this chapter with these resources on MyPoliSciLab.

Read on mypoliscilab.com

eText: Chapter 3

Study and **Review** on mypoliscilab.com

Pre-Test
Post-Test
Chapter Exam
Flashcards

Watch on mypoliscilab.com

Video: Proposition 8
Video: The Real ID
Video: Water Wars

Explore on mypoliscilab.com

Simulation: You Are a Federal Judge
Simulation: You Are an Informed Voter Helping Your Classmates
Simulation: You Are a Restaurant Owner
Comparative: Comparing Federal and Unitary Systems
Timeline: Federalism and the Supreme Court
Visual Literacy: Federalism and Regulations

Key Terms

Barron v. *Baltimore* (1833), p. 89
bill of attainder, p. 85
block grant, p. 95
categorical grant, p. 94
concurrent powers, p. 84
cooperative federalism, p. 93
Dred Scott v. *Sandford* (1857), p. 90
dual federalism, p. 90
ex post facto law, p. 85

extradition clause, p. 85
federal system, p. 82
full faith and credit clause, p. 85
Gibbons v. *Ogden* (1824), p. 88
interstate compacts, p. 86
McCulloch v. *Maryland* (1819), p. 87
New Deal, p. 92
New Federalism, p. 94
nullification, p. 90

preemption, p. 97
privileges and immunities clause, p. 85
progressive federalism, p. 100
reserved (or police) powers, p. 84
Seventeenth Amendment, p. 91
Sixteenth Amendment, p. 91
Tenth Amendment, p. 84
unfunded mandates, p. 95
unitary system, p. 82

To Learn More on Federalism
In the Library

Chemerinsky, Erwin. *Enhancing Government: Federalism for the 21st Century*. Stanford, CA: Stanford Law Books, 2008.

Elazar, Daniel J., and John Kincaid, eds. *The Covenant Connection: From Federal Theology to Modern Federalism*. Lexington, MA: Lexington Books, 2000.

Gerston, Larry N. *American Federalism: A Concise Introduction*. Armonk, NY: M.E. Sharpe, 2007.

Grodzins, Morton. *The American System: A View of Government in the United States*. Chicago: Rand McNally, 1966.

LaCroix, Alison. *The Ideological Origins of American Federalism*. Cambridge, MA: Harvard University Press, 2010.

Manna, Paul. *School's In: Federalism and the National Education Agenda*. Washington, DC: Georgetown University Press, 2006.

Mayer, M.H. *Homeland Security and Federalism: Protecting America from Outside the Beltway*. New York: Praeger, 2009.

Nagel, Robert F. *The Implosion of American Federalism*. New York: Oxford University Press, 2002.

Nugent, John D. *Safeguarding Federalism: How States Protect their Interests in National Policymaking*. Norman: University of Oklahoma Press, 2009.

O'Toole, Laurence L., ed. *American Intergovernmental Relations: Foundations, Perspectives, and Issues*, 4th ed. Washington, DC: CQ Press, 2007.

Peterson, Paul E. *The Price of Federalism*. Washington, DC: Brookings Institution, 1995.

Purcell, Edward, A. *Originalism, Federalism, and the American Constitutional Enterprises: A Historical Inquiry*. New Haven: Yale University Press, 2007.

Rivlin, Alice, Timothy J. Conlan, and Paul Posner. *Intergovernmental Management for the 21st Century*. Washington. DC: Brookings Institution, 2007.

Schapiro, Robert. *Polyphonic Federalism: Toward the Protection of Fundamental Rights*. Chicago: University of Chicago Press, 2009.

Stephens, G. Ross, and Nelson Wikstrom. *American Intergovernmental Relations: A Fragmented Federal Polity*. New York: Oxford University Press, 2006.

On the Web

To learn more about federalism, go to the American Council on Intergovernmental Relations at **govinfo.library.unt.edu/amcouncil/federalism.html.**

To learn more about state and local governments, go to State and Local Government on the Net at **www.statelocalgov.net/.**

To learn more about the landmark Supreme Court cases *McCulloch v. Maryland* (1819), *Gibbons v. Ogden* (1824), and *Barron v. Baltimore* (1833), go to Landmark Supreme Court Cases at **www.landmarkcases.org.**

To learn more about recent Supreme Court cases on federalism, go to the Oyez Project at **www.oyez.org.**

LIVE SAFELY...LIVE HAPPILY!

How to Clean a Gun and Keep Your Head...

4 Civil Liberties

Unlike most constitutional amendments dealing with civil liberties, the Second Amendment, concerning the right to bear arms, historically has received relatively little attention from the U.S. Supreme Court. In fact, before 2008, the Court had not directly considered the Second Amendment in nearly seventy years, although gun control was a hot-button issue in the national and state legislatures. The federal government for its part, was active in legislating on firearms issues, placing a waiting period on the purchase of weapons and prohibiting the ownership of certain types of automatic and semi-automatic weapons. And, many states have enacted similar restrictions. Washington, D.C., for example, passed a total ban on handgun ownership in 1976.

For much of its history, this law went relatively unchallenged. But, in 2003, Robert A. Levy, a lawyer who worked as a constitutional fellow at the libertarian Cato Institute, decided it was time to test the legality of the statute. Levy, who had never owned a gun personally, financed the litigation, recruited co-counsel, and hand-picked six plaintiffs who were willing to bring suit against the D.C. government. To illustrate the scope of the effects of the law, Levy made certain that the plaintiffs were diverse in many ways. They included three men and three women, whose ages varied from twenty to sixty. Four of the plaintiffs were white; two were black. They lived in a variety of neighborhoods and had a wide range of jobs, from lawyer to security guard.[1]

The case took five years to weave its way through the federal judicial system, eventually reaching the U.S. Supreme Court in time for its 2007–2008 term. The justices set the case for oral arguments and in June 2008 handed down a 5–4 decision. Writing for the majority in *D.C.* v. *Heller*, Justice Antonin Scalia acknowledged the problem that gun violence poses in American cities but declared that D.C.'s ban on handgun ownership was unconstitutional.

The right to bear arms is an enduring civil liberty established by the Second Amendment. At left, a gun safety pamphlet from the 1950s references the recreational aspects of hunting that were once taken for granted in the United States. At right, Dick Heller, the lead plaintiff in *D.C.* v. *Heller* (2008), awaits the Supreme Court's ruling, with pro- and anti-gun protesters surrounding him.

The Court's majority opinion also included language declaring that the Second Amendment guaranteed "the right of law abiding, responsible citizens to use arms in defense of hearth and home." This statement clarified a long-standing dispute about whether the amendment had been written to assure the preservation of a well-trained militia or whether the right to own a weapon also extended to ownership for private use. The majority's view was not well received by the four dissenting justices, who charged that the opinion of the Court created a "dramatic upheaval in the law."[2]

The case, however, put Second Amendment rights on the national agenda. During the Court's 2009–2010 term, it again considered the boundaries of this civil liberty. In the case of *McDonald* v. *City of Chicago* (2010) the Court extended its decision in *Heller*, binding state governments to the Second Amendment and broadening citizens' rights to bear arms. Wrote Justice Samuel A. Alito Jr. in the Court's majority

opinion, "It is clear that the Framers . . . counted the right to keep and bear arms among those fundamental rights necessary to our system of ordered liberty."[3]

What Should I Know About . . .

After reading this chapter, you should be able to:

★ **4.1** Trace the constitutional roots of civil liberties, p. 106.

★ **4.2** Describe the First Amendment guarantee of freedom of religion, p. 109.

★ **4.3** Outline the First Amendment guarantees of and limitations on freedom of speech, press, assembly, and petition, p. 111.

★ **4.4** Summarize changes in the interpretation of the Second Amendment right to keep and bear arms, p. 115.

★ **4.5** Analyze the rights of criminal defendants found in the Bill of Rights, p. 116.

★ **4.6** Explain the origin and significance of the right to privacy, p. 123.

★ **4.7** Evaluate how reforms to combat terrorism have affected civil liberties, p. 127.

civil liberties
The personal guarantees and freedoms that the government cannot abridge by law, constitution, or judicial interpretation.

civil rights
The government-protected rights of individuals against arbitrary or discriminatory treatment by governments or individuals.

Civil liberties are the personal guarantees and freedoms that the government cannot abridge, either by law, constitution, or judicial interpretation. As guarantees of "freedom to" action, they place limitations on the power of the government to restrain or dictate an individual's actions. **Civil rights,** in contrast, provide freedom against arbitrary or discriminatory treatment by government or individuals. (To learn more about civil rights, see **chapter 5.**)

Questions of civil liberties often present complex problems. We must decide how to determine the boundaries of speech and assembly. We must also consider how much infringement on our personal liberties we want to give the police or other government actors. Moreover, during times of war, it is important to consider what liberties should be accorded to those who oppose war or are suspected of anti-government activities.

Resolution of civil liberties questions often falls to the judiciary, which must balance the competing interests of the government and the people. Thus, in many of the cases discussed in this chapter, there is a conflict between an individual or group of individuals seeking to exercise what they believe to be a liberty, and the government, be it local, state, or national, seeking to control the exercise of that liberty in an attempt to keep order and preserve the rights (and safety) of others. In other cases, two liberties are in conflict, such as a physician's and her patients' rights to easy access to a medical clinic versus a pro-life advocate's liberty to picket that clinic. In this chapter, we will explore the various dimensions of civil liberties guarantees contained in the U.S. Constitution and the Bill of Rights.

- First, we will discuss *the roots of civil liberties* and *the Bill of Rights.*
- Second, we will survey the meaning of one of the *First Amendment guarantees: freedom of religion.*
- Third, we will consider the meanings of other *First Amendment guarantees: freedoms of speech, press, assembly, and petition.*
- Fourth, we will review *the Second Amendment and the right to keep and bear arms.*
- Fifth, we will analyze *the rights of criminal defendants.*
- Sixth, we will explore *the right to privacy.*
- Finally, we will examine how *reforms to combat terrorism have affected civil liberties.*

ROOTS OF Civil Liberties: The Bill of Rights

⭐ **4.1 . . . Trace the constitutional roots of civil liberties.**

As discussed in **chapter 2,** recognition of the increased power that would be held by the new national government led Anti-Federalists to stress the need for a bill of rights in the new Constitution. Anti-Federalists and many others were confident that they could control the actions of their own state legislators, but they did not trust the national government to be so protective of their civil liberties.

The notion of adding a bill of rights to the Constitution was not a popular one at the Constitutional Convention. When George Mason of Virginia proposed that such a bill be added to the preface of the proposed Constitution, his resolution was defeated unanimously.[4] In the subsequent ratification debates, Federalists argued that a bill of rights was unnecessary, putting forward three main arguments in opposition.

1. A bill of rights was unnecessary in a constitutional republic founded on the idea of popular sovereignty and inalienable, natural rights. Moreover, most state constitutions contained bills of rights, so federal guarantees were unnecessary.

2. A bill of rights would be dangerous. According to Alexander Hamilton in *Federalist No. 84*, since the national government was a government of enumerated powers (that is, it had only the powers listed in the Constitution), "Why declare that things shall not be done which there is no power to do?"

3. A national bill of rights would be impractical to enforce. Its validity would largely depend on public opinion and the spirit of the people and government.

Some Federalists, however, grew to support the idea. After the Philadelphia convention, James Madison found himself in a close race against James Monroe for a seat in the House of Representatives in the First Congress. The district was largely Anti-Federalist. In an act of political expediency, Madison issued a new series of public letters similar to *The Federalist Papers* in which he vowed to support a bill of rights. Once elected to the House, Madison made good on his promise and became the prime author of the Bill of Rights. Still, he considered Congress to have far more important matters to handle and viewed his work on the Bill of Rights as "a nauseous project."[5]

With fear of political instability running high, Congress worked quickly to approve Madison's draft. The proposed Bill of Rights was sent to the states for ratification in 1789, the same year the first Congress convened. By 1791, most of its provisions had been approved by the states.

The **Bill of Rights,** the first ten amendments to the Constitution, contains numerous specific guarantees against the encroachment of the new government, including those of free speech, press, and religion. (To learn more about the full text, see the Annotated Constitution that begins on page 52.) The Ninth and Tenth Amendments, favored by the Federalists, note that the Bill of Rights is not exclusive. The **Ninth Amendment** makes it clear that this special listing of rights does not mean that others do not exist. The **Tenth Amendment** reiterates that powers not delegated to the national government are reserved to the states or to the people.

The Incorporation Doctrine: The Bill of Rights Made Applicable to the States

The Bill of Rights was intended to limit the powers of the national government to infringe on the rights and liberties of the citizenry. In *Barron* v. *Baltimore* (1833), the Supreme Court ruled that the national Bill of Rights limited only the actions of the U.S. government and not those of the states.[6] In 1868, however, the Fourteenth Amendment was added to the U.S. Constitution. Its language suggested the possibility that some or even all of the protections guaranteed in the Bill of Rights might be interpreted to prevent state infringement of those rights. Section 1 of the Fourteenth Amendment reads: "No State shall . . . deprive any person of life, liberty, or property, without due process of law." Questions about the scope of "liberty" as well

Bill of Rights

The first ten amendments to the U.S. Constitution, which largely guarantee specific rights and liberties.

Ninth Amendment

Part of the Bill of Rights that makes it clear that enumerating rights in the Constitution or Bill of Rights does not mean that others do not exist.

Tenth Amendment

The final part of the Bill of Rights that defines the basic principle of American federalism in stating that the powers not delegated to the national government are reserved to the states or to the people.

due process clause

Clause contained in the Fifth and Fourteenth Amendments; over the years, it has been construed to guarantee to individuals a variety of rights ranging from economic liberty to criminal procedural rights to protection from arbitrary governmental action.

substantive due process

Judicial interpretation of the Fifth and Fourteenth Amendments' due process clauses that protects citizens from arbitrary or unjust state or federal laws.

incorporation doctrine

An interpretation of the Constitution that holds that the due process clause of the Fourteenth Amendment requires that state and local governments must also guarantee the rights stated in the Bill of Rights.

selective incorporation

A judicial doctrine whereby most but not all of the protections found in the Bill of Rights are made applicable to the states via the Fourteenth Amendment.

fundamental freedoms

Those rights defined by the Court to be essential to order, liberty, and justice and therefore entitled to the highest standard of review.

as the meaning of "due process of law" continue even today to engage legal scholars and jurists.

Until nearly the turn of the century, the Supreme Court steadfastly rejected numerous arguments urging it to interpret the **due process clause** found in the Fourteenth Amendment as making various provisions contained in the Bill of Rights applicable to the states. In 1897, however, the Court began to increase its jurisdiction over the states.[7] It began to hold states to a **substantive due process** standard whereby states had the legal burden to prove that their laws were a valid exercise of their power to regulate the health, welfare, or public morals of their citizens.

Interferences with state power, however, were rare, and states passed sedition laws (laws that made it illegal to speak or write any political criticism that threatened to diminish respect for the government, its laws, or public officials), anticipating that the U.S. Supreme Court would uphold their constitutionality. When Benjamin Gitlow, a member of the Socialist Party, printed 16,000 copies of a manifesto in which he urged workers to overthrow the U.S. government, he was convicted of violating a New York state law that prohibited such advocacy. Although his conviction was upheld, in *Gitlow* v. *New York* (1925), the U.S. Supreme Court noted that the states were not completely free to limit forms of political expression. The Court argued that certain "fundamental personal rights and liberties" were protected from impairment by the Fourteenth Amendment's due process clause.[8]

Gitlow, with its finding that states could not abridge free speech protections, was the first step in the slow development of what is called the **incorporation doctrine.** In *Near* v. *Minnesota* (1931), the U.S. Supreme Court specifically reiterated that a state law violated the U.S. Constitution's freedom of the press.[9]

Selective Incorporation and Fundamental Freedoms

Not all of the specific guarantees in the Bill of Rights have been made applicable to the states through the due process clause of the Fourteenth Amendment, as revealed in Table 4.1. Instead, the Court has used the process of **selective incorporation** to limit the rights of states by protecting against abridgement of **fundamental freedoms.** Fundamental freedoms are those liberties defined by the Court as essential to order, liberty, and justice. These freedoms are subject to the Court's most rigorous standard of review.

The rationale for selective incorporation was set out by the Court in *Palko* v. *Connecticut* (1937).[10] Frank Palko was charged with first-degree murder for killing two Connecticut police officers, found guilty of a lesser charge of second-degree murder, and sentenced to life imprisonment. Connecticut appealed. Palko was retried, found guilty of first-degree murder, and sentenced to death. Palko then appealed his second conviction, arguing that it violated the Fifth Amendment's prohibition against double jeopardy because the Fifth Amendment had been made applicable to the states by the due process clause of the Fourteenth Amendment.

The Supreme Court disagreed. In an opinion written by Justice Benjamin Cardozo, the Court ruled that the due process clause bound states only to those rights that were "of the very essence of a scheme of ordered liberty." The Fifth Amendment's double jeopardy clause was not, in the Court's view, among these rights. The Court's decision was overruled in 1969.

Today selective incorporation requires the states to respect freedoms of press, speech, and assembly, among other liberties. Other guarantees, such as those contained in the Third and Seventh Amendments (housing of soldiers and jury trials in civil cases), have not been incorporated because the Court has yet to consider them sufficiently fundamental to national notions of liberty and justice.

Table 4.1 *How has selective incorporation made the Bill of Rights applicable to the states?*

Amendment	Right	Date	Case Incorporated
I	Speech	1925	*Gitlow* v. *New York*
	Press	1931	*Near* v. *Minnesota*
	Assembly	1937	*DeJonge* v. *Oregon*
	Religion	1940	*Cantwell* v. *Connecticut*
II	Bear arms	2010	*McDonald* v. *City of Chicago*
III	No quartering of soldiers		Not incorporated
IV	No unreasonable searches or seizures	1949	*Wolf* v. *Colorado*
	Exclusionary rule	1961	*Mapp* v. *Ohio*
V	Just compensation	1897	*Chicago, B&Q R.R. Co.* v. *Chicago*
	Self-incrimination	1964	*Malloy* v. *Hogan*
	Double jeopardy	1969	*Benton* v. *Maryland*
	Grand jury indictment		Not incorporated
VI	Right to counsel	1963	*Gideon* v. *Wainwright*
	Public trial	1948	*In re Oliver*
	Confrontation of witnesses	1965	*Pointer* v. *Texas*
	Impartial trial	1966	*Parker* v. *Gladden*
	Speedy trial	1967	*Klopfer* v. *North Carolina*
	Compulsory trial	1967	*Washington* v. *Texas*
	Criminal jury trial	1968	*Duncan* v. *Louisiana*
VII	Civil jury trial		Not incorporated
VIII	No cruel and unusual punishment	1962	*Robinson* v. *California*
	No excessive fines or bail		Not incorporated

First Amendment Guarantees: Freedom of Religion

★ **4.2 . . . Describe the First Amendment guarantee of freedom of religion.**

The Framers' distaste for a national church or religion was also reflected in the Constitution. Article VI, for example, provides that "no religious Test shall ever be required as a Qualification to any Office or Public Trust under the United States." This simple statement, however, did not completely reassure those who feared the new Constitution would curtail individual liberty. Thus, the First Amendment to the Constitution soon was ratified to allay those fears.

The **First Amendment** to the Constitution begins, "Congress shall make no law respecting an establishment of religion, or prohibiting the free exercise thereof." This statement sets the boundaries of governmental action. The **establishment clause** directs the national government not to sanction an official religion. The **free exercise clause** ("or prohibiting the free exercise thereof") guarantees citizens that the national government will not interfere with their practice of religion. These guarantees, however, are not absolute.

The Establishment Clause

Over the years, the Court has been divided over how to interpret the establishment clause. Does this clause erect a total wall between church and state, as favored by Thomas Jefferson, or is some governmental accommodation of religion allowed? While the Supreme Court has upheld the constitutionality of many kinds of church/state entanglements such as public funding to provide sign language interpreters for deaf students in religious schools,[11] the Court has held fast to the rule of strict separation between church and state when issues of mandatory prayer in school are involved. In *Engel* v. *Vitale* (1962), for example, the Court ruled that the recitation in public school

First Amendment

Part of the Bill of Rights that imposes a number of restrictions on the federal government with respect to civil liberties, including freedom of religion, speech, press, assembly, and petition.

establishment clause

The first clause of the First Amendment; it directs the national government not to sanction an official religion.

free exercise clause

The second clause of the First Amendment; it prohibits the U.S. government from interfering with a citizen's right to practice his or her religion.

Should children be required to pray in public schools? This is just one of the thorny questions the Supreme Court has addressed under the establishment clause.

Photo courtesy: Bettmann/Corbis

Lemon test

Three-part test created by the Supreme Court for examining the constitutionality of religious establishment issues.

classrooms of a brief nondenominational prayer drafted by the local school board was unconstitutional.[12] One year later, in *Abington School District* v. *Schempp* (1963), the Court ruled that state-mandated Bible reading or recitation of the Lord's Prayer in public schools was also unconstitutional.[13]

The Court has gone back and forth in its effort to come up with a workable way to deal with church/state questions. In 1971, in *Lemon* v. *Kurtzman*, the Court tried to carve out a three-part test for laws dealing with religious establishment issues. According to the *Lemon* **test,** a practice or policy was constitutional if it: (1) had a legitimate secular purpose; (2) neither advanced nor inhibited religion; and, (3) did not foster an excessive government entanglement with religion.[14] But, the Supreme Court often has sidestepped the *Lemon* test altogether and has appeared more willing to lower the wall between church and state so long as school prayer is not involved. In 1981, for example, the Court ruled unconstitutional a Missouri law prohibiting the use of state university buildings and grounds for "purposes of religious worship." The law had been used to ban religious groups from using school facilities.[15]

In 1995, the Court signaled that it was willing to lower the wall even further. In a case involving the University of Virginia, a 5–4 majority held that the university violated the free speech rights of a fundamentalist Christian group when it refused to fund the group's student magazine. The importance of this decision was highlighted by Justice David Souter, who noted in dissent: "The Court today, for the first time, approves direct funding of core religious activities by an arm of the state."[16] The Roberts Court, however, has demonstrated that there are boundaries to these accommodations. In 2010, in *Christian Legal Society* v. *Martinez*, the Court ruled that the University of California Hastings College of Law could deny recognition and therefore funding to the Christian Legal Society because the group limited its membership to those who shared a common faith orientation.

For more than a quarter-century, the Supreme Court basically allowed "books only" as an aid to religious schools, noting that the books go to children, not to the schools. But, in 2000, the Court voted 6–3 to uphold the constitutionality of a federal aid provision that allowed the government to lend books and computers to religious schools.[17] And, in 2002, by a bitterly divided 5–4 vote, the Supreme Court concluded that governments can give money to parents to allow them to send their children to private or religious schools.[18] Basically, the Court now appears willing to support programs so long as they provide aid to religious and nonreligious schools alike, and the money goes to persons who exercise free choice over how it is used.

Prayer in school also continues to be an issue. In 1992, the Court continued its unwillingness to allow organized prayer in public schools by finding unconstitutional the saying of prayer at a middle school graduation.[19] And, in 2000, the Court ruled that student-led, student-initiated prayer at high school football games violated the establishment clause.

Establishment issues, however, do not always focus on education. In 2005, for example, the Supreme Court in a 5–4 decision narrowly upheld the continued vitality of the *Lemon* test in holding that a privately donated courthouse display, which included the Ten Commandments and 300 other historical documents illustrating the evolution of American law, was a violation of the First Amendment's establishment clause.[20] But, in 2010, the Court appeared to reverse course. In a 5–4 decision, the Court ruled that a white cross erected on a World War I memorial on federal lands in the Mojave Desert was constitutional. This opinion leaves state and local governments to ponder what kind of religious displays in public settings will be constitutional.[21]

The Free Exercise Clause

The free exercise clause of the First Amendment proclaims that "Congress shall make no law . . . prohibiting the free exercise [of religion]." Although the free exercise clause of the First Amendment guarantees individuals the right to be free from governmental interference in the exercise of their religion, this guarantee, like other First Amendment freedoms, is not absolute.

In 1990, for example, the Supreme Court ruled that the free exercise clause allowed Oregon to ban the use of sacramental peyote (an illegal hallucinogenic drug) in some Native American tribes' traditional religious services.[22] This decision prompted a dramatic outcry. Congressional response was passage of the Religious Freedom Restoration Act, which makes it harder for states to interfere with how citizens practice their religion. Although the Supreme Court ruled portions of the act unconstitutional in 1997, it continues to have some effect.[23] For example, in 2006, the U.S. Supreme Court found that the use of Hosasea tea, which contains the controlled substance dimethyltryptamine (DMT), well-known for its hallucinogenic properties, was permissible free exercise of religion for members of the Brazilian-based O Centro Espiritia Beneficente União do Vegetal church.[24]

First Amendment Guarantees: Freedoms of Speech, Press, Assembly, and Petition

★ **4.3** . . . Outline the First Amendment guarantees of and limitations on freedom of speech, press, assembly, and petition.

The remaining guarantees protected by the First Amendment have been subject to varying degrees of scrutiny by the Supreme Court. During times of war, for example, the Court generally has allowed Congress and the chief executive extraordinary leeway in limiting First Amendment freedoms. Below, we provide historical background and current judicial interpretations of the freedoms of speech, press, assembly, and petition.

Freedoms of Speech and the Press

A democracy depends on a free exchange of ideas, and the First Amendment shows that the Framers were well aware of this fact. Historically, one of the most volatile areas of constitutional interpretation has been in the interpretation of the First Amendment's mandate that "Congress shall make no law ... abridging the freedom of speech or of the press." Like the establishment and free exercise clauses of the First Amendment, the speech and press clauses have not been interpreted as absolute bans against government regulation. A lack of absolute meaning has led to thousands of cases seeking both broader and narrower judicial interpretations of the scope of the amendment. Over the years, the Court has employed a hierarchical approach in determining what the government can and cannot regulate, with some liberties getting greater protection than others. Generally, thoughts have received the greatest protection, and actions or deeds the least. Words have come somewhere in the middle, depending on their content and purpose.

THE ALIEN AND SEDITION ACTS   When the First Amendment was ratified in 1791, it was considered to protect against **prior restraint** of speech or expression, or to guard against the prohibition of speech or publication before the fact. However, in 1798, the Federalist Congress with President John Adams's blessing enacted the Alien and Sedition Acts, which were designed to ban any criticism of the Federalist

prior restraint
Constitutional doctrine that prevents the government from prohibiting speech or publication before the fact; generally held to be in violation of the First Amendment.

government by the growing numbers of Democratic-Republicans. These acts made the publication of "any false, scandalous writing against the government of the United States" a criminal offense. Although the law clearly ran in the face of the First Amendment's ban on prior restraint, the Adams administration and partisan Federalist judges successfully prosecuted and imposed fines and jail terms on at least ten Democratic-Republican newspaper editors. The acts became a major issue in the 1800 presidential election campaign, which led to the election of Thomas Jefferson, a vocal opponent of the acts. He quickly pardoned all who had been convicted under their provisions and the Democratic-Republican Congress allowed the acts to expire.

SLAVERY, THE CIVIL WAR, AND RIGHTS CURTAILMENTS   After the public outcry over the Alien and Sedition Acts, the national government largely refrained from regulating speech. But, in its place, the states, which were not yet bound by the Bill of Rights through selective incorporation, began to prosecute those who published articles critical of governmental policies. In the 1830s, at the urging of abolitionists (those who sought an end to slavery), the publication or dissemination of any positive information about slavery became a punishable offense in the North. In the opposite vein, in the South, supporters of slavery enacted laws to prohibit publication of any antislavery sentiments. Southern postmasters, for example, refused to deliver northern abolitionist newspapers, a step that amounted to censorship of the U.S. mail.

During the Civil War, President Abraham Lincoln took several steps that actually were unconstitutional. He made it unlawful to print any criticisms of the national government or of the Civil War, effectively suspending the free press protections of the First Amendment. Lincoln went so far as to order the arrest of several newspaper editors critical of his conduct of the war and ignored a Supreme Court decision saying that these practices were unconstitutional.

After the Civil War, states also began to prosecute individuals for seditious speech if they uttered or printed statements critical of the government. Between 1890 and 1900, for example, there were more than one hundred state prosecutions for sedition.[25] Moreover, by the dawn of the twentieth century, public opinion in the United States had grown increasingly hostile toward the commentary of Socialists and Communists who attempted to appeal to growing immigrant populations. Groups espousing socialism and communism became the targets of state laws curtailing speech and the written word. By the end of World War I, over thirty states had passed laws to punish seditious speech, and more than 1,900 individuals and over one hundred newspapers were prosecuted for violations.[26] In 1925, however, states' authority to regulate speech was severely restricted by the Court's decision to incorporate the free press provision of the First Amendment in *Gitlow* v. *New York*, discussed earlier in this chapter.

WORLD WAR I AND ANTI-GOVERNMENTAL SPEECH   The next major national efforts to restrict freedom of speech and the press did not occur until Congress, at the urging of President Woodrow Wilson during World War I, passed the Espionage Act in 1917. Nearly 2,000 Americans were convicted of violating its various provisions, especially those that made it illegal to urge resistance to the draft or to prohibit the distribution of anti-war leaflets. In *Schenck* v. *U.S.* (1919), the Supreme Court upheld this act, ruling that Congress had a right to restrict speech "of such a nature as to create a clear and present danger that will bring about the substantive evils that Congress has a right to prevent."[27] Under this **clear and present danger test,** the circumstances surrounding an incident are important. Anti-war leaflets, for example, may be permissible during peacetime, but during World War I they were considered to pose too much of a danger to be permissible.

For decades, the Supreme Court wrestled with what constituted a danger. Finally, in *Brandenburg* v. *Ohio* (1969), the Court fashioned a new test for deciding whether certain kinds of speech could be regulated by the government: the **direct incitement test.** Now, the government could punish the advocacy of illegal action only if "such advocacy

clear and present danger test
Test articulated by the Supreme Court in *Schenck* v. *U.S.* (1919) to draw the line between protected and unprotected speech; the Court looks to see "whether the words used" could "create a clear and present danger that they will bring about substantive evils" that Congress seeks "to prevent."

direct incitement test
Test articulated by the Supreme Court in *Brandenburg* v. *Ohio* (1969) that holds that advocacy of illegal action is protected by the First Amendment unless imminent lawless action is intended and likely to occur.

is directed to inciting or producing imminent lawless action and is likely to incite or produce such action."[28] The requirement of "imminent lawless action" makes it more difficult for the government to punish speech and publication and is consistent with the Framers' notion of the special role played by these elements in a democratic society.

Protected Speech and Press

The expression of ideas through speech and the press is the cornerstone of a free society. As a result, the U.S. Supreme Court has accorded constitutional protection to a number of aspects of speech and the press, even though the content of such expression may be objectionable to some citizens or the government. Here, we discuss the implications of this protection with respect to prior restraint, symbolic speech, and hate speech.

LIMITING PRIOR RESTRAINT   As we have seen with the Alien and Sedition Acts, although Congress attempted to limit speech before the fact as early as 1798, the U.S. Supreme Court did not take a firm position on this issue until the 1970s (but see *Near* v. *Minnesota* [1931] on page 108). In *New York Times Co.* v. *U.S.* (1971) (also called the Pentagon Papers case), the Supreme Court ruled that the U.S. government could not block the publication of secret Department of Defense documents illegally furnished to the *Times* by anti-war activists.[29] In 1976, the U.S. Supreme Court went even further, noting in *Nebraska Press Association* v. *Stuart* that any attempt by the government to prevent expression carried "'a heavy presumption' against its constitutionality."[30]

SYMBOLIC SPEECH   In addition to the general protection accorded to pure speech, the Supreme Court has extended the reach of the First Amendment to **symbolic speech,** a means of expression that includes symbols or signs. In the words of Justice John Marshall Harlan, these kinds of speech are part of the "free trade in ideas."[31]

symbolic speech

Symbols, signs, and other methods of expression generally also considered to be protected by the First Amendment.

The Supreme Court first acknowledged that symbolic speech was entitled to First Amendment protection in *Stromberg* v. *California* (1931).[32] There, the Court overturned a communist youth camp director's conviction under a state statute prohibiting the display of a red flag, a symbol of opposition to the U.S. government. In a similar vein, the right of high school students to wear black armbands to protest the Vietnam War was upheld in *Tinker* v. *Des Moines Independent Community School District* (1969).[33]

In recent years, however, the Court has appeared less willing to support some types of symbolic speech. In a case commonly referred to as the "Bong Hits 4 Jesus" case, the Court ruled that a student's free speech rights were not violated when he was suspended for displaying what the Court characterized as a "sophomoric" banner at an Olympic torch relay parade.[34]

HATE SPEECH   In the 1990s, a particularly thorny First Amendment issue emerged as cities and universities attempted to prohibit what they viewed as offensive hate speech. In *R.A.V.* v. *City of St. Paul* (1992), a St. Paul, Minnesota, ordinance that made it a crime to engage in speech or action likely to arouse "anger," "alarm," or "resentment" on the basis of race, color, creed, religion, or gender was at issue. The Court ruled 5–4 that a white teenager who burned a cross on a black family's front lawn, thereby committing a hate crime under the ordinance, could not be charged under that law because the First Amendment prevents governments from "silencing speech on the basis of its content."[35] In 2003, the Court narrowed this definition, ruling that state

How broad is the right to symbolic speech? In a 2007 case, the Supreme Court ruled that a school district was within its rights to suspend a student for displaying this banner, because it was intended to promote illegal drug use, even though it occurred off school property.

Photo courtesy: Clay Good/ZUMA

governments could constitutionally restrict cross burning when it occurred with the intent of racial intimidation.[36]

Unprotected Speech and Press

Although the Supreme Court has allowed few governmental bans on most types of speech, some forms of expression are not protected. In 1942, the Supreme Court set out the rationale by which it would distinguish between protected and unprotected speech. According to the Court, libel, fighting words, obscenity, and lewdness are not protected by the First Amendment because "such expressions are no essential part of any exposition of ideals, and are of such slight social value as a step to truth that any benefit that may be derived from them is clearly outweighed by the social interest in order and morality."[37]

LIBEL AND SLANDER   **Libel** is a written statement that defames the character of a person. If the statement is spoken, it is **slander.** In many nations—such as Great Britain, for example—it is relatively easy to sue someone for libel. In the United States, however, the standards of proof are much higher. A person who believes that he or she has been a victim of libel must show that the statements made were untrue. Truth is an absolute defense against the charge of libel, no matter how painful or embarrassing the revelations.

It is often more difficult for individuals the U.S. Supreme Court considers "public persons or public officials" to sue for libel or slander. *New York Times Co.* **v.** *Sullivan* **(1964)** was the first major libel case considered by the Supreme Court.[38] An Alabama state court found the *Times* guilty of libel for printing a full-page advertisement accusing Alabama officials of physically abusing African Americans during various civil rights protests. (The ad was paid for by civil rights activists, including former First Lady Eleanor Roosevelt.) The Supreme Court overturned the conviction and established that a finding of libel against a public official could stand only if there was a showing of "actual malice," or a knowing disregard for the truth. Proof that the statements were false or negligent was not sufficient to prove actual malice.

FIGHTING WORDS   In the 1942 case of *Chaplinsky* v. *New Hampshire*, the Court stated that **fighting words,** or words that "by their very utterance inflict injury or tend or incite an immediate breach of peace," are not subject to the restrictions of the First Amendment.[39] Fighting words, which include "Profanity, obscenity, and threats," are therefore able to be regulated by the federal and state governments. These words do not necessarily have to be spoken; fighting words can also come in the form of symbolic expression.

OBSCENITY   The current standard by which the Court judges obscenity was laid out by Chief Justice Warren E. Burger, who wrote the opinion in *Miller* v. *California* (1973). There, the Court set out a test that redefined obscenity. To make it easier for states to regulate obscene materials, the justices concluded that lower courts must ask "whether the work depicts or describes, in a patently offensive way, sexual conduct specifically defined by state law." The courts also were to determine "whether the work, taken as a whole, lacks serious literary, artistic, political, or scientific value." And, in place of the contemporary community standards gauge used in *Roth*, the Court defined community standards to refer to the locality in question, under the rationale that what is acceptable in New York City might not be acceptable in Maine or Mississippi.[40]

Time and contexts clearly have altered the Court's and, indeed, much of America's perceptions of what works are obscene. But, the Supreme Court has allowed communities great leeway in drafting statutes to deal with obscenity and, even more importantly, other forms of questionable expression. In 1991, for example, the Court voted 5–4

libel
Written statement that defames a person's character.

slander
Untrue spoken statements that defame the character of a person.

New York Times Co. v. *Sullivan* (1964)
Case in which the Supreme Court concluded that "actual malice" must be proved to support a finding of libel against a public figure.

fighting words
Words that, "by their very utterance inflict injury or tend to incite an immediate breach of peace." Fighting words are not subject to the restrictions of the First Amendment.

to allow Indiana to ban totally nude erotic dancing, concluding that the statute furthered a substantial governmental interest, and therefore was not in violation of the First Amendment.[41]

While lawmakers have been fairly effective in restricting the sale and distribution of obscene materials, monitoring the Internet has proven difficult for Congress. Since 1996, Congress has passed several laws designed to prohibit the transmission of obscene or "harmful" materials over the Internet to anyone under age eighteen. For many years, the Supreme Court repeatedly found these laws unconstitutional.[42] But, in 2008, a seven-justice majority decided that the PROTECT Act, which outlawed the sale or transmission of child pornography, was not overly broad and did not abridge the freedom of speech guaranteed by the First Amendment.[43]

Freedoms of Assembly and Petition

"Peaceful assembly for lawful discussion cannot be made a crime," Chief Justice Charles Evans Hughes wrote in the 1937 case of *DeJonge* v. *Oregon*, which incorporated the First Amendment's freedom of assembly clause to apply to the states.[44] Despite this clear declaration, and an even more ringing declaration in the First Amendment, the fundamental freedoms of assembly and petition have been among the most controversial, especially in times of war. As with other First Amendment freedoms, the Supreme Court often has become the arbiter between the freedom of the people to express dissent and government's authority to limit controversy in the name of national security.

Because the freedom to assemble is hinged on peaceful conduct, the freedoms of assembly and petition are related directly to the freedoms of speech and of the press. If the words or actions taken at any event cross the line of constitutionality, events such as parades or protests may no longer be protected by the Constitution. Absent that protection, leaders and attendees may be subject to governmental regulation and even criminal arrest, incarceration, or civil fines.

The Second Amendment: The Right to Keep and Bear Arms

★ 4.4 ... Summarize changes in the interpretation of the Second Amendment right to keep and bear arms.

Most colonies required all white men to keep and bear arms, and all white men in whole sections of the colonies were deputized to defend their settlements against Indians and European powers. These local militias were viewed as the best way to keep order and protect liberty.

The Second Amendment was added to the Constitution to ensure that Congress could not pass laws to disarm state militias. This amendment appeased Anti-Federalists, who feared that the new Constitution would cause them to lose the right to "keep and bear arms." It also preserved an unstated right—the right to revolt against governmental tyranny.

Through the early 1920s, few state statutes were passed to regulate firearms (and generally these laws dealt with the possession of firearms by slaves). The Supreme Court's decision in *Barron* v. *Baltimore* (1833), which refused to incorporate the Bill of Rights to the state governments, prevented federal review of those state laws.[45] Moreover, in *Dred Scott* v. *Sandford* (1857), Chief Justice Roger B. Taney listed the right to own and carry arms as a basic right of citizenship.[46]

Gun Control

Many countries have very strict laws governing gun ownership. In Great Britain, it is illegal to own a handgun. In France, citizens may apply for a three-year permit only after demonstrating a clear need and undergoing an exhaustive background check. In Mexico, citizens may own only low-caliber guns after petitioning the Ministry of Defense for permission. A major problem that Mexico faces in controlling drug trafficking along the U.S.-Mexico border is that drug cartel members can cross into the United States and purchase guns legally.

■ Why is the issue of gun control so polarizing in the United States but not in some other countries?

■ What type of international action, if any, should be taken to reduce the flow of guns across borders?

■ To what extent should U.S. laws or policies on gun control be influenced by the laws and policies of other countries?

In 1934, Congress passed the National Firearms Act in response to the increase in organized crime that occurred in the 1920s and 1930s as a result of Prohibition. The act imposed taxes on automatic weapons and sawed-off shotguns. In *U.S.* v. *Miller* (1939), a unanimous Court upheld the constitutionality of the act, stating that the Second Amendment was intended to protect a citizen's right to own ordinary militia weapons and not sawed-off shotguns.[47] For nearly seventy years following *Miller*, the Court did not directly address the Second Amendment. Then, as detailed in our opening vignette about *D.C.* v. *Heller* (2008), the Court ruled that the Second Amendment protected an individual's right to own a firearm for personal use in Washington, D.C.[48]

In light of the Court's ruling, the D.C. City Council adopted new gun control laws requiring gun registration and prohibiting assault weapons and large-capacity magazines. A U.S. District Court ruled that these laws were valid and within the scope of the *Heller* decision.[49] And, in 2010, the Supreme Court broadened the ownership rights in *Heller* to include citizens of all states. It also incorporated the Second Amendment.[50]

The Rights of Criminal Defendants

★ **4.5** . . . Analyze the rights of criminal defendants found in the Bill of Rights.

writs of *habeas corpus*
Court orders in which a judge requires authorities to prove that a prisoner is being held lawfully and that allow the prisoner to be freed if the judge is not persuaded by the government's case. *Habeas corpus* rights imply that prisoners have a right to know what charges are being made against them.

ex post facto law
Law that makes an act punishable as a crime even if the action was legal at the time it was committed.

bill of attainder
A law declaring an act illegal without a judicial trial.

Fourth Amendment
Part of the Bill of Rights that reads: "The right of the people to be secure in their persons, houses, papers, and effects, against unreasonable searches and seizures, shall not be violated, and no Warrants shall issue, but upon probable cause, supported by Oath or affirmation, and particularly describing the place to be searched, and the persons or things to be seized."

Article I of the Constitution guarantees a number of rights for those accused of crimes. The Constitution guarantees **writs of *habeas corpus***, court orders in which a judge requires authorities to prove that a prisoner is being held lawfully and that allow the prisoner to be freed if the judge is not persuaded by the government's case. *Habeas corpus* rights also imply that prisoners have a right to know what charges are being made against them.

Article I of the Constitution also prohibits ***ex post facto* laws,** or laws that make an act punishable as a crime even if the action was legal at the time it was committed. And, Article I prohibits **bills of attainder,** laws declaring an act illegal without a judicial trial.

The Fourth, Fifth, Sixth, and Eighth Amendments supplement these rights with a variety of procedural guarantees, often called due process rights. In this section, we examine how the courts have interpreted and applied these guarantees in an attempt to balance personal liberty and national safety and security.

The Fourth Amendment and Searches and Seizures

The **Fourth Amendment** to the Constitution protects people from unreasonable searches by the federal government. Moreover, in some detail, it sets out what may not be searched unless a warrant is issued, underscoring the Framers' concern with preventing government abuses.

The purpose of this amendment was to deny the national government the authority to make general searches. Over the years, in a number of decisions, the Supreme Court has interpreted the Fourth Amendment to allow the police to search: (1) the person arrested; (2) things in plain view of the accused person; and, (3) places or things that the arrested person could touch or reach or are otherwise in the arrestee's immediate control.

Warrantless searches often occur if police suspect that someone is committing or is about to commit a crime. In these situations, police may stop and frisk the individual under suspicion. In 1989, the Court ruled that there need be only a "reasonable suspicion" for stopping a suspect—a much lower standard than probable cause.[51]

Searches can also be made without a warrant if consent is obtained. In the case of homes, this consent must come from all occupants present at the time of the search; the police cannot conduct a warrantless search of a home if one of the occupants objects.[52] In contrast, under the open fields doctrine first articulated by the Supreme Court in 1924, if you own a field, and even if you post "No Trespassing" signs, the police can search your field without a warrant to see if you are engaging in illegal activity such as growing marijuana, because you cannot reasonably expect privacy in an open field.[53]

In situations where no arrest occurs, police must obtain search warrants from a "neutral and detached magistrate" ⋯⋯ to conducting more extensive searches of houses, cars, offices, or an⋯ ⋯⋯here an individual would reasonably have some expectation of ⋯⋯ ⋯⋯hters can enter your home to fight a fire without a warrant. ⋯⋯ ⋯stigate the cause of the fire, they must obtain a warrant befo⋯

Cars have proven ⋯⋯ the courts because of their mobile nature. As noted by Ch⋯ ⋯s early as 1925, "the vehicle can quickly be moved out of ⋯⋯ in which the warrant must be sought."[56] Over the years, t⋯ ⋯ingly lenient about the scope of automobile searches. In 20⋯ ⋯nanimous Court ruled that when evaluating if a border pa⋯ ⋯pping a suspicious mini-van, the totality of the circun⋯ ⋯. Wrote Chief Justice William H. Rehnquist, the "bala⋯ ⋯ and the individual's right to personal security," tilts in ⋯⋯ ⋯able cause in brief investigatory stops." This ruling gave⋯ ⋯ore leeway to pull over suspicious motorists.[57] And, courts ⋯ ⋯arrants in possible drunk driving situations. Thus, the police in ⋯ ⋯e you to take a Breatha-lyzer test to determine whether you have ⋯ ⋯s of legal limits.[58]

Testing for drugs, too, is an especia⋯ ⋯ and seizure issue. While many private employers and professional a⋯ ⋯ganizations routinely require drug tests upon application or as a condition of employment, governmental requirements present constitutional questions about the scope of permissible searches and seizures. In 1989, the Supreme Court ruled that mandatory drug and alcohol testing of employees involved in accidents was constitutional.[59] In 1995, the Court upheld the constitutionality of random drug testing of public high school athletes.[60] And, in 2002, the Court upheld the constitutionality of a Tecumseh, Oklahoma, policy that required mandatory drug testing of high school students participating in any extracurricular activities. Thus, prospective band, choir, debate, or drama club members may be subject to the same kind of random drug testing as athletes.[61]

The Fifth Amendment: Self-Incrimination and Double Jeopardy

The **Fifth Amendment** provides a variety of guarantees that protect those who have been charged with a crime. It requires, for example, that individuals who are accused in the most serious cases are to be allowed to present their case before a grand jury, a group of citizens charged with determining whether there is enough evidence for a case to go to trial. The Fifth Amendment also provides that "No person shall be . . . compelled in any criminal case to be a witness against himself." "Taking the Fifth" is shorthand for

Fifth Amendment
Part of the Bill of Rights that imposes a number of restrictions on the federal government with respect to the rights of persons suspected of committing a crime. It provides for indictment by a grand jury and protection against self-incrimination, and prevents the national government from denying a person life, liberty, or property without the due process of law. It also prevents the national government from taking property without just compensation.

Who was Ernesto Miranda? Even though Ernesto Miranda's confession was not admitted as evidence at his retrial, the testimony of his ex-girlfriend and the victim were enough to convince the jury of his guilt. He served nine years in prison before he was paroled. After his release, he routinely sold autographed cards inscribed with what are called the *Miranda* rights now read to all suspects. In 1976, four years after his release, Miranda was stabbed to death in a Phoenix bar fight during a card game. Two *Miranda* cards were found on his body, and the person who killed him was read his *Miranda* rights upon his arrest.

Photo courtesy: AP/Wide World Photos

Miranda v. Arizona (1966)

A landmark Supreme Court ruling that held the Fifth Amendment requires that individuals arrested for a crime must be advised of their right to remain silent and to have counsel present.

Miranda rights

Statements that must be made by the police informing a suspect of his or her constitutional rights protected by the Fifth Amendment, including the right to an attorney provided by the court if the suspect cannot afford one.

double jeopardy clause

Part of the Fifth Amendment that protects individuals from being tried twice for the same offense in the same jurisdiction.

exercising one's constitutional right not to self-incriminate. The Supreme Court has interpreted this guarantee to be "as broad as the mischief against which it seeks to guard," finding that criminal defendants do not have to take the stand at trial to answer questions, nor can a judge make mention of their failure to do so as evidence of guilt.[62] Moreover, lawyers cannot imply that a defendant who refuses to take the stand must be guilty or have something to hide.

This right not to incriminate oneself also means that prosecutors cannot use as evidence in a trial any of a defendant's statements or confessions that were not made voluntarily. As is the case in many areas of the law, however, judicial interpretation of the term voluntary has changed over time. In earlier times, it was not unusual for police to beat defendants to obtain their confessions. In 1936, however, the Supreme Court ruled that convictions for murder based solely on confessions given after physical beatings were unconstitutional.[63] Police then began to resort to other measures to force confessions. Defendants, for example, were questioned for hours on end with no sleep or food, or threatened with physical violence until they were mentally beaten into giving confessions.

Miranda v. *Arizona* **(1966)** was the Supreme Court's response to these coercive efforts to obtain confessions that were not truly voluntary. On March 3, 1963, an eighteen-year-old girl was kidnapped and raped on the outskirts of Phoenix, Arizona. Ten days later, police arrested Ernesto Miranda, a poor, mentally disturbed man with a ninth-grade education. In a police-station lineup, the victim identified Miranda as her attacker. Police then took Miranda to a separate room and questioned him for two hours. At first he denied guilt. Eventually, however, he confessed to the crime and wrote and signed a brief statement describing the crime and admitting his guilt. At no time was he told that he did not have to answer any questions or that he could be represented by an attorney.

After Miranda's conviction, his case was appealed on the grounds that his Fifth Amendment right not to incriminate himself had been violated because his confession had been coerced. Writing for the Court, Chief Justice Earl Warren, himself a former district attorney and a former California state attorney general, noted that because police have a tremendous advantage in any interrogation situation, criminal suspects must be given greater protection. A confession obtained in the manner of Miranda's was not truly voluntary; thus, it was inadmissible at trial.

To provide guidelines for police to implement *Miranda*, the Court mandated that: "Prior to any questioning, the person must be warned that he has a right to remain silent, that any statements he does make may be used as evidence against him, and that he has a right to the presence of an attorney, either retained or appointed."[64] In response to this mandate from the Court, police routinely began to read suspects what are now called their *Miranda* **rights,** a practice you undoubtedly have seen repeated over and over in movies and TV police dramas.

Although the Burger Court did not enforce the reading of *Miranda* rights as vehemently as had the Warren Court, Chief Justice Warren E. Burger, Warren's successor, acknowledged that they had become an integral part of established police procedures.[65] The more conservative Rehnquist and Roberts Courts, however, have been more willing to weaken *Miranda* rights, allowing coerced confessions and employing a much more flexible standard.[66] (To learn more about a Roberts Court ruling that scales back *Miranda* rights, see Politics Now: Suspects Must Assert Right to Silence.)

The Fifth Amendment also mandates: "nor shall any person be subject for the same offense to be twice put in jeopardy of life or limb." This is called the **double jeopardy clause** and it protects individuals from being tried twice for the same crime in the same jurisdiction. Thus, if a defendant is acquitted by a jury of a charge of murder, he or she cannot be retried in that jurisdiction for the offense even if new information is unearthed that could further point to guilt. But, if a defendant was tried in a state court, he or she could still face charges in a federal court or vice versa.

Suspects Must Assert Right to Silence

By Joan Biskupic

June 2, 2010
USA Today
www.usatoday.com

A divided Supreme Court scaled back the well-known *Miranda* right Tuesday and enhanced prosecutors' ability to assert that a suspect waived his right to remain silent even when he did not say so.

By a 5-4 vote, the justices said that once rights have been read and questioning begun, a suspect must clearly declare that he wants to remain silent and cannot simply be silent.

The decision in a Michigan case broke along ideological lines, with Justice Anthony Kennedy writing the opinion, joined by fellow conservatives. The four liberals dissented in an opinion by Justice Sonia Sotomayor, a former Manhattan prosecutor who warned that the decision "turns *Miranda* upside down."

She said defendants often use equivocal or colloquial language in attempting to invoke their right to silence and that requiring a clear declaration would weaken the right.

"There is no question that this decision authorizes lower courts to construe ambiguous situations in favor of police and prosecutors," said Stanford University law professor Robert Weisberg. . . .

Tuesday's case did not involve when a suspect should be read rights. Rather, it addressed what happens when a suspect declines to answer hours of questions, then makes a potentially incriminating statement and later says he had wanted to remain silent and that his statement was not made freely. . . .

"Where the prosecution shows that a *Miranda* warning was given and that it was understood by the accused, an accused's uncoerced statement establishes an implied waiver of the right to remain silent," Kennedy wrote. He said [the defendant] waived his right by answering the detective's questions . . .

Sotomayor called their decision "a substantial retreat from the protection against compelled self-incrimination." She said it undercuts the "heavy burden" the government should have to show that a defendant gave up his right against self-incrimination. . . .

Critical Thinking Questions
1. Should a suspect have to signal their choice to remain silent? Why or why not?
2. How does this decision erode the protections of the *Miranda* decision?
3. How do you expect criminal rights to change in the coming years? Do you expect that *Miranda* rights will be eliminated? Why or why not?

The Fourth and Fifth Amendments and the Exclusionary Rule

In *Weeks* v. *U.S.* (1914), the U.S. Supreme Court adopted the **exclusionary rule,** which bars the use of illegally seized evidence at trial. Thus, although the Fourth and Fifth Amendments do not prohibit the use of evidence obtained in violation of their provisions, the exclusionary rule is a judicially created remedy to deter constitutional violations. In *Weeks*, for example, the Court reasoned that allowing police and prosecutors to use the "fruits of a poisonous tree" (a tainted search) would only encourage that activity.[67]

In balancing the need to deter police misconduct against the possibility that guilty individuals could go free, the Warren Court decided that deterring police misconduct was most important. In *Mapp* v. *Ohio* (1961), the Warren Court ruled that "all evidence obtained by searches and seizures in violation of the Constitution, is inadmissible in a state court."[68] This historic and controversial case put law enforcement officers on notice that if they found evidence in violation of any constitutional rights, those efforts would be for naught because the tainted evidence could not be used in federal or state trials.

In 1976, the Court noted that the exclusionary rule "deflects the truth-finding process and often frees the guilty."[69] Since then, the Court has carved out a variety

exclusionary rule
Judicially created rule that prohibits police from using illegally seized evidence at trial.

of limited "good faith exceptions" to the exclusionary rule, allowing the use of tainted evidence in a variety of situations, especially when police have a search warrant and, in good faith, conduct the search on the assumption that the warrant is valid even though it is subsequently found invalid. Since the purpose of the exclusionary rule is to deter police misconduct, and in this situation there is no police misconduct, the courts have permitted the introduction at trial of the seized evidence. Another exception to the exclusionary rule is "inevitable discovery." Illegally seized evidence may be introduced if it would have been likely to be discovered in the course of continuing investigation.

The Sixth Amendment and the Right to Counsel

Sixth Amendment
Part of the Bill of Rights that sets out the basic requirements of procedural due process for federal courts to follow in criminal trials. These include speedy and public trials, impartial juries, trials in the state where crime was committed, notice of the charges, the right to confront and obtain favorable witnesses, and the right to counsel.

The **Sixth Amendment** guarantees to an accused person "the Assistance of Counsel in his defense." In the past, this provision meant only that an individual could hire an attorney to represent him or her in court. Since most criminal defendants are too poor to hire private lawyers, this provision was of little assistance to many who found themselves on trial. Recognizing this, Congress required federal courts to provide an attorney for defendants who could not to afford one. This was first required in capital cases (where the death penalty is a possibility);[70] eventually, attorneys were provided to the poor in all federal criminal cases.[71] The Court also began to expand the right to counsel to other state offenses but did so in a piecemeal fashion that gave the states little direction. Given the high cost of providing legal counsel, this ambiguity often made it cost-effective for the states not to provide counsel at all.

These ambiguities came to an end with the Court's decision in *Gideon* v. *Wainwright* (1963).[72] Writing for the Court, Justice Hugo Black explained that "lawyers in criminal courts are necessities, not luxuries." Therefore, the Court concluded, the state must provide an attorney to indigent defendants in felony cases. Underscoring the Court's point, Gideon was acquitted when he was retried with a lawyer to argue his case.

The Burger and Rehnquist Courts gradually expanded the *Gideon* rule. The justices first applied this standard to cases that were not felonies[73] and, later, to many cases where probation and future penalties were possibilities. In 2008, the Court also ruled that the right to counsel began at the accused's first appearance before a judge.[74]

The issue of legal representation also extends to questions of competence. Various courts have held that lawyers who fell asleep during trial, failed to put on a defense, or were drunk during the proceedings were "adequate." In 2005, however, the Supreme Court ruled that the Sixth Amendment's guarantees required lawyers to take reasonable steps to prepare for their clients' trial and sentencing, including examining their prior criminal history.[75]

The Sixth Amendment and Jury Trials

The Sixth Amendment (and, to a lesser extent, Article III of the Constitution) provides that a person accused of a crime shall enjoy the right to a speedy and public trial by an impartial jury—that is, a trial in which a group of the accused's peers act as a fact-finding, deliberative body to determine guilt or innocence. It also provides defendants the right to confront witnesses against them. The Supreme Court has held that jury trials must be available if a prison sentence of six or more months is possible.

Impartiality is a requirement of jury trials that has undergone significant change, with the method of selecting jurors being the most frequently challenged part of the process. Historically, lawyers had used peremptory challenges (those for which no cause needs to be given) to exclude minorities from juries, especially when the defendant was a member of a minority group. In 1954, for example, the U.S. Supreme Court ruled that Hispanics were entitled to a jury trial that included other Hispanics.[76] And, in 1986, the Court ruled that the use of peremptory challenges specifically to exclude African American jurors violated the equal protection clause of the Fourteenth Amendment.[77]

In 1994, the Supreme Court answered the major remaining unanswered question about jury selection: can lawyers exclude women from juries through their use of peremptory challenges? This question came up frequently because in rape trials and sex discrimination cases, one side or another often considers it advantageous to select jurors on the basis of their sex. The Supreme Court ruled that the equal protection clause prohibits discrimination in jury selection on the basis of gender. Thus, lawyers cannot strike all potential male jurors based on the belief that males might be more sympathetic to the arguments of a man charged in a paternity suit, a rape trial, or a domestic violence suit, for example.[78]

The right to confront witnesses at trial also is protected by the Sixth Amendment. In 1990, however, the Supreme Court ruled that this right was not absolute and the testimony of a six-year-old alleged child abuse victim via one-way closed circuit television was permissible. The clause's central purpose, said the Court, was to ensure the reliability of testimony by subjecting it to rigorous examination in an adversarial proceeding.[79] In this case, the child was questioned out of the presence of the defendant, who was in communication with his defense and prosecuting attorneys. The defendant, along with the judge and jury, watched the testimony.

The Eighth Amendment and Cruel and Unusual Punishment

Among its protections, the **Eighth Amendment** prohibits "cruel and unusual punishments," a concept rooted in the English common-law tradition. Interestingly, today the United States is the only western nation to put people to death for committing crimes. Not surprisingly, there are tremendous regional differences in the imposition of the death penalty, with the South leading in the number of men and women executed each year.

In the 1960s, the NAACP Legal Defense and Educational Fund (LDF), believing that the death penalty was applied more frequently to African Americans than to members of other groups, orchestrated a carefully designed legal attack on its constitutionality.[80] Public opinion polls revealed that in 1971, on the eve of the LDF's first major death sentence case to reach the Supreme Court, public support for the death penalty had fallen below 50 percent. With the timing just right, in *Furman* v. *Georgia* (1972), the Supreme Court effectively put an end to capital punishment, at least in the short run.[81] The Court ruled that because the death penalty often was imposed in an arbitrary manner, it constituted cruel and unusual punishment in violation of the Eighth and Fourteenth Amendments. Following *Furman*, several state legislatures enacted new laws designed to meet the Court's objections to the arbitrary nature of the sentence. In 1976, in *Gregg* v. *Georgia*, Georgia's rewritten death penalty statute was ruled constitutional by the Supreme Court in a 7–2 decision.[82] (To learn more about the controversy over the death penalty, see Join the Debate: Should the Death Penalty Be Abolished?)

Although the Supreme Court as recently as 2008 has upheld the constitutionality of the death penalty by lethal injection,[83] it has made some exceptions to this view. The Court, for example, has exempted two key classes of people from the death penalty: those who are mentally retarded and those under the age of eighteen.[84]

PROTECTING THE WRONGFULLY CONVICTED   At the state level, a move to at least stay executions took on momentum in March 2000 when Governor George Ryan (R–IL) ordered a moratorium on all executions. Ryan, a death penalty proponent, became disturbed by new evidence collected as a class project by Northwestern University students. The students unearthed information that led to the release of thirteen men on the state's death row. The specter of allowing death sentences

Eighth Amendment
Part of the Bill of Rights that states: "Excessive bail shall not be required, nor excessive fines imposed, nor cruel and unusual punishments inflicted."

Join the DEBATE | Should the Death Penalty Be Abolished?

The use of capital punishment, otherwise known as the death penalty, has declined considerably in the United States since its peak in 1999. Although there were almost 3,300 people on death row in 2009, only 106 people were sentenced to death, and 52 people were executed. According to a 2009 Gallup poll, public support for the death penalty has declined, with only 65 percent of the general public supporting the use of the death penalty today versus 80 percent in 1994.[a] The debate over the death penalty raises issues about the fundamental fairness of the U.S. system of justice. Many Americans worry that innocent people might be put to death, despite all the procedural safeguards in the court system to prevent mistakes. The Innocence Project, a nonprofit organization, has been working since 1992 to use DNA evidence to exonerate those wrongly convicted of crimes. As of February 2010, the group's efforts led to the release of 250 people, 16 of them on death row.

Supporters of the death penalty believe the consequence for taking someone else's life should be the loss of the criminal's life, and that doing so will deter other people from committing murder. However, while Texas executes more people than all of the rest of the states combined, it consistently has one of the highest murder rates in the country. Given these challenges, does the death penalty constitute cruel and unusual punishment? Is the death penalty fair? Should the death penalty be abolished?

To develop an ARGUMENT FOR abolition of the death penalty, think about how:

- **The death penalty seems to be cruel and unusual punishment.** Why is the United States alone among Western countries in its continued use of the death penalty? Do constitutional prohibitions against cruel and unusual punishment take on new meaning in a global context?
- **Innocent people may be put to death for crimes they did not commit.** How can an imperfect system ensure that only guilty people are executed? What are the consequences of executing an innocent person? Are the constitutional guarantees provided for criminal defendants sufficient to ensure a fair trial and just decision?
- **The death penalty has been applied unevenly with respect to race and gender.** How much more likely are minorities to be sentenced to death than whites for committing the same types of crimes? Does uneven application of the death penalty constitute a violation of the equal protection clause? Do gender and racial disparities in executions suggest that the death penalty is fundamentally unfair?

How do states vary in their application of the death penalty? This cartoon offers a social commentary on the administration of the death penalty in Texas, which leads the nation in the number of executions.

To develop an ARGUMENT AGAINST abolition of the death penalty, think about how:

- **Since 1976, the Supreme Court has repeatedly upheld the constitutionality of the death penalty.** Did the Framers of the U.S. Constitution view the death penalty as cruel and unusual punishment? With almost 3,300 people on death row in 37 states, can the death penalty be considered an unusual punishment? Doesn't the use of lethal injection limit the cruelness of the punishment as defined by the Eighth Amendment?
- **The availability of DNA testing and careful application of the rule of law can ensure that only guilty people are put to death.** In what ways do the constitutional guarantees provided to criminal defendants under the Fourth, Fifth, Sixth, and Eighth Amendments ensure that death penalty cases are fair and just? How do the decisions of the U.S. Supreme Court in cases dealing with the mentally retarded and minors ensure the fair application of the death penalty?
- **The death penalty is a cost-effective way to deter capital offenses.** How does the death penalty help to deter criminal activity? In what ways does the death penalty help states conserve money?

[a]Lydia Saad, "Four Moral Issues Sharply Divide Americans," www.gallup.com.

to continue in light of evidence showing so many men were wrongly convicted prompted Ryan's much publicized action. Soon thereafter, the Democratic governor of Maryland followed suit after receiving evidence that blacks were much more likely to be sentenced to death than whites; however, the Republican governor who succeeded him lifted the stay. Before leaving office in January 2003, Illinois Governor Ryan continued his anti-death-penalty crusade by commuting the sentences of 167 death-row inmates, giving them life in prison instead. This action constituted the single largest anti-death-penalty action since the Court's decision in *Gregg*, and it spurred national conversation on the death penalty, which, in recent polls, has seen its lowest levels of support since 1978.

   In another effort to verify that those on death row are not there wrongly, several states offer free DNA testing to death-row inmates. The U.S. Supreme Court recognized the potential exculpatory power of DNA evidence in *House* v. *Bell* (2006). In this case, the Court ruled a Tennessee death-row inmate who had exhausted other federal appeals was entitled to an exception to more stringent federal appeals rules due to DNA and related evidence suggesting his innocence.[85] However, the Court decided in 2009 that convicted inmates do not have a constitutional right to DNA testing.[86]

The Right to Privacy

⭐ **4.6 . . . Explain the origin and significance of the right to privacy.**

To this point, we have discussed rights and freedoms that have been derived fairly directly from specific guarantees contained in the Bill of Rights. However, the U.S. Supreme Court also has given protection to rights not enumerated specifically in the Constitution. Although silent about the **right to privacy,** the Bill of Rights contains many indications that the Framers expected that some areas of life were off limits to governmental regulation. As early as 1928, Justice Louis Brandeis hailed privacy as "the right to be left alone—the most comprehensive of rights and the right most valued by civilized men."[87] It was not until 1965, however, that the Court attempted to explain the origins of this right. (To learn more about the right to privacy, see The Living Constitution: Ninth Amendment.)

right to privacy
The right to be left alone; a judicially created principle encompassing a variety of individual actions protected by the penumbras or shadows cast by several constitutional amendments, including the First, Third, Fourth, Ninth, and Fourteenth Amendments.

Birth Control

Today, most Americans take access to birth control as a matter of course. Condoms are sold in the grocery store, and some television stations air ads for them. Easy access to birth control, however, wasn't always the case. *Griswold* v. *Connecticut* (1965) involved a challenge to the constitutionality of an 1879 Connecticut law prohibiting the dissemination of information about and/or the sale of contraceptives.[88] In *Griswold*, seven justices decided that various portions of the Bill of Rights, including the First, Third, Fourth, Ninth, and Fourteenth Amendments, cast what the Court called "penumbras" (unstated liberties on the fringes or in the shadow of more explicitly stated rights), thereby creating zones of privacy, including a married couple's right to plan a family. Thus, the Connecticut statute was ruled unconstitutional because it violated marital privacy, a right the Court concluded could be read into the U.S. Constitution through interpreting several amendments.

   Later, the Court expanded the right of privacy to include the right of unmarried individuals to have access to contraceptives. "If the right of privacy means anything," wrote Justice William J. Brennan Jr., "it is the right of the individual, married or single, to be free from unwarranted governmental intrusion into matters

TIMELINE: The Supreme Court and the Right to Privacy

1965 *Griswold* v. *Connecticut*— The right to privacy is explained by the Court and used to justify striking down a Connecticut statute prohibiting married couples' access to birth control.

1980 *Harris* v. *McRae*—The Court upholds the Hyde Amendment, ruling that federal funds cannot be used to pay for poor women's abortions.

1973 *Roe* v. *Wade*—The Court finds that a woman has a right to have an abortion based on her right to privacy.

1986 *Bowers* v. *Hardwick*— The Court upholds a Georgia sodomy law, finding that gay men and lesbians have no privacy rights.

so fundamentally affecting a person as the decision to bear or beget a child."[89] This right to privacy was to be the basis for later decisions from the Court, including the right to secure an abortion.

What was the outcome of Griswold v. Connecticut *(1965)?* In this photo, Estelle Griswold (left), executive director of the Planned Parenthood League of Connecticut, and Cornelia Jahncke, its president, celebrate the Supreme Court's ruling in *Griswold* v. *Connecticut* (1965). *Griswold* invalidated a Connecticut law that made selling contraceptives or disseminating information about contraception to married couples illegal.

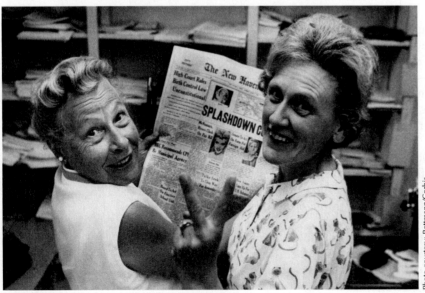

Abortion

In 1973, the Supreme Court handed down one of its most controversial decisions. The case involved Norma McCorvey, an itinerant circus worker and the mother of a toddler she was unable to care for. McCorvey could not leave another child in her mother's care. So, she decided to terminate her second pregnancy. She was unable to secure a legal abortion and was frightened by the conditions she found when she sought an illegal abortion. McCorvey turned to two young Texas lawyers who were looking for a plaintiff to bring a lawsuit to challenge Texas's restrictive statute. McCorvey, who was unable to obtain a legal abortion, later gave birth and put the baby up for adoption. Nevertheless, she allowed her

1989 *Webster v. Reproductive Health Services*— The Court comes close to overruling *Roe*; invites states to fashion abortion restrictions.

Photo courtesy: Greg Gibson/Agence France Presse/Getty Images

2003 *Lawrence v. Texas*—In overruling *Bowers*, the Court, for the first time, concludes that the right to privacy applies to homosexuals.

1992 *Planned Parenthood of Southeastern Pennsylvania v. Casey*—By the narrowest of margins, the Court limits *Roe* by abolishing its trimester approach.

2007 *Gonzales v. Carhart*—Supreme Court upholds the federal Partial Birth Abortion Ban Act.

lawyers to proceed with the case using her as their plaintiff. Her lawyers used the pseudonym Jane Roe for McCorvey as they challenged the Texas law as enforced by Henry Wade, the district attorney for Dallas County, Texas.

When the case finally came before the Supreme Court, Justice Harry A. Blackmun, a former lawyer at the Mayo Clinic, relied heavily on medical evidence to rule that the Texas law violated a woman's constitutionally guaranteed right to privacy, which he argued included her decision to terminate a pregnancy. Writing for the majority in **Roe v. Wade (1973),** Blackmun divided pregnancy into three stages. In the first trimester, a woman's right to privacy gave her an absolute right (in consultation with her physician), free from state interference, to terminate her pregnancy. In the second trimester, the state's interest in the health of the mother gave it the right to regulate abortions—but only to protect the woman's health. Only in the third trimester—when the fetus becomes potentially viable—did the Court find that the state's interest in potential life outweighed a woman's privacy interests. Even in the third trimester, however, abortions to save the life or health of the mother were to be legal.[90]

From the 1970s through the present, the right to an abortion and its constitutional underpinnings in the right to privacy have been under attack by well-organized pro-life groups. The administrations of Ronald Reagan and George Bush were strong abortion opponents, and their Justice Departments regularly urged the Court to overrule *Roe*. They came close to victory in *Webster* v. *Reproductive Health Services* (1989).[91] In *Webster*, the Court upheld state-required fetal viability tests in the second trimester, even though these tests increased the cost of an abortion considerably. The Court also upheld Missouri's refusal to allow abortions to be performed in state-supported hospitals or by state-funded doctors or nurses. Perhaps most noteworthy, however, was that four justices seemed willing to overrule *Roe v. Wade* and that Justice Antonin Scalia publicly rebuked his colleague, Justice Sandra Day O'Connor, then the only woman on the Court, for failing to provide the critical fifth vote to overrule *Roe*.

Roe v. Wade (1973)

The Supreme Court found that a woman's right to an abortion was protected by the right to privacy that could be implied from specific guarantees found in the Bill of Rights applied to the states through the Fourteenth Amendment.

The Living Constitution

The enumeration in the Constitution, of certain rights, shall not be construed to deny or disparage others retained by the people.

—NINTH AMENDMENT

This amendment simply reiterates the belief that rights not specifically enumerated in the Bill of Rights exist and are retained by the people. It was added to assuage the concerns of Federalists, such as James Madison, who feared that the enumeration of so many rights and liberties in the first eight amendments to the Constitution would result in the denial of rights that were not enumerated.

Until 1965, the Ninth Amendment was rarely mentioned by the Court. In that year, however, it was used for the first time by the Court as a positive affirmation of a particular liberty—marital privacy. Although privacy is not mentioned in the Constitution, it was—according to the Court—one of those fundamental freedoms that the drafters of the Bill of Rights implied as retained. Since 1965, the Court

has ruled in favor of a host of fundamental liberties guaranteed by the Ninth Amendment, often in combination with other specific guarantees, including the right to have an abortion.

CRITICAL THINKING QUESTIONS

1. How can the U.S. justice system dictate the definition of a fundamental right if the Constitution does not specifically enumerate that right?
2. How might public opinion affect judicial interpretations of the Ninth Amendment?
3. What other implied rights should be protected by the Ninth Amendment?

After *Webster*, states began to enact more restrictive legislation. In *Planned Parenthood of Southeastern Pennsylvania v. Casey* (1992), Justices O'Connor, Anthony Kennedy, and David Souter, in a jointly authored opinion, wrote that Pennsylvania could limit abortions so long as its regulations did not pose "an undue burden" on pregnant women.[92] The narrowly supported standard, by which the Court upheld a twenty-four-hour waiting period and parental consent requirements, did not overrule *Roe*, but clearly limited its scope by abolishing its trimester approach and substituting the undue burden standard for the trimester approach used in *Roe*.

Meanwhile, Republican-controlled Congresses made repeated attempts to restrict abortion rights. In March 1996 and again in 1998, Congress passed and sent to President Clinton a bill to ban—for the first time—a specific procedure used in late-term abortions. The president repeatedly vetoed the federal Partial Birth Abortion Act. Many state legislatures, nonetheless, passed their own versions of the law. In 2000, the Supreme Court, however, ruled 5–4 in *Stenberg* v. *Carhart* that a Nebraska partial birth abortion statute was unconstitutionally vague because it failed to contain an exemption for a woman's health. The law, therefore, was unenforceable and called into question the partial birth abortion laws of twenty-nine other states.[93]

But, by October 2003, Republican control of the White House and both houses of Congress facilitated passage of the federal Partial Birth Abortion Ban Act. Pro-choice groups immediately filed lawsuits challenging the constitutionality of this law. The Supreme Court heard oral arguments on the challenge to the federal ban the day after the 2006 midterm elections. In a 5–4 decision, *Gonzales* v. *Carhart*

(2007), the Roberts Court revealed the direction it was heading in abortion cases. Over the strong objections of Justice Ginsburg, Justice Kennedy's opinion for the majority upheld the federal act although, like the law at issue in *Stenberg*, it contained no exceptions for the health of the mother. This ruling was viewed as a significant step toward reversing *Roe* v. *Wade* altogether.

The Court's decision in *Gonzales* has empowered states to enact abortion regulations with new gusto. In 2010, for example, Nebraska enacted legislation prohibiting most abortions after 20 weeks. Other states, such as Oklahoma, have laws or are considering legislation that require doctors to show women an ultrasound image of the fetus before they are allowed to abort. And, in Utah, a new law categorizes self-induced abortions as homicide.[94]

Homosexuality

It was not until 2003 that the U.S. Supreme Court ruled that an individual's constitutional right to privacy, which provided the basis for the *Griswold* (contraceptives) and *Roe* (abortion) decisions, prevented states from criminalizing private sexual behavior. This monumental decision invalidated the laws of fourteen states.

In *Lawrence* v. *Texas* (2003), six members of the Court overruled its decision in *Bowers* v. *Hardwick* (1986) which had upheld anti-sodomy laws—and found that a Texas law banning sodomy was unconstitutional; five justices found it violated fundamental privacy rights.[95] Justice Sandra Day O'Connor agreed that the law was unconstitutional, but concluded that it was an equal protection violation. (To learn more about the equal protection clause of the Fourteenth Amendment, see **chapter 5**.) Although Justice Antonin Scalia issued a stinging dissent, charging that "the Court has largely signed on to the so-called homosexual agenda," the majority of the Court was unswayed.

Do all Americans deserve the same freedoms and liberties? Tyron Garner (left) and John Geddes Lawrence (center), the plaintiffs in *Lawrence* v. *Texas* (2003), are shown here with their attorney. The ruling in this case proved to be a huge victory for advocates of gay rights, as it deemed anti-sodomy laws unconstitutional.

Photo courtesy: AP/Wide World Photos

TOWARD REFORM: Civil Liberties and Combating Terrorism

⭐ **4.7 . . . Evaluate how reforms to combat terrorism have affected civil liberties.**

After September 11, 2001, the George W. Bush administration, Congress, and the courts all began to operate in what Secretary of State Condoleezza Rice dubbed "an alternate reality," where Bill of Rights guarantees were suspended in a time of war, just as they had been in the Civil War and in World Wars I and II.[96] The USA PATRIOT Act, the Military Commissions Act, and a series of secret Department of Justice memos all altered the state of civil liberties in the United States. Here, we detail the provisions of these actions, as well as subsequent actions by the Barack Obama administration, and explain how they have affected the civil liberties discussed in this chapter.

The First Amendment

The USA PATRIOT Act violates the First Amendment's free speech guarantees by barring those who have been subject to search orders from telling anyone about those orders, even in situations where no need for secrecy can be proven. It also authorizes the Federal Bureau of Investigation to investigate citizens who choose to exercise their freedom of speech with no need to prove that any parts of their speech might be labeled illegal.

In addition, respect for religious practices has fallen by the wayside during the war on terrorism. For example, many Muslim detainees captured in Iraq and Afghanistan have been fed pork, a violation of basic Islamic dietary laws. Some have also been stripped naked in front of members of the opposite sex, another religious violation.

The Fourth Amendment

The USA PATRIOT Act enhances the ability of the government to curtail specific search and seizure restrictions in four areas. First, it allows the government to examine an individual's private records held by third parties. This includes allowing the FBI to force anyone, including physicians, libraries, bookshops, colleges and universities, and Internet service providers, to turn over all records they have on a particular individual. Second, it expands the government's right to search private property without notice to the owner. Third, according to the American Civil Liberties Union, the act "expands a narrow exception to the Fourth Amendment that had been created for the collection of foreign intelligence information."[97] Finally, the act expands an exception for spying that collects "addressing information" about where and to whom communications are going, as opposed to what is contained in the documents.

Judicial oversight of these governmental powers is virtually nonexistent. Proper governmental authorities need only certify to a judge, without any evidence, that the requested search meets the statute's broad criteria. Moreover, the legislation deprives judges of the authority to reject such applications.

Due Process Rights

Illegal incarceration and torture are federal crimes, and the Supreme Court ruled in 2004 that detainees have a right of *habeas corpus*.[98] However, the Bush administration argued that under the Military Commissions Act of 2006, alien victims of torture had significantly reduced rights of *habeas corpus*. The Military Commissions Act also eliminated the right to bring any challenge to "detention, transfer, treatment, trial, or conditions of confinement" of detainees. It allowed the government to declare permanent resident aliens to be enemy combatants and enabled the government to jail these people indefinitely without any opportunity to file a writ of *habeas corpus*. In 2008, in a surprising setback for the Bush administration, the Roberts Court ruled parts of the act unconstitutional, finding that any detainees could challenge their extended incarceration in federal court.[99]

Many suspected terrorists have also been held against their will in secret offshore prisons, known as black sites. In September 2006, President Bush acknowledged the existence of these facilities, moving fourteen such detainees to the detention facility at Guantanamo Bay, Cuba. The conditions of this facility sparked intense debate, as opponents cited numerous accusations of torture as well as possible violations of human rights. Those in support of the continued use of Guantanamo said that the detainees were unlawful combatants and not war criminals subject to the provisions of the Geneva Convention. After President Barack Obama took office in 2009, he vowed to close Guantanamo by January 2010 and move detainees to a facility in Illinois.

ANALYZING VISUALS

Trying Suspected Terrorists

This political cartoon was published in November 2009, just days after Attorney General Eric Holder announced that Khalid Shaikh Mohammed would be tried in a Manhattan federal courthouse for his role in the September 11, 2001, terrorist attacks on the World Trade Center in New York City. Look at the cartoon and consider the questions.

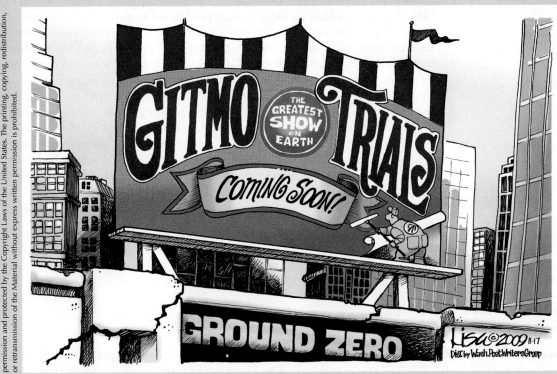

- To what is the trial of Khalid Shaikh Mohammed being compared?
- Based on what is depicted in this cartoon, do you think the cartoonist supports plans to hold the trial in a federal courthouse located in New York City? Why or why not?
- Why might someone be opposed to trying suspected terrorists in courts so close to where the terrorist attacks occurred? Why might someone support such trials?
- Should Americans worry about protecting the civil liberties of non-U.S. citizens who have been accused of committing heinous attacks against the United States? Why or why not?

While Obama did not meet that deadline, he appears to have made some efforts to change the policies enforced by the Bush administration by holding criminal trials and military tribunals for several existing Guantanamo detainees. (To learn more about the trials of Guantanamo detainees, see Analyzing Visuals: Trying Suspected Terrorists.)

The Sixth Amendment right to trial by jury has also been curtailed by recent federal activity. Although those declared enemy combatants can no longer be held indefinitely for trial by military tribunals, they still do not have access to the evidence against them, and additional evidence may be obtained through coercion or torture. Trials of enemy combatants are closed, and people tried in these courts do not have a right to an attorney of their choosing. The federal government's activity in these tribunals was limited by the Supreme Court,[100] but the Military Commissions Act returned these powers to the executive branch. The Obama administration, to the surprise of many observers, has done little to restore the rights revoked by these acts.

Finally, the Eighth Amendment's prohibition on cruel and unusual punishment has been the subject of great controversy. Since shortly after the terrorist attacks of September 11, 2001, there were rumors that many of the prisoners detained by the U.S. government were being treated in inhumane ways. In 2004, for example, photos of cruel treatment of prisoners held by the U.S. military in Abu Ghraib prison in Iraq surfaced. These photos led to calls for investigations at all levels of government. On the heels of this incident, the Justice Department declared torture "abhorrent" in a December 2004 legal memo. That position lasted but a short time. After Alberto Gonzales was sworn in as attorney general in February 2005, the department issued a secret memo endorsing harsh interrogation techniques. According to one Justice Department memo, interrogation practices were not to be considered illegal unless they produced pain equivalent to organ failure or death. Among the techniques authorized by the government were combinations of "painful physical and psychological tactics, including head-slapping, simulated drowning, and frigid temperatures."[101] The most controversial of these techniques is water-boarding, which simulates drowning. Although the Obama administration has harshly attacked the use of these kinds of tactics and techniques, it announced that those who committed these acts during the Bush administration would not be prosecuted.[102]

What Should I Have LEARNED?

Now that you have read this chapter, you should be able to:

⭐ **4.1 Trace the constitutional roots of civil liberties, p. 106.**

Most of the Framers originally opposed the Bill of Rights. Anti-Federalists, however, continued to stress the need for a bill of rights during the drive for ratification of the Constitution, and some states tried to make their ratification contingent on the addition of a bill of rights. Thus, during its first session, Congress sent the first ten amendments to the Constitution, the Bill of Rights, to the states for their ratification. Later, the addition of the Fourteenth Amendment allowed the Supreme Court to apply some of the amendments to the states through a process called selective incorporation.

⭐ **4.2 Describe the First Amendment guarantee of freedom of religion, p. 109.**

The First Amendment guarantees freedom of religion. The establishment clause, which prohibits the national government from establishing a religion, does not, according to Supreme Court interpretation, create an absolute wall between church and state. While the national and state governments may generally not give direct aid to religious groups, many forms of aid, especially many that benefit children, have been held to be constitutionally permissible. In contrast, the Court

has generally barred mandatory prayer in public schools. The Court has allowed some governmental regulation of religious practices under the free exercise clause.

⭐ **4.3 Outline the First Amendment guarantees of and limitations on freedom of speech, press, assembly, and petition, p. 111.**

Historically, one of the most volatile areas of constitutional interpretation has been in the interpretation of the First Amendment's mandate that "Congress shall make no law . . . abridging the freedom of speech or of the press." Like the establishment and free exercise clauses of the First Amendment, the speech and press clauses have not been interpreted as absolute bans against government regulation. The Supreme Court has ruled against prior restraint, thus protecting freedom of the press. The Court has also protected symbolic speech and hate speech as long as it does not become action. Areas of speech and publication unprotected by the First Amendment include libel, fighting words, and obscenity and pornography. The freedoms of peaceable assembly and petition are directly related to the freedoms of speech and of the press. As with other First Amendment rights, the Supreme Court has often become the arbiter between the people's right to dissent and government's need to promote security.

★ 4.4 Summarize changes in the interpretation of the Second Amendment right to keep and bear arms, p. 115.

Initially, the right to bear arms was envisioned as dealing with state militias. Over the years, states and Congress have enacted various gun ownership restrictions with little Supreme Court interpretation. However, the Court ruled in *D.C.* v. *Heller* (2008) and *McDonald* v. *City of Chicago* (2010) that the Second Amendment protects an individual's right to own a firearm.

★ 4.5 Analyze the rights of criminal defendants found in the Bill of Rights, p. 116.

The Fourth, Fifth, Sixth, and Eighth Amendments provide a variety of procedural guarantees to individuals accused of crimes. The Fourth Amendment prohibits unreasonable searches and seizures, and the Court has generally refused to allow evidence seized in violation of this safeguard to be used at trial. The Fifth Amendment protects those who have been charged with crimes. It mandates the use of grand juries in cases of serious crimes. It also guarantees that "no person shall be compelled to be a witness against himself." The Supreme Court has interpreted this provision to require that the government inform the accused of his or her right to remain silent. This provision has also been interpreted to require that illegally obtained confessions must be excluded at trial. Finally, the Fifth Amendment's double jeopardy clause protects individuals from being tried twice for the same crimes in the same jurisdiction. The Sixth Amendment's guarantee of "assistance of counsel" has been interpreted by the Court to require that the government provide counsel to defendants unable to pay for it in cases where prison sentences may be imposed. The Sixth Amendment also requires an impartial jury, although the meaning of impartial continues to evolve through judicial interpretation. The Eighth Amendment's ban against "cruel and unusual punishments" has been held not to bar imposition of the death penalty.

★ 4.6 Explain the origin and significance of the right to privacy, p. 123.

The right to privacy is a judicially created right carved from the penumbras (unstated liberties implied by more explicitly stated rights) of several amendments, including the First, Third, Fourth, Ninth, and Fourteenth Amendments. The court has found unconstitutional statutes that limit access to birth control, prohibit abortion, and ban homosexual acts.

★ 4.7 Evaluate how reforms to combat terrorism have affected civil liberties, p. 127.

After the terrorist attacks of September 11, 2001, reforms enacted by Congress and the executive branch dramatically altered civil liberties in the United States. Critics charge that a host of constitutional guarantees have been significantly compromised, while supporters say that these reforms are necessary to protect national security in a time of war.

Test Yourself: Civil Liberties

★ 4.1 Trace the constitutional roots of civil liberties, p. 106.

Which of the following amendments makes some of the provisions of the Bill of Rights applicable to the states?
A. Fifth
B. Tenth
C. Eleventh
D. Fourteenth
E. Fifteenth

★ 4.2 Describe the First Amendment guarantee of freedom of religion, p. 109.

The U.S. Supreme Court has interpreted the establishment clause to mean that
A. reciting prayer in classrooms is constitutional, as long as the prayer is nondenominational.
B. state university grounds cannot be used for worship.
C. a privately owned display of the Ten Commandments in a courthouse is unconstitutional.
D. student-led, student-initiated prayer at high school football games is constitutional.
E. allowing the government to lend books and computers to religious schools is in violation of the First Amendment.

★ 4.3 Outline the First Amendment guarantees of and limitations on freedom of speech, press, assembly, and petition, p. 111.

Which of the following is considered a protected form of speech?
A. Carrying a "Bong Hits 4 Jesus" banner during a school-sanctioned parade
B. Wearing black armbands to protest a war
C. Burning a cross with the intent to intimidate a member of a racial minority
D. Writing a libelous article about another person
E. Child pornography

★ 4.4 Summarize changes in the interpretation of the Second Amendment right to keep and bear arms, p. 115.

The U.S. Supreme Court first ruled that the Second Amendment protects an individual's right to own a firearm in certain jurisdictions
A. in the early 1800s, when laws were passed to limit possession of firearms by slaves.
B. when Justice Roger B. Taney considered the right to own and carry arms a basic right of citizenship.
C. in *D.C.* v. *Heller* in 2008.
D. when a law that made sawed-off shotguns illegal was overturned in the 1930s.
E. in *Barron* v. *Baltimore* in 1833.

★ **4.5 Analyze the rights of criminal defendants found in the Bill of Rights, p. 116.**

When suspects are arrested and read their *Miranda* rights, the authorities are informing them of their rights established by the _____ Amendment of the U.S. Constitution.
  A. Second
  B. Third
  C. Fourth
  D. Fifth
  E. Seventh

★ **4.6 Explain the origin and significance of the right to privacy, p. 123.**

The U.S. Supreme Court deemed the controversial 2003 federal Partial Birth Abortion Ban Act
  A. a law that could only be passed by the states.
  B. unconstitutional because it contained no health exceptions for the mother.
  C. constitutional despite its lack of health exceptions for the mother.
  D. unconstitutional because it violated the three-trimester rule created by *Roe* v. *Wade* (1973).
  E. constitutional based on the precedent of *Harris* v. *McRae* (1980).

★ **4.7 Evaluate how reforms to combat terrorism have affected civil liberties, p. 127.**

Why has the USA PATRIOT Act been considered unconstitutional by groups such as the American Civil Liberties Union?
  A. It curtails protections against illegal search and seizure.
  B. The act violates Second Amendment rights.
  C. Non-U.S. citizens have no right to bring challenge to "detention, transfer, treatment, trial, or conditions of confinement" under provisions of the act.
  D. It eliminates a right to trial by jury.
  E. The act legalizes harsh punishment of prisoners of war.

Essay Questions
  1. What freedoms are guaranteed by the First Amendment to the U.S. Constitution? How have they been interpreted by the Supreme Court?
  2. Who was Clarence Earl Gideon, and what impact did he have on the rights of the accused?
  3. How does the U.S. Constitution imply a right to privacy?

PEARSON
mypoliscilab Exercises

Apply what you learned in this chapter on MyPoliSciLab.

📖 **Read** on **mypoliscilab.com**

  eText: Chapter 4

✔ **Study** and **Review** on **mypoliscilab.com**

  Pre-Test
  Post-Test
  Chapter Exam
  Flashcards

👁 **Watch** on **mypoliscilab.com**

  Video: Funeral Protestors Push the Limits of Free Speech
  Video: D.C.'s Right to Bear Arms

✛ **Explore** on **mypoliscilab.com**

  Simulation: You Are a Police Officer
  Simulation: You Are a Supreme Court Justice Deciding a Free Speech Case
  Simulation: Balancing Liberty and Security in a Time of War
  Comparative: Comparing Civil Liberties
  Timeline: Civil Liberties and National Security

Key Terms

bill of attainder, p. 116
Bill of Rights, p. 107
civil liberties, p. 106
civil rights, p. 106
clear and present danger test,
    p. 112
direct incitement test, p. 112
double jeopardy clause, p. 118
due process clause, p. 108
Eighth Amendment, p. 121
establishment clause, p. 109
exclusionary rule, p. 119
ex post facto law, p. 116

Fifth Amendment, p. 117
fighting words, p. 114
First Amendment, p. 109
Fourth Amendment, p. 116
free exercise clause, p. 109
fundamental freedoms, p. 108
incorporation doctrine, p. 108
Lemon test, p. 110
libel, p. 114
Miranda rights, p. 118
Miranda v. *Arizona* (1966), p. 118
New York Times Co. v. *Sullivan* (1964),
    p. 114

Ninth Amendment, p. 107
prior restraint, p. 111
right to privacy, p. 123
Roe v. *Wade* (1973), p. 125
selective incorporation, p. 108
Sixth Amendment, p. 120
slander, p. 114
substantive due process, p. 108
symbolic speech, p. 113
Tenth Amendment, p. 107
writ of *habeas corpus*, p. 116

To Learn More on Civil Liberties

In the Library

Abrams, Floyd. *Trials of the First Amendment*. New York: Viking, 2006.

Ackerman, Bruce. *Before the Next Attack: Preserving Civil Liberties in an Age of Terrorism*. New Haven, CT: Yale University Press, 2007.

Baird, Robert M., and Stuart E. Rosenbaum. *Death Penalty: Debating the Moral, Legal, and Political Issues*. Amherst, NY: Prometheus Books, 2010.

Cole, David, and James X. Dempsey. *Terrorism and the Constitution: Sacrificing Civil Liberties in the Name of National Security*, 3rd ed. Washington, DC: First Amendment Foundation, 2006.

Darmer, M. Katherine B., Robert M. Baird, and Stuart E. Rosenbaum, eds. *Civil Liberties vs. National Security in a Post 9/11 World*. Amherst, NY: Prometheus Books, 2004.

Ehrlich, Howard J. *Hate Crimes and Ethnoviolence: The History, Current Affairs, and Future of Discrimination in America*. Boulder, CO: Westview Press, 2009.

Fiss, Owen M. *The Irony of Free Speech*, reprint ed. Cambridge, MA: Harvard University Press, 1998.

Gates, Henry Louis, Jr., ed. *Speaking of Race, Speaking of Sex: Hate Speech, Civil Rights, and Civil Liberties*. New York: New York University Press, 1995.

Ivers, Gregg, and Kevin T. McGuire, eds. *Creating Constitutional Change*. Charlottesville: University Press of Virginia, 2004.

Lane, Frederick S. *American Privacy: The 400-Year History of Our Most Contested Right*. Boston: Beacon Press, 2009.

Lewis, Anthony. *Gideon's Trumpet*, reissue ed. New York: Vintage Books, 1989.

———. *Make No Law: The Sullivan Case and the First Amendment*, reprint ed. New York: Random House, 1992.

Lichtblau, Eric. *Bush's Law: The Remaking of American Justice*. New York: Pantheon, 2008.

O'Connor, Karen. *No Neutral Ground: Abortion Politics in an Age of Absolutes*. Boulder, CO: Westview, 1996.

Romero, Anthony D., and Dina Temple-Raston. *In Defense of Our America: The Fight for Civil Liberties in the Age of Terror*. New York: William Morrow, 2007.

Sando, Philippe. *Torture Teams: Rumsfeld's Memo and the Betrayal of American Values*. New York: Palgrave Macmillan, 2008.

On the Web

To learn more about differing views on civil liberties, including debates related to the war on terrorism, go to the home pages for the following groups:
American Civil Liberties Union at **www.aclu.org.**
People for the American Way, **www.pfaw.org.**
American Center for Law and Justice at **www.aclj.org.**
The Federalist Society at **www.fed-soc.org.**

To learn more about the Supreme Court cases discussed in this chapter, go to Oyez: U.S. Supreme Court Media at **www.oyez.org,** and search on the case name. Or, go to the Legal Information Institute of Cornell University's Law School at **www.law.cornell.edu/supet/cases/topic.htm,** where you can search cases by topic.

To learn more about the different sides of the abortion debate, go to FLITE (Federal Legal Information Through Electronics) at **www.fedworld.gov/supcourt/.**

To learn more about civil liberties protections for homosexuals, go to Human Rights Campaign at **www.hrc.org,** and Lambda Legal at **www.lambdalegal.org.**

5 Civil Rights

In 2006, during the presidency of George W. Bush, the Civil Rights Division of the U.S. Department of Justice was in turmoil. Almost 20 percent of its lawyers, a record number, left in 2005 when many took advantage of a buyout program that allowed them to retire early; other career lawyers took positions elsewhere because they were upset by what they perceived as the politicization of the division. Many of the lawyers, all career civil servants, believed they were being pressured to leave because they "did not share the administration's conservative view on civil rights laws." Veteran lawyers charged that the political appointees in the division made hiring and policy decisions without consulting staff members with more expertise. Their allegations were supported when it was revealed in 2007 that Attorney General Alberto Gonzales, along with the White House, had interfered in the work of regional U.S. attorneys. Eight of these attorneys appeared to have been fired without just cause, spurring congressional hearings and the indictment of a Gonzales aide. Moreover, after President Bush took office and appointed those who shared his beliefs to key division spots, prosecutions of race and sex discrimination decreased by 40 percent. Many division lawyers found their workloads shifted to immigration and deportation cases.[1]

The U.S. government, however, has long played an important role in enforcing civil rights in the nation. The passage of the Thirteenth, Fourteenth, and Fifteenth Amendments, for example, abolished slavery, guaranteed citizens equal protection of the laws, and granted the right to vote to newly freed male slaves, a right eventually extended to women by the Nineteenth Amendment.

Who protects the civil rights of American citizens? At left, nonviolent protestors demanding voting rights for African Americans march across the Edmund Pettus Bridge on their way from Selma to Montgomery, Alabama, in March 1965. At right, some of the U.S. attorneys who were fired by the Department of Justice in 2006. The firings raised questions about the extent to which partisan politics rather than the rule of law was the guiding force during Alberto Gonzales's tenure as attorney general.

Later, after a prolonged civil rights movement sparked by years of discrimination against African Americans, particularly in the South, the U.S. Congress passed sweeping anti-discrimination legislation in the Civil Rights Act of 1964 and the Voting Rights Act of 1965. The Civil Rights Act, in particular, banned discrimination in employment, public accommodations, and education based on race, creed, color, religion, national origin, or sex. Over the years, Congress has added prohibitions based on pregnancy and disability to the act.

Under President Barack Obama, civil rights enforcement has once again become a focus within the Department of Justice. The administration has increased funding to the division and hired fifty new attorneys. It continues to prosecute the immigration and human trafficking cases that were priorities of the Bush administration and also has returned to handling traditional concerns such as race and sex discrimination in employment and housing.

What Should I Know About . . .

After reading this chapter, you should be able to:

★ **5.1** Trace the efforts from 1800 to 1890 of African Americans and women to win the vote, p. 136.

★ **5.2** Outline developments in African Americans' and women's push for equality from 1890 to 1954, p. 140.

★ **5.3** Analyze the civil rights movement and the effects of the Civil Rights Act of 1964, p. 143.

★ **5.4** Assess statutory and constitutional remedies for discrimination pursued and achieved by the women's rights movement, p. 147.

★ **5.5** Describe how other groups have mobilized in pursuit of their own civil rights, p. 151.

★ **5.6** Evaluate the ongoing debate concerning civil rights and affirmative action, p. 161.

civil rights
The government-protected rights of individuals against arbitrary or discriminatory treatment by governments or individuals.

Since the Constitution was written, concepts of **civil rights**, the government-protected rights of individuals against arbitrary or discriminatory treatment by governments or individuals based on categories such as race, sex, national origin, age, religion, or sexual orientation, have changed dramatically. The Fourteenth Amendment, one of three Civil War Amendments ratified from 1865 to 1870, introduced the notion of equality into the Constitution by specifying that a state could not deny "any person within its jurisdiction equal protection of the laws." Throughout history, the Fourteenth Amendment's equal protection guarantees have been the linchpin of efforts to expand upon the original intent of the amendment. Today, this amendment protects a variety of groups from discrimination.

Since passage of the Civil War Amendments, there has been a fairly consistent pattern of expansion of civil rights to more and more groups. In this chapter, we will explore how notions of equality and civil rights have changed in the United States.

- First, we will discuss *the roots of suffrage from 1800 to 1890.*

- Second, we will examine African Americans' and women's *push for equality from 1890 to 1954,* using two of the Supreme Court's most famous decisions, *Plessy* v. *Ferguson* (1896) and *Brown* v. *Board of Education* (1954), as bookends for our discussion.

- Third, we will analyze *the civil rights movement* as well as the Civil Rights Act of 1964 and its effects.

- Fourth, we will discuss the development of a new *women's rights movement* and its push for an equal rights amendment to the U.S. Constitution.

- Fifth, we will present the efforts of *other groups,* including Hispanic Americans, American Indians, Asian and Pacific Island Americans, gays and lesbians, and Americans with disabilities, to *mobilize for rights.*

- Finally, we will explore *reform efforts related to civil rights and affirmative action.*

ROOTS OF Suffrage: 1800–1890

★ **5.1** . . . Trace the efforts from 1800 to 1890 of African Americans and women to win the vote.

The period from 1800 to 1890 was one of tremendous change and upheaval in America. Despite the Civil War and the freeing of the slaves, the promise of equality guaranteed to African Americans by the Civil War Amendments failed to become a reality. Women's rights activists also began to make claims for equality, often using the arguments enunciated for the abolition of slavery, but they too fell far short of their goals.

Slavery and Congress

As the nation grew westward in the early 1800s, conflicts between northern and southern states intensified over the admission of new states to the union with free or slave status. The first major crisis occurred in 1820, when Missouri applied for admission to the union as a slave state—that is, one in which slavery would be legal. Missouri's admission would have weighted the Senate in favor of slavery and therefore was opposed by northern senators. To resolve this conflict, Congress passed the Missouri

Compromise of 1820. The Compromise prohibited slavery north of the geographical boundary at 36 degrees latitude. This act allowed Missouri to be admitted to the union as a slave state, and to maintain the balance of slave and free states, Maine was carved out of a portion of Massachusetts.

The First Civil Rights Movements: Abolition and Women's Rights

The Missouri Compromise solidified the South in its determination to keep slavery legal, but it also fueled the fervor of those who opposed slavery. William Lloyd Garrison, a white New Englander, galvanized the abolitionist movement in the early 1830s. Garrison, a newspaper editor, founded the American Anti-Slavery Society in 1833; by 1838, it had more than 250,000 members.

Slavery was not the only practice that people began to question in the decades following the Missouri Compromise. In 1840, for example, Elizabeth Cady Stanton and Lucretia Mott, who were to found the first women's rights movement, attended the 1840 meeting of the World Anti-Slavery Society in London with their husbands. After their long journey, they were not allowed to participate in the convention because they were women. As they sat apart from the male delegates, they paused to compare their status to that of the slaves they sought to free. They concluded that women were not much better off than slaves, and they resolved to meet to address these issues.

The Seneca Falls Convention in 1848 attracted people from both New York state and other states. Attendees passed resolutions calling for the abolition of legal, economic, and social discrimination against women. All of the resolutions reflected the attendees' dissatisfaction with contemporary moral codes, divorce and criminal laws, and the limited opportunities for women in education, the church, medicine, law, and politics. Ironically, only the call for "woman suffrage" (a call to give women the right to vote) failed to win unanimous approval. Most who attended the Seneca Falls Convention continued to press for women's rights along with the abolition of slavery. Similar conventions were later held across the Northeast and Midwest. At an 1851 meeting in Akron, Ohio, for example, former slave Sojourner Truth delivered her famous "Ain't I a Woman?" speech calling on women to recognize the plight of their black sisters.

The 1850s: The Calm Before the Storm

By 1850, much had changed in America: the Gold Rush had spurred westward migration, cities grew as people were lured from their farms, railroads and the telegraph increased mobility and communication, and immigrants flooded into the United States. The woman's movement gained momentum, and slavery continued to tear the nation apart. Harriet Beecher Stowe's *Uncle Tom's Cabin*, a novel that depicted the evils of slavery, further inflamed the country. *Uncle Tom's Cabin* sold more than 300,000 copies in 1852. Equivalent sales today would top 4 million copies.

The tremendous national reaction to Stowe's work, which later prompted President Abraham Lincoln to call Stowe "the little woman who started the big war," had not yet faded when a new controversy over the Missouri Compromise became the lightning rod for the first major civil rights case to be addressed by the U.S. Supreme Court. As discussed in **chapter 3**, in *Dred Scott* v. *Sandford* (1857), the Court ruled that the Missouri Compromise, which prohibited slavery north of a set geographical boundary, was unconstitutional. Furthermore, the Court went on to add that slaves were not U.S. citizens, and as a consequence, could not bring suits in federal court.

What was the Seneca Falls Convention? This is the announcement placed in a local newspaper about the convention to be held in Seneca Falls to discuss the civil and political rights of women.

Photo courtesy: Reproduced from the collections of the Library of Congress

THE FIRST CONVENTION

EVER CALLED TO DISCUSS THE

Civil and Political Rights of Women,

SENECA FALLS, N. Y., JULY 19, 20, 1848.

———

WOMAN'S RIGHTS CONVENTION.

———

A Convention to discuss the social, civil, and religious condition and rights of woman will be held in the Wesleyan Chapel, at Seneca Falls, N. Y., on Wednesday and Thursday, the 19th and 20th of July current; commencing at 10 o'clock A. M. During the first day the meeting will be exclusively for women, who are earnestly invited to attend. The public generally are invited to be present on the second day, when Lucretia Mott, of Philadelphia, and other ladies and gentlemen, will address the Convention.*

———

* This call was published in the *Seneca County Courier*, July 14, 1848, without any signatures. The movers of this Convention, who drafted the call, the declaration and resolutions were Elizabeth Cady Stanton, Lucretia Mott, Martha C. Wright, Mary Ann McClintock, and Jane C. Hunt.

The Civil War and its Aftermath: Civil Rights Laws and Constitutional Amendments

The Civil War had many causes, but slavery was clearly a key issue. During the war (1861–1865), abolitionists continued to press for an end to slavery. They were partially rewarded when President Abraham Lincoln issued the Emancipation Proclamation, which provided that all slaves in states still in active rebellion against the United States would be freed automatically on January 1, 1863. Designed as a measure to gain favor for the war in the North, the Emancipation Proclamation did not free all slaves—it freed only those who lived in the Confederacy. Complete abolition of slavery did not occur until congressional passage and ultimate ratification of the Thirteenth Amendment in 1865.

Thirteenth Amendment
One of the three Civil War Amendments; specifically bans slavery in the United States.

The **Thirteenth Amendment** was the first of the three Civil War Amendments. It banned all forms of "slavery [and] involuntary servitude." (To learn more about the Thirteenth Amendment, see The Living Constitution: Thirteenth Amendment, Section 1.) Although southern states were required to ratify the Thirteenth Amendment as a condition of their readmission to the United States after the war, most of the former Confederate states passed laws that were designed to restrict opportunities for newly freed slaves. These **Black Codes** denied most legal rights to newly freed slaves by prohibiting African Americans from voting, sitting on juries, or even appearing in public places. Although Black Codes differed from state to state, all empowered local law-enforcement officials to arrest unemployed blacks, fine them for vagrancy, and hire them out to employers to satisfy their fines. Some state codes went so far as to require African Americans to work on plantations or to be domestics. The Black Codes laid the groundwork for Jim Crow laws, which later would institute segregation in all walks of life in the South.

Black Codes
Laws denying most legal rights to newly freed slaves; passed by southern states following the Civil War.

An outraged Congress enacted the Civil Rights Act of 1866 to invalidate some state Black Codes. President Andrew Johnson vetoed the legislation, but—for the first time in history—Congress overrode a presidential veto. The Civil Rights Act formally made African Americans citizens of the United States and gave the Congress and the federal courts the power to intervene when states attempted to restrict the citizenship rights of male African Americans in matters such as voting. Congress reasoned that African Americans were unlikely to fare well if they had to file discrimination complaints in state courts, where most judges were elected. Passage of a federal law allowed African Americans to challenge discriminatory state practices in the federal courts, where judges were appointed for life by the president.

Fourteenth Amendment
One of the three Civil War Amendments; guarantees equal protection and due process of the law to all U.S. citizens.

equal protection clause
Section of the Fourteenth Amendment that guarantees that all citizens receive "equal protection of the laws."

Fifteenth Amendment
One of the three Civil War Amendments; specifically enfranchised newly freed male slaves.

Because controversy remained over the constitutionality of the act (since the Constitution gives states the right to determine qualifications of voters), the **Fourteenth Amendment** was proposed simultaneously with the Civil Rights Act to guarantee, among other things, citizenship to all freed slaves. Other key provisions of the Fourteenth Amendment barred states from abridging "the privileges or immunities of citizenship" or depriving "any person of life, liberty, or property, without due process of law." Finally, the Fourteenth Amendment includes the **equal protection clause** that prohibits states from denying "any person within its jurisdiction the equal protection of the laws." Unlike the Thirteenth Amendment, which had near-unanimous support in the North, the Fourteenth Amendment was opposed by many women because it failed to guarantee suffrage for women. The **Fifteenth Amendment** was also passed by Congress in early 1869. It guaranteed the "right of citizens" to vote regardless of their "race, color or previous condition of servitude." Sex was not mentioned.

Civil Rights, Congress, and the Supreme Court

Continued southern resistance to African American equality led Congress to pass the Civil Rights Act of 1875, designed to grant equal access to public accommodations

The Living Constitution

Neither slavery nor involuntary servitude, except as a punishment for crime whereof the party shall have been duly convicted, shall exist within the United States, or any place subject to their jurisdiction.

—THIRTEENTH AMENDMENT, SECTION 1

This amendment, the first of three Civil War Amendments, abolished slavery throughout the United States and its territories. It also prohibited involuntary servitude.

Based on his wartime authority, in 1863, President Abraham Lincoln issued the Emancipation Proclamation abolishing slavery in the states that were in rebellion against the United States. Abolishing slavery in the union, however, proved more challenging. Congress could not by statute end this practice. Thus, the proposed Thirteenth Amendment was forwarded to the states on February 1, 1865. With its adoption, said one of its sponsors, it relieved Congress "of sectional strifes."

Initially, some doubted if any groups other than newly freed African slaves were protected by the provisions of the amendment. Soon, however, the Supreme Court went on to clarify this question by noting: "If Mexican peonage or the Chinese coolie labor system shall develop slavery of the Mexican or Chinese race within our territory, this amendment may safely be trusted to make it void."

In the early 1900s, the Supreme Court was called on several times to interpret section 1 of the amendment, especially in regard to involuntary servitude. Thus, provisions of an Alabama law that called for criminal sanctions and jail time for defaulting sharecroppers were considered unconstitutional, and Congress enacted a law banning this kind of involuntary servitude. More recently, the Court has found that compulsory high school community service programs do not violate the ban on involuntary servitude.

The Supreme Court and a host of lower federal and state courts have also upheld criminal convictions of those who coerced mentally retarded farm laborers into service or who lured foreign workers to the United States with promises of jobs and then forced them to work long hours at little or no pay. Human trafficking, in fact, was targeted by the George W. Bush administration as an especially onerous form of involuntary servitude. The U.S. Department of Justice began hundreds of investigations in an attempt to end this system.

CRITICAL THINKING QUESTIONS

1. Why would the Supreme Court rule that compulsory high school community service programs do not violate the Thirteenth Amendment?
2. Is forcing prison inmates to work as part of a "chain gang" a form of involuntary servitude? Why or why not?
3. What other actions might be banned by the Thirteenth Amendment?

such as theaters, restaurants, and transportation. The act also prohibited the exclusion of African Americans from jury service. But, after federal occupation of the South (Reconstruction) ended in 1877, southern states quickly moved to limit African Americans' access to the ballot. Other forms of discrimination also were allowed by judicial decisions upholding **Jim Crow laws,** which required segregation in public schools and facilities, including railroads, restaurants, and theaters.

All these laws, at first glance, appeared to conflict with the Civil Rights Act of 1875. In 1883, however, a series of cases decided by the Supreme Court severely

Jim Crow laws
Laws enacted by southern states that required segregation in public schools, theaters, hotels, and other public accommodations.

Civil Rights Cases (1883)
Name attached to five cases brought under the Civil Rights Act of 1875. In 1883, the Supreme Court decided that discrimination in a variety of public accommodations, including theaters, hotels, and railroads, could not be prohibited by the act because such discrimination was private discrimination and not state discrimination.

poll tax
A tax levied in many southern states and localities that had to be paid before an eligible voter could cast a ballot.

grandfather clause
Voter qualification provision in many southern states that allowed only those citizens whose grandfathers had voted before Reconstruction to vote unless they passed a wealth or literacy test.

damaged the vitality of the 1875 act. The **Civil Rights Cases (1883)** were five separate cases involving the convictions of private individuals found to have violated the Civil Rights Act by refusing to extend accommodations to African Americans in theaters, a hotel, and a railroad.[2] In deciding these cases, the Supreme Court ruled that Congress could prohibit only state or governmental action but not private acts of discrimination. The Court thus concluded that Congress had no authority to prohibit private discrimination in public accommodations. The Court's opinion in the *Civil Rights Cases* provided a moral reinforcement for the Jim Crow system. Southern states viewed the Court's ruling as an invitation to gut the reach and intent of the Thirteenth, Fourteenth, and Fifteenth Amendments.

In devising ways to make certain that African Americans did not vote, southern states had to avoid the intent of the Fifteenth Amendment. This amendment did not guarantee suffrage; it simply said that states could not deny anyone the right to vote on account of race or color. To exclude African Americans in a seemingly racially neutral way, southern states used three devices before the 1890s: (1) **poll taxes** (small taxes on the right to vote that often came due when poor African American sharecroppers had the least amount of money on hand); (2) some form of property-owning qualifications; and, (3) "literacy" or "understanding" tests, which allowed local voter registration officials to administer difficult reading-comprehension tests to potential voters whom they did not know.

These voting restrictions had an immediate impact. By the late 1890s, black voting fell by 62 percent from the Reconstruction period, while white voting fell by only 26 percent. To make certain that these laws did not further reduce the numbers of poor or uneducated white voters, many southern states added a **grandfather clause** to their voting qualification provisions, granting voting privileges to those citizens who failed to pass a wealth or literacy test only if their grandfathers had voted before Reconstruction. Grandfather clauses effectively denied the descendents of slaves the right to vote.

The Push for Equality, 1890–1954

★ **5.2** . . . Outline developments in African Americans' and women's push for equality from 1890 to 1954.

The Progressive era (1890–1920) was characterized by a concerted effort to reform political, economic, and social affairs. Evils such as child labor, the concentration of economic power in the hands of a few industrialists, limited suffrage, political corruption, business monopolies, and prejudice against African Americans all were targets of progressive reform efforts. Distress over the inferior legal status of African Americans was aggravated by the U.S. Supreme Court's decision in *Plessy* v. *Ferguson* **(1896),** a case that some commentators point to as the Court's darkest hour.[3]

In *Plessy,* the Court upheld the constitutionality of a Louisiana law mandating racial segregation on all public trains. The justices based their decision on their belief that separate facilities for blacks and whites provided equal protection of the laws. After all, they reasoned, Plessy was not prevented from riding the train; the Louisiana statute required only that the races travel separately. Justice John Marshall Harlan was the lone dissenter. He argued that "the Constitution is colorblind" and that it was senseless to hold constitutional a law "which, practically, puts the badge of servitude and degradation upon a large class of our fellow citizens."

Not surprisingly, the separate-but-equal doctrine enunciated in *Plessy* v. *Ferguson* soon came to mean only separate, as new legal avenues to discriminate against African Americans were enacted into law throughout the South. By 1900, equality for African Americans was far from the promise first offered by the Civil War Amendments. Again and again, the Supreme Court nullified the intent of the amendments and sanctioned racial segregation while the states avidly followed its lead.[4]

Plessy v. Ferguson (1896)
Supreme Court case that challenged a Louisiana statute requiring that railroads provide separate accommodations for blacks and whites. The Court found that separate but equal accommodations did not violate the equal protection clause of the Fourteenth Amendment.

The Founding of Key Groups

In 1909, a handful of individuals active in a variety of progressive causes, including woman suffrage and the fight for better working conditions for women and children, met to discuss the idea of a group devoted to the problems of the "Negro." Major race riots had occurred in several American cities, and progressive reformers were concerned about these outbreaks of violence and the possibility of others. Oswald Garrison Villard, the influential publisher of the *New York Evening Post*—and the grandson of William Lloyd Garrison—called a conference to discuss the problem. This group soon evolved into the National Association for the Advancement of Colored People (NAACP).

The NAACP was not the only new group. The struggle for woman's rights was revitalized in 1890 when the National and American Woman Suffrage Associations merged. The new organization, the National American Woman Suffrage Association (NAWSA), was headed by Susan B. Anthony. This new association was devoted largely to securing woman suffrage. Its task was greatly facilitated by the proliferation of woman's groups that emerged during the Progressive era. In addition to the rapidly growing temperance movement—the move to ban the sale of alcohol, which many women blamed for a variety of social ills—woman's groups were created to seek maximum hour or minimum wage laws for women and to work for improved sanitation, public morals, education, and the like.

NAWSA based its claim to the right to vote largely on the fact that women, as mothers, should be enfranchised. The new woman's movement—called the **suffrage movement** because of its focus on the vote alone—soon took on racist overtones. Suffragists argued that if undereducated African American men could vote, why couldn't women?

By 1917, the new movement had more than 2 million members. In 1920, a coalition of women's groups, led by NAWSA and the newer, more radical National Woman's Party, was able to secure ratification of the **Nineteenth Amendment** to the Constitution through rallies, protest marches, and the support of President Woodrow Wilson. The Nineteenth Amendment guaranteed all women the right to vote—fifty years after African American males were enfranchised by the Fifteenth Amendment.

After passage of the suffrage amendment in 1920, the fragile alliance of diverse woman's groups that had come together to fight for the vote quickly disintegrated. Widespread organized activity on behalf of woman's rights did not reemerge until the 1960s. In the meantime, the NAACP continued to fight racism and racial segregation. Its activities and those of others in the civil rights movement would later give impetus to a new women's movement.

What was the Niagara Movement? This Niagara Movement was the predecessor to the NAACP. It was comprised of a group of African American intellectuals whose leaders included W.E.B. Du Bois (second from the left in the second row, facing right). They met to discuss the injustices suffered by African Americans and took their name from their first meeting in Niagara Falls, Ontario, Canada. This 1905 photo was taken on the Canadian side of Niagara Falls because no hotel on the American side would accommodate the group's African American members.

Photo courtesy: The New York Public Library Photographic Services/Art Resource, NY

suffrage movement
The drive for voting rights for women that took place in the United States from 1890 to 1920.

Nineteenth Amendment
Amendment to the Constitution that guaranteed women the right to vote.

Litigating for Equality

During the 1930s, leaders of the NAACP began to sense that the time was right to launch a full-scale challenge in the federal courts to the constitutionality of *Plessy*'s separate-but-equal doctrine. Clearly, the separate-but-equal doctrine and the proliferation of Jim Crow laws were a bar to any hope of full equality for African Americans. Traditional legislative channels were unlikely to work, given African Americans' limited or nonexistent political power. Thus, the federal courts and a litigation strategy were the NAACP's only hopes. The NAACP mapped out a long-range plan that would first target segregation in professional and graduate education.

TEST CASES   The NAACP opted first to challenge the constitutionality of Jim Crow law schools. In 1935, all southern states maintained fully segregated elementary and secondary schools. Colleges and universities also were segregated, and most states did not provide for postgraduate education for African Americans. NAACP lawyers chose to target law schools because they were institutions that judges could well understand, and integration there would prove less threatening to most whites.

Lloyd Gaines, a graduate of Missouri's all-black Lincoln University, sought admission to the all-white University of Missouri Law School in 1936. He was immediately rejected. In the separate-but-equal spirit, the state offered to build a law school at Lincoln (although no funds were allocated for the project) or, if he didn't want to wait, to pay his tuition at an out-of-state law school. Gaines rejected the offer, sued, lost in the lower courts, and appealed to the U.S. Supreme Court.

Gaines's case was filed at a promising time. As discussed in **chapter 3,** a constitutional revolution of sorts occurred in Supreme Court decision making in 1937. Before this time, the Court was most receptive to and interested in the protection of economic liberties. In 1937, however, the Court reversed itself in a series of cases and began to place individual freedoms and personal liberties on a more protected footing. Thus, in 1938, Gaines's lawyers pleaded his appeal to a far more sympathetic Supreme Court. NAACP attorneys argued that the creation of a separate law school of a lesser caliber than that of the University of Missouri would not and could not afford Gaines an equal education. The justices agreed and ruled that Missouri had failed to meet the separate-but-equal requirements of *Plessy*. The Court ordered Missouri either to admit Gaines to the school or to set up a law school for him.[5]

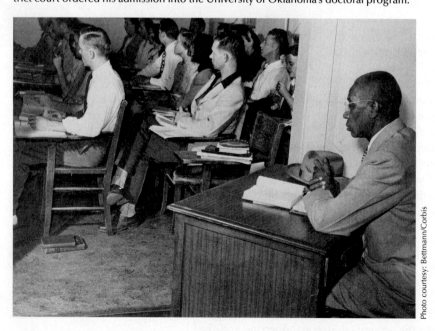

What did "separate but equal" look like? Here, George McLaurin, the plaintiff in one of the NAACP LDF's challenges to the separate-but-equal-doctrine, is shown outside his classroom. This was the university's shameful accommodation when a federal district court ordered his admission into the University of Oklahoma's doctoral program.

Photo courtesy: Bettmann/Corbis

Recognizing the importance of the Court's ruling, in 1939 the NAACP created a separate, tax-exempt legal defense fund to devise a strategy that would build on the Missouri case and bring about equal educational opportunities for all African American children. The first head of the NAACP Legal Defense and Educational Fund, commonly referred to as the LDF, was Thurgood Marshall, who later became the first African American to serve on the U.S. Supreme Court. Sensing that the Court would be more amenable to the NAACP's broader goals if it were first forced to address a variety of less threatening claims to educational opportunity, Marshall and the LDF brought a series of carefully crafted test cases to the Court.

The first case involved H. M. Sweatt, a forty-six-year-old African American mail carrier, who applied for admission to the all-white University of Texas Law School in 1946. Rejected on racial grounds, Sweatt sued. The judge gave the state six months to establish a law school or to admit Sweatt to the university. The state legislature saw the handwriting on the wall and authorized $3 million for the creation of the Texas State University for Negroes. One hundred thousand dollars of that money was to be for a new law school in Austin across the street from the state capitol building. It consisted of three small basement rooms, a library of 10,000 books, access to the state law library, and three part-time first-year instructors as the faculty. Sweatt declined the opportunity to obtain an education there and instead chose to continue his legal challenge.

The Supreme Court handled this case together with another LDF case involving graduate education.[6] The eleven southern states filed an *amicus curiae* (friend of the court) brief, in which they argued that *Plessy* should govern both cases. The LDF received assistance, however, from an unexpected source—the U.S. government. In a dramatic departure from the past, the administration of President Harry S Truman filed an *amicus* brief, urging the Court to overrule *Plessy*.

Although the Court did not overrule *Plessy*, the justices found that the measures taken by the states in each case failed to live up to the strictures of the separate-but-equal doctrine. The Court unanimously ruled that the remedies to each situation were inadequate to afford a sound education.

In 1950, after these decisions were handed down, the LDF concluded that the time had come to launch a full-scale attack on the separate-but-equal doctrine. The decisions of the Court were encouraging, and the position of the U.S. government and the population in general appeared to be more receptive to an outright overruling of *Plessy*.

BROWN v. BOARD OF EDUCATION   *Brown* v. *Board of Education* (1954) actually was four cases brought from different areas of the South and border states involving public elementary or high school systems that mandated separate schools for blacks and whites.[7] In *Brown*, LDF lawyers, again led by Thurgood Marshall, argued that *Plessy*'s separate-but-equal doctrine was unconstitutional under the equal protection clause of the Fourteenth Amendment, and that if the Court was still reluctant to overrule *Plessy*, the only way to equalize the schools was to integrate them. A major component of the LDF's strategy was to prove that the intellectual, psychological, and financial damage that befell African Americans as a result of segregation prevented any court from finding that equality was served by the separate-but-equal policy.

On May 17, 1954, Chief Justice Earl Warren delivered the fourth opinion of the day, *Brown* v. *Board of Education*. Writing for the Court, Warren stated:

> To separate [some school children] from others . . . solely because of their race generates a feeling of inferiority as to their status in the community that may affect their hearts and minds in a way very unlikely ever to be undone. We conclude, unanimously, that in the field of public education the doctrine of "separate but equal" has no place.

There can be no doubt that *Brown* was the most important civil rights case decided in the twentieth century.[8] It immediately evoked an uproar that shook the nation. Some segregationists called the day the decision was handed down Black Monday. The governor of South Carolina denounced the decision, saying, "Ending segregation would mark the beginning of the end of civilization in the South as we know it."[9]

Brown v. Board of Education (1954)
U.S. Supreme Court decision holding that school segregation is inherently unconstitutional because it violates the Fourteenth Amendment's guarantee of equal protection.

The Civil Rights Movement

★ **5.3 . . . Analyze the civil rights movement and the effects of the Civil Rights Act of 1964.**

Brown served as a catalyst for change, sparking the development of the modern civil rights movement. Women's work in that movement and the student protest movement that arose in reaction to the U.S. government's involvement in the Vietnam War gave women the experience needed to form their own organizations to press for full equality.

How did Emmett Till's murder awaken a nation to racial injustice? The brutal 1955 murder of Emmett Till, a fourteen-year-old boy from Chicago, Illinois, heightened awareness of the injustices of the Jim Crow system in the South and helped to coalesce the nascent civil rights movement. Till, who was visiting relatives in Mississippi, was accused of whistling at a white woman. He was kidnapped, beaten, mutilated, shot, and thrown in a river. His mother insisted on an open-casket funeral, so that news media and mourners would understand the violence visited upon her child. Two suspects were acquitted of the killings but later confessed their crime to a reporter.

Photo courtesy: The Chicago Defender

School Desegregation After *Brown*

One year after *Brown*, in a case referred to as *Brown* v. *Board of Education II* (1955), the Court ruled that racially segregated systems must be dismantled "with all deliberate speed."[10] Many politicians in the South entered into a near conspiracy to avoid the mandates of *Brown II*. In Arkansas, for example, Governor Orval Faubus, who was facing a reelection bid, announced that he would not "be a party to any attempt to force acceptance of change to which people are overwhelmingly opposed."[11] The day before school was to begin, he announced that National Guardsmen would surround Little Rock's Central High School to prevent African American students from entering. While the federal courts in Arkansas continued to order the admission of African American children, the governor remained adamant. Finally, President Dwight D. Eisenhower sent federal troops to Little Rock to protect the rights of the nine students attending Central High.

In reaction to the governor's outrageous conduct, the Court broke with tradition and issued a unanimous decision in *Cooper* v. *Aaron* (1958), which was filed by the Little Rock School Board asking the federal district court for a two-and-one-half-year delay in implementation of its desegregation plans. Each justice signed the opinion individually, underscoring his individual support for the notion that "no state legislator or executive or judicial officer can war against the Constitution without violating his undertaking to support it."[12] The state's actions thus were ruled unconstitutional and its "evasive schemes" illegal.

A New Move for African American Rights

In 1955, soon after *Brown II*, the civil rights movement took another step forward—this time in Montgomery, Alabama. Rosa Parks, the local NAACP's Youth Council adviser, decided to challenge the constitutionality of the segregated bus system. First, Parks and other NAACP officials began to raise money for litigation and made speeches around town to garner public support. Then, on December 1, 1955, Rosa Parks made history when she refused to leave her seat in the front of a bus to make room for a white male passenger. She was arrested for violating an Alabama law banning integration of public facilities, including buses. After she was freed on bond, Parks and the NAACP decided to enlist city clergy to help her cause. At the same time, they distributed 35,000 handbills calling for African Americans to boycott the Montgomery bus system on the day of Parks's trial. Black ministers used Sunday services to urge their members to support the boycott. On Monday morning, African Americans walked, carpooled, or used black-owned taxicabs. That night, local ministers decided that the boycott should be continued. A new, twenty-six-year-old minister, the Reverend Martin Luther King Jr., was selected to lead the newly formed Montgomery Improvement Association.

As the boycott dragged on, Montgomery officials and local business owners began to harass the city's African American citizens. The residents held out, despite suffering personal hardship for their actions, ranging from harassment to job loss to bankruptcy. In 1956, a federal court ruled that the segregated bus system violated the equal protection clause of the Fourteenth Amendment. After a year-long boycott, black Montgomery residents ended their protest when city buses were ordered to integrate. The first effort at nonviolent protest had been successful. Organized boycotts and other forms of nonviolent protest, including sit-ins at segregated restaurants and bus stations, were to follow.

Formation of New Groups

The recognition and respect that the Reverend Martin Luther King Jr. earned within the African American community helped him to launch the Southern Christian Leadership Conference (SCLC) in 1957, soon after the end of the Montgomery bus boycott. Unlike the NAACP, which had northern origins and had come to rely largely on litigation as a means of achieving expanded equality, the SCLC had a southern base and was rooted more closely in black religious culture. The SCLC's philosophy reflected King's growing belief in the importance of nonviolent protest and civil disobedience.

Eventually, the SCLC and the Student Non-violent Coordinating Committee (SNCC), largely made up of activist college students, dominated the new civil rights movement. Whereas the SCLC generally worked with church leaders in a community, SNCC was much more of a grassroots organization. Always perceived as more radical than the SCLC, SNCC tended to focus its organizing activities on the young, both black and white.

In addition to joining the sit-in bandwagon, SNCC also came to lead what were called freedom rides, designed to focus attention on segregated public accommodations. Bands of college students and other civil rights activists traveled by bus throughout the South in an effort to force bus stations to desegregate.

While SNCC continued to sponsor sit-ins and freedom rides, in 1963 the Reverend Martin Luther King Jr. launched a series of massive nonviolent demonstrations in Birmingham, Alabama, long considered a major stronghold of segregation. Thousands of blacks and whites marched to Birmingham in a show of solidarity. Peaceful marchers were met there by the Birmingham police commissioner, who ordered his officers to use dogs, clubs, and fire hoses on the marchers. Americans across the nation were horrified as they witnessed on television the brutality and abuse heaped on the protesters. As the marchers hoped, the shocking scenes helped convince President John F. Kennedy to propose important civil rights legislation. (To learn more about the role of the media in the civil rights movement, see Analyzing Visuals: Police Confront Civil Rights Demonstrators in Birmingham.)

The Civil Rights Act of 1964

Both the SCLC and SNCC sought full implementation of U.S. Supreme Court decisions dealing with race and an end to racial segregation and discrimination. The cumulative effect of collective actions including sit-ins, boycotts, marches, and freedom rides—as well as the tragic bombings lynchings, and other deaths inflicted in retaliation—led Congress

ANALYZING VISUALS

Police Confront Civil Rights Demonstrators in Birmingham

During the spring of 1963, civil rights demonstrators descended on Birmingham, Alabama, to challenge racial segregation. This famous photograph, taken by Charles Moore in May 1963, was frequently reprinted and also discussed on the floor of Congress during the debate over the Civil Rights Act of 1964. After examining the photograph, answer the questions.

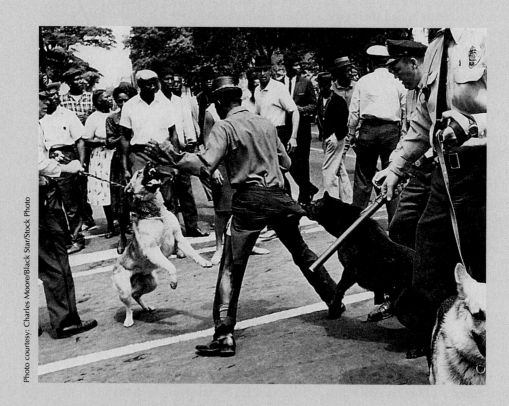

Photo courtesy: Charles Moore/Black Star/Stock Photo

- What is happening in this photograph?
- Which part of this image do you find most disturbing? Why?
- Why do you think this image became an effective tool in the struggle for African Americans' civil rights?

to pass the first major piece of civil rights legislation since the post–Civil War era, the Civil Rights Act of 1964, followed the next year by the Voting Rights Act of 1965. Several events led to the consideration of the two pieces of legislation.

In 1963, President John F. Kennedy requested that Congress pass a law banning discrimination in public accommodations. Seizing the moment, the Reverend Martin Luther King Jr. called for a monumental march on Washington, D.C., to demonstrate widespread support for far-ranging anti-discrimination legislation. It was clear that national legislation outlawing discrimination was the only answer: southern legislators would never vote to repeal Jim Crow laws. The March on Washington for Jobs and Freedom was held in August 1963, only a few months after the Birmingham demonstrations. More than 250,000 people heard King deliver his famous "I Have a Dream" speech from the Lincoln Memorial. Before Congress had the opportunity to vote on any legislation, however, President Kennedy was assassinated on November 22, 1963, in Dallas, Texas.

When Vice President Lyndon B. Johnson, a southern-born, former Senate majority leader, succeeded Kennedy as president, he put civil rights reform at the top of his legislative priority list, and civil rights activists gained a critical ally. Thus, through the 1960s, the movement subtly changed in focus from peaceful protest and litigation to legislative lobbying. Its focus broadened from integration of school and public facilities and voting rights to preventing housing and job discrimination and alleviating poverty.

In spite of strong presidential support and the sway of public opinion, the Civil Rights Act of 1964 did not sail through Congress. Southern senators, led by South Carolina's Strom Thurmond, a Democrat who later switched to the Republican Party, conducted the longest filibuster in the history of the Senate. For eight weeks, Thurmond led the effort to hold up voting on the civil rights bill. Once passed, the **Civil Rights Act of 1964:**

- Outlawed arbitrary discrimination in voter registration and expedited voting rights lawsuits.
- Barred discrimination in public accommodations engaged in interstate commerce.
- Authorized the Department of Justice to initiate lawsuits to desegregate public facilities and schools.
- Provided for the withholding of federal funds from discriminatory state and local programs.
- Prohibited discrimination in employment on grounds of race, creed, color, religion, national origin, or sex.
- Created the Equal Employment Opportunity Commission (EEOC) to monitor and enforce the bans on employment discrimination.

As challenges were made to the Civil Rights Act of 1964, other changes continued to sweep the United States. African Americans in the North, who believed that their brothers and sisters in the South were making progress against discrimination, found themselves frustrated. Northern blacks were experiencing high unemployment, poverty, discrimination, and little political clout. Some, including African American Muslim leader Malcolm X, even argued that, to survive, African Americans must separate themselves from white culture in every way. These increased tensions resulted in riots in many major cities from 1964 to 1968, when many African Americans in the North took to the streets, burning and looting to vent their rage. The assassination of the Reverend Martin Luther King Jr. in 1968 triggered a new epidemic of race riots.

Civil Rights Act of 1964
Wide-ranging legislation passed by Congress to outlaw segregation in public facilities and discrimination in employment, education, and voting; created the Equal Employment Opportunity Commission.

The Women's Rights Movement

★ **5.4** . . . **Assess statutory and constitutional remedies for discrimination pursued and achieved by the women's rights movement.**

Just as in the abolition movement in the 1800s, women from all walks of life participated in the civil rights movement. Women were important members of new groups such as SNCC and the SCLC as well as more traditional groups such as the NAACP, yet they often found themselves treated as second-class citizens. At one point during a SNCC national meeting, its chair proclaimed: "The only position for women in

SNCC is prone."[13] Statements and attitudes such as these led some women to found early women's liberation groups that generally were quite radical but small in membership. Others founded more traditional groups such as the National Organization for Women (NOW).

The Equal Rights Amendment

Not all women agreed with the notion of full equality for women. Nevertheless, from 1923 to 1972, a proposal for an equal rights amendment was made in every session of every Congress. Every president between Harry S Truman and Richard M. Nixon backed it, and by 1972 public opinion favored its ratification.

Equal Rights Amendment

Proposed amendment to the Constitution that states "Equality of rights under the law shall not be denied or abridged by the United States or any state on account of sex."

Finally, in 1972, in response to pressure from NOW, the National Women's Political Caucus, and a wide variety of other feminist groups, Congress voted in favor of the **Equal Rights Amendment** (ERA) by overwhelming majorities (84–8 in the Senate; 354–24 in the House). The amendment provided that:

Equality of rights under the law shall not be denied or abridged by the United States or by any state on account of sex.

The Congress shall have the power to enforce, by appropriate legislation, the provisions of this article.

Within a year, twenty-two states ratified the amendment, most by overwhelming margins, but the tide soon turned. In 1974 and 1975, the amendment only squeaked through the Montana and North Dakota legislatures, and two states—Nebraska and Tennessee—voted to rescind their earlier ratifications. By 1978, one year before the deadline for ratification was to expire, thirty-five states had voted for the amendment—three short of the three-fourths necessary for ratification. Efforts in key states such as Illinois and Florida failed as opposition to the ERA intensified. Faced with the prospect of defeat, ERA supporters heavily lobbied Congress to extend the deadline for ratification. Congress extended the ratification period by three years, but to no avail. No additional states ratified the amendment, and three more rescinded their votes.

What began as a simple correction to the Constitution turned into a highly controversial proposed change. Even though large percentages of the public favored the ERA, opponents needed to stall ratification in only thirteen states while supporters had to convince legislators in thirty-eight. The success that women's rights activists were having in the courts was hurting the effort. When women first sought the ERA in the late 1960s, the Supreme Court had yet to rule that women were

Who continues to fight for the ERA? Members of Congress led by Representative Carolyn B. Maloney (D–NY) have reintroduced the Equal Rights Amendment in all recent sessions of Congress. Here, Representative Maloney (at podium), her co-sponsors, and women's group leaders hold a press conference in July 2009 announcing the reintroduction of the ERA in the 111th Congress.

Photo courtesy: Office of Congresswoman Carolyn Maloney

protected by the Fourteenth Amendment's equal protection clause from any kind of discrimination, thus highlighting the need for an amendment. But, as the Court widened its interpretation of the Constitution to protect women from some sorts of discrimination, many felt the need for a new amendment was less urgent. The proposed amendment died without being ratified on June 30, 1982. Since 1982, the amendment has been reintroduced in every session of Congress.

The Equal Protection Clause and Constitutional Standards of Review

The Fourteenth Amendment protects all U.S. citizens from state action that violates equal protection of the laws. Most laws, however, are subject to what is called the rational basis or minimum rationality test. This lowest level of scrutiny means that governments must allege a rational foundation for any distinctions they make. As early as 1937, however, the Supreme Court recognized that certain freedoms were so fundamental that a very heavy burden would be placed on any government that sought to restrict those rights. As discussed in **chapter 4,** when fundamental freedoms such as those guaranteed by the First Amendment or **suspect classifications** such as race are involved, the Court uses a heightened standard of review called **strict scrutiny** to determine the constitutional validity of the challenged practices, as detailed in Table 5.1.

In legal terms, this means that if a statute or governmental practice makes a classification based on race, the statute is presumed to be unconstitutional unless the state can provide "compelling affirmative justifications": that is, unless the state can prove the law in question is necessary to accomplish a permissible goal and that it is the least restrictive means through which that goal can be accomplished.

During the 1960s and into the 1970s, the Court routinely struck down as unconstitutional practices and statutes that discriminated on the basis of race. "Whites-only" public parks and recreational facilities, tax-exempt status for private schools that discriminated, and statutes prohibiting interracial marriage were

suspect classification
Category or class, such as race, that triggers the highest standard of scrutiny from the Supreme Court.

strict scrutiny
A heightened standard of review used by the Supreme Court to determine the constitutional validity of a challenged practice.

Table 5.1 *What are the standards of review fashioned by the Court under the equal protection clause?*

Type of Classification: *What kind of statutory classification is at issue?*	Standard of Review: *What standard of review will be used?*	Test: *What does the Court ask?*	Example: *How does the Court apply the test?*
Fundamental freedoms (including religion, speech, assembly, press, Suspect classifications (including race, alien, age, and national origin)	Strict scrutiny or heightened standard	Is the classification necessary to the accomplishment of a permissible state goal? Is it the least restrictive way to reach that goal?	*Brown* v. *Board of Education* (1954): Racial segregation not necessary to accomplish the state's goal of educating its students.
Gender	Intermediate standard	Does the classification serve an important governmental objective, and is it substantially related to those ends?	*Craig* v. *Boren* (1976): Keeping drunk drivers off the roads may be an important governmental objective, but allowing eighteen-to twenty-one-year-old women to drink alcoholic beverages while prohibiting men of the same age from drinking is not substantially related to that goal.
Others (including age, wealth, mental retardation, and sexual orientation)	Minimum rationality standard	Is there any rational foundation for the discrimination?	*Romer* v. *Evans* (1996): Colorado state constitutional amendment denying equal rights to homosexuals is unconstitutional.

declared unconstitutional. In contrast, the Court refused to consider whether the equal protection clause might apply to discrimination against women. Finally, in a case argued in 1971 by Ruth Bader Ginsburg (later an associate justice of the Supreme Court) as director of the Women's Rights Project of the ACLU, the Supreme Court ruled that an Idaho law granting a male parent automatic preference over a female parent as the administrator of their deceased child's estate violated the equal protection clause of the Fourteenth Amendment. *Reed* v. *Reed* (1971), the Idaho case, turned the tide in terms of constitutional litigation. Although the Court did not rule that sex was a suspect classification, it concluded that the equal protection clause of the Fourteenth Amendment prohibited unreasonable classifications based on sex.[14]

In *Craig* v. *Boren* (1976), the Court carved out a new test to be used in examining claims of sex discrimination alleged to violate the U.S. Constitution: "to withstand constitutional challenge, . . . classifications by gender must serve important governmental objectives and must be substantially related to achievement of those objectives."[15]

Since 1976, the Court has applied the intermediate standard of constitutional review to most claims that it has heard involving gender. Thus, the following practices have been found to violate the Fourteenth Amendment:

- Single-sex public nursing schools.[16]
- Laws that consider males adults at twenty-one years but females at eighteen years.[17]
- Laws that allow women but not men to receive alimony.[18]
- State prosecutors' use of peremptory challenges to reject male or female potential jurors to create more sympathetic juries.[19]
- Virginia's maintenance of an all-male military college, the Virginia Military Institute.[20]

In contrast, the Court has upheld the following governmental practices and laws:

- Draft registration provisions for males only.[21]
- State statutory rape laws that apply only to female victims.[22]
- Different requirements for a child's acquisition of citizenship based on whether the citizen parent is a mother or a father.[23]

The level of review used by the Court is crucial. Clearly, a statute excluding African Americans from draft registration would be unconstitutional. But, because gender is not subject to the same higher standard of review that is used in racial discrimination cases, the exclusion of women from the requirements of the Military Selective Service Act was ruled permissible because the government policy was considered to serve "important governmental objectives."[24]

This history has perhaps clarified why women's rights activists continue to argue that until the passage of the Equal Rights Amendment, women will never enjoy the same rights as men. An amendment would raise the level of scrutiny that the Court applies to gender-based claims, although there are clear indications that the Supreme Court of late favors requiring states to show "exceedingly persuasive justifications" for their actions.[25]

Statutory Remedies for Sex Discrimination

Equal Pay Act of 1963
Legislation that requires employers to pay men and women equal pay for equal work.

In part because of the limits of the intermediate standard of review and the fact that the equal protection clause applies only to governmental discrimination, women's rights activists began to look for statutory solutions to discrimination. The **Equal Pay Act of 1963,** the first such piece of legislation, requires employers to pay women and men equal pay for equal work. Women have won important victories under the act, but a large wage gap between women and men continues to exist. Women's earnings in 2010 equaled only 75 to 80 percent of their male counterparts' earnings, depending on location and occupation.

In 2007, the boundaries of the Equal Pay Act were tested in the U.S. Supreme Court. The justices heard the case of Lilly Ledbetter, the lone female supervisor at a Goodyear tire factory in Alabama. Ledbetter charged that sex discrimination throughout her career had led her to earn substantially less than her male counterparts. In a 5–4 decision, the Court ruled that Ledbetter and other women could not seek redress of grievances for discrimination that had occurred over a period of years under the provisions of the Equal Pay Act. Justice Ruth Bader Ginsburg, the only woman on the Court at the time, took the uncommon action of reading her dissent from the bench. Speaking for herself and Justices David Souter, John Paul Stevens, and Stephen Breyer, she noted, "In our view, the Court does not comprehend, or is indifferent to, the insidious way in which women can be victims of pay discrimination."[26] In 2009, the first official act of President Barack Obama was to sign the Lilly Ledbetter Fair Pay Act, which overruled the Court's decision bearing her name.

Another important piece of legislation is Title VII of the Civil Rights Act of 1964, which prohibits gender discrimination by private (and, after 1972, public) employers. This act, too, has been the subject of much litigation. Key victories under Title VII include:

- Consideration of sexual harassment as sex discrimination.[27]
- Inclusion of law firms, which many argued were private partnerships, in the coverage of the act.[28]
- A broad definition of what can be considered sexual harassment, including same-sex harassment.[29]
- Allowance of voluntary programs to redress historical discrimination against women.[30]

Finally, **Title IX** of the Education Amendments of 1972 bars educational institutions receiving federal funds from discriminating against female students. Title IX, which parallels Title VII, greatly expanded the opportunities for women in elementary, secondary, and postsecondary institutions. Most of today's college students do not go through school being excluded from home economics or technology education classes because of their sex. Nor, probably do many attend schools that have no team sports for females. Yet, this was commonly the case in the United States prior to passage of Title IX.[31] Nevertheless, sport facilities, access to premium playing times, and quality equipment remain unequal in many high schools and colleges. Major rulings by the U.S. Supreme Court that uphold the provisions of Title IX include the following:

- Holding school boards or districts responsible for both student-on-student harassment and harassment of students by teachers.[32]
- Allowing retaliatory lawsuits by coaches on behalf of their sports teams denied equal treatment by school boards.[33]

Title IX

Provision of the Education Amendments of 1972 that bars educational institutions receiving federal funds from discriminating against female students.

Other Groups Mobilize for Rights

★ **5.5** . . . **Describe how other groups have mobilized in pursuit of their own civil rights.**

African Americans and women are not the only groups that have suffered unequal treatment under the law. Denial of civil rights has led many other disadvantaged groups to mobilize. Their efforts have many parallels to the efforts made by African Americans and women.

TIMELINE: Important Moments in Hispanic Rights

1910 Mexican Revolution—Political turmoil during the Mexican Revolution forces Mexicans to seek safety and employment in the United States.

1929 League of United Latin American Citizens Formed—Several service organizations unite, creating LULAC, the largest Hispanic service organization in the country.

1954 *Hernandez* v. *Texas*—Supreme Court rules that the Fourteenth Amendment's equal protection rights apply to other racial groups, including Hispanics.

1916 New Mexico Becomes a State—New Mexico is granted statehood as an officially bilingual member of the union.

1939 *Grapes of Wrath* Published—John Steinbeck's novel draws attention to the plight of migrant farm workers.

How did citizens learn about the plight of migrant farmers? John Steinbeck's *The Grapes of Wrath*, published in 1939, focused national attention on the plight of migrant workers in California's grape-growing industry.

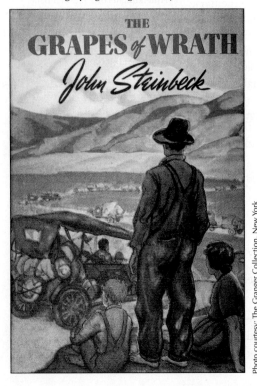

Hispanic Americans

Hispanics are the largest and fastest growing minority group in the United States. But, Hispanic population growth in the United States is not a new phenomenon. In 1910, the Mexican Revolution forced Mexicans seeking safety and employment into the United States. And, in 1916, New Mexico entered the union as an officially bilingual state—the only one in the United States.

These early Hispanic immigrants, many of whom were from families who had owned land when parts of the Southwest were still in Mexico's control, formed the League of United Latin American Citizens (LULAC) in 1929. LULAC continues to be the largest Hispanic organization in the United States, with local councils in every state and Puerto Rico.

As large numbers of immigrants from Mexico and Puerto Rico came to the United States, they quickly became a source of cheap labor, with Mexicans initially tending to settle in the Southwest, where they most frequently were employed as migratory farm workers, and Puerto Ricans mainly moving to New York City. Both groups tended to live in their own neighborhoods, where life was centered around the Roman Catholic Church and the customs of their homeland, and both groups largely lived in poverty. Still, in 1954, the same year as *Brown*, Hispanics won a major victory when in *Hernandez* v. *Texas*, the Supreme Court struck down discrimination based on ethnicity and class.[34] In *Hernandez*, the Court ruled unanimously that Mexican Americans were entitled to a jury that included other Mexican Americans.

A push for greater Hispanic rights began in the mid-1960s, just as a wave of Cuban immigrants began to establish homes in Florida,

1965 **Voting Rights Act of 1965**—The Voting Rights Act of 1965, among other innovations, requires bilingual ballots in Spanish speaking communities.

1973 *San Antonio Independent School District v. Rodriguez*— MALDEF fails to convince the Supreme Court that educational funds should be distributed equally among school districts.

1965 **United Farm Workers Union Founded**— The United Farm Workers Union, the largest farm workers union in the United States is well-known for coordinating strikes in California.

1968 **Legal Lobbying Groups Created**—MALDEF and the Puerto Rican Legal Defense and Education Fund are founded in the image of the NAACP LDF.

2006 *LULAC v. Perry*— The Supreme Court decides that a Texas redistricting plan does not intentionally limit Hispanic representation.

dramatically altering the political and social climate of Miami and other neighboring towns and cities. This new movement, marked by the establishment of the National Council of La Raza in 1968, included many tactics drawn from the African American civil rights movement, including sit-ins, boycotts, marches, and other activities designed to attract publicity to their cause. In one earlier example, in 1965, Cesar Chavez and Dolores Huerta organized migrant workers into the United Farm Workers Union, which would become the largest farm workers union in the nation, and led them in a strike against produce growers in California. This strike was eventually coupled with a national boycott of several farm products.

Hispanics also have relied heavily on litigation to secure legal change. Key groups are the Mexican American Legal Defense and Educational Fund (MALDEF) and the Puerto Rican Legal Defense and Educational Fund (renamed LatinoJustice PRLDEF). MALDEF was founded in 1968 after members of LULAC met with NAACP LDF leaders and, with their assistance, secured a $2.2-million start-up grant from the Ford Foundation. MALDEF was originally created to bring test cases before the Supreme Court to force school districts to allocate more funds to schools with predominantly low-income minority populations, to implement bilingual education programs, to force employers to hire Hispanics, and to challenge election rules and apportionment plans that undercount or dilute Hispanic voting power.

MALDEF has been successful in its efforts to expand voting rights and electoral opportunities to Hispanic Americans under the Voting Rights Act of 1965 (renewed in 2006 for ten years) and the U.S. Constitution's equal protection clause. In 1973, for example, it won a major victory when the Supreme Court ruled that multimember electoral districts (in which more than one person represents a single district) in Texas discriminated against African Americans and Hispanics.[35] In multimember systems, legislatures generally add members to larger districts instead of drawing smaller districts in which a minority candidate could get a majority of the votes necessary to win.

MALDEF's success in educational equity cases came more slowly. In 1973, for example, in *San Antonio Independent School District* v. *Rodriguez*, the Supreme Court refused to find that a Texas law under which the state appropriated a set dollar amount to each school district per pupil, while allowing wealthier districts to enrich educational programs from other funds, violated the equal protection clause of the Fourteenth Amendment.[36] In 1989, however, MALDEF won a case in which a state district judge elected by the voters of only a single county declared the state's entire method of financing public schools to be unconstitutional under the state constitution.[37] And, in 2004, it entered into a settlement with the state of California in a case brought four years earlier to address, in MALDEF's words, "the shocking inequities facing public school children across the state."[38]

MALDEF continues to litigate in a wide range of areas of concern to Hispanics. High on its agenda today are affirmative action, the admission of Hispanic students to state colleges and universities, health care for undocumented immigrants, and challenging redistricting practices that make it more difficult to elect Hispanic legislators. It also litigates to challenge many state redistricting plans to ensure that Hispanics are adequately represented. In 2006, for example, MALDEF and other Hispanic rights groups played a major role in *LULAC* v. *Perry*, challenging a redistricting plan created by the Texas Legislature, charging that the legislature's plan was designed intentionally to limit Hispanic representation in South Texas. The U.S. Supreme Court, however, disagreed.[39]

MALDEF is also at the fore of legislative lobbying for expanded rights. Since 2002, it has worked to oppose restrictions concerning driver's license requirements for undocumented immigrants, to gain greater rights for Hispanic workers, and to ensure that redistricting plans do not silence Hispanic voters. MALDEF also focuses on the rights of Hispanic immigrants and workers. (To learn more about a controversial state law designed to combat illegal immigration, see Politics Now: Brewer Signs Sweeping Immigration Measure.)

American Indians

American Indians are the first true Americans, and their status under U.S. law is unique. Under the U.S. Constitution, Indian tribes are considered distinct governments, a situation that has affected American Indians' treatment by Congress and the Supreme Court.

For years, Congress and the courts manipulated the law to promote the westward expansion of the United States. The Northwest Ordinance of 1787, passed by the Continental Congress, specified that "good faith should always be observed toward the Indians; their lands and property shall never be taken from them without their consent, and their property rights, and liberty, they shall never be invaded or disturbed, unless in just and lawful wars authorized by Congress." These strictures were not followed. During the eighteenth and nineteenth centuries, the U.S. government isolated Indians on reservations as it confiscated their lands and denied them basic political rights. Indian reservations were administered by the federal government, and American Indians often lived in squalid conditions.

With passage of the Dawes Act in 1887, however, the government switched policies to promote assimilation over separation. Each Indian family was given land within the reservation; the rest was sold to whites, thus reducing Indian lands from about 140 million acres to about 47 million. Moreover, to encourage American Indians to assimilate, their children were sent to boarding schools off the reservation, and native languages and rituals were banned. American Indians did not become U.S. citizens nor were they given the right to vote until 1924.

At least in part because tribes were small and scattered (and the number of Indians declining), American Indians formed no protest movement in reaction to these drastic policy changes. It was not until the 1960s that Indians began to mobilize. During this time, Indian activists, many trained by the American Indian Law Center at the University of New Mexico, began to file hundreds of test cases in the federal courts involving tribal fishing rights, tribal land claims, and the taxation of tribal profits. The Native American Rights Fund (NARF), founded in 1970, became the NAACP LDF of the Indian rights movement.

American Indians have won some very important victories concerning hunting, fishing, and land rights. American Indian tribes all over America have sued to reclaim lands they say were stolen from them by the United States, often more than 200 years ago. Today, these land rights allow American Indians to play host to a number of casinos across the country, a phenomenon that has resulted in billions of dollars for Indian tribes. These improvements in Indians' economic affairs have helped to increase their political clout. Tribes are donating to political campaigns of candidates predisposed to policies favorable to tribes. The Agua Caliente Band of Cahuilla Indians, for example, donated $7.5 million to political campaigns in just one year alone. These large expenditures, Indians claim, are legal, because as sovereign nations they are immune from federal and state campaign finance disclosure laws. It is likely that the political involvement of Indian tribes will continue to grow as their casinos—and the profits of those ventures—continue to proliferate.

Like the civil rights and women's rights movements, the movement for American Indian rights has had a radical as well as a more traditional branch. In 1973, for example, national attention was drawn to the plight of Indians when members of the radical American Indian Movement took over Wounded Knee, South Dakota, the site of the massacre of 150 Indians by the U.S. Army in 1890. Just two years before the protest, the treatment of Indians had been highlighted in Dee Brown's best-selling *Bury My Heart at Wounded Knee*, which in many ways served to mobilize public opinion against the oppression of American Indians in the same way *Uncle Tom's Cabin* had against slavery.[40] (To learn more about another controversy related to American Indians, see Join the Debate: Should Sports Teams Use American Indian Names and Mascots?)

THINKING GLOBALLY

Indigenous Rights

Chiapas is one of the poorest states in Mexico; it also boasts one of the largest concentrations of indigenous peoples, those people whose descendants were the original settlers of the region. In 1994, a rebel movement known as the Zapatistas took control of several Chiapas cities. Its leaders demanded better treatment by the federal government for the Chiapas people. The rebels' actions focused the world's attention on the plight of many indigenous groups in Central and South America.

The Mexican government met the Zapatista movement with a show of military force. However, the Roman Catholic Church helped arrange a cease-fire that held until 1995, when the military overran the Zapatista-controlled territory and the rebels fled into the mountains. Since then, an uneasy truce has returned, and the Zapatistas have moved away from violence and entered the political arena, calling for better public health clinics and schools. They have also sponsored an international meeting of indigenous groups from the western hemisphere. For its part, the Mexican government has undertaken some development programs, but critics refer to them as "pacification" programs designed to quiet the opposition rather than to solve social problems.

- What is a country's responsibility to its indigenous people?
- Should indigenous peoples enjoy any distinct or special rights? Why or why not?
- In thinking about the rights of indigenous peoples (including American Indians), should the priority be given to individual rights or group rights?

Asian and Pacific Island Americans

One of the most significant difficulties for Asian and Pacific Island Americans has been finding a Pan-Asian identity. Originally, Asian and Pacific Island Americans were far more likely to identify with their individual Japanese, Chinese, Korean, or Filipino heritage.[41] It was not until 1977 that the U.S. government decided to use "Asian and Pacific Island" for all of these origins. Even this identity has been challenged by

POLITICSNOW

Brewer Signs Sweeping Immigration Measure

April 24, 2010
Arizona Daily Star
azstarnet.com

By Doug Kreutz and Phil Villarreal

Defending its legality, Gov. Jan Brewer on Friday signed the toughest state law in the country designed to combat illegal immigration.

The governor rejected claims that the legislation, which gives police more power to stop and detain those not in this country legally, amounts to legalized racial profiling. She said the measure contains sufficient protections to individual constitutional rights. . . .

The governor pointed out in her statement that the new law prohibits police from using race or ethnicity as the sole factor in determining whether to pursue an inquiry.

But she conceded that it does permit either to be used as one factor for an officer's consideration. And she defended the language. . . .

"Police officers are going to be respectful," the governor continued. "They know what their jobs are, they've taken an oath. And racial profiling is illegal."

But Phoenix attorney David Selden, who was involved in unsuccessfully challenging a 2006 state law aimed at companies that knowingly hire illegal immigrants, said allowing race to be used as a factor at all is unconstitutional.

"That was a strategy used by white segregationists when they were trying to gut the (federal) civil-rights bill," he said. Selden suggested the same logic may be at work here.

"If they're not going to allow racial profiling, let's get 'race' out of it entirely," he said, rather than continuing to let police consider it. . . .

Attorney General Terry Goddard said those who challenge the law may have a case. . . .

Brewer brushed aside concerns that illegal immigrants who are crime victims or witnesses won't come forward, for fear of being questioned about their immigration status. That is based on language saying that when police officers make an official contact with anyone, a "reasonable attempt shall be made, when practicable, to determine the immigration status of the person." . . .

Critical Thinking Questions

1. Is this law a necessary step to combat illegal immigration? Explain your answer.
2. Should officers be allowed to consider race or ethnicity in immigration and border control cases? Why or why not?
3. How should the government balance immigration control and civil rights?

---

some subgroups; in the 1990s, native Hawaiians unsuccessfully requested to be categorized with American Indians, with whom they felt greater affinity.

Discrimination against Asian and Pacific Island immigrants developed over time in the United States. In 1868, Congress passed a law allowing free migration from China, but in 1882, Congress passed the Chinese Exclusion Act, which was the first act to restrict the immigration of any identifiable nationality. This legislation implicitly invited more discriminatory laws against the Chinese, which closely paralleled the Jim Crow laws affecting African Americans.

Several Supreme Court cases also slowed the progress of Asian and Pacific Island Americans. This began to change in 1886, when the Court decided the landmark case of *Yick Wo* v. *Hopkins* using the rational basis test highlighted in Table 5.1. A number of events precipitated this decision. Discriminatory provisions in the California Constitution prevented Chinese people from practicing many professions. However, the Chinese in California were allowed to open laundries. And, many immigrants did. In response to this growing trend, the city of San Francisco passed a ban on cleaners operating in wooden buildings, two-thirds of which

Join the DEBATE | Should Sports Teams Use American Indian Names and Mascots?

In November 2009, the U.S. Supreme Court refused to hear an appeal by a group of American Indians who had sued to force the National Football League's Washington Redskins to rename their team. The case was the most recent phase of a long struggle by American Indian groups to highlight the use of team names and mascots that they consider derogatory racial stereotypes or slurs. At the professional sports level, several other teams use similar names, including the Chicago Blackhawks, Atlanta Braves, and Kansas City Chiefs.

Across the United States, an estimated 2,500 schools and universities use American Indian mascots, including the University of Hawaii Rainbow Warriors, the University of North Dakota Fighting Sioux, and the University of Utah Utes. Facing pressure from the National Collegiate Athletic Association (NCAA), some schools have changed their names and mascots. St. John's University changed its team nickname from "the Redmen" to "the Red Storm" in 1995. In 2009, the College of William and Mary decided to keep "the Tribe" as its team nickname but dropped its American Indian mascot, choosing instead to use the griffin, a mythological figure. Florida State University sought and received permission from the Seminole tribe to use the Seminole name for their sports teams and mascot; the school emphasized that their use of the name was intended to honor and celebrate American Indian culture. However, some schools, including the University of Wisconsin–Madison and the University of Iowa, have refused to schedule games against schools with American Indian mascots. In addition, NCAA rules prohibit teams with offensive names or mascots from participating in post-season play.

Does the battle over sports teams' use of American Indian names and mascots represent political correctness run amok? Or does the use of American Indian names and mascots by sports teams perpetuate racial stereotypes? Should sports teams use American Indian names and mascots?

To develop an ARGUMENT FOR the use of American Indian names and mascots by sports teams, think about how:

■ **The use of American Indian names and mascots is a sign of respect and honor.** In what ways do using American Indian names and mascots promote awareness of and respect for American Indian culture?

■ **Many American Indians approve of the use of American Indian names for sports teams, as evidenced by the Florida State Seminoles.** If some American Indians approve of their use, is there any reason to change team names or mascots?

■ **The use of American Indian names for sports teams and mascots does not violate the civil rights of American Indians.** Does the use of symbols and names rise to a level of discrimination that necessitates governmental intervention or regulation? Even if some groups find the use of American Indian names and symbols offensive, does that constitute grounds to force teams to rename themselves?

To develop an ARGUMENT AGAINST the use of American Indian names and mascots by sports teams, think about how:

■ **The use of American Indian team names and mascots perpetuates racial stereotypes.** How do symbols like face paint and feathers feed into misperceptions about American Indian culture?

■ **American Indian leaders have campaigned against the use of American Indian names for sports teams and mascots since the 1960s.** Who should determine how symbols for a people or culture are used? Should American Indians have a right to determine how profit-making groups use names and symbols that represent them?

■ **No other racial groups are used as team names or mascots.** How would people react if a sports team called itself "the Asians," "the African Americans," or "the Hispanics"? If it is not acceptable to use these names, why is it acceptable to use "Indians," or worse, "Redskins"? How is using the name of an ethnic group, such as the "Fighting Irish" different (or not) from using the name of a racial group?

How were Japanese Americans treated during World War II? The internment of Japanese Americans during World War II was a low point in American history. In *Korematsu* v. *U.S.* (1944), the U.S. Supreme Court upheld the constitutionality of this action.

Photo courtesy: Russell Lee/Corbis

were owned by persons of Chinese ancestry. The Court in *Yick Wo* found that the law violated the Fourteenth Amendment in its application.[42]

In 1922, the Court took a step backward, ruling that Asian and Pacific Island Americans were not white and therefore not entitled to full citizenship rights.[43] Conditions became even worse, especially for those of Japanese descent, after the Japanese invasion of Pearl Harbor in 1941. In response to this action, President Franklin D. Roosevelt issued Executive Order 9066, which led to the internment of over 130,000 Japanese Americans, Italian Americans, and German Americans, some of whom were Jewish refugees. Over two-thirds of those confined to internment camps were U.S. citizens. The Supreme Court upheld the constitutionality of these camps in *Korematsu* v. *U.S.* (1944).[44]

During the 1960s and 1970s, Asian and Pacific Island Americans, like many other groups discussed in this chapter, began to organize for equal rights. Filipino farm workers, for example, joined with Mexicans to form the United Farm Workers Union. In 1973, the Movement for a Free Philippines emerged to oppose the government of Ferdinand Marcos, the president of the Philippines. Soon, it joined forces with the Friends of Filipino People, which ultimately established the Congress Education Project, a Washington, D.C.-based lobbying group. The Congress Education Project and other Asian and Pacific Island American organizations largely were opposed to the Vietnam War.

In the 1970s and 1980s, Japanese Americans mobilized, lobbying the courts and Congress for reparations for their treatment during World War II. In 1988, Congress passed the Civil Liberties Act, which apologized to the interned and their descendants and offered reparations to them and their families.

Today, myriad Asian and Pacific Island American groups target diverse political venues. In California, in particular, they have been successful in seeing more men and women elected at the local and state levels.

Gays and Lesbians

Until very recently, gays and lesbians have had an even harder time than other groups in achieving anything approximating equal rights.[45] However, gays and lesbians have, on average, far higher household incomes and educational levels than other minority groups, and they are beginning to convert these advantages into political clout at the ballot box. They have also recently benefited from changes in public opinion. Like African Americans and women, gays and lesbians have worked through the courts to achieve incremental legal change. In the late 1970s, the Lambda Legal Defense and Education Fund, the Lesbian Rights Project, and Gay and Lesbian Advocates and Defenders were founded by gay and lesbian activists dedicated to ending legal restrictions on the civil rights of homosexuals.[46] Although these groups have won important legal victories concerning HIV/AIDS discrimination, insurance policy survivor benefits, and even some employment issues, their progress has been slower in other areas.[47]

In 1993, for example, President Bill Clinton tried to ban discrimination against homosexuals in the armed services. Eventually, Clinton compromised with congressional and military leaders on what was called the "Don't Ask, Don't Tell" policy. Gays and lesbians would no longer be asked if they were homosexual, but they were barred from revealing their sexual orientation under threat of discharge from the service. Despite the compromise, thousands were discharged for their sexual orientation. The policy was called into question as the wars in Iraq and Afghanistan increased America's need for active-duty military personnel. In 2010, President Barack Obama's secretary of defense, Robert Gates, a holdover from the Bush administration, announced a more tolerant approach supported by many in the military.

In 2010, a federal district court judge ruled that the "Don't Ask" policy was unconstitutional. She also issued an injunction directing the Department of Defense to refrain from enforcing the policy. This injunction was reversed by the Ninth Circuit Court of Appeals and litigation continues.

The public's views toward homosexuality have also changed, as signaled by the Court's 1996 decision in *Romer* v. *Evans*.[48] In this case, the Court ruled that an amendment to the Colorado Constitution that denied homosexuals the right to seek protection from discrimination was unconstitutional under the equal protection clause of the Fourteenth Amendment. This paved the way for further legislative lobbying and litigation for gay rights.

The Supreme Court's decision in *Lawrence* v. *Texas* (2003) really put homosexual rights on the public agenda. (To learn more about *Lawrence,* see **chapter 4**.) In this case, the Court reversed an earlier ruling by finding a Texas state court that found a statute banning sodomy to be unconstitutional. Writing for the majority, Justice Anthony Kennedy stated, "[homosexuals'] right to liberty under the due process clause gives them the full right to engage in their conduct without intervention of the government."[49]

Following the Court's ruling in *Lawrence,* many Americans were quick to call for additional rights for homosexuals. Many corporations responded to this amplified call for equal rights. For example, Wal-Mart announced it would ban job discrimination based on sexual orientation. In addition, editorial pages across the country praised the Court's ruling, arguing that the national view toward homosexuality had changed.[50] In November 2003, the Massachusetts Supreme Court further agreed when it ruled that denying homosexuals the right to civil marriage was unconstitutional under the state's constitution. The U.S. Supreme Court later refused to hear an appeal of this case, paving the way for the legality of same-sex marriage.

While voters, legislators, and courts in more liberal states took action to legalize these unions, the right mobilized against them. In 2004, many conservative groups and Republican politicians made same-sex marriage a key issue. Initiatives or referenda prohibiting same-sex marriage were placed on eleven state ballots, and all were passed overwhelmingly by voters. Same-sex marriage bans were also on several state ballots in the 2006 midterm elections, but the issue seemed to lack the emotional punch of the 2004 effort in the context of plummeting presidential approval and the ongoing war in Iraq.

In 2008, California and Connecticut joined Massachusetts in legalizing same-sex marriages. Same-sex couples traveled to California, especially, to legally marry. But, in November 2008, California voters passed a ballot proposition amending the state constitution to make same-sex marriages illegal again. This provision continues to be litigated in federal court.

Americans with Disabilities

In the aftermath of World War II, many veterans returned to a nation unequipped to handle their disabilities. The Korean and Vietnam Wars made the problems of disabled veterans all the more clear. These veterans saw the successes of African Americans, women, and other minorities, and they too began to lobby for greater protection against discrimination.[51] In 1990, in coalition with other disabled people, veterans finally were able to convince Congress to pass the Americans with Disabilities Act (ADA). The statute defines a disabled person as someone with a physical or mental impairment that limits one or more "life activities," or who has a record of such impairment. It thus extends the protections of the Civil Rights Act of 1964 to all citizens with physical or mental disabilities. It guarantees access to public facilities, employment, and communication services. It also requires employers to acquire or modify work equipment, adjust work schedules, and make existing facilities accessible to those with disabilities.

In 1999, the U.S. Supreme Court issued a series of four decisions redefining and limiting the scope of the ADA. The cumulative impact of these decisions was to limit dramatically the number of people who can claim coverage under the act. Moreover, these cases "could profoundly affect individuals with a range of impairments—from diabetes and hypertension to severe nearsightedness and hearing loss—who are able to function in society with the help of medicines or aids but whose impairments may still make employers consider them ineligible for certain jobs."[52] Thus, pilots who need glasses to correct their vision cannot claim discrimination when employers fail to hire them even though their vision is correctable.[53] In the 2004 case of *Tennessee* v. *Lane*, however, the Court ruled 5–4 that disabled persons could sue states that failed to make reasonable accommodations to assure that courthouses are handicapped accessible.[54]

The largest national nonprofit organization lobbying for expanded civil rights for the disabled is the American Association of People with Disabilities (AAPD). Acting on behalf of the over 56 million Americans who suffer from some form of disability, it works in coalition with other disability organizations to assure that the ADA is implemented fully. AAPD was founded by activists who lobbied for the ADA and who recognized that "beyond national unity for ADA and our civil rights, people with disabilities did not have a venue or vehicle for working together for common goals."[55]

Who does the Americans with Disabilities Act protect? George Lane was the appellant in *Tennessee* v. *Lane* (2004), concerning the scope of the Americans with Disabilities Act, which guarantees the disabled access to public buildings among other protections. Lane was forced to crawl up two flights of stairs to attend a state court hearing on a misdemeanor charge. Had he not, he could have been jailed.

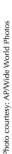

Photo courtesy: AP/Wide World Photos

TOWARD REFORM: Civil Rights and Affirmative Action

⭐ **5.6 . . . Evaluate the ongoing debate concerning civil rights and affirmative action.**

Many civil rights debates center on the question of equality of opportunity versus equality of results. Most civil rights and women's rights organizations argue that the lingering and pervasive burdens of racism and sexism can be overcome only by taking race or gender into account in fashioning remedies for discrimination. They argue that the U.S. Constitution is not and should not be blind to color or sex.

Other groups believe that if it was once wrong to use labels to discriminate against a group, it should be wrong to use those same labels to help a group. They argue that laws should be neutral, or color-blind. According to this view, quotas and other forms of **affirmative action,** policies designed to give special attention or compensatory treatment to members of a previously disadvantaged group, are unconstitutional.

The debate over affirmative action and equality of opportunity became particularly intense during the presidential administration of Ronald Reagan. Shortly before his election, in 1978, the Supreme Court for the first time fully addressed the issue of affirmative action. In *Regents of the University of California* v. *Bakke* (1978), a sharply divided Court concluded that Bakke's rejection for admission to the university of California at Davis' medical school had been illegal because the use of strict quotas was inappropriate.[56] The medical school, however, was free to "take race into account," said the Court.

Bakke was followed by a 1979 case in which the Court ruled that a factory and a union could voluntarily adopt a quota system in selecting black workers over more senior white workers for a training program.[57] These kinds of programs outraged blue-collar Americans who traditionally had voted for the Democratic Party. In 1980, they abandoned the party in droves to support Ronald Reagan, an ardent foe of affirmative action.

For a while, despite the addition of Reagan-appointed Justice Sandra Day O'Connor to the Court, the justices continued to uphold affirmative action plans, especially when there was clear-cut evidence of prior discrimination. In 1987, for example, the Court ruled for the first time that a public employer could use a voluntary plan to promote women even if there was no judicial finding of prior discrimination.[58]

In all these affirmative action cases, the Reagan administration strongly urged the Court to invalidate the plans in question, but to no avail. Changes on the Court, however, including the 1986 elevation of William H. Rehnquist, a strong opponent of affirmative action, to chief justice, signaled an end to the advances in civil rights law. In a three-month period in 1989, the Supreme Court handed down five civil rights decisions limiting affirmative action programs and making it harder to prove employment discrimination.

In February 1990, congressional and civil rights leaders unveiled legislation designed to overrule the Court's rulings, which, according to the bill's sponsor, "were an abrupt and unfortunate departure from its historic vigilance in protecting the rights of minorities."[59] The bill passed both houses of Congress but was vetoed by President Reagan's successor, George Bush, and Congress failed to override the veto. In late 1991, however, Congress and the White House reached a compromise on a weaker version of the civil rights bill, which was passed by overwhelming majorities in both houses of Congress. The Civil Rights Act of 1991 overruled all five Supreme Court rulings.

By 2002, the U.S. Supreme Court once again found the affirmative action issue ripe for review. In *Grutter* v. *Bollinger* (2003), the Court voted to uphold the

affirmative action
Policies designed to give special attention or compensatory treatment to members of a previously disadvantaged group.

constitutionality of the University of Michigan's law school admissions policy, which gave preference to minority applicants.[60] However, in a companion case, *Gratz* v. *Bollinger* (2003), the Court struck down Michigan's undergraduate point system, which gave minority applicants twenty automatic points simply because they were minorities.[61]

Taken together, these cases set the stage for a new era in affirmative action in the United States. Although the use of strict quotas and automatic points is not constitutional, the Court clearly believes that there is a place for some preferential treatment, at least until greater racial and ethnic parity is achieved. However, as Justice Sandra Day O'Connor noted in *Grutter*, "a program must remain flexible enough to ensure that each applicant is evaluated as an individual and not in a way that makes an applicant's race or ethnicity the defining feature of his or her application."

What Should I Have LEARNED?

Now that you have read this chapter, you should be able to:

⭐ **5.1 Trace the efforts from 1800 to 1890 of African Americans and women to win the vote, p. 136.**

When the Framers tried to compromise on the issue of slavery, they only postponed dealing with a volatile question that eventually would rip the nation apart. Ultimately, the Civil War brought an end to slavery. Among its results were the triumph of the abolitionist position and the adoption of the Thirteenth, Fourteenth, and Fifteenth Amendments. During this period, women also sought expanded rights, especially the right to vote, but to no avail.

⭐ **5.2 Outline developments in African Americans' and women's push for equality from 1890 to 1954, p. 140.**

Although the Civil War Amendments were added to the Constitution, the Supreme Court limited their application. As Jim Crow laws were passed throughout the South, the NAACP was founded in the early 1900s to press for equal rights for African Americans. Woman's groups also were active during this period, successfully lobbying for passage of the Nineteenth Amendment, which assured them the right to vote.

⭐ **5.3 Analyze the civil rights movement and the effects of the Civil Rights Act of 1964, p. 143.**

In 1954, the U.S. Supreme Court ruled in *Brown* v. *Board of Education* that racially segregated state school systems were unconstitutional. This victory empowered African Americans as they sought an end to other forms of pervasive discrimination. Bus boycotts, sit-ins, freedom rides, pressure for voting rights, and massive nonviolent demonstrations became common tactics. This culminated

in passage of the Civil Rights Act of 1964, which gave African Americans another weapon in their legal arsenal.

⭐ **5.4 Assess statutory and constitutional remedies for discrimination pursued and achieved by the women's rights movement, p. 147.**

After passage of the Equal Pay Act of 1963 and the Civil Rights Act of 1964, a new women's rights movement arose. Several women's rights groups were created. Some sought a constitutional amendment (the Equal Rights Amendment) as a remedy for discrimination; they felt this would elevate the standard of review for sex-based claims. In general, strict scrutiny, the most stringent standard, is applied to race-based claims and cases involving fundamental freedoms. An intermediate standard of review was developed to assess the constitutionality of sex discrimination claims. All other claims are subject to the rational basis test.

⭐ **5.5 Describe how other groups have mobilized in pursuit of their own civil rights, p. 151.**

Building on the successes of African Americans and women, other groups, including Hispanics, American Indians, Asian and Pacific Island Americans, gays and lesbians, and those with disabilities, organized to litigate for expanded civil rights and to lobby for anti-discrimination laws.

⭐ **5.6 Evaluate the ongoing debate concerning civil rights and affirmative action, p. 161.**

All of the groups discussed in this chapter have yet to reach full equality. One policy, affirmative action, which was designed to remedy education and employment discrimination, continues to be very controversial.

Test Yourself: Civil Rights

⭐ **5.1 Trace the efforts from 1800 to 1890 of African Americans and women to win the vote, p. 136.**

Why did Elizabeth Cady Stanton and Lucretia Mott found the first woman's rights movement in the nineteenth century?
  A. They escaped from slavery and joined forces with William Lloyd Garrison.
  B. After attending an abolitionist meeting, they concluded that women were not much better off than slaves.
  C. They were jailed for attempting to hold a women's rights convention in Seneca Falls in 1848.
  D. William Lloyd Garrison and Frederick Douglass left the Anti-Slavery Society after it did not allow women to participate in activities equally with men and encouraged them to pursue a new movement.
  E. The abolitionist publication *North Star* made comments implying women were undeserving of suffrage rights.

⭐ **5.2 Outline developments in African Americans' and women's push for equality from 1890 to 1954, p. 140.**

Which of the following strategies was NOT used by the NAACP Legal Defense and Educational Fund to extend civil rights to African Americans?
  A. Test case litigation
  B. *Amicus curiae* briefs
  C. Arguing cases such as *Brown* v. *Board of Education* before the Supreme Court
  D. Slowing the efforts of NAWSA to make rights of African Americans a top priority
  E. Mapping out a long-term plan that first targeted segregation in professional and graduate education

⭐ **5.3 Analyze the civil rights movement and the effects of the Civil Rights Act of 1964, p. 143.**

The Civil Rights Act of 1964 did all of the following EXCEPT
  A. create the Equal Employment Opportunity Commission.
  B. prohibit discrimination in employment because of a person's race, creed, color, religion, national origin, or sex.
  C. ban discrimination in public facilities.
  D. ban discrimination in private facilities.
  E. expedite voting rights lawsuits.

⭐ **5.4 Assess statutory and constitutional remedies for discrimination pursued and achieved by the women's rights movement, p. 147.**

What standard of review does the U.S. Supreme Court apply to practices involving alleged gender discrimination?
  A. Strict scrutiny
  B. Heightened standard
  C. Intermediate standard
  D. Minimum rationality
  E. Suspect class scrutiny

⭐ **5.5 Describe how other groups have mobilized in pursuit of their own civil rights, p. 151.**

Why has the extension of rights to Asian and Pacific Island Americans been difficult?
  A. The lack of a Pan-Asian identity has prevented a strong, cohesive movement from forming.
  B. Cases such as *Yick Wo* v. *Hopkins* (1886) gave some rights on the surface and seemed sufficient.
  C. Asian and Pacific Island Americans did not immigrate into the United States until after the turn of the twentieth century.
  D. The Vietnam War caused many Americans to view Asian and Pacific Island Americans negatively.
  E. There are too few Asian and Pacific Island Americans in the United States to have much national visibility.

⭐ **5.6 Evaluate the ongoing debate concerning civil rights and affirmative action, p. 161.**

Which of the following statements is true about the constitutionality of affirmative action programs in the United States?
  A. Affirmative action programs are widespread with virtually no limitations.
  B. Affirmative action programs have been deemed unconstitutional.
  C. Affirmative action programs can be used, but they must pass the strict scrutiny test.
  D. Numerical quotas are the only means by which affirmative action can be applied.
  E. The Supreme Court ruled that racial and ethnic parity have made affirmative action programs obsolete.

Essay Questions
  1. What is the significance of the Fourteenth Amendment of the U.S. Constitution in the fight for civil rights for racial minorities?
  2. How has test case litigation been used to guarantee civil rights for different groups in the United States?
  3. Why did the proposed Equal Rights Amendment spark such contentious debate?
  4. What are legal defense funds, and how have various defense funds worked for rights for minority groups?

mypoliscilab Exercises

Apply what you learned in this chapter on MyPoliSciLab.

Read on **mypoliscilab.com**

eText: Chapter 5

Study and **Review** on **mypoliscilab.com**

Pre-Test
Post-Test
Chapter Exam
Flashcards

Watch on **mypoliscilab.com**

Video: Supreme Court: No Race-Based Admissions
Video: Teen Sues for Equal Protection
Video: Should Don't Ask Don't Tell Go Away?

Explore on **mypoliscilab.com**

Simulation: You are the Mayor and Need to Make Civil
  Rights Decisions
Comparative: Comparing Civil Rights
Timeline: The Civil Rights Movement
Timeline: Women's Struggle for Equality
Timeline: The Mexican-American Civil Rights Movement
Timeline: The Struggle for Equal Protection
Visual Literacy: Race and the Death Penalty

Key Terms

affirmative action, p. 161
Black Codes, p. 138
Brown v. *Board of Education*
  (1954), p. 143
civil rights, p. 136
Civil Rights Act of 1964, p. 147
Civil Rights Cases (1883), p. 140
Equal Pay Act of 1963, p. 150

equal protection clause, p. 138
Equal Rights Amendment, p. 148
Fifteenth Amendment, p. 138
Fourteenth Amendment, p. 138
grandfather clause, p. 140
Jim Crow laws, p. 139
Nineteenth Amendment, p. 141
Plessy v. *Ferguson* (1896), p. 140

poll tax, p. 140
strict scrutiny, p. 149
suffrage movement, p. 141
suspect classification, p. 149
Thirteenth Amendment, p. 138
Title IX, p. 151

To Learn More on Civil Rights

In the Library

Anderson, Terry H. *The Pursuit of Fairness: A History of Affirmative Action.* New York: Oxford University Press, 2005.

Delgado, Richard. *Justice at War: Civil Liberties and Civil Rights During Times of Crisis.* New York: New York University Press, 2005.

Freeman, Jo. *The Politics of Women's Liberation.* New York: Backinprint.com, 2000.

Guinier, Lani, and Susan Sturm. *Who's Qualified?* Boston: Beacon, 2001.

Longmore, Paul, and Lauri Umansky. *The New Disability History: American Perspectives.* New York: New York University Press, 2001.

Mansbridge, Jane J. *Why We Lost the ERA.* Chicago: University of Chicago Press, 1986.

McClain, Paula D., and Joseph Stewart Jr. *"Can We All Get Along?": Racial and Ethnic Minorities in American Politics,* 4th ed. Boulder, CO: Westview, 2005.

McGlen, Nancy E., Karen J. O'Connor, Laura Van Assendelft, and Wendy Gunther-Canada. *Women, Politics, and American Society,* 5th ed. New York: Longman, 2010.

Reed, Adolph, Jr., ed. *Without Justice for All: The New Liberalism and Our Retreat from Racial Equity.* Boulder, CO: Westview, 2001.

Rodriguez, Clara E. *Changing Race: Latinos, the Census, and the History of Ethnicity in the United States.* New York: New York University Press, 2000.

Rosales, F. Arturo. *Chicano! The History of the Mexican American Civil Rights Movement.* Houston, TX: Arte Publico, 1996.

Wilkins, David E. *American Indian Politics and the American Political System.* New York: Rowman and Littlefield, 2006.

Williams, Juan. *Eyes on the Prize: America's Civil Rights Years, 1954–1965.* New York: Penguin, 1987.

Wilson, William Julius. *The Bridge over the Racial Divide: Rising Inequality and Coalition Politics*, 2nd ed. Berkeley: University of California Press, 2001.

Zia, Hellen. *Asian American Dreams: The Emergence of an American People*. New York: Farrar, Straus and Giroux, 2000.

On the Web

To learn more about the Civil Rights Division of the Department of Justice and its priorities, go to **www.usdoj.gov/crt/**.

To learn more about civil rights issues in the United States, go to **www.civilrights.org**, where a coalition of 150 civil rights organizations provides coverage of a host of civil rights issues as well as links to breaking news related to civil rights.

To learn more about the ACLU Women's Rights Project, go to **www.aclu.org/womensrights/index.html.**

To learn more about disability advocacy groups, go to the Web site for the American Association of People with Disabilities, **www.aapd.com.**

6 Congress

In March 2010, President Barack Obama signed into law the Patient Protection and Affordable Care Act. More commonly referred to as the health care reform bill, the legislation was one of the most aggressive attempts at health care reform in over forty years and the culmination of a journey that began on the campaign trail, with presidential candidate Obama and many Democratic members of Congress promising to pass a bill that would reform health care and provide health insurance to the more than 45 million Americans without medical coverage. This campaign promise, however, was not an easy one to fulfill.

From the beginning, Republicans universally opposed President Obama and the Democratic leadership's plan to reform health care. Even some moderate and conservative Democrats feared that supporting comprehensive reform

would hurt their chances of keeping their seats in the 2010 midterm elections. In order to assure that the legislation had enough votes to pass both houses of Congress, Speaker of the House Nancy Pelosi (D–CA) and Senate Majority Leader Harry Reid (D–NV) worked diligently to broker compromises between members. Proposals to provide universal health care coverage and provisions regarding public funding of abortions were contentious from the start; in the end, universal coverage did not survive the legislative process, and pro-life Democrats signed onto the bill only after President Obama promised to take action to assure that federal funds would not be used to pay for abortion procedures.

Throughout the legislative process, the president played an important role as a lobbyist. He sent prominent White House officials, including Chief of Staff Rahm

Congress has played a key role in enacting many of the major social policy reforms of the last century. At left, President Franklin D. Roosevelt signs a bill creating the Social Security program in 1935. At right, President Barack Obama signs the Patient Protection and Affordable Care Act of 2010.

Emanuel, to Capitol Hill to speak with members about the importance of reforming health care. The president also held a national summit addressing the major flaws in the American system of care and traveled around the country to build the grassroots support necessary to convince on-the-fence moderate Democrats to vote in favor of the bill.[1]

One reason it was so difficult to garner the necessary votes to pass this legislation is that members of Congress constantly worry about voting "incorrectly" or in ways that do not appeal to their constituencies. With the media and interest groups following every move and every vote, members know that constituents will find out if they are "out of step" with public opinion. And, ultimately, members of Congress depend on citizen approval if they wish to win reelection and stay in office.[2]

What Should I Know About . . .

After reading this chapter, you should be able to:

★ **6.1** Trace the roots of the legislative branch outlined by the U.S. Constitution, p. 168.

★ **6.2** Characterize the demographic attributes of members of Congress, and identify factors that affect their chances for reelection, p. 170.

★ **6.3** Assess the role of the committee system, political parties, and congressional leadership in organizing Congress, p. 174.

★ **6.4** Identify three of the most significant powers of Congress, p. 180.

★ **6.5** Analyze the factors that influence how members of Congress make decisions, p. 188.

★ **6.6** Evaluate the strategic interactions between Congress, the president, and the courts, p. 193.

The Framers' original conception of Congress's authority was much narrower than it is today. Those in attendance at the Constitutional Convention were concerned with creating a legislative body that would be able to make laws and raise and spend revenues. Over time, Congress has attempted to maintain these roles, but changes in the demands made on the national government have allowed the executive and judicial branches to gain powers at the expense of the legislative branch. Moreover, the power and the importance of individual members has grown.

Today, members of Congress must combine and balance the roles of lawmaker, budgeter, and policy maker with being a representative of their district, their state, their party, and sometimes their race, ethnicity, or gender. Not surprisingly, this balancing act often results in role conflict.

In this chapter, we will analyze the powers of Congress and the competing roles members of Congress play as they represent the interests of their constituents, make laws, and oversee the actions of the other two branches of government. We will also see that as these functions have changed throughout U.S. history, so has Congress itself.

- First, we will examine *the roots of the legislative branch of government.*

- Second, we will look at who *the members of Congress* are, including how members get elected and remain in office.

- Third, we will describe *how Congress is organized,* including the differences in House and Senate leadership and the way the committee system operates.

- Fourth, we will outline the three most significant *powers of Congress.*

- Fifth, we will analyze the factors that influence *how members make decisions.*

- Finally, we will investigate the ways that Congress, the president, and the judiciary *balance institutional power.*

ROOTS OF the Legislative Branch of Government

★ **6.1 . . . Trace the roots of the legislative branch outlined by the U.S. Constitution.**

Article I of the Constitution describes the structure of the legislative branch of government. As discussed in **chapter 2**, the Great Compromise at the Constitutional Convention resulted in the creation of an upper house, the Senate, and a lower house, the House of Representatives. Any two-house legislature, such as the one created by the Framers, is called a **bicameral legislature.** Each state is represented in the Senate by two senators, regardless of the state's population. The number of representatives each state sends to the House of Representatives, in contrast, is determined by that state's population.

bicameral legislature
A two-house legislature.

The U.S. Constitution sets out the formal, or legal, requirements for membership in the House and Senate. As agreed to at the Constitutional Convention, House members must be at least twenty-five years of age; senators, thirty. Members of the House are required to be citizens of the United States for at least seven years; those elected to the Senate must have been citizens for at least nine years. Both representatives and senators must be legal residents of the states from which they are elected.

Senators are elected for six-year terms, and originally they were chosen by state legislatures because the Framers intended for senators to represent their states' interests in the Senate. State legislators lost this influence over the Senate with the ratification of the Seventeenth Amendment in 1913, which provides for the direct election of senators by voters. Then, as now, one-third of all senators are up for reelection every two years.

Members of the House of Representatives are elected to two-year terms by a vote of the eligible electorate in each congressional district. The Framers expected that House members would be more responsible to the people, both because they were elected directly by them and because they were up for reelection every two years.

The U.S. Constitution requires that a census, which entails the counting of all Americans, be conducted every ten years. Until the first census could be taken, the Constitution fixed the number of representatives in the House of Representatives at sixty-five. In 1790, one member represented about 30,000 people. But, as the population of the new nation grew and states were added to the union, the House became larger and larger. In 1910, it expanded to 435 members, and in 1929, its size was fixed at that number by statute.

Each state is allotted its share of these 435 representatives based on its population. After each U.S. Census, the number of seats allotted to each state is adjusted by a constitutionally mandated process called **apportionment.** After seats are apportioned, congressional districts must be redrawn by state legislatures to reflect population shifts to ensure that each member in Congress represents approximately the same number of residents. This process of redrawing congressional districts to reflect increases or decreases in the number of seats allotted to a state, as well as population shifts within a state, is called redistricting. It is discussed in greater detail later in this chapter.

The Constitution specifically gives Congress its most important powers: the authorities to make laws and raise and spend revenues. No **bill,** or proposed law, can become law without the consent of both houses. Examples of other powers shared by both houses include the power to declare war, raise an army and navy, coin money, regulate commerce, establish the federal courts and their jurisdiction, establish rules of immigration and naturalization, and "make all Laws which shall be necessary and proper for carrying into Execution the foregoing Powers." As interpreted by the U.S. Supreme Court, the necessary and proper clause, found at the end of Article I, section 8, when coupled with one or more of the specific powers enumerated in Article I, section 8, has allowed Congress to increase the scope of its authority, often at the expense of the states.

Reflecting the different constituencies and size of each house of Congress (as well as the Framers' intentions), Article I gives special, exclusive powers to each house in addition to their shared role in law-making. For example, as noted in Table 6.1, the Constitution specifies that all revenue bills must originate in the House of Representatives. Over the years, however, this mandate has been blurred, and it is not unusual to see

One House or Two?

Among the nations of the world, the most common legislative model is the bicameral parliament, congress, or assembly, with a lower chamber and an upper chamber—as in the United Kingdom, Canada, Australia, and United States. However, a unicameral system—a single legislative body—is used in several industrialized democracies, including Denmark, Sweden, Israel, New Zealand, South Korea, and Singapore. Debate over which system promotes better governance continues today.

- What are the potential weaknesses of a unicameral system? Of a bicameral system?

- Why might some countries choose a unicameral system?

- How would replacing the U.S. House and Senate with a single body affect the legislative process?

apportionment
The process of allotting congressional seats to each state following the decennial census according to their proportion of the population.

bill
A proposed law.

Table 6.1 *What are the key differences between the House of Representatives and the Senate?*

Constitutional Differences	
House	**Senate**
435 voting members (apportioned by population)	100 voting members (two from each state)
Two-year terms	Six-year terms (one-third up for reelection every two years)
Initiates all revenue bills	Offers "advice and consent" on many major presidential appointments
Initiates impeachment procedures and passes articles of impeachment	Tries impeached officials
	Approves treaties

Differences in Operation	
House	**Senate**
More centralized, more formal; stronger leadership	Less centralized, less formal; weaker leadership
Committee on Rules fairly powerful in controlling time and rules of debate (in conjunction with the Speaker of the House)	No rules committee; limits on debate come through unanimous consent or cloture of filibuster
More impersonal	More personal
Power distributed less evenly	Power distributed more evenly
Members are highly specialized	Members are generalists
Emphasizes tax and revenue policy	Emphasizes foreign policy

Changes in the Institution	
House	**Senate**
Power centralized in the Speaker's inner circle of advisers	Senate workload increasing and institution becoming more formal; threat of filibusters more frequent than in the past
House procedures becoming more efficient	Becoming more difficult to pass legislation
Turnover is relatively high, although those seeking reelection almost always win	Turnover is moderate

impeachment

The power delegated to the House of Representatives in the Constitution to charge the president, vice president, or other "civil officers," including federal judges, with "Treason, Bribery, or other high Crimes and Misdemeanors." This is the first step in the constitutional process of removing government officials from office.

Who were the first sisters in Congress? U.S. Representatives Loretta and Linda Sanchez are the first sisters to serve in Congress. Many members come from political families.

Photo courtesy: George Bridges/KRT/Newscom

budget bills being considered simultaneously in both houses, especially since, ultimately, each house must approve all bills. The House also has the power of **impeachment,** or to charge the president, vice president, or other "civil Officers," including federal judges, with "Treason, Bribery, or other high Crimes and Misdemeanors." But, only the Senate is authorized to conduct impeachment trials, with a two-thirds yea vote being necessary before a federal official can be removed from office.

The Senate has the sole authority to approve major presidential appointments, including federal judges, ambassadors, and Cabinet- and sub-Cabinet-level positions. The Senate, too, must approve all presidential treaties by a two-thirds vote.

The Members of Congress

★ **6.2** . . . **Characterize the demographic attributes of members of Congress, and identify factors that affect their chances for reelection.**

Members must attempt to appease several constituencies—party leaders, colleagues, and lobbyists in Washington, D.C., and constituents at home.[3] In attempting to do so, members spend full days at home as well as in D.C. According to one study of House members, average representatives made about forty trips back home to their districts each year.[4] One journalist has aptly

Table 6.2 *What is a typical day like for a member of Congress?*

5:00 a.m.	Arrive at office.
7:00 a.m.	Give a tour of the U.S. Capitol to constituents.
8:00 a.m.	Eat breakfast with the House Shipbuilding Caucus.
9:00 a.m.	Meet with Speaker of the House and other members of Congress.
10:00 a.m.	Attend House Armed Services Committee hearing.
11:00 a.m.	Prepare for afternoon press conference, return phone calls, and sign constituent mail.
12:00 p.m.	Meet with constituents who want the member to join a caucus that may benefit the district.
1:00 p.m.	Read one of nine newspapers to keep track of current events.
2:00 p.m.	Attend Homeland Security Subcommittee hearing.
3:00 p.m.	Attend floor vote.
3:30 p.m.	Meet with group of high school students on front steps of Capitol.
4:15 p.m.	Return to office to sign more constituent mail and to meet with the American Heart Association.
5:00 p.m.	Attend Sustainable Energy and Environment Caucus meeting.
7:00 p.m.	Eat dinner with fellow members.
9:00 p.m.	Return to office to sign more constituent mail and read more newspapers.
11:00 p.m.	Leave office to go home.

Source: Adapted from Bob Clark, "A Day in the Life . . ." *Evening Tribune* (October 7, 2009).
www.eveningtribune.com Access date: October 20, 2010

described a member's days as a "kaleidoscopic jumble: breakfast with reporters, morning staff meetings, simultaneous committee hearings to juggle, back-to-back sessions with lobbyists and constituents, phone calls, briefings, constant buzzers interrupting office work to make quorum calls and votes on the run, afternoon speeches, evening meetings, receptions, fund-raisers, all crammed into four days so they can race home for a weekend gauntlet of campaigning. It's a rat race."[5] (To learn more about a day in the life of a member of Congress, see Table 6.2.)

Congressional Demographics

Congress is better educated, richer, more male, and more white than the general population. Over two-thirds of the members of the House and Senate also hold advanced degrees.[6]

Almost 250 members of Congress are millionaires. The Senate, in fact, is often called the Millionaires Club. The median net worth of a senator in 2010 was $1.7 million, while the median net worth of a House member was $75,000.[7] Many members of both houses have significant inherited wealth, but given their educational attainment, which is far higher than the average American's, it is not surprising to find so many wealthy members of Congress.

The average age of senators in the 112th Congress is sixty-three. Michael Lee (R–UT) is the youngest senator. The average age of House members is fifty-seven; Representative Aaron Schock (R–IL) was first elected to the House in 2008 and is still the youngest member of Congress.

As revealed in Figure 6.1, the 1992 elections saw a record number of women, African Americans, and

Figure 6.1 *How many women and minorities serve in Congress?*

Source: Data compiled by the authors.

other minorities elected to Congress. By the 112th Congress, the total number of women members decreased for the first time in recent history, with seventy in the House and seventeen in the Senate. The number of African Americans in the House increased to forty-two, including two African American Republicans. No African Americans served in the Senate. Twenty-seven Hispanics served in the House. Also serving in the 112th Congress are seven members of Asian or Pacific Island American heritage, and one American Indian, Tom Cole (R–OK). A record number—four—of openly homosexual members served in the House. Jewish members saw their numbers decrease about 10 percent to forty down from a historic high of forty-five in the last Congress.

Running For and Staying In Office

Despite the long hours and hard work required of senators and representatives, thousands of people aspire to these jobs every year. Yet, only 535 men and women (plus seven non-voting members) actually serve in the U.S. Congress. Membership in one of the two major political parties is almost always a prerequisite for election, because election laws in various states often discriminate against independents (those without party affiliation) and minor-party candidates. As discussed in **chapter 12**, the ability to raise money often is key to any member's victory, and many members spend nearly all of their free time on the phone dialing for dollars or attending fundraisers. Incumbency and redistricting also affect members' chances at reelection.

incumbency
Already holding an office.

INCUMBENCY   **Incumbency** helps members stay in office once they are elected.[8] It is often very difficult for outsiders to win because they don't have the advantages enjoyed by incumbents, including name recognition, access to free media, an inside track on fund-raising, and a district drawn to favor the incumbent. (To learn more about incumbency, see Table 6.3.) It is not surprising, then, that an average of 96 percent of the incumbents who seek reelection win their primary and general election races.[9] In 2010, only 87 percent of House members were reelected. Almost all who lost were Democrats, and this was the lowest reelection percentage since 1970.[10] In the Senate, however, 90 percent were reelected, the highest rate since 2004.

redistricting
The process of redrawing congressional districts to reflect increases or decreases in seats allotted to the states, as well as population shifts within a state.

REDISTRICTING   The process of redrawing congressional districts to reflect increases or decreases in seats allotted to the states, as well as population shifts within a state, is called **redistricting**. Redistricting is a largely political process. In most states, districts lines are drawn by partisan state legislatures. As a result, the majority party in the state legislature uses the redistricting process as an opportunity to ensure

Table 6.3 *What are the advantages of incumbency?*

- **Name recognition.** Members' names have been on the ballot before, and voters may associate their names with programs or social services they have brought to the district.
- **Credit claiming.** Members may claim to be responsible for federal money brought to the district.
- **Casework.** Members and their staffs help constituents solve problems with the government, including navigating red tape and tracking down federal aid.
- **Franking privilege.** Members may send mail or newsletters for free by using their signature in place of a stamp.
- **Access to media.** Members and their staffs may have relationships with reporters and be easily able to spin stories or give quotes.
- **Ease in fund-raising.** Incumbents' high reelection rates make them a safe bet for individuals or groups wanting to give donations in exchange for access.
- **Experience in running a campaign.** Members have already put together a campaign staff, made speeches, and come to understand constituent concerns.
- **Redistricting.** In the House, a member's district may be drawn to enhance electability.

formation of voting districts that protect their majority. Hoping to avoid this type of political conflict, some states, including Iowa and Arizona, appoint nonpartisan commissions or use some other independent means of drawing district lines. Although the processes vary in detail, most states require legislative approval of redistricting plans.

The redistricting process often involves **gerrymandering**—the drawing of congressional districts to produce a particular electoral outcome without regard to the shape of the district. Because of enormous population growth, the partisan implications of redistricting, and the requirement under the Voting Rights Act of 1965 for minorities to get an equal chance to elect candidates of their choice, legislators end up drawing oddly shaped districts to elect more members of their party.[11] (To learn more about gerrymandering, see Figure 6.2.)

The U. S. Supreme Court for a long time considered redistricting based on partisan considerations to be a political question that was not a matter of constitutional law, but rather a question to be worked out through the regular political process.[12] But, in recent years the Supreme Court has involved itself in some such cases and has ruled that:

- Congressional as well as state legislative districts must be apportioned on the basis of population.[13]

- District lines must be contiguous; you must be able to draw the boundaries of the district with one unbroken line.[14]

- Purposeful gerrymandering of a congressional district to dilute minority strength is illegal under the Voting Rights Act of 1965.[15]

- Redrawing districts to enhance minority representation is constitutional if race is not the "predominate" factor.[16]

- States may redistrict more than every ten years.[17]

gerrymandering
The drawing of congressional districts to produce a particular electoral outcome without regard to the shape of the district.

Figure 6.2 *What is gerrymandering?*

Two drawings—one a mocking cartoon, the other all too real—show the bizarre geographical contortions that result from gerrymandering. The term was coined by combining the last name of the Massachusetts governor first credited with politicizing the redistricting process, Elbridge Gerry, and the word "salamander," which looked like the oddly shaped district that Gerry created.

Sources: David Van Biema, "Snakes or Ladders?" *Time* (July 12, 1993) © 1993, Time Inc. Reprinted by permission. Illinois General Assembly.

How Congress Is Organized

⭐ **6.3 . . . Assess the role of the committee system, political parties, and congressional leadership in organizing Congress.**

majority party

The political party in each house of Congress with the most members.

minority party

The political party in each house of Congress with the second most members.

party caucus or conference

A formal gathering of all party members.

As demonstrated in Figure 6.3, the organization of both houses of Congress is closely tied to political parties and their strength in each house. The basic division in Congress is between majority and minority parties. The **majority party** is the political party in each house with the most members. The **minority party** is the political party in each house with the second most members. (To learn more about the partisan composition of the 112th Congress, see Figure 6.4.)

At the beginning of each new Congress—the 112th Congress, for example, will sit in two sessions, one in 2011 and one in 2012—the members of each party formally gather in their **party caucus or conference.** Historically, these caucuses have enjoyed varied powers, but today the party caucuses—now called caucus by the Democrats and conference by the Republicans—have several roles, including nominating or electing party officers, reviewing committee assignments, discussing party policy, imposing party discipline, setting party themes, and coordinating media, including talk radio. Conference and caucus chairs are recognized party leaders who work with other leaders in the House or Senate.[18]

Figure 6.3 *How are the House of Representatives and the Senate organized?*

Source: Adapted from Roger H. Davidson and Walter J. Oleszek, *Congress and its Members,* 10th ed. (Washington, DC: CQ Press, 2006.) Updated by the authors.

Figure 6.4 *What is the partisan composition of the 112th Congress?*

Senate
- Democratic
- Republican
- Split

Total
Democrats 51
Republicans 46
Independents 3

House of Representatives
- Republican seats
- Democratic seats
- Undecided seats*
- Republican majority
- Democratic majority
- Equal party membership

Total
Republicans 239
Democrats 189
Undecided 7*

*As of mid-November 2010.

Each caucus or conference has specialized committees that fulfill certain tasks. Senate Republicans, for example, have a Committee on Committees that makes committee assignments. The Democrats' Steering Committee performs this function. Each party also has House and Senate campaign committees to assist members in their reelection bids.

Leadership in the House of Representatives

Even in the first Congress in 1789, the House of Representatives was almost three times larger than the Senate. It is not surprising, then, that from the beginning the House has been organized more tightly, structured more elaborately, and governed by stricter rules. Traditionally, loyalty to the party leadership and voting along party lines has been more common in the House than in the Senate. House leaders also play a key role in moving the business of the House along. Historically, the Speaker of the House, the majority and minority leaders, and the Republican and Democratic House whips have made up the party leadership that runs the institution. This group now has been expanded to include deputy whips of both parties, as well as those who head the Democratic Caucus and the Republican Conference.

Speaker of the House

The only officer of the House of Representatives specifically mentioned in the Constitution; the chamber's most powerful position; traditionally a member of the majority party.

THE SPEAKER OF THE HOUSE   The **Speaker of the House** is the only officer of the House of Representatives specifically mentioned in the Constitution. The entire House of Representatives elects the Speaker at the beginning of each new Congress. Traditionally, the Speaker is a member of the majority party. Although typically not the member with the longest service, the Speaker generally has served in the House for a long time and in other House leadership positions as an apprenticeship.

The Speaker presides over the House of Representatives, oversees House business, and is the official spokesperson for the House, as well as being second in the line of presidential succession. Moreover, the Speaker is the House liaison with the president and generally has great political influence within the chamber. The Speaker is also expected to smooth the passage of party-backed legislation through the House.

majority leader

The head of the party controlling the most seats in the House of Representatives or the Senate; is second in authority to the Speaker of the House and in the Senate is regarded as its most powerful member.

minority leader

The head of the party with the second highest number of elected representatives in the House of Representatives or the Senate.

whip

Party leader who keeps close contact with all members of his or her party, takes vote counts on key legislation, prepares summaries of bills, and acts as a communications link within a party.

LEADERSHIP TEAMS   After the Speaker, the next most powerful people in the House are the majority and minority leaders, who are elected in their individual party caucuses or conferences. The **majority leader** is the head of the party controlling the most seats in the House; his or her counterpart in the party with the second highest number of seats is the **minority leader.** The majority leader helps the Speaker schedule proposed legislation for debate on the House floor.

The Republican and Democratic **whips,** who are elected by party members in caucuses, assist the Speaker and majority and minority leaders in their leadership efforts. The position of whip originated in the British House of Commons, where it was named after the "whipper in," the rider who keeps the hounds together in a fox hunt. Party whips—who were first designated in the U.S. House of Representatives in 1899—do, as their name suggests, try to whip fellow Democrats or Republicans into line on partisan issues. They try to maintain close contact with all members on important votes, prepare summaries of content and implications of bills, take vote counts during debates and votes, and in general get members to toe the party line. Whips and their deputy whips also serve as communications links, distributing word of the party line from leaders to rank-and-file members and alerting leaders to concerns in the ranks.

Leadership in the Senate

Organization and formal rules never have played the same role in the Senate that they do in the House. Through the 1960s, the Senate was a gentlemen's club whose folkways—unwritten rules of behavior—governed its operation. In the 1960s and 1970s, senators became more and more active on a variety of issues on and off the Senate floor, and extended debates often occurred on the floor without the rigid rules of courtesy that had once been the hallmark of the body. These changes have made the majority leader's role as coalition-builder extraordinarily challenging.[19]

president pro tempore

The official chair of the Senate; usually the most senior member of the majority party.

PRESIDING OFFICER   The Constitution specifies that the presiding officer of the Senate is the vice president of the United States. Because he is not a member of the Senate, he votes only in the case of a tie.

The official chair of the Senate is the **president pro tempore,** or pro tem, who is selected by the majority party and presides over the Senate in the absence of the vice president. The position of pro tem today is primarily an honorific office that generally goes to the most senior senator of the majority party. Once elected, the pro tem stays in that office until there is a change in the majority party in the Senate. Since presiding over the Senate can be a rather perfunctory duty, neither the vice president nor the president pro tempore actually perform the task very often. Instead, the duty of presiding over the Senate rotates among junior members of the majority party of the chamber, allowing more senior members to attend more important meetings.

MAJORITY LEADER   The true leader of the Senate is the majority leader, elected to the position by the majority party. Because the Senate is a smaller and more collegial body, the majority leader is not nearly as powerful as the Speaker of the House. Senate Majority Leader Harry Reid (D–NV) discovered the many difficulties that may face a Senate leader trying to coordinate members of his party and assure party loyalty, even in times of unified government. Most of these troubles were the result of struggles to assure loyalty of moderate Democratic members on important votes dealing with economic recovery and health care reform. As a result of these challenges, but also due to high unemployment and foreclosure rates in his home state of Nevada, Reid was thought to be one of the most vulnerable members of the Senate during the 2010 election. He ultimately was able to defeat tea party member Sharron Angle with help from many labor unions.

LEADERSHIP TEAMS   The minority leader and the Republican and Democratic whips round out the leadership positions in the Senate and perform functions similar to those of their House counterparts. But, leading and whipping in the Senate can be quite a challenge. Senate rules always have given tremendous power to individual senators; in most cases senators can offer any kind of amendments to legislation on the floor, and an individual senator can bring all work on the floor to a halt indefinitely through a filibuster unless three-fifths of the senators vote to cut him or her off.[20]

The Committee System

The saying "Congress in session is Congress on exhibition, whilst Congress in its committee rooms is Congress at work" may not be as true today as it was when Woodrow Wilson wrote it in 1885.[21] Still, "the work that takes place in the committee and subcommittee rooms of Capitol Hill is critical to the productivity and effectiveness of Congress."[22] Standing committees are the first and last places to which most bills go. Usually committee members play key roles in floor debate about the merits of bills that have been introduced. When different versions of a bill are passed in the House and Senate, a conference committee with members of both houses meets to iron out the differences. Committee organization and specialization are especially important in the House of Representatives because of its size. The establishment of subcommittees allows for even greater specialization.

TYPES OF COMMITTEES   There are four types of congressional committees: (1) standing; (2) joint; (3) conference; and, (4) select (or special).[23]

1. **Standing committees** are the committees to which bills are referred for consideration; they are so called because they continue from one Congress to the next.

2. **Joint committees** are standing committees that include members from both houses of Congress and are set up to conduct investigations or special studies. They focus public attention on major matters, such as the economy, taxation, or scandals.

3. **Conference committees** are special joint committees created to reconcile differences in bills passed by the House and Senate. A conference committee is made up of members from the House and Senate committees that originally considered the bill.

4. **Select (or special) committees** are temporary committees appointed for specific purposes, such as investigating the September 11, 2001, terrorist attacks.

standing committee
Committee to which proposed bills are referred; continues from one Congress to the next.

joint committee
Standing committee that includes members from both houses of Congress; set up to conduct investigations or special studies.

conference committee
Special joint committee created to reconcile differences in bills passed by the House and Senate.

select (or special) committee
Temporary committee appointed for a specific purpose.

In the 111th Congress, the House had nineteen standing committees, as shown in Table 6.4, each with an average of thirty-one members. Together, these standing committees had roughly ninety subcommittees that collectively acted as the eyes, ears, and hands of the House. They considered issues roughly parallel to those of the departments represented in the president's Cabinet.

Although most committees in one house parallel those in the other, the House Committee on Rules, for which there is no counterpart in the Senate, plays a key role in the House's law-making process. Indicative of the importance of the Committee on Rules, majority party members are appointed directly by the Speaker. This committee reviews most bills after they come from a committee and before they go to the full chamber for consideration. Performing a traffic cop function, the Committee on Rules gives each bill what is called a rule, which contains the date the bill will come up for debate and the time that will be allotted for discussion, and often specifies what kinds of amendments can be offered. Bills considered under a closed rule cannot be amended.

Standing committees have considerable power. They can kill bills, amend them radically, or hurry them through the process. In the words of former President Woodrow Wilson, once a bill is referred to a committee, it "crosses a parliamentary bridge of sighs to dim dungeons of silence from whence it never will return."[24]

Table 6.4 *What were the committees of the 111th Congress?*

Standing Committees	
House	**Senate**
Agriculture	Agriculture, Nutrition, & Forestry
Appropriations	Appropriations
Armed Services	Armed Services
Budget	Banking, Housing, & Urban Affairs
Education & Labor	Budget
Energy & Commerce	Commerce, Science, & Transportation
Financial Services	Energy & Natural Resources
Foreign Affairs	Environment & Public Works
Homeland Security	Finance
House Administration	Foreign Relations
Judiciary	Health, Education, Labor, & Pensions
Commercial & Administrative Law	Homeland Security & Governmental Affairs
The Constitution, Civil Rights, & Civil Liberties	Indian Affairs
Courts & Competition Policy	Judiciary
Crime, Terrorism, & Homeland Security	*Administrative Oversight & the Courts*
Immigration, Citizenship, Refugees, Border	*Antitrust, Competition Policy, & Consumer*
Security, & International Law	*Rights*
Task Force on Antitrust	*The Constitution*
Natural Resources	*Crime & Drugs*
Oversight & Government Reform	*Human Rights & the Law*
Rules	*Immigration, Refugees, & Border Security*
Science & Technology	*Terrorism, Technology, & Homeland Security*
Small Business	Rules & Administration
Standards of Official Conduct	Small Business & Entrepreneurship
Transportation & Infrastructure	Veterans Affairs
Veterans Affairs	
Ways & Means	

Select, Special, and Other Committees		
House	**Senate**	**Joint Committees**
Permanent Select Intelligence	Select Ethics	Economics
Select Committee on Energy	Select Intelligence	Taxation
Independence & Global Warming	Special Aging	Library of Congress
		Printing

Note: The subcommittees of the House and Senate Judiciary Committees during the 111th Congress are listed in italics.

Committees report out to the full House or Senate only a small fraction of the bills assigned to them. Bills can be forced out of a House committee by a **discharge petition** signed by a majority (218) of the House membership.

In the 111th Congress, the Senate had seventeen standing committees ranging in size from fifteen to twenty-nine members. It also had roughly seventy subcommittees, which allowed all majority party senators to chair at least one.

In contrast to the House, whose members hold few committee assignments (an average of 1.8 standing and three subcommittees), senators each serve on an average of three to four committees and seven subcommittees. Whereas the committee system allows House members to become policy or issue specialists, Senate members often are generalists. In the 111th Congress, Senator John Cornyn (R–TX), for example, served on several committees, including Finance, Judiciary, Budget, and Agriculture. He also served on several subcommittees and was a member of the Senate Republican leadership as chairman of the National Republican Senatorial Committee (NRSC).

Senate committees enjoy the same power over framing legislation that House committees do, but the Senate, being an institution more open to individual input than the House, gives less deference to the work done in committees. In the Senate, legislation is more likely to be rewritten on the floor, where all senators can generally participate and add amendments.

COMMITTEE CHAIRS   Committee chairs enjoy tremendous power and prestige. They are authorized to select all subcommittee chairs, call meetings, and recommend majority members to sit on conference committees. Committee chairs may even opt to kill a bill by refusing to schedule hearings on it. They also have a large committee staff at their disposal and are often recipients of favors from lobbyists, who recognize the chair's unique position of power. Personal skill, influence, and expertise are a chair's best allies.

Historically, committee chairs were the majority party members with the longest continuous service on the committee. Committee chairs in the House, unlike the Senate, are no longer selected by **seniority,** or time of continuous service on the committee. Instead, potential chairs are interviewed by party leaders to ensure that candidates demonstrate loyalty to the party. All committee chairs are limited to six years of service on a particular committee.

COMMITTEE MEMBERSHIP   Many newly elected members of Congress come into the body with their sights set on certain committee assignments. Others are more flexible. Many legislators seeking committee assignments inform their party's selection committee of their preferences. They often request assignments based on their own interests or expertise or on a particular committee's ability to help their prospects for reelection. One political scientist has noted that committee assignments are to members what stocks are to investors—they seek to acquire those that will add to the value of their portfolios.[25]

Some committees, such as Energy and Commerce, facilitate reelection by giving House members influence over decisions that affect large campaign contributors. Other committees, such as Education and the Workforce or Judiciary, attract members eager to work on the policy responsibilities assigned to the committee even

Why are senators policy generalists? One reason why senators must have such a broad base of knowledge is their many committee assignments. In the 111th Congress, Senator John Cornyn (R–TX), shown here, served on four different committees.

Photo courtesy: Office of Senator John Cornyn

discharge petition
Petition that gives a majority of the House of Representatives the authority to bring an issue to the floor in the face of committee inaction.

seniority
Time of continuous service on a committee.

if the appointment does them little good at the ballot box. Another motivator for certain committee assignments is the desire to have power and influence within the chamber. The Appropriations and Budget Committees provide that kind of reward for some members, given the monetary impact of the committees. Congress can approve programs, but unless money for them is appropriated in the budget, they are largely symbolic.

In both the House and the Senate, committee membership generally reflects the party distribution within that chamber. For example, at the outset of the 112th Congress, Republicans held a majority of House seats and thus claimed about a 56 percent share of the seats on several committees. On committees more critical to the operation of the House or to the setting of national policy, the majority often takes a disproportionate share of the slots. Since the Committee on Rules regulates access to the floor for legislation approved by other standing committees, control by the majority party is essential for it to manage the flow of legislation. For this reason, no matter how narrow the majority party's margin in the chamber, it makes up more than two-thirds of the Committee on Rules' membership.

Powers of Congress

⭐ **6.4 . . . Identify three of the most significant powers of Congress.**

As discussed in **chapter 2**, the Framers were interested in assuring that the national government had sufficient power to govern the states. Thus, Article I, section 7, of the Constitution details the procedures by which Congress can make laws and raise revenues. Article I, section 8, also details Congress's power to tax, spend, regulate commerce, coin money, and make "all Laws which shall be necessary and proper for carrying into Execution" those powers. (To learn more about Congress's powers over naturalization, see The Living Constitution: Article I, Section 8, Clause 4.)

Today, Congress not only makes laws dealing with substantive policy, but it also spends significant time negotiating and passing the nation's budget. In addition, in accordance with the system of checks and balances, it has a key oversight role. Through the War Powers Act, congressional review, approval of nominations, and impeachment, Congress can check the power of the executive and judicial branches.

The Law-Making Function

Congress's law-making power allows it to affect the day-to-day lives of all Americans and set policy for the future. Although proposals for legislation—be they about terrorism, Medicare, or tax policy—can come from the president, executive agencies, committee staffs, interest groups, or even private individuals, only members of the House or Senate can formally submit a bill for congressional consideration (although many are initially drafted by lobbyists). Once a bill is introduced by a member of Congress, it usually reaches a dead end. Of the approximately 10,000 bills introduced during the 111th session of Congress, fewer than 5 percent were made into law.

A bill must survive several stages or roadblocks before it becomes a law. It must be approved by one or more standing committees and both chambers, and, if House and Senate versions differ, each house must accept a conference report resolving those differences. These multiple points of approval provide many opportunities for members to revise the content of legislation and may lead representatives to alter their views on a particular piece of legislation several times over. Thus, it is much easier to defeat a bill than it is to get one passed. (To learn more about how a bill becomes a law, see Figure 6.5.)

The Living Constitution

The Congress shall have power . . . . to establish a uniform Rule of Naturalization.

—ARTICLE I, SECTION 8, CLAUSE 4

This clause places authority to draft laws concerning naturalization in the hands of Congress. Congress's power over naturalization is exclusive—meaning that no state can bestow U.S. citizenship on anyone. Citizenship is a privilege and Congress may make laws limiting or expanding the criteria.

The word *citizen* was not defined constitutionally until ratification in 1868 of the Fourteenth Amendment, which sets forth two kinds of citizenship: by birth and through naturalization. Throughout American history, Congress has imposed a variety of limits on naturalization, originally restricting it to "free, white persons." "Orientals" were excluded from eligibility in 1882. At one time, those affiliated with the Communist Party and those who lacked "good moral character" (a phrase that was construed to bar homosexuals, drunkards, gamblers, and adulterers) were deemed unfit for citizenship. These restrictions no longer carry the force of law, but they do underscore the power of Congress in this matter.

Congress continues to retain the right to naturalize large classes of individuals, as it did in 2000 when it granted automatic citizenship rights to all minor children adopted abroad as long as at least one adoptive parent was an American citizen. Naturalized citizens, however, do not necessarily enjoy the full rights of citizenship enjoyed by other Americans. Congress at any time, subject only to Supreme Court review, can limit the rights and liberties of naturalized citizens, especially in times of national crisis. In the wake of the September 11, 2001, terrorist attacks, when it was revealed that one-third of the forty-eight al-Qaeda-linked operatives who took part in some sort of terrorist activities against the United States were lawful permanent residents or naturalized citizens, Congress called for greater screening by the U.S. Bureau of Citizenship and Immigration Services for potential terrorists.

CRITICAL THINKING QUESTIONS

1. Is Congress the appropriate institution to have the power over immigration and naturalization? Why or why not?
2. Is racial profiling by the U.S. Bureau of Citizenship and Immigration Services and other government entities an appropriate action in the name of national security? Why or why not?
3. What action should Congress take to regulate immigration and naturalization in light of restrictive state laws such as the one adopted in Arizona (see **chapter 3**)?

COMMITTEE REFERRAL   The House and Senate have parallel processes, and often the same bill is introduced in each chamber at the same time. A bill must be introduced by a member of Congress, but, in an attempt to show support for the aims of the bill, it is often sponsored by several other members (called co-sponsors). Once introduced, the bill is sent to the clerk of the chamber, who gives it a number (for example, HR 1 or S 1—indicating House or Senate bill number one). The bill is then printed, distributed, and sent to the appropriate committee or committees for consideration.

The committee usually refers the bill to one of its subcommittees, which researches the bill and decides whether to hold hearings on it. The subcommittee

Figure 6.5 *How does a bill become a law?*

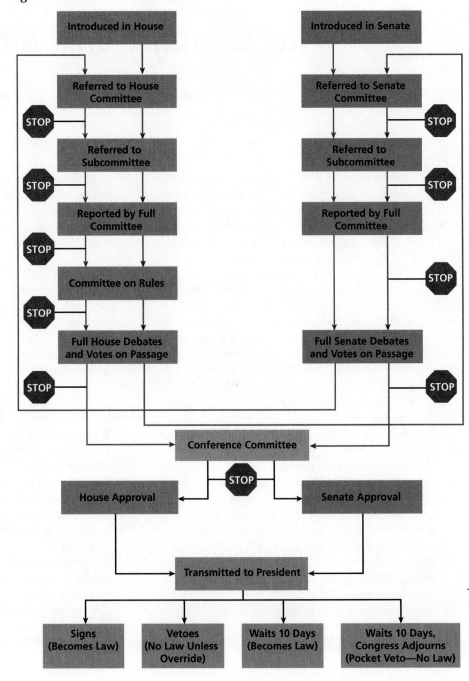

hearings provide the opportunity for those on both sides of the issue to voice their opinions. Since the passage of sunshine laws in the 1970s, most of these hearings are now open to the public. After the hearings, the bill is revised in subcommittee, and then the subcommittee votes to approve or defeat the bill. If the subcommittee votes in favor of the bill, it is returned to the full committee. There, it goes through **markup,** a session during which committee members can offer changes to a bill before it goes to the floor. The full committee may also reject the bill before it goes to the floor in either house.

THE WAR POWERS ACT   After years of playing second fiddle to a series of presidents from Theodore Roosevelt to Richard M. Nixon, a "snoozing Congress" was "aroused" and seized for itself the authority and expertise necessary to exercise its full foreign policy oversight powers over the chief executive.[26] In a delayed response to Lyndon B. Johnson's conduct of the Vietnam War, in 1973 Congress passed the **War Powers Act** over President Nixon's veto. This act requires presidents to obtain congressional approval before committing U.S. forces to a combat zone. It also requires them to notify Congress within forty-eight hours of committing troops to foreign soil. In addition, the president must withdraw troops within sixty days unless Congress votes to declare war. The president also is required to consult with Congress, if at all possible, prior to committing troops.

The War Powers Act, however, has been of limited effectiveness in claiming an oversight role for Congress in international crisis situations. Presidents Gerald R. Ford, Jimmy Carter, and Ronald Reagan never consulted Congress in advance of committing troops, citing the need for secrecy and swift movement, although each president did notify Congress shortly after the deployment of troops abroad. They contended that the War Powers Act was probably unconstitutional because it limits presidential prerogatives as commander in chief, as discussed in greater detail in **chapter 7**.

CONGRESSIONAL REVIEW   The Congressional Review Act of 1996 allows Congress to exercise its oversight powers by nullifying agency regulations. Under the home rule charter of the District of Columbia, the House and Senate may also nullify actions of the Washington, D.C. City Council. This process is called **congressional review**.[27] If Congress uses this oversight power, it has sixty days after the implementation of an administrative action to pass a joint resolution of legislative disapproval. The resolution must also be signed by the president.

CONFIRMATION OF PRESIDENTIAL APPOINTMENTS   The Senate plays a special oversight function through its ability to confirm key members of the executive branch, as well as presidential appointments to the federal courts. As discussed in **chapters 7 and 8**, although the Senate generally confirms most presidential nominees, it does not always do so. A wise president considers senatorial reaction before nominating potentially controversial individuals to his administration or to the federal courts.

In the case of federal district court appointments, senators often have considerable say in the nomination of judges from their states through **senatorial courtesy,** a process by which presidents generally defer to the senators who represent the state where the vacancy occurs. Despite this procedure, the judicial nominees of recent presidents have encountered particularly hostile Senates. "Appointments have always been the battleground for policy disputes," says one political scientist. But now, "what's new is the rawness of it—all of the veneer is off."[28]

IMPEACHMENT   As discussed earlier, the impeachment process is Congress's ultimate oversight of the U.S. president and federal court judges. The U.S. Constitution is quite vague about the impeachment process, and much of the debate about it concerns what constitutes an impeachable offense. The Constitution specifies that a president can be impeached for treason, bribery, or other "high crimes and misdemeanors." Most commentators agree that this phrase was intended to mean significant abuses of power.

House and Senate rules control how the impeachment process operates. Yet, because the process is used so rarely, and under such disparate circumstances, there are few hard and fast rules. The U.S. House of Representatives has voted to impeach only seventeen federal officials. Of those, seven were convicted and removed from office and three resigned before the process was completed.

War Powers Act
Passed by Congress in 1973; the president is limited in the deployment of troops overseas to a sixty-day period in peacetime (which can be extended for an extra thirty days to permit withdrawal) unless Congress explicitly gives its approval for a longer period.

congressional review
A process whereby Congress can nullify agency regulations by a joint resolution of legislative disapproval.

senatorial courtesy
A process by which presidents, when selecting district court judges, defer to the senators in whose state the vacancy occurs.

How Members Make Decisions

⭐ **6.5 . . . Analyze the factors that influence how members of Congress make decisions.**

Over the years, political theorists have offered various ideas about how constituents' interests are best represented in any legislative body. Does it make a difference if the members of Congress come from or are members of a particular group? Are they bound to vote the way their constituents expect them to vote even if they personally favor another policy? Your answer to these questions may depend on your view of the representative function of legislators.

British political philosopher Edmund Burke (1729–1797), who also served in the British Parliament, believed that although he was elected from Bristol, it was his duty to represent the interests of the entire nation. He reasoned that elected officials were obliged to vote as they personally thought best. According to Burke, a representative should be a **trustee** who listens to the opinions of constituents and then can be trusted to use his or her own best judgment to make final decisions.

A second theory of representation holds that a representative should be a **delegate.** True delegates are representatives who vote the way their constituents would want them to regardless of their own opinions. Delegates, therefore, must be ready and willing to vote against their conscience or personal policy preferences if they know how their constituents feel about a particular issue.

Not surprisingly, members of Congress and other legislative bodies generally don't fall neatly into either category. It is often unclear how constituents feel about a particular issue, or there may be conflicting opinions within a single constituency. With these difficulties in mind, a third theory of representation holds that a **politico** alternately dons the hat of a trustee or delegate, depending on the issue. On issues of great concern to their constituents, representatives most likely will vote as delegates; on other issues, perhaps those that are less visible, representatives will act as trustees and use their own best judgment.[29]

In addition to weighing their representational role, members of Congress consider a number of other factors when deciding how to vote on a piece of legislation. Among these are political parties, constituents, interest groups and lobbyists, and staff and support agencies.

trustee

Role played by an elected representative who listens to constituents' opinions and then uses his or her best judgment to make a final decision.

delegate

Role played by an elected representative who votes the way his or her constituents would want him or her to, regardless of his or her own opinions.

politico

Role played by an elected representative who acts as a trustee or as a delegate, depending on the issue.

Political Parties

The influence of political parties on members' votes cannot be underestimated. In fact, congressional party unity, a measure of the solidarity of the members of a political party, has reached historically high levels in recent years. As discussed in **chapter 11**, members of both the Democratic and Republican Parties in the House and Senate vote together on approximately 90 percent of all legislation considered by those bodies. (To learn more about the issue of partisanship, see Join the Debate: Is Partisanship Good for Democracy?)

The incentives for members to vote with their party also rarely have been higher—or more creative. In addition to offering members campaign support through party organizations or member-to-member political action committees (PACs), leadership in both houses may also offer committee assignments or chairs as rewards to members who toe the party line.

Constituents

Constituents—the people who live and vote in a representative's home district or state—are always in a member's mind when casting votes. It is rare for a legislator to vote against the wishes of his or her constituents regularly, particularly on issues of

Join the DEBATE | Is Partisanship Good for Democracy?

In recent years, bipartisanship has become a mantra used by many in American politics. In the 2008 presidential elections, both Senators John McCain and Barack Obama attempted to lay claim to the label, emphasizing their ability to work across the aisle. And, after he won the presidency, Barack Obama appointed Republicans to several high-profile positions. However, many observers criticized his claims of bipartisanship when he failed to consult in a meaningful way with Republicans in Congress on significant policy issues, such as health care reform. Meanwhile, although both the Republican and Democratic leadership have repeatedly emphasized their bipartisan credentials, members of Congress have voted with their parties about 90 percent of the time in recent Congresses.

But, bipartisanship may not always be a good thing. For example, when Representative Tom DeLay (R–TX) announced his retirement as House majority leader, he said, "You show me a nation without partisanship, and I'll show you a tyranny. For all its faults, it is partisanship, based on core principles, that clarifies our debates, that prevents one party from straying too far from the mainstream, and that constantly refreshes our politics with new ideas and new leaders."[a] Is partisanship good for democracy? Or, should the president and members of Congress strive for bipartisanship?

To develop an ARGUMENT FOR partisanship, think about how:

- **Partisanship produces stronger policies.** How might bipartisanship lead to watered down public policy? In what ways can partisanship improve legislative and policy proposals?
- **Partisanship protects democracy.** In what ways were the Framers' fears about partisanship unfounded? How are the rights of the minority, in particular, protected as a result of partisan divisions?
- **Partisanship reflects the will of the people.** How does the composition of Congress reflect the composition of the electorate? Should citizens have an absolute right to choose their representatives?

To develop an ARGUMENT AGAINST partisanship, think about how:

- **Partisanship results in political gridlock.** How do the rules of Congress, particularly the Senate, discourage partisanship? In what ways does the filibuster necessitate bipartisanship?
- **Partisanship is undemocratic.** With low voter turnout, how can a party that wins control of Congress be said to enjoy a popular mandate? In what ways does emphasizing bipartisanship in the political process increase the inclusiveness of the legislative process?
- **Partisanship does not reflect the will of the people.** How do public opinion polls demonstrate the American public's frustration with political bickering? In what ways would less partisanship improve political discourse in the country?

"Stop laughing."

Photo courtesy: Clay Bennett, Chattanooga Times Free Press

Is Congress making efforts to be less partisan? This cartoon expresses the opinion that, despite all the talk about a need for greater bipartisanship in Congress, in practice, Congress is as partisan as it has ever been.

---

[a]"Party Unity: An Ever Thicker Dividing Line," *CQ Weekly* (January 11, 2010): library.cqpress.com.

social welfare, domestic policy, or other highly salient issues. (To learn more about how constituents view their representatives, see Analyzing Visuals: Approval Ratings of Congress and Individual Representatives.)

Gauging how voters feel about any particular issue often is not easy. Because it is virtually impossible to know how the folks back home feel on all issues, a representative's perception of their constituents' preferences is important. Even when voters have opinions, legislators may get little guidance if their district is narrowly divided. Abortion is an issue about which many voters feel passionately, but a legislator whose district has roughly equal numbers of pro-choice and pro-life advocates can satisfy only a portion of his or her constituents.

Colleagues and Caucuses

logrolling
Vote trading; voting to support a colleague's bill in return for a promise of future support.

The range and complexity of issues confronting Congress means that no one can be up to speed on more than a few topics. When members must vote on bills about issues on which they know very little, they often turn for advice to colleagues who have served on the committee that handled the legislation. On issues that are of little interest to a legislator, **logrolling,** or vote trading, often occurs. Logrolling often takes place on specialized bills targeting money or projects to selected congressional districts. An unaffected member may exchange a yea vote now for the promise of a future yea vote on a similar piece of specialized legislation.

ANALYZING VISUALS

Approval Ratings of Congress and Individual Representatives

The line graph shows poll data from the Roper Center for Public Opinion. Poll respondents were asked: (1) "Do you approve or disapprove of the way Congress is handling its job?" and; (2) "Do you approve or disapprove of the way the representative from your district is handling his or her job?" Examine the line graph and then answer the questions.

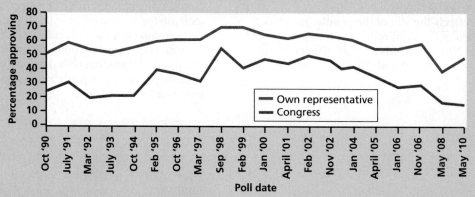

Source: Data derived from Lexis-Nexis RPOLL, Roper Center for Public Opinion.

■ What is the general trend for approval of Congress over the length of the graph? What about for approval of one's own representative?

■ Which factors might account for the differences in the ratings of Congress as a whole and one's own representative?

■ Why might approval ratings for Congress be significantly lower than those for individual members?

Members may also look to other representatives who share common interests. Special-interest caucuses created around issues, home states, regions, congressional class, or other commonalities facilitate this communication. Prior to 1995, these groups were more powerful. Several caucuses enjoyed formal status and were provided staff, office space, and budgets, which were ended by the Republican takeover. Today, however, all caucuses are informal in nature, although some, such as the Black and Hispanic Caucuses, are far more organized than others. The Congressional Caucus for Women's Issues, for example, has formal elections of its Republican and Democratic co-chairs and vice chairs, its members provide staff to work on issues of common concern to caucus members, and staffers meet regularly to facilitate support for legislation of interest to women. (To learn more about caucuses, see Politics Now: Congressional Caucus Puts Its Heft to Work on Behalf of Coal.)

Interest Groups, Lobbyists, and Political Action Committees

A primary function of most lobbyists, whether they work for interest groups, trade associations, or large corporations, is to provide information to supportive or potentially supportive legislators, committees, and their staffs. Organized interests can win over undecided legislators or confirm the support of their friends by providing information that legislators use to justify the position they have embraced. They also can supply direct campaign contributions, volunteers, and publicity to members seeking reelection.

The high cost of campaigning has made members of Congress, especially those without huge personal fortunes, attentive to those who help pay the tab for the high cost of many campaigns. Political action committees (PACs) organized by interest groups are a major source of most members' campaign funding. When an issue comes up that is of little consequence to a member's constituents, there is, not surprisingly, a tendency to support the positions of those interests who helped pay for the last campaign. After all, who wants to bite the hand that feeds him or her? (To learn more about PACs and interest groups, see **chapter 11**.)

Interest groups also use grass-roots appeals to pressure legislators by urging their members in a particular state or district to call, write, fax, e-mail, text, or tweet their senators or representatives. Lobbyists can't vote, but constituents back home can and do.

Staff and Support Agencies

Members of Congress rely heavily on their staffs for information on pending legislation.[30] House members have an average of seventeen staffers; senators have an average of forty. Staff are divided between D.C. and district offices. When a bill is nonideological or one on which the member has no real position, staff members can be very influential. In

How do staffers affect congressional decision making? Members of the Congressional Muslim Staffers Association such as Sarah Bassal (left) and Amina Rubin (right) work to educate policy makers about Islam and Islamic beliefs.

Photo courtesy: Jamie Rose/The New York Times/Redux

POLITICS**NOW**

| WORLD | NATION | LOCAL | **POLITICS** | OPINION | HEALTH & SCIENCE | ARTS | SPORTS | LEISURE |

Congressional Caucus Puts Its Heft to Work on Behalf of Coal

June 1, 2010
Pittsburgh Tribune-Review
www.pittsburghlive.com

By Debra Erdley

Under assault over safety and environmental issues, King Coal may have found a few friends: 81 members of Congress who came together last week for the first meeting of the new Congressional Coal Caucus.

The bipartisan caucus, co-chaired by McCandless Democrat Rep. Jason Altmire and West Virginia Republican Rep. Shelley Moore Capito, formed in January to provide a voice for coal-producing districts, a spokeswoman for Capito said.

That its first meeting took place one day after a congressional panel took testimony on the April 5 Upper Big Branch Mine explosion that killed 29 West Virginia coal miners was coincidental, Capito spokeswoman AshLee Strong said.

"The meeting had been in the planning before Upper Big Branch," she said.

Capito and Altmire attended the Upper Big Branch hearing in Beckley, W.Va. Altmire, who took part in questioning at the hearing, said the caucus will focus on coal's economic impact on states where the industry is active.

"I helped form this caucus because I wanted to provide a forum through which Republicans and Democrats could work together to advance policies that will capitalize on our nation's coal resources in a safe way," he said in a prepared statement.

The caucus' first meeting showcased a roundtable discussion among speakers from the mining, transportation and energy sectors, as well as a representative from the United Mine Workers of America.

Industry critics say the group is the coal industry's attempt to stave off proposed environmental regulations and shift public attention from questions about workplace safety as the Upper Big Branch investigation ramps up.

"What you're seeing now is the entire coal industrial complex trying to protect its stake, to buff up its image. Clearly, the coal industry is going to have to do a lot of public relations to find its way around Big Branch. . . . They are clearly circling the wagons, to sell a green image of coal," said Kert Davies of Greenpeace.

Lisa Camuso Miller, vice president of media affairs for the American Coalition for Clean Coal Electricity, an advocacy organization of coal, energy and transportation groups, said the group indeed is working to heighten public awareness of coal's primacy in the American energy market—and of the impact regulations could have on the industry and consumers.

The group's $30 million ad blitz includes highway billboards and TV spots.

"We're the guys who say we can be for the bill, as long as it is the right bill and it doesn't impose high energy rates on consumers. The consensus among our members is we want to develop legislation that is supportive of the industry," she said.

And not a day too soon, Mike Caputo said.

Caputo, 52, lives near Fairmont, W.Va., and went to work in the mines after high school. Today, he is a West Virginia legislator and international official with the UMWA.

Industry and labor need to work together to promote coal, Caputo said.

"Coal is certainly a focus right now, whether you're for it or against it," he said. "There are several environmental groups that would like to see the use of coal lessened or eliminated. Over 50 percent of this nation's energy is supplied by coal. Jobs are at stake. And No. 2, a much higher cost of energy for consumers is at stake."

Even so, Caputo said health and safety issues come first. "Not one pound of coal is worth one human life," he said.

Altmire insisted the caucus will not overlook safety.

"Given the fact that our caucus represents states where thousands of people go to work in the mines each day, mine safety issues are always at the forefront of our minds," he said.

Critical Thinking Questions

1. What are the advantages to forming congressional caucuses to work on particular policy issues? What are the disadvantages?

2. How important do you think caucuses are to members' decision-making processes?

3. Does the formation of congressional caucuses increase interest groups' access to the law-making process? Is this input beneficial?

many offices, they are the greatest influence on their boss's votes, and lobbyists are just as likely to contact key staffers as they are members.

Congressional committees and subcommittees also have their own dedicated staff to assist committee members. Additional support for members comes from support personnel at the Congressional Research Service (CRS) at the Library of Congress, the Government Accountability Office (GAO), and the Congressional Budget Office (CBO).

TOWARD REFORM: Balancing Institutional Power

★ **6.6 ... Evaluate the strategic interactions between Congress, the president, and the courts.**

The Constitution envisioned that the Congress, the president, and the judiciary would have discrete powers, and that one branch would be able to hold the other in check. Over the years, and especially since the 1930s, the president often has held the upper hand. In times of crisis or simply when it was unable to meet public demands for solutions, Congress willingly has handed over its authority to the chief executive. Even though the chief executive has been granted greater latitude, Congress does, of course, retain ultimate legislative authority to question executive actions and to halt administration activities by cutting off funds for programs a president wants. Similar checks and balances affect relations between Congress and the courts.

Congress and the Executive

The balance of power between Congress and the president has seesawed over time. The post–Civil War Congress attempted to regain control of the vast executive powers that President Abraham Lincoln, recently slain, had assumed. Angered at the refusal of Lincoln's successor, Andrew Johnson, to go along with its radical "reforms" of the South, Congress passed the Tenure of Office Act, which prevented the president, under the threat of civil penalty, from removing any Cabinet-level appointees of the previous administration. Johnson accepted the challenge and fired Lincoln's secretary of war, who many believed was guilty of heinous war crimes. The House voted to impeach Johnson, but the desertion of a handful of Republican senators prevented him from being removed from office. (The effort fell short by one vote.) Nonetheless, the president's power had been greatly weakened, and the Congress again became the center of power and authority in the federal government.

Beginning in the early 1900s, however, a series of strong presidents acted at the expense of congressional power. Theodore Roosevelt, Franklin D. Roosevelt, and Lyndon B. Johnson viewed the presidency as carrying with it enormous powers. Especially since the presidency of Franklin D. Roosevelt, Congress has ceded to the president a major role in the legislative process. Today, Congress often finds itself responding to executive-branch proposals.

Presidents George W. Bush and Barack Obama both had tremendous success in setting the congressional agenda and lobbying members of Congress to support their policy proposals. A variety of political circumstances aided them in these efforts. For example, for much of the last ten years, one party—first the Republicans and later the Democrats—controlled government. In addition, national emergencies such as the September 11, 2001, terrorist attacks and the 2008 economic crisis necessitated swift action by both Congress and the executive branch.

Congress and the Judiciary

As part of our system of checks and balances, the power of judicial review (discussed in **chapters 2 and 9**) gives the Supreme Court the ability to review the constitutionality of acts of Congress. Historically, the Court has used this power very carefully. From 1787 to 1987, the Supreme Court struck down only 127 federal laws for an average of less than one law per term. However, in recent years, the Court has been more willing to strike down congressional legislation; from 1987 to 2005, the Rehnquist Court invalidated thirty-three statutes, for an average of nearly two laws per term. Thus, Congress must be increasingly mindful of the Court's reaction when it enacts new laws for the nation.[31]

Congress also interacts with the judiciary in a number of other ways. No matter how busy federal judges are, it is ultimately up to Congress to determine the number of judges on each court, as well as the boundaries of judicial districts and circuits. Congress also sets the jurisdiction of the federal courts. During recent Congresses, for example, several members, unhappy with Supreme Court actions on abortion and gay rights, pushed for a bill to prevent federal courts from hearing challenges related to these civil liberties issues. When Congress rears the ugly head of jurisdiction, it is signaling to the federal courts that it believes federal judges have gone too far.

What Should I Have LEARNED?

Now that you have read this chapter, you should be able to:

★ 6.1 Trace the roots of the legislative branch outlined by the U.S. Constitution, p. 168.

The Constitution created a bicameral legislature with members of each body to be elected differently, and thus to represent different constituencies. Article I of the Constitution sets forth qualifications for office, states age minimums, and specifies how legislators are to be distributed among the states. The Constitution also requires seats in the House of Representatives to be apportioned by population. Thus, after every U.S. Census, district lines must be redrawn to reflect population shifts. The Constitution also provides a vast array of enumerated and implied powers to Congress. Some, such as law-making and oversight, are shared by both houses of Congress; others, such as confirmation of presidential appointees, are not.

★ 6.2 Characterize the demographic attributes of members of Congress, and identify factors that affect their chances for reelection, p. 170.

Members of Congress live in two worlds—in their home districts and in the District of Columbia. They must attempt to appease two constituencies—party leaders, colleagues, and lobbyists in Washington, D.C., and constituents in their home districts. In general, members of Congress are better educated, richer, more likely to be male, and more likely to be white than the makeup of the general population, and membership in one of the two major parties is almost always a prerequisite for election, as is the ability to raise money. When it comes to reelection, incumbency and redistricting also affect members' chances.

★ 6.3 Assess the role of the committee system, political parties, and congressional leadership in organizing Congress, p. 174.

Political parties play a major role in the way Congress is organized. The Speaker of the House is traditionally a member of the majority party, and other leadership roles such as majority and minority leaders and whips are also controlled by the parties. In addition to the party leaders, Congress has a labyrinth of committees and subcommittees that cover the entire range of government policies, often with a confusing tangle of shared responsibilities. It is in these environments that many policies are shaped and that members make their primary contributions to solving public problems.

★ 6.4 Identify three of the most significant powers of Congress, p. 180.

The three most significant powers of Congress are its law-making, budgetary, and oversight functions. The road to enacting a bill into law is long and strewn with obstacles, and only a small share of the proposals introduced become law. The Congressional Budget Act of 1974 solidified Congress's role in the budget process. Congress conducts oversight in a number of ways, including through hearings. Congress also offers advice and consent on executive and judicial branch nominees and has the power to impeach federal officials and remove them from office.

★ 6.5 Analyze the factors that influence how members of Congress make decisions, p. 188.

Members' view of their representational role—as trustees, delegates, or politicos—influences how they make policy decisions. Legislators may also consider a number of other factors, including political party, constituents, colleagues and caucuses, staff and support agencies, and interest groups, lobbyists, and political action committees. When a bill is nonideological or one on which a member has no real position, staff members may be the greatest influence on how a member of Congress votes.

★ **6.6 Evaluate the strategic interactions between Congress, the president, and the courts, p. 193.**

The balance of power between Congress and the executive branch has fluctuated tremendously over time. Although Congress was most powerful in the early years of U.S. history, since the New Deal, the president has played an important role in proposing legislation and spending. Congress and the judiciary also have an ongoing power struggle. Although the judiciary can declare acts of Congress unconstitutional, Congress also exercises control over the judiciary in a variety of ways. It has the constitutional authority to establish the size of the Supreme Court, its appellate jurisdiction, and the structure of the federal court system.

Test Yourself: Congress

★ **6.1 Trace the roots of the legislative branch outlined by the U.S. Constitution, p. 168.**

The structure of the legislative branch of government is set out in _____ of the Constitution.
A. Article I
B. Article II
C. Article III
D. Article IV
E. Article VII

★ **6.2 Characterize the demographic attributes of members of Congress, and identify factors that affect their chances for reelection, p. 170.**

Which of the following is NOT an advantage of incumbency?
A. Franking privilege
B. Name recognition
C. Access to the media
D. Easier fund-raising
E. Guaranteed reelection

★ **6.3 Assess the role of the committee system, political parties, and congressional leadership in organizing Congress, p. 174.**

Which of the following is the main organizational vehicle in the House and Senate?
A. Political parties
B. Factions formed of multiparty coalitions
C. Strong nonpartisan leaders
D. Interest group alliances
E. Subcommittees

★ **6.4 Identify three of the most significant powers of Congress, p. 180.**

The practice that allows for unlimited debate in the Senate is called
A. a hold.
B. senatorial courtesy.
C. a filibuster.
D. cloture.
E. grandstanding.

★ **6.5 Analyze the factors that influence how members of Congress make decisions, p. 188.**

When members of Congress must vote on a bill that is nonideological or one on which they have no specific position, what are the most powerful influences?
A. Interest groups
B. Aides or staff members
C. Support agencies
D. Constituents
E. Media

★ **6.6 Evaluate the strategic interactions between Congress, the president, and the courts, p. 193.**

With regard to the federal judiciary, both houses of Congress have the power to do all of the following EXCEPT
A. establish the size of the Supreme Court.
B. set federal jurisdiction.
C. modify the Supreme Court's appellate jurisdiction.
D. approve or reject presidential appointments.
E. determine the number of judges on lower federal courts.

Essay Questions
1. What are the key differences between the House and Senate?
2. What are the roles of the leaders in the House and Senate, and how do they differ from one another?
3. How is the budget passed in Congress?
4. What is the role and importance of congressional oversight?

mypɵliscilab Exercises

Apply what you learned in this chapter on MyPoliSciLab.

Read on **mypolisilab.com**

eText: Chapter 6

Study and **Review** on **mypoliscilab.com**

Pre-Test
Post-Test
Chapter Exam
Flashcards

Watch on **mypolisilab.com**

Video: Unknown Wins South Carolina Senate Primary
Video: Kagan Hearing

Explore on **mypoliscilab.com**

Simulation: How a Bill Becomes a Law
Simulation: You Are a Member of Congress
Comparative: Comparing Legislatures
Timeline: The Power of the Speaker of the House
Visual Literacy: Congressional Redistricting
Visual Literacy: Why is it So Hard to Defeat an Incumbent?

Key Terms

apportionment, p. 169
bicameral legislature, p. 168
bill, p. 169
cloture, p. 183
conference committee, p. 177
Congressional Budget Act of 1974, p. 184
congressional review, p. 187
delegate, p. 188
discharge petition, p. 179
earmark, p. 186
filibuster, p. 183
gerrymandering, p. 173
hold, p. 183

impeachment, p. 170
incumbency, p. 172
joint committee, p. 177
logrolling, p. 190
majority leader, p. 176
majority party, p. 174
markup, p. 182
minority leader, p. 176
minority party, p. 174
party caucus or conference, p. 174
pocket veto, p. 183
politico, p. 188
pork, p. 185
president pro tempore, p. 176

reconciliation, p. 185
redistricting, p. 172
select (or special) committee, p. 177
senatorial courtesy, p. 187
seniority, p. 179
Speaker of the House, p. 176
standing committee, p. 177
trustee, p. 188
veto, p. 183
War Powers Act, p. 187
whip, p. 176

To Learn More on Congress

In the Library

Adler, E. Scott, and John S. Lapinski, eds., *The Macropolitics of Congress.* Princeton, NJ: Princeton University Press, 2006.

Binder, Sarah A. *Stalemate: Causes and Consequences of Legislative Gridlock.* Washington, DC: Brookings Institution, 2003.

Cox, Gary W., and Mathew D. McCubbins. *Setting the Agenda: Responsible Party Government in the U.S. House of Representatives.* New York: Cambridge University Press, 2005.

Davidson, Roger H., Walter J. Oleszek, and Frances E. Lee. *Congress and Its Members,* 12th ed. Washington, DC: CQ Press, 2009.

Dodd, Lawrence C. *Thinking About Congress: Essays on Congressional Change.* New York: Routledge, 2011.

Dodd, Lawrence C., and Bruce I. Oppenheimer, eds. *Congress Reconsidered,* 9th ed. Washington, DC: CQ Press, 2008.

Evans, Diana. *Greasing the Wheels: Using Pork Barrel Projects to Build Majority Coalitions in Congress.* New York: Cambridge University Press, 2004.

Fenno, Richard F., Jr. *Home Style: House Members in Their Districts,* reprint ed. New York: Longman, 2002.

Mayhew, David R. *Congress: The Electoral Connection,* 2nd ed. New Haven, CT: Yale University Press, 2004.

Miler, Kristina C. *Constituency Representation in Congress: The View from Capitol Hill.* New York: Cambridge University Press, 2010.

Oleszek, Walter J. *Congressional Procedures and the Policy Process,* 8th ed. Washington, DC: CQ Press, 2010.

Price, David E. *The Congressional Experience: A View from the Hill,* 3rd ed. Boulder, CO: Westview Press, 2005.

Quirk, Paul J., and Sarah A. Binder, eds. *Institutions of American Democracy: The Legislative Branch*. New York: Oxford University Press, 2006.

Smith, Steven S. *Party Influence in Congress*. New York: Cambridge University Press, 2007.

Theriault, Sean M. *Party Polarization in Congress*. New York: Cambridge University Press, 2008.

On the Web

To learn more about the Senate, go to its official Web site at **www.senate.gov**.

To learn more about the House of Representatives, go to its official Web site at **www.house.gov**.

To learn more about the legislative branch, go to the Library of Congress's home page, named Thomas, in honor of President Thomas Jefferson, at **thomas.loc.gov**.

To learn more about members of Congress, go to Project Vote Smart at **www.votesmart.org**. Project Vote Smart is a nonpartisan group dedicated to providing U.S. citizens with the factual information they need to be informed voters.

THE NATION MOURNS.

7 The Presidency

When Ronald Reagan died on June 5, 2004, many Americans, first in California and then in Washington, D.C., lined up for hours to pay their respects to the man who had been the fortieth president of the United States. Many people were able to see, for the first time in recent memory, the grandeur of a presidential state funeral. Reagan was the first president to lie in state in the Rotunda of the Capitol since Lyndon B. Johnson died in January 1973, and one of only nine American presidents to receive that honor.

Presidential funerals underscore the esteem with which most Americans accord the office of the president, regardless of its occupant. Just before the first president, George Washington, died, he made it known that he wanted his burial to be a quiet one, "without parade or funeral oration." He also asked that he not be buried for three days; at that time, it was not without precedent to make this kind of request out of fear of being buried alive. Despite these requests, Washington's funeral was a state occasion as hundreds of soldiers, with their rifles held backward, marched to Mount Vernon, Virginia, where he was interred. Across the nation, imitation funerals were held, and the military wore black armbands for six months.[1]

When President Abraham Lincoln was assassinated in 1865, his funeral became a nationwide event. He laid in state in the East Room of the White House, where more than 25,000 mourners came to pay their respects. The room was draped in black cloth, and two dozen Union soldiers formed an honor guard. Following the funeral, a parade to the Capitol was held in Washington, D.C. Thousands of free blacks escorted the body to the Rotunda, where Lincoln laid in state for another day. The body of the deceased president then embarked on a national train tour to Springfield, Illinois, allowing Americans across the country an opportunity to grieve.

Presidential funerals have been occasions for national mourning since the death of the first president, George Washington. At left, the nation mourns President Abraham Lincoln, the first American president to be assassinated. At right, former presidents and vice presidents and their wives attend a funeral service for President Ronald Reagan in the National Cathedral in Washington, D.C. prior to his interment in California.

Today, one of the first things a president is asked to do upon taking office is to consider funeral plans. The military has a 138-page long book devoted to the kind of ceremony and traditions that were so evident in the Reagan funeral: a horse-drawn caisson; a riderless horse with boots hung backward in the stirrups to indicate that the deceased will ride no more; a twenty-one-gun salute; and a flyover by military aircraft. Each president's family, however, has personalized their private, yet also public opportunity to mourn. The Reagan family, for example, filed a 300-page plan for the funeral in 1989 and updated it regularly. Former president Gerald R. Ford filed a plan that was implemented after his death in 2006. Presidents Jimmy Carter and George Bush have also filed formal plans; Bill Clinton, George W. Bush, and Barack Obama have yet to do so.

The Reagan funeral also created a national time-out from the news of war, and even presidential campaigns were halted in respect for the deceased president. One historian commented that the event gave Americans the opportunity to "rediscover . . . what holds us together instead of what pulls us apart."[2] This is often the role of presidents—in life or in death.

What Should I Know About . . .

After reading this chapter, you should be able to:

★ 7.1 Trace the development of the presidency and the provisions for choosing and replacing presidents, p. 200.

★ 7.2 Identify and describe the constitutional powers of the president, p. 203.

★ 7.3 Evaluate the development and expansion of presidential power, p. 209.

★ 7.4 Outline the structure of the presidential establishment and the functions of each of its components, p. 212.

★ 7.5 Explain the concept of presidential leadership, and analyze the importance of public opinion, p. 214.

★ 7.6 Assess the president's role as policy maker, p. 217.

The authority granted to the president by the U.S. Constitution and through subsequent congressional legislation makes it a position with awesome power and responsibility. Not only did the Framers not envision such a powerful role for the president, but they could not have foreseen the skepticism with which many presidential actions are now greeted in the press, on talk radio, and on the Internet.

The modern media, used by successful presidents to help advance their agendas, have brought us closer to our presidents and made them seem more human, a mixed blessing for those trying to lead. Only two photographs exist of President Franklin D. Roosevelt in a wheelchair; his paralysis was a closely guarded secret. Five decades later, presidential candidate Bill Clinton was asked on national TV what kind of underwear he preferred (briefs).

Public opinion and confidence are key components of a president's ability to get his programs adopted and his vision of the nation implemented. As one political scientist has noted, the president's power often rests on his power to persuade.[3] To persuade, he not only must be able to forge links with members of Congress, but he also must have the support of the American people and the respect of foreign leaders.

The tension between public expectations about the presidency and the formal powers of the president permeate our discussion of how the office has evolved from its humble origins in Article II of the Constitution to its current stature. In this chapter:

- First, we will examine *the roots of the office of president of the United States* and discuss how the Framers created a chief executive officer for the new nation.

- Second, we will discuss *the constitutional powers of the president.*

- Third, we will explore *the development and expansion of presidential power* and a more personalized presidency.

- Fourth, we will investigate the development of *the presidential establishment,* the myriad departments, special assistants, and advisers who help the president.

- Fifth, we will examine *presidential leadership and the importance of public opinion,* including the effect that public opinion has on the American presidency.

- Finally, we will explore *the president's role as policy maker.*

ROOTS OF the Office of President of the United States

★ **7.1 . . . Trace the development of the presidency and the provisions for choosing and replacing presidents.**

Under the Articles of Confederation, there was no executive branch of government; the eighteen different men who served as the president of the Continental Congress of the United States of America were president in name only—they held no actual authority or power in the new nation. When the delegates to the Constitutional Convention met in Philadelphia to fashion a new government, there was little dissention about the need for an executive branch to implement the laws made by Congress. Although some delegates suggested there should be multiple executives, eventually the Framers agreed that executive authority should be vested in one person. This agreement was relatively seamless because the Framers were sure that George Washington—whom they had trusted with their lives during the Revolutionary War—would become the first president of the new nation.

The manner of the president's election haunted the Framers for some time, and their solution to the dilemma—the creation of the Electoral College—is described in detail in **chapter 12**. We leave the resolution of that issue aside for now and turn instead to details of the issues the Framers resolved quickly.

Presidential Qualifications and Terms of Office

The Constitution requires that the president (and the vice president, whose major function is to succeed the president in the event of his death or disability) be a natural-born citizen of the United States, at least thirty-five years old, and a resident of the United States for at least fourteen years.

At one time the length of a president's term was controversial. Four-, seven-, and eleven-year terms with no eligibility for reelection were suggested by various delegates to the Constitutional Convention. The Framers ultimately reached agreement on a four-year term with eligibility for reelection. In the 1930s and 1940s, however, Franklin D. Roosevelt ran successfully in four elections as Americans fought first the Great Depression and then World War II. Despite Roosevelt's popularity, negative reaction to his long tenure in office ultimately led to passage (and ratification in 1951) of the **Twenty-Second Amendment.** It limits presidents to two four-year terms. A vice president who succeeds a president due to death, resignation, or impeachment is eligible for a total of ten years in office: two years of a president's remaining term and two elected terms, or more than two years of a president's term followed by one elected term.

During the Constitutional Convention, Benjamin Franklin was a staunch supporter of including a provision allowing for **impeachment,** the first step in a formal process to remove a specified official from office. He noted that "historically, the lack of power to impeach had necessitated recourse to assassination."[4] Not surprisingly, then, Franklin urged the rest of the delegates to formulate a legal mechanism to remove the president and vice president.

The impeachment provision ultimately included in Article II was adopted as a check on the power of the president. As we discussed in detail in **chapter 6**, each house of Congress was given a role to play in the impeachment process to assure that the chief executive could be removed only for "Treason, Bribery, or other high Crimes and Misdemeanors." The House is empowered to vote to impeach the president by a simple majority vote. The Senate then acts as a court of law and tries

Twenty-Second Amendment
Adopted in 1951; prevents a president from serving more than two terms, or more than ten years if he came to office via the death, resignation, or impeachment of his predecessor.

impeachment
The power delegated to the House of Representatives in the Constitution to charge the president, vice president, or other "civil officers," including federal judges, with "Treason, Bribery, or other high Crimes and Misdemeanors." This is the first step in the constitutional process of removing government officials from office.

Who serves as president of the United States? Before Barack Obama, all of the people who served as president were white men. Here, five former presidents—Richard M. Nixon, Gerald R. Ford, Jimmy Carter, Ronald Reagan, and George Bush—gather to celebrate the opening of the Reagan Presidential Library in 1991.

Photo courtesy: AP/Wide World Photos

Presidential Term Limits

In the United States, presidents are limited to two four-year terms in office. This is not true everywhere. Presidential terms in office vary from country to country. And, some countries have additional restrictions on the presidency. The table shows the presidential term limits and special conditions present in various countries.

Country	Length of Term	Term Limits
Italy	7 years	none
Iceland	4 years	none
Mexico	6 years	1 term
Russia	4 years	2 terms
Brazil	4 years	2 terms

- How long should a president's term be?

- Why do some countries place limits on the number of terms that a president can serve while others do not?

- Should the U.S. Constitution be amended to allow presidents to serve more than two terms? Why or why not?

executive privilege

An implied presidential power that allows the president to refuse to disclose information regarding confidential conversations or national security to Congress or the judiciary.

U.S. v. Nixon (1974)

Supreme Court ruling on power of the president, holding that there is no absolute constitutional executive privilege allowing a president to refuse to comply with a court order to produce information needed in a criminal trial.

Twenty-Fifth Amendment

Adopted in 1967 to establish procedures for filling vacancies in the office of president and vice president as well as providing for procedures to deal with the disability of a president.

the president for the charged offenses with the chief justice of the U.S. Supreme Court presiding. A two-thirds majority vote in the Senate on any count contained in the articles of impeachment is necessary to remove the president from office.

In 1974, President Richard M. Nixon resigned from office rather than face the certainty of impeachment, trial, and removal from office for his role in covering up details about a break-in at the Democratic Party's national headquarters in the Watergate office complex. What came to be known simply as Watergate also produced a major decision from the Supreme Court on the scope of what is termed **executive privilege**. In **U.S. v. Nixon (1974)**, the Supreme Court ruled unanimously that there was no overriding executive privilege that sanctioned the president's refusal to comply with a court order to produce information for use in the trial of the Watergate defendants.

Rules of Succession

Through 2010, eight presidents have died in office from illness or assassination. William H. Harrison was the first president to die in office—he caught a cold at his inauguration in 1841 and died one month later. John Tyler thus became the first vice president to succeed to the presidency. In 1865, Abraham Lincoln became the first president to be assassinated.

The Framers were aware that a system of orderly transfer of power was necessary; this was the primary reason they created the office of the vice president. To further clarify the order of presidential succession, in 1947, Congress passed the Presidential Succession Act, which lists—in order—those in line (after the vice president) to succeed the president. (To learn more about the order of succession, see Table 7.1.)

The Succession Act has never been used because there has always been a vice president to take over when a president died in office. The **Twenty-Fifth Amendment,** in fact, was added to the Constitution in 1967 to assure that this will continue to be the case. Should a vacancy occur in the office of the vice president, the Twenty-Fifth Amendment directs the president to appoint a new vice president, subject to the approval (by a simple majority) of both houses of Congress. (To learn more, see The Living Constitution: Twenty-Fifth Amendment, Section 2.)

Table 7.1 *What is the presidential line of succession?*

1. Vice President	10. Secretary of Commerce
2. Speaker of the House	11. Secretary of Labor
3. President Pro Tempore of the Senate	12. Secretary of Health and Human Services
4. Secretary of State	13. Secretary of Housing and Urban Development
5. Secretary of the Treasury	14. Secretary of Transportation
6. Secretary of Defense	15. Secretary of Energy
7. Attorney General	16. Secretary of Education
8. Secretary of the Interior	17. Secretary of Veterans Affairs
9. Secretary of Agriculture	18. Secretary of Homeland Security

The Living Constitution

Whenever there is a vacancy in the office of the Vice President, the President shall nominate a Vice President who shall take office upon confirmation by a majority vote of both Houses of Congress.

—TWENTY-FIFTH AMENDMENT, SECTION 2

This clause of the Twenty-Fifth Amendment allows a president to fill a vacancy in the office of vice president with the consent of a simple majority of both Houses of Congress. The purpose of this amendment, which also deals with vacancies in the office of the president, was to remedy some structural flaws in Article II. When this amendment to the Constitution was proposed in 1965 (it was ratified in 1967), seven vice presidents had died in office and one had resigned. For over 20 percent of the nation's history there had been no vice president to assume the office of the president in case of his death or infirmity. When John F. Kennedy was assassinated, Vice President Lyndon B. Johnson became president and the office of vice president was vacant. Since Johnson had suffered a heart attack as vice president, members of Congress were anxious to remedy the problems that might occur should there be no vice president.

Richard M. Nixon followed Johnson as president, and during Nixon's presidency, the office of the vice president became empty twice. First, Vice President Spiro T. Agnew was forced to resign in the wake of charges of bribe taking, corruption, and income-tax evasion while an elected official in Maryland. He was replaced by popular House Minority Leader Gerald R. Ford (R–MI), who had no trouble getting a majority vote in both houses of Congress to confirm his nomination. When Nixon resigned rather than face sure impeachment, Ford became president and selected the former governor of New York, Nelson A. Rockefeller, to be his vice president. This chain of events set up for the first time in U.S. history a situation in which neither the president nor the vice president had been elected to those positions.

CRITICAL THINKING QUESTIONS

1. Why wasn't the Twenty-Fifth Amendment proposed until 1965? Why might a vice president be more necessary today than in the past?
2. Is it appropriate in a representative democracy to ever have a situation where both the president and the vice president have not been popularly elected?
3. What could be an alternative method by which a person could become vice president in the event of a vacancy? How would this method be an improvement over the current constitutional protocol?

The Constitutional Powers of the President

★ 7.2 . . . **Identify and describe the constitutional powers of the president.**

In contrast to Article I's laundry list of enumerated powers for the Congress, Article II details few presidential powers. Perhaps the most important section of Article II is its first sentence: "The executive Power shall be vested in a President of the United States of America." Nonetheless, the sum total of the president's powers, enumerated below, allows him to become a major player in the policy process.

The Appointment Power

To help the president enforce laws passed by Congress, the Constitution authorizes him to appoint, with the advice and consent of the Senate, "Ambassadors, other public Ministers and Consuls, judges of the supreme Court, and all other Officers of the United

How do presidents choose their political appointees? Presidents look for loyalty, honesty, and integrity when making appointments. Often they rely on friends and advisors to fill vacant positions. Here Vice President Joe Biden and President Barack Obama celebrate the nomination of Solicitor General Elena Kagan to the Supreme Court.

Photo courtesy: Win McNamee/Getty Images

States, whose Appointments are not herein otherwise provided for, and which shall be established by Law." Although this section of the Constitution deals only with appointments, behind that language is a powerful policy-making tool. The president has the authority to make nearly 3,500 appointments to his administration (of which just over 1,000 require Senate confirmation). He also has the power to remove many of his appointees at will. In addition, he technically appoints more than 75,000 military personnel. Many of these appointees are in positions to wield substantial authority over the course and direction of public policy. And, especially in the context of his ability to make appointments to the federal courts, his influence can be felt far past his term of office.

It is not surprising, then, that selecting the right people is often one of a president's most important tasks. Presidents look for a blend of loyalty, competence, and integrity. Identifying these qualities in people is a major challenge that every new president faces. Recent presidents have made an effort to create staffs that, in President Bill Clinton's words, look "more like America."

In the past, when a president forwarded a nomination to the Senate for its approval, his selections traditionally were given great respect—especially those for the **Cabinet,** an advisory group selected by the president to help him make decisions and execute the laws. In fact, until recently, the vast majority (97 percent) of all presidential nominations were confirmed.[5] This is no longer the case, as investigations into nominees' pasts and political wrangling in the Senate can delay the approval of nominees for months.

Delay or rejection of nominees can have a major impact on the course of an administration. Rejections leave a president without first choices, affect a president's relationship with the Senate, and affect how the president is perceived by the public. One method presidents have for persuading Congress to approve or disapprove nominees quickly is to make temporary appointments while Congress is in recess (thus, without congressional approval). For example, President Barack Obama's threats to use recess appointments after Congress delayed confirmation of sixty-three of his nominees led Congress to confirm twenty-seven nominees in one day.

Cabinet

The formal body of presidential advisers who head the fifteen executive departments. Presidents often add others to this body of formal advisers.

The Power to Convene Congress

The Constitution requires the president to inform the Congress periodically of "the State of the Union," and authorizes the president to convene either one or both houses of Congress on "extraordinary Occasions." In *Federalist No. 77*, Hamilton justified the latter by noting that because the Senate and the chief executive enjoy concurrent powers to make treaties, "It might often be necessary to call it together with a view to this object, when it would be unnecessary and improper to convene the House of Representatives." The power to convene Congress was more important when Congress did not sit in nearly year-round sessions.

THE PRESIDENT'S MANY ROLES

Chief law enforcer: Troops sent by President Dwight D. Eisenhower enforce a federal court decision ordering the integration of public schools in Little Rock, Arkansas.

Photo courtesy: Getty Images

Leader of the party: President Ronald Reagan mobilized conservatives and changed the nature of the Republican Party.

Photo courtesy: Bettmann/Corbis

Commander in chief: President George. W. Bush speaks about the war in Iraq on aircraft carrier *USS Abraham Lincoln.*

Photo courtesy: AP/Wide World Photos

Shaper of public policy: President Richard M. Nixon cheers on the efforts of Apollo 11 astronauts as he celebrates U.S. space policy.

Key player in the legislative process: President Bill Clinton celebrates newly passed legislation at a bill signing ceremony.

Photo courtesy: AP/Wide World Photos

Chief of state: President John F. Kennedy and his wife Jacqueline pose for cameras with the president of France and his wife during the Kennedys' widely publicized 1961 trip to that nation.

Photo courtesy: Bettmann/Corbis

Photo courtesy: MPI/Getty Images

The Power to Make Treaties

The president's power to make treaties with foreign nations is checked by the Constitution's stipulation that all treaties must be approved by at least two-thirds of the members of the Senate. The chief executive can also "receive ambassadors," wording that has been interpreted to allow the president to recognize the existence of other nations.

The Senate also may require substantial amendment of a treaty prior to its consent. When President Jimmy Carter proposed the controversial Panama Canal Treaty in 1977 to turn the canal over to Panama, for example, the Senate required several conditions to be ironed out before approving the canal's return.

Presidents may also "unsign" treaties, a practice often met with dismay from other signatories. For example, the George W. Bush administration formally withdrew its support for the International Criminal Court (ICC), the first permanent court to prosecute war crimes, genocide, and other crimes against humanity. Critics of the treaty argued that it could lead to politically motivated charges against U.S. troops in Afghanistan and Iraq.[6]

executive agreements

Formal international agreements entered into by the president that do not require the advice and consent of the U.S. Senate.

Presidents also often try to get around the constitutional "advice and consent" of the Senate requirement for ratification of treaties and the congressional approval requirement for trade agreements by entering into **executive agreements,** which allow the president to form secret and highly sensitive arrangements with foreign nations without Senate approval. Presidents have used these agreements since the days of George Washington, and their use has been upheld by the courts. Although executive agreements are not binding on subsequent administrations, since 1900 they have been used far more frequently than treaties, further cementing the role of the president in foreign affairs. (To learn more about the president's attempts to juggle relations with other nations, see Politics Now: With Home Trouble, Obama Faces Hard Choices on Trips.)

Veto Power

veto power

The formal, constitutional authority of the president to reject bills passed by both houses of Congress, thus preventing them from becoming law without further congressional action.

In keeping with the system of checks and balances, then, the president was given the **veto power,** but only as a "qualified negative." Although the president was given the authority to veto any act of Congress (with the exception of joint resolutions that propose constitutional amendments), Congress was given the authority to override an executive veto by a two-thirds vote in each house. Congress, however, cannot usually muster enough votes to override a veto. Thus, in over 200 years, there have been approximately 2,500 presidential vetoes and only about a hundred have been overridden.

The Power to Preside over the Military as Commander in Chief

One of the most important executive powers is the president's authority over the military. Article II states that the president is "Commander in Chief of the Army and Navy of the United States." While the Constitution specifically grants Congress the authority to declare war, presidents since Abraham Lincoln have used the commander in chief clause in conjunction with the chief executive's duty to "take Care that the Laws be faithfully executed" to wage war (and to broaden various powers).

Modern presidents continually clash with Congress over the ability to commence hostilities. The Vietnam War, in which 58,000 American soldiers were killed and 300,000 were wounded, was conducted (at a cost of $150 billion) without a congressional declaration of war.

WORLD | NATION | LOCAL | **POLITICS** | OPINION | HEALTH & SCIENCE | ARTS | SPORTS | LEISURE

With Home Trouble, Obama Faces Hard Choices on Trips

By Shaun Tandon

June 5, 2010
Agence France-Presse
www.afp.com

Faced with mounting challenges at home, President Barack Obama will soon have to choose between jamming foreign trips onto this year's tightening schedule or neglecting key U.S. partners.

Obama, who traveled overseas more than any other president in his first year, on Thursday called off a visit to Australia and Indonesia for the second time to focus on curbing a major oil leak in the Gulf of Mexico. . . .

Obama earlier delayed the Pacific trip to lead his top legislative priority of health care reform. His domestic calendar will remain busy, with his Democratic Party fighting to keep control of Congress in November 2 elections.

"I wouldn't be surprised if more of these foreign visits are canceled between now and the mid-term elections," said Brian Katulis, an expert on national security at the left-leaning Center for American Progress.

"Sometimes I think foreign policy issues go over the heads of most ordinary Americans and they're going to vote, it seems, on the bread-and-butter issues here at home," he said.

But, even in an age of instant communications, Obama can send a powerful message that another nation is important when he heads overseas, Katulis said. . . .

Obama said Thursday he would head in November to India, which has warming ties with the United States but where some policymakers worried Obama was too focused on fellow rising power China, which he visited last year, and Pakistan.

Obama is also committed to travel in November to back-to-back summits of the Group of 20 economic powers in South Korea and of the Asia-Pacific Economic Cooperation forum in Japan. . . .

Critical Thinking Questions

1. How does a visit from another country's head of state affect diplomatic relations?
2. How does this article illustrate the difficulties presidents face in balancing their many roles?
3. Should midterm elections play a role in determining a president's travel schedule? Why or why not?

During that highly controversial war, Presidents Johnson and Nixon routinely assured members of Congress that victory was near. In 1971, however, publication of what were called The Pentagon Papers revealed what many people had suspected all along: the Johnson administration had systematically altered casualty figures and distorted key facts to place the progress of the war in a more positive light. Realizing that this misinformation had led Congress to defer to the executive in the conduct of the Vietnam War, in 1973 Congress passed the **War Powers Act** to limit the president's authority to introduce American troops into hostile foreign lands without congressional approval. President Nixon vetoed the act, but it was overridden by a two-thirds majority in both houses of Congress.

Presidents since Nixon have continued to insist that the War Powers Act is an unconstitutional infringement of their executive power. Still, in 2001, President George W. Bush complied with the act when he sought, and both houses of Congress approved, a joint resolution authorizing the use of force against "those responsible for the recent [September 11] attacks launched against the United States." This resolution actually gave the president more open-ended authority to wage war than President Johnson had received from the Gulf of Tonkin Resolution in 1964. In October 2002, after President Bush declared Iraq to be a "grave threat to peace," the House (296–133) and Senate (77–23) also voted overwhelmingly to allow the president to use force in Iraq "as he determines to be necessary and appropriate," thereby conferring tremendous authority on the president to wage war. (To learn more about the controversies related to this law, see Join the Debate: The War Powers Act.)

War Powers Act

Passed by Congress in 1973; the president is limited in the deployment of troops overseas to a sixty-day period in peacetime (which can be extended for an extra thirty days to permit withdrawal) unless Congress explicitly gives its approval for a longer period.

Join the DEBATE | Is the War Powers Act Constitutional?

The Constitution gives Congress the authority to declare war, to make the rules that govern the military, and to provide appropriations to the armed services, but the Constitution also designates the president commander in chief of the armed services. Since the nation's founding, the president's constitutional jurisdiction over war powers has steadily increased.

Passed in the aftermath of the Vietnam War, the War Powers Act of 1973 was an attempt to rein in the war-making authority of the president by demanding, among other things, that the executive notify Congress within forty-eight hours after deploying the armed forces in combat. The stated purpose of the act was to "fulfill the intent of the framers . . . and insure that the collective judgment of both the Congress and the president will apply to the introduction of United States Armed Forces into hostilities . . . and to the continued use of such forces."

While generally complying with the requirements of the War Powers Act, every presidential administration since Nixon's has argued that the act infringes on the president's constitutional duty as commander in chief. Consequently, the constitutionality of the War Powers Act remains contested. Some constitutional scholars maintain that Congress is within its right to exercise oversight in foreign policy matters, reining in the executive where necessary. Other scholars side with executive-branch officials who consider the War Powers Act an infringement on the president's constitutional authority. Does the War Powers Act undermine the ability of the executive to make foreign policy? Is the War Powers Act constitutional?

To develop an ARGUMENT FOR the constitutionality of the War Powers Act, think about how:

- **The War Powers Act attempts to restore the balance of shared control of the military.** How does the Constitution balance the powers of the president and Congress with respect to the power to make war? How does the act return to the constitutional principle that waging war is to be shared by both branches of government?
- **The United States has not officially declared war since World War II.** Does the constitutional separation of powers function in the context of undeclared wars? Could the Framers have anticipated the changing nature of warfare in the twentieth century?
- **The War Powers Act reflects the will of the American people.** In what ways does the act place ultimate war-making authority with the American people? What role should Congress, as a representative of the American people, play in overseeing the use of force by the executive?

To develop an ARGUMENT AGAINST the constitutionality of the War Powers Act, think about how:

- **The Constitution clearly defines the role of the president in foreign policy.** Why did the Framers grant primary responsibility for foreign and military affairs to the president?
- **The Constitution clearly defines the role of Congress in military action.** How does the War Powers Act unnecessarily expand congressional authority in foreign policy? What other constitutional powers does Congress have to check the actions of the executive?
- **The Supreme Court has upheld an expanded interpretation of the president's authority in matters of foreign policy.** How does the nature of international politics, including the need to act quickly to respond to threats in a time of crisis, necessitate a greater concentration of power in the executive?

What authority do presidents have during wartime? President Lyndon B. Johnson's action during the Vietnam War led to the passage of the War Powers Act, which, at least in theory, restricts presidential power to deploy troops.

Photo courtesy: Yoichi R. Okamoto/Picture History

The Pardoning Power

Presidents can exercise a check on judicial power through their constitutional authority to grant reprieves or pardons. A **pardon** is an executive grant releasing an individual from the punishment or legal consequences of a crime before or after conviction, and restores all rights and privileges of citizenship. Presidents exercise complete pardoning power for federal offenses except in cases of impeachment, which cannot be pardoned. President Gerald R. Ford granted the most famous presidential pardon when he pardoned former President Richard M. Nixon—who had not been formally charged with any crime—"for any offenses against the United States, which he, Richard Nixon, has committed or may have committed while in office." This unilateral, absolute pardon unleashed a torrent of public criticism against Ford and questions about whether Nixon had discussed the pardon with Ford before Nixon's resignation. Many analysts attribute Ford's defeat in the 1976 election to that pardon.

pardon

An executive grant providing restoration of all rights and privileges of citizenship to a specific individual charged or convicted of a crime.

The Development and Expansion of Presidential Power

⭐ **7.3 . . . Evaluate the development and expansion of presidential power.**

Every president brings to the position not only a vision of America, but also expectations about how to use presidential authority. But, most presidents find accomplishing their goals much more difficult than they envisioned. After President John F. Kennedy was in office two years, for example, he noted publicly that there were "greater limitations upon our ability to bring about a favorable result than I had imagined."[7] Similarly, as he was leaving office, President Harry S Truman mused about what surprises awaited his successor, Dwight D. Eisenhower, a former general: "He'll sit here and he'll say, 'Do this! Do that!' And nothing will happen. Poor Ike—it won't be a bit like the army. He'll find it very frustrating."[8]

A president's authority is limited by the formal powers enumerated in Article II of the Constitution and by the Supreme Court's interpretation of those constitutional provisions. How a president wields these powers is affected by the times in which the president serves, his confidantes and advisers, and the president's personality and leadership abilities. The 1950s postwar Era of Good Feelings and economic prosperity presided over by the grandfatherly Eisenhower, for instance, called for a very different leader from the one needed by the Civil War–torn nation governed by Abraham Lincoln.

During the Civil War, Lincoln argued that he needed to act quickly for the very survival of the union. Thus, he frequently took action without first obtaining the approval of Congress. Among many of Lincoln's legally questionable acts:

- He suspended the writ of *habeas corpus*, which allows those in prison to petition to be released, citing the need to jail persons suspected of disloyal practices.
- He expanded the size of the U.S. Army above congressionally mandated ceilings.
- He ordered a blockade of southern ports without the approval of Congress.
- He closed the U.S. mail to treasonable correspondence.

Lincoln argued that the **inherent powers** of his office, or powers that belong to the president because they can be inferred from the Constitution, allowed him to circumvent the Constitution in a time of war or national crisis. Since the Constitution conferred on the president the duty to make sure that the laws of the United States are faithfully executed, reasoned Lincoln, the acts enumerated above were constitutional. He simply refused to allow the nation to crumble because of what he viewed as technical

inherent powers

Powers that belong to the president because they can be inferred from the Constitution.

TIMELINE: The Development of Presidential Power

1787 Office Created— Article II of the Constitution includes provisions for a chief executive known as the president.

1829 Chief of Party— President Andrew Jackson uses his personal popularity to buttress the president's role as chief of party.

1861 Using Inherent Powers— President Abraham Lincoln takes a number of legally questionable actions during the Civil War. He claims these actions are justified by the inherent powers of the presidency.

1789 President George Washington Takes Office— As the first president, Washington establishes the Cabinet, sets a precedent for the president's role in foreign affairs, and claims inherent powers for the office.

requirements of the Constitution. Because of his leadership during this crisis, Lincoln is generally ranked as one of the best presidents. (To learn more about presidential rankings, see Table 7.2.)

Presidential leadership has also become more important with the development of new technology. Before the days of instantaneous communication, the nation could afford to allow Congress, with its relatively slow deliberative processes, to make most decisions. Furthermore, decision making might have been left to Congress because its members, and not the president, were closest to the people. As times and technology have changed, however, so have the public's expectations of anyone who becomes president. The breakneck speed with which so many cable news networks and Web sites report national and international events has intensified the public's expectation that, in a crisis, the president will be the individual to act quickly and decisively on behalf of the entire nation. Congress often is unable to respond to fast-changing events—especially in foreign affairs.

Since the 1930s, the general trend has been for presidential—as opposed to congressional—decision making to be more and more important. The start of this trend can be traced to the four-term presidency of Franklin D. Roosevelt (FDR), who led the nation through several crises.

Table 7.2 *Who were the best and worst U.S. presidents?*

Five Best Presidents	Five Worst Presidents
1. Lincoln (best)	1. Buchanan (worst)
2. Washington	2. A. Johnson
3. F. Roosevelt	3. Pierce
4. T. Roosevelt	4. W. H. Harrison
5. Truman	5. Harding

Source: C-SPAN 2009 Historians Survey of Presidential Leadership, www.cspan.com.

1939 Bureau of the Budget—FDR creates this office, now called the Office of Management and Budget, to enhance the president's role in the budget process.

1964 Chief Legislator—President Lyndon B. Johnson establishes an even greater role for the president in the legislative process.

1933 Modern Presidency—President Franklin D. Roosevelt ushers in a new era marked by a growing federal bureaucracy and an active role for the president in the legislative process.

2009 Chief of State— As the world becomes more globalized, the president's role as ambassador and diplomat becomes increasingly important.

FDR took office in 1933 in the midst of a major crisis—the Great Depression—during which a substantial portion of the U.S. workforce was unemployed. Noting the sorry state of the national economy in his Inaugural Address, FDR concluded: "This nation asks for action and action now." To jump-start the American economy, FDR asked Congress for and was given "broad executive powers to wage a war against the emergency, as great as the power that would be given to me if we were in fact invaded by a foreign foe."[9]

Just as Abraham Lincoln had taken bold steps upon his inauguration, Roosevelt also acted quickly. He immediately fashioned a plan for national recovery called the **New Deal,** a package of bold and controversial programs designed to invigorate the failing American economy (To learn more about the New Deal, see **chapter 3**).

Roosevelt served an unprecedented twelve years in office; he was elected to four terms but died shortly after the beginning of this fourth term. During his years in office, the nation went from the economic war of the Great Depression to the real international conflict of World War II. The institution of the presidency changed profoundly and permanently as new federal agencies were created to implement the New Deal.

Not only did FDR create a new bureaucracy to implement his pet programs, but he also personalized the presidency by establishing a new relationship between the president and the people. In his radio addresses, or fireside chats, as he liked to call them, he spoke directly to the public in a relaxed and informal manner about serious issues.

To his successors, FDR left the modern presidency, including a burgeoning federal bureaucracy, an active and usually leading role in both domestic and foreign policy and legislation, and a nationalized executive office that used technology—first radio, then television, and now the Internet—to bring the president closer to the public than ever before.

New Deal

The name given to the program of "Relief, Recovery, Reform" begun by President Franklin D. Roosevelt in 1933 to bring the United States out of the Great Depression.

The Presidential Establishment

⭐ **7.4 . . . Outline the structure of the presidential establishment and the functions of each of its components.**

As the responsibilities and scope of presidential authority grew over the years, so did the executive branch, including the number of people working directly for the president in the White House. The vice president and his staff, the Cabinet, the first lady and her staff, the Executive Office of the President, and the White House staff all help the president fulfill his duties as chief executive.

The Vice President

Historically, presidents chose their vice presidents largely to balance—politically, geographically, or otherwise—the presidential ticket, with little thought given to the possibility that the vice president would become president. Franklin D. Roosevelt, for example, a liberal New Yorker, selected John Nance Garner, a conservative Texan, to be his running mate in 1932. After serving two terms, Garner—who openly disagreed with Roosevelt over many policies, including Roosevelt's decision to seek a third term—unsuccessfully sought the 1940 presidential nomination himself.

In 2008, Senator John McCain surprised most commentators when he selected Alaska Governor Sarah Palin to be his running mate. Palin, a virtual unknown outside her home state, energized social conservatives who had not been firmly behind McCain. Barack Obama, who was accused of lacking foreign policy experience, chose Senator Joe Biden (D–DE) to provide balance to the Democratic ticket.

How much power a vice president has depends on how much the president is willing to give. Jimmy Carter was the first president to give his vice president, Walter Mondale, more than ceremonial duties. In fact, Mondale was the first vice president to have an office in the White House. The last two vice presidents, Dick Cheney and Joe Biden, have been given significant powers and access to the president, elevating the office to new heights.

What guides the selection of a running mate? Governor Sarah Palin (R–AK) and Senator Joe Biden (D–DE) were chosen as vice presidential nominees for very different reasons. Both, however, helped to balance two historic presidential tickets.

Photo courtesy: Steve Kelley/Cartoonist Group

The Cabinet

The Cabinet, which has no official basis in the Constitution but is implied by Article II, section 2, is an informal institution based on practice and precedent whose membership is determined by tradition and presidential discretion. By custom, this advisory group selected by the president includes the heads of major executive departments. Presidents today also include their vice presidents in Cabinet meetings, as well as any other agency heads or officials to whom they would like to accord Cabinet-level status. As a body, the Cabinet's major function is to help the president execute the laws and assist him in making decisions.

Over the years, the Cabinet has grown alongside the responsibilities of the national government. As interest groups, in particular, pressured Congress and the president to recognize their demands for services and governmental action, they often were rewarded by the creation of an executive department. Since each was headed by a secretary who automatically became a member of the president's Cabinet, powerful clientele groups including farmers

(Agriculture), business people (Commerce), workers (Labor), and teachers (Education) saw the creation of a department as increasing their access to the president.

While the size of the president's Cabinet has increased over the years, most presidents' reliance on their Cabinet secretaries has decreased. Some individual members of a president's Cabinet, however, may be very influential. (To learn more about the Cabinet's role in executing U.S. policy, see **chapter 8**.)

The First Lady

From the time of Martha Washington, first ladies (a term coined in 1849) have assisted presidents as informal advisers while making other, more public, and significant contributions to American society. Edith Bolling Galt Wilson was probably the most powerful first lady. When President Woodrow Wilson collapsed and was left partly paralyzed in 1919, she became his surrogate and decided whom and what the stricken president saw. Her detractors dubbed her "Acting First Man."

Eleanor Roosevelt also played a powerful and much criticized role in national affairs. Not only did she write a nationally syndicated daily newspaper column, but she traveled and lectured widely, worked tirelessly on countless Democratic Party matters, and raised six children. After FDR's death, she shone in her own right as U.S. delegate to the United Nations, where she headed the commission that drafted the covenant on human rights. Later, she headed President John F. Kennedy's Commission on the Status of Women.

More recently, First Lady Michelle Obama, a lawyer who was an administrator at the University of Chicago Medical Center, has prioritized health and physical fitness. From planting an organic White House vegetable garden to visiting schools around the country, she has stressed the importance of healthy lunches and encouraged children to make nutritious choices, viewing childhood obesity as a serious problem and policy priority.

The Executive Office of the President (EOP)

The **Executive Office of the President (EOP)** was established by FDR in 1939 to oversee his New Deal programs. It was created to provide the president with a general staff to help him direct the diverse activities of the executive branch. In fact, it is a mini-bureaucracy of several advisers and offices located in the ornate Eisenhower Executive Office Building next to the White House on Pennsylvania Avenue, as well as in the White House itself, where the president's closest advisers often are located.

The EOP has expanded to include several advisory and policy-making agencies and task forces. Over time, the units of the EOP have become the prime policy makers in their fields of expertise as they play key roles in advancing the president's policy preferences. Among the EOP's most important members are the National Security Council, the Council of Economic Advisers, the Office of Management and Budget, the Office of the Vice President, and the Office of the U.S. Trade Representative.

The National Security Council (NSC) was established in 1947 to advise the president on American military affairs and foreign policy. The NSC is composed of the president, the vice president, and the secretaries of state, defense, and treasury. The chair of the Joint Chiefs of Staff and the director of the Central Intelligence Agency also participate. Others such as the White House chief of staff and the general counsel may attend. The national security adviser runs the staff of the NSC, coordinates information and options, and advises the president.

Presidents can give clear indications of their policy preferences by the kinds of offices they include in the EOP. President Barack Obama's addition of an Economic Recovery Advisory Board to the EOP showed his concern about the economy and a desire to find ways to bring the country out of recession.

Executive Office of the President (EOP)

A mini-bureaucracy created in 1939 to help the president oversee the executive branch bureaucracy.

The White House Staff

Although presidents organize the White House staff in different ways, they typically have a chief of staff whose job is to facilitate the smooth running of the staff and the executive branch of government. Successful chiefs of staff also have protected the president from mistakes and helped implement policies to obtain the maximum political advantage for the president. Other key White House aides include domestic, foreign, and economic policy strategists; the communications staff; the White House counsel; and a lobbyist who acts as a liaison between the president and Congress.

As presidents have tried to consolidate power in the White House, and as public demands on the president have grown, the size of the White House staff has increased—from fifty-one in 1943, to 247 in 1953, to a high of 583 in 1972. Since that time, staffs have been trimmed, generally running around 500. The Obama White House has approximately 490 staffers.

Presidential Leadership and the Importance of Public Opinion

★ 7.5 . . . Explain the concept of presidential leadership, and analyze the importance of public opinion.

A president's ability to get his programs adopted or implemented depends on many factors, including his leadership abilities, his personality and powers of persuasion, his ability to mobilize public opinion to support his actions, the public's perception of his performance, and Congress's perception of his public support.

Presidential Leadership

Leadership is not an easy thing to exercise, and it remains an elusive concept for scholars to identify and measure, but it is important to all presidents seeking support for their programs and policies. Moreover, ideas about the importance of effective leaders have deep roots in our political culture. The leadership abilities of the great presidents—Washington, Jefferson, Lincoln, and FDR—have been extolled over and over again, leading us to fault modern presidents who fail to cloak themselves in the armor of leadership. Americans thus have come to believe that "if presidential leadership works some of the time, why not all of the time?"[10] This attitude, in turn, directly influences what we expect presidents to do and how we evaluate them.

Research by political scientists shows that presidents can exercise leadership by increasing public attention to particular issues. Analyses of presidential State of the Union Addresses, for example, reveal that mentions of particular policies translate into more Americans mentioning those policies as the most important problems facing the nation.[11] Political scientist Richard E. Neustadt calls the president's ability to influence members of Congress and the public "the power to persuade." Neustadt believes this power is crucial to presidential leadership.[12]

Frequently, the difference between great and mediocre presidents centers on their ability to grasp the importance of leadership style. Truly great presidents, such as Lincoln and FDR, understood that the White House was a seat of power from which decisions could flow to shape the national destiny. They recognized that their day-to-day activities and how they went about them should be designed to bolster support for their policies and to secure congressional and popular backing that could translate their intuitive judgment into meaningful action. Mediocre presidents, on the other

Table 7.3 *What can we learn from presidential personalities?*

	Active	Passive
Positive	F. Roosevelt	Taft
	Truman	Harding
	Kennedy	Reagan
	Ford	
	Carter[a]	
	Bush	
Negative	Wilson	Coolidge
	Hoover	Eisenhower
	L. Johnson	
	Nixon	

[a] Some scholars think that Carter better fits the active-negative typology.

Source: James David Barber, *The Presidential Character: Predicting Performance in the White House*, 5th ed. (New York: Longman, 2009).

hand, have tended to regard the White House as "a stage for the presentation of performances to the public" or a fitting honor to cap a career.[13]

Political scientist James David Barber characterized presidents based on their energy level (active or passive) and their attitude toward their job (positive or negative). He argues that active-positive presidents are most successful due to their drive to lead and succeed positively. In stark contrast, Barber contends that passive-negative presidents are reactive and likely to follow the lead of others, thus failing to make full use of their resources as president. (To learn more about these personalities, see Table 7.3.)

Going Public: Mobilizing Public Opinion

Even before radio, television, and the Internet, presidents tried to reach out to the public to gain support for their programs through what President Theodore Roosevelt called the bully pulpit. The development of commercial air travel and radio, newsreels, television, computers, and cell phones have made direct communication to larger numbers of voters easier. Presidents, first ladies, and other presidential advisers travel all over the world to publicize their views and to build personal support as well as support for administration programs.

Direct, presidential appeals to the electorate like those often made by recent presidents are referred to as "going public."[14] Going public means that a president goes over the heads of members of Congress to gain support from the people, who can then place pressure on their elected officials in Washington.

The Public's Perception of Presidential Performance

For presidents and other public figures, approval ratings are often used as tacit measures of their political capital: their ability to enact public policy simply because of their name and their office. Presidents who have high approval ratings, as President George W. Bush did in the immediate aftermath of the September 11, 2001, terrorist attacks, are assumed to be more powerful leaders with a mandate for action that comes largely by virtue of high levels of public support. They are often able to use their clout to push controversial legislation, such as the USA

How important is public opinion to presidential success? Public support can be essential to presidents' policy making power, both at home and abroad. Here, President Barack Obama speaks to Chinese youth on a state visit to China.

Photo courtesy: AP/Wide World Photos

ANALYZING VISUALS

Presidential Approval Ratings Since 1981

Examine the line graph, which shows the percentage of the American public approving of the president's performance from 1981 through 2010, and answer the questions.

- Which president left office with the highest approval ratings? The lowest approval ratings?
- What pattern do you notice in the approval ratings of each president?
- How would you explain the changes in the approval ratings of President Barack Obama?

Source: Gallup.com

PATRIOT Act, through Congress. A public appearance from a popular president can even deliver a hotly contested congressional seat or gubernatorial contest to the president's party.

In sharp contrast, presidents with low approval ratings are often crippled in the policy arena. Their low ratings can actually prevent favored policies from being enacted on Capitol Hill, even when their party controls the legislature, as many of their partisans locked in close elections shy away from being seen or affiliated with an unpopular president.

Presidential popularity, however, generally follows a cyclical pattern. These cycles have been recorded since 1938, when pollsters first began to track presidential popularity. Typically, presidents enjoy their highest level of public approval at the beginning of their terms and try to take advantage of this honeymoon period to get their programs passed by Congress as soon as possible. Each action a president takes, however, is divisive—some people will approve, and others will disapprove. Disapproval tends to have a negative cumulative effect on a president's approval rating. (To learn more, see Analyzing Visuals: Presidential Approval Ratings Since 1981.)

TOWARD REFORM: The President as Policy Maker

⭐ **7.6** . . . Assess the president's role as policy maker.

When President Franklin D. Roosevelt sent his first legislative package to Congress, he broke the traditional model of law-making.[15] As envisioned by the Framers, it was to be Congress that made the laws. Now FDR was claiming a leadership role for the president in the legislative process. Said the president of this new relationship: "It is the duty of the President to propose and it is the privilege of the Congress to dispose."[16] With those words and the actions that followed, FDR shifted the presidency into a law- and policy-maker role. Now the president and the executive branch not only executed the laws but generally suggested them and proposed budgets to Congress to fund those proposals (see **chapter 6**).

The President's Role in Proposing and Facilitating Legislation

From FDR's presidency to the Republican-controlled 104th Congress, the public looked routinely to the president to formulate concrete legislative plans to propose to Congress, which subsequently adopted, modified, or rejected his plans for the nation. Then, in 1994, it appeared for a while that the electorate wanted Congress to reassert itself in the legislative process. In fact, the Contract with America was a Republican call for Congress to take the reins of the law-making process. But, several Republican Congresses failed to pass many of the items of the Contract, and President Bill Clinton's continued forceful presence in the budgetary and legislative processes made a resurgent role for Congress largely illusory.

On the whole, presidents have a hard time getting Congress to pass their programs. Recent research by political scientists, however, shows that presidents are much more likely to win on bills central to their announced agendas, such as President Barack Obama's victory on health care reform, than to secure passage of legislation proposed by others.[17]

Because presidents generally experience declining support for policies they advocate throughout their terms, it is important that a president propose key plans early in his administration. Even President Lyndon B. Johnson, who was able to get nearly 60 percent of his programs through Congress, noted: "You've got to give it all you can, that first year . . . before they start worrying about themselves. . . . You can't put anything through when half the Congress is thinking how to beat you."[18]

Another way a president can bolster support for his legislative package is to call on his political party. As the informal leader of his party, he should be able to use that position to his advantage to build coalitions in Congress, where party loyalty is very important. This strategy works best when the president has carried members of his party into office on his coattails as well as when his party has a majority in the legislature.

How did the president become a policy maker? President Franklin D. Roosevelt's strong leadership of Congress throughout the Great Depression and World War II helped cement the powers of the modern presidency. Here, Roosevelt gives a "fireside chat" radio broadcast to the American people.

Photo courtesy: Bettman/Corbis

The Budgetary Process and Legislative Implementation

Closely associated with a president's ability to pass legislation is his ability to secure funding for new and existing programs. A president sets national policy and priorities through his budget proposals and his continued insistence on their congressional passage. The budget proposal not only outlines the programs he wants but indicates the importance of each program by the amount of funding requested for each and for its associated agency or department.

Because the Framers gave Congress the power of the purse, Congress had primary responsibility for the budget process until 1930. The economic disaster set off by the stock market crash of 1929, however, gave FDR the opportunity to assert himself in the congressional budgetary process, just as he inserted himself in the legislative process. In 1939, the Bureau of the Budget, which had been created in 1921 to help the president tell Congress how much money it would take to run the executive branch of government, was made part of the newly created Executive Office of the President. In 1970, President Nixon changed its name to the **Office of Management and Budget (OMB)** to clarify its function in the executive branch.

The OMB works exclusively for the president and employs hundreds of budget and policy experts. Key OMB responsibilities include preparing the president's annual budget proposal, designing the president's program, and reviewing the progress, budget, and program proposals of the executive department agencies. It also supplies economic forecasts to the president and conducts detailed analyses of proposed bills and agency rules. OMB reports allow the president to attach price tags to his legislative proposals and defend the presidential budget. The OMB budget is a huge document, and even those who prepare it have a hard time deciphering all of its provisions. Even so, the expertise of the OMB directors often gives them an advantage over members of Congress.

Office of Management and Budget (OMB)

The office that prepares the president's annual budget proposal, reviews the budget and programs of the executive departments, supplies economic forecasts, and conducts detailed analyses of proposed bills and agency rules.

Policy Making Through Executive Order

Proposing legislation and using the budget to advance policy priorities are not the only ways that presidents can affect the policy process, especially in times of highly divided government when the policies of the president and Congress may differ.

How important is a balanced budget? President Bill Clinton and Vice President Al Gore celebrate the first balanced budget in years, a feat not likely to be repeated soon.

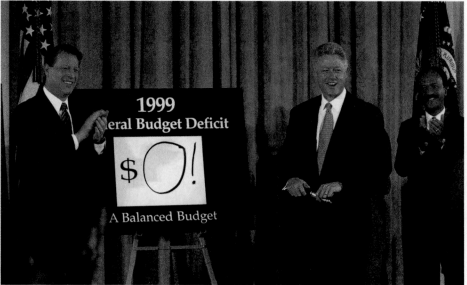

Photo courtesy: AP/Wide World Photos

Major policy changes may be instituted when a president has issued an **executive order,** a rule or regulation issued by the president that has the effect of law without congressional approval. Presidents Franklin D. Roosevelt and Harry S Truman used executive orders to seize mills, mines, and factories whose production was crucial to World War II and the Korean War efforts. Roosevelt and Truman argued that these actions were necessary to preserve national security. The Supreme Court, however, eventually disagreed with the Truman administration in *Youngstown Sheet and Tube* v. *Sawyer* (1952). In that case, the Court unequivocally stated that Truman had overstepped the boundaries of his office as provided by the Constitution.[19]

Presidents may also issue "signing statements" when signing legislation. Often these written statements merely comment on the bill signed, but they sometimes include controversial claims by the president that some part of the legislation is unconstitutional and that he intends to disregard it or to implement it in other ways.

President George W. Bush used signing statements to express his belief that portions of more than 1,200 laws were unconstitutional. "Among the laws Bush said he can ignore are military rules and regulations, affirmative action provisions, requirements that Congress be told about immigration services problems, 'whistle-blower' protections for nuclear regulator officials, and safeguards against political interference in federally funded research."[20]

After taking office, President Barack Obama issued a memorandum instructing agencies not to follow directives from previous administrations without first seeking the approval of the Department of Justice.[21] And yet, much like Bush, Obama has issued several signing statements raising constitutional concerns about bills he signed into law, including several sections of the $447-billion budget bill in 2009.[22]

Signing statements, thus, have become another way for the president to use his informal powers to make and influence public policy. For example, these statements invite litigation and may delay policy implementation. Because signing statements happen at the end of the legislative process, they are also a largely unchecked way for the president to assert himself in the ongoing power struggle with Congress.

executive order

Rule or regulation issued by the president that has the effect of law. All executive orders must be published in the *Federal Register*.

What Should I Have LEARNED?

Now that you have read this chapter, you should be able to:

★ **7.1 Trace the development of the presidency and the provisions for choosing and replacing presidents, p. 200.**

Distrust of a too powerful leader led the Framers to create an executive office with limited powers. They mandated that a president be at least thirty-five years old, a natural-born citizen, and a resident of the United States for at least fourteen years, and they opted not to limit the president's term of office. To further guard against tyranny, they made provisions for the removal of the president.

★ **7.2 Identify and describe the constitutional powers of the president, p. 203.**

The Framers gave the president a variety of specific constitutional powers in Article II, including the appointment power, the power to convene Congress, and the power to make treaties. The Constitution also gives the president the power to grant pardons and to veto acts of Congress. In addition, the president derives considerable power from being commander in chief of the military.

★ **7.3 Evaluate the development and expansion of presidential power, p. 209.**

The development of presidential power has depended on the personal force of those who have held the office. Abraham Lincoln, in particular, took several actions to establish the inherent powers of the presidency. Franklin D. Roosevelt (FDR) also took significant steps to increase the policy-making power of the president, and presidential decision making became more important in national and foreign affairs.

★ **7.4 Outline the structure of the presidential establishment and the functions of each of its components, p. 212.**

As the responsibilities of the president have grown, so has the executive branch of government. FDR established the Executive Office of the President to help him govern. Perhaps the most important policy advisers are those closest to the president: the vice president, the White

House staff, some members of the Executive Office of the President, and the first lady.

⭐ **7.5 Explain the concept of presidential leadership, and analyze the importance of public opinion, p. 214.**

To gain support for his programs or proposed budget, the president uses a variety of skills, including personal leadership and direct appeals to the public. How the president goes about winning support is determined by his leadership and personal style, which are affected by his character and his ability to persuade. Since the 1970s,

however, the American public has been increasingly skeptical of presidential actions, and few presidents have enjoyed the extended periods of popularity needed to help win support for programmatic change.

⭐ **7.6 Assess the president's role as policy maker, p. 217.**

Since FDR, the public has looked to the president to propose legislation to Congress. Through proposing legislation, advancing budgets, involvement in the regulatory process, and executive orders, presidents make policy.

Test Yourself: The Presidency

⭐ **7.1 Trace the development of the presidency and the provisions for choosing and replacing presidents, p. 200.**

After Franklin D. Roosevelt's election to four terms as president, which constitutional amendment was passed to limit the number of terms a president could serve?
A. Twentieth
B. Twenty-First
C. Twenty-Second
D. Twenty-Third
E. Twenty-Fourth

⭐ **7.2 Identify and describe the constitutional powers of the president, p. 203.**

Which of the following is NOT considered a constitutional power of the president?
A. Power to make appointments
B. Power to convene Congress
C. Power to make laws
D. Power to issue a line-item veto
E. Power to pardon

⭐ **7.3 Evaluate the development and expansion of presidential power, p. 209.**

President Franklin D. Roosevelt expanded the powers of the presidency largely as a result of
A. World War I.
B. the Great Depression.
C. his continued successes during his five terms as president.
D. increasing the size of the U.S. Supreme Court.
E. closing the U.S. mail to supposedly treasonous correspondence.

⭐ **7.4 Outline the structure of the presidential establishment and the functions of each of its components, p. 212.**

What is the primary purpose of the Executive Office of the President?
A. Check the powers of the president
B. Act as a liaison between Congress and the president

C. Decide who should be appointed to the Cabinet
D. Help the president oversee the bureaucracy
E. Serve as spokespeople for the White House

⭐ **7.5 Explain the concept of presidential leadership, and analyze the importance of public opinion, p. 214.**

Presidents often leave office with approval ratings
A. higher than those of Congress.
B. that rival those ratings experienced during their honeymoon period.
C. below 50 percent.
D. similar to ratings during times of national crisis.
E. at their lowest levels.

⭐ **7.6 Assess the president's role as policy maker, p. 217.**

Presidents have a particularly difficult time getting Congress to pass their programs if
A. they have unusually high approval ratings.
B. proposals are consistent with their announced agenda.
C. proposals are accompanied by signing statements.
D. they are no longer in their honeymoon period.
E. political parties have disagreements over the language of the bills.

Essay Questions

1. How did *U.S. v. Nixon* (1974) affect a president's claim to executive privilege?
2. Discuss the various roles a president must play while in office.
3. How does a president's leadership style affect the way he governs?
4. Describe the roles of the first lady.

mypoliscilab Exercises

Apply what you learned in this chapter on MyPoliSciLab.

Read on **mypoliscilab.com**

eText: Chapter 7

Study and **Review** on **mypoliscilab.com**

Pre-Test
Post-Test
Chapter Exam
Flashcards

Watch on **mypoliscilab.com**

Video: Bush and Congress
Video: The Government Bails Out Automakers

Explore on **mypoliscilab.com**

Simulation: Presidential Leadership: Which Hat Do You Wear?
Simulation: You Are a President During a Nuclear Meltdown
Comparative: Comparing Chief Executives
Timeline: The Executive Order Over Time
Visual Literacy: Presidential Success in Polls and Congress

Key Terms

Cabinet, p. 204
executive agreements, p. 206
Executive Office of the President (EOP), p. 213
executive order, p. 219
executive privilege, p. 202

impeachment, p. 201
inherent powers, p. 209
New Deal, p. 211
Office of Management and Budget (OMB), p. 218
pardon, p. 209

Twenty-Fifth Amendment, p. 202
Twenty-Second Amendment, p. 201
U.S. v. Nixon (1974), p. 202
veto power, p. 205
War Powers Act, p. 207

To Learn More on the Presidency

In the Library

Barber, James David. *The Presidential Character: Predicting Presidential Performance in the White House*, 5th ed. New York: Longman, 2008.

Cooper, Philip J. *By Order of the President: The Use and Abuse of Executive Direct Action*. Lawrence: University Press of Kansas, 2002.

Cronin, Thomas E., and Michael A. Genovese. *The Paradoxes of the American Presidency*, 3rd ed. New York: Oxford University Press, 2009.

Greenstein, Fred I. *The Presidential Difference: Leadership Style from FDR to George W. Bush*, 2nd ed. Princeton, NJ: Princeton University Press, 2004.

Han, Lori Cox. *New Directions in the American Presidency*. New York: Routledge, 2010.

Neustadt, Richard E. *Presidential Power and the Modern Presidents*. New York: Free Press, 1991.

Pfiffner, James P. *The Character Factor: How We Judge America's Presidents*. College Station: Texas A&M University Press, 2004.

———. *The Modern Presidency*, 6th ed. Belmont, CA: Wadsworth, 2010.

Pika, Joseph A., and John Anthony Maltese. *The Politics of the Presidency*, 7th ed. Washington, DC: CQ Press, 2009.

Rozell, Mark J. *Executive Privilege: Presidential Power, Secrecy, and Accountability*. Lawrence: University Press of Kansas, 2010.

Schier, Steven E. *Panorama of a Presidency: How George W. Bush Acquired and Spent His Political Capital*. Armonk, NY: M.E. Sharpe, 2008.

Shesol, Jeff. *Supreme Power: Franklin Roosevelt vs. the Supreme Court*. New York: W.W. Norton, 2010.

Skowronek, Stephen. *The Politics Presidents Make: Leadership from John Adams to Bill Clinton*. Cambridge, MA: Harvard University Press, 1997.

Warshaw, Shirley Anne. *The Keys to Power: Managing the Presidency*, 2nd ed. New York: Longman, 2005.

Wood, B. Dan. *The Politics of Economic Leadership: The Causes and Consequences of Presidential Rhetoric*. Princeton, NJ: Princeton University Press, 2007.

On the Web

To learn more about the office of the president, go to the official White House Web site at **www.whitehouse.gov.** There you can track current presidential initiatives and legislative priorities, read press briefings, and learn more about presidential nominations and executive orders.

To learn more about past presidents, go to the National Archives Web site at **www.archives.gov/index.html** where you can learn about presidential libraries, view presidential documents, and hear audio of presidents speaking.

To learn more about the office of the vice president, go to **www.whitehouse.gov/vicepresident.**

To learn more about the initiatives favored by the first lady, go to **www.whitehouse.gov/firstlady.**

The Executive Branch and the Federal Bureaucracy

Following the terrorist attacks on The World Trade Center the Pentagon on September 11, 2001, homeland security became a top priority for the executive branch and the federal bureaucracy. President George W. Bush responded by tightening airline security and launching his War on Terror. Over the next eight years, the public's attention drifted away from terrorism prevention as the country became mired in two wars, was struck by natural disasters such as Hurricane Katrina, and plunged into the worst recession since the Great Depression.

On Christmas Day 2009, however, the U.S. government's responsibility to prevent terrorist attacks was thrust back to the forefront. Twenty-three-year-old Nigerian national Umar Farouk Abdulmutallab, who had ties to al-Qaeda's branch in Yemen, attempted but failed to ignite explosives concealed in his underwear as Northwest Airlines Flight 253 prepared to land in Detroit, Michigan. Although no one except Abdulmutallab was injured in the incident, the nation was rattled and looked to their government, specifically President Barack Obama, to explain how such an incident could have happened and to take actions that would prevent anything similar from happening in the future.

It was soon revealed that Abdulmutallab's father had warned the U.S. Embassy in Nigeria about his son's extremism. But, Abdulmutallab

Presidents have significant support in dealing with international crises. At left, President John F. Kennedy meets with aides during the 1962 Cuban Missile Crisis. At right, President Barack Obama and his advisors devise a strategic response to the 2009 Christmas Day bombing attempt.

was not placed on the no-fly list. Homeland Security Advisor John O. Brennan had received reports of a possible attack on the United States from al-Qaeda in Yemen, but the young Nigerian was able to pass through airport security and board the Northwest plane in Amsterdam, The Netherlands.

President Obama and his intelligence agencies came under heavy fire from critics for a lack of communication and preparation, and the public wanted to know which bureaucrats to blame. The president, however, said the intelligence failures resulted from systemic problems and added, "I'm less interested in passing out blame. . . . than correcting the mistakes."

To discover exactly what went wrong, the president met with the chiefs of the sixteen U.S. intelligence agencies on January 5, 2010, in the White House situation room. In the meeting, President Obama dressed down the officials, telling them, "We dodged a bullet but

just barely. It was averted by brave individuals, not because the system worked." Obama's words struck a chord with many of the officials in attendance. Almost immediately after the meeting, measures were taken to reduce the risk of similar terrorist attacks. For example, passengers to the United States embarking from fourteen high-risk countries must now go through enhanced screening. President Obama also pledged an additional $1 billion for improving airport security across the nation.

What Should I Know About . . .

After reading this chapter, you should be able to:

★ 8.1 Trace the growth and development of the federal bureaucracy, p. 224.

★ 8.2 Describe modern bureaucrats, and outline the structure of the modern bureaucracy, p. 227.

★ 8.3 Determine how the bureaucracy makes policy, p. 235.

★ 8.4 Evaluate controls designed to make agencies more accountable, p. 237.

bureaucracy
The thousands of federal government agencies and institutions that implement and administer federal laws and programs.

The federal **bureaucracy,** or the thousands of federal government agencies and institutions that implement and administer federal laws and programs, frequently is called the "fourth branch of government." Critics often charge that the bureaucracy is too large, too powerful, and too unaccountable to the people or even to elected officials. Many politicians, elected officials, and voters complain that the federal bureaucracy is too wasteful. However, few critics discuss the fact that laws and policies also are implemented by state and local bureaucracies and bureaucrats whose numbers are proportionally far larger, and often far less accountable, than those working for the federal government.

Many Americans are uncomfortable with the large role of the federal government in policy making. Nevertheless, recent studies show that most users of federal agencies rate quite favorably the agencies and the services they receive. Most of those polled drew sharp distinctions between particular agencies and the government as a whole. For example, only 20 percent of Americans in one poll expressed positive views toward federal agencies, whereas 61 percent of respondents were satisfied with the agencies with which they have dealt.[1]

Harold D. Lasswell once defined political science as the "study of who gets what, when, and how."[2] It is by studying the bureaucracy that those questions can perhaps best be answered. To help you to understand the role of the bureaucracy, this chapter explores the following issues:

- First, we will examine *the roots of the federal bureaucracy.*

- Second, we will explore the key characteristics of *the modern bureaucracy,* including bureaucrats and the formal organization of the bureaucracy.

- Third, we will investigate *how the bureaucracy works* and its role in making policy.

- Finally, we will discuss the controls intended to *make agencies more accountable.*

ROOTS OF the Federal Bureaucracy

★ 8.1 . . . Trace the growth and development of the federal bureaucracy.

Only three executive departments existed under the Articles of Confederation: Foreign Affairs, War, and Treasury, which President George Washington inherited as his Cabinet. The head of each department was called its secretary, and Foreign Affairs was renamed the Department of State. To provide the president with legal advice, Congress also created the office of attorney general. From the beginning, individuals appointed as Cabinet secretaries (as well as the attorney general) were subject to approval by the U.S. Senate, but they could be removed from office by the president alone. Even the first Congress realized how important it was that a president be surrounded by those in whom he had complete confidence and trust.

The Civil War and the Growth of Government

As discussed in **chapter 3,** the Civil War (1861–1865) permanently changed the nature of the federal bureaucracy. As the nation geared up for war, thousands of additional employees were added to existing departments. The Civil War also spawned the need for new government agencies. A series of poor harvests and distribution problems led President

Abraham Lincoln (who understood that well-fed troops are necessary to conduct a war) to create the Department of Agriculture in 1862, although it was not given full Cabinet-level status until more than twenty years later.

The Pension Office was established in 1866 to pay benefits to the thousands of Union veterans who had fought in the war (more than 127,000 veterans initially were eligible for benefits). Justice, headed by the attorney general, was made a Cabinet department in 1870, and other departments were added through 1900.

From the Spoils System to the Merit System

In 1831, describing President Andrew Jackson's populating the federal government with his political cronies, a New York senator commented, "To the victor belong the spoils." From his statement derives the term **spoils system** to describe the firing of public office holders of the defeated political party and their replacement with loyalists of a new administration. The spoils system was a form of **patronage:** that is jobs, grants, or other special favors given as rewards to friends and political allies for their support. Political patronage often is defended as an essential element of the party system because it provides rewards and inducements for party workers. This system reached a high-water mark during Abraham Lincoln's presidency. By the time James A. Garfield, a former distinguished Civil War officer, was elected president in 1880, many reformers were calling for changes in the patronage system. On his election, thousands pressed Garfield for positions. Garfield resolved to reform the civil service, but his life was cut short by the bullets of an assassin who, ironically, was a frustrated job seeker.

Public reaction to Garfield's death and increasing criticism of the spoils system prompted Congress to pass the Civil Service Reform Act in 1883, more commonly known as the **Pendleton Act.** It established a **merit system** of federal employment on the basis of open, competitive exams and created a bipartisan three-member Civil Service Commission, which operated until 1978. Initially, only about 10 percent of the positions in the federal **civil service system** were covered by the law, but later laws and executive orders extended coverage of the act to over 90 percent of all federal employees.

Regulating Commerce

As the nation grew, so did the bureaucracy. (To learn more, about the growth of the bureaucracy see Analyzing Visuals: Federal Employees in the Executive Branch.) In the wake of the tremendous growth of big business (especially railroads), widespread price fixing, and other unfair business practices that occurred after the Civil War, Congress created the Interstate Commerce Commission (ICC) in 1887. In creating the ICC, Congress was reacting to public outcries over the exorbitant rates charged by railroad companies for hauling freight. It became the first **independent regulatory commission,** an entity outside a major executive department. Independent regulatory commissions such as the ICC are created by Congress and generally are concerned with particular aspects of the economy. Commission members are appointed by the president and hold their jobs for fixed terms, but they cannot be removed by the president unless they fail to uphold their oaths of office. The creation of the ICC also marked a shift in the focus of the bureaucracy from service to regulation. Its creation gave the government—in the shape of the bureaucracy—vast powers over individual and property rights.

As discussed in **chapter 3,** the ratification of the Sixteenth Amendment to the Constitution in 1913 also affected the size and growth potential of government. It gave

Which U.S. president popularized the spoils system? Here, a political cartoonist depicts how President Andrew Jackson might have been immortalized for his use of the spoils system.

Photo courtesy: Bettmann/Corbis

spoils system
The firing of public-office holders of a defeated political party to replace them with loyalists of the newly elected party.

patronage
Jobs, grants, or other special favors that are given as rewards to friends and political allies for their support.

Pendleton Act
Reform measure that established the principle of federal employment on the basis of open, competitive exams and created the Civil Service Commission.

civil service system
The merit system by which many federal bureaucrats are selected.

merit system
A system of employment based on qualifications, test scores, and ability, rather than party loyalty.

independent regulatory commission
An entity created by Congress outside a major executive department.

ANALYZING VISUALS

Federal Employees in the Executive Branch

This line graph tracks the number of federal employees in the executive branch of the U.S. government from the eighteenth to the twenty-first century. Review the figure, and then answer the questions.

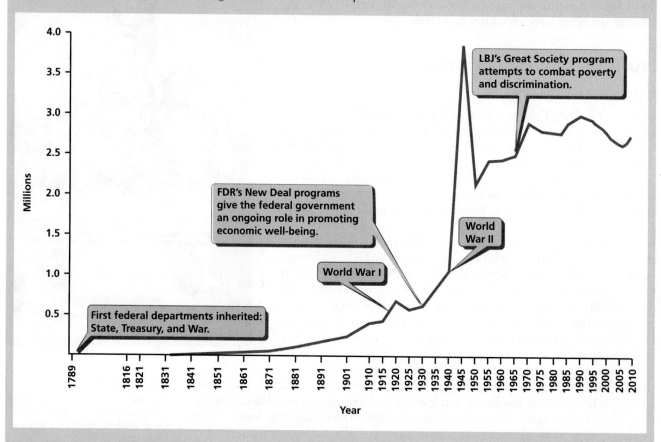

- Between which years did the number of federal employees increase the most rapidly? What do you think were the principal reasons for the increase?
- Between which years did the number of federal employees decrease the most rapidly? What do you think were the principal reasons for the decrease?
- What might explain the modest declines in the number of federal employees after 1970 and after 1990?
- In the next five years, would you expect the number of federal employees to increase, decrease, or stay the same? Why? What sorts of factors might influence the number of federal employment positions in the future?

Source: Office of Personnel Management, *The Fact Book,* www.opm.gov/feddata/factbook/2007/2007factbook.pdf; www.fedscope.opm.gov/employment.asp.

Congress the authority to implement a federal income tax to supplement the national treasury and provided a huge infusion of funds to support new federal agencies, services, and programs.

The World Wars and the Growth of Government

The economy appeared to boom as U.S. involvement in World War I caused an increase in manufacturing, but ominous events were just over the horizon. Farmers were in trouble after a series of bad harvests, the nation experienced a severe slump in agricultural prices, the construction industry went into decline, and, throughout the 1920s, bank failures became common. After stock prices crashed in 1929, the nation plunged into the Great Depression. To combat the resultant high unemployment and weak financial markets, President Franklin D. Roosevelt created hundreds of new government agencies to regulate business practices and various aspects of the national economy. Roosevelt believed that a national economic depression called for national intervention. Thus, the president proposed, and the Congress enacted, far-ranging economic legislation. The desperate mood of the nation supported these moves, as most Americans began to reconsider their ideas about the proper role of government and the provision of governmental services. Formerly, most Americans had believed in a hands-off approach; now they considered it the federal government's job to get the economy going and get Americans back to work.

World War II also prompted an expansion of the federal bureaucracy. Tax rates were increased to support the war, and they never again fell to prewar levels. After the war, this infusion of new monies and veterans' demands for services led to a variety of new programs and a much bigger government. The G.I. (Government Issue) Bill, for example, provided college loans for returning veterans and reduced mortgage rates to allow them to buy homes. The national government's involvement in these programs not only affected more people but also led to its greater involvement in more regulation. Homes bought with Veterans Housing Authority loans, for example, had to meet certain specifications. With these programs, Americans became increasingly accustomed to the national government's role in entirely new areas such as affordable middle-class housing and scholarships that allowed lower- and middle-class men who fought in World War II their first opportunities for higher education.

Within two decades after World War II, the civil rights movement and President Lyndon B. Johnson's Great Society program produced additional growth in the bureaucracy. The Equal Employment Opportunity Commission (EEOC) was created in 1965 by the Civil Rights Act of 1964. The Departments of Housing and Urban Development (HUD) and Transportation were created in 1965 and 1966, respectively. These expansions of the bureaucracy corresponded to increases in the president's power and his ability to persuade Congress that new commissions and departments would be an effective way to solve pressing social problems.

The Modern Bureaucracy

★ 8.2 . . . Describe modern bureaucrats, and outline the structure of the modern bureaucracy.

The national government differs from private business in numerous ways. Governments exist for the public good, not to make money. Businesses are driven by a profit motive; government leaders, but not bureaucrats, are driven by reelection. Businesses earn their money from customers; the national government raises revenue from taxpayers. Another difference between a bureaucracy and a business is that it is difficult to determine to whom bureaucracies are responsible. Is it the president? Congress? The people?

The different natures of government and business have a tremendous impact on the way the bureaucracy operates. Because all of the incentive in government "is in the direction of not making mistakes," public employees view risks and rewards very differently from their private-sector counterparts.[3] There is little reason for government employees to take risks or go beyond their assigned job tasks. In contrast, private employers are far more likely to reward ambition. The key to the modern bureaucracy is to understand who bureaucrats are, how the bureaucracy is organized, how organization and personnel affect each other, and how bureaucrats act within the political process. It also is important to understand that government cannot be run entirely like a business. An understanding of these facts and factors can help in the search for ways to motivate positive change in the bureaucracy.

Who Are Bureaucrats?

Federal bureaucrats are career government employees who work in the Cabinet-level departments and independent agencies that comprise more than 2,000 bureaus, divisions, branches, offices, services, and other subunits of the federal government. There are more than 2.7 million federal workers. Over one-quarter of all civilian employees work in the U.S. Postal Service. Small percentages work as legislative and judicial staff. The remaining federal civilian workers are spread out among the various executive departments and agencies throughout the United States. Most of these federal employees are paid according to what is called the "General Schedule" (GS). They advance within fifteen GS grades (as well as steps within those grades), moving into higher GS levels and salaries as their careers progress.

At the lower levels of the U.S. Civil Service, most positions are filled by competitive examinations. These usually involve a written test. Mid-level to upper ranges of federal positions do not normally require tests; instead, applicants submit résumés online. Personnel departments then evaluate potential candidates and rank candidates according to how well they fit a particular job opening. Only the names of those deemed "qualified" are then forwarded to the official filling the vacancy. This can be a time-consuming process; it often takes six to nine months before a position can be filled in this manner.

The remaining 10 percent of the federal workforce is made up of persons not covered by the civil service system. These positions generally fall into three categories:

1. *Appointive policy-making positions.* Nearly 3,500 people are presidential appointees. Some of these, including Cabinet secretaries and under- and assistant secretaries, are subject to Senate confirmation. These appointees, in turn, are responsible for appointing high-level policy-making assistants who form the top of the bureaucratic hierarchy. These are called "Schedule C" political appointees.

2. *Independent regulatory commissioners.* Although each president gets to appoint as many as one hundred commissioners, they become independent of his direct political influence once they take office.

3. *Low-level, nonpolicy patronage positions.* These types of positions generally concern secretarial assistants to policy makers.

More than 15,000 job skills are represented in the federal government. Government employees, whose average age is forty-seven, have an average length of service of sixteen years. They include forest rangers, FBI agents, foreign service officers, computer programmers, security guards, librarians, administrators, engineers, plumbers, lawyers, doctors, postal carriers, and zoologists, among others. The diversity of government jobs mirrors the diversity of jobs in the private sector. The federal workforce, itself, is also diverse but under-represents Hispanics, in particular, and the overall employment of women lags behind that of men. Women make up 64 percent of the lowest GS levels but only 34 percent of the highest GS levels.[4] (To learn more about the distribution of the federal workforce, see Figure 8.1.)

There are about 344,400 federal workers in the nation's capital; the rest are located in regional, state, and local offices scattered throughout the country. To enhance efficiency, the United States is broken up into several regions, with most agencies having regional offices in at least one city in that region. The decentralization of the bureaucracy facilitates accessibility to the public. The Social Security Administration, for example, has numerous offices so that its clients can have a place nearby to take their paperwork,

Figure 8.1 *What are the characteristics of federal civilian employees?*

This figure depicts the percentage of the federal civilian workforce in several categories. As you review the data displayed in the graph, consider the trends you observe across GS levels and overall.

Source: Office of Personnel Management, *The Fact Book,* www.opm.gov/feddata/factbook/2007/2007factbook.pdf.

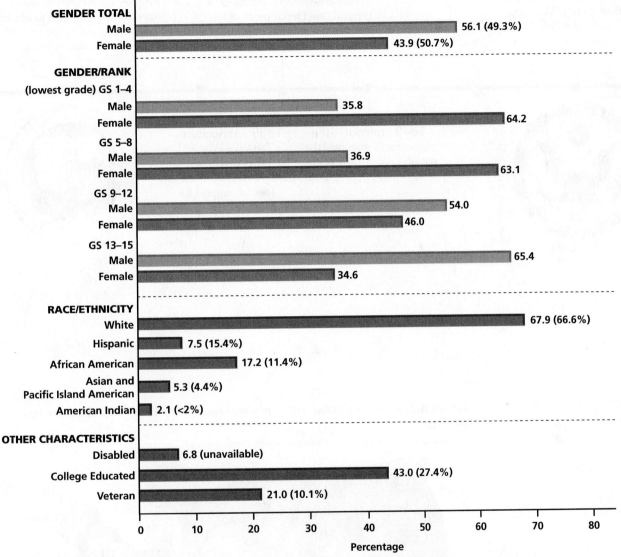

* Percentages in parentheses indicate each group's representation in the general population.

questions, and problems. Decentralization also helps distribute jobs and incomes across the country. (To learn more about agency regions, see Figure 8.2.)

One of the major concerns about the federal workforce is the high rates of turnover in many of the most important positions. This has become especially true in the Department of Homeland Security. Many employees of its Transportation Security Administration, for example, leave after only a short time on the job for more lucrative careers outside government. At the Department of State, which once had many of the most highly coveted jobs in the federal bureaucracy, the dangers associated with postings in Iraq and Afghanistan, as well as elsewhere in the Middle East, are making it harder to find well-qualified people to staff critical positions.[5] Consequently, the military has enlisted private contractors at unprecedented rates to fill many bureaucratic positions in Iraq and other dangerous sites. Many of these private contractors are former government employees who can make much more money working for private

TIMELINE: Establishing U.S. Cabinet Departments

1789 State, Treasury, and Defense—Soon after the creation of the new nation, President George Washington creates the first three Cabinet departments.

1870 Justice—Although there had always been an attorney general, the Department of Justice did not attain Cabinet status until after the Civil War.

1903 Commerce and Labor—Progressive reforms illustrate the need for departments to aid both employers and employees; they are divided in 1913.

Photo courtesy: United States Department of State

1849 Interior—The department manages the nation's natural resources, wildlife, and public lands.

1889 Agriculture—The Civil War and Reconstruction underscore the need for federal support for agricultural programs.

Photo courtesy: United States Department of Agriculture

Figure 8.2 *What are the federal agency regions, and where are their headquarters located?*

Source: Department of Health and Human Services, www.hhs.gov/images/regions.gif.

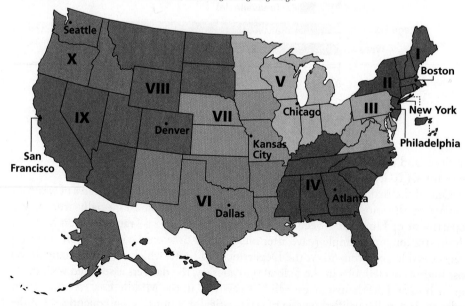

companies. While the exact number of private contractors is unknown, it is estimated that $538 billion of the federal budget was spent on government contractors in 2008.[6]

1960s Housing and Transportation— Increased federal activity in social programs necessitates the creation of these departments.

1989 Veterans Affairs— This department is established to administer benefits to veterans and their families.

2002 Homeland Security— Following the September 11, 2001, terrorist attacks, the nation identifies a need for greater coordination of domestic security activities.

1953 Health and Human Services—Originally called the Department of Health, Education, and Welfare, this department is created to administer health, welfare and Social Security. Until 1979, it also handles education.

1970s Energy and Education—The energy crisis and growing federal role in education make the creation of these departments important.

Formal Organization

While even experts cannot agree on the exact number of separate governmental agencies, commissions, and departments that make up the federal bureaucracy, there are at least 1,150 civilian agencies.[7] A distinctive feature of the executive bureaucracy is its traditional division into areas of specialization. For example, the Occupational Safety and Health Administration (OSHA) handles occupational safety, and the Department of State specializes in foreign affairs. It is not unusual, however, for more than one agency to be involved in a particular issue or for one agency to be involved in many issues. The vast authority and range of activities of the Department of Homeland Security are probably the best examples of this phenomenon. In fact, numerous agencies often have authority in the same issue areas, making administration even more difficult. (To learn more about how different bureaucratic agencies interact, see Politics Now: Pediatricians Call for a Choke Proof Hot Dog.)

Agencies fall into four general types: (1) Cabinet departments; (2) government corporations; (3) independent executive agencies; and, (4) independent regulatory commissions.

CABINET DEPARTMENTS The fifteen Cabinet **departments** are major administrative units that have responsibility for conducting broad areas of government operations. Cabinet departments account for about 60 percent of the federal workforce. The vice president, the heads of all of the departments, as well as the heads of the Environmental Protection Agency (EPA), Office of Management and Budget (OMB), the U.S. Trade Representative, the Council of Economic Advisors, the U.S. Ambassador to the United Nations, and the president's chief of staff make up his formal Cabinet. (To learn more about the Cabinet, see The Living Constitution: Article II: Section 2, Clause 1.)

Executive branch departments are headed by Cabinet members called secretaries (except the Department of Justice, which is headed by the attorney general). Secretaries are responsible for establishing their department's general policy and overseeing its operations. As discussed in **chapter 7**, Cabinet secretaries are directly responsible

departments

Major administrative units with responsibility for a broad area of government operations. Departmental status usually indicates a permanent national interest in a particular governmental function, such as defense, commerce, or agriculture.

POLITICS NOW

Pediatricians Call for a Choke Proof Hot Dog

February 22, 2010
USA Today
www.usatoday.com

Critical Thinking Questions

1. Should bureaucratic agencies be responsible for warning parents when foods might be a choking hazard for children? How severe should the problem have to become before it necessitates government action?

2. How might government agencies such as the Consumer Product Safety Commission and Food and Drug Administration take action to encourage greater food safety?

3. How does this article illustrate the role interest groups play in the regulatory process?

By Liz Szabo

. . . The American Academy of Pediatrics wants foods like hot dogs to come with a warning label—not because of their nutritional risks but because they pose a choking hazard to babies and children.

Better yet, the academy would like to see foods such as hot dogs "redesigned" so their size, shape and texture make them less likely to lodge in a youngster's throat. . . .

"If you were to take the best engineers in the world and try to design the perfect plug for a child's airway, it would be a hot dog," says statement author Gary Smith, director of the Center for Injury Research and Policy at Nationwide Children's Hospital in Columbus, Ohio. "I'm a pediatric emergency doctor, and to try to get them out once they're wedged in, it's almost impossible."

The Consumer Product Safety Commission requires labels on toys with small parts alerting people not to give them to kids under 3. Yet there are no required warnings on food, though more than half of non-fatal choking episodes involve food, Smith says. . . .

Janet Riley, president of the National Hot Dog & Sausage Council, supports the academy's call to better educate parents and caregivers about choking prevention. "Ensuring the safety of the foods we service to children is critically important for us," Riley says.

But Riley questions whether warning labels are needed. She notes that more than half of hot dogs sold in stores already have choking-prevention tips on their packages, advising parents to cut them into small pieces. "As a mother who has fed toddlers cylindrical foods like grapes, bananas, hot dogs and carrots, I 'redesigned' them in my kitchen by cutting them with a paring knife until my children were old enough to manage on their own," Riley says.

The Food and Drug Administration, which has authority to recall products it considers "unfit for food," plans to review the new statement, spokeswoman Rita Chappelle says. . . .

to the president but are often viewed as having two masters—the president and citizens affected by the business of their departments. Cabinet secretaries also are tied to Congress, through the appropriations process and their role in implementing legislation and making rules and policy.

Most departments are subdivided into bureaus, divisions, sections, or other smaller units, and it is at this level that the real work of each agency is done. Most departments are subdivided along functional lines, but the basis for division may be geography, work processes (for example, the Transportation Security Administration is housed in the Department of Homeland Security), or clientele (such as the Bureau of Indian Affairs in the Department of the Interior). Clientele agencies representing clearly defined interests are particularly subject to outside lobbying. These organized interests are also active at the regional level where the agencies conduct most of their program implementation.

INDEPENDENT EXECUTIVE AGENCIES   **Independent executive agencies** closely resemble Cabinet departments but have narrower areas of responsibility. Generally speaking, independent agencies perform services rather than regulatory functions. The heads of these agencies are appointed by the president and serve, like Cabinet secretaries, at his pleasure.

Independent agencies exist apart from executive departments for practical or symbolic reasons. The National Aeronautics and Space Administration (NASA), for example, could have been placed within the Department of Defense. Such positioning, however, could have conjured up thoughts of a space program dedicated solely to military

independent executive agencies
Governmental units that closely resemble a Cabinet department but have narrower areas of responsibility, and perform services rather than regulatory functions.

The Living Constitution

The President . . . may require the Opinion, in writing, of the principal Officer in each of the executive Departments, upon any subject relating to the Duties of their respective Office.

—ARTICLE II, SECTION 2, CLAUSE 1

This clause, along with additional language designating that the president shall be the commander in chief, notes that the heads of departments are to serve as advisers to the president. There is no direct mention of the Cabinet in the Constitution.

This meager language is all that remains of the Framers' initial efforts to create a council to guide the president. Those in attendance at the Constitutional Convention largely favored the idea of a council but could not agree on who should be a part of that body. Some actually wanted to follow the British parliamentary model and create the Cabinet from members of the House and Senate, who would rotate into the bureaucracy; most, however, appeared to support the idea of the heads of departments along with the chief justice, who would preside when the president was unavailable. The resulting language above depicts a one-sided arrangement whereby the heads of executive departments must simply answer in writing questions put to them by the president.

The Cabinet of today differs totally from the structure envisioned by the Framers.

George Washington was the first to convene a meeting of what he called his Cabinet. Some presidents have used their Cabinets as trusted advisers; others have used them to demonstrate that they are committed to political, racial, ethnic, or gender diversity, and have relied more on White House aides than particular Cabinet members. Who is included in the Cabinet, as well as how it is used, is solely up to the discretion of the sitting president with the approval of the U.S. Senate, although executive departments cannot be created or abolished without approval of both houses of Congress.

CRITICAL THINKING QUESTIONS

1. What are the advantages and disadvantages of having a Cabinet composed of heads of the departments?
2. What issues arise from requiring senatorial approval for Cabinet positions, and how does the Constitution remedy these issues?
3. Why has the composition and role of the president's Cabinet changed over the years?

purposes, rather than to civilian satellite communication or scientific exploration. Similarly, the Environmental Protection Agency (EPA) could have been created within the Department of the Interior but instead was created as an independent agency in 1970 to administer federal programs aimed at controlling pollution and protecting the nation's environment. As an independent agency, the EPA is less indebted to the president on a day-to-day basis than it would be if it were within a Cabinet department, although the president still has the ability to appoint its director and often intervenes on high-profile environmental issues and decisions.

INDEPENDENT REGULATORY COMMISSIONS As noted earlier, independent regulatory commissions are agencies created by Congress to exist outside the major departments to regulate a specific economic activity or interest. Because of the complexity of modern economic issues, Congress sought to create commissions that could develop expertise and provide continuity of policy with respect to economic issues because neither Congress nor the courts have the time or specific talents to do so. Examples include the National Labor Relations Board (NLRB), the Federal Reserve Board, the Federal Communications Commission (FCC), and the Securities and Exchange Commission (SEC).[8]

What do government corporations do? Amtrak provides train service across the United States. Its most profitable line runs through the Northeast Corridor from Boston to Washington, D.C. Vice President Joe Biden frequently takes the train from the nation's capital to his home in Wilmington, Delaware.

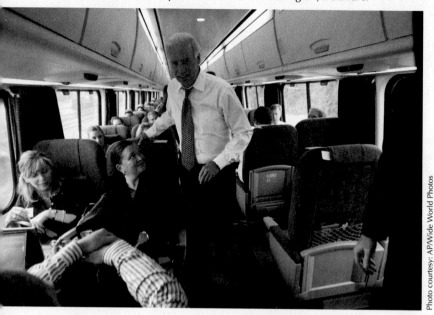

Photo courtesy: AP/Wide World Photos

Older boards and commissions, such as the SEC and the Federal Reserve Board, generally are charged with overseeing a certain industry. Most were created specifically to be free from partisan political pressure. Each is headed by a board composed of five to seven members (always an odd number, to avoid tie votes) who are selected by the president and confirmed by the Senate for fixed, staggered terms to increase the chances of a bipartisan board. Unlike executive department heads, they cannot easily be removed by the president.

Newer regulatory boards are more concerned with how the business sector relates to public health and safety. The Occupational Safety and Health Administration (OSHA), for example, promotes job safety. These boards and commissions often lack autonomy and freedom from political pressures; they are generally headed by a single administrator who can be removed by the president. Thus, they are far more susceptible to the political wishes of the president who appoints them.

government corporations
Businesses established by Congress to perform functions that could be provided by private businesses.

GOVERNMENT CORPORATIONS **Government corporations** are the most recent addition to the bureaucracy. Dating from the early 1930s, they are businesses established by Congress to perform functions that could be provided by private businesses. Some of the better-known government corporations include Amtrak and the Federal Deposit Insurance Corporation (FDIC). Unlike other governmental agencies, government corporations charge a fee for their services.

Government corporations are often formed when the financial incentives for private industry to provide services are minimal. The area served by the TVA demonstrates this point; it is a poor region of Appalachia that had failed to attract private companies. In other cases, Congress steps in to salvage valuable public assets. For example, when passenger rail service in the United States became unprofitable, Congress stepped in to create Amtrak, nationalizing the passenger-train industry to keep passenger trains running, especially in the Northeast corridor.

Government Workers and Political Involvement

As the number of federal employees and agencies grew during the 1930s, many Americans began to fear that the members of the civil service would play major roles not only in implementing public policy but also in electing members of Congress and even the president. Consequently, Congress enacted the Political Activities Act of 1939, commonly known as the **Hatch Act.** It was designed to prohibit federal employees from becoming directly involved in working for political candidates. Although this act allayed many critics' fears, other people argued that the Hatch Act was too extreme.

Hatch Act
The 1939 act to prohibit civil servants from taking activist roles in partisan campaigns. This act prohibited federal employees from making political contributions, working for a particular party, or campaigning for a particular candidate.

Federal Employees Political Activities Act of 1993
The 1993 liberalization of the Hatch Act. Federal employees are now allowed to run for office in nonpartisan elections and to contribute money to campaigns in partisan elections.

Today, government employees' political activity is regulated by the **Federal Employees Political Activities Act of 1993.** This liberalization of the Hatch Act allows employees to run for public office in nonpartisan elections, contribute money to political organizations, and campaign for or against candidates in partisan elections. Federal employees still, however, are prohibited from engaging in political activity while on duty, soliciting contributions from the general public, or running for office in partisan elections. (To learn more about the Federal Employees Political Activities Act, see Table 8.1.)

Table 8.1 *What does the Federal Employees Political Activities Act of 1993 stipulate?*

Federal Employees May	Federal Employees May Not
■ Be candidates for public office in nonpartisan elections	■ Use their official authority or influence to interfere with an election
■ Assist in voter registration drives	■ Collect political contributions unless both individuals are members of the same federal labor organization or employee organization and the one solicited is not a subordinate employee
■ Express opinions about candidates and issues	
■ Contribute money to political organizations	
■ Attend political fund-raising functions	■ Knowingly solicit or discourage the political activity of any person who has business before the agency
■ Attend and be active at political rallies and meetings	
■ Join and be active members of a political party or club	■ Engage in political activity while on duty
■ Sign nominating petitions	■ Engage in political activity in any government office
■ Campaign for or against referendum questions, constitutional amendments, and municipal ordinances	■ Engage in political activity while wearing an official uniform
■ Campaign for or against candidates in partisan elections	■ Engage in political activity while using a government vehicle
■ Make campaign speeches for candidates in partisan elections	■ Solicit political contributions from the general public
■ Distribute campaign literature in partisan elections	■ Be candidates for public office in partisan elections
■ Hold office in political clubs or parties	

Source: U.S. Special Counsel's Office.

How the Bureaucracy Works

★ **8.3 . . . Determine how the bureaucracy makes policy.**

German sociologist Max Weber believed bureaucracies were a rational way for complex societies to organize themselves. Model bureaucracies, said Weber, are characterized by certain features, including:

1. A chain of command in which authority flows from top to bottom.

2. A division of labor whereby work is apportioned among specialized workers to increase productivity.

3. Clear lines of authority among workers and their superiors.

4. A goal orientation that determines structure, authority, and rules.

5. Impersonality, whereby all employees are treated fairly based on merit and all clients are served equally, without discrimination, according to established rules.

6. Productivity, whereby all work and actions are evaluated according to established rules.[9]

Clearly, this Weberian idea is somewhat idealistic, and even the best-run government agencies don't always work this way, but most are trying.

When Congress creates any kind of department, agency, or commission, it is actually delegating some of its powers listed in Article I, section 8, of the U.S. Constitution. Therefore, the laws creating departments, agencies, corporations, or commissions carefully describe their purpose and give them the authority to make numerous policy decisions, which have the effect of law. Congress recognizes that it does not have the

Figure 8.3 *What is an iron triangle?*

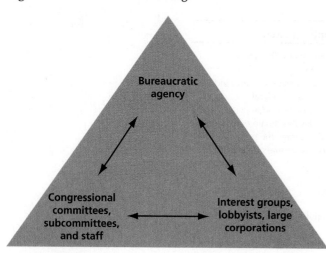

implementation

The process by which a law or policy is put into operation.

iron triangles

The relatively stable relationships and patterns of interaction that occur among agencies, interest groups, and congressional committees or subcommittees.

issue networks

The loose and informal relationships that exist among a large number of actors who work in broad policy areas.

interagency councils

Working groups created to facilitate coordination of policy making and implementation across a host of governmental agencies.

time, expertise, or ability to involve itself in every detail of every program; therefore, it sets general guidelines for agency action and leaves it to the agency to work out the details. How agencies execute congressional wishes is called **implementation,** the process by which a law or policy is put into operation.

Historically, political scientists attempting to study how the bureaucracy made policy investigated what they termed **iron triangles,** the relatively stable relationships and patterns of interaction that occur among federal workers in agencies or departments, interest groups, and relevant congressional committees and subcommittees. Today, iron triangles no longer dominate most policy processes. Some do persist, however, such as the relationship between the Department of Veterans Affairs, the House Committee on Veterans Affairs, and the American Legion and the Veterans of Foreign Wars, the two largest veterans groups. (To learn more about iron triangles, see Figure 8.3.)

Many political scientists examining external influences on the modern bureaucracy prefer to examine **issue networks.** In general, issue networks, like iron triangles, include agency officials, members of Congress (and committee staffers), and interest group lobbyists. But, they also include lawyers, consultants, academics, public relations specialists, and sometimes even the courts. Unlike iron triangles, issue networks constantly are changing as members with technical expertise or newly interested parties become involved in issue areas.

As a result of the increasing complexity of many policy domains, many alliances have also been created within the bureaucracy. One such example is **interagency councils,** working groups created to facilitate the coordination of policy making and implementation across a host of agencies. Depending on how well these councils are funded, they can be the prime movers of administration policy in any area where an interagency council exists. The U.S. Interagency Council on Homelessness, for example, was created in 1987 to coordinate the activities of the more than fifty governmental agencies and programs that work to alleviate homelessness.

In areas where there are extraordinarily complex policy problems, recent presidential administrations have created policy coordinating committees (PCCs) to facilitate interaction among agencies and departments at the subcabinet level. These PCCs gained increasing favor after the September 11, 2001, terrorist attacks. For example, the Homeland Security Council PCC oversees multiple agencies and executive departments to ensure that consistent, effective homeland security policies are developed and carried out, and that such policies are coordinated with state and local agencies. It is composed of representatives from various executive departments as well as the Federal Bureau of Investigation, Central Intelligence Agency, Federal Emergency Management Agency, and the vice president's office, among others.

Making Policy

The main purpose of all of these decision-making bodies is policy making. Policy making and implementation take place on both informal and formal levels. Practically, many decisions are left to individual government employees on a day-to-day basis. Department of Justice lawyers, for example, make daily decisions about whether or not to prosecute suspects. Similarly, street-level Internal Revenue Service agents make many decisions during personal audits. These street-level bureaucrats make policy on two levels. First, they exercise broad judgment in decisions concerning citizens with whom they interact. Second, taken together, their individual actions add up to agency behavior.[10] Thus, how bureaucrats interpret and how they apply (or choose not to apply) various policies are equally important parts of the policy-making process.

Administrative discretion, the ability of bureaucrats to make choices concerning the best way to implement congressional or executive intentions, also allows decision makers (whether they are in a Cabinet-level position or at the lowest GS levels) a tremendous amount of leeway. It is exercised through two formal administrative procedures: rule making and administrative adjudication.

RULE MAKING   **Rule making** is a quasi-legislative process that results in regulations that have the characteristics of a legislative act. **Regulations** are the rules that govern the operation of all government programs and have the force of law. In essence, then, bureaucratic rule makers often act as lawmakers as well as law enforcers when they make rules or draft regulations to implement various congressional statutes. Some political scientists say that rule making "is the single most important function performed by agencies of government."[11]

Because regulations often involve political conflict, the 1946 Administrative Procedures Act established rule-making procedures to give everyone the chance to participate in the process. The act requires that: (1) public notice of the time, place, and nature of the rule-making proceedings be provided in the *Federal Register*; (2) interested parties be given the opportunity to submit written arguments and facts relevant to the rule; and, (3) the statutory purpose and basis of the rule be stated. Once rules are written, thirty days generally must elapse before they take effect.

Sometimes an agency is required by law to conduct a formal hearing before issuing rules. Evidence is gathered, and witnesses testify and are cross-examined by opposing interests. The process can take weeks, months, or even years, at the end of which agency administrators must review the entire record and then justify the new rules. Although cumbersome, the process has reduced criticism of some rules and bolstered the deference given by the courts to agency decisions. Many Americans are unaware of their opportunity to influence government at this stage.

ADMINISTRATIVE ADJUDICATION   Agencies regularly find that persons or businesses are not in compliance with the federal laws the agencies are charged with enforcing, or that they are in violation of an agency rule or regulation. To force compliance, some agencies resort to **administrative adjudication,** a quasi-judicial process in which a bureaucratic agency settles disputes between two parties in a manner similar to the way courts resolve disputes. Administrative adjudication is referred to as quasi judicial, because adjudication by any body other than the judiciary would be a violation of the constitutional principle of separation of powers.

Several agencies and boards employ administrative law judges to conduct hearings. Although these judges are employed by the agencies, they are strictly independent and cannot be removed except for gross misconduct. Their actions, however, are reviewable in the federal courts, as are the findings of the Equal Employment Opportunity Commission and Social Security Administration judges.

administrative discretion
The ability of bureaucrats to make choices concerning the best way to implement congressional or executive intentions.

rule making
A quasi-legislative process that results in regulations that have the characteristics of a legislative act.

regulations
Rules that govern the operation of all government programs that have the force of law.

administrative adjudication
A quasi-judicial process in which a bureaucratic agency settles disputes between two parties in a manner similar to the way courts resolve disputes.

TOWARD REFORM: Making Agencies Accountable

★ **8.4 . . . Evaluate controls designed to make agencies more accountable.**

Although many critics of the bureaucracy argue that federal employees should be responsive to the public interest, the public interest is difficult to define. As it turns out, several factors work to control the power of the bureaucracy, and to some degree, the same kinds of checks and balances that operate among the three branches of government serve to check the bureaucracy.

Join the DEBATE | Should the Federal Bureaucracy Play a Role in Funding Higher Education?

Over the past decade, college tuition has increased an average of 4.9 percent per year, meaning that a student who paid $3,000 per year in tuition in 2000 would pay $4,840 in 2010 for the same education.[a] With these rising costs come increasing concerns about how many middle-class families will be able to pay for their children's higher education.

Some educational policy experts argue that the best way to address this educational funding dilemma is to increase the federal Department of Education's role in providing student loans, Pell Grants (grants sponsored by the U.S. Department of Education, which are given based on financial need and do not need to be repaid), and other programs designed to help students finance their educational aspirations. These observers note that the federal bureaucracy has unique knowledge and resources in the area of educational policy that make it well-suited to providing and administering a wide array of higher education programs.

Other observers maintain that it should not be the federal bureaucracy's responsibility to administer programs to defray the costs of higher education. They argue that the federal bureaucracy is already too large and that expanding the purview of the federal bureaucracy will negatively impact American society. Is the federal bureaucracy well-suited to equitably distribute education benefits to all Americans? Should the Department of Education be responsible for assuring that higher education is affordable for all Americans? If not, where should this responsibility fall?

To develop an ARGUMENT FOR the federal bureaucracy's role in funding higher education, think about how:

- **The federal bureaucracy is best suited to offer certain services.** Do state governments or the private sector have the resources and expertise to ensure that higher education is widely available to all students? In what ways is higher education a public good that the Department of Education should provide?
- **The federal bureaucracy has a responsibility to help citizens.** If the Department of Education can offer student loans at a lower cost than private industry, should it do so? How is the idea of equality of opportunity undermined by restricting access to higher education to only those who can pay for it themselves?
- **The federal bureaucracy does not focus on earning a profit.** How does the Department of Education's funding of higher education facilitate the development of basic scientific and social inquiry? In what ways does it encourage students to give back to their communities and society?

To develop an ARGUMENT AGAINST the federal bureaucracy's role in funding higher education, think about how:

- **Private banks and corporations can provide services more efficiently and less expensively than the federal bureaucracy.** Why might banks be better equipped to responsibly distribute loans than the Department of Education? How can banks and other corporations operate more efficiently than the federal bureaucracy?
- **It is not the federal bureaucracy's job to administer higher education programs.** Who should be responsible for education policy under the Constitution? What other goals should the federal government be exploring instead?
- **Students receive monetary benefits from their education.** Why should the Department of Education subsidize students' higher education, when a college degree is likely to increase students' earning potential over their lifetimes? In what ways is it fairer to privatize the costs of education, since its benefits are already privatized?

---

[a]All student loan data here are taken from the College Board's *Trends in Higher Education 2009*, www.trends-collegeboard.com/.

Executive Control

As the size and scope of the American national government, in general, and of the executive branch and the bureaucracy, in particular, have grown, presidents have delegated more and more power to bureaucrats. But, most presidents have continued to try to exercise some control over the bureaucracy. They have often found that task more difficult than they first envisioned. President John F. Kennedy, for example, once lamented that to give anyone at the Department of State an instruction was comparable to putting your request in a dead-letter box.[20] No response would ever be forthcoming.

Recognizing these potential problems, presidents try to appoint the best possible people to carry out their wishes and policy preferences. Presidents make hundreds of appointments to the executive branch; in doing so, they have the opportunity to appoint individuals who share their views on a range of policies. Although presidential appointments make up a very small proportion of all federal jobs, presidents or the Cabinet secretaries usually fill most top policy-making positions.

Presidents, with the approval of Congress, can reorganize the bureaucracy. They also can make changes in an agency's annual budget requests and ignore legislative initiatives originating within the bureaucracy.

As discussed in **chapter 7**, presidents also can shape policy and provide direction to bureaucrats by issuing executive orders.[12] **Executive orders** are rules or regulations issued by the president that have the effect of law; all executive orders must be published in the *Federal Register*. For example, even before Congress acted to protect women from discrimination by the federal government, the National Organization for Women convinced President Lyndon B. Johnson to sign a 1967 executive order that added the category of "gender" to an earlier order prohibiting discrimination on the basis of race, color, religion, or national origin in the awarding of federal contracts. Although the president signed the order, the Office of Federal Contract Compliance, part of the Department of Labor's Employment Standards Administration, failed to draft appropriate guidelines for implementation of the order until several years later.[13]

How does the government oversee environmental disasters? The U.S. Coast Guard worked together with the Environmental Protection Agency, the National Oceanic and Atmospheric Administration, and numerous other executive agencies to design ways to minimize the effects of a massive oil spill in the Gulf of Mexico in May 2010. While British Petroleum was deemed responsible for the spill and handled much of the cleanup, these agencies oversaw the process and contributed to the efforts to minimize the damage to the environment.

Photo courtesy: John Moore/Getty Images

executive order
Rule or regulation issued by the president that has the effect of law. All executive orders must be published in the *Federal Register*.

Congressional Control

Congress, can confirm (or reject) nominees to top bureaucratic positions and has also played an important role in checking the power of the bureaucracy. Constitutionally, it possesses the authority to create or abolish departments and agencies. It may also transfer agency functions, and expand or contract bureaucratic discretion as was the case in the creation of the Department of Homeland Security.

Congress can also use its investigatory powers to conduct program evaluations or hold oversight hearings. It is not at all unusual for a congressional committee or

Globalization and Bureaucracy

Globalization has created new problems for controlling and over-seeing the decisions of bureaucrats. It has led to ever-increasing demands for international uniformity and standardization not only in trade and investment policies but also in health and safety standards, environmental regulations, labor policies, and more. Most of these standards and regulations are negotiated at international conferences, and they are implemented by international organizations such as the World Trade Organization and World Bank.

But, who controls the actions of bureaucrats in these settings, especially when the need to reach a global agreement is great and compromises of national standards are almost inevitable? If an elected official for a particular country acts contrary to the wishes of citizens, he or she can be voted out of office. Bureaucrats working for the World Trade Organization or UNICEF, however, cannot be voted out of office, and elected officials have no real control over them. As globalization continues, many believe that more and more key decisions in areas such as health and the environment will be made by bureaucrats working beyond the effective reach of citizens. This challenge is referred to as a "democratic deficit."

- To what extent does globalization undermine national control over the bureaucracy?

- What can the United States do if its rules or policies are not accepted as the international standards?

- Does the United States need to create a new bureaucracy to manage international standards? What might such a bureaucracy look like?

subcommittee to hold hearings on a particular problem and then direct the relevant agency to study the problem or find ways to remedy it. Representatives of the agencies also appear before these committees on a regular basis to inform members about agency activities, ongoing investigations, and budget requests.

Congress also has the power of the purse. To control the bureaucracy, Congress uses its abilities to authorize spending and appropriate funds for an agency's activities much like the proverbial carrot and sticks. Money can be a powerful tool to coerce bureaucrats to make particular policies.

In addition, legislators augment their formal oversight of the executive branch by allowing citizens to appeal adverse bureaucratic decisions to agencies, Congress, and even the courts. Congressional review, a procedure adopted by the 104th Congress, by which agency regulations can be nullified by joint resolutions of legislative disapproval, is another method of exercising congressional oversight. This form of oversight is discussed in greater detail in **chapter 6**.

Judicial Control

Whereas the president's and Congress's ongoing control over the actions of the bureaucracy are direct, the judiciary's oversight function is less apparent. Still, federal judges, for example, can issue injunctions or orders to an executive agency even before a rule is publicized, giving the federal judiciary a potent check on the bureaucracy.

The courts also have ruled that agencies must give all affected individuals their due process rights guaranteed by the U.S. Constitution. A Social Security recipient's checks cannot be stopped, for example, unless that individual is provided with reasonable notice and an opportunity for a hearing. On a more informal, indirect level, litigation, or even the threat of litigation, often exerts a strong influence on bureaucrats. Injured parties can bring suit against agencies for their failure to enforce a law and can challenge agency interpretations of any law. In general, however, the courts give great weight to the opinions of bureaucrats and usually defer to their expertise.[14]

The development of specialized courts, however, has altered the relationship of some agencies with the federal courts, apparently resulting in less judicial deference to agency rulings. Research by political scientists reveals that specialized courts such as the Court of International Trade, because of its jurists' expertise, defer less to agency decisions than do more generalized federal courts. Conversely, decisions from executive agencies are more likely to be reversed than those from more specialized independent regulatory commissions.[15]

What Should I Have LEARNED?

Now that you have read this chapter, you should be able to:

⭐ **8.1 Trace the growth and development of the federal bureaucracy, p. 224.**

The federal bureaucracy has changed dramatically since President George Washington's time, when the executive branch had only three departments—State, War, and Treasury. Significant gains occurred in the size of the federal bureaucracy following the Civil War. As employment opportunities within the federal government increased, concurrent reforms in the civil service system assured that more and more jobs were filled according to merit and not by patronage. By the late 1800s, reform efforts led to further increases in the size of the bureaucracy, as independent regulatory commissions were created. In the wake of the Great Depression, many new agencies were created to get the national economy back on course as part of President Franklin D. Roosevelt's New Deal.

⭐ **8.2 Describe modern bureaucrats, and outline the structure of the modern bureaucracy, p. 227.**

The modern bureaucracy is composed of more than 2.7 million civilian workers from all walks of life. In general,

bureaucratic agencies fall into four categories: departments, independent agencies, independent regulatory commissions, and government corporations. The political activity of employees in the federal government is regulated by the Federal Employees Political Activities Act of 1993.

⭐ **8.3 Determine how the bureaucracy makes policy, p. 235.**

The bureaucracy is responsible for implementing many laws passed by Congress. A variety of formal and informal mechanisms, such as rule making and administrative adjudication, help the bureaucracy and bureaucrats make policy.

⭐ **8.4 Evaluate controls designed to make agencies more accountable, p. 237.**

Agencies enjoy considerable discretion, but they are also subject to many formal controls to help make them more accountable. The president, Congress, and the judiciary all exercise various degrees of control over the bureaucracy through oversight, funding, or litigation.

Test Yourself: The Executive Branch and the Federal Bureaucracy

⭐ **8.1 Trace the growth and development of the federal bureaucracy, p. 224.**

"To the victors belong the spoils" was a comment regarding President Andrew Jackson's use of what?
A. Patronage
B. The merit system
C. The Pendleton Act
D. Legislative programs such as the G.I. Bill
E. Administrative adjudication

⭐ **8.2 Describe modern bureaucrats, and outline the structure of the modern bureaucracy, p. 227.**

Which of the following is true about Cabinet departments?
A. Their heads always support the president.
B. They represent areas of permanent national interest.
C. They must be established by constitutional amendment.
D. They are for-profit entities.
E. All employees are paid on the merit system.

⭐ **8.3 Determine how the bureaucracy makes policy, p. 235.**

Relatively stable relationships and patterns of interaction that occur among agencies, interest groups, and congressional committees or subcommittees are known as
A. interagency councils.
B. iron triangles.
C. independent networks.

D. issue networks.
E. regulatory task forces.

⭐ **8.4 Evaluate controls designed to make agencies more accountable, p. 237.**

Which of the following is NOT a power the president has to make agencies accountable for their actions?
A. Issuing executive orders
B. Ignoring legislative initiatives originating within the bureaucracy
C. Appointing and removing agency heads and other top bureaucrats
D. Ordering Congress to hold investigational hearings about the actions of the bureaucracy
E. Making changes in an agency's annual budget proposals

Essay Questions

1. What factors led to the development of the merit system?
2. Describe the primary functions of government corporations and independent executive agencies.
3. What are some of the basic provisions of the Federal Employees Political Activities Act of 1993?
4. How is a regulation made?
5. How does the bureaucracy exercise quasi-judicial authority?
6. In what ways does Congress have oversight over the bureaucracy?

myp●liscilab Exercises
Apply what you learned in this chapter on MyPoliSciLab.

📖 Read on **mypoliscilab.com**

eText: Chapter 8

✓ Study and Review on **mypoliscilab.com**

Pre-Test
Post-Test
Chapter Exam
Flashcards

👁 Watch on **mypoliscilab.com**

Video: The CDC and the Swine Flu
Video: Internal Problems at the FDA

✦ Explore on **mypoliscilab.com**

Simulation: You Are Deputy Director of the Census Bureau
Simulation: You Are a Federal Administrator
Simulation: You Are the Head of FEMA
Simulation: You Are the President of MEDICORP
Comparative: Comparing Bureaucracies
Timeline: The Evolution of the Federal Bureaucracy
Visual Literacy: The Changing Face of the Federal Bureaucracy

Key Terms

administrative adjudication, p. 237
administrative discretion, p. 237
bureaucracy, p. 224
civil service system, p. 225
departments, p. 231
executive order, p. 239
Federal Employees Political Activities Act of 1993, p. 234

government corporations, p. 234
Hatch Act, p. 234
implementation, p. 236
independent executive agencies, p. 231
independent regulatory commission, p. 225
interagency councils, p. 236
iron triangles, p. 236

issue networks, p. 236
merit system, p. 225
patronage, p. 225
Pendleton Act, p. 225
regulations, p. 237
rule making, p. 237
spoils system, p. 225

To Learn More on the Executive Branch and the Federal Bureaucracy

In the Library

Anderson, James E. *Public Policymaking: An Introduction*, 7th ed. Belmont, CA: Wadsworth Publishing, 2010.

Borrelli, MaryAnne. *The President's Cabinet: Gender, Power, and Representation*. Boulder, CO: Lynne Rienner, 2002.

Dolan, Julie A., and David H. Rosenbloom. *Representative Bureaucracy: Classic Readings and Continuing Controversies*. Armonk, NY: M. E. Sharpe, 2003.

Durant, Robert F., ed. *The Oxford Handbook of American Bureaucracy*. New York: Oxford University Press, 2010.

Etzioni-Halevy, Eva. *Bureaucracy and Democracy*. New York: Routledge, 2009.

Goodsell, Charles T. *The Case for Bureaucracy: A Public Administration Polemic*, 4th ed. Washington, DC: CQ Press, 2003.

Hood, Christopher. *The Blame Game? Spin, Bureaucracy, and Self-Preservation in Government*. Princeton, NJ: Princeton University Press, 2010.

Ingraham, Patricia Wallace, and Laurence E. Lynn Jr. *The Art of Governance: Analyzing Management and Administration*. Washington, DC: Georgetown University Press, 2004.

Kerwin, Cornelius M. *Rulemaking: How Government Agencies Write Law and Make Policy*, 3rd ed. Washington, DC: CQ Press, 2003.

Meier, Kenneth J., and Laurence O'Toole. *Bureaucracy in a Democratic State: A Governance Perspective*. Baltimore: Johns Hopkins University Press, 2006.

Nigro, Lloyd G., Felix A. Nigro, and J. Edward Kellough. *The New Public Personnel Administration*, 6th ed. Belmont, CA: Wadsworth, 2006.

Peters, B. Guy. *The Politics of Bureaucracy*, 6th ed. New York: Routledge, 2009.

Stivers, Camilla. *Gender Images in Public Administration: Legitimacy and the Administrative State*, 2nd ed. Thousand Oaks, CA: Sage, 2002.

Twight, Charlotte. *Dependent on DC: The Rise of Federal Control over the Lives of Ordinary Americans*. New York: Palgrave Macmillan, 2002.

Wilson, James Q. *Bureaucracy: What Government Agencies Do and Why They Do It*, reprint ed. New York: Basic Books, 2000.

On the Web

To learn more about federal employees, go to the Office of Personnel Management Web site at **www.opm.gov** or to the page listing demographic information, **www.opm.gov/feddata/factbook/.**

To learn more about rules, proposed rules, and notices of federal agencies and organizations, go to the Web site of the *Federal Register* at **www.gpoaccess.gov/fr/index.html.**

To learn more about the Government Accountability Office, go to **www.gao.gov.**

To learn more about the Congressional Budget Office, go to **www.cbo.gov.**

The Judiciary

In July, 2005, Justice Sandra Day O'Connor, the first woman to serve on the U.S. Supreme Court, announced her retirement from the bench. A few short months later, in September, Chief Justice William H. Rehnquist passed away, leaving another seat on the Court unoccupied. These two events—the first vacancies on the Court in fourteen years—combined to give President George W. Bush an extraordinary opportunity to change the course and direction of the Court for years to come.

President Bush chose to replace Chief Justice Rehnquist with an appeals court judge named John G. Roberts Jr. Roberts's record in the lower courts had been conservative, and observers expected that his ideology would deviate little from that of his predecessor. President Bush's appointee to replace Justice O'Connor, another appeals court judge named Samuel A. Alito Jr., was another story. Justice O'Connor had long been known as the conservative-to-moderate "swing justice" on

the Court; at one time her ideology had led Court-watchers to call her "the most powerful woman in America." Justice Alito, however, was expected to maintain a more conservative political ideology, moving the Court, and perhaps American society, further to the right.

Five years after the appointments of Roberts and Alito, the Roberts Court has been declared the most conservative Supreme Court in nearly 100 years, a mantle it carries despite the addition of two moderate-to-liberal female justices to the Court in 2009 and 2010. Unlike Alito, whose ideology deviated significantly from that of the justice he replaced, Justices Sonia Sotomayor and Elena Kagan have replaced two similarly liberal judges, Justices David Souter and John Paul Stevens.

The conservatism of the Roberts Court can be seen in its decisions on a range of issues. In 2007, for example, it ruled in *Gonzales* v. *Carhart* that the federal Partial Birth Abortion Ban Act was constitutional. This decision was a

The Supreme Court's power has increased markedly since the founding of the United States. At left, the Warren Court (1953–1969) greatly expanded civil rights and liberties as well as the powers of the judiciary and the national government. At right, members of the Roberts Court during the 2010–2011 term.

dramatic reversal of the Rehnquist Court's 2003 decision in *Stenberg* v. *Carhart*. In that case, the Court declared unconstitutional an almost identical Nebraska partial birth abortion law. The major difference between the two decisions, according to legal scholars, was the departure of Justice O'Connor, who had been a reliable advocate for abortion in narrowly tailored circumstances.

Similarly, in 2010, the Court heard the case of *Citizens United* v. *FEC*. In this case, the Court was asked to decide whether the Bipartisan Campaign Reform Act's ban on certain campaign spending by businesses and unions passed constitutional muster. The Court ruled that limits on campaign spending—even by corporations—amounted to prohibitions on free speech. This decision reversed a 2003 ruling by the Court in *McConnell* v. *FEC*. Justice O'Connor had been one of the main authors of the Court's opinion in *McConnell*, which upheld the restrictions on corporate

electioneering. When asked about the Court's opinion in *Citizens United*, O'Connor expressed obvious displeasure, saying that if reporters wanted her opinion on campaign financing, they should read the Court's opinion in *McConnell*.[1]

What Should I Know About . . .

After reading this chapter, you should be able to:

★ **9.1** Trace the development of the federal judiciary and the origins of judicial review, p. 246.

★ **9.2** Describe the structure and main components of the American legal system, p. 252.

★ **9.3** Explain the organization of the federal court system, p. 254.

★ **9.4** Outline the criteria and process used to select federal court judges, p. 256.

★ **9.5** Evaluate the Supreme Court's process for accepting, hearing, and deciding cases, p. 261.

★ **9.6** Analyze the factors that influence judicial decision making, p. 268.

★ **9.7** Assess the role of the Supreme Court in the policy-making process, p. 270.

I n 1787, when Alexander Hamilton wrote *The Federalist Papers* urging support for the U.S. Constitution, he firmly believed that the judiciary would prove to be the weakest of the three branches of government. In its formative years, the judiciary was, in Hamilton's words, "the least dangerous" branch. The judicial branch seemed so inconsequential that when the young national government made its move to the District of Columbia in 1800, Congress actually forgot to include any space to house the justices of the Supreme Court!

Today, the role of the courts, particularly the Supreme Court of the United States, is significantly different from that envisioned when the national government came into being. The "least dangerous branch" now is perceived by many as having too much power.

In this chapter, we will explore the scope and development of judicial power:

- First, we will look at *the roots of the federal judiciary*.

- Second, we will explore the structure of *the American legal system* and the concepts of civil and criminal law.

- Third, we will discuss the organization of *the federal court system*, including that of specialized courts, district courts, courts of appeals, and the Supreme Court.

- Fourth, we will examine *how federal court judges are selected*, including the nomination criteria and the confirmation process.

- Fifth, we will look at *the Supreme Court today* and how cases make their way to the Supreme Court through the lengthy appellate process.

- Sixth, we will analyze *judicial philosophy and decision making* and their basis in a variety of legal and extra-legal factors.

- Finally, we will investigate *the judiciary's power to affect policy* and efforts at reform.

A note on terminology: When we refer to the "Supreme Court," the "Court," or the "high Court" here, we always mean the U.S. Supreme Court, which sits at the pinnacle of the federal and state court systems. The Supreme Court is referred to by the name of the chief justice who presided over it during a particular period. For example, the Marshall Court is the Court presided over by John Marshall from 1801 to 1835, and the Roberts Court is the current Court that began in 2005. When we use the term "courts," we refer to all federal or state courts unless otherwise noted.

ROOTS OF the Federal Judiciary

⭐ **9.1 . . . Trace the development of the federal judiciary and the origins of judicial review.**

The detailed notes James Madison took at the Constitutional Convention in Philadelphia make it clear that the Framers devoted little time to writing Article III, which created the judicial branch of government. The Framers believed that a federal judiciary posed little threat of tyranny. One scholar has even suggested that, for at least some delegates to the Constitutional Convention, "provision for a national judiciary was a matter of theoretical necessity . . . more in deference to the maxim of separation [of powers] than in response to clearly formulated ideas about the role of a national judicial system and its indispensability."[2]

As discussed in **chapter 2**, the Framers also debated the need for any federal courts below the Supreme Court. Some argued in favor of deciding all cases in state courts, with only appeals going before the Supreme Court. Others argued for a system of federal courts. A compromise left the final choice to Congress, and Article III, section 1, begins simply by vesting "The judicial Power of the United States . . . in one supreme Court, and in such inferior Courts as the Congress may from time to time ordain and establish."

Article III, section 2 specifies the judicial power of the Supreme Court. It also discusses the Court's original and appellate jurisdiction. This section also specifies that all federal crimes, except those involving impeachment, shall be tried by jury in the state in which the crime was committed. The third section of the article defines treason, and mandates that at least two witnesses appear in such cases. (To learn more about the Court's jurisdiction, see Table 9.1.)

Had the Supreme Court been viewed as the potential policy maker it is today, it is highly unlikely that the Framers would have provided for life tenure with "good behavior" for all federal judges in Article III. This feature was agreed on because the Framers did not want the justices (or any federal judges) subject to the whims of politics, the public, or politicians. Moreover, Alexander Hamilton argued in *Federalist No. 78* (see Appendix XX) that the "independence of judges" was needed "to guard the Constitution and the rights of individuals." (To learn more about Article III and judicial compensation, see The Living Constitution: Article III, Section 1.)

Some checks on the power of the judiciary were nonetheless included in the Constitution. The Constitution gives Congress the authority to alter the Court's jurisdiction (its ability to hear certain kinds of cases). Congress can also propose constitutional amendments that, if ratified, can effectively reverse judicial decisions, and it can impeach and remove federal judges. In one further check, it is the president who, with the "advice and consent" of the Senate, appoints all federal judges.

The Court can, in turn, check the presidency by presiding over presidential impeachment. Article I, section 3, notes in discussing impeachment, "When the President of the United States is tried, the Chief Justice shall preside."

The Constitution, however, is silent on the Court's power of **judicial review,** which allows the judiciary to review acts of the other branches of government and the state. This question was not resolved until *Marbury* v. *Madison* (1803), regarding acts of the national government, and *Martin* v. *Hunter's Lessee* (1816), regarding state law.[3]

judicial review
Power of the courts to review acts of other branches of government and the states.

Table 9.1 *What kinds of cases does the U.S. Supreme Court hear?*

The following are the types of cases the Supreme Court was given the jurisdiction to hear as initially specified in Article III, section 2, of the Constitution:
- All cases arising under the Constitution and laws or treaties of the United States
- All cases of admiralty or maritime jurisdiction
- Cases in which the United States is a party
- Controversies between a state and citizens of another state (later modified by the Eleventh Amendment)
- Controversies between two or more states
- Controversies between citizens of different states
- Controversies between citizens of the same state claiming lands under grants in different states
- Controversies between a state, or the citizens thereof, and foreign states or citizens thereof
- All cases affecting ambassadors or other public ministers

The Living Constitution

The Judges both of the supreme and inferior Courts, shall . . . receive for their services, a compensation, which shall not be diminished during their continuance in office.

—ARTICLE III, SECTION 1

This section of Article III guarantees that the salaries of all federal judges will not be reduced during their service on the bench. During the Constitutional Convention, there was considerable debate over how to treat the payment of federal judges. Some believed that Congress should have an extra check on the judiciary by being able to reduce their salaries. This provision was a compromise after James Madison suggested that Congress have the authority to bar increases as well as decreases in the salaries of these unelected jurists. The delegates recognized that decreases, as well as no opportunity for raises, could negatively affect the perks associated with life tenure.

There has not been much controversy over this clause of the Constitution. When the federal income tax was first enacted, some judges unsuccessfully challenged it as a diminution of their salaries. Much more recently, Chief Justices William H. Rehnquist and John G. Roberts Jr. repeatedly urged Congress to increase salaries for federal judges. As early as 1989, Rehnquist noted that "judicial salaries are the single greatest problem facing the federal judiciary today." Roberts, in his first state of the judiciary message, pointed out that the comparatively low salaries earned by federal judges drive away many well-qualified and diverse lawyers, compromising the independence of the American judiciary.

More and more federal judges are leaving the bench for more lucrative private practice. While a salary of $223,500 (for the chief justice) or $213,900 (for the other justices) may sound like a lot to most people, lawyers in large urban practices routinely earn more than double and triple that amount annually. Supreme Court clerks, moreover, now regularly receive $250,000 signing bonuses (in addition to large salaries) from law firms anxious to pay for their expertise.

CRITICAL THINKING QUESTIONS

1. How does prohibiting Congress from diminishing the salaries of judges reduce political influences in the judiciary?
2. What other checks on judicial power does Congress have?
3. Do you agree with Chief Justice Roberts's contention that judges are underpaid? Why or why not?

The Judiciary Act of 1789 and the Creation of the Federal Judicial System

In spite of the Framers' intentions, the pervasive role of politics in the judicial branch quickly became evident with the passage of the Judiciary Act of 1789. Congress spent nearly the entire second half of its first session deliberating the various provisions of the act to give form and substance to the federal judiciary.

The **Judiciary Act of 1789** established the basic three-tiered structure of the federal court system. At the bottom were the federal district courts—at least one in each state. If the people participating in a lawsuit (called litigants) were unhappy with the district court's verdict, they could appeal their case to the circuit courts. Each circuit court, initially created to function as a trial court for important cases, was originally composed of one district court judge and two Supreme Court justices who met as a

Judiciary Act of 1789

Legislative act that established the basic three-tiered structure of the federal court system.

circuit court twice a year. It wasn't until 1891 that circuit courts (or, as we know them today, courts of appeals) took on their exclusively appellate function and began to focus solely on reviewing the findings of lower courts. The third tier of the federal judicial system defined by the Judiciary Act of 1789 was the Supreme Court of the United States. Although the Constitution mentions "the supreme Court," it was silent on its size. In the Judiciary Act, Congress set the size of the Supreme Court at six—the chief justice plus five associate justices. After being reduced to five members in 1801, it later expanded and contracted, and finally the Court's size was fixed at nine in 1869.

When the justices met in their first public session in New York City in 1790, they were garbed magnificently in black and scarlet robes in the English fashion. The elegance of their attire, however, could not make up for the relative ineffectiveness of the Court. Its first session—presided over by John Jay, who was appointed chief justice of the United States by President George Washington—initially had to be adjourned when less than half the justices attended. Later, once a sufficient number of justices assembled, the Court decided only one major case. Moreover, as an indication of its lowly status, one associate justice left the Court to become chief justice of the South Carolina Supreme Court.

In its first decade, the Court took several actions to mold the new nation. First, by declining to give George Washington advice on the legality of some of his actions, the justices attempted to establish the Supreme Court as an independent, nonpolitical branch of government. The early Court also tried to advance principles of nationalism and to maintain the national government's supremacy over the states. Finally, in a series of circuit and Supreme Court decisions, the justices paved the way for announcement of the doctrine of judicial review by the third chief justice, John Marshall.

Who was John Marshall? A single person can make a major difference in the development of an institution. Such was the case with John Marshall (1755–1835), who dominated the Supreme Court during his thirty-four years as chief justice. More of a politician than a lawyer, Marshall served as a delegate to the Virginia legislature and played an instrumental role in Virginia's ratification of the U.S. Constitution in 1787. He became secretary of state in 1800 under John Adams. When Oliver Ellsworth resigned as chief justice of the United States in 1800, Adams nominated Marshall. Marshall served on the Court until the day he died, participating in more than 1,000 decisions and authoring more than 500 opinions.

Photo courtesy: The Boston Athenaeum

The Marshall Court: *Marbury* v. *Madison* (1803) and Judicial Review

John Marshall was appointed chief justice by President John Adams in 1800, three years after he declined to accept a nomination as associate justice. An ardent Federalist, Marshall is considered the most important justice to serve on the high Court. Part of his reputation is the result of the duration of his service and the historical significance of this period in our nation's history.

As chief justice, Marshall helped to establish the role and power of the Court. The Marshall Court, for example, discontinued the practice of *seriatim* (Latin for "in a series") opinions, which was the custom of the King's Bench in Great Britain. Prior to the Marshall Court, the justices delivered their individual opinions in order. For the Court to take its place as an equal branch of government, Marshall believed, the justices needed to speak as a Court and not as six individuals. In fact, during Marshall's first four years in office, the Court routinely spoke as one, and the chief justice wrote twenty-four of its twenty-six opinions.

The Marshall Court also established the authority of the Supreme Court over the judiciaries of the various states.[4] In

TIMELINE: The Development of the Supreme Court

1787 Writing a Constitution—The U.S. Constitution makes provisions for a federal judiciary in Article III.

1790 First Supreme Court Session—The Court meets for the first time in New York City.

Photo courtesy: The Granger Collection, New York

1803 *Marbury* v. *Madison*—The Court asserts that the power of judicial review can be implied from the Constitution's supremacy clause.

1789 Judiciary Act—The act gives form and substance to the federal judiciary, establishing the three-tiered system that exists today.

1801 John Marshall becomes Chief Justice—The Marshall Court increases the power of the Court, discontinues the practice of *seriatim* opinions, and expands the power of the Court over the states.

addition, the Court established the supremacy of the federal government and Congress over state governments through a broad interpretation of the necessary and proper clause in *McCulloch* v. *Maryland* (1819), discussed in detail in **chapter 3**.[5]

Finally, the Marshall Court claimed the right of judicial review, from which the Supreme Court derives much of its day-to-day power and impact on the policy process. This established the Court as the final arbiter of constitutional questions, with the right to declare congressional acts void.[6]

Alexander Hamilton first publicly endorsed the idea of judicial review in *Federalist No. 78,* noting, "Whenever a particular statute contravenes the Constitution, it will be the duty of the judicial tribunals to adhere to the latter and disregard the former." Nonetheless, because judicial review is not mentioned in the U.S. Constitution, the actual authority of the Supreme Court to review the constitutionality of acts of Congress was an unsettled question. But, in ***Marbury* v. *Madison* (1803),** Chief Justice John Marshall claimed this sweeping authority for the Court by asserting that the right of judicial review could be implied from the Constitution's supremacy clause.[7]

Marbury v. *Madison* arose amid a sea of political controversy. In the final hours of the Adams administration, William Marbury was appointed a justice of the peace for the District of Columbia. But, in the confusion of winding up matters, Adams's secretary of state failed to deliver Marbury's commission. Marbury then asked James Madison, Thomas Jefferson's secretary of state, for the commission. Under direct orders from Jefferson, who was irate over the Adams administration's last-minute appointment of several Federalist judges (quickly confirmed by the Federalist Senate), Madison refused to turn over the commission. Marbury and three other Adams appointees who were in the same situation then filed a writ of *mandamus* (a legal motion) asking the Supreme Court to order Madison to deliver their commissions.

Marbury v. *Madison* (1803)

Case in which the Supreme Court first asserted the power of judicial review by finding that the congressional statute extending the Court's original jurisdiction was unconstitutional.

1935 Supreme Court Building Opens—The Court moves into its own building located behind the U.S. Capitol.

1882 Justice Horace Gray Hires a Clerk—Clerks greatly facilitate the work of the justices; today each justice has four clerks.

1953 Earl Warren becomes Chief Justice—The Warren Court is noted for its broad expansions of civil rights and liberties.

2005 John G. Roberts Jr. becomes Chief Justice—The current Court is viewed as generally conservative.

Political tensions ran high as the Court met to hear the case. Jefferson threatened to ignore any order of the Court. Marshall realized that he and the prestige of the Court could be devastated by any refusal of the executive branch to comply with the decision. Responding to this challenge, in a brilliant opinion that in many sections reads more like a lecture to Jefferson than a discussion of the merits of Marbury's claim, Marshall concluded that although Marbury and the others were entitled to their commissions, the Court lacked the power to issue the writ sought by Marbury. In *Marbury* v. *Madison,* Marshall further ruled that the parts of the Judiciary Act of 1789 that extended the original jurisdiction of the Court to allow it to issue writs of *mandamus* were inconsistent with the Constitution and therefore unconstitutional.

Although the immediate effect of the decision was to deny power to the Court, its long-term effect was to establish the implied power of judicial review. Said Marshall, writing for the Court, "it is emphatically the province and duty of the judicial department to say what the law is." Since *Marbury,* the Court has routinely exercised the power of judicial review to determine the constitutionality of acts of Congress, the executive branch, and the states.

THINKING GLOBALLY

Advisory Opinions

The U.S. Supreme Court cannot be asked by presidents or other policy makers to give a nonbinding advisory opinion on issues that might come before it. This is not true everywhere. In Canada, under the terms of the Supreme Court Act, the national government may ask Canada's supreme court for an advisory opinion about the legality or constitutionality of a pending piece of legislation. While its decision is not legally binding, no Canadian government has ever ignored the court's advisory opinions. As of 2010, over seventy questions have been "referenced" to the court, including ones involving language rights, an independent Quebec, and same-sex marriage.

- For what types of cases might advisory opinions be most useful?

- Why might a president or legislative body want a supreme court to issue an advisory opinion?

- Should the U.S. Supreme Court be asked to give advisory opinions? Why or why not?

The American Legal System

★ **9.2** ... Describe the structure and main components of the American legal system.

trial court

Court of original jurisdiction where cases begin.

appellate court

Court that generally reviews only findings of law made by lower courts.

The judicial system in the United States can best be described as a dual system consisting of the federal court system and the judicial systems of the fifty states. Cases may arise in either system. Both systems are basically three-tiered. At the bottom of the system are **trial courts,** where litigation begins. In the middle are **appellate courts;** these courts generally review only findings of law made by trial courts. At the top of each pyramid sits a court of last resort. (To learn more about the structure of the judicial system, see Figure 9.1.)

Figure 9.1 *How is the American judicial system structured?*

FEDERAL COURT SYSTEM

STATE COURT SYSTEM

Original Jurisdiction   *Appellate Jurisdiction*

U.S. Supreme Court
(hears 75–90 cases per term)

The Supreme Court rarely exercises its original jurisdiction (1–3 percent of cases heard). Cases are heard by the Supreme Court first when they involve:
- Two or more states
- The United States and a state
- Foreign ambassadors and other diplomats
- A state and a citizen of another state (if the action is begun by the state)

Most cases heard by the Supreme Court are under its appellate jurisdiction (97–99 percent of cases heard). The Supreme Court can agree to hear cases involving appeals from:
- U.S. courts of appeals
- Highest state courts (only in cases involving federal questions)
- Court of Military Appeals

Highest State Courts
(52 courts handling 95,000 cases per year)

U.S. Courts of Appeals
(13 courts handling 60,000 cases per year)

No original jurisdiction

Hear appeals of cases from:
- Lower federal courts
- U.S. regulatory commissions
- Legislative courts, including the U.S. Court of Federal Claims and U.S. Court of Veterans Appeals

State Intermediate Appellate Courts
(found in 39 states; handling 300,000 cases per year)

U.S. District Courts
(94 courts handling 350,000 cases per year)

Cases are heard in U.S. district courts when they involve:
- The federal government as a party
- Civil suits under federal law
- Civil suits between citizens of different states if the amount at issue is more than $75,000
- Admiralty or maritime disputes
- Bankruptcy
- Other matters assigned to them by Congress

No appellate jurisdiction

State Trial Courts
(100 million filings per year)

Jurisdiction

Before a state or federal court can hear a case, it must have **jurisdiction,** or the authority to hear and decide the issues in that case. The jurisdiction of the federal courts is controlled by the U.S. Constitution and by statute. Jurisdiction is conferred based on issues, the amount of money involved in a dispute, or the type of offense. Procedurally, we speak of two types of jurisdiction: original and appellate. **Original jurisdiction** refers to a court's authority to hear disputes as a trial court; these courts determine the facts of a case. For example, the child custody case between Bristol Palin and Levi Johnston began in an Alaska state trial court of original jurisdiction. In contrast, the legal battle over the constitutionality of the federal Partial Birth Abortion Ban Act began in several federal district courts. More than 90 percent of all cases, whether state or federal, end in a court of original jurisdiction. **Appellate jurisdiction** refers to a court's ability to review and/or revise cases already decided by a trial court. Appellate courts ordinarily do not review the factual record. Instead, they review legal procedures to make certain that the law was applied properly to the issues presented in the case, generally in panels of three.

jurisdiction
Authority vested in a particular court to hear and decide the issues in a particular case.

original jurisdiction
The jurisdiction of courts that hear a case first, usually in a trial. These courts determine the facts of a case.

appellate jurisdiction
The power vested in particular courts to review and/or revise the decision of a lower court.

Criminal and Civil Law

Criminal law is the body of law that relates to the protection of property and individual safety.[8] Crimes are graded as felonies, misdemeanors, or offenses, according to their severity. Some acts—for example, murder, rape, and robbery—are considered crimes in all states. Although all states outlaw murder, their penal, or criminal, codes treat the crime quite differently; some states, for example, allow the death penalty for murder, while others prohibit the use of capital punishment. Other practices—such as gambling—are illegal only in some states.

Criminal law assumes that society itself is the victim of the illegal act; therefore, the government prosecutes, or brings an action, on behalf of an injured party (acting as a plaintiff) in criminal cases. Criminal cases are traditionally in the purview of the states. But, a burgeoning set of federal criminal laws is contributing significantly to delays in the federal courts.

Civil law is the body of law that regulates the conduct and relationships between individuals or groups. While national, state, or local governments may file civil lawsuits, it is more common for individuals to do so. People who believe they have been injured by another party must take action to seek judicial relief. Civil cases, then, involve lawsuits filed to recover something of value, whether it is the right to vote, fair treatment, or monetary compensation for an item or service that cannot be recovered.

Each civil or criminal case has a plaintiff, or petitioner, who brings charges against a defendant, or respondent. Sometimes the government is the plaintiff. The government may bring civil charges on behalf of the citizens of the state or the national government against a person or corporation for violating the law, but it is always the government that brings a criminal case. When cases are initiated, they are known first by the name of the petitioner. For example, in *Marbury* v. *Madison*, William Marbury was the petitioner, suing the respondents, the U.S. government and James Madison as its secretary of state, for not delivering Marbury's judicial commission.

During trials, judges often must interpret the intent of laws enacted by Congress and state legislatures. To do so, they read reports, testimony, and debates on the relevant legislation and study the results of other similar legal cases. They also rely on the presentations made by lawyers in their briefs and at trial.

Another important component of most civil and criminal cases is the jury. This body acts as the ultimate finder of fact and plays an important role in determining the culpability of the individual on trial.

criminal law
Codes of behavior related to the protection of property and individual safety.

civil law
Codes of behavior related to the conduct and relationships between individuals or groups.

The Federal Court System

⭐ **9.3 . . . Explain the organization of the federal court system.**

The federal district courts, courts of appeals, and the Supreme Court are called **constitutional** (or Article III) **courts** because Article III of the Constitution either established them or authorized Congress to establish them. Judges who preside over these courts are nominated by the president (with the advice and consent of the Senate), and they serve lifetime terms, as long as they engage in "good behavior."

In addition to constitutional courts, **legislative courts** are set up by Congress, under its implied powers, generally for special purposes. The U.S. territorial courts (which hear federal cases in the territories) and the U.S. Court of Appeals for Veterans Claims are examples of legislative courts, or what some call Article I courts. The judges who preside over these federal courts are appointed by the president (subject to Senate confirmation) and serve fixed, limited terms.

constitutional courts
Federal courts specifically created by the U.S. Constitution or by Congress pursuant to its authority in Article III.

legislative courts
Courts established by Congress for specialized purposes, such as the Court of Appeals for Veterans Claims.

District Courts

As we have seen, Congress created U.S. district courts when it enacted the Judiciary Act of 1789. District courts are federal trial courts. There are currently ninety-four federal district courts. No district court cuts across state lines. Every state has at least one federal district court, and the most populous states—California, Texas, and New York—each have four.[9]

Federal district courts, where the bulk of the judicial work takes place in the federal system, have original jurisdiction over only specific types of cases. Although the rules governing district court jurisdiction can be complex, cases heard in federal district courts by a single judge (with or without a jury) generally fall into one of three categories:

1. They involve the federal government as a party.
2. They present a federal question based on a claim under the U.S. Constitution, a treaty with another nation, or a federal statute. This is called federal question jurisdiction and it can involve criminal or civil law.
3. They involve civil suits in which citizens are from different states, and the amount of money at issue is more than $75,000.[10]

Each federal judicial district has a U.S. attorney, nominated by the president and confirmed by the Senate. The U.S. attorney in each district is that district's chief law enforcement officer. U.S. attorneys have a considerable amount of discretion as to whether they pursue criminal or civil investigations or file charges against individuals or corporations. They also have several assistants to help them in their work. The number of U.S. attorneys in each district depends on the amount of litigation.

The Courts of Appeals

The losing party in a case heard and decided in a federal district court can appeal the decision to the appropriate court of appeals. The U.S. courts of appeals (known as the circuit courts of appeals prior to 1948) are the intermediate appellate courts in the federal system and were established in 1789 to hear appeals from federal district courts. There are currently eleven numbered courts of appeals. A twelfth, U.S. Court of Appeals for the D.C. Circuit, handles most appeals involving federal regulatory commissions and agencies, including, for example, the National Labor Relations Board and the Securities and Exchange Commission. The thirteenth federal appeals court is the U.S. Court of Appeals for the Federal Circuit, which deals with patents and contract and financial claims against the federal government.

The number of judges within each court of appeals varies—depending on the workload and the complexity of the cases—and ranges from six to nearly thirty. Each court is supervised by a chief judge, the most senior judge in terms of service below the age of sixty-five, who can serve no more than seven years. In deciding cases, judges are divided into rotating three-judge panels, made up of the active judges within the court of appeals, visiting judges (primarily district judges from the same court), and retired judges. In rare cases, all the judges in a court of appeals may choose to sit together (*en banc*) to decide a case of special importance by majority vote.

The courts of appeals have no original jurisdiction. Rather, Congress has granted these courts appellate jurisdiction over two general categories of cases: appeals from criminal and civil cases from the district courts, and appeals from administrative agencies. Once a decision is made by a federal court of appeals, a litigant no longer has an automatic right to an appeal. The losing party may submit a petition to the U.S. Supreme Court to hear the case, but the Court grants few of these requests.

In general, courts of appeals try to correct errors of law and procedure that have occurred in lower courts or administrative agencies. Courts of appeals hear no new testimony; instead, lawyers submit written arguments in what is called a **brief** (also submitted in trial courts), and they then appear to present and argue the case orally to the court.

Decisions of any court of appeals are binding on only the courts within its geographic confines. Decisions of the U.S. Supreme Court, however, are binding throughout the nation and establish national **precedents,** or rules for settling subsequent cases of similar nature. This reliance on past decisions or precedents to formulate decisions in new cases is called ***stare decisis*** (a Latin phrase meaning "let the decision stand"). The principle of *stare decisis* allows for continuity and predictability in our judicial system. Although *stare decisis* can be helpful in predicting decisions, at times judges carve out new ground and ignore, decline to follow, or even overrule precedents to reach a different conclusion in a case involving similar circumstances. This is a major reason why so much litigation exists in America today. Parties to a suit know that the outcome of a case is not always predictable; if such prediction were possible, there would be little reason to go to court.

brief
A document containing the legal written arguments in a case filed with a court by a party prior to a hearing or trial.

precedent
A prior judicial decision that serves as a rule for settling subsequent cases of a similar nature.

stare decisis
In court rulings, a reliance on past decisions or precedents to formulate decisions in new cases.

The Supreme Court

The U.S. Supreme Court, as we saw in the opening vignette, is often at the center of highly controversial issues that have yet to be resolved successfully in the political process. It reviews cases from the U.S. courts of appeals and state supreme courts (as well as other courts of last resort) and acts as the final interpreter of the U.S. Constitution. The Court not only decides a number of major cases with tremendous policy significance, but it also ensures uniformity in the interpretation of national laws and the Constitution, resolves conflicts among the states, and maintains the supremacy of national law in the federal system.

Since 1869, the U.S. Supreme Court has consisted of eight associate justices and one chief justice, who is nominated by the president specifically for that position. There is no special significance about the number nine, and the Constitution is silent about the size of the Court. Between 1789 and 1869, Congress periodically altered the size of the Court. The lowest number of justices on the Court was six; the most, ten. Through December 2010, only 112 justices had served on the Court, and there had been seventeen chief justices. (To learn more about chief justices of the Supreme Court, see Appendix IV.)

How Federal Court Judges Are Selected

★ **9.4** . . . Outline the criteria and process used to select federal court judges.

The selection of federal judges is often a very political process with important political ramifications because judges are nominated by the president and must be confirmed by the U.S. Senate. Presidents, in general, try to select well-qualified men and women for the bench. But, these appointments also provide a president with the opportunity to put his philosophical stamp on the federal courts. Nominees, however, while generally members of the nominating president's party, usually are vetted through the senators' offices of the states where the district court or court of appeals vacancy occurs. In the absence of a senator from the president's party, the president may look to members of the House from that state. He may also turn to advisors, confidantes, or other high-ranking party officials.[11] This process by which presidents generally defer selection of district court judges to the choice of senators of their own party who represent the state where the vacancy occurs is known as **senatorial courtesy.** (To learn more about how presidents affect the judiciary, see Table 9.2.)

senatorial courtesy
Process by which presidents generally defer selection of district court judges to the choice of senators of their own party who represent the state where the vacancy occurs.

Who Are Federal Judges?

Typically, federal district court judges have held other political offices, such as state court judge or prosecutor. Most have been involved in politics, which is what usually brings them into consideration for a position on the federal bench.

Most recent nominees have had prior judicial experience. White males continue to dominate the federal courts, but since the 1970s, most presidents have pledged (with varying degrees of success) to do their best to appoint more African Americans, Hispanics, women, and other underrepresented groups to the federal bench. (To learn more, see Analyzing Visuals: Race, Gender, and Ethnicity of Federal Court Appointees.)

Nomination Criteria

Justice Sandra Day O'Connor once remarked that "You have to be lucky" to be appointed to the judiciary.[12] Although luck is certainly important, over the years nominations to the bench have been made for a variety of reasons. Depending on the timing of a vacancy, a president may or may not have a list of possible candidates or even a specific individual in mind. Until recently, presidents often looked within their circle of friends or their administration to fill a vacancy. Nevertheless, whether the nominee

Table 9.2 *How does a president affect the federal judiciary?*

President	Appointed to Supreme Court	Appointed to Courts of Appeals[a]	Appointed to District Courts[b]	Total Appointed	Total Number of Judgeships[c]	Percentage of Judgeships Filled by President
Carter (1977–1981)	0	56	203	259	657	39
Reagan (1981–1989)	3	83	290	376	740	50
Bush (1989–1993)	2	42	148	192	825	22
Clinton (1993–2001)	2	66	305	373	841	44
G. W. Bush (2001–2009)	2	61	261	324	866	37
Obama (2009–)[d]	2	11	30	43	866	5

[a]Does not include the U. S. Court of Appeals for the Federal Circuit.
[b]Includes district courts in the territories.
[c]Total judgeships authorized in president's last year in office.
[d]Barack Obama data through September 20, 2010.
Source: "Imprints on the Bench," *CQ Weekly Report* (January 19, 2001): 173. Reprinted by permission of Copyright Clearance Center on behalf of Congressional Quarterly, Inc. Updated by authors.

ANALYZING VISUALS

Race, Gender, and Ethnicity of Federal Court Appointees

Examine the bar graphs, which show some of the characteristics of federal court appointees from President Jimmy Carter to President Barack Obama, and consider the questions.

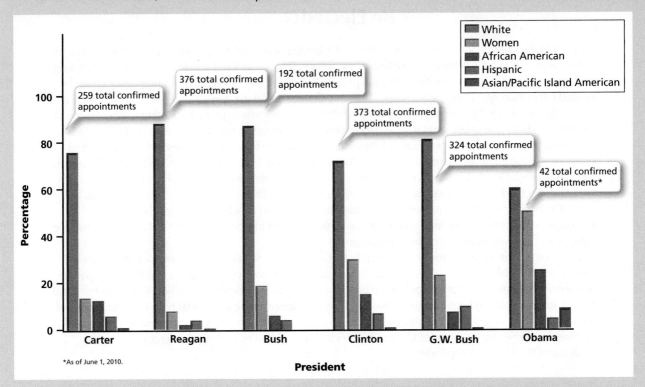

*As of June 1, 2010.

- Overall, which groups are most underrepresented in federal court appointments?
- What differences, if any, are there between judicial appointments made by Democratic presidents and those made by Republican presidents?
- Should race, gender, and ethnicity matter in judicial appointments? Why or why not?

Source: Federal Judges Biographical database, www.fjc.gov/public/home.nsf/hisj.

is a friend or someone known to the president only by reputation, at least six criteria are especially important: competence, ideology or policy preferences, rewards, pursuit of political support, religion, and race and gender. (To learn more about the debate over selecting Supreme Court justices, see Join the Debate: Should U.S. Supreme Court Justices Be Elected?)

COMPETENCE   Most nominees have had at least some judicial, legal, or governmental experience. For example, John Jay, the first chief justice, was one of the authors of *The Federalist Papers* and was active in New York politics. In 2010, all nine sitting Supreme Court justices but one—former solicitor general Elena Kagan—had prior judicial experience. (To learn more about the current Court, see Table 9.3.)

IDEOLOGY OR POLICY PREFERENCES   Most presidents seek to appoint individuals who share their policy preferences, and almost all have political goals in mind when

Join the DEBATE | Should U.S. Supreme Court Justices Be Elected?

Article II of the Constitution grants the president of the United States authority to make judicial appointments to federal courts with the advice and consent of the Senate. Thus, judges serving on federal courts, including the U.S. Supreme Court, are not elected by the people. But, at the state level, it is common for judges to be elected rather than appointed. Seven states (Alabama, Illinois, Louisiana, New York, Pennsylvania, Texas, and West Virginia) elect judges in partisan elections, while twenty-nine others provide for other forms of election (nonpartisan ballots or gubernatorial appointment with confirmation or retention through popular election).

These judicial elections have received a great deal of criticism in recent years. As their price tags and controversy have escalated, many observers, including former Supreme Court Justice Sandra Day O'Connor, have charged that judicial elections compromise judicial independence and the ideal of blind justice. "We all expect judges to be accountable to the law rather than political supporters or special interests," writes O'Connor, "But elected judges in many states are compelled to solicit money for their election campaigns . . . whether or not those contributions tilt the scales of justice, three-fourths of Americans believe campaign contributions affect courtroom decisions."[a]

But, other observers contend that judicial elections are an excellent way to assure that judges remain accountable to the people. They further argue that electing judges assures that the positions are not political plums to be handed out to the biggest supporters and ideological allies. How can our legal system strike a balance between guaranteeing judicial independence and equality in the application of the law and the democratic accountability of the Supreme Court? Should U.S. Supreme Court justices be directly elected by the people? Or, would the election of justices undermine the application of justice and the Court's independence?

To develop an ARGUMENT FOR the election of U.S. Supreme Court justices, think about how:

- **The decisions of the U.S. Supreme Court impact public policy.** Should public policy be made by a group of nine individuals who are not directly elected by the people? How might electing judges help judicial decisions reflect the times?
- **The U.S. Supreme Court is often perceived as unresponsive to public opinion.** How would the direct election of justices force them to be more responsive to public opinion? In what ways would the direct election of justices limit judicial activism on the Court?
- **The U.S. Supreme Court does not represent the diversity of the American people.** Why is diversity on the Supreme Court important? How might the direct election of justices yield a Court that is more ideologically, racially, and gender representative of the United States?

To develop an ARGUMENT AGAINST the election of U.S. Supreme Court justices, think about how:

- **The U.S. Supreme Court provides stability to the entire court system.** What would happen to the principle of *stare decisis* if Supreme Court justices were regularly voted out of office? What role would legal precedent play in such a system?
- **Justice requires a Supreme Court that is willing to defy popular opinion.** Would the Supreme Court have reached the same decisions in controversial cases like *Brown* v. *Board of Education* (1954), *Texas* v. *Johnson* (1990), or *Lawrence* v. *Texas* (2003), if its members were popularly elected? Can justices concerned with reelection make the right decisions, even if they are unpopular?
- **Donors play a central role in financing expensive election campaigns.** In what ways would Supreme Court justices be responsive to the special interests that helped finance their campaigns? Would elected Supreme Court justices apply justice evenly?

---

[a] Brennan Center for Justice, "The New Politics of Judicial Elections." www.brennancenter.org.

Table 9.3 *Who are the justices of the Supreme Court in 2010?*

	Year of Birth	Year Appointed	Political Party	Law School	Appointing President	Religion	Prior Judicial Experience	Prior Government Experience
John G. Roberts Jr.	1955	2005	R	Harvard	G. W. Bush	Roman Catholic	U.S. Court of Appeals	Dept. of Justice, associate White House counsel
Antonin Scalia	1936	1986	R	Harvard	Reagan	Roman Catholic	U.S. Court of Appeals	Assistant attorney general, Office of Legal Counsel
Anthony Kennedy	1936	1988	R	Harvard	Reagan	Roman Catholic	U.S. Court of Appeals	None
Clarence Thomas	1948	1991	R	Yale	Bush	Roman Catholic	U.S. Court of Appeals	Chair, Equal Employment Opportunity Commission
Ruth Bader Ginsburg	1933	1993	D	Columbia/ Harvard	Clinton	Jewish	U.S. Court of Appeals	None
Stephen Breyer	1938	1994	D	Harvard	Clinton	Jewish	U.S. Court of Appeals	Chief counsel, Senate Judiciary Committee
Samuel A. Alito Jr.	1950	2006	R	Yale	G. W. Bush	Roman Catholic	U.S. Court of Appeals	Dept. of Justice, U.S. attorney
Sonia Sotomayor	1954	2009	D	Yale	Obama	Roman Catholic	U.S. Court of Appeals	Assistant attorney general, City of New York
Elena Kagan	1960	2010	D	Harvard	Obama	Jewish	None	U.S. solicitor general, associate White House counsel

they appoint a judge or justice. Presidents Franklin D. Roosevelt, Richard M. Nixon, and Ronald Reagan were successful in molding the courts to their own political beliefs.

REWARDS   Historically, many of those appointed to the judiciary have been personal friends of presidents. Abraham Lincoln, for example, appointed one of his key political advisors to the Supreme Court. Lyndon B. Johnson appointed his longtime friend Abe Fortas to the bench. Most presidents also select judges and justices of their own party affiliation. Chief Justice John G. Roberts Jr. and Justice Samuel A. Alito Jr., for example, both Republicans, worked in the Department of Justice during the Reagan and George Bush administrations. Roberts also served as associate White House counsel under Reagan.

PURSUIT OF POLITICAL SUPPORT   During Ronald Reagan's successful campaign for the presidency in 1980, some of his advisors feared that the gender gap would hurt him. Polls repeatedly showed that he was far less popular with female voters than with men. To gain support from women, Reagan announced during his campaign that should he win, he would appoint a woman to fill the first vacancy on the Supreme Court. When Justice Potter Stewart, a moderate, announced his retirement from the bench, under pressure from women's rights groups, President Reagan nominated Sandra Day O'Connor of the Arizona Court of Appeals to fill the vacancy. Similarly, it probably did not hurt President Barack Obama's popularity with Hispanic voters that his first appointment, Sonia Sotomayor, was Hispanic.

RELIGION   Through late 2010, of the 112 justices who have served on the Court, almost all have been members of traditional Protestant faiths. Only twelve have been Roman Catholic and only eight have been Jewish.[13] Today, more Catholics—Roberts, Scalia, Kennedy, Thomas, Alito, and Sotomayor—serve on the Court than at any other point in history. Ironically, there was a time when no one could have imagined that Catholics would someday make up a majority of the Court, or that no members of any Protestant faiths would serve.

How do demographic characteristics affect judicial nomination and confirmation? Ethnicity and gender were important issues during the confirmation hearings of Justice Sonia Sotomayor. Other issues, such as lack of judicial experience, took precedence in the confirmation of Justice Elena Kagan.

RACE, ETHNICITY, AND GENDER   Through 2010, only two African Americans and three women have served on the Court. Race was undoubtedly a critical issue in the appointment of Clarence Thomas to replace Thurgood Marshall, the first African American justice. But, President George Bush refused to acknowledge his wish to retain a black seat on the Court. Instead, he announced that he was "picking the best man for the job on the merits," a claim that was met with considerable skepticism by many observers.

The Confirmation Process

The Constitution gives the Senate the authority to approve all nominees to the federal bench. Ordinarily, nominations are referred to the Senate Judiciary Committee. This committee investigates the nominees, holds hearings, and votes on its recommendation for Senate action. At this stage, the committee may reject a nominee or send the nomination to the full Senate for a vote. The full Senate then deliberates on the nominee before voting. A simple majority vote is required for confirmation.

INVESTIGATION   As a president begins to narrow the list of possible nominees for a judicial vacancy, those names are sent to the Federal Bureau of Investigation for background checks. After a formal nomination is made and sent to the Senate, the Senate Judiciary Committee begins its own investigation.

LOBBYING BY INTEREST GROUPS   Many organized interests are keenly interested in the nomination process. Interest groups are particularly active in Supreme Court nominations. In 1987, for example, the nomination of Judge Robert H. Bork to the

Supreme Court led liberal groups to launch an extensive radio, television, and print media campaign against the nominee. These interest groups decried Bork's actions as solicitor general, especially his firing of the Watergate special prosecutor at the request of President Richard M. Nixon, as well as his political beliefs.

More and more, interest groups are also getting involved in district court and court of appeals nominations. They recognize that these appointments often pave the way for future nominees to the Supreme Court.

THE SENATE COMMITTEE HEARINGS AND SENATE VOTE   After hearings are concluded, the Senate Judiciary Committee usually makes a recommendation to the full Senate. Any rejections of presidential nominees to the Supreme Court generally occur only after the Senate Judiciary Committee has recommended against a nominee's appointment. Few recent confirmations have been close, although current Supreme Court Justices Clarence Thomas and Samuel A. Alito Jr. were confirmed by margins of less than ten votes.

Appointments to the U.S. Supreme Court

Like other federal court judges, the justices of the Supreme Court are nominated by the president and must be confirmed by the Senate. Historically, because of the special place the Supreme Court enjoys in our constitutional system, its nominees have encountered more opposition than have district court or court of appeals nominees. As the role of the Court has increased over time, so too has the amount of attention given to nominees. With this increased attention has come greater opposition, especially to nominees with controversial views. (To learn more about the role that interest groups play in the nomination and confirmation processes of Supreme Court justices, see Politics Now: Gun Rights Could Pose Problem for Kagan.)

The Supreme Court Today

★ **9.5 . . . Evaluate the Supreme Court's process for accepting, hearing, and deciding cases.**

Given the judicial system's vast size and substantial, although often indirect, power over so many aspects of our lives, it is surprising that so many Americans know next to nothing about the judicial system in general and the U.S. Supreme Court in particular.

Even after the attention the Court received during the recent nomination hearings, 80 percent of those Americans surveyed in 2010 could not name one member of the Court; virtually no one could name all nine members of the Court. As revealed in Table 9.4, Clarence Thomas was the most well-known justice. Still, only about 20 percent of those polled could name him.

While much of this ignorance can be blamed on the American public's lack of interest, the Court has also taken great pains to ensure its privacy and sense of decorum. Its rites and rituals contribute to the Court's mystique and encourage a "cult of the robe."[14] Consider, for example, the way Supreme Court proceedings are conducted. Oral arguments are not televised, and deliberations concerning the outcome of cases are conducted in utmost secrecy. In contrast, C-SPAN brings us daily coverage of various congressional hearings and floor debate on bills and important national issues, and CNN and sometimes other networks provide extensive coverage of many important state court trials. The Supreme Court, however, remains adamant in its refusal to televise

Table 9.4 *Can Americans name the justices of the Supreme Court?*

Supreme Court Justice	Percentage Who Could Name
Clarence Thomas	19
John G. Roberts Jr.	16
Sonia Sotomayor	15
Ruth Bader Ginsburg	13
Antonin Scalia	10
Samuel A. Alito Jr.	8
John Paul Stevens	8
Anthony Kennedy	6
Stephen Breyer	3

Source: Findlaw.com Poll, June 2, 2010.

POLITICS**NOW**

| WORLD | NATION | LOCAL | **POLITICS** | OPINION | HEALTH & SCIENCE | ARTS | SPORTS | LEISURE |

Gun Rights Could Pose Problem for Kagan

May 27, 2010
Los Angeles Times
www.latimes.com

By James Oliphant

In her first weeks as dean of Harvard Law School in 2003, Elena Kagan put the warring sides of the gun rights debate in a room and let them fight it out.

The debate between gun control advocates and 2nd Amendment purists was sponsored by the law school's target shooting club, and Kagan showed her support by moderating the exchange. But her own views on gun rights went unaired.

With her Supreme Court confirmation pending, those views have become of extreme interest to pro-gun groups such as the National Rifle Assn. The NRA is already skeptical that it can support Kagan—and in Washington, when the NRA gets worried, senators become nervous.

"There are serious problems," said Andrew Arulanandam, public affairs director for the NRA. "We will work with senators to make sure tough questions are asked during hearings."

A concerted effort by the NRA to scuttle Kagan's confirmation could prove problematic for Republicans and moderate Democrats who fear falling from its good graces.

There appears to be enough evidence to stoke the NRA's concerns. Kagan worked in the Clinton administration for four years, first as a lawyer in the White House and later as a senior domestic policy advisor. Gun rights advocates already have locked in on a 1997 Kagan memo that paved the way for an executive order banning dozens of semiautomatic weapons as an example of the nominee's anti-gun views.

They also point to Kagan's background working for judges, such as federal Judge Abner Mikva, who later brought Kagan into the White House to serve as his deputy and who once likened the NRA to a "street-crime lobby."

But Kagan more recently has pledged her fidelity to the Supreme Court's 2008 decision in the case, *District of Columbia* vs. *Heller,* that found a constitutional right to own a handgun for personal protection. The White House maintains that Kagan would view her role as a justice differently from that of a policy-crafter in the Clinton White House. . . .

Critical Thinking Questions

1. To what extent should interest groups such as the NRA be involved in judicial nominations?
2. Should interest groups be able to use the paper trails of potential judges to lobby for or against their nomination?
3. What other issues might be the subject of substantial interest group involvement in judicial nominations?

---

its proceedings—including public oral arguments, although it now allows the release of same-day audio tapes of oral arguments.

Deciding to Hear a Case

Over 8,150 cases were filed at the Supreme Court during its 2009–2010 term; 82 were heard, and 81 decisions were issued. In contrast, from 1790 to 1801, the Court received only 87 total cases under its appellate jurisdiction. In the Court's early years, most of the justices' workload involved their circuit-riding duties.[15] As recently as the 1940s, fewer than 1,000 cases were filed annually. Filings increased at a dramatic rate until the mid-1990s, shot up again in the late 1990s, and generally have now leveled off. (To learn more about the Court's caseload, see Figure 9.2.)

The content of the Court's docket is every bit as significant as its size. During the 1930s, cases requiring the interpretation of constitutional law began to take a growing portion of the Court's workload, leading the Court to take a more important role in the policy-making process. At that time, only 5 percent of the Court's cases involved questions concerning the Bill of Rights. By the late 1950s, one-third of filed cases involved such questions; by the 1960s, half did.[16]

Figure 9.2 *How many cases does the Supreme Court handle?*
Cases the Supreme Court chooses to hear (represented by brown bars) represent a tiny fraction of the total number of cases filed with the Court (represented by green bars).
Source: Administrative Office of the Courts; Supreme Court Public Information Office.

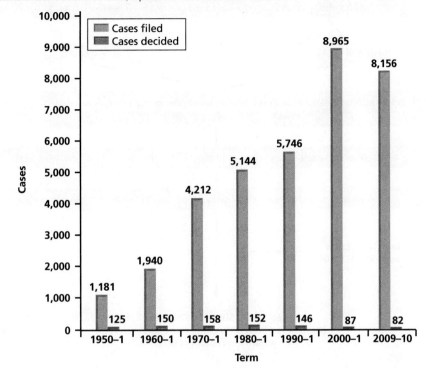

As discussed earlier in the chapter, the Court has two types of jurisdiction. The Court has original jurisdiction in "all Cases affecting Ambassadors, other public Ministers and Consuls, and those in which a State shall be a party." It is rare for more than four or five of these cases to come to the Court in a year. The second kind of jurisdiction enjoyed by the Court is its appellate jurisdiction. The Court is not expected to exercise its appellate jurisdiction simply to correct errors of other courts. Instead, appeal to the Supreme Court should be taken only if the case presents important issues of law, or what is termed "a substantial federal question." Since 1988, nearly all appellate cases that have gone to the Supreme Court arrived there on a petition for a **writ of *certiorari*** (from the Latin "to be informed"), which is a request for the Supreme Court—at its discretion—to order up the records of the lower courts for purposes of review. (To learn more about this process, see Figure 9.3.)

writ of *certiorari*
A request for the Supreme Court to order up the records from a lower court to review the case.

WRITS OF *CERTIORARI* AND THE RULE OF FOUR   The Supreme Court controls its own caseload through the *certiorari* process, deciding which cases it wants to hear, and rejecting most cases that come to it. All petitions, or writs of *certiorari*, must meet two criteria:

1. The case must come from either a U.S. court of appeals, a special three-judge court of military appeals, district court, or a state court of last resort.
2. The case must involve a federal question. Thus, the case must present questions of federal constitutional law or involve a federal statute, action, or treaty. The reasons that the Court should accept the case for review and legal argument supporting that position are set out in the petitioner's writ of *certiorari*.

Figure 9.3 *How does a case get to the Supreme Court?*
This figure illustrates both how cases get on the Court's docket and what happens after a case is accepted for review.

The clerk of the Court transmits petitions for writs of *certiorari* first to the chief justice's office, where clerks review the petitions, and then to the individual justices' offices. On the Roberts Court, all of the justices except Justice Samuel A. Alito Jr. (who allows his clerks great individual authority in selecting the cases for him to review) participate in what is called the *cert* pool. Pool participants review their assigned fraction of petitions and share their notes with each other. Those cases that the justices deem noteworthy are then placed on what is called the discuss list prepared by the chief justice's clerks and circulated to the chambers of the other justices. All others are dead listed and go no further. Only about 30 percent of submitted petitions make it to the discuss list. During one of the justices' weekly conference meetings, the cases on the discuss list are reviewed. The chief justice speaks first, then the rest of the justices, according to seniority. The decision process ends when the justices vote, and by custom, *certiorari* is granted according to the **Rule of Four**— when at least four justices vote to hear a case.

THE ROLE OF CLERKS   As early as 1850, the justices of the Supreme Court beseeched Congress to approve the hiring of a clerk to assist each justice. Congress denied the request, so when Justice Horace Gray hired the first law clerk in 1882, he paid the clerk himself. Justice Gray's clerk was a top graduate of Harvard Law School whose duties included cutting Justice Gray's hair and running personal errands. Finally, in 1886, Congress authorized each justice to hire a stenographer clerk for $1,600 a year.

Clerks typically are selected from candidates at the top of the graduating classes of prestigious law schools. They perform a variety of tasks, ranging from searching for arcane facts to playing tennis or taking walks with the justices. Clerks spend most of their time researching material, reading and summarizing cases, and helping justices write opinions. Clerks also make the first pass through the petitions that come to the Court, undoubtedly influencing which cases get a second look. Just how much help they provide in the writing of opinions is unknown.[17] (To learn more about what clerks do, see Table 9.5.)

Over time, the number of clerks employed by the justices has increased. Through the 1946 to 1969 terms, most justices employed two clerks. By 1970, most had three clerks, and by 1980, all but three justices had four clerks. In 2010, the nine active justices and three retired justices employed approximately forty clerks. This growth in the number of clerks has had many interesting ramifications for the Court. As the number of clerks has grown, so have the number and length of the Court's opinions.[18] And, until recently, the number of cases decided annually increased as more help was available to the justices.

The relationship between clerks and the justices for whom they work is close and confidential, and many aspects of the relationship are kept secret.[19] Clerks may sometimes talk among themselves about the views and personalities of their justices, but rarely has a clerk leaked such information to the press. In 1998, a former clerk to Justice Harry A. Blackmun broke the silence. Edward Lazarus published an insider's account of how the Court really works.[20] He argued that the justices give their young, often ideological, clerks far too much power.

How Does a Case Survive the Process?

It can be difficult to determine why the Court decides to hear a particular case. The Court does not offer reasons, and "the standards by which the justices decide to grant or deny review are highly personalized and necessarily discretionary," noted former Chief Justice Earl Warren.[21] Political scientists nonetheless have attempted to determine the characteristics of the cases the Court accepts. Among the cues are the following:

- The federal government is the party asking for review.
- The case involves conflict among the courts of appeals.
- The case presents a civil rights or civil liberties question.
- The case involves the ideological or policy preferences of the justices.
- The case has significant social or political interest, as evidenced by the presence of interest group *amicus curiae* briefs.

Table 9.5 *What do Supreme Court clerks do?*

Supreme Court clerks are among the best and brightest recent law school graduates. Almost all first clerk for a judge on one of the courts of appeals. After their Supreme Court clerkship, former clerks are in high demand. Firms often pay signing bonuses of up to $250,000 to attract clerks, who can earn $200,000 their first year in private practice.

Tasks of a Supreme Court clerk include the following:
- Perform initial screening of the 8,000 or so petitions that come to the Court each term
- Draft memos to summarize the facts and issues in each case, recommending whether the case should be accepted by the Court for full review
- Write "bench memos" summarizing an accepted case and suggesting questions for oral argument
- Write the first draft of an opinion
- Serve as informal conduit for communicating and negotiating with other justices' chambers as to the final wording of an opinion

Rule of Four
At least four justices of the Supreme Court must vote to consider a case before it can be heard.

solicitor general
The fourth-ranking member of the Department of Justice; responsible for handling nearly all appeals on behalf of the U.S. government to the Supreme Court.

amicus curiae
"Friend of the court"; *amici* may file briefs or even appear to argue their interests orally before the court.

FEDERAL GOVERNMENT   One of the most important cues for predicting whether the Court will hear a case is the solicitor general's position. The **solicitor general,** appointed by the president, is the fourth-ranking member of the Department of Justice and is responsible for handling nearly all appeals on behalf of the U.S. government to the Supreme Court. The solicitor's staff resembles a small, specialized law firm within the Department of Justice. But, because this office has such a special relationship with the Supreme Court, even having a suite of offices within the Supreme Court building, the solicitor general often is referred to as the Court's "ninth and a half member."[22] Moreover, the solicitor general, on behalf of the U.S. government, appears as a party or as an ***amicus curiae*** or friend of the court, in more than 50 percent of the cases heard by the Court each term. *Amici* may file briefs or even appear to argue their interests orally before the Court. This special relationship helps to explain the overwhelming success the solicitor general's office enjoys before the Supreme Court. The Court generally accepts 70 to 80 percent of the cases where the U.S. government is the petitioning party, compared with about 5 percent of all others.[23]

CONFLICT AMONG THE COURTS OF APPEALS   Conflict among the lower courts is another reason that the justices take cases. When interpretations of constitutional or federal law are involved, the justices seem to want consistency throughout the federal court system. Often these conflicts occur when important civil rights or civil liberties questions arise. Political scientists have noted that the justices' ideological leanings play a role.[24] It is not uncommon to see conservative justices voting to hear cases to overrule liberal lower court decisions, or vice versa. Justices also take cases when several circuit courts are in disagreement over a main issue.

INTEREST GROUP PARTICIPATION   A quick way for the justices to gauge the ideological ramifications of a particular civil rights or liberties case is by the nature and amount of interest group participation. Richard C. Cortner has noted that "cases do not arrive on the doorstep of the Supreme Court like orphans in the night."[25] Instead, most cases heard by the Supreme Court involve either the government or an interest group—either as the sponsoring party or as an *amicus curiae.*

How does the Supreme Court interact with the courts of appeals? Each year, the Supreme Court reviews a small number of court of appeals decisions; granting *certiorari* is more common in cases where there is conflict between the circuits. Many Supreme Court justices, including Justice Sonia Sotomayor and Chief Justice John G. Roberts Jr., shown below at Sotomayor's swearing in, also served as appeals court judges.

Photo courtesy: AP/Wide World Photos

Liberal groups, such as the American Civil Liberties Union, People for the American Way, or the NAACP Legal Defense and Educational Fund, and conservative groups, including the Washington Legal Foundation, Concerned Women for America, and the American Center for Law and Justice, routinely sponsor cases before the Supreme Court.

The positions of both parties in a case are often echoed or expanded in *amicus curiae* briefs filed by interested parties, especially interest groups or other parties potentially affected by the outcome of the case. Interest groups also provide the Court with information not necessarily contained in the party briefs, help write briefs, and assist in practice oral arguments during mock court sessions. In these sessions, the lawyer who will argue the case before the justices goes through several complete rehearsals, with prominent lawyers and law professors role playing the various justices.

Research by political scientists has found that "not only does [an *amicus*] brief in favor of *certiorari* significantly improve the chances of a case being accepted, but two, three, and four briefs improve the chances even more."[26] Clearly, it's the more the merrier, whether the briefs are filed for or against granting review.

Hearing and Deciding the Case

Once a case is accepted for review, a flurry of activity begins. Lawyers on both sides of the case begin to prepare their written arguments for submission to the Court. In these briefs, lawyers cite prior case law and make arguments as to why the Court should find in favor of their client.

ORAL ARGUMENTS   Once a case is accepted by the Court for full review, and after briefs and *amicus* briefs are submitted on each side, oral argument takes place. Oral argument generally is limited to the immediate parties in the case, although it is not uncommon for the U.S. solicitor general to appear to argue orally as an *amicus curiae*. Oral argument at the Court is fraught with time-honored tradition and ceremony. At precisely ten o'clock every morning when the Court is in session, the Court marshal, dressed in a formal morning coat, emerges to intone "Oyez! Oyez! Oyez!" as the nine justices emerge from behind a reddish-purple velvet curtain to take their places on the raised and slightly angled bench. The chief justice sits in the middle. The remaining justices sit to the left and right alternating in seniority.

Almost all attorneys are allotted one half hour to present their cases, and this time includes that required to answer questions from the bench. Although many Court watchers have tried to figure out how a particular justice will vote based on the questioning at oral argument, most researchers find that the nature and number of questions asked do not help much in predicting the outcome of a case.

THE CONFERENCE AND THE VOTE   The justices meet in closed conference twice a week when the Court is hearing oral arguments. Since the ascendancy of Chief Justice Roger B. Taney to the Court in 1836, the justices have begun each conference session with a round of handshaking. Once the door to the conference room closes, no others are allowed to enter. The justice with the least seniority acts as the doorkeeper for the other eight, communicating with those waiting outside to fill requests for documents, water, and any other necessities.

Conferences highlight the importance and power of the chief justice, who presides over them and makes the initial presentation of each case. Each individual justice then discusses the case in order of his or her seniority on the Court, with the most senior justice speaking next. Most accounts of the decision-making process reveal that at this point some justices try to change the minds of others, but that most enter the conference room with a clear idea of how they will vote on each case.

WRITING OPINIONS   After the Court has reached a decision in conference, the justices must formulate a formal opinion of the Court. If the chief justice is in the majority, he selects the justice who will write the opinion. This privilege enables him to wield tremendous power and is a very important strategic decision. If the chief justice is in the minority, the assignment falls to the most senior justice in the majority.

The opinion of the Court can take several different forms. Most decisions are reached by a majority opinion written by one member of the Court to reflect the views of at least five of the justices. This opinion usually sets out the legal reasoning justifying the decision, and this legal reasoning becomes a precedent for deciding future cases. The reasoning behind any decision is often as important as the outcome. Under the system of *stare decisis,* both are likely to be relied on as precedent later by lower courts confronted with cases involving similar issues.

In the process of creating the final opinion of the Court, informal caucusing and negotiation often take place, as justices may hold out for word changes or other modifications as a condition of their continued support of the majority opinion. This negotiation process can lead to divisions in the Court's majority. When this occurs, the Court may be forced to decide cases by plurality opinions, which attract the support of three or four justices. While these decisions do not have the precedential value of majority opinions, they nonetheless have been used by the Court to decide many major cases. Justices who agree with the outcome of the case but not with the legal rationale for the decision may file concurring opinions to express their differing approach. Justices who do not agree with the outcome of a case file dissenting opinions. Although these opinions have little direct legal value, they can be an important indicator of legal thought on the Court and are an excellent platform for justices to note their personal and legal disagreements with other members of the Court.

Judicial Philosophy and Decision Making

★ **9.6** . . . Analyze the factors that influence judicial decision making.

Justices do not make decisions in a vacuum. Principles of *stare decisis* dictate that the justices follow the law of previous cases in deciding cases at hand. But, a variety of legal and extra-legal factors have also been found to affect Supreme Court decision making.

Judicial Philosophy, Original Intent, and Ideology

judicial restraint

A philosophy of judicial decision making that posits courts should allow the decisions of other branches of government to stand, even when they offend a judge's own principles.

judicial activism

A philosophy of judicial decision making that posits judges should use their power broadly to further justice.

strict constructionist

An approach to constitutional interpretation that emphasizes interpreting the Constitution as it was written and intended by the Framers.

One of the primary issues concerning judicial decision making focuses on what is called the activism/restraint debate. Advocates of **judicial restraint** argue that courts should allow the decisions of other branches to stand, even when they offend a judge's own principles. Restraintists defend their position by asserting that the federal courts are composed of unelected judges, which makes the judicial branch the least democratic branch of government. Consequently, the courts should defer policy making to other branches of government as much as possible.

Restraintists refer to *Roe* v. *Wade* (1973), the case that liberalized abortion laws, as a classic example of **judicial activism** run amok. They maintain that the Court should have deferred policy making on this sensitive issue to the states or to the elected branches of the federal government.

Advocates of judicial restraint generally agree that judges should be **strict constructionists;** that is, they should interpret the Constitution as it was written and intended by the Framers. They argue that in determining the constitutionality of a statute or policy, the Court should rely on the explicit meanings of the clauses in the document, which can be clarified by looking at founding documents.

Advocates of judicial activism contend that judges should use their power broadly to further justice. Activists argue that it is appropriate for the courts to correct injustices committed by the other branches of government. Implicit in this argument is the notion that courts need to protect oppressed minorities.[27]

Although judicial activists are often considered politically liberal and restraintists politically conservative, in recent years a new brand of conservative judicial activism has become prevalent. Liberal activist decisions often expanded the rights of political and legal minorities. But, conservative activist judges view their positions as an opportunity to issue broad rulings that impose their own political beliefs and policies on the country at large.

Some scholars argue that this increased conservative judicial activism has had an effect on the Court's reliance on *stare decisis* and adherence to precedent. Chief Justice William H. Rehnquist noted that while "*stare decisis* is a cornerstone of our legal system . . . it has less power in constitutional cases."[28]

Models of Judicial Decision Making

Most political scientists who study judicial behavior conclude that a variety of forces shape judicial decision making. Many have attempted to explain how judges vote by integrating a variety of models to offer a more complete picture of how judges make decisions.[29] Many of those models attempt to take into account justices' individual behavioral characteristics and attitudes as well as the fact patterns of the case.

BEHAVIORAL CHARACTERISTICS   Some political scientists argue that social background differences, including childhood experiences, religious values, education, earlier political and legal careers, and political party loyalties, are likely to influence how a judge evaluates the facts and legal issues presented in any given case.

THE ATTITUDINAL MODEL   The attitudinal model holds that Supreme Court justices decide cases according to their personal preferences toward issues of public policy.[30] Among some of the factors used to derive attitudes are a justice's party identification, the party of the appointing president, and the liberal/conservative leanings of a justice.[31]

THE STRATEGIC MODEL   The strategic model argues that justices temper legal doctrine and their own policy beliefs with concerns about how other internal and external variables will affect and be affected by their decision. In sharp contrast to the attitudinal model, the strategic model suggests that justices are prospective thinkers who act to achieve and preserve their policy and personal goals over the long term. Scholars have accumulated a body of evidence in support of the strategic model. They have found, for example, that justices are strategic in their votes for *certiorari*.[32] Justices may not vote to hear a case, no matter how interesting, if they suspect they will lose in the final decision.

Other internal and external factors may influence strategic decisions. Evidence shows that the chief justice often assigns final opinions to justices based on the organizational needs of the Court.[33] And, at least under some conditions, justices pay attention to their colleagues' preferences in crafting majority opinions.[34] Finally, the Supreme Court appears to be responsive to public opinion,[35] other courts,[36] and other institutions.[37]

Public Opinion

Many political scientists have examined the role of public opinion in Supreme Court decision making. Not only do the justices read legal briefs and hear oral arguments, but they also read newspapers, watch television, and have some knowledge of public opinion—especially on controversial issues.

Whether or not public opinion actually influences justices, it can act as a check on the power of the courts and as an energizing factor. Activist periods on the Supreme Court generally have corresponded to periods of social or economic crisis. For example, the Marshall Court supported a strong national government, much to the chagrin of a series of pro-states' rights Democratic-Republican presidents in the early crisis-ridden years of the republic. Similarly, the Court capitulated to political pressures and public opinion when, after 1936, it reversed many of its earlier decisions that had blocked President Franklin D. Roosevelt's New Deal programs.

The courts, especially the Supreme Court, also can be the direct target of public opinion. When *Webster* v. *Reproductive Health Services* (1989) was about to come before the Supreme Court, the Court was subjected to unprecedented lobbying as groups and individuals on both sides of the abortion issue marched and sent appeals to the Court. Mail at the Court, which usually averaged about 1,000 pieces a day, rose to an astronomical 46,000 pieces per day, virtually paralyzing normal lines of communication.

The Supreme Court also appears to affect public opinion. Political scientists have found that the Court's initial rulings on controversial issues such as abortion or capital punishment positively influence public opinion in the direction of the Court's opinion. However, this research also finds that subsequent decisions have little effect.[38]

The Court also is dependent on the public for its prestige as well as for compliance with its decisions. In times of war and other emergencies, for example, the Court frequently has decided cases in ways that commentators have attributed to the sway of public opinion and political exigencies. In *Korematsu* v. *U.S.* (1944), for example, the high Court upheld the obviously unconstitutional internment of Japanese, Italian, and German American citizens during World War II.[39] Moreover, Chief Justice William H. Rehnquist once suggested that the Court's restriction on presidential authority in *Youngstown Sheet & Tube Co.* v. *Sawyer* (1952), which invalidated President Harry S Truman's seizure of the nation's steel mills, was largely attributable to Truman's unpopularity in light of the Korean War.[40]

Public confidence in the Court, as with other institutions of government, has ebbed and flowed. Public support for the Court was highest after the Court issued *U.S.* v. *Nixon* (1974).[41] At a time when Americans lost faith in the presidency due to the Watergate scandal, they could at least look to the Supreme Court to do the right thing. Although the numbers of Americans with confidence in the courts has fluctuated over time, in 2009, 61 percent of those sampled by Gallup International approved of the way the Supreme Court was doing its job.[42]

TOWARD REFORM: Power, Policy Making, and the Court

★ 9.7 . . . Assess the role of the Supreme Court in the policy-making process.

All judges, whether they recognize it or not, make policy. The decisions of the Supreme Court, in particular, have a tremendous impact on American politics and policy. Over the last 250 years, the justices have helped to codify many of the major rights and liberties guaranteed to the citizens of the United States. Although justices need the cooperation of the executive and legislative branches to implement and enforce many of their decisions, it is safe to say that many policies we take for granted in the United States would not have come to fruition without the support of the Supreme Court.[43]

Several Courts have played particularly notable roles in the development of the judiciary's policy-making role. As discussed earlier in the chapter, the Marshall Court played an important role in establishing the role and power of the Supreme Court, including establishing the power of judicial review in *Marbury* v. *Madison* (1803). The Warren Court decided a number of civil rights cases that broadly expanded civil and political rights. These decisions drew a great deal of criticism but played a major role in broadening public understanding of the Court as a policy maker. The Rehnquist Court made numerous decisions related to federalism (see **chapter 3**), which caused observers to take note of the Court's ability to referee conflicts between the federal government and the states. And, the Roberts Court reversed the general trend of the Court agreeing with executive actions during times of war by finding in 2008 that the Bush administration's denial of *habeas corpus* rights to prisoners being held at Guantanamo Bay was an unconstitutional exercise of presidential power.[44]

Policy Making

One measure of the power of the courts and their ability to make policy is that more than one hundred federal laws have been declared unconstitutional. Although many of these laws have not been particularly significant, others have.

Another measure of the policy-making power of the Supreme Court is its ability to overrule itself. Although the Court generally abides by the informal rule of *stare decisis*, by one count, it has overruled itself in more than 200 cases.[45] Moreover, in the past few years, the Court repeatedly has reversed earlier decisions in the areas of criminal defendants' rights, reproductive rights, and free speech, revealing its powerful role in determining national policy. The modern Supreme Court also handles a number of issues that had been considered political questions more appropriately left to the other branches of government to decide.

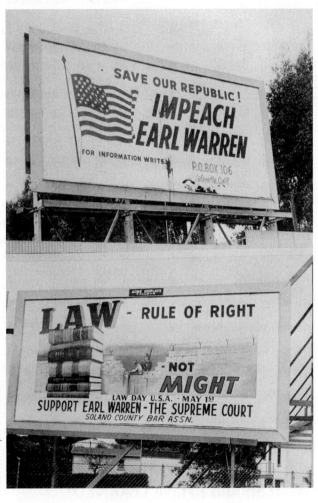

Do unpopular Supreme Court rulings threaten the nation? The Warren Court's broad expansions of civil and political rights led to a great deal of criticism, including a movement to impeach the chief justice. Here, two California billboards present contrasting views of Warren's performance.

Photo courtesy: Bettmann/Corbis

Implementing Court Decisions

President Andrew Jackson, annoyed about a particular decision handed down by the Marshall Court, is alleged to have said, "John Marshall has made his decision; now let him enforce it." Jackson's statement raises a question: how do Supreme Court rulings translate into public policy? In fact, although judicial decisions carry legal and even moral authority, all courts must rely on other units of government to carry out their directives. If the president or members of Congress, for example, don't like a particular Supreme Court ruling, they can underfund programs needed to implement a decision or seek only lax enforcement. **Judicial implementation** refers to how and whether judicial decisions are translated into actual public policies affecting more than the immediate parties to the lawsuit.

How well a decision is implemented often depends on how well crafted or popular it is. Hostile reaction in the South to *Brown* v. *Board of Education* (1954) and the

judicial implementation
How and whether judicial decisions are translated into actual public policies affecting more than the immediate parties to a lawsuit.

absence of precise guidelines to implement the decision meant that the ruling went largely unenforced for years. The *Brown* experience also highlights how much the Supreme Court needs the support of both federal and state courts as well as other governmental agencies to carry out its judgments. For example, you probably graduated from high school after 1992, when the Supreme Court ruled that public middle school and high school graduations could not include a prayer, yet your own commencement ceremony may have included one.[46]

For effective implementation of a judicial decision, the first requirement is that the members of the implementing population must act to show that they understand the original decision. For example, the Supreme Court ruled in *Reynolds* v. *Sims* (1964) that every person should have an equally weighted vote in electing governmental representatives.[47] This "one person, one vote" rule might seem simple enough at first glance, but in practice it can be very difficult to understand.

The second requirement is that the implementing population actually must follow Court policy. Thus, when the Court ruled that men could not be denied admission to a state-sponsored nursing school, the implementing population—in this case, university administrators and the state board of regents governing the nursing school—had to enroll qualified male students.[48]

Judicial decisions are most likely to be implemented smoothly if responsibility for implementation is concentrated in the hands of a few highly visible public officials, such as the president or a governor. By the same token, these officials also can thwart or impede judicial intentions. Recall from **chapter 5**, for example, the effect of Governor Orval Faubus's initial refusal to allow black children to attend all-white public schools in Little Rock, Arkansas.

The third requirement for implementation is that the consumer population must be aware of the rights that a decision grants or denies them. Teenagers seeking an abortion, for example, are consumers of the Supreme Court's decisions on abortion. They need to know that most states require them to inform their parents of their intention to have an abortion or to get parental permission to do so.

What Should I Have LEARNED?
Now that you have read this chapter, you should be able to:

⭐ **9.1 Trace the development of the federal judiciary and the origins of judicial review, p. 246.**

Many of the Framers viewed the judicial branch of government as little more than a minor check on the other two branches, ignoring Anti-Federalist concerns about an unelected judiciary and its potential for tyranny. The Judiciary Act of 1789 established the basic federal court system we have today. It was the Marshall Court (1801–1835), however, that interpreted the Constitution to include the Court's major power, that of judicial review.

⭐ **9.2 Describe the structure and main components of the American legal system, p. 252.**

The American legal system is a dual judicial system consisting of the federal court system and the separate judicial systems of the fifty states. In each system are two

basic types of courts: trial courts and appellate courts. Each type deals with cases involving criminal and civil law. Original jurisdiction refers to a court's ability to hear a case as a trial court; appellate jurisdiction refers to a court's ability to review cases already decided by a trial court.

⭐ **9.3 Explain the organization of the federal court system, p. 254.**

The federal court system is made up of constitutional and legislative courts. Federal district courts, courts of appeals, and the Supreme Court are constitutional courts.

⭐ **9.4 Outline the criteria and process used to select federal court judges, p. 256.**

District court, court of appeals, and Supreme Court justices are nominated by the president and must also win Senate confirmation. Important criteria for selection include competence, ideology, rewards, pursuit of political support, religion, race, ethnicity, and gender.

★ **9.5 Evaluate the Supreme Court's process for accepting, hearing, and deciding cases, p. 261.**

Several factors influence the Court's decision to hear a case. Not only must the Court have jurisdiction, but at least four justices must vote to hear the case. Cases with certain characteristics are most likely to be heard. Once a case is set for review, briefs and *amicus curiae* briefs are filed and oral argument is scheduled. The justices meet in conference after oral argument to discuss the case, votes are taken, and opinions are written, circulated, and then announced.

★ **9.6 Analyze the factors that influence judicial decision making, p. 268.**

Judges do not make decisions in a vacuum. In addition to following the law of previous cases, other factors

including judges' philosophy and ideology have an extraordinary impact on how they decide cases. Political scientists have identified three models of how judges make decisions: behavioral—based on social background; attitudinal—based on personal preferences about policy; and strategic—based on long-term personal and policy goals.

★ **9.7 Assess the role of the Supreme Court in the policy-making process, p. 270.**

The Supreme Court is an important participant in the policy-making process. The power to interpret the laws gives the Court tremendous policy-making power never envisioned by the Framers. However, if the president or members of Congress oppose a particular Supreme Court ruling, they can underfund programs needed to implement a decision or seek only lax enforcement.

Test Yourself: The Judiciary

★ **9.1 Trace the development of the federal judiciary and the origins of judicial review, p. 246.**

The basic principles of the American judiciary can be found primarily in which Article of the U.S. Constitution?
A. I
B. II
C. III
D. IV
E. V

★ **9.2 Describe the structure and main components of the American legal system, p. 252.**

In criminal law, who or what is considered the victim of illegal acts?
A. The injured party
B. The government
C. The perpetrator
D. Society at large
E. Families of the parties involved

★ **9.3 Explain the organization of the federal court system, p. 254.**

How are the Supreme Court and the court of appeals similar?
A. Both have original jurisdiction.
B. Both are appellate courts.
C. Both are legislative courts.
D. Both have elected judges.
E. Both use judges on three judge panels.

★ **9.4 Outline the criteria and process used to select federal court judges, p. 256.**

Which of the following is NOT generally an important factor in selecting a modern Supreme Court nominees?
A. Competence
B. Race
C. Ethnicity
D. Gender
E. Geography

★ **9.5 Evaluate the Supreme Court's process for accepting, hearing, and deciding cases, p. 261.**

To what does the Rule of Four refer?
A. If at least four senators object to a Supreme Court nominee, then the justice generally is not confirmed.
B. Four justices must vote to consider a case before it can be heard.
C. The average number of clerks assigned to Supreme Court justices.
D. The number of months that must transpire before a case is granted writ of *certiorari*.
E. The way cases are bundled in *cert* pools.

★ **9.6 Analyze the factors that influence judicial decision making, p. 268.**

Those who believe that judges should be strict constructionists are generally advocates of
A. liberalized abortion laws.
B. judicial activism.
C. broad rights of the accused.
D. judicial restraint.
E. the Supreme Court acting as an instrument of social change.

⭐ **9.7 Assess the role of the Supreme Court in the policy-making process, p. 270.**

Which of the following is an example of the Supreme Court's ability to act as a policy maker?
A. Its ability to overrule itself in later decisions
B. The ideological split of the Court
C. The length of oral arguments before the Court
D. The decision of a Court to issue *amicus* briefs
E. The traditional presence of some justices during the president's State of the Union message

Essay Questions
1. Why was *Marbury* v. *Madison* (1803) a critical case in shaping the development of the Supreme Court?
2. What factors influence the probability that the Supreme Court will hear a case?
3. Describe the relationship between the Court and public opinion.

---

mypoliscilab Exercises
Apply what you learned in this chapter on MyPoliSciLab.

📖─┤**Read** on **mypoliscilab.com**

eText: Chapter 9

✓─┤**Study** and **Review** on **mypoliscilab.com**

Pre-Test
Post-Test
Chapter Exam
Flashcards

👁─┤**Watch** on **mypoliscilab.com**

Video: Court Rules on Hazelton's Immigration Laws
Video: Prosecuting Corruption
Video: Most Significant Abortion Ruling in 30 Years
Video: Prosecuting Cyber Crime

⊕─┤**Explore** on **mypoliscilab.com**

Simulation: You Are a Young Lawyer
Simulation: You Are the President and Need to Appoint a Supreme Court Justice
Simulation: You Are a Clerk to Supreme Court Justice Judith Gray
Comparative: Comparing Judiciaries
Timeline: Chief Justices of the Supreme Court
Visual Literacy: Case Overload

Key Terms

amicus curiae, p. 266
appellate court, p. 252
appellate jurisdiction, p. 253
brief, p. 255
civil law, p. 253
constitutional courts, p. 254
criminal law, p. 253
judicial activism, p. 268

judicial implementation, p. 271
judicial restraint, p. 268
judicial review, p. 247
Judiciary Act of 1789, p. 248
jurisdiction, p. 253
legislative courts, p. 254
Marbury v. *Madison* (1803), p. 250
original jurisdiction, p. 253

precedent, p. 255
Rule of Four, p. 265
senatorial courtesy, p. 256
solicitor general, p. 266
stare decisis, p. 255
strict constructionist, p. 268
trial court, p. 252
writ of *certiorari*, p. 263

To Learn More on the Judiciary
In the Library

Baird, Vanessa. *Answering the Call of the Court: How Justices and Litigants Set the Supreme Court Agenda.* Charlottesville: University of Virginia Press, 2008.

Baum, Lawrence. *Judges and Their Audiences: A Perspective on Judicial Behavior.* Princeton, NJ: Princeton University Press, 2005.

Bonneau, Chris W., and Melinda Gann Hall. *In Defense of Judicial Elections.* New York: Routledge, 2009.

Collins Paul M., Jr. *Friends of the Supreme Court: Interest Groups and Decision Making.* New York: Oxford University Press, 2008.

Epstein, Lee, and Jeffrey A. Segal. *Advice and Consent: The Politics of Judicial Appointments.* New York: Oxford University Press, 2005.

Epstein, Lee, Jeffrey A. Segal, Harold J. Spaeth, and Thomas G. Walker. *The Supreme Court Compendium,* 5th ed. Washington, DC: CQ Press, 2010.

Hall, Kermit L., ed. *The Oxford Companion to the Supreme Court of the United States,* 2nd ed. New York: Oxford University Press, 2005.

Hall, Kermit L., and Kevin T. McGuire, eds. *Institutions of American Democracy: The Judicial Branch.* New York: Oxford University Press, 2005.

Lazarus, Edward. *Closed Chambers: The First Eyewitness Account of the Epic Struggles Inside the Supreme Court.* New York: Times Books, 1998.

O'Brien, David M. *Storm Center: The Supreme Court in American Politics,* 8th ed. New York: Norton, 2008.

Perry, H. W. *Deciding to Decide: Agenda Setting in the United States Supreme Court,* reprint ed. Cambridge, MA: Harvard University Press, 2005.

Segal, Jeffrey A., and Harold J. Spaeth. *The Supreme Court and the Attitudinal Model Revisited.* New York: Cambridge University Press, 2002.

Sunstein, Cass R., David Schkade, Lisa M. Ellman, and Andres Sawicki. *Are Judges Political? An Empirical Analysis of the Federal Judiciary.* Washington, DC: Brookings Institution, 2006.

Ward, Artemus, and David L. Weiden. *Sorcerer's Apprentices: 100 Years of Law Clerks at the United States Supreme Court.* New York: New York University Press, 2006.

Whittington, Keith E. *Political Foundations of Judicial Supremacy: The Presidency, the Supreme Court, and Constitutional Leadership in U.S. History.* Princeton, NJ: Princeton University Press, 2007.

Woodward, Bob, and Scott Armstrong. *The Brethren: Inside the Supreme Court,* 2nd reprint ed. New York: Avon, 2005.

On the Web

To learn more about the U.S. Supreme Court and examine current cases on the Court's docket, go to **www.supremecourtus.gov.**

To learn more about the workings of the U.S. justice system, go to the Department of Justice's Web site at **www.usdoj.gov.**

To learn more about the U.S. Senate Judiciary Committee and judicial nominations currently under review, go to the Senate's Web site at **www.senate.gov.**

To learn more about past and current U.S. Supreme Court cases, go to **www.oyez.org** to hear streaming audio of oral arguments before the Court.

10 Public Opinion and The News Media

Exit polls have long received attention for their ability to help media outlets predict the outcome of elections before state agencies completely tabulate the results. But, during the 2008 Iowa Caucuses, a different, related way to gauge public opinion—the entrance poll—gained prevalence. In an entrance poll, voters are asked about which candidate they are going to vote for and why before they walk into the actual caucus. These polls are favored in caucuses because their results can be released immediately after they are collected. This allows networks to predict what might happen in a caucus while the event is actually occurring.

During the 2008 Iowa Caucuses, five major television and cable networks (ABC, CBS, NBC, CNN, and FOX News) and the Associated Press banded together to collect information through an agency known as the National Election Pool. This agency sent pollsters to 40 caucuses for each political party, a total of 80 different meetings. Polls were conducted in a very short period of time—as voters arrived at their precincts in the 60- to 90-minute window before the start of the caucus. This allowed their results to be quickly tabulated and analyzed while the caucuses were occurring.

Entrance polls in Iowa immediately set the tone for the 2008 contest, showing record numbers of first-time caucus-goers and young voters. They emphasized the importance of independent voters and correctly predicted strong support for Democratic candidate Barack Obama and Republican candidate Mike Huckabee, both of whom won their party's caucuses.

The 2008 entrance polls were notable for a number of other reasons as well. First,

Polling has been used to gauge public opinion on presidential elections since the early twentieth century. At left, George Gallup, the godfather of scientific polling, appears on a television program in 1948. At right, Iowa Caucus-goers register inside Waukee High School in Waukee, Iowa, in 2008. Many had first been surveyed by entrance pollers.

they were the first entrance polls to include a correction to take into account caucus-goers who refused to participate in the survey. This correction, which had previously been implemented in exit polls, required pollsters to collect the demographic information of all of the people who elected not to participate in the poll. This information was used to weight the collected data to accurately represent the population that came to the party caucus.

Second, the polling firms charged with conducting the entrance poll made a concerted effort to recruit and train a broader cross-section of interviewers. This, too, was directed at improving the representativeness of the sample; pollsters believed that people would be more likely to participate in a poll conducted by someone like them. In addition, two

interviewers attended each caucus, an attempt to increase both diversity and ability to efficiently collect accurate data.

What Should I Know About . . .

After reading this chapter, you should be able to:

★ **10.1** Trace the development of modern public opinion research, p. 278.

★ **10.2** Describe the methods for conducting and analyzing different types of public opinion polls, p. 280.

★ **10.3** Analyze the process by which people form political opinions, p. 286.

★ **10.4** Trace the historical development of the news media in the United States, p. 290.

★ **10.5** Summarize the ethical standards and federal regulations that govern the news media, p. 298.

★ **10.6** Assess how the news media cover politics, p. 300.

★ **10.7** Evaluate the influence of the news media on public policy and the impact of media bias, p. 303.

The television news networks, many major newspapers, and polling organizations routinely report on and often attempt to gauge public opinion about a wide array of events. Still, many citizens question the fairness or bias of the media in all of its forms as well as the accuracy of public opinion polls. Often, as reported by or even commissioned by the media, polls reveal much about what "the public" is thinking. The complex interaction of the media and public opinion is the focus of this chapter:

- First, we will examine *the roots of public opinion research*.

- Second, we will explore how *public opinion polls are conducted and analyzed*.

- Third, we will consider how citizens *form political opinions*.

- Fourth, we will discuss *news media in the United States*.

- Fifth, we will consider *rules governing the news media*, including both self-imposed rules of conduct and government regulations.

- Sixth, we will discuss *how the news media cover politics*.

- Finally, we will explore reforms pertaining to *news media influence and bias, as well as public confidence* in the news media.

ROOTS OF Public Opinion Research

⭐ **10.1 . . . Trace the development of modern public opinion research.**

public opinion
What the public thinks about a particular issue or set of issues at any point in time.

public opinion polls
Interviews or surveys with samples of citizens that are used to estimate the feelings and beliefs of the entire population.

At first glance, **public opinion** seems to be a very straightforward concept: it is what the public thinks about a particular issue or set of issues at any point in time. Since the 1930s, governmental decision makers have relied heavily on **public opinion polls**—interviews with samples of citizens that are used to estimate the feelings and beliefs of the entire population. According to George Gallup (1901–1983), an Iowan who is considered the founder of modern-day polling, polls have played a key role in defining issues of concern to the public, shaping administrative decisions, and helping "speed up the process of democracy" in the United States.[1]

Early Public Opinion Research

As early as 1824, one Pennsylvania newspaper tried to predict the winner of that year's presidential contest, showing Andrew Jackson leading over John Quincy Adams. In 1883, the *Boston Globe* sent reporters to selected election precincts to poll voters as they exited voting booths in an effort to predict the results of key contests. But, public opinion polling as we know it today did not begin to develop until the 1930s. Much of this growth was prompted by Walter Lippmann's seminal work, *Public Opinion* (1922). In this book, Lippmann observed that research on public opinion was far too limited, especially in light of its importance. Researchers in a variety of disciplines, including political science, heeded Lippmann's call to learn more about public opinion. Some tried to use scientific methods to measure political thought through the use of surveys or polls. As methods for gathering and interpreting data improved, survey data began to play an increasingly important role in all walks of life, from politics to retailing.

Literary Digest, a popular magazine that first began national presidential polling in 1916, was a pioneer in the use of the **straw poll,** an unscientific survey used to gauge public opinion, to predict the popular vote, which it did in a victory for Woodrow Wilson. Its polling methods were hailed widely as "amazingly right" and "uncannily accurate."[2] In 1936, however, its luck ran out. *Literary Digest* predicted that Republican Alfred M. Landon would beat incumbent President Franklin D. Roosevelt by a margin of 57 percent to 43 percent of the popular vote. Roosevelt, however, won in a landslide election, receiving 62.5 percent of the popular vote and carrying all but two states.

Literary Digest's 1936 straw poll had three fatal errors. First, its **sample,** a subset of the whole population selected to be questioned for the purposes of prediction or gauging opinion, was drawn from telephone directories and lists of automobile owners. This technique oversampled the upper middle class and the wealthy, groups heavily Republican in political orientation. Moreover, in 1936, voting polarized along class lines. Thus, the oversampling of wealthy Republicans was particularly problematic because it severely underestimated the Democratic vote.

Literary Digest's second problem was timing. Questionnaires were mailed in early September. It did not measure the changes in public sentiment that occurred as the election drew closer.

Its third error occurred because of a problem we now call self-selection. Only highly motivated individuals sent back the cards—a mere 22 percent of those surveyed responded. Those who respond to mail surveys (or today, online surveys) are quite different from the general electorate; they often are wealthier and better educated and care more fervently about issues. *Literary Digest*, then, failed to observe one of the now well-known cardinal rules of survey sampling: "One cannot allow the respondents to select themselves into the sample."[3]

straw poll
Unscientific survey used to gauge public opinion on a variety of issues and policies.

sample
A subset of the whole population selected to be questioned for the purposes of prediction or gauging opinion.

The Gallup Organization

At least one pollster, however, correctly predicted the results of the 1936 election: George Gallup. Gallup had written his dissertation in psychology at the University of Iowa on how to measure the readership of newspapers. He then expanded his research to study public opinion about politics. He was so confident about his methods that he gave all of his newspaper clients a money-back guarantee: if his poll predictions weren't closer to the actual election outcome than those of the highly acclaimed *Literary Digest*, he would refund their money. Although Gallup underpredicted Roosevelt's victory by nearly 7 percent, the fact that he got the winner right was what everyone remembered, especially given *Literary Digest*'s dramatic miscalculation.

Through the late 1940s, polling techniques became more sophisticated. The number of polling groups also dramatically increased, as businesses and politicians began to rely on polling information to market products and candidates. But, in 1948, the polling industry suffered a severe, although fleeting, setback when Gallup and many other pollsters incorrectly predicted that Thomas E. Dewey would defeat President Harry S Truman.

Nevertheless, as revealed in Figure 10.1, the Gallup Organization continues to predict the winners of the presidential popular vote successfully. In 2008, for example, Gallup correctly predicted not only the winner but also Barack Obama's share of the popular vote.

Figure 10.1 *How successful has the Gallup Poll been?*

As seen here, Gallup's final predictions have been remarkably accurate. Furthermore, in each of the years where there is a significant discrepancy between Gallup's prediction and the election's outcome, there was a prominent third candidate. In 1948, Strom Thurmond ran on the Dixiecrat ticket; in 1980, John Anderson ran as the American Independent Party candidate; in 1992, Ross Perot ran as an independent.

Sources: Marty Baumann, "How One Polling Firm Stacks Up," *USA Today* (October 27, 1992): 13A; 1996 data from Mike Mokrzycki, "Pre-election Polls' Accuracy Varied," *Atlanta Journal and Constitution* (November 8, 1996): A12; 2000 data from Gallup Organization, "Poll Releases," November 7, 2000; 2004 and 2008 data from *USA Today* and CNN/Gallup Tracking Poll, www.usatoday.com.

Conducting and Analyzing Public Opinion Polls

⭐ **10.2 . . . Describe the methods for conducting and analyzing different types of public opinion polls.**

The polling process most often begins when someone says, "Let's find out about X and Y." Potential candidates for local office may want to know how many people have heard of them (the device used to find out is called a name recognition survey). Better-known candidates contemplating running for higher office might want to know how they might fare against an incumbent. Polls also can be used to gauge how effective particular ads are or if a candidate is being well (or negatively) perceived by the public.

Types of Polls

As polling has become increasingly sophisticated and networks, newspapers, and magazines compete with each other to report the most up-to-the-minute changes in public opinion on issues or politicians, new types of polls have been suggested and put into use. Each type of poll has contributed to our knowledge of public opinion and its role in the political process. In addition to traditional telephone polls, organizations may use exit polls, tracking polls, Internet polls, and the entrance polls described in the opening vignette. In addition, some political operatives use polls called push polls to try to influence public opinion.

TRADITIONAL TELEPHONE POLLS   As landline telephones became common in most American homes, pollsters saw a tremendous opportunity to conduct surveys in an expeditious manner. Early on, most people were excited to be asked about their views on political issues, and they welcomed phone calls to this end. In recent years, however, telephone polls have been more difficult to conduct, both due to the growth in cell phones and peoples' increasing unwillingness to be contacted by outsiders. Today, many pollsters use random-digit dialing with the help of computers to contact both listed and unlisted landline and cell phone numbers. Results are generally adjusted to make sure the sample accurately reflects the demographic factors of the actual population.

EXIT POLLS   **Exit polls** are conducted as voters leave selected polling places on Election Day. Generally, large news organizations send pollsters to selected precincts to sample every tenth voter as he or she emerges from the polling site. The results of these polls are used to help the media predict the outcome of key races, often just a few minutes after the polls close in a particular state and generally before voters in other areas—sometimes in a later time zone—have cast their ballots. They also provide an independent assessment of why voters supported particular candidates by asking a series of demographic and issue questions.

exit polls
Polls conducted as voters leave selected polling places on Election Day.

TRACKING POLLS   During the 1992 presidential elections, **tracking polls,** which were taken on a daily basis by some news organizations, were first introduced to allow presidential candidates to monitor short-term campaign developments and the effects of their campaign strategies. Today, tracking polls involve small samples (usually of registered voters contacted at certain times of day) and are conducted every twenty-four hours. The results are then combined into moving three- to five-day averages. (To learn more about tracking polls, see Figure 10.2.)

tracking polls
Continuous surveys that enable a campaign or news organization to chart a candidate's daily rise or fall in support.

INTERNET POLLS   Well-established pollster John Zogby was among the first to use a scientific Internet survey. Zogby regularly queries over 3,000 representative volunteers (selected using the sampling techniques discussed later in this chapter) on a host of issues. Zogby, Harris Interactive, and other Internet pollsters using scientific sampling

Figure 10.2 *What does a daily tracking poll look like?*
Day-to-day fluctuations in public opinion on election contests are often shown through tracking polls. This figure shows the ups and downs of the 2008 presidential election.
Source: USA Today and CNN/Gallup Poll results, www.usatoday.com/news/politicselections/nation/polls/usatodaypolls.htm.

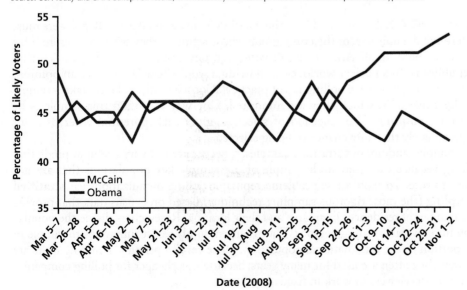

strategies have had relatively successful records in predicting election outcomes and gauging opinions on numerous issues of importance to the American public.

PUSH POLLS   All good polls for political candidates contain questions intended to produce information that helps campaigns judge their own strengths and weaknesses as well as those of their opponents. They might, for example, ask if you would be more likely to vote for candidate X if you knew that candidate was a strong environmentalist. These kinds of questions are accepted as an essential part of any poll, but there are concerns as to where to draw the line. Questions that go over the line are called **push polls** and often are a result of ulterior motives.[4] Push polls are designed to give respondents some negative or even untruthful information about a candidate's opponent to push them away from that candidate and toward the one paying for the poll.

push polls

Polls taken for the purpose of providing information on an opponent that would lead respondents to vote against that candidate.

Conducting Polls

Pollsters or polling firms must make several decisions before polling the public. These include determining the content and phrasing of the questions, selecting the sample, and deciding how to go about contacting respondents. (To learn more about a newer method for contacting respondents, see Politics Now: Gubernatorial "Robo-Poll" Turns Out to Be the Only Right Poll.)

DETERMINING THE CONTENT AND PHRASING THE QUESTIONS   The first thing candidates, political groups, or news organizations must consider when deciding to use a poll is what questions they want answered. Determining the content of a survey is critical to obtaining the desired results, and for that reason, candidates, companies, and news organizations generally rely on pollsters. Polls may ask, for example, about job performance, demographics, and specific issue areas. Special care must be taken in constructing the questions to be asked. For example, if your professor asked you, "Do you think my grading procedures are fair?" rather than asking, "In general, how fair do you think the grading is in your American Politics course?" you might give a slightly different answer. The wording of the first question tends to put you on the spot and personalize the grading style; the second question is more neutral. Even more obvious differences appear in the real world of polling, especially when interested groups want a poll to yield particular results. Responses to highly emotional issues such as abortion, same-sex marriage, and affirmative action often are skewed depending on the wording of a particular question.

SELECTING THE SAMPLE   Once the decision is made to take a poll, pollsters must determine the universe, or the entire group whose attitudes they wish to measure. This universe could be all Americans, all voters, all city residents, all Hispanics, or all Republicans. In a perfect world, each individual would be asked to give an opinion, but such comprehensive polling is not practical. Consequently, pollsters take a sample of the universe in which they are interested. One way to obtain this sample is by **random sampling.** This method of selection gives each potential voter or adult approximately the same chance of being selected.

random sampling

A method of poll selection that gives each person in a group the same chance of being selected.

Simple random, nonstratified samples, however are not very useful at predicting voting because they may undersample or oversample key populations that are not likely to vote. To avoid these problems, reputable polling organizations use **stratified sampling** (the most rigorous sampling technique) based on census data that provide the number of residences in an area and their location. Researchers divide the population into several sampling regions. They then randomly select subgroups to sample in proportion to the total national population. Once certain primary sampling units are chosen, they often are used for many years, because it is cheaper for polling companies to train interviewers to work in fixed areas.

stratified sampling

A variation of random sampling; the population is divided into subgroups and weighted based on demographic characteristics of the national population.

Gubernatorial "Robo-Poll" Turns Out to Be the Only Right Poll

By Aaron Deslatte

August 27, 2010
Orlando Sentinel
www.orlandosentinel.com

Political watchers have been bombarded with polls this summer, but most of them failed to predict Rick Scott's upset win in the Republican gubernatorial primary.

Despite all the fingers on the pulse of the state's unique electorate, the only public polling firm that accurately predicted Scott's win in the final week was a Democratic-allied firm from North Carolina called Public Policy Polling (which does the dreaded "robo calls.")

PPP put out the only survey over the weekend that showed Scott leading, 47 percent-to-40 percent. The final tally: Scott 46.4 percent, Bill McCollum 43.4 percent.

Now, conventional pollsters argue that robo-polling—"Press 1 for McCollum, 2 for Scott"—is flawed because you don't know who's pushing the buttons, though live interviewers can introduce their own bias in survey results . . .

Yet, in the end, PPP was more accurate than conventional pollsters. PPP director Tim Jensen said his best guess was he got better results because his shop used a looser screen for the voters it sampled, calling general election GOP voters instead of past primary voters.

"If the folks who voted [Tuesday] had been exactly the same as the folks who voted in the 2006 primary, I imagine McCollum would have won," Jensen said. . . "But there were hundreds of thousands more people voting . . . than in 2006 and my sense is the newbies went strongly for Scott. . ."

Brad Coker, managing director of Mason-Dixon Polling & Research, is one of several pollsters whose surveys failed to correctly call the race. Coker's last poll, released on the Saturday before election day and based on interviews with 500 likely Republican primary voters between Aug. 17 and 19, had McCollum up by 9 points, 45-to-36 . . .

. . . We asked Coker where he thought he went wrong. After noting that this was the first time in 26 years that the leader in his final poll didn't win, Coker said a final cash infusion from Scott may have played a role in influencing undecided voters in the five days between when the poll was in the field and the election.

"Going into the final weekend, many voters remained conflicted. This was reflected by the high negatives each candidate had," Coker told us. "Many couldn't seem to settle on which one was the lesser of two evils, as the ugly tone of the campaign had turned them off . . ."

Critical Thinking Questions

1. Are observers' concerns about "robo polls" justified? Why or why not?
2. How does this poll demonstrate the importance of selecting a sample when conducting a public opinion poll?
3. What survey questions could researchers have asked to better understand citizens' uncertainty in the final days of the election?

About twenty respondents from each primary sampling unit are picked to be interviewed; this total is 600 to 1,000 respondents. Large, sophisticated surveys such as the National Election Studies and in the University of Chicago's General Social Survey attempt to sample from lists of persons living in each household in a sampling unit. The key to the success of the stratified sampling method is not to let people volunteer to be interviewed—volunteers as a group often have different opinions from those who do not volunteer.

CONTACTING RESPONDENTS After selecting the methodology to conduct the poll, the next question is how to contact those to be surveyed. Telephone polls are the most frequently used mechanism by which to gauge the temper of the electorate. The most common form of telephone polls are random-digit dialing surveys, in which a computer randomly selects telephone numbers to be dialed. In spite of some problems (such as the fact that many people do not want to be bothered or do not have landline phones), most polls done for newspapers and news magazines are conducted in this way. Pollsters are exempt from federal and state do-not-call lists because poll-taking is a form of constitutionally protected speech.

Individual, person-to-person interviews are conducted by some groups, such as the National Election Studies. Some analysts favor such in-person surveys, but others argue that the unintended influence of the questioner or pollster is an important source of errors. How the pollster dresses, relates to the person being interviewed, and asks the questions can affect responses. Some of these factors, such as tone of voice or accent, can also affect the results of telephone surveys.

Analyzing the Data

Analyzing the collected data is a critical step in the polling process. The analysis reveals the implications of the data for public policy and political campaigns. When conducting their analysis, a polling group must consider how the choices they made throughout the process have affected their ultimate results. Two of the most serious concerns are the margin of error and sampling error.

margin of error
A measure of the accuracy of a public opinion poll.

MARGIN OF ERROR   All polls contain errors. Typically, the margin of error in a sample of 1,000 will be about 4 percent. If you ask 1,000 people "Do you like ice cream?" and 52 percent say yes and 48 percent say no, the results are too close to tell whether more people like ice cream than not. Why? Because the **margin of error** implies that somewhere between 56 percent (52 + 4) and 48 percent (52 − 4) of the people like ice cream, while between 52 percent (48 + 4) and 44 percent (48 − 4) do not. The margin of error in a close election makes predictions very difficult.

SAMPLING ERROR   The accuracy of any poll depends on the quality of the sample that was drawn. Small samples, if properly drawn, can be very accurate if each unit in the universe has an equal opportunity to be sampled. If a pollster, for example, fails to sample certain populations, his or her results may reflect that shortcoming. Often the opinions of the poor and homeless are under-represented because insufficient attention is given to making certain that these groups are sampled representatively.

How can sampling affect polling results? This cartoon pokes fun at a serious shortcoming of polling—sampling error.

Peter Steiner

THE LATEST POLL SHOWS THE PEOPLE DON'T TRUST STATISTICAL SAMPLING. OF COURSE, THE LATEST POLL IS STATISTICAL SAMPLING.

Shortcomings of Polling

The information derived from public opinion polls has become an important part of governance. When the results of a poll are accurate, they express the feelings of the electorate and help guide policy makers. However, when the results of a poll are inaccurate, disastrous consequences often result.

LIMITED RESPONDENT OPTIONS   Famed political scientist V. O. Key Jr. was among the first social scientists to note the problem of limited respondent options. He cautioned students of public opinion to take care that their questions adequately allowed respondents the appropriate range for which they could register their opinions. Simple yes-no (or approve-disapprove) questions may not be sufficient to measure the temperature of the public. For example, if you are asked "How do you like this class?" and are given only like or dislike options, your full sentiments may not be tapped if you like the class very much or feel only so-so about it.

LACK OF INFORMATION   Public opinion polls may also be inaccurate when they attempt to gauge attitudes toward issues about which the public has little information. Most academic public opinion research organizations, such as the National Election Studies, use some kind of filter question that first asks respondents whether or not they have thought about the question. These screening procedures generally allow survey researchers to exclude as many as 20 percent of their respondents, especially on complex issues such as the federal budget. Questions on more personal issues such as moral values, drugs, crime, race, and women's role in society get far fewer "no opinion" or "don't know" responses.

DIFFICULTY MEASURING INTENSITY   Another shortcoming of polls concerns their inability to measure intensity of feeling about particular issues. Whereas a respondent might answer affirmatively to any question, it is likely that his or her feelings about issues such as abortion, the death penalty, or support for the wars in Afghanistan and Iraq are much more intense than are his or her feelings about the Electoral College or types of voting machines used. (To learn more about public opinion on the Iraq War, see Analyzing Visuals: Public Opinion on the Iraq War.)

ANALYZING VISUALS

Public Opinion on the Iraq War

The Gallup Organization periodically conducts a telephone poll on the subject of the war in Iraq. Pollsters interview adults age eighteen and older (dialing both landline and cell-phone numbers). Among the questions asked of respondents is, "In view of the developments since we first sent our troops to Iraq, do you think the United States made a mistake in sending troops to Iraq, or not?" Examine this graph showing the results of the polls conducted since the war first began, and answer the questions.

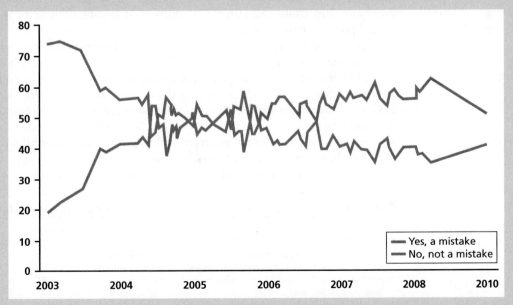

Source: Gallup Poll, April 2010, www.gallup.com. www.pollingreport.com/iraq.htm

- In which year was support for sending American troops to Iraq the highest? In which year was support the lowest?
- What events might explain the shift in public opinion between 2003 and 2010?
- In what ways, if any, do you think these poll results influenced the outcome of the 2008 presidential election?

Forming Political Opinions

★ **10.3** ... Analyze the process by which people form political opinions.

political socialization

The process through which individuals acquire their political beliefs and values.

Political scientists believe that many of our attitudes about issues are grounded in our political values. The process through which individuals acquire their beliefs is known as **political socialization.**[5] Demographic characteristics, family, school, peers, the mass media, and political leaders are often important influences or agents of political socialization.

Demographic Characteristics

Most demographic characteristics are ones over which individuals have little control. But, at birth, demographic characteristics begin to affect you and your political values. Below, we discuss some of the major demographic characteristics that pollsters routinely query. These include gender, race and ethnicity, age, and religion.

GENDER   From the time that the earliest public opinion polls were taken, women have held more liberal attitudes than men about social welfare issues such as education, juvenile justice, capital punishment, and the environment. Public opinion polls have also found that women hold more negative views about war and military intervention than men. Some analysts suggest that women's more nurturing nature and their prominent role as mothers lead women to have more liberal attitudes on issues affecting the family or children. Research by political scientists, however, finds no support for a maternal explanation.[6] (To learn more about the gender gap, see Table 10.1.)

RACE AND ETHNICITY   Differences in political socialization appear at a very early age. Young African American children, for example, generally show very positive feelings about American society and political processes, but this attachment lessens considerably over time. Historically, black children have had less positive views of the president than white children.[7] The election of Barack Obama to the presidency should produce dramatic changes in these views.

Race and ethnicity are exceptionally important factors in the study of public opinion. The direction and intensity of African American and Hispanic opinions on a variety of hot-button issues often are quite different from those of whites. For example, whites are much more likely to support the war in Iraq than are blacks or Hispanics. Likewise, differences can be seen in other issue areas. Guaranteeing government-sponsored health insurance, for example, is a hot-button issue with Hispanic voters; 61 percent favor government involvement.[8] Hispanics also favor bilingual education and liberalized immigration policies.[9] Asian and Pacific Island Americans, as well as American Indians, often respond differently to issues than do whites.

Table 10.1 *Do men and women think differently about political issues?*

	Men (%)	Women (%)
Favor a woman's ability to obtain an abortion as a matter of choice	36	43
Approve of the way the U.S. government is handling the war in Iraq	26	17
Agree that controlling and reducing illegal immigration is an important policy goal	93	91
Favor allowing people to put a portion of Social Security payroll taxes into personal retirement accounts that would be invested in stocks and bonds	36	29
Agree that newer lifestyles are breaking down society	62	64
Voted for Barack Obama in 2008	49*	56*

Source: Data compiled and analyzed by Jon L. Weakley from the 2008 American National Election Study.
*From CNN exit polling data, November 5, 2008.

AGE   Age seems to have a decided effect on political socialization. Our view of the proper role of government, for example, often depends on the era in which we were born and our individual experiences with a variety of social, political, and economic forces. Older people, for example, continue to be affected by having lived through the Great Depression and World War II.

One political scientist predicts that as Baby Boomers age, the age gap in political beliefs about political issues, especially governmental programs, will increase.[10] Young people, for example, resist higher taxes to fund Medicare, while the elderly resist all efforts to limit Medicare or Social Security. In states such as Florida, to which many northern retirees have flocked seeking relief from cold winters and high taxes, the elderly have voted as a bloc to defeat school tax increases and to pass tax breaks for themselves.

RELIGION   Political scientists have found significant evidence that religion affects the political beliefs and behaviors of the American citizenry. As discussed in **chapter 1**, many American ideals, including hard work and personal responsibility, are rooted in our nation's Protestant heritage. These ideals have affected the public policies adopted by our government; they may be one reason why the United States has a less developed welfare state than many other industrialized democracies.

Our individual attitudes toward political issues are also shaped by our religious beliefs. Evangelical Christians and Catholics, for example, may be more supportive of programs that provide aid to parochial schools, even if it comes at the expense of lowering the wall of separation between church and state. Similarly, Jewish Americans are likely to be more supportive of aid to Israel—a policy that is at odds with Muslim Americans' support for a Palestinian state.

Family, Peers, and School

The influence of the family on political socialization can be traced to two factors: communication and receptivity. Children, especially during their preschool years, spend tremendous amounts of time with their parents; early on, they learn their parents' political values, even though these concepts may be vague. One study found that the most important visible public figures for children under the age of ten were police officers and, to a much lesser extent, the president.[11] Young children almost uniformly view both as "helpful." But, by the age of ten or eleven, children become more selective in their perceptions of the president. By this age, children raised in Democratic households are much more likely to be critical of a Republican president than are those raised in Republican households, and vice versa.

A child's peers—that is, children about the same age—also seem to have an important effect on the socialization process. While parental influences are greatest from birth to age five, a child's peer group becomes increasingly important as the child gets older, especially as he or she gets into middle school or high school.

There is no question that, in elementary school, children are taught respect for their nation and its symbols. Most school days begin with the Pledge of Allegiance, and patriotism and respect for country are important components of most school curricula. Support for flag and country create a foundation for national allegiance that prevails despite the negative views about politicians and government institutions that many Americans develop later in life.

High schools also can be important agents of political socialization. They continue the elementary school tradition of building good citizens and often reinforce textbook learning with trips to the state or national

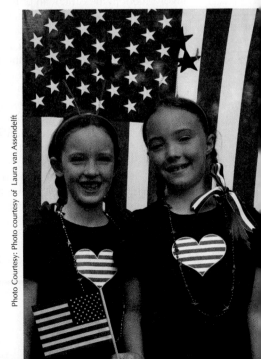

When are political values shaped?
Political values begin to form during childhood.

Photo Courtesy: Photo courtesy of Laura van Assendelft

Join the DEBATE | Should Civics Be Taught in American High Schools?

A civic education is an essential component of political socialization. Most democratic societies have some form of civic education, if only to teach citizens social norms, virtues, and the "rules of the game" of the democratic process. From the time you entered the first grade, you received elements of a civic education: reciting the Pledge of Allegiance every morning, learning about the Revolutionary War, the founding of our country, the Constitution, the struggle for civil rights, and so on. But in spite of these efforts, the effectiveness of civic education in the United States has been questioned. According to one study, only about one-quarter of all high school seniors reached proficiency in their American political knowledge.[a]

French political commentator Alexis de Tocqueville argued that without common values and virtues, there can be no common action or social stability. Thinking about your own experiences, how effective were the civics courses you took in school? Did they expand your knowledge and understanding of democratic processes and political participation? Or were they token courses of little relevance or help in understanding the American political system? What is the best way to teach American history, government, and political principles so that all who have contributed to the American experiment are recognized? Is a common civic education necessary, or should political socialization be left to the family? What can be done to increase interest in democratic politics and participation, and how can civic knowledge be restored to the American electorate?

To develop an ARGUMENT FOR teaching civics in American high schools, think about how:

- **Political participation, political socialization, and civic education are related.** In what ways does knowledge of democratic institutions and processes increase involvement in the American political process? How did your civic education in elementary and high school affect your understanding of the political process and increase your political engagement?
- **Civic education plays an important role in a democratic society.** How does civic education increase cooperation, tolerance of dissent and opposing views, and political compromise? How might this prepare students for the realities of pluralistic democratic life?
- **Civic education complements political socialization.** If schools do not provide for a common, basic understanding of political processes in the United States, who will? How would the common myths and beliefs that provide the foundation for political culture be transmitted outside of the schools?

To develop an ARGUMENT AGAINST teaching civics in American high schools, think about how:

- **Civic education is innately biased.** In a free, multicultural society, should certain values and social views be pressed upon individuals? Should schools determine what social values are central to a civic education? How might teaching one viewpoint stifle the diversity of cultures and political views that strengthen American democracy?
- **Schools have more important responsibilities.** Given the competing demands placed on schools today, including budgetary constraints, growing enrollments, and standardized testing, can schools realistically be expected to also focus on civic education? Given these constraints, can schools do an effective job of civic education?
- **Responsibility for teaching civics should fall to the family.** Should something as important as civic education be left to schools, which have to balance a number of competing educational goals? Why might other agents of political socialization, such as the family or religious establishments, be better suited to bear primary responsibility for civic education?

[a] National Assessment of Educational Progress (NAEP), www.nces.ed.gov/nationsreportcard/civics/.

capital. They also offer courses on current U.S. affairs. Many high schools impose a compulsory service learning requirement, which some studies report positively affects later political participation.[12] (To learn more about schools and the socialization process, see Join the Debate: Should Civics Be Taught in American High Schools?).

At the college level, teaching style often changes. Many college courses and texts like this one are designed in part to provide you with the information necessary to think critically about issues of major political consequence. It is common in college for students to be called on to question the appropriateness of certain political actions or to discuss underlying reasons for certain political or policy decisions. Therefore, most researchers believe that college has a liberalizing effect on students. Since the 1920s, studies have shown that students become more liberal each year they are in college. (To learn more about the ideology of first-year college students, see Figure 10.3.)

The Mass Media

The media have taken on a growing role as socialization agents. Adult Americans spend over thirty-five hours a week in front of their television sets; children spend more than fifty-three hours. And, Americans spend an average of thirteen hours a week on the Internet.[13] Television has a tremendous impact on how people view politics, government, and politicians. Television can serve to enlighten voters and encourage voter turnout. MTV began coverage of presidential campaigns in 1992. Its "Choose or Lose" and "Rock the Vote" campaigns are designed to change the usually abysmal turnout rates of young voters.

Figure 10.3 *What are the ideological self-identifications of first-year college students?*
A majority of entering first-year college students describe themselves as middle of the road; this number was fairly consistent in the 1990s but decreased beginning in the early 2000s. The number of students identifying themselves as liberal and far left declined dramatically during the 1970s and early 1980s but is currently on the rise. The number of students identifying themselves as conservative and far right has also increased since the 1970s, but at a slower rate.

Sources: Reprinted from Harold W. Stanley and Richard G. Niemi, *Vital Statistics on American Politics, 2009–2010* (Washington, DC: CQ Press, 2009), 124.

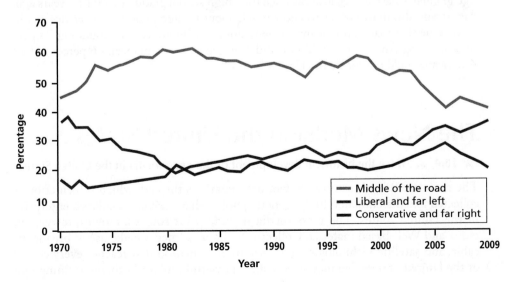

Over the years, more and more Americans have turned away from traditional sources of news such as nightly news broadcasts on the major networks and daily newspapers in favor of different outlets. In 2008, one study estimated that the same percentage of viewers watched alternative sources such as *The Tonight Show, The Late Show,* or *The Daily Show* as watched more traditional cable news such as CNN or FOX News.[14] TV talk shows, talk radio, online magazines, and blogs are important sources of information about politics for many, yet the information that people get from these sources often is skewed. This may affect the way that these citizens process political information and form opinions on public policy, as well as their receptiveness to new ideas.

Cues from Leaders or Opinion Makers

Given the visibility of political leaders and their access to the media, it is easy to see the important role they play in influencing value formation. Political leaders, members of the news media, and a host of other experts have regular opportunities to influence public opinion because of the lack of deep conviction with which most Americans hold many of their political beliefs.

The president, especially, is often in a position to mold public opinion through effective use of the bully pulpit, as discussed in **chapter 7**. One political commentator emphasizes the support of a group of citizens—called followers—who are inclined to rally to the support of the president no matter what he does.[15]

Political Knowledge

Political knowledge and political participation have a reciprocal effect on one another—an increase in one will increase the other. Knowledge about the political system is essential to successful political involvement, which, in turn, teaches citizens about politics and increases their interest in public affairs. And, although few citizens know everything about all of the candidates and issues in a particular election, they can, and often do, know enough to impose their views and values as to the general direction the nation should take.

This is true despite the fact that most Americans' level of knowledge about history and politics is quite low. According to the Department of Education, today's college graduates have less civic knowledge than high school graduates did fifty years ago. Americans also don't appear to know much about foreign policy; some critics would even argue that many Americans are geographically illiterate. An astounding 88 percent of young Americans could not find Afghanistan on a map, and 6 percent of all Americans could not locate the United States.[16]

The News Media in the United States

⭐ **10.4** . . . Trace the historical development of the news media in the United States.

mass media
The entire array of organizations through which information is collected and disseminated to the general public.

The **mass media**—the entire array of organizations through which information is collected and disseminated to the general public—have become a colossal enterprise in the United States. The mass media include print sources, movies, television, radio, and Web-based material. Collectively the mass media make use of broadcast, cable, and satellite technologies to distribute information that reaches every corner of the United States. The mass media are a powerful tool for both entertaining and informing the public. They reflect American society, but they are also the primary lens through which citizens view American culture and American politics. The **news media,** which are one component of the larger mass media, provide the public with new information about subjects of public interest and play a vital role in the political process.[17]

Print Media

The first example of news media in America came in the form of newspapers, which were published in the colonies as early as 1690. The number of newspapers grew throughout the 1700s, as colonists began to realize the value of a press free from government oversight and censorship. The battle between Federalists and Anti-Federalists over ratification of the Constitution, discussed in **chapter 2**, played out in various partisan newspapers in the late eighteenth century. Thus, it was not surprising that one of the Anti-Federalists' demands was a constitutional amendment guaranteeing the freedom of the press. (To learn more about freedom of the press, see The Living Constitution: First Amendment.)

The partisan press eventually gave way to the penny press. In 1833, Benjamin Day founded the *New York Sun,* which cost a penny at the newsstand. Beyond its low price, the *Sun* sought to expand its audience by freeing itself from the grip of a single political party. Inexpensive and politically independent, the *Sun* was the forerunner of modern newspapers, which rely on mass circulation and commercial advertising to produce profit. By 1861, the penny press had so supplanted partisan papers that President Abraham Lincoln announced his administration would have no favored or sponsored newspaper.

Although the print media were becoming less partisan, they were not necessarily becoming more respectable. Mass-circulation dailies sought wide readership, attracting readers with the sensational and the scandalous. The sordid side of politics became the entertainment of the times. One of the best-known examples occurred in the presidential campaign of 1884, when the *Buffalo Evening Telegraph* headlined "A Terrible Tale" about Grover Cleveland, the Democratic nominee.[18] The story alleged that Cleveland, an unmarried man, had fathered a child in 1871, while sheriff of Buffalo, New York. Even though paternity was indeterminate because the child's mother had been seeing other men, Cleveland willingly accepted responsibility, since all the other men were married, and he had dutifully paid child support for years. The strict Victorian moral code that dominated American values at the time made the story even more shocking than it would be today. Fortunately for Cleveland, another newspaper, the *Democratic Sentinel,* broke a story that helped to offset this scandal: Republican presidential nominee James G. Blaine and his wife's first child had been born just three months after their wedding.

Throughout the nineteenth century, payoffs to the press were common. Andrew Jackson, for instance, gave one in ten of his early appointments to loyal reporters.[19] During the 1872 presidential campaign, the Republicans slipped cash to about 300 newsmen.[20] Wealthy industrialists also sometimes purchased investigative cease-fires for tens of thousands of dollars.

In the late 1800s and early 1900s, prominent publishers such as William Randolph Hearst and Joseph Pulitzer expanded the reach of newspapers in their control by practicing what became known as **yellow journalism**—a form of newspaper publishing that featured pictures, comics, color, and sensationalized news coverage. These innovations were designed to increase readership and capture a share of the burgeoning immigrant population.

The Progressive movement gave rise to a new type of journalism in the early 1920s. **Muckraking** journalists—so named by President Theodore Roosevelt after

TIMELINE: The Development of the American News Media

1833 **Rise of the Penny Press**—Benjamin Day founds the *New York Sun*; it costs a penny at the newsstand and is politically independent.

1920 **KDKA in Pittsburgh**—First commercial radio station launches and provides detailed campaign coverage.

1893 **Joseph Pulitzer Launches** *New York World*—Known for its sensationalism and progressive crusades, Pulitzer's approach is nicknamed "yellow journalism."

1963 **Television News Grows**—NBC becomes first network to have a 30-minute nightly national news broadcast.

a special rake designed to collect manure—were devoted to exposing misconduct by government, business, and individual politicians.[21] For Roosevelt, muckraking was a derogatory term used to describe reporters who focused on the carnal underbelly of politics rather than its more lofty pursuits. Nevertheless, much good came from these efforts. Muckrakers stimulated demands for anti-trust regulations—laws that prohibit companies, like large steel companies, from controlling an entire industry—and exposed deplorable working conditions in factories, as well as outright exploitation of workers by business owners. An unfortunate side effect of this emphasis on crusades and investigations, however, was the frequent publication of gossip and rumor without sufficient proof.

As the news business grew, so did the focus on increasing its profitability. Newspapers became more careful and less adversarial in their reporting to avoid alienating the advertisers and readers who produced their revenues.

Radio News

The advent of radio in the early part of the twentieth century was a media revolution and a revelation to the average American who rarely, if ever, had heard the voice of a president, governor, or senator. The radio became the center of most homes in the evening, when national networks broadcast the news as well as entertainment shows. Calvin Coolidge was the first president to appear on radio on a regular basis, but President Franklin D. Roosevelt made the radio appearance a must-listen by presenting "fireside chats" to promote his New Deal.

News radio, which had begun to take a back seat to television by the mid-1950s, regained popularity with the development of AM talk radio in the mid-1980s. Controversial radio host Rush Limbaugh began the trend with his unabashed conservative

1980 Cable News Network (CNN)—Founded by media mogul Ted Turner, CNN makes national and international events available instantaneously around the globe.

2009 Death of Newspapers—In the face of declining circulation and revenues, several daily newspapers close their newsrooms and cease all publication, a trend that continues today.

1996 Candidate Home Pages Appear on the Web—Internet sites contain candidate profiles, issue positions, campaign strategy and slogans, and more.

2006 Social Networking and Video Sharing Explode—Online social networks and video-sharing Web sites transform political campaigns.

views, opening the door for other conservative commentators such as Laura Ingraham, Sean Hannity, and Glenn Beck. Statistics show that these conservative radio hosts resurrected the radio as a news medium by giving the information that they broadcast a strong ideological bent.

Television News

Television was first demonstrated in the United States at the 1939 World's Fair in New York, but it did not take off as a news source until after World War II. While most homes had televisions by the early 1960s, it took several years more for television to replace print and radio as the nation's chief news provider. In 1963, most networks provided only fifteen minutes of news per day; only two major networks provided thirty minutes of news coverage. During this period, a substantial majority of Americans still received most of their news from newspapers. But, on a typical day in 2010, only 50 percent read a local newspaper and 17 percent read a national newspaper. (To learn more about Americans' news sources, see Figure 10.4.)

An important distinction exists between network and cable news stations. Network news has lost viewers in every year since 1980. Cable news, however, has seen rapid increases in viewership, due in large part to the increased availability of cable and satellite services providing twenty-four-hour news channels.

Cable and satellite providers give consumers access to a less glitzy and more unfiltered source of news, C-SPAN, a basic cable channel that offers gavel-to-gavel coverage of congressional proceedings, as well as major political events when Congress is not in session. It also produces some of its own programming, such as *Washington Journal*, which invites scholars and journalists to speak about topics pertaining to their areas of expertise. Because the content of C-SPAN can be erudite, technical, and sometimes

Figure 10.4 *Where do Americans get their news?*

Source: Pew Internet and Public Life Project, "Understanding the Participatory News Consumer." (March 1, 2010): www.pewinternet.org/Reports/2010/online-news.aspx.

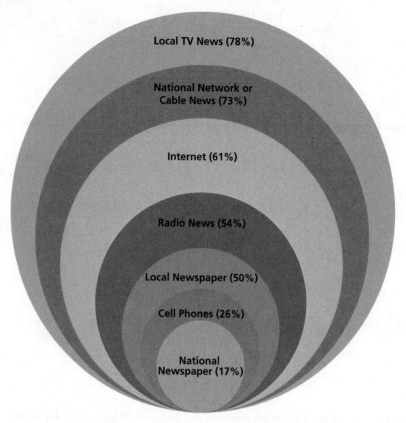

Local TV News (78%)

National Network or Cable News (73%)

Internet (61%)

Radio News (54%)

Local Newspaper (50%)

Cell Phones (26%)

National Newspaper (17%)

downright tedious (such as the fixed camera shot of the Senate during a roll-call vote), audiences tend to be very small, but they are very loyal and give C-SPAN its place as a truly content-driven news source.

What is C-SPAN? C-SPAN, shown here, is a public access channel that (through the main channel and its affiliates) provides gavel to gavel coverage of the House and Senate. It also airs a variety of other public affairs programming.

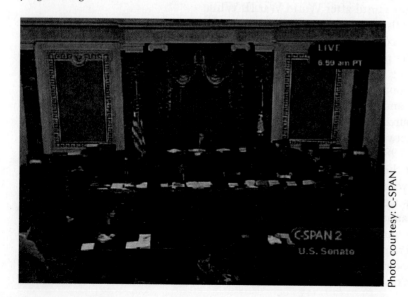

Photo courtesy: C-SPAN

A recent development in television news is the growth in popularity of comedy news programs. While *Saturday Night Live* and other late-night comedy programs, like those hosted by Jay Leno and David Letterman, have mocked politicians and the news for years, more recent programs like Jon Stewart's *The Daily Show* and Stephen Colbert's *The Colbert Report*—a satire of FOX News's *The O'Reilly Factor*—dedicate their entire program to poking fun at world leaders and current issues. One study conducted by the Annenberg Public Policy Center of the University of Pennsylvania revealed comedy programs actually inform viewers as well as entertain them. Regular viewers of *The Daily Show* were found to know more about world events than nonviewers, even when education, party identification, watching cable news, and other factors were taken into consideration.[22]

The Living Constitution

Congress shall make no law respecting an establishment of religion, or prohibiting the free exercise thereof; or abridging the freedom of speech, or of the press; or the right of the people peaceably to assemble, and to petition the Government for a redress of grievances.

—FIRST AMENDMENT

The Framers knew that democracy is not easy, that a republic requires a continuous battle for rights and responsibilities. One of those rights is the freedom of the press, preserved in the First Amendment to the Constitution. The Framers' view of the press, and its required freedom, however, was almost certainly less broad than our conception of press freedom today.

It is difficult to appreciate what a leap of faith it was for the Framers to grant freedom of the press when James Madison brought the Bill of Rights before Congress. Newspapers were largely run by disreputable people, since at the time editors and reporters were judged as purveyors of rumor and scandal.

But, the printed word was one of the few mediums of political communication in the young nation—it was critical for keeping Americans informed about issues. Therefore, the Framers hoped that giving the press freedom to print all content, although certain to give rise to sensational stories, would also produce high-quality, objective reporting.

Not much has changed since the Framers instituted the free press. We still have tabloids and partisan publications in which politicians attack each other, and we still rely on the press to give us important political information that we use to make voting decisions. The simple, enduring protection the Framers created in the First Amendment continues to make possible the flow of ideas that a democratic society relies upon.

CRITICAL THINKING QUESTIONS

1. While the First Amendment guarantees the rights of a free press, it is silent about the media's responsibilities to the public. What should the responsibilities of the news media and individual journalists be?
2. Should television news, which relies on the spoken word, be afforded the same protections given to the written word? Why or why not?
3. How relevant are the guarantees enshrined in the First Amendment to new media? Do bloggers, for example, deserve the same constitutional protections as traditional journalists?

New Media

Increasingly, media consumers, especially those under the age of thirty-five, are abandoning traditional media outlets in favor of other sources. While television networks are still the most regularly viewed, new media, including Internet news, blogs, and social networking sites, are gaining ground. These outlets are also transforming the relationship between the media and citizens, even challenging our perceptions of what is defined as "media." They also remove many of the traditional filters—such as editors and journalistic standards—that lend credibility to professional news outlets.

THE INTERNET   The Internet, which began as a Department of Defense project named Advanced Research Projects Agency Network (ARPANET) in the late 1960s, has grown into an unprecedented source of public information for people throughout the world. In 2010, for example, 61 percent of Americans claimed to get some of their news online.

The current debate among scholars is whether all the information available on the Web will be good for politics and society or not. Most observers believe that the availability of all this information makes for a better-informed and more active electorate.[23] Others are concerned that only the more educated and affluent will benefit from a greater reliance on technology and that this will produce new inequalities. There also is concern that the ability to view only those news sources that support one's existing views and ideological preferences and a tendency to communicate only with like-minded people will polarize Americans further, rather than allowing them to bridge differences and identify common ground.[24] A crucial question for the future is whether citizens will devote the time necessary to find valid and balanced data amidst the almost unlimited information available through the Internet.

BLOGS   Blogs, which have rapidly grown in popularity in recent years, are Web-based journal entries that provide an editorial and news outlet for citizens. They have become important informational tools, linking together people with common ideological or issue-specific interests.

Many blogs are devoted to ideological rabble-rousing and rumor mongering, while others provide reasoned discourse. The right-leaning Drudge Report (www.drudgereport.com) pioneered the spreading of newsworthy rumors during the Clinton administration. Other well-known right-leaning political Web sites include Red State (www.redstate.org) and Townhall (www.townhall.com). On the left are the Daily Kos (www.dailykos.com), the Huffington Post (www.huffingtonpost.com), and Talking Points Memo (www.talkingpointsmemo.com).

While blogs and their user-generated content seem to offer the public a more democratic means of engaging in public discussion, there is growing concern that the blogosphere has become dominated by a small elite. While there are over 70 million blogs on the Web, only a very small number of sites have a sizeable audience and, thus, attract most of the advertising dollars available. Moreover, most of the bloggers on the "A-list" are graduates of the nation's top colleges, and many have post-graduate degrees.

SOCIAL NETWORKING SITES   Another new form of news dissemination on the Internet is social networking sites such as Facebook, MySpace, and Twitter. Although not necessarily created to spread political news, they have been effective in doing just that. During the 2008 election, for example, Facebook was home to a great deal of political debate. Supporters of presidential candidate Barack Obama, especially, established fan pages with millions of Facebook friends. These sites were then used to organize activists, raise money, and energize young voters.

A growing number of political leaders have also turned to Twitter to reach out to supporters. Among these are Senator John McCain (@SenJohnMcCain) and Representative Maxine Waters (@MaxineWaters). The White House, too, has its own Twitter feed (@whitehouse). Sites such as these fundamentally change the media. No longer do politicians have to rely on the older forms of media to disseminate their message. As a consequence, articles in traditional media publications or Web sites might cite a leader's Twitter page as an authoritative source. Though this may seem more democratic, critics worry that a growing reliance on social networking sites will weaken the media's role as a filter, educator, and watchdog.

Average citizens, too, have used Twitter to spread political news. Users have tweeted from political rallies, offered commentary on the president's State of the Union Address, and used the #hcr hash tag to make health care a trending topic during congressional debates on that issue. Although most tweeps probably do not consider these actions political, they are in fact, a part of politics.

Current News Media Trends

A number of major changes define the news media today. Among these are the increasing consolidation of media ownership and the targeting of programming at specific populations. The people who deliver the news, too, have changed. Media news coverage today increasingly relies not only on subject-matter experts but also on average citizens.

MEDIA CONSOLIDATION   The news media in the United States are multibillion-dollar, for-profit businesses that ultimately are driven by the bottom line. As with all free-market enterprises, the pressure in privately owned media is to increasingly consolidate media ownership, so as to reap the benefits that come from larger market shares and fewer large-scale competitors.

Unlike traditional industries, where the primary concern associated with consolidation is the manipulation of prices made possible by monopolies or near monopolies, the consolidation of the media poses far greater potential risks. Should the news media become dominated by a few mega-corporations, the fear is that these groups could limit the flow of information and ideas that form the very essence of a free society and that make democracy possible.

NARROWCASTING   In recent years, fierce competition to attract viewers and the availability of additional television channels made possible by cable and satellite television have led media outlets to move toward **narrowcasting**—targeting media programming at specific populations within society. Within the realm of cable news, MSNBC and FOX News have begun engaging in this form of niche journalism. The

narrowcasting
Targeting media programming at specific populations within society.

What are the consequences of narrowcasting? Narrowcasting, such as that seen on conservative FOX News, can lead to polarization in political opinion.

Photo courtesy: Jennifer Taylor/Corbis

two stations divide audiences by ideology. FOX News emphasizes a conservative viewpoint and MSNBC increasingly stresses a more liberal perspective, although the FOX view is often more pronounced.[25]

While narrowcasting can help to promote the interests of parts of the population, especially racial and ethnic minorities who may ordinarily be left out of mainstream media coverage, it comes with a social cost. Narrowcasting increases the chance that group members will rely on news that is appealing to their preexisting views. By limiting one's exposure to a broad range of information or competing views, narrowcasting could result in the further polarization of public opinion. The polarization made possible by narrowcasting is particularly problematic when it comes to programs that are narrowcasted in a specific ideological direction.[26]

INCREASING USE OF EXPERTS   Most journalists know a little bit about many subjects but do not specialize in any one area and certainly do not possess enough knowledge to fill the hours of airtime made possible by cable television's twenty-four-hour news cycle. Therefore, especially on cable stations, the news media employ expert consultants from a number of different disciplines ranging from medical ethics to political campaigning. These experts, also referred to as pundits, or the more derogatory term "talking heads," are hired to discuss the dominant issues of the day.

One study about how experts affect citizens' views on political issues says that "news from experts or research studies is estimated to have almost as great an impact" as anchorpersons, reporters in the field, or special commentators. Such findings are both good and bad for Americans. On the one hand, the "strong effects by commentators and experts are compatible with a picture of a public that engages in collective deliberation and takes expertise seriously." On the other, "one might argue that the potency of media commentators and of ostensibly nonpartisan TV 'experts' is disturbing. Who elected them to shape our views of the world? Who says they are insightful or even unbiased?"[27]

CITIZEN JOURNALISTS   In the past, news reports were filed only by professionals who covered current events as an occupation. Today, however, much of what we call "news" content is written and filmed by amateur **citizen journalists,** ordinary individuals who collect, report, and analyze news content. Although some citizen journalists are paid for their work, many are unpaid and work for pleasure.

Media scholars have hotly debated the value of citizen journalism. On one hand, citizen journalism can be a democratizing force, allowing more people to participate in setting the agenda and framing issues. It can also provide more instantaneous coverage than traditional media. On the other hand, citizen journalists are often not trained in the rules and standards of journalism. They may not treat their sources with the same respect or fact-check as thoroughly as professional reporters. Citizen journalists may also compromise the objectivity of their coverage.

citizen journalists
Ordinary individuals who collect, report, and analyze news content.

Rules Governing the News Media

⭐ **10.5** . . . **Summarize the ethical standards and federal regulations that govern the news media.**

Professional journalists may obtain and publish information in a number of ways. There are, however, boundaries to this action. Journalists are primarily limited by the ethical standards of their profession. In some cases, however, additional governmental regulations may apply.

Journalistic Standards

The heaviest restrictions placed on reporters come from the industry's own professional norms and each journalist's level of integrity, as well as from the oversight provided by editors who are ultimately responsible for the accuracy of the news they produce. To help guide the ethical behavior of journalists, the Society of Professional Journalists publishes a detailed "Code of Ethics" that includes principles and standards governing issues such as avoiding conflicts of interest and verifying the information being reported.

One dilemma reporters face is how to deal ethically with sources. These informants may speak to reporters in a number of ways. If a session is **on the record,** as in a formal press conference, every word an official utters can be printed. In contrast, a journalist may obtain information **off the record,** which means that nothing the official says may be printed. Reporters may also obtain information **on background**—meaning that none of the information can be attributed to the source by name. Whereas background talks can be euphemistically attributed to sources, such as "unnamed senior officials," information on **deep background** must be completely unsourced, with the reporter giving the reader no hint about the origin. When information is obtained in any of these ways, reporters must be careful to respect their source's wishes. Otherwise, not only might that person refuse to talk to them in the future, but other potential sources may do the same.

Journalists also grapple with the competitive nature of the news business. The pressure to get the story right is often weighed against the pressure to get the story first, or at the very least to get the story finished before the next deadline. The twenty-four-hour news cycle, brought to life by cable news stations and nourished by the expansion of Web-based media, has only heightened the pressure to produce interesting copy in a timely manner.

on the record
Information provided to a journalist that can be released and attributed by name to the source.

off the record
Information provided to a journalist that will not be released to the public.

on background
Information provided to a journalist that will not be attributed to a named source.

deep background
Information provided to a journalist that will not be attributed to any source.

Government Regulations

The U.S. government regulates media in a number of ways. Some of these regulations apply to all forms of media. Libel and slander, for example, are illegal in all cases. The Constitution also places a limit on prior restraint—that is, the government may not limit any speech or publications before they actually occur. This principle was clearly affirmed in *New York Times Co.* v. *U.S.* (1971).[28] In this case, the Supreme Court ruled that the government could not prevent publication by the *New York Times* of the Pentagon Papers, classified government documents about the Vietnam War that had been photocopied and sent to the *Times* and the *Washington Post* by Daniel Ellsberg, a government employee. "Only a free and unrestrained press can effectively expose deception in the government," Justice Hugo Black wrote in a concurring opinion for the Court. "To find that the President has 'inherent power' to halt the publication of news by resort to the courts would wipe out the First Amendment."

Government can, however, regulate electronic media such as radio or television more heavily than print content. There are two reasons for this unequal treatment. First, the airwaves used by the electronic media are considered public property and are leased by the federal government to private broadcasters. Second, those airwaves are in limited supply; without some regulation, the nation's many radio and television stations would interfere with one another's frequency signals. These government regulations of the electronic media apply in two major areas: ownership and content.

MEDIA OWNERSHIP   In 1996, Congress passed the sweeping Telecommunications Act, deregulating whole segments of the electronic media. The Telecommunications Act sought to provide an optimal balance of competing corporate interests, technological innovations, and consumer needs. It appeared to offer limitless opportunities for entrepreneurial companies to provide enhanced services to consumers. The result of this deregulation was the sudden merger of previously distinct kinds of media in order to create a more "multimedia" approach to communicating information and entertainment. This paved the way for the creation of multimedia corporations such as Viacom, Time Warner, and Comcast.

Since the initial passage of this act, the Federal Communications Commission (FCC) has continued to relax ownership standards, leading to greater media consolidation (discussed earlier in this chapter). Today, a single company may own up to 45 percent of media in a given market. Companies may now also own both newspapers and television stations in a single market. In addition, the FCC no longer reviews broadcast licenses to ensure that broadcasters are serving the public interest.

content regulations
Limitations on the substance of the mass media.

equal time rule
The rule that requires broadcast stations to sell air time equally to all candidates in a political campaign if they choose to sell it to any.

CONTENT   The government also subjects the electronic media to substantial **content regulations,** or limitations on the substance of the mass media. In order to ensure that the airwaves "serve the public interest, convenience, and necessity," the FCC has attempted to promote equity in broadcasting. For example, the **equal time rule** requires that broadcast stations sell air time equally to all candidates in a political campaign if they choose to sell it to any, which they are under no obligation to do. An exception to this rule is a political debate: stations may exclude from this event less well-known and minor-party candidates.

One controversy over regulation of electronic media content involves the communications industry and Internet service providers. Common carriers as defined by the Communications Act of 1934, such as telephone companies, are required to be neutral in the content they carry over their networks and cannot limit or censor individuals or organizations they may disagree with. Internet service providers (ISPs), including telephone and cable companies that offer Internet service, are not subject to the common carrier definition and therefore may legally block transmission through their networks of content they find objectionable.

In addition to blocking objectionable content, however, ISPs such as Comcast and Verizon have used this policy as a way to slow the Internet connections of individuals using peer-to-peer file sharing programs. The federal courts have upheld the legality of this action. Many free speech advocates and Web-based businesses (including Google and Yahoo) take issue with this decision. They argue that Internet providers are both censoring content and using the policy as a way to charge high-volume Internet users more money. Such actions, advocates believe, constitute an infringement on users' First Amendment rights. Thus, these Web-based companies have spent millions of dollars lobbying Congress and the FCC to adopt a policy of "net neutrality." This policy would overturn the existing restrictions on Internet access and require ISPs to allow all users access to any content they desire at one flat-rate cost.

How the News Media Cover Politics

★ 10.6 . . . Assess how the news media cover politics.

The news media focus an extraordinary amount of attention on politicians and the day-to-day operations of government. In 2010, over 1,300 reporters were accredited to sit in Congress's press gallery.[29] The media have a visible presence at the White House as well; in 2010, about eighty journalists were credentialed as daily White House correspondents. These reporters come from traditional and new media outlets and hail from across the country and, increasingly, around the world. Consequently, a politician's every public utterance is reported and intensively scrutinized and interpreted in the media.

How the Press and Public Figures Interact

Communication between elected officials or public figures and the media takes a number of different forms. A **press release** is a written document offering an official comment or position on an issue or news event; it is usually faxed, e-mailed, or handed directly to reporters. A **press briefing** is a relatively restricted live engagement with the press, with the range of questions limited to one or two specific topics. In a press briefing, a press secretary or aide represents the elected official or public figure, who does not appear in person. In a full-blown **press conference,** an elected official appears in person to talk with the press at great length about an unrestricted range of topics. Press conferences provide a field on which reporters struggle to get the answers they need and public figures attempt to retain control of their message and spin the news and issues in ways favorable to them.

Politicians and media interact in a variety of other ways as well. Politicians hire campaign consultants who use focus groups and polling in an attempt to gauge how to present the candidate to the media and to the public. Additionally, politicians can attempt to bypass the national news media through paid advertising and by appearing on talk shows and local news programs. (Some of these and other techniques for dealing with the media during a campaign are discussed in greater detail in **chapter 12.**) Politicians also use the media to attempt to retain a high level of name recognition and to build support for their ideological and policy ideas.

press release
A document offering an official comment or position.

press briefing
A relatively restricted session between a press secretary or aide and the press.

press conference
An unrestricted session between an elected official and the press.

Covering the Presidency

The three branches of the U.S. government—the executive, the legislative, and the judicial—are roughly equal in power and authority. But, in the world of media coverage, the president is first among equals. The White House beat is one of the most prestigious posts a political reporter can hold. Many of the most famous network news anchors, including NBC's Brian Williams, got their start covering the presidency.

What does the White House press secretary do? The press secretary is the conduit of daily communications between the president and the news media. Here, Press Secretary Robert Gibbs holds a daily press briefing.

Photo courtesy: AP/Wide World Photos

The attention of the press to the White House enables a president to appear even on very short notice and to televise live, interrupting regular programming. The White House's press briefing room is a familiar sight on the evening news, not just because presidents use it fairly often, but also because the presidential press secretary has almost daily question and answer sessions there.

The post of press secretary to the president has existed only since Herbert Hoover's administration (1929–1933). The press secretary's power, however, has grown tremendously over that time. Presidents increasingly resist facing the media on their own and leave this task to their press secretary. As a result, press secretaries have a difficult job; they must convince the media of the importance of the president's policy decisions as well as defend any actions taken by the executive office. In many ways, the prestige and power of the presidency depends on the "spin" of the press secretary and his or her ability to win over the media. Thus, many presidents choose close aides with whom they have worked previously and who are familiar with their thinking. For example, President Barack Obama's press secretary, Robert Gibbs, worked on Obama's Senate and presidential campaigns as well as in his Senate office before being appointed press secretary in 2009.

Covering Congress

With 535 voting members representing distinct geographic areas, covering Congress poses a difficult challenge for the media. Most news organizations solve the size and decentralization problems inherent in covering news developments in the legislative branch by concentrating coverage on three groups of individuals. First, the leaders of both parties in both houses receive the lion's share of attention because only they can speak for a majority of their party's members. Usually the majority and minority leaders in each house and the Speaker of the House are the preferred spokespersons, but the whips also receive a substantial share of air time and column inches. Second, key committee chairs command center stage when subjects in their domain are newsworthy. Heads of the most prominent committees (such as Appropriations or Judiciary) are guaranteed frequent coverage, but even the chairs and members of minor committees or subcommittees can achieve fame when the time and issue are right. For example, a sensational scandal like steroid use in Major League Baseball may lead to congressional committee hearings that receive extensive media coverage. Third, local newspapers and broadcast stations normally devote some resources to covering their local senators and representatives, even when these legislators are junior and relatively lacking in influence.

As with coverage of the president, media coverage of Congress is disproportionately negative. A significant portion of the media attention given to the House and Senate focuses on conflict among members. Some political scientists believe that such reporting is at least partially responsible for the public's negative perceptions of Congress.[30]

Covering the Supreme Court

While the president and Congress interact with the media on a regular basis, the Supreme Court remains a virtual media vacuum. Television cameras have never been permitted to record Supreme Court proceedings. Print and broadcast reporters, however, are granted access to the Court. Still, there are fewer than a dozen full-time reporters covering the Supreme Court, and the amount of space dedicated to Court-related stories has continued to shrink. Stories involving complex legal issues are not as easy to sell as well-illustrated stories related to the Congress or president.[31]

The justices, citing the need to protect the public's perception of the Supreme Court as a nonpolitical and autonomous entity, have given little evidence to suggest that they are eager to become more media friendly. Many veteran reporters have criticized this decision. As longtime Court reporter Tony Mauro noted, "Of course we don't want the Supreme Court playing to the crowd, ruling to please the majority. But that does not mean the [C]ourt should be invisible and unaccountable. Clarence Thomas on *Face the Nation*? John Roberts taking questions posted on YouTube? Sam Alito blogging? Why not? Really, why not?"[32]

TOWARD REFORM: News Media Influence, News Media Bias, and Public Confidence

⭐ **10.7** . . . **Evaluate the influence of the news media on public policy and the impact of media bias.**

There are many important questions concerning the news media's relationship with the public. For instance, how much influence do the media actually have on the public's understanding of political issues? Do the media have a discernable ideological bent or bias, as some people suggest? Are people able to resist information that is inconsistent with their preexisting beliefs? And, how much confidence does the public have in the news media?

News Media Influence

Some political scientists argue that the content of news coverage accounts for a large portion of the volatility and changes in public opinion and voting preferences of Americans, when measured over relatively short periods of time.[33] These changes are called **media effects.** These effects may be visible in a number of ways.

First, reporting can sway the public opinion and votes of people who lack strong political beliefs. So, for example, the media have a greater influence on political independents than on strong partisans.[34] That said, the sort of politically unmotivated individual who is subject to media effects may be less likely to engage in political affairs, in which case the media's influence may be more limited.

Second, it is likely that the media have a greater impact on topics far removed from the lives and experiences of readers and viewers. News reports can probably shape public opinion about events in foreign countries fairly easily. Yet, what the media say about domestic issues such as rising food or gas prices, neighborhood crime, or child rearing may have relatively little effect, because most citizens have personal experience of and well-formed ideas about these subjects.

Third, the media can influence the list of issues to be addressed by government through a process known as **agenda setting.** Significant media attention to an issue often increases the salience of that issue with average citizens. These citizens then pressure the government to take action.

Fourth, the media influence public opinion through **framing**—the process by which a news organization defines a political issue and consequently affects opinion about the issue. Finally, the media have the power to indirectly influence the way the public views politicians and government.

media effects
The influence of news sources on public opinion.

agenda setting
The constant process of forming the list of issues to be addressed by government.

framing
The process by which a news organization defines a political issue and consequently affects opinion about the issue.

Al-Jazeera and Media Bias

Al-Jazeera is an independent television station founded in 1996 that broadcasts from the tiny, oil-rich Islamic country of Qatar—an important U.S. ally. Unlike its regional competitors, al-Jazeera offers more than state propaganda and limited news content. Over the years, al-Jazeera's broadcasts have caused international controversy. Saudi Arabia, Libya, Algeria, and Kuwait have all expressed outrage over the station's coverage of domestic events, while the United States has criticized al-Jazeera for broadcasting interviews with Osama bin Laden and for referring to Palestinians killed by Israeli forces as martyrs.

■ Go to al-Jazeera's English-language Web site, english .aljazeera.net. How does its coverage of world news compare with that of American media outlets?

■ Why would media coverage of the United States in some parts of the world tend to be highly critical?

■ Think about the media outlets you rely on for news. How objective or balanced are they in their coverage? In what ways, if any, are they biased?

News Media Bias

Are journalists biased? The answer is simple and unavoidable. Of course they are. Journalists, like all human beings, have values, preferences, and attitudes galore—some conscious, others subconscious, but all reflected at one time or another in the subjects selected for coverage or the portrayal of events or content communicated. Given that the press is biased, in what ways is it biased and when and how are the biases shown?

For much of the 1980s and 1990s, the argument was that the media had a liberal bias because of the sheer number of journalists who self identified as liberal Democrats.[35] This argument still holds today; journalists are substantially Democratic in party affiliation and voting habits, progressive and anti-establishment in political orientation, and to the left of the general public on many economic, foreign policy, and social issues.

But, more recently, other analysts have argued that a conservative bias in the media is even more pervasive. They point to the elite background of the typical journalist, who tends to be white, male, highly educated, and relatively affluent. As a result, many of these journalists may unconsciously ignore reporting on issues that are important to racial and ethnic minorities, the poor, and others who might be critical of government and big business.[36]

At the end of the day, the deepest bias among political journalists is the desire to get a good story. News people know that if they report on a story with spice and drama, they will increase their audience. The fear of missing a good story shapes how media outlets develop headlines and frame their stories.

Public Confidence

Americans' general assessment of the news media is considerably unfavorable and has been in a downward trend since the 1980s. According to a 2009 survey by the Pew Research Center for the People and the Press, a majority of the public gives the media low ratings on a number of indicators. Pew, for example, found that just 29 percent of respondents said news organizations get the facts straight, and 63 percent believed the press was often inaccurate.[37] These figures were at their lowest levels in two decades.

Despite the increasing displeasure that the majority of Americans express about political bias and other shortcomings, traditional media have managed to maintain a reputation as an authoritative source for news in an ever-expanding media market. The nightly news anchors regularly are rated as the most trusted journalists, while tabloid-style journalists are ranked at the bottom.[38] Moreover, the majority of Americans who access Internet news say they also rely on at least one traditional form of news media, and 75 percent of the most visited news and information sites are produced by established news organizations.[39]

Still, Americans continue to value the media's watchdog role, with 62 percent believing that press scrutiny keeps political leaders from doing things they should not do.[40]

Thus, while public confidence in media organizations has declined and reforms are certainly warranted, Americans have not wavered in their support for a vigorous free press and the role that the media play in a democratic society.

What Should I Have LEARNED?

Now that you have read this chapter, you should be able to:

★ 10.1 Trace the development of modern public opinion research, p. 278.

Public opinion is what the public thinks about an issue or a particular set of issues. Polls are used to estimate public opinion. Almost since the beginning of the United States, various attempts have been made to influence public opinion about particular issues or to sway elections. *Literary Digest* first began national presidential polling in 1916, using unscientific straw polls. Modern-day polling did not begin until the 1930s. George Gallup was the first to use scientific polling methods to determine public opinion.

★ 10.2 Describe the methods for conducting and analyzing different types of public opinion polls, p. 280.

The different types of polls include traditional telephone polls, entrance and exit polls, tracking polls, Internet polls, and push polls. Those who conduct polls must first determine what questions they want answered and how those questions should be phrased. Then they must determine the sample, or subset of the group whose attitudes they wish to measure, and finally they must determine the method for contacting respondents. Once the poll results are in, they must be analyzed, which includes determining the margin of error and the sampling error of the poll. Polls may have several shortcomings that lead them to be inaccurate.

★ 10.3 Analyze the process by which people form political opinions, p. 286.

The first step in forming opinions occurs through a process known as political socialization. Demographic characteristics—including gender, race, ethnicity, age, and religion—as well as family, school, and peers all affect how we view political events and issues. The views of other people, the media, and cues from leaders and opinion makers also affect our ultimate opinions about political matters.

★ 10.4 Trace the historical development of the news media in the United States, p. 290.

News media, a component of the larger mass media, provide the public with key information about subjects of public interest and play a crucial role in the political process. The news media consist of print, broadcast, and new media. The nation's first newspaper was published in 1690. Until the mid- to late 1800s, when independent papers first appeared, newspapers were partisan; that is, they openly supported a particular party. In the twentieth century, first radio in the late 1920s and then television in the late 1940s revolutionized

the transmission of political information. The growth of new media such as the Internet, blogs, and social networking sites continues to transform the relationship between media and citizens. Four trends affecting the modern media are: (1) the growth of media conglomerates; (2) narrowcasting; (3) the increasing use of experts; and, (4) the growth of citizen journalists.

★ 10.5 Summarize the ethical standards and federal regulations that govern the news media, p. 298.

Journalists are guided in ethical behavior by a detailed "Code of Ethics" published by the Society of Professional Journalists, which includes principles and standards concerning issues such as avoiding conflicts of interest, verifying the information being reported, and dealing ethically with sources. In addition, the U.S. government regulates both media ownership and content. The Telecommunications Act of 1996 deregulated whole segments of the electronic media, paving the way for greater media consolidation. Content regulation such as network neutrality has also been a subject of significant government attention.

★ 10.6 Assess how the news media cover politics, p. 300.

The news media cover every aspect of the political process, including the executive, legislative, and judicial branches of government, though the bulk of attention focuses on the president. Congress, with its 535 members and complex committee system, poses a challenge to the modern media, as does the Supreme Court, with its legal rulings and aversion to media attention. Politicians have developed a symbiotic relationship with the media, both feeding the media a steady supply of news and occasionally being devoured by the latest media feeding frenzy.

★ 10.7 Evaluate the influence of the news media on public policy and the impact of media bias, p. 303.

By controlling the flow of information, framing issues in a particular manner, and setting the agenda, the media have the potential to exert influence over the public, though generally they have far less influence than people believe. While the media do possess biases, a wide variety of news options are available in the United States, providing news consumers with an unprecedented amount of information from which to choose. Public opinion regarding the media is largely critical, although Americans continue to value the news media's watchdog role.

Test Yourself: Public Opinion and the News Media

⭐ **10.1 Trace the development of modern public opinion research, p. 278.**

Which of the following was NOT a primary reason that early public opinion polling was inaccurate?
A. Samples were compiled from telephone directories.
B. Self-selection created survey bias.
C. Newspaper clients received monetary benefits from survey miscalculations, driving them to skew results.
D. The timing of surveys prevented measurement of public sentiment closer to elections.
E. Only automobile owners were sampled in surveys, creating an unrepresentative sample of the general population.

⭐ **10.2 Describe the methods for conducting and analyzing different types of public opinion polls, p. 280.**

The method of selection that gives each person in a group an equal chance of being selected for a survey is known as
A. random sampling.
B. stratified sampling.
C. self-selection.
D. tracking survey samples.
E. margin of error.

⭐ **10.3 Analyze the process by which people form political opinions, p. 286.**

Which of the following is a major weakness of public opinion polls?
A. Only elite opinion is measured.
B. Polls are unable to measure the intensity of respondent's opinions.
C. Polls have very large margins of error.
D. Polls have too many respondent options.
E. Minority groups are often over-sampled.

⭐ **10.4 Trace the historical development of the news media in the United States, p. 290.**

Most people get their information about politics from
A. the radio.
B. newspapers and news magazines.
C. scholarly journals.
D. the Internet.
E. television.

⭐ **10.5 Summarize the ethical standards and federal regulations that govern the news media, p. 298.**

Television and radio are regulated by the federal government because
A. there is an unlimited supply of broadcast stations.
B. television and radio are considered dangerous to the spirit of democracy.
C. the airwaves are public property.
D. the Constitution allows it specifically.
E. media profits are not legally allowed to exceed certain levels.

⭐ **10.6 Assess how the news media cover politics, p. 300.**

Much of the news media's attention to government focuses on
A. the president.
B. Congress.
C. the Supreme Court.
D. the bureaucracy.
E. interest groups.

⭐ **10.7 Evaluate the influence of the news media on public policy and the impact of media bias, p. 303.**

When covering campaigns, most journalists' deepest bias is
A. a liberal bias.
B. a conservative bias.
C. a libertarian bias.
D. a bias to get a good story.
E. total objectivity.

Essay Questions

1. What are some of the driving forces behind a person's political socialization?
2. How do journalistic standards influence the conduct of the news media?
3. What are media effects and how do they affect the policy preferences of the American electorate?

myp⚫liscilab Exercises

Apply what you learned in this chapter on MyPoliSciLab.

📖—**Read** on **mypoliscilab.com**

    eText: Chapter 10

✔—**Study** and **Review** on **mypoliscilab.com**

    Pre-Test
    Post-Test
    Chapter Exam
    Flashcards

👁—**Watch** on **mypoliscilab.com**

    Videos: Opinion Poll on the U.S. Economy
    Videos: YouTube Politics
    Videos: The Pentagon's Media Message

✛—**Explore** on **mypoliscilab.com**

    Simulation: You Are a Polling Consultant
    Simulation: You Are the News Editor
    Comparative: Comparing Governments and Public Opinion
    Comparative: Comparing News Media
    Timeline: War, Peace, and Public Opinion
    Visual Literacy: Three Hundred Years of American Mass Media

Key Terms

agenda setting, p. 303
citizen journalists, p. 298
content regulations, p. 300
deep background, p. 299
equal time rule, p. 300
exit polls, p. 281
framing, p. 303
margin of error, p. 284
mass media, p. 290
media effects, p. 303

muckraking, p. 291
narrowcasting, p. 297
news media, p. 291
off the record, p. 299
on background, p. 299
on the record, p. 299
political socialization, p. 286
press briefing, p. 301
press conference, p. 301
press release, p. 301

public opinion, p. 278
public opinion polls, p. 278
push polls, p. 282
random sampling, p. 282
sample, p. 279
stratified sampling, p. 282
straw poll, p. 279
tracking polls, p. 281
yellow journalism, p. 291

To Learn More on Public Opinion and the News Media

In the Library

Alvarez, R. Michael, and John Brehm. *Hard Choices, Easy Answers: Values, Information, and American Public Opinion.* Princeton, NJ: Princeton University Press, 2002.

Clawson, Rosalee A., and Zoe M. Oxley. *Public Opinion: Democratic Ideals, Democratic Practice.* Washington, DC: CQ Press, 2008.

Dagnes, Alison D. *Politics on Demand: The Effects of 24-Hour News on American Politics.* New York: Praeger, 2010.

Erikson, Robert S., James A. Stimson, and Michael B. Mackuen. *The Macro Polity.* New York: Cambridge University Press, 2002.

Erikson, Robert S., James A. Stimson, and Micheal B. Mackuen. *American Public Opinion: Its Origins, Contents, and Impact*, 8th ed. New York: Longman, 2010.

Graber, Doris A. *Mass Media and American Politics*, 8th ed. Washington, DC: CQ Press, 2009.

Hamilton, James T. *All the News That's Fit to Sell.* Princeton, NJ: Princeton University Press, 2004.

Iyengar, Shanto, and Jennifer A. McGrady. *Media Politics: A Citizen's Guide.* New York: Norton, 2007.

Jamieson, Kathleen Hall, and Joseph N. Cappella. *Echo Chamber: Rush Limbaugh and the Conservative Media Establishment,* reprint ed. New York: Oxford University Press, 2010.

Key, V. O., Jr. *Public Opinion and American Democracy.* New York: Knopf, 1961.

McChesney, Robert W. *The Problem of the Media: U.S. Communication Politics in the Twenty-First Century.* New York: Monthly Review, 2004.

Norrander, Barbara, and Clyde Wilcox. *Understanding Public Opinion.* Washington, DC: CQ Press, 2009.

Rosenstiel, Tom, Marion Just, Todd Belt, Atiba Pertilla, Walter Dean, and Dante Chinni. *We Interrupt This Newscast: How to Improve Local News and Win Ratings, Too.* New York: Cambridge University Press, 2007.

Stimson, James A. *Tides of Consent: How Public Opinion Shapes American Politics.* New York: Cambridge University Press, 2004.

Zaller, John. *The Nature and Origins of Mass Opinions.* New York: Cambridge University Press, 1992.

On the Web

To learn more about the history of the Gallup Organization and poll trends, go to **www.gallup.com.**

To learn more about the National Election Studies (NES), including the history of this public opinion research project, go to **www.electionstudies.org.**

To learn more about the public's attitudes about the news media, go to the Pew Research Center for the People and the Press at **www.people-press.org.**

To learn more about the front pages of over a hundred daily newspapers from around the world in their original, unedited form, go to the Web site of the Newseum at **www.newseum.org.**

11 Political Parties and Interest Groups

In 1773, the British Parliament passed the Tea Act. This legislation was designed to rescue the British East India Tea Company from financial ruin. In order to do so, it granted the company a monopoly on the tea trade to all British colonies, including those in the new world. American colonists were outraged by this action; they considered it to be an act of governmental oppression. To show their disgust with King George III new policy, they held a protest known as the Boston Tea Party. Late on the evening of December 16th, the colonists boarded ships docked in Boston Harbor and threw overboard all of the imported tea stored on the boats. Similar tea parties were held in other colonies.

More than two hundred years later, in 2008, the U.S. Congress enacted legislation creating the Troubled Asset Relief Program (TARP). This program, also known as the "bailout bill," was designed to rescue American banks from

financial ruin. In order to do so, it used billions of federal taxpayers' dollars to purchase troubled assets and equity from financial institutions. Many Americans were outraged by this action; they considered it to be an act of governmental oppression. To show their disgust with the new policy, on February 27, 2009, thousands of Americans held organized protests around the country. These protestors soon became known as the tea party movement.

Members of this social movement seek to influence the direction of governmental policy. Of particular interest to tea party members is opposing federal government intervention in the financial sector. They believe in a free market economy and states' rights to govern themselves without undue involvement from the national government. They value lower taxes and fewer so-called governmental handouts. To communicate this message to legislators and other policymakers, they have held additional

Interest groups play an important role in protesting governmental policies. At left, colonists protest the Tea Act of 1773 by throwing tea in the Boston Harbor. At right, members of the modern tea party movement protest in Indiana against high taxes and government intervention by lowering a giant tea bag into the Broad Ripple Canal.

protests on occasions such as Tax Day (April 15) and Independence Day (July 4). They have also garnered significant media attention and gained access to members of Congress who are interested in addressing the concerns of the growing number of tea party identifiers among their constituents.

More recently, the tea party movement has shown some interest in becoming a political party and running candidates for a wide array of local, state, and national offices. In 2010, it vetted potential candidates to challenge congressional Democrats in the midterm elections, but many of these candidates, including visible Senate candidate Rand Paul (KY), ran under the Republican Party label. Members of the tea party also devised the beginnings of a party platform, known as the Contract from America. Among a number of other conservative public policy goals, this document called for protecting the Constitution, balancing the federal budget, reforming taxes, limiting government spending, and repealing the 2010 health care reform bill.

It was signed by more than 300 candidates and elected officials. Although more than thirty of its endorsed candidates for Congress won, to date, the movement's greatest successes have come from its protests and lobbying—actions that are more typical of an interest group than a political party.

What Should I Know About . . .

After reading this chapter, you should be able to:

★ **11.1** Trace the evolution of the two-party system in the United States, p. 310.

★ **11.2** Outline the structure of American political parties at the national, state, and local levels, p. 316.

★ **11.3** Identify the functions performed by American political parties, p. 319.

★ **11.4** Analyze how political socialization and group affiliations shape party identification, p. 322.

★ **11.5** Trace the roots of the American interest group system, p. 325.

★ **11.6** Identify several strategies and tactics used by organized interests, p. 330.

★ **11.7** Explain reform efforts geared toward regulating interest groups and lobbyists, p. 333.

political party

A group of office holders, candidates, activists, and voters who identify with a group label and seek to elect to public office individuals who run under that label.

interest group

An organized group that tries to influence public policy.

W hen James Madison warned of the dangers of faction in *Federalist No. 10*, he never envisioned the development of political parties, or the role that organized interests would eventually play in politics and policy making. It was not long after the ink was dry on the new constitution that factions arose concerning the desirability to the new system of government that it created. And, soon after, political parties were formed to reflect those political divisions.

At the most basic level, a **political party** is a group of office holders, candidates, activists, and voters who identify with a group label and seek to elect to public office individuals who run under the label. Notice that the goal is to *win* office, not just compete for it. This objective is in keeping with the practical nature of Americans and the country's historical aversion to most ideologically driven, purist politics. Nevertheless, the group label—also called party identification—can carry with it clear messages about ideology and issue positions. Although these especially exist for minor, less broad-based parties that have little chance of electoral success, they also apply to the Democrats and the Republicans, the two national, dominant political parties in the United States.

In contrast to political parties, **interest groups,** which go by a variety of names— special interests, pressure groups, organized interests, political groups, lobby groups, and public interest groups—are organizations that "seek or claim to represent people or organizations which share one or more common interests or ideals."[1] Distinguished political scientist V. O. Key Jr. tried to differentiate political parties from interest groups by arguing that "interest groups promote their interests by attempting to influence government rather than by nominating candidates and seeking responsibility for the management of government."[2]

In this chapter, we trace the evolution of the role of political parties and interest groups in America.

- First, we will trace *the roots of the two-party system* from the development of political parties in the late 1700s to the present day.

- Second, we will explore *the organization of American political parties* at the national, state, and local levels.

- Third, we will examine the multitude of *activities of American political parties in* our political system.

- Fourth, we will analyze *party identification* and explain how it is shaped by political socialization and group affiliations.

- Fifth, we will explore *the roots of the American interest group system.*

- Sixth, we will investigate *what interest groups do.*

- Finally, we will discuss reform efforts geared toward *regulating interest groups and lobbyists.*

ROOTS OF the Two-Party System

⭐ **11.1 . . . Trace the evolution of the two-party system in the United States.**

The broad structure and pragmatic purpose of political parties have been features of the American party system since the founding of the republic. By tracing the history and development of political parties in the United States, we will see that another prominent feature is a competitive two-party system, even as there have been dramatic shifts in party coalitions and reforms to democratize the system.

The Development of Political Parties, 1800–1824

It is one of the great ironies of the early republic that George Washington's public farewell, which warned the nation against parties, marked the effective beginning of party competition in the United States. (To learn more about American party history, see Figure 11.1.) Washington's unifying influence ebbed as he stepped off the national stage, and his vice president and successor, John Adams, occupied a much less exalted position. To win the presidency in 1796, Adams narrowly defeated his arch-rival Thomas Jefferson, who according to the existing rules of the Constitution became vice president. Over the course of Adams's single term, two competing congressional factions, the Federalists and Democratic-Republicans, gradually organized around these clashing men and their principles: Adams and his Federalist allies supported a strong central government; the Democratic-Republicans of Thomas Jefferson and his allies preferred a federal system in which the states retained the balance of power. In the presidential election of 1800, the Federalists supported Adams's bid for a second term, but this time the Democratic-Republicans prevailed with their nominee, Jefferson, who became the first U.S. president elected as the nominee of a political party.

Jefferson was deeply committed to the ideas of his party but not nearly as devoted to the idea of a party system. He regarded his party as a temporary measure necessary to defeat Adams, not a long-term political tool or an essential element of democracy. As a result, Jefferson's party never achieved widespread loyalty among the citizenry. Although Southerners were overwhelmingly partial to the Democratic-Republicans and New Englanders favored the Federalists, no broad-based party organizations existed to mobilize popular support.[3] Just as the nation was in its infancy, so, too, was the party system.

Figure 11.1 *How has the two-party system developed?*

Source: Harold W. Stanley and Richard G. Niemi, *Vital Statistics on American Politics, 2007–2008* (Washington, DC: CQ Press, 2007). Updated by the authors.

MAJOR PARTIES

Jacksonian Democracy, 1824–1860

What is sometimes called the second party system began around 1824, when Andrew Jackson ran for president. He lost to John Quincy Adams, but he was successful when he ran again in 1828. Around this time, party membership broadened along with the electorate. After receiving criticism for being elitist and undemocratic, the small caucuses of congressional party leaders that had nominated candidates gave way to nominations at large party conventions. In 1832, the Democratic Party, which succeeded the old Jeffersonian Democratic-Republicans, held the first national presidential nomination convention. Formed around President Andrew Jackson's popularity, the Democratic Party attracted most of the newly enfranchised voters, who were drawn to Jackson's charismatic style. Jackson's strong personality polarized many people, and opposition to the president coalesced into the Whig Party. Among the Whig Party's early leaders was Henry Clay, the Speaker of the House from 1811 to 1820. The incumbent Jackson, having won a first term as president in 1828, defeated Clay in the 1832 presidential contest. Jackson was the first chief executive who won the White House as the nominee of a truly national, popularly based political party.

The Whigs and the Democrats continued to strengthen after 1832. Their competition was usually fierce and closely matched, and they brought the United States the first broadly supported two-party system in the Western world.[4] Unfortunately for the Whigs, the issue of slavery sharpened the many divisive tensions within the party, which led to its gradual dissolution and replacement by the new Republican

TIMELINE: Political Parties in the United States

1796 Federalists and Democratic-Republicans Emerge—The new nation's first political parties emerge and usher in the first American party system.

1828 Second Party System Emerges—The disappearance of the Federalists and a split among Democratic-Republicans pits the Whigs against the modern Democratic Party.

1856 Whig Party Dissolves—The new Republican Party, which opposes slavery, nominates John C. Frémont as their first presidential candidate.

1800 Jefferson Elected President—Voters reject the Federalists' agenda of a strong centralized government by electing Thomas Jefferson to the presidency and a majority of Democratic-Republicans to Congress.

1832 First Presidential Nomination Convention—The Democratic Party holds the first presidential nomination convention, renominating President Andrew Jackson for president.

Party. Formed in 1854 by anti-slavery activists, the Republican Party set its sights on the abolition (or at least the containment) of slavery. After a losing presidential effort for John C. Frémont in 1856, the party was able to assemble enough support primarily from former Whigs and anti-slavery northern Democrats to win the presidency for Abraham Lincoln in a fragmented 1860 vote. In that year, the South voted solidly Democratic, beginning a tradition so strong that not a single southern state voted Republican for president again until 1920.

The Golden Age, 1860–1932

From the presidential election of 1860 to this day, the same two major parties, the Republicans and the Democrats, have dominated elections in the United States, and control of an electoral majority has seesawed between them. Party stability, the dominance of party organizations in local and state governments, and the impact of those organizations on the lives of millions of voters were the central traits of the era called the "Golden Age" of political parties.

Emigration from Europe (particularly from Ireland, Italy, and Germany) fueled the development in America of big-city **political machines** that gained control of local and state government during this time. A political machine is a party organization that uses tangible incentives such as jobs and favors to win loyalty among voters. Machines also are characterized by a high degree of leadership control over member activity. Party machines were a central element of life for millions of people in the United States during the Golden Age. For city-dwellers, their party and their government were virtually interchangeable during this time.

Political parties thus not only served the underlying political needs of the society, but also supplemented the population's desire for important social services. In

political machine

A party organization that recruits voter loyalty with tangible incentives and is characterized by a high degree of control over member activity.

1870s Party Machines Form—Party machines enforce voters' party loyalty by providing jobs and services in exchange for votes.

1992 Ross Perot Runs for President—Perot wins 19 percent of the popular vote in his independent campaign.

1932 New Deal Coalition Forms—A new coalition of voters rallies behind President Franklin D. Roosevelt to form the group that continues to be the Democratic Party's base today.

2010 Party Unity Rising—Though party ties have weakened in the electorate, they have never been stronger in Congress.

addition to providing housing, employment, and even food to many voters, parties in most major cities provided entertainment by organizing torchlight parades, weekend picnics, socials, and other community events. Many citizens—even those who weren't particularly "political"—attended, thereby gaining some allegiance to one party or the other. The parties offered immigrants not just services but also the opportunity for upward social mobility as they rose in the organization. As a result, parties generated intense loyalty and devotion among their supporters and office holders that helped to produce startlingly high voter turnouts—75 percent or better in all presidential elections from 1876 to 1900—compared with today's 50–60 percent.[5]

The Modern Era

Many social, political, technological, and governmental changes have contributed to changes in the nature of the national parties. The government's gradual assumption of important functions previously performed by the parties, such as printing ballots, conducting elections, and providing social welfare services, for example, had a major impact on party loyalty and strength. Beginning in the 1930s with Franklin D. Roosevelt's New Deal, social services began to be seen as a right of citizenship rather than as a privilege extended in exchange for a person's support of a party. Also, as the flow of immigrants slowed dramatically in the 1920s, party machines lost power in many places.

In the post–World War II era, extensive social changes also contributed to the move away from strong parties. A weakening of the party system gave rise to **candidate-centered politics,** which focuses on candidates, their particular issues, and character rather than party affiliation. Parties' diminished control over issues and campaigns also have given candidates considerable power in how they conduct themselves during

candidate-centered politics

Politics that focuses on the candidates, their particular issues, and character rather than party affiliation.

Where did the party symbols originate? This Thomas Nast cartoon is the first to depict the Democratic donkey and Republican elephant together in a common scene.

STRANGER THINGS HAVE HAPPENED.
HOLD ON, AND YOU MAY WALK OVER THE SLUGGISH ANIMAL UP THERE YET.

Photo courtesy: The Granger Collection, New York

party realignment
Dramatic shifts in partisan preferences that drastically alter the political landscape.

critical election
An election that signals a party realignment through voter polarization around new issues and personalities.

secular realignment
The gradual rearrangement of party coalitions, based more on demographic shifts than on shocks to the political system.

election season and how they seek resources. Interest groups and lobbyists have stepped into the void that weaker parties have left behind. Candidates compete for endorsements and contributions from a variety of multi-issue as well as single-issue organizations.

Another post–World War II social change that affected the parties is the population shift from urban to suburban locales. Millions of people moved from the cities to the suburbs, where a sense of privacy and detachment can deter even the most energetic party organizers. In addition, population growth in the last half-century has created legislative districts with far more people, making it less feasible to knock on every door or shake every hand.

Citizen Support and Party Realignment

Periodically, voters make dramatic shifts in partisan preference that drastically alter the political landscape. During these **party realignments,** existing party affiliations are subject to upheaval: many voters may change parties, and the youngest age group of voters may permanently adopt the label of the newly dominant party.[6]

Preceding a major realignment are one or more **critical elections,** which may polarize voters around new issues and personalities in reaction to crucial developments, such as a war or an economic depression. Three tumultuous eras in particular have produced significant critical elections. First, Thomas Jefferson, in reaction against the Federalist Party's agenda of a strong, centralized federal government, formed the Democratic-Republican Party, which won the presidency and Congress in 1800. Second, in reaction to the growing crisis over slavery, the Whig Party gradually dissolved and the Republican Party gained strength and ultimately won the presidency in 1860. Third, the Great Depression caused large numbers of voters to repudiate Republican Party policies and embrace the Democratic Party in 1932. Each of these cases resulted in fundamental and enduring alterations in the party equation.

A critical election is not the only occasion when changes in partisan affiliation are accommodated. More gradual shifts in party coalitions, called **secular realignments,** may also change voters' loyalties.[7] This piecemeal process depends not on convulsive shocks to the political system but on slow, almost barely discernible demographic shifts—the shrinking of one party's base of support and the enlargement of the other's, for example—or simple generational replacement (that is, the dying off of the older generation and the maturing of the younger generation).

The most significant recent example of this phenomenon occurred during the late 1980s and early 1990s, when the southern states, traditionally Democratic stalwarts since the Civil War, shifted dramatically toward the Republican Party. Many factors contributed to this gradual regional shift in party allegiance. Southern Democrats were the most conservative of the New Deal coalition, favoring the social status quo and opposing civil rights reform and affirmative action. As the Democratic Party turned toward more liberal social causes such as civil rights and social spending, many southern voters and politicians shifted their allegiance toward the Republicans.[8]

Dealignment

Over the past two decades, numerous political scientists as well as other observers, journalists, and party activists have become increasingly anxious about **dealignment,** a general decline in partisan identification and loyalty in the electorate.[9] Since parties traditionally provide political information and serve as an engine of political participation, it has been feared that weakening party attachments are undermining political involvement. The Center for Political Studies/Survey Research Center (CPS/SRC) of the University of Michigan has charted the rise of self-described independents from a low of 19 percent in 1958 to a peak of 40 percent in 2000, with percentages in recent years consistently hovering just below the high-water mark of 40 percent.

dealignment
A general decline in party identification and loyalty in the electorate.

Currently, the Democratic and Republican Parties can claim a roughly equal percentage of self-identified partisans, with levels fluctuating around one-third of the population each. This can seem inconsistent with voting behavior and election results, but one must pay close attention to the manner in which these data are collected. When pollsters ask for party identification information, they generally proceed in two stages. First, they inquire whether a respondent considers himself or herself to be a Democrat, Republican, or independent. Then the party identifiers are asked to categorize themselves as "strong" or "not very strong" supporters, while the independents are pushed to reveal their "leanings" with a question such as "Which party do you normally support in elections, the Democrats or the Republicans?" It may be true that some independent respondents are thereby prodded to pick a party under the pressure of the interview situation, regardless of their true feelings. But, research has demonstrated that independent "leaners" in fact vote very much like real partisans, in some elections more so than the "not very strong" party identifiers.[10] There is reason to count the independent leaners as closet partisans, though voting behavior is not the equivalent of real partisan identification.

In fact, the reluctance of leaners to admit their real party identities reveals a significant change in attitudes about political parties and their role in our society. The reasons for these anti-party attitudes are not hard to find. The growth of issue-oriented politics that cut across party lines for voters who feel intensely about certain policy matters is partly the cause. So, too, is the emphasis on personality politics by the mass media and political consultants. Despite these challenges, the parties' decline can easily be exaggerated. When we view parties in the broad sweep of U.S. history, several strengths of parties become clear.

First, although political parties have evolved considerably, they usually have been reliable vehicles for mass participation in a representative democracy. In fact, parties orchestrated the gradual but steady expansion of suffrage in order to incorporate new supporters into the party fold.[11]

Second, the parties' journeys through U.S. history have been characterized by the same ability to adapt to prevailing conditions that is often cited as the genius of the Constitution. Both major parties exhibit flexibility and pragmatism, which help ensure their survival and the success of the society they serve.

Third, despite massive changes in political conditions and frequent dramatic shifts in the electorate's mood, the two major parties not only have achieved remarkable longevity but also have almost always provided strong competition for each other and the voters at the national level. Of the thirty presidential elections from 1884 to 2008, for instance, the Republicans won seventeen and the Democrats fifteen.

Fourth, while party identification may be waning, the party in government and the party organizations are stronger than ever. The sharp rise in party unity scores in Congress discussed in more detail later in the chapter suggests that the party in government is alive and well. The unprecedented fund-raising of the party organizations suggests, moreover, that political parties are here to stay.

Table 11.1 *What are some of America's major third parties?*

Third Party	Year Founded	Primary Purpose
Liberty/Free-Soil	1840	Abolition of slavery
Prohibition	1880	Prohibition of alcohol sale and consumption
Progressive/Bull Moose	1912	Factionalism in Republican Party; gave Theodore Roosevelt the platform to run for the presidency
American Independent	1968	States' rights; opposition to desegregation
Libertarian	1971	Opposition to governmental intervention in economic and social policy
Reform	1996	Economic issues; tax reform, national debt, federal deficit
Green	2000	Environmentalism and social justice

Third Parties in the Two Party System

Minor parties based on causes often neglected by the major parties have significantly affected American politics. Third parties find their roots in sectionalism (as did the Southern states' rights Dixiecrats, who broke away from the Democrats in 1948), in economic protest (such as the agrarian revolt that fueled the Populists, an 1892 prairie-states party), in specific issues (such as the Green Party's support of the environment), in ideology (the Socialist, Communist, and Libertarian Parties are examples), and in appealing, charismatic personalities (Theodore Roosevelt's affiliation with the Bull Moose Party in 1912 is perhaps the best case). (To learn more about third parties in the United States, see Table 11.1.)

Third parties achieve their greatest successes when they incorporate new ideas or alienated groups or nominate attractive candidates as their standard-bearers. Third parties do best when declining trust in the two major political parties plagues the electorate. Usually, though, third parties' ideas are eventually co-opted by one of the two major parties, each of them eager to take the politically popular issue that gave rise to the third party and make it theirs in order to secure the allegiance of the third party's supporters. For example, the Republicans of the 1970s absorbed many of the states' rights planks of George Wallace's 1968 presidential bid. Both major parties have also more recently attempted to attract independent voters by sponsoring reforms of the governmental process, such as the ongoing attempts to reform the nation's campaign finance laws. (To learn more about the role of third parties, see Join the Debate: Are Third Parties Good for American Politics?)

The Organization of American Political Parties

⭐ **11.2 . . . Outline the structure of American political parties at the national, state, and local levels.**

Although the distinctions might not be as clear today as they were two or three decades ago, the two major parties remain fairly well organized. The different levels of each party represent diverse interests in Washington, D.C., state capitals, and local governments throughout the nation. (To learn more about political party organization, see Figure 11.2.)

The National Party

The national party organization sits at the pinnacle of the party system in the United States. Its primary function is to establish a cohesive vision for partisan identifiers nationwide and to disseminate that vision to party members and voters. A chairperson,

Join the DEBATE | Are Third Parties Good for the American Political System?

Third parties are a recurring political phenomenon in the United States, and they generally originate for one of two reasons: (1) to express an alternative political platform from those held by the major parties, such as when the Dixiecrats, who believed in continued racial segregation, broke from the Democratic Party in 1948; or, (2) to launch an alternative candidate for public office, such as when Ross Perot founded the Reform Party in 1996, with the sole purpose of running for president.

These third parties and the candidates that bear their standard, gain popularity and support based on dissatisfaction with the candidates and trends in the two major parties at the time. Despite their failures at the ballot box, they exert pressure on the major parties, and most influence election outcomes to some extent. Should we encourage greater involvement by third parties? Or do third parties undermine American political values?

To develop an ARGUMENT FOR third parties in American politics, think about how:

- **Third parties allow for a greater diversity of opinions.** In what ways do third parties promote diversity of viewpoints and opinions? How do the issues promoted by third parties and the candidates that represent them change the political discourse?
- **Third parties can provide useful solutions to political problems on the local and regional level.** How might the smaller scale of third parties allow them to address specific local and regional issues better than the major parties? Does the election of third-party state governors, such as Jesse Ventura in Minnesota and Angus King in Maine, suggest that third parties could be more successful on the state and local level than on the national level?
- **Third parties encourage greater participation in the American political system.** How does the current electoral system undermine participation by voters who might be inclined to support third parties, such as the Green Party or the Libertarian Party? Are electoral outcomes representative of the interests and preferences of voters who support third parties?

To develop an ARGUMENT AGAINST third parties in American politics, think about how:

- **Third parties act as spoilers rather than as issue definers.** How realistic is it that a third-party candidate would get elected at the national level? How does the voting system used in the United States undermine the ability of third parties to affect the national agenda?
- **Third parties are often composed of political extremists who seek to undermine real politics.** How might the rise of third parties like the Dixiecrats or the American Communist Party undermine the ideal of compromise that characterizes the American political system? In what ways do emotional appeals used by political extremists result in disenfranchisement and less participation in the political process?
- **Third parties undermine the stability of the American political system.** In what ways are political systems with large numbers of third parties more unstable than two-party systems? How might greater instability in the political system lead to lower levels of participation, higher levels of voter apathy, and greater polarization in American politics?

How did Ross Perot influence American politics? Reform Party candidate Ross Perot advocated for tax reform and a balanced budget.

Photo courtesy: AP/Wide World Photos

Figure 11.2 *How are political parties organized?*

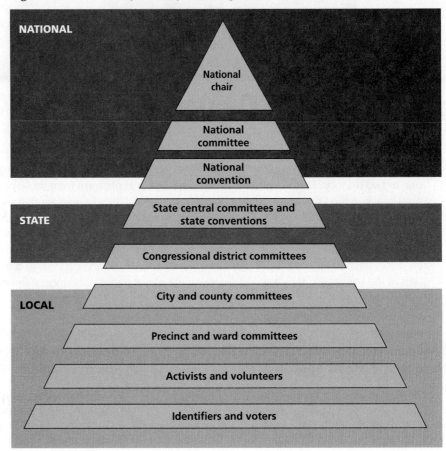

NATIONAL

National chair

National committee

National convention

STATE

State central committees and state conventions

Congressional district committees

LOCAL

City and county committees

Precinct and ward committees

Activists and volunteers

Identifiers and voters

who serves as the head of the national committee, leads the national party. Every four years, the national committee organizes a convention designed to reevaluate policies and nominate a candidate for the presidency.

THE NATIONAL CHAIRPERSON   The key national party official is the chair of the national committee. The chair is usually selected by the sitting president or newly nominated presidential candidate, who is accorded the right to name the individual for at least the duration of his or her campaign. The chair may also be chosen by the national committee when the election has ended and the party has been defeated. The chair is the prime spokesperson and arbitrator for the party during the four years between elections. He or she is called on to damp down factionalism, negotiate candidate disputes, and prepare the machinery for the next presidential election. Perhaps most critically, the chair is called upon to raise funds and keep the party financially strong. Balancing the interests of all potential party candidates is a particularly difficult job, and strict neutrality is normally expected from the chair.

THE NATIONAL COMMITTEE   The first national party committees were skeletal and formed some years after the first presidential nominating conventions in the 1830s. First the Democrats in 1848 and then the Republicans in 1856 established national governing bodies—the Democratic National Committee, or DNC, and the Republican National Committee, or RNC—to make arrangements for the national conventions and to coordinate the subsequent presidential campaigns. In addition, to serve their interests, the congressional party caucuses in both houses organized their own national committees, loosely allied with the DNC and RNC.

There is an informal division of labor among the national committees. Whereas the DNC and RNC focus primarily on aiding presidential campaigns and conducting general party-building activities, the congressional campaign committees work primarily to maximize the number of seats held by their respective parties in Congress. In the past two decades, all of these national party committees have become major, service-oriented organizations in American politics.[12]

The National Convention

Every four years, each party holds a **national convention** to nominate its presidential and vice presidential candidates. The convention also fulfills its role as the ultimate governing body for the party. The rules adopted and the party platform that is passed serve as durable guidelines that steer the party until the next convention.

national convention
A party meeting held in the presidential election year for the purposes of nominating a presidential and vice presidential ticket and adopting a platform.

States and Localities

Although national committee activities attract most of the media attention, the party is structurally based not in Washington, D.C., but in the states and localities. Virtually all government regulation of political parties is left to the states. Most importantly, the vast majority of party leadership positions are filled at subnational levels.

The arrangement of party committees provides for a broad base of support. The smallest voting unit, the precinct, usually takes in a few adjacent neighborhoods and is the fundamental building block of the party. There are more than 100,000 precincts in the United States. The precinct committee members are the foot soldiers of any party, and their efforts are supplemented by party committees above them in the wards, cities, counties, towns, villages, and congressional districts.

The state governing body supervising this collection of local party organizations is usually called the state central (or executive) committee. Its members come from all major geographic units, as determined by and selected under state law. Generally, state parties are free to act within the limits set by their state legislatures without interference from the national party, except in the selection and seating of presidential convention delegates.

Activities of American Political Parties

★ **11.3 . . . Identify the functions performed by American political parties.**

For over 200 years, the two-party system has served as the mechanism American society uses to organize and resolve social and political conflict. Political parties often are the chief agents of change in our political system. They provide vital services to society, and it would be difficult to envision political life without them.

Running Candidates for Office

The election, proclaimed author H. G. Wells, is "democracy's ceremonial, its feast, its great function," and the political parties assist in this ceremony in essential ways. First, the parties help to raise money for candidates. Second, parties help to recruit candidates, mobilize public support, and get out the vote.

Figure 11.3 *How much money do parties raise?*

Sources: 2003–2010 from Center for Responsive Politics www.opensecrets.org, and earlier years from Harold W. Stanley and Richard Niemi, *Vital Statistics on American Politics, 2003–2004* (Washington, DC: CQ Press, 2004), November 2010 FEC data.

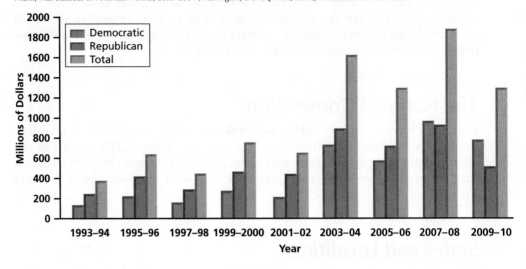

RAISING MONEY   Political parties, particularly during midterm and presidential election years, spend a great deal of time raising and disseminating money for candidates. Historically, Republicans have enjoyed greater fund-raising success than Democrats due in large part to a significant number of wealthy identifiers and donors. However, in recent years, Democrats have caught up, even out-raising Republicans during the 2008 presidential election. (To learn more about party finances, see Figure 11.3.)

The parties raise so much money because they have developed networks of donors reached by a variety of methods. Both parties have highly successful mail solicitation lists. The Republican effort to reach donors through the mail dates back to the early 1960s and accelerated in the mid-1970s, when postage and production costs were relatively low. Today, both the Republican and Democratic National Committees have expanded their mailing, emailing, and phone lists of proven donors to several million people.

How do parties help mobilize support for candidates? One common method of gathering support and raising enthusiasm for candidates is to hold campaign rallies. This photo shows such a rally for Senator John McCain's (AZ) 2008 Presidential election bid.

Photo courtesy: William Thomas Cain/Getty Images

MOBILIZING SUPPORT AND GETTING OUT THE VOTE   The parties take a number of steps to broaden citizens' knowledge of candidates and campaigns in the days leading up to the election. Parties, for example, spend millions of dollars for national, state, and local public opinion surveys. Both parties also operate sophisticated media divisions that specialize in the design and production of television advertisements for party nominees at all levels. And, both parties train the armies of political volunteers and paid operatives who run the candidates' campaigns.

Finally, both parties place a large emphasis on their duty to "get out the vote" (GOTV) on Election Day. The Republican Party has been a pioneer in the use of "micro-targeting," a practice derived from the field of consumer behavior. With data obtained from a growing volume of government census records and marketing firms, Republicans have used advanced computer models to identify potential GOP voters based on consumer preferences, personal habits, and past voting behavior. Once identified, these voters' names are stored in a database—Voter Vault—and shared with individual campaigns, whose volunteers contact voters by phone and personal visits.

Because Democrats have been suspicious of using corporate techniques and traditionally have relied on labor unions and other interest groups to carry out voter mobilization, they have been slower in creating similar programs. They have, however, embraced the Internet and other technology as methods of reaching voters.

Formulating and Promoting Policy

As discussed at the beginning of this chapter, the **national party platform** is the most visible instrument that parties use to formulate, convey, and promote public policy. Every four years, each party writes a lengthy platform explaining its positions on key issues. Typically, about two-thirds of the promises in the victorious party's presidential platform have been completely or mostly implemented. Moreover, about one-half or more of the pledges of the losing party also tend to find their way into public policy, a trend that no doubt reflects the effort of both parties to support broad policy positions that enjoy widespread support in the general public.[13]

national party platform
A statement of the general and specific philosophy and policy goals of a political party, usually promulgated at the national convention.

Parties in Congress

Nowhere is the party more visible or vital than in the Congress. In this century, political parties have dramatically increased the sophistication and impact of their internal congressional organizations. Prior to the beginning of every session, the parties in both houses of Congress gather (or "caucus") separately to select party leaders and to arrange for the appointment of members of each chamber's committees. In effect, then, the parties organize and operate the Congress.

Perhaps as a result, party labels have become the most powerful predictor of congressional roll-call voting. In the last few years, party-line voting has increased noticeably, as reflected in the upward trend in both Democrats' and Republicans' party unity shown in Figure 11.4. Although not invariably predictive, a member's party affiliation proved to be the best indicator of his or her votes; in 2009 the average representative

Figure 11.4 *How have party unity scores changed?*
Source: Congressional Quarterly.

or senator sided with his or her party on about 88 percent of the votes that divided a majority of Democrats from a majority of Republicans that year.[14]

Furthering Unity, Linkage, and Accountability

Parties, finally, are the glue that holds together the disparate elements of the U.S. governmental and political apparatus. The Framers designed a system that divides and subdivides power, making it possible to preserve individual liberty but difficult to coordinate and produce action in a timely fashion. Parties help compensate for this drawback by linking the branches of government. Although rivalry between the branches is inevitable, the partisan and ideological affiliations of the leaders of each branch constitute a common basis for cooperation, as the president and his fellow party members in Congress usually demonstrate daily.

Even within each branch, the party helps narrow the differences between the House of Representatives and the Senate, or between the president and the department heads in the bureaucracy. Similarly, the division of national, state, and local governments, while always an invitation to conflict, is made more workable and more easily coordinated by the intersecting party relationships that exist among office holders at all levels. Party affiliation, in other words, is a basis for mediation and negotiation laterally among the branches of government and vertically among national, state, and local layers.

The party's linkage function does not end there. Party identification and organization foster communication between the voter and the candidate, as well as between the voter and the office holder. The party connection is one means of increasing accountability in election campaigns and in government. Candidates on the campaign trail and elected party leaders are required from time to time to account for their performance at party-sponsored forums, nominating primaries, and on Election Day.

Party Identification

⭐ 11.4 . . . Analyze how political socialization and group affiliations shape party identification.

party identification
A citizen's personal affinity for a political party, usually expressed by a tendency to vote for the candidates of that party.

The party in the electorate—the mass of potential voters who identify with a party label—is a crucial element of the political party. But, in some respects, it is the weakest of the components of the U.S. political party system. Although **party identification,** or a citizen's affinity for a political party, tends to be a reliable indicator of likely voting choices, the trend is for fewer voters to declare loyalty to a party; 29 percent of voters called themselves independents on Election Day in 2008.

For those Americans who do firmly adopt a party label, their party often becomes a central political reference symbol and perceptual screen. For these partisans, party identification is a significant aspect of their political personality and a way of defining and explaining themselves to others. The loyalty generated by the label can be as intense as any enjoyed by sports teams and alma maters.

Political Socialization

Not surprisingly, parents are the single greatest influence in establishing a person's first party identification. Parents who are politically active and share the same party identification raise children who will be strong party identifiers, whereas parents without party affiliations or with mixed affiliations produce offspring more likely to be independents. (To learn more about political socialization, see **chapter 10**.)

Early socialization is hardly the last step in an individual's acquisition and maintenance of a party identity; marriage, economic status, and other aspects of adult life can change one's loyalty. Charismatic political personalities, particularly at the national level (such as Franklin D. Roosevelt and Ronald Reagan) can influence party identification, as can cataclysmic events (the Civil War and the Great Depression are the best examples). Hot-button social issues (for instance, abortion and same-sex marriage), sectionalism, and candidate-oriented politics, may also influence party ties.

Group Affiliations

Just as individuals vary in the strength of their partisan choice, so do groups vary in the degree to which they identify with the Democratic Party or the Republican Party. Variations in party identification are particularly noticeable when geographic region, gender, race and ethnicity, age, social and economic status, religion, marital status, and ideology are examined. (To learn more about the party identifications of various groups, see Table 11.2.)

GEOGRAPHIC REGION   In modern American politics, the geographic regions are relatively closely contested between the parties. The South, which was solidly Democratic as a result of party attachments that were cultivated in the nineteenth century and

Table 11.2 Who identifies as a Democrat? A Republican?

		Democratic Identifiers	Independents	Republican Identifiers
Region	Northeast	33	45	23
	Midwest	35	44	21
	South	34	41	26
	West	33	39	29
Gender	Male	30	45	25
	Female	37	39	24
Race	Black	66	31	3
	Hispanic	37	47	17
	White	27	42	30
Age	<30	35	46	19
	30–49	30	42	28
	50+	36	40	24
Income	<30,000	41	15	44
	30,000–74,999	31	30	39
	75,000+	39	32	39
Education	High School or Less	34	24	43
	College	28	32	40
	Advanced Degree	39	22	39
Union Member	Yes	47	22	32
Military Veteran	Yes	29	27	45
Religion	Protestant	34	39	37
	Catholic	34	23	43
	Jewish	48	18	34
Evangelical Christian	Yes	31	33	36
Marital Status	Married	28	31	41
	Not Currently Married	39	19	42
Ideology	Conservative	21	33	45
	Moderate	35	48	17
	Liberal	53	42	6

Note: In this table, independent leaners are collapsed into the independent column. Partisans and strong partisans are collapsed into the party columns. Due to rounding, not all rows equal 100 percent.
Source: Pew Research Center, *Political Landscape More Favorable to Democrats: Trends in Political Values and Core Attitudes, 1987–2007.*

Regional Parties in India

In the United States, national elections are contested by national parties. This is not true everywhere. India's political party system combines national parties with a large number of regional parties. In the 2009 election, national parties won 377 seats in the Parliament of India, while regional parties won 144 seats.

The graph shows the distribution of seats won by Indian national and regional parties from 1975 to 2009. In 1996, the strength of regional parties jumped as the dominance of the Indian National Congress Party came to an end and an era of coalition governments began. Coalition governments are ones in which political parties cooperate with one another to form majorities because no single political party has a majority on its own. The rise of coalition governments in India led regional parties to be seen as potentially important political forces, which in turn led to increased support for their candidates. Prior to 1996, regional parties won more than 12 percent of the seats in parliament only once. Since then, they have won at least 18 percent of the seats and as many as 29 percent of them.

Percentage of National Parliamentary Seats Won by National and Regional Parties, 1975–2009

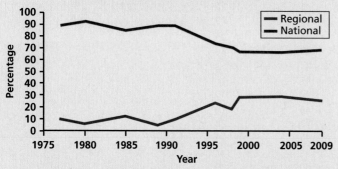

- Under what conditions might regional parties emerge in the United States? Have we seen anything like this in the past?

- Would the Democrats or Republicans be harmed the most by regional parties? Why?

- If regional parties arose in the United States, would you expect them to become well established or to last for only an election or two? Why?

hardened in the fires of the Civil War, is now a two-party region. Since the 1994 elections, Southerners have elected Republicans to a majority of the Senate and U.S. House seats representing the states of the old Confederacy, and Republican presidential candidates have come to rely on strong support in southern states.[15]

GENDER   Some political scientists argue that the difference in the way men and women vote first emerged in 1920, when newly enfranchised women registered overwhelmingly as Republicans. It was not until the 1980 presidential election, however, that a noticeable and possibly significant gender gap in party identification emerged. This pattern continues to play an important role in politics. Today, 37 percent of women identify as Democrats, and 25 percent identify as Republicans.

RACE AND ETHNICITY   African Americans are the most dramatically split population subgroup in party terms. The 60-percent-plus advantage they offer the Democrats in party affiliation dwarfs the edge given to either party by any other significant segment of the electorate, and their proportion of strong Democrats (about 40 percent) is three times that of whites.

Hispanics supplement African Americans as Democratic stalwarts; by more than two-thirds, Hispanics prefer the Democratic Party. Voting patterns of Puerto Ricans are very similar to those of African Americans, while Mexican Americans favor the Democrats by smaller margins. An exception is the Cuban American population, whose anti–Fidel Castro tilt leads to support for the Republican Party.

AGE   Political socialization creates a strong relationship between age and party identification. Today, generally the youngest and oldest voters tend to prefer the Democratic Party, while middle-aged voters disproportionately favor the Republican Party. The Democratic Party's more liberal positions on social issues tend to resonate with today's moderate but socially progressive young adults. The nation's oldest voters, who were alive during the Great Depression, tend to favor the Democratic Party's support for social insurance programs. Middle-aged voters, often at the height of their careers and consequently at the height of their earnings potential, tend to favor the low taxes championed by Republicans.[16]

SOCIAL AND ECONOMIC FACTORS   Occupation, income, and education are closely related, so many of the same partisan patterns appear in all three classifications. Democratic support drops as one climbs the income scale. Those with a college education tend to support the Republican Party, although those with advanced degrees tend to be Democrats.[17] The GOP remains predominant among executives, professionals, and white-collar workers, whereas the Democrats lead substantially among trial lawyers, educators, and blue-collar workers. Labor union members are also Democrats by nearly two to one.

Women who do not work outside the home tend to be conservative and favor the Republicans.

RELIGION   White Protestants—especially Methodists, Presbyterians, and Episcopalians— favor the Republicans, whereas Catholics and, even more so, Jewish voters tend to favor the Democratic Party. Decreased polarization is apparent all around, however. Democrats have made inroads among many liberal Protestant denominations over the past three decades, and Republicans claim increasing percentages of Jewish and Catholic identifiers. Evangelical Christians are somewhat less Republican than commonly believed. The GOP usually has just a 5 percent edge among them, primarily because so many African Americans, who are strongly pro-Democratic, are also members of this group.[18]

MARITAL STATUS   Even marital status reveals something about partisan affiliation. People who are married tend to favor the Republican Party, while single people who have never married tend to favor the Democratic Party. Taken as a group, the widowed lean toward the Democrats, probably because there are many more widows than widowers; here, the gender gap is again expressing itself. The divorced and the separated, who may be experiencing economic hardship, appear to be more liberal than the married population.[19]

Roots of the American Interest Group System

★ **11.5 . . . Trace the roots of the American interest group system.**

The face of interest group politics in the United States is changing as quickly as laws, political consultants, and technology allow. Big business and trade groups are increasing their activities and engagement in the political system at the same time that there is conflicting evidence concerning whether ordinary citizens join political groups. Political scientist Robert Putnam, for example, has argued that fewer Americans are joining groups, a phenomenon he labeled "bowling alone."[20] Others have faulted Putnam, concluding that America is in the midst of an "explosion of voluntary groups, activities and charitable donations [that] is transforming our towns and cities."[21] Although bowling leagues, which were once a very common means of bringing people together, have withered, other organizations such as volunteer groups, soccer associations, health clubs, and environmental groups are flourishing. Older organizations, such as the Elks Club and the League of Women Voters, whose membership was tracked by Putnam, are attracting few new members, but this does not mean that people are not joining groups; they are simply joining different groups and online social networks.

Why is this debate so important? Political scientists believe that involvement in community groups and activities with others of like interests enhances the level of **social capital,** "the web of cooperative relationships between citizens that facilitates resolution of collective action problems."[22] The more social capital that exists in a given community, the more citizens are engaged in its governance and well-being, and the more likely they are to work for the collective good.[23] This tendency to form small-scale associations for the public good, or **civic virtue,** as Putnam calls it, creates fertile ground within communities for improved political and economic development.[24] Thus, if Americans truly are joining fewer groups, overall citizen engagement in government and the government's provision of services may suffer. New groups, such as the tea party movement, place increased demands on government, even when the demands are for less government.

social capital
Cooperative relationships that facilitate the resolution of collective problems.

civic virtue
The tendency to form small-scale associations for the public good.

Interest groups are also important because they give the unrepresented or underrepresented an opportunity to have their voices heard, thereby making the government and its policy-making process more representative of diverse populations and perspectives.

Theories of Interest Group Formation

pluralist theory

The theory that political power is distributed among a wide array of diverse and competing interest groups.

disturbance theory

The theory that interest groups form as a result of changes in the political system.

transactions theory

The theory that public policies are the result of narrowly defined exchanges among political actors.

collective good

Something of value that cannot be withheld from a nonmember of a group, for example, a tax write-off or a better environment.

population ecology theory

The theory that the formation of political organizations is conditional on the resources allocated to a given issue area.

Interest group theorists use a variety of theories to explain how interest groups form and how they influence public policy. **Pluralist theory** argues that political power is distributed among a wide array of diverse and competing interest groups. Pluralist theorists such as David B. Truman explain the formation of interest groups through **disturbance theory.** According to this approach, groups form as a result of changes in the political system. Moreover, one wave of groups will give way to another wave of groups representing a contrary perspective (a countermovement). Thus, Truman would argue, all salient issues will be represented in government. The government, in turn, should provide a forum in which the competing demands of groups and the majority of the U.S. population can be heard and balanced.[25]

Transactions theory arose out of criticisms of the pluralist approach. Transactions theory argues that public policies are the result of narrowly defined exchanges among political actors. Transactions theorists offer two main contentions: it is not rational for people to mobilize into groups, and therefore, the groups that do mobilize will represent elites.

The idea that individuals will not mobilize into groups arises from economist Mancur Olson's *The Logic of Collective Action.*[26] In this work, Olson assumes that individuals are rational and have perfect information upon which to make informed decisions. He uses these assumptions to argue that, especially in the case of **collective goods,** or things of value that may not be withheld from nonmembers, such as a better environment, it makes little sense for individuals to join a group, if they can gain the benefits secured by others at no cost and become "free riders."

The elite bias that transactionists expect in the interest group system is the result of differences in the relative cost of mobilization for elite and nonelite citizens. Individuals who have greater amounts of time or money available simply have lower transaction costs. Thus, according to one political scientist, "The flaw in the pluralist heaven is that the heavenly chorus sings with a strong upper-class bias."[27]

More recently, a new wave of political scientists called neopluralists have evaluated previous theories and data to find a middle ground. For example, one neopluralist perspective, **population ecology theory,** argues that the formation of political organizations is conditional on the resources allocated to a given issue area. This theory builds on the biological idea that the resources of an ecosystem can only support a certain number of any one species (or groups). Growth of these species usually proceeds in an "s" curve, with a slow period of initial growth followed by a rapid increase in population and an eventual leveling off when the population has reached its maximum carrying capacity.[28]

How do special interests develop? Geography often determines the kinds of special interests that are most common in a given region.

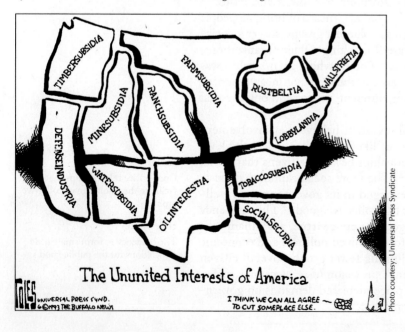

The Ununited Interests of America

Photo courtesy: Universal Press Syndicate

Interest Group Maintenance

All interest groups require adequate funding to build their memberships as well as to advance their policy objectives. Governments, foundations, and wealthy individuals can serve as **patrons,** providing crucial start-up funds for groups, especially public interest groups.[29] Advertising, litigating, and lobbying are expensive. Without financiers, few public interest groups could survive their initial start-up period.

patron
A person who finances a group or individual activity.

Organizations usually are composed of three kinds of members. At the top are a relatively small number of leaders who devote most of their energies to the single group. The second tier of members generally is involved psychologically as well as organizationally. They are the workers of the group—they attend meetings, pay dues, and chair committees to see that things get done. In the bottom tier are the rank and file members who don't actively participate. They pay their dues and call themselves group members, but they do little more. Most group members fall into this last category.

Groups vary tremendously in their ability to enroll what are called potential members. According to Mancur Olson, all groups provide a collective good.[30] If one union member at a factory gets a raise, for example, all other workers at that factory will, too. Therefore, those who don't join or work for the benefit of the group still reap the rewards of the group's activity. The downside of this phenomenon is called the **free rider problem.** As Olson asserts, potential members may be unlikely to join a group because they realize that they will receive many of the benefits the group achieves, regardless of their participation. Not only is it irrational for free riders to join any group, but the bigger the group, the greater the free rider problem. Thus, groups provide a variety of material benefits to convince potential members to join. These can be newsletters, discounts, or simply a good feeling.

free rider problem
Potential members fail to join a group because they can get the benefit, or collective good, sought by the group without contributing the effort.

The Development of American Interest Groups

Although all kinds of local groups proliferated throughout the colonies and in the new states, it was not until the 1830s, as communications networks improved, that the first national groups emerged. Many of these groups were single-issue groups deeply rooted in the Christian religious revivalism that was sweeping the nation. Concern with humanitarian issues such as temperance, peace, education, slavery, and women's rights led to the founding of numerous associations dedicated to solving these problems. Among the first of these groups was the American Anti-Slavery Society, founded in 1833 by William Lloyd Garrison. (To learn more about group formation, see The Living Constitution: First Amendment.)

After the Civil War, more groups were founded. For example, the Women's Christian Temperance Union (WCTU) was created in 1874 with the goal of outlawing the sale of liquor. Its members, many of them quite religious, believed that the consumption of alcohol was an evil injurious to family life because many men drank away their paychecks, leaving no money to feed or clothe their families.

Business interests also began to play even larger roles in both state and national politics during the late 1800s. A popular saying of the day noted that the Standard Oil Company did everything to the Pennsylvania legislature except refine it. Increasingly large trusts, monopolies, business partnerships, and corporate conglomerations in the oil, steel, and sugar industries became sufficiently powerful to control the votes of many representatives in the state and national legislatures.

Perhaps the most effective organized interest of the day was the railroad industry. In a move that couldn't take place today because of its clear impropriety, the Central Pacific Railroad sent its own **lobbyist** to Washington, D.C., in 1861, where he eventually became the clerk (staff administrator) of the committees of both houses of Congress that were charged with overseeing regulation of the railroad industry.

lobbyist
Interest group representative who seeks to influence legislation that will benefit his or her organization or client through political and/or financial persuasion.

The Living Constitution

Congress shall make no law respecting…the right of the people peaceably to assemble, and to petition the Government for a redress of grievances.

—FIRST AMENDMENT

This section of the First Amendment prohibits the national government from enacting laws dealing with the right of individuals to join together to make their voices known about their positions on a range of political issues. There was little debate on this clause in the U.S. House of Representatives, and none was recorded in the Senate. James Madison, however, warned of the perils of "discussing and proposing abstract propositions," which this clause was for many years.

Freedom of association, a key concept that allows Americans to organize and join a host of political groups, grew out of a series of cases decided by the Supreme Court in the 1950s and 1960s when many southern states were trying to limit the activities of the National Association for the Advancement of Colored People (NAACP). From the right to assemble and petition the government, along with the freedom of speech, the Supreme Court construed the right of people to come together to support or to protest government actions. First, the Court ruled that states could not compel interest groups to provide their membership lists to state officials. Later, the Court ruled that Alabama could not prohibit the NAACP from urging its members and others to file lawsuits challenging state discriminatory practices. Today, although states and localities can require organized interests to apply for permits to picket or protest, they cannot in any way infringe on their ability to assemble and petition in peaceable ways.

CRITICAL THINKING QUESTIONS

1. What role has protest played in American history?
2. Does requiring a government permit infringe on the right to protest? Under what conditions could a government permit be declined?
3. What is meant by "peaceable" protest? Should these words be strictly interpreted to prohibit physical violence, or could behaviors that are not physical be interpreted as nonpeaceable?

Subsequently, Congress awarded the Central Pacific Railroad (later called the Southern Pacific) vast grants of lands along its route and large subsidized loans. The railroad company became so powerful that it later went on to have nearly total political control of the California legislature.

By the 1890s, a profound change had occurred in the nation's political and social outlook. Rapid industrialization, an influx of immigrants, and monopolistic business practices created a host of problems including crime, poverty, squalid and unsafe working conditions, and widespread political corruption. Many Americans began to believe that new measures would be necessary to impose order on this growing chaos and to curb some of the more glaring problems in society. The political and social movement that grew out of these concerns was called the Progressive movement.

In response to the pressure applied by Progressive-era groups, the national government began to regulate business. Because businesses had a vested interest in keeping wages low and costs down, more business groups organized to consolidate their strength and to counter Progressive moves. Not only did governments have to mediate Progressive and business demands, but they also had to accommodate the role of organized labor, which often allied itself with Progressive groups against big business.

Until the creation of the American Federation of Labor (AFL) in 1886, there was not any real national activity on behalf of organized labor. The AFL brought skilled workers from several trades together into one stronger national organization for the first time. As the AFL grew in power, many business owners began to press individually or collectively to quash the unions. As business interests pushed states for what are called open shop laws to outlaw unions in their factories, the AFL became increasingly political. It also was forced to react to the success of big businesses' use of legal injunctions to prohibit union organization. In 1914, massive lobbying by the AFL and its members led to passage of the Clayton Act, which labor leader Samuel Gompers hailed as the Magna Carta of the labor movement. This law allowed unions to organize free from prosecution and also guaranteed their right to strike, a powerful weapon against employers.

The National Association of Manufacturers (NAM) was founded in 1895 by manufacturers who had suffered business losses in the economic panic of 1893 and who believed that they were being affected adversely by the growth of organized labor. The second major business organization came into being in 1912, when the U.S. Chamber of Commerce was created with the assistance of the federal government. NAM, the Chamber of Commerce, and other **trade associations,** groups representing specific industries, were effective spokespersons for their member companies. They were unable to defeat passage of the Clayton Act, but organized interests such as cotton manufacturers planned elaborate and successful campaigns to overturn key provisions of the act in the courts.[31] Aside from the Clayton Act, innumerable pieces of pro-business legislation were passed by Congress, whose members continued to insist that they had never been contacted by business groups.

trade association
A group that represents a specific industry.

In 1928, the bubble burst for some business interests. At the Senate's request, the Federal Trade Commission (FTC) undertook a massive investigation of the lobbying tactics of the business community. The FTC's examination of Congress revealed extensive illegal lobbying by yet another group, the National Electric Light Association (NELA). Not only did NELA lavishly entertain members of Congress, but it also went to great expense to educate the public on the virtues of electric lighting. Books and pamphlets were produced and donated to schools and public libraries to sway public opinion. Needy teachers and ministers who were willing to advocate electricity were helped with financial grants. Many considered these tactics unethical and held business in disfavor. These kinds of activities also led the public to view lobbyists in a negative light.

The Rise of the Interest Group State

During the 1960s and 1970s, the Progressive spirit reappeared in the rise of public interest groups. Generally, these groups devoted themselves to representing the interests of African Americans, women, the elderly, the poor, and consumers, or to working on behalf of the environment. Many of their leaders and members had been active in the civil rights and anti–Vietnam War movements of the 1960s. Other groups formed during the Progressive era, such as the American Civil Liberties Union (ACLU) and the NAACP, gained renewed vigor. Many of them had as their patron the liberal Ford Foundation, which helped to bankroll numerous groups, including the Women's Rights Project of the ACLU, the Mexican American Legal Defense and Educational Fund, the Puerto Rican Legal Defense and Education Fund (now called LatinoJustice PRLDEF), and the Native American Rights Fund.[32] The American Association of Retired Persons, now simply called AARP, also came to prominence in this era.

The civil rights and anti-war struggles left many Americans feeling cynical about a government that they believed failed to respond to the will of the majority. They also believed that if citizens banded together, they could make a difference. Thus, two major new public interest groups—Common Cause and Public Citizen—were founded. Common Cause, a good-government group that acts as a watchdog over the federal government, is similar to some of the early Progressive movement's public interest groups. Public

Citizen is the collection of groups founded by Ralph Nader (who went on to run as a candidate for president in 1996 and subsequent elections). In 1965, the publication of Nader's *Unsafe at Any Speed* thrust the young lawyer into the limelight. In this book, he charged that the Corvair, a General Motors (GM) car, was unsafe to drive; he produced voluminous evidence of how the car could flip over at average speeds on curved roads. In 1966, he testified about auto safety before Congress and then learned that GM had spied on him in an effort to discredit his work. The $250,000 that GM subsequently paid to Nader in an out-of-court settlement allowed him to establish a public citizen litigation center in 1971.

Conservatives, concerned by the activities of these liberal public interest groups founded during the 1960s and 1970s, responded by forming religious and ideological groups that became a potent force in U.S. politics. In 1978, the Reverend Jerry Falwell founded the first major new religious group, the Moral Majority. The Moral Majority was widely credited with assisting in the election of Ronald Reagan as president in 1980 as well as with the defeats of several liberal Democratic senators that same year. Falwell claimed to have sent 3 to 4 million newly registered voters to the polls.[33]

Pat Robertson, a televangelist, formed the Christian Coalition in 1990. Since then, it has grown in power and influence. The Christian Coalition played an important role in the Republicans winning control of the Congress in 1994. In 2008, the group distributed millions of voter guides in churches throughout the United States.

The Christian Coalition is not the only conservative interest group to play an important role in the policy process as well as in elections at the state and national level. The National Rifle Association (NRA), an active opponent of gun control legislation, saw its membership rise in recent years, as well as its importance in Washington, D.C. The NRA and its political action committee spent more than $11 million trying to elect John McCain president in 2008. And, conservative groups such as Students for Academic Freedom have made their views known in the area of higher education.

What Do Interest Groups Do?

★ **11.6** . . . **Identify several strategies and tactics used by organized interests.**

Whether good or bad, interest groups play an important role in U.S. politics. In addition to enhancing the democratic process by providing increased representation and participation, they increase public awareness about important issues, help frame the public agenda, and often monitor programs to guarantee effective implementation. Most often, they accomplish these things through some sort of lobbying activities as well as participating in elections.

Lobbying

lobbying
The activities of a group or organization that seek to persuade political leaders to support the group's position.

Most interest groups put lobbying at the top of their agendas. **Lobbying** is the activities of a group or organization that seek to persuade political leaders to support the group's position. There are multiple legal ways for organizations to lobby at the state and national level. Almost all interest groups lobby by testifying at hearings and contacting legislators. Other groups also provide information that decision makers might not have the time, opportunity, or interest to gather on their own. Interest groups also file lawsuits or friend of the court briefs to lobby the courts, and some even engage in protests or demonstrations as a form of lobbying public opinion or decision makers.

LOBBYING CONGRESS   Members of Congress are the targets of a wide variety of lobbying activities: congressional testimony on behalf of a group, individual letters from interested constituents, campaign contributions, or the outright payment of money for votes. Of course, the last item is illegal, but there are numerous documented instances of money changing hands for votes.

Today, many effective lobbyists are former members of Congress, staff aides, or other Washington insiders. These connections help them to develop close relationships with senators and House members in an effort to enhance their access to the policy-making process. (To learn more about why lobbying firms seek to hire former members of Congress, see Politics Now: Wall St. Ramps Up Lobbying on Hill.)

LOBBYING THE EXECUTIVE BRANCH   Groups often target one or more levels of the executive branch because there are so many potential access points, including the president, White House staff, and the numerous levels of the executive branch bureaucracy. Groups try to work closely with the administration to influence policy decisions at their formulation and later implementation stages. As with congressional lobbying, the effectiveness of a group often depends on its ability to provide decision makers with important information and a sense of where the public stands on the issue.

What role do lobbyists play in Congress? This cartoon presents one popular, although not always correct, view of how legislation gets enacted on Capitol Hill.

Photo courtesy: Creators Syndicate, Inc.

LOBBYING THE COURTS   The courts, too, have proved a useful target for interest groups.[34] Although you might think that the courts decide cases that affect only the parties involved or that they should be immune from political pressures, interest groups for years have recognized the value of lobbying the courts, especially the U.S. Supreme Court, and many political scientists view it as a form of political participation.[35]

Generally, interest group lobbying of the courts can take two forms: direct sponsorship or the filing of *amicus curiae* briefs. Sponsorship involves providing resources (financial, human, or otherwise) to shepherd a case through the judicial system. When a case a group is interested in but not actually sponsoring comes before a court, the organization often will file an *amicus* brief—either alone or with other like-minded groups—to inform the justices of the group's policy preference, generally offered in the guise of legal arguments. Over the years, as the number of both liberal and conservative groups viewing litigation as a useful tactic has increased, so has the number of briefs submitted to the courts. Most major U.S. Supreme Court cases noted in this book have been sponsored by an interest group, or one or both of the parties in the case have been supported by an *amicus curiae* brief.[36] Interest groups also file *amicus* briefs in lower federal and state supreme courts, but in much lower numbers.

GRASSROOTS LOBBYING   Interest groups regularly try to inspire their members to engage in grassroots lobbying, hoping that lawmakers will respond to those pressures and the attendant publicity.[37] In essence, the goal of many organizations is to persuade ordinary voters to serve as their advocates. In the world of lobbying, there are few things more useful than a list of committed supporters. Radio and television talk-show hosts such as Rush Limbaugh and Glenn Beck try to stir up their listeners by urging them to contact their representatives in Washington, D.C. Other interest groups use petition drives and carefully targeted and costly television advertisements pitching one side of an argument. It is also routine for interest groups to e-mail or text message their members and to provide a direct Web link as well as suggested text that citizens can use to lobby their legislators.

POLITICS NOW

| WORLD | NATION | LOCAL | **POLITICS** | OPINION | HEALTH & SCIENCE | ARTS | SPORTS | LEISURE |

Wall St. Ramps Up Lobbying on Hill

June 3, 2010
POLITICO
www.politico.com

By Erika Lovley

Wall Street has dramatically expanded its influence on Capitol Hill over the past year, using a lobbying army that includes nearly 1,500 former federal employees and 73 former members of Congress who have been deployed during debate on financial reform legislation.

Citigroup, Visa, the American Bankers Association, Prudential Financial and Goldman Sachs have drawn some of the top experts from Capitol Hill—with each organization registering nearly 50 people who formerly worked in the government, according to a joint report released today by the Center for Responsive Politics and Public Citizen. . . .

Of the 73 lawmakers-turned-lobbyists touting Wall Street's interests, 17 served on congressional banking committees during their time in office, including former House Financial Services Committee Chairman Michael Oxley (R–Ohio), a co-author of the Sarbanes-Oxley Act. . . .

"Wall Street hires former members of Congress and their staff for a reason," said Public Citizen Congress Watch Division Director David Arkush. "These people are influential because they have personal relationships with current members and staff. It's hard to say no to your friends."

Besides members of Congress, Wall Street bankers have also snapped up some of the brightest former staffers from financial committees.

At least 66 registered financial lobbyists previously worked as staffers on either a House or Senate banking committee, and 82 worked for members of Congress who sat on one of the banking committees. Another 42 served at some point in the Treasury Department with at least seven serving in some form in the Office of the Comptroller of the Currency. . . .

Even more intriguing, dozens of current banking lobbyists have previously worked for members of Congress who are still serving on the Senate or House Banking Committees— a key relationship connection. . . .

"Companies pay a premium for lobbyists who've spun through the revolving door because it can be a small price to pay relative to the huge payoff if they can shape legislation," said Center for Responsive Politics Executive Director Sheila Krumholz. "Without a doubt, the goal is to weaken the legislation.". . .

Critical Thinking Questions

1. What other reasons might lobbying firms have for hiring former members and staffers?
2. Former members and staffers must currently wait one year before they can become lobbyists. Should this waiting period be extended? What other limitations, if any, might be necessary?
3. How might the relationships discussed in this article affect public policy outcomes?

PROTESTS AND RADICAL ACTIVISM   An occasional though highly visible tactic used by some groups is protest activity. Although it is much more usual for a group's members to opt for more conventional forms of lobbying or to influence policy through the electoral process, when these forms of pressure-group activities are unsuccessful, some groups (or individuals within groups) resort to more forceful measures to attract attention to their cause. Since the Revolutionary War, violent, illegal protest has been one tactic of organized interests. The Boston Tea Party, for example, involved breaking all sorts of laws, although no one was hurt physically. Other forms of protest, such as the Whiskey Rebellion, ended in tragedy for some participants.

Election Activities

In addition to trying to achieve their goals (or at least draw attention to them) by lobbying, many interest groups also become involved more directly in the electoral process.

CANDIDATE RECRUITMENT AND ENDORSEMENTS   Some interest groups recruit, endorse, and/or provide financial or other forms of support for political candidates. EMILY's List (EMILY stands for "Early money is like yeast—it makes the dough rise") was founded to support pro-choice Democratic women candidates, especially during party primary election contests. It now also recruits and trains candidates. In 2008, EMILY's List not only provided over $30 million in direct contributions to candidates, but also mobilized volunteers, provided campaign consultants, and paid for some direct media.

GETTING OUT THE VOTE   Many interest groups believe they can influence public policy by putting like-minded representatives in office. To that end, many groups across the ideological spectrum launch massive get-out-the-vote (GOTV) efforts. These include identifying prospective voters and getting them to the polls on Election Day. Well-financed interest groups such as the liberal MoveOn.org and its conservative counterpart, Progress for America, often produce issue-oriented ads for newspapers, radio, television, and the Internet designed to educate the public as well as increase voter interest in election outcomes. (To learn more about the efforts of parties and candidates to turn out voters, see **chapter 12**.)

RATING THE CANDIDATES OR OFFICE HOLDERS   Many ideological groups rate candidates to help their members (and the general public) evaluate the voting records of members of Congress. The American Conservative Union (conservative) and Americans for Democratic Action (liberal)—two groups at ideological polar extremes—routinely rate candidates and members of Congress based on their votes on key issues. (To learn more about interest group ratings, see Analyzing Visuals: Interest Group Ratings of Selected Members of Congress.)

CAMPAIGN CONTRIBUTIONS   As discussed in **chapter 12**, corporations, labor unions, and interest groups may give money to political candidates in a number of ways. Organized interests are allowed to form **political action committees (PACs)** to raise money to contribute directly to political candidates in national elections. PAC money plays a significant role in the campaigns of many congressional incumbents, often averaging over half a House candidate's total campaign spending. PACs generally contribute to those who have helped them before and who serve on committees or subcommittees that routinely consider legislation of concern to that group. In 2008, the average Senate candidate received $2 million from PACs, and the average House candidate received $600,000.

    Some organized interests may also prefer to make campaign expenditures through soft money groups such as 527s or 501(c) groups. Money raised by these groups may not be given to or spent in coordination with a candidate's campaign. However, it may be used for issue advocacy, which may help a group's preferred candidate indirectly. Soft money groups have been major players in recent elections, spending over $400 million in 2008.

political action committee (PAC)
Officially registered fund-raising organization that represents interest groups in the political process.

TOWARD REFORM: Regulating Interest Groups and Lobbyists

★ **11.7** . . . **Explain reform efforts geared toward regulating interest groups and lobbyists.**

For the first 150 years of our nation's history, federal lobbying practices went unregulated. While the courts remain largely free of lobbying regulations, reforms have altered the state of affairs in Congress and the executive branch.

ANALYZING VISUALS

Interest Group Ratings of Selected Members of Congress

Many organized interests rate members of Congress based on the way legislators vote on issues important to the interest group. They use these ratings to help their members and other voters make informed voting decisions. The table displays the 2010 ratings of selected members of Congress by six interest groups that vary greatly in their ideology. Examine the table, and then answer the questions.

Member	ACU	ACLU	ADA	AFL-CIO*	CC*	CoC
Senate						
Mitch McConnell (R–KY)	96	0	10	20	100	71
Dianne Feinstein (D–CA)	0	100	100	100	10	43
John Cornyn (R–TX)	100	0	5	11	100	71
Charles Schumer (D–NY)	0	100	95	100	0	43
House						
John Boehner (R–OH)	96	9	0	0	100	80
Sheila Jackson Lee (D–TX)	0	91	95	100	0	33
Ileana Ros-Lehtinen (R–FL)	72	31	40	67	70	73
Henry Waxman (D–CA)	0	100	100	100	0	33

Key
ACU = American Conservative Union
ACLU = American Civil Liberties Union
ADA = Americans for Democratic Action
AFL-CIO = American Federation of Labor-Congress of Industrial Organizations
CC = Christian Coalition
CoC = Chamber of Commerce

Members are rated on a scale of 1 to 100 with 1 being the lowest and 100 being the highest support of a particular group's policies.

*2008 ratings.

- Which members of Congress listed in this table would you consider the most liberal? What about the most conservative? Which groups' ratings did you use to reach your conclusion?
- Is it important to know the specific issues or pieces of legislation an interest group uses to determine the ratings of members of Congress? Why or why not?
- Do you think voters should use interest group ratings to help them determine which candidates to vote for in elections? Why or why not?

Regulating Congressional Lobbyists

In 1946, in an effort to limit the power of lobbyists, Congress passed the Federal Regulation of Lobbying Act, which required anyone hired to lobby any member of Congress to register and file quarterly financial reports. For years, few lobbyists actually filed these reports and numerous good government groups continued to argue for the strengthening of lobbying laws.

By 1995, public opinion polls began to show that Americans believed the votes of members of Congress were available to the highest bidder. Thus, in late 1995, Congress passed the first effort to regulate lobbying since the 1946 act. The Lobbying

Disclosure Act employed a strict definition of lobbyist (one who devotes at least 20 percent of a client's or employer's time to lobbying activities). It also required lobbyists to: (1) register with the clerk of the House and the secretary of the Senate; (2) report their clients and issues and the agency or house they lobbied; and, (3) estimate the amount they are paid by each client. These reporting requirements made it easier for watchdog groups or the media to monitor lobbying activities.

After lobbyist Jack Abramoff pleaded guilty to extensive corruption charges in 2006, Congress pledged to reexamine the role of lobbyists in the legislative process. After the Democrats took control of both houses of Congress in 2007 in the wake of a variety of lobbying scandals, they were able to pass the **Honest Leadership and Open Government Act of 2007.** Among the act's key provisions were a ban on gifts and honoraria to members of Congress and their staffs, tougher disclosure requirements, and longer time limits on moving from the federal government to the private lobbying sector. Many observers complained, however that the law did not go far enough. In particular, many commentators were critical of the fact that the ban on gifts applied only to private lobbyists. Thus, state and local agencies and public universities, which spent over $130 million in 2006 to obtain earmarks, are still free to offer tickets for football and basketball games, and provide meals and travel.[38]

Honest Leadership and Open Government Act of 2007
Lobbying reform banning gifts to members of Congress and their staffs, toughening disclosure requirements, and increasing time limits on moving from the federal government to the private sector.

Regulating Executive Branch Lobbyists

Formal lobbying of the executive branch is governed by some restrictions in the 1995 Lobbying Disclosure Act as well as updates contained in the Honest Leadership and Open Government Act of 2007. Executive branch employees are also constrained by the 1978 Ethics in Government Act. (To learn more about the Ethics in Government Act, see Table 11.3.) Enacted in the wake of the Watergate scandal, this act attempted to curtail questionable moves by barring members of the executive branch from representing any clients before their agency for two years after leaving governmental service. Thus, someone who worked in air pollution policy for the Environmental Protection Agency and then went to work for the Environmental Defense Fund would have to wait two years before lobbying his or her old agency.

More recently, the Obama administration has implemented reforms that bring congressional-style lobbying regulation to the executive branch. In regulations put into place on his first day on the job, Barack Obama limited aides leaving the White House from lobbying executive agencies within two years. He also banned members of the administration from accepting gifts from lobbyists.

Table 11.3 *What are the key provisions of the Ethics in Government Act?*

1. **Financial disclosure** The president, vice president, and top-ranking executive employees must file annual public financial disclosure reports that list:
   ■ The source and amount of all earned income; all income from stocks, bonds, and property; any investments or large debts; the source of a spouse's income, if any.
   ■ Any position or offices held in any business, labor, or nonprofit organizations.

2. **Employment after government service** Former executive branch employees may not:
   ■ Represent anyone before an agency for two years after leaving government service on matters that came within the former employees' sphere or responsibility (even if they were not personally involved in the matter).
   ■ Represent anyone on any matter before their former agency for one year after leaving it, even if the former employees had no connection with the matter while in the government.

Source: Congressional Quarterly Weekly Report (October 28, 1978): 3121.

What Should I Have LEARNED?

Now that you have read this chapter, you should be able to:

⭐ **11.1 Trace the evolution of the two-party system in the United States, p. 310.**

Political parties have been a presence in American politics since the nation's infancy. The Federalists and the Democratic-Republicans were the first two parties to emerge in the late 1700s. In 1832, the Democratic Party (which succeeded the Democratic-Republicans) held the first national presidential nomination convention to nominate Andrew Jackson, and the Whig Party formed around opposition to the president. The Democratic and Whig Parties strengthened for several years until the issue of slavery led to the Whig Party's gradual dissolution and replacement by the Republican Party (formed by anti-slavery activists to push for the containment of slavery). From 1860 to this day, the same two political parties, Democratic and Republican, have dominated elections in the United States.

⭐ **11.2 Outline the structure of American political parties at the national, state, and local levels, p. 316.**

The national party organization sits at the top of the party system. A chairperson leads the national party, and every four years the national committee of each party organizes a national convention to nominate a candidate for the presidency. The state and local parties are the heart of party activism, as virtually all government regulation of political parties is left to the states. The state governing body, generally called the state central or executive committee, supervises the collection of local party organizations.

⭐ **11.3 Identify the functions performed by American political parties, p. 319.**

For over 200 years, the two-party system has served as the mechanism American society uses to organize and resolve social and political conflict. The two major parties provide vital services to society, including running candidates for office, proposing and formulating policy, organizing Congress, and furthering unity, linkage, and accountability.

⭐ **11.4 Analyze how political socialization and group affiliations shape party identification, p. 322.**

Most American voters have a personal affinity for a political party, which summarizes their political views and preferences and is expressed by a tendency to vote for the candidates of that party. This party identification begins with political socialization; parents are the single greatest influence on a person's political leanings. However, different group affiliations including geographic region, gender, race and ethnicity, age, social and economic factors, religion,

and marital status also impact individuals' loyalties to political parties, and these may change over the course of a lifetime.

⭐ **11.5 Trace the roots of the American interest group system, p. 325.**

An organized interest is a collection of people or groups with shared attitudes who make claims on government. Political scientists approach the development of interest groups from a number of theoretical perspectives, including pluralist theory, the transactions approach, and neopluralist theories such as population ecology. Interest groups did not begin to emerge in the United States until the 1830s. From 1890 to 1920, the Progressive movement dominated. The 1960s saw the rise of a wide variety of liberal interest groups. During the 1970s and 1980s, legions of conservatives formed new groups to counteract those efforts.

⭐ **11.6 Identify several strategies and tactics used by organized interests, p. 330.**

Interest groups often fill voids left by the major political parties and give Americans opportunities to make organized claims on government. The most common activity of interest groups is lobbying, which takes many forms. Groups routinely pressure members of Congress and their staffs, the president and the bureaucracy, and the courts; they use a variety of techniques to educate and stimulate the public to pressure key governmental decision makers. Interest groups also attempt to influence the outcome of elections. Others rate elected officials to inform their members how particular legislators stand on issues of importance to them. Political action committees (PACs), a way for some groups to contribute money to candidates for office, are another method of gaining support from elected officials and ensuring that supportive officials stay in office.

⭐ **11.7 Explain reform efforts geared toward regulating interest groups and lobbyists, p. 333.**

It was not until 1946 that Congress passed any laws regulating federal lobbying. Those laws were largely ineffective and were successfully challenged as violations of the First Amendment. In 1995, Congress passed the Lobbying Disclosure Act that required lobbyists to register with both houses of Congress. By 2007, a rash of scandals resulted in the sweeping reforms of the Honest Leadership and Open Government Act, which dramatically limited what lobbyists can do. The executive branch is also regulated by the 1978 Ethics in Government Act.

Test Yourself: Political Parties and Interest Groups

⭐ **11.1 Trace the evolution of the two-party system in the United States, p. 310.**

Parties have been affected, and in general weakened, by
A. the movement of people to urban areas.
B. a decline in the number of lobbyists.
C. decreases in district size.
D. candidate-centered politics.
E. voters deemphasizing the importance of a candidate's personality.

⭐ **11.2 Outline the structure of American political parties at the national, state, and local levels, p. 316.**

The key national party official is the
A. most recently defeated presidential candidate of his party.
B. secretary of the party.
C. national convention chair.
D. former president of the United States.
E. chair of the national committee.

⭐ **11.3 Identify the functions performed by American political parties, p. 319.**

One of the main functions of a party is electioneering, which includes
A. recruiting candidates.
B. determining the constitutionality of election laws.
C. advising the president.
D. negotiating with Congress.
E. creating linkages between the state and federal governments.

⭐ **11.4 Analyze how political socialization and group affiliations shape party identification, p. 322.**

The single greatest influence on an individual's first party identification is
A. parents.
B. age.
C. race.
D. gender.
E. income.

⭐ **11.5 Trace the roots of the American interest group system, p. 325.**

Which political and social movement started in the 1890s and grew out of concerns about the effects of rapid industrialization, an influx of immigrants, and monopolistic business practices?

A. The Progressive movement
B. The Industrial Revolution
C. The labor movement
D. The Grange
E. The Christian revivalism movement

⭐ **11.6 Identify several strategies and tactics used by organized interests, p. 330.**

An interest group files an *amicus curiae* brief to
A. sponsor a case heard before the Court.
B. respond to a ruling against the interests of the group.
C. inform the courts of its policy preferences.
D. respond to a judicial request for additional information on the implications of decisions.
E. to seek clarification on a ruling of the Court.

⭐ **11.7 Explain reform efforts geared toward regulating interest groups and lobbyists, p. 333.**

The Honest Leadership and Open Government Act of 2007 was passed in large part due to
A. Republicans seeking to limit the influence of interest groups.
B. the lack of any previous efforts to control the activities of lobbyists.
C. lobbying scandals that came to light around the 2006 midterm elections.
D. complaints about the ban on gifts that applied only to private lobbyists.
E. the desire to make lobbying registration more efficient for lobbyists.

Essay Questions

1. Explain the major party realignments that have occurred in the United States. Why have we not seen a major realignment in recent years?
2. How are political parties organized in America? What effect does this have on the political system?
3. How do lobbyists seek to influence the different branches of government?

mypoliscilab Exercises

Apply what you learned in this chapter on MyPoliSciLab.

Read on **mypoliscilab.com**

eText: Chapter 11

Study and **Review** on **mypoliscilab.com**

Pre-Test
Post-Test
Chapter Exam
Flashcards

Watch on **mypoliscilab.com**

Video: New Ballots Bring New Complications in New York
Video: Green Party Candidates Stay on Ballot
Video: Republicans and Democrats Divide on Tax Cut
Video: Senator Specter Switches Parties

Video: American Cancer Society Recommendation
Video: California Teachers Stage Sit-Ins
Video: Chicago Worker Protest
Video: Murtha and the PMA Lobbyists

Explore on **mypoliscilab.com**

Simulation: You Are a Campaign Manager: Help McCain Win Swing States and Swing Voters
Simulation: You Are a Lobbyist
Simulation: You Are the Leader of Concerned Citizens for World Justice
Comparative: Comparing Interest Groups
Timeline: The Evolution of Political Parties in the United States
Visual Literacy: State Control and National Platforms

Key Terms

candidate-centered politics, p. 313
civic virtue, p. 325
collective good, p. 326
critical election, p. 314
dealignment, p. 315
disturbance theory, p. 326
free rider problem, p. 327
Honest Leadership and Open Government Act of 2007, p. 335

interest group, p. 310
lobbying, p. 330
lobbyist, p. 327
national convention, p. 319
national party platform, p. 321
party identification, p. 322
party realignment, p. 314
patron, p. 327
pluralist theory, p. 326

political action committee (PAC), p. 333
political machine, p. 312
political party, p. 310
population ecology theory, p. 326
secular realignment, p. 314
social capital, p. 325
trade association, p. 329
transactions theory, p. 326

To Learn More on Political Parties and Interest Groups

In the Library

Abramowitz, Alan I. *The Disappearing Center: Engaged Citizens, Polarization, and American Democracy.* New Haven, CT: Yale University Press, 2010.

Aldrich, John H. *Why Parties? The Origin and Transformation of Political Parties in America.* Chicago: University of Chicago Press, 1995.

Baumgartner, Frank R., Jeffrey M. Berry, Marie Hojnacki, David C. Kimball, and Beth L. Leech. *Lobbying and Policy Change: Who Wins, Who Loses, and Why.* Chicago: University of Chicago Press, 2009.

Berry, Jeffrey M., and Clyde Wilcox. *The Interest Group Society,* 5th ed. New York: Longman, 2008.

Bibby, John F., and Brian Schaffner. *Politics, Parties, and Elections in America.* Boston, MA: Thomson Wadsworth, 2008.

Cigler, Allan J., and Burdett A. Loomis, eds. *Interest Group Politics,* 8th ed. Washington, DC: CQ Press, 2007.

Green, Donald J. *Third Party Matters: Politics, Presidents, and Third Parties in American History.* New York: Praeger, 2010.

Hershey, Marjorie Randon. *Party Politics in America,* 14th ed. New York: Pearson Longman, 2010.

Key, V.O., Jr. *Southern Politics in State and Nation,* new edition. Knoxville: University of Tennessee Press, 1984.

Maisel, L. Sandy, Jeffrey M. Berry, and George C. Edwards III, eds. *The Oxford Handbook of American Political Parties and Interest Groups.* New York: Oxford University Press, 2010.

Nownes, Anthony J. *Total Lobbying: What Lobbyists Want (and How They Try to Get It).* New York: Cambridge University Press, 2006.

Olson, Mancur. *The Logic of Collective Action: Public Goods and the Theory of Groups.* Cambridge, MA: Harvard University Press, 1965.

Sabato, Larry J., and Howard R. Ernst. *Encyclopedia of American Political Parties and Elections.* New York: Facts on File, 2005.

Schattschneider, E. E. *Party Government.* New York: Holt, Rinehart and Winston, 1942.

Truman, David B. *The Governmental Process: Political Interests and Public Opinion.* New York: Knopf, 1951.

On the Web

To learn more about the Democratic and Republican Parties, visit **www.dnc.org** and **www. rnc.org.**

To learn more about the ideology and party identification of the American electorate, visit the Web site of the Pew Research Center for the People and the Press at **www.people-press.org.**

To learn more about how interest groups grade your political representatives, go to Project Vote Smart at **www.votesmart.org** and click "Interest Group Ratings" on the home page.

To learn more about specific interest groups discussed in this chapter, type the name of the group into an Internet search engine and ask yourself the following questions as you explore the group's Web site:

- What are this group's stated goals?
- What are the requirements to become a member of the group?
- Does the group provide information that can be used by anyone, even someone not interested in formally joining the group?

12 Campaigns, Elections, and Voting

By the time Senator Barack Obama secured his party's nomination in June, 2008 the electoral environment looked favorable for the Democrats. President George W. Bush's approval rating was around 25 percent, the Democratic base was energized, and a hunger for change was sweeping the nation. Obama's path to the presidency was not assured, however. Democrats worried that not enough white Americans would be willing to vote for an African American for president. And, Obama's Republican opponent, Senator John McCain, was a more experienced candidate with a distinguished war record and history of breaking with his own party's policies. The decision awaiting both campaigns was how best to accumulate a majority of Electoral College votes, given the advantages and disadvantages at hand.

The Obama campaign decided to pursue electors in the key battleground states of

Florida and Ohio, as well as to compete vigorously in a number of reliably Republican states, most notably Virginia, which had not voted for a Democrat for president since 1964. While this plan seemed risky to many seasoned observers, the Obama campaign was confident in its decision to pursue this strategy, which also included grassroots organizing in all fifty states, extensive use of technology, including social networking sites such as Twitter, and opting out of the public financing system, which would allow it to raise and spend unprecedented sums of money.

McCain's campaign, in contrast, planned to hold all the states George W. Bush had won in 2004 and to target one or more states that generally did not vote Republican. This was a difficult challenge in an unfavorable political climate. McCain's challenge was made more difficult by his decisions to limit his campaign spending in return for federal financing and to

Presidential campaigns leave indelible marks on the nation. At left, Theodore Roosevelt gives a campaign speech from the back of a train in 1912. At right, President Barack Obama and his family wave to over 100,000 supporters in Chicago's Grant Park after Obama was declared the winner of the 2008 presidential election.

focus his early attention and scarce resources only on key battleground states.

On Election Day, the Obama campaign's strategy proved to be decisive. Obama won early victories in liberal northeastern states and was competitive in a number of traditionally Republican states. The outcomes in Indiana, Georgia, North Carolina, and Virginia, for example, remained in doubt for most of the evening.

A similar pattern soon became apparent in the West, with the networks unwilling to make early calls on the outcomes in traditionally Republican Montana, North Dakota, and even McCain's home state of Arizona.

In the end, McCain won states in the South, Midwest, Southwest, and Mountain West, which were large in landmass, but small in population and electoral votes. Ultimately, his strategy to target only Republican strongholds proved to be a poor one.

In contrast, Obama was able to develop a broad national base of support, and he even energized many young voters, who are often unwilling or uninterested in going to the polls. As a result, Obama not only held on to all of the states the Democrats had won in 2004, but he also won Florida, Ohio, Virginia, North Carolina, and Indiana, for a total of 364 electoral votes and a victory in the Electoral College.

What Should I Know About . . .

After reading this chapter, you should be able to:

★ 12.1 Trace the evolution of political campaigns in the United States, p. 342.

★ 12.2 Assess the role of candidates and their staff in the campaign process, p. 343.

★ 12.3 Evaluate the ways campaigns raise money, p. 346.

★ 12.4 Identify the ways campaigns use the media to reach potential voters, p. 351.

★ 12.5 Describe the electoral procedures used in presidential elections, p. 354.

★ 12.6 Explain the incumbency advantage in congressional elections, p. 359.

★ 12.7 Assess the effects of several factors that affect voter turnout and voter choice, p. 363.

M odern campaigns and elections have become high-stakes, high-priced extravaganzas, but the basic purpose of modern electioneering remains intact: one person asking another for support. The art of electoral politics involves the management of a large campaign budget and staff, the coordination of voter outreach efforts, and the creation of sophisticated Internet sites that provide continuous communication updates and organize voter and donor support. Campaigning also involves the diplomatic skill of unifying disparate individuals and groups to achieve a fragile electoral majority. How candidates perform these exquisitely difficult tasks in order to win voters' support in presidential and congressional elections is the subject of this chapter, in which we will discuss the following topics:

- First, we will explore *the roots of modern political campaigns*, including the nomination and general election campaigns.

- Second, we will examine the process of *assembling a campaign staff.*

- Third, we will investigate the ways campaigns *raise money*, including the rules that govern campaign finances and the sources of funding.

- Fourth, we will analyze how campaigns *reach voters*.

- Fifth, we will discuss the mechanics of *presidential elections*.

- Sixth, we will explore *congressional elections*.

- Finally, we will investigate the range of factors that affect *voter choice and turnout*.

ROOTS OF Modern Political Campaigns

★ **12.1 . . . Trace the evolution of political campaigns in the United States.**

No two political campaigns are the same. Each aspect of the campaign interacts with the other aspects to create a dynamic set of circumstances that make campaigns unpredictable and add to their excitement. Despite the unique qualities of each race, however, most electoral contests are similar in structure, consisting of a nomination campaign and a general election.

The Nomination Campaign

nomination campaign
Phase of a political campaign aimed at winning a primary election.

primary election
Election in which voters decide which of the candidates will represent the party in the general election.

The **nomination campaign,** the phase of a political campaign aimed at winning a **primary election,** begins as soon as the candidate has decided to run for office. This may be years prior to the actual election. During the nomination campaign, the candidates target party leaders and interest groups. They test out themes, slogans, and strategies, and learn to adjust to the pressure of being in the spotlight day in and day out. This is the time for the candidates to learn that a single careless phrase could end the campaign or guarantee a defeat. The press and public take much less notice of gaffes at this time than they will later, in the general election campaign.

A danger not always heeded by candidates during the nomination campaign is that, in the quest to win the party's nomination, a candidate can move too far to the right or left and appear too extreme to the electorate in November. Party activists are generally more ideologically extreme than party-identified voters in the general electorate, and activists participate in primaries and caucuses at a relatively high rate. If a candidate tries too hard to appeal to the interests of party elites, he or she jeopardizes the ultimate goal of winning the election.

The General Election Campaign

After earning the party's nomination, candidates embark on the **general election campaign,** or the phase of a political campaign aimed at winning a **general election.** Unlike the nomination campaign, where candidates must run against members of their own political party, during the general election campaign, candidates in partisan elections run against nominees from other political parties. All eligible voters, regardless of political party, have the opportunity to vote in these elections. For this reason, most political scientists suggest that candidates running in general elections have an incentive to move their positions on political issues toward the ideological center. These scholars argue that candidates representing the two major parties are unlikely to lose the votes of party loyalists. The citizens whose votes are "up for grabs" are often political moderates, and choosing middle-of-the-road positions on controversial issues may help to attract these individuals' votes.

  The length of the general election campaign varies widely from state to state, depending on the date of the primary elections. In states that hold primary elections in March, the general election campaign can be quite long. However, in states that hold primary elections in September, the general election campaign is quite short. The length of this campaign season affects how candidates structure their campaigns, how they raise money, whom they meet along the campaign trail, and even their advertising strategy.

general election campaign
Phase of a political campaign aimed at winning election to office.

general election
Election in which voters decide which candidates will actually fill elective public offices.

Assembling a Campaign Staff

⭐ **12.2 . . . Assess the role of candidates and their staff in the campaign process.**

Candidates are the center of political campaigns. While a candidate may not make all of the decisions, or even have the expertise or knowledge to handle the wide variety of issues and concerns that affect the campaign, it is ultimately the candidate's name that appears on the ballot. And, on Election Day, voters hold only the candidate truly accountable.

  Candidates employ a wide variety of people in order to help them run an effective campaign. Most candidates for higher offices hire a campaign manager, finance chair, and communications staff. They may also contract the assistance of a variety of

Length of Legislative Campaigns

There is no official campaign season in the United States, although to the public, it may seem as if legislators and legislative candidates are always campaigning. Election campaigns in other established democracies, however, vary greatly in length, with most being only thirty to sixty days. The table lists the lengths of the legislative campaigns in several countries.

  Japanese law, for example, establishes different official campaign periods for election to the Lower House (12 days) and to the Upper House (17 days) of its legislature. Japanese law also imposes a number of highly restrictive conditions on candidates during this period. Campaign rallies are only permitted between 8:00 a.m. and 8:00 p.m. Direct mailing or e-mailing of campaign materials to voters is prohibited. Candidates are also limited in the number of campaign vehicles they may place on the streets, and there are restrictions on the number, size, and location of campaign posters and newspaper advertisements.

Country	Length of Legislative Campaign
Israel	101 days
Germany	60 days
Australia	42 days
Canada	36 days (minimum length and average)
Great Britain	17 days
Japan	17 days (upper house)
	12 days (lower house)
South Korea	15 days

- What are the advantages of shorter campaigns for candidates? What about the advantages for the public?

- Are there any disadvantages for the public when a campaign is less than a month long? Explain your answer.

- Would the types of campaign restrictions imposed on legislative candidates in Japan work in the United States? Why or why not?

Markey Rallies Longmont Campaign Volunteers

May 16, 2010
Longmont Times-Call
www.timescall.com

By John Fryar

Maintaining Longmont voters' support will play a crucial role in U.S. Rep. Betsy Markey's campaign for a second term in Congress, she said Saturday.

Markey further noted that those Longmont voters' support represented nearly 15 percent of the total votes she got two years ago from the 4th District, which sprawls across all or parts of 18 northern and eastern Colorado counties.

This year, she said, "it's really critical that we get everybody out" again to vote in next fall's general election.

Markey's Saturday morning Longmont event was a kickoff of her volunteers' door-to-door efforts to identify probable or possible supporters in this year's congressional contest.

She emphasized the importance that such traditional grass-roots campaign techniques will have for her re-election.

"If the voter doesn't know me, if they see ugly ads on both sides and they don't know what to believe, it's that one-on-one contact with the voters that makes the difference," Markey said. . . .

Markey told her Collyer Park crowd that two years ago, "because of you, we knocked on every door" in Longmont "for every Democrat, every independent, a lot of moderate Republicans."

That, rather than million-dollar TV advertising buys, "is what makes the difference in campaigns," Markey said.

"We need to keep this seat in Democratic hands," Markey said, but "it's going to be a difficult year, as we know."

Markey told of the need, again this year, of taking her message to 4th Congressional District voters who are unaffiliated with either major political party, a group she said comprises about a third of the district's total registered voters.

In 2008, those unaffiliated voters "went with us," Markey said. But she joked that someone had told her that "we don't own them. They're like renters."

In 2010, "we've got to earn their votes" all over again, Markey said, "but we have a good story to tell."

Critical Thinking Questions

1. This article was written in May 2010. Why might a member of Congress need to organize and mobilize volunteer campaign staff six months before the election?
2. Do you agree with Representative Markey's contention that face-to-face contact is more important than campaign advertising? Why or why not?
3. Why does Representative Markey appear to be so concerned with get-out-the-vote efforts?

political consultants. In addition, candidates rely on networks of grassroots volunteers to spread the campaign's message and to get out the vote. (To learn more about one U.S. representative's get-out-the-vote efforts, see Politics Now: Markey Rallies Longmont Campaign Volunteers.)

The Candidate

Before there can be a campaign, there must be a candidate. Candidates run for office for any number of reasons, including personal ambition, the desire to promote ideological objectives or pursue specific public policies, or simply because they think they can do a better job than their opponents.[1] In any case, to be successful, candidates must spend a considerable amount of time and energy in pursuit of their desired office, and all candidates must be prepared to expose themselves and often their families to public scrutiny and the chance of rejection by the voters.

The Campaign Staff

Paid staff, political consultants, and dedicated volunteers work behind the scenes to support the candidate. Collectively, they plan general strategy, conduct polls, write speeches, craft the campaign's message, and design a communications plan to disseminate that message in the form of television advertisements, radio spots, Web sites, and direct mail pieces. Others are responsible for organizing fund-raising events, campaign rallies, and direct voter contacts.

It is important to note that the size and nature of the campaign staff varies significantly depending on the type of race. Presidential, senatorial, and gubernatorial races employ large professional staffs and a number of different consultants and pollsters. In contrast, races for state legislatures will likely have only a paid campaign manager and rely heavily on volunteer workers.

CAMPAIGN MANAGER   A **campaign manager** runs nearly every campaign at the state and national level. The campaign manager travels with the candidate and coordinates the campaign. He or she is the person closest to the candidate who makes the essential day-to-day decisions, such as whom to hire and when to air television and radio advertisements. The campaign manager also helps to determine the campaign's overall strategy and works to keep the campaign on message throughout the race.

campaign manager
The individual who travels with the candidate and coordinates the campaign.

FINANCE CHAIR   The major role of the **finance chair** is to coordinate the financial efforts of the campaign. This job includes raising money, keeping records of funds received and spent, and filing the required paperwork with the Federal Election Commission, the bureaucratic agency in charge of monitoring campaign activity. As the cost of campaigns has risen and fund-raising has become increasingly important, the prestige and significance of the finance chair has also grown.

finance chair
The individual who coordinates the financial business of the campaign.

COMMUNICATIONS STAFF   A **communications director,** who develops the overall media strategy for the campaign, heads the communications staff. It is the communications director's job to stay apprised of newspaper, television, radio, and Internet coverage, as well as supervise media consultants who craft campaign advertisements. Coordinating these many media sources can be challenging, as we will discuss later in this chapter.

communications director
The person who develops the overall media strategy for the candidate.

In many campaigns, the communications director works closely with the **press secretary.** The press secretary interacts and communicates with journalists on a daily basis and acts as the spokesperson for the campaign. It is the press secretary's job to be quoted in news coverage, to explain the candidate's issue positions, and to react to the actions of opposing candidates. They also have the job of delivering bad news and responding to attacks from opponents or interest groups. (It is better not to have the candidate doing the dirty work of the campaign.)

press secretary
The individual charged with interacting and communicating with journalists on a daily basis.

An increasingly important part of a campaign's communications staff is the Internet team, which manages the campaign's online communications, outreach, and fund-raising. Members of the Internet team post on blogs advocating for the candidate and create candidate profiles on social networking sites. They may organize Web chats or real-world meet-ups and grassroots events. They also act as important liaisons with the campaign's volunteers.

CAMPAIGN CONSULTANTS   **Campaign consultants** are the private-sector professionals and firms who sell the technologies, services, and strategies many candidates need to get elected. Consultants' numbers have grown exponentially since they first appeared in the 1930s, and their specialties and responsibilities have increased accordingly, to the point that campaign consultants are now an important part of many campaigns at the state and national level.[2]

campaign consultant
A private-sector professional who sells to a candidate the technologies, services, and strategies required to get that candidate elected.

Candidates generally hire specialized consultants who focus on only one or two areas, such as fund-raising, polling, media relations, Internet outreach, and speech

What do campaign volunteers do? Campaign volunteers often run phone banks, calling other citizens and encouraging them to turn out to vote. Here, Senator Harry Reid (D–NV) signs an autograph for phone bankers at one of his campaign offices.

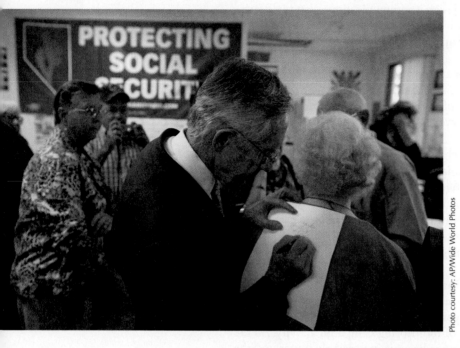

Photo courtesy: AP/Wide World Photos

writing. **Pollsters,** for example, are campaign consultants who conduct public opinion surveys. These studies gather opinions from a candidate's potential constituents. They are useful because they can tell a candidate where he or she stands relative to their opponent, or provide useful information about the issues and positions that are important to voters (see **chapter 10**).

VOLUNTEERS Volunteers are the lifeblood of every national, state, and local campaign. Volunteers answer phone calls, staff candidate booths at festivals and county fairs, copy and distribute campaign literature, and serve as the public face of the campaign. They go door to door to solicit votes, or use computerized telephone banks to call targeted voters with scripted messages, two basic methods of **voter canvass.** Most canvassing, or direct solicitation of support, takes place in the month before the election, when voters are most likely to be paying attention. Closer to Election

pollster

A campaign consultant who conducts public opinion surveys.

voter canvass

The process by which a campaign reaches individual voters, either by door-to-door solicitation or by telephone.

get-out-the-vote (GOTV)

A push at the end of a political campaign to encourage supporters to go to the polls.

Day, volunteers begin vital **get-out-the-vote (GOTV)** efforts, calling and e-mailing supporters to encourage them to vote and arranging for their transportation to the polls if necessary. In recent years, the Internet and social networking sites such as Facebook have been important tools used by volunteers to get out the vote and energize supporters.

Raising Money

⭐ **12.3 . . . Evaluate the ways campaigns raise money.**

Successful campaigns require a great deal of money. In 2008, for example, nearly $2 billion was raised by the Democratic and Republican parties. Presidential candidates raised more than $1.1 billion in additional support for their campaigns. And, the 29 incumbents in the Senate running for reelection raised an average of $9.7 million. Their challengers, in contrast, raised an average of $2.7 million.[3]

Efforts to regulate this type of campaign spending are nothing new. They are also far from settled. As spending from individuals, political parties, political action committees, and other sources continues to rise, it is likely that calls for reform will also continue. The sections that follow detail the current regulations and their implications for candidates for political office.

Regulating Campaign Finance

Serious, broad campaign finance regulation, was not enacted in the United States until the 1970s, in the wake of the Watergate scandal. The Federal Election Campaign Act (FECA) and its amendments established disclosure requirements; the

Presidential Public Funding Program, which provides partial public funding for presidential candidates who meet certain criteria; and the Federal Election Commission (FEC), an independent federal agency tasked with enforcing the nation's election laws. Although these provisions altered the campaign landscape, by 2002, it became clear that they were insufficient to regulate ever increasing campaign expenditures in the United States. Behind the leadership of Senators John McCain (R–AZ) and Russell Feingold (D–WI), Congress enacted and President George W. Bush signed into law a new set of campaign finance regulations known as the Bipartisan Campaign Reform Act (BCRA).

BCRA regulates political advertising and funding. The act limits the broadcast of issue advocacy ads within thirty days of a primary election and sixty days of a general election, and it regulates campaign contributions from a number of sources. Campaign contributions that are clearly regulated by the Federal Election Commission are known as **hard money.** Campaign funds may also come from public sources or from sources that are not regulated or limited by the Federal Election Commission; these funds are known as **soft money.** Soft money may not be given directly to the candidate, but it may be used for indirect issue advocacy on the candidate's behalf, as long as such advocacy does not directly mention the candidate's name and does not occur in coordination with the campaign.

hard money
Campaign contributions that are regulated and limited by the Federal Election Commission.

soft money
Campaign contributions that are not regulated or limited by the Federal Election Commission.

Opponents of BCRA, including Senator Mitch McConnell (R–KY) and the National Rifle Association, wasted little time in challenging its limits as an infringement on their right to free speech. In a 2003 decision, the Supreme Court disagreed, holding that the government's interest in preventing corruption overrides the free speech rights to which the parties would otherwise be entitled. Thus, BCRA's restrictions on soft-money donations and political advertising did not violate free speech rights.[4]

The Supreme Court, however, has declared other sections of BCRA unconstitutional. In 2007, for example, the Court held that the thirty- and sixty-day limits placed on issue advocacy ads were unconstitutional, thus opening the door to these electioneering communications throughout the election cycle.[5] And, in 2008, the Court overturned another provision of the act that had attempted to limit the amount of a candidate's own money that could be spent running for office.[6]

Most recently, in 2010, the Court handed down a decision in *Citizens United* v. *FEC* that declared unconstitutional BCRA's ban on electioneering communications made by corporations and unions.[7] This decision struck a significant blow to BCRA's provisions and is likely to dramatically increase the power of interest groups and corporations in campaigns and elections. As a result of these rulings, businesses and special interests surpassed all recent records, spending 2 billion in the 2010 election. (To learn more about the debate over campaign financing, see Join the Debate: Should the Government Regulate Campaign Spending?)

Sources of Campaign Funding

As mentioned previously, the Bipartisan Campaign Reform Act regulates campaign contributions from a number of sources, including individuals, political parties, political action committees, members of Congress, and personal savings. The Federal Election Commission regulates, records, and discloses these expenditures. The FEC also monitors infractions of campaign finance rules and acts as a quasi-judicial arbiter of conflicts.

Candidates may also receive some outside assistance from soft money groups. These groups include 527 political committees and 501(c) groups. Both of these types of groups have played increasingly active roles since the passage of BCRA.

INDIVIDUALS   Individual contributions are donations from independent citizens. The maximum allowable contribution under federal law for congressional and presidential elections was $2,400 per election to each candidate in 2009–2010, with

Join the DEBATE | Should the Government Regulate Campaign Spending?

In its January 2010 decision in *Citizens United* v. *FEC*, the U.S. Supreme Court narrowly struck down several components of the Bipartisan Campaign Reform Act of 2002, ruling that limitations on corporate election spending were unconstitutional restrictions on freedom of speech. The Court's decision provoked a flurry of debate and discussion around the need for and wisdom of campaign finance restrictions.

In his 2010 State of the Union Address, President Barack Obama condemned the decision as a blow to American democracy, giving "the special interests and their lobbyists even more power in Washington—while undermining the influence of average Americans who make small contributions to support their preferred candidates." But, many observers concur with the Court's decision, arguing that contributions make a statement about the donor's political beliefs. According to Jan Baran, a member of the Commission on Federal Ethics Law Reform, "The history of campaign finance reform is the history of incumbent politicians seeking to muzzle speakers, any speakers, particularly those who might publicly criticize them and their legislation. It is a lot easier to legislate against unions, gun owners, 'fat cat' bankers, health insurance companies and any other industry or 'special interest' group when they can't talk back."[a]

The controversy surrounding the Supreme Court's decision in *Citizens United* reignited debates about whether the government should regulate campaign spending. Do campaign finance regulations serve to prevent political corruption, or do they interfere with the right to free speech that belongs to all Americans?

To develop an ARGUMENT FOR government regulation of campaign spending, think about how:

- **Regulation of campaign finance prevents special interests, such as unions and corporations, from controlling candidate agendas.** What would happen if members of government were beholden to wealthy and mobilized interests? Would candidates, once elected, represent the ordinary constituents or the campaign donors they depend on for reelection?

- **Regulation of campaign finance creates a more even playing field for candidates.** How does curbing the influence of wealthy interests open the door for new challengers? In what ways would incumbents become more accountable if they had to run against strong challengers?

- **Regulation of campaign finance expands the marketplace of ideas.** How do campaign finance laws expand the diversity of voices and positions heard on an issue? In what ways might the removal of campaign finance laws permit a handful of voices or positions to dominate public discourse?

To develop an ARGUMENT AGAINST government regulation of campaign spending, think about how:

- **Regulation of campaign finance limits political speech protected by the First Amendment.** In what ways are campaign contributions a form of political speech? If organizations such as the National Rifle Association or American Civil Liberties Union wish to air political ads on behalf of an issue that is important to them, shouldn't they be able to under the First Amendment?

- **Regulation of campaign finance creates an uneven playing field for candidates.** How does money assist challengers in overcoming the many benefits enjoyed by incumbents? In what ways does regulation of campaign spending limit a challenger's competitiveness?

- **Regulation of campaign finance limits the marketplace of ideas.** How would groups such as unions and corporations be limited in their ability to raise their concerns? In what ways might the marketplace of ideas be expanded by removing limits on campaign spending?

---

[a]Jan Witold Baran, "Stampede Toward Democracy," *New York Times* (January 25, 2010); www.nytimes.com.

Table 12.1 *What are the individual contribution limits under BCRA?*

	Before	After[a]
To candidate, per election	$ 1,000	$ 2,400
To national party committee, per year	$20,000	$ 30,400
To state/local party committee, per year		$ 10,000
To other political committee, per year		$ 5,000
Total contributions, per 2-year cycle	$50,000	$115,500

[a] These limits are for 2009–2010. BCRA limits are adjusted in odd-numbered years to account for inflation.
Source: Federal Election Commission, www.fec.gov.

primary and general elections considered separately. Individuals in 2009–2010 were also limited to a total of $115,500 in gifts to all candidates, political action committees, and parties combined per two-year election cycle. These limits will rise at the rate of inflation in subsequent cycles. (To learn more about individual contribution limits, see Table 12.1.)

Most candidates receive a majority of all funds directly from individuals, and most individual gifts are well below the maximum level. In one recent election, researchers found that individual donors accounted for 60 percent of contributions to candidates for the House of Representatives, 75 percent of contributions to candidates for the Senate, and 85 percent of contributions to presidential candidates.[8] In 2008, 90 percent of Barack Obama's record-breaking $745 million fund-raising effort came from individuals. Of those donations, almost 50 percent came from small money donors of less than $200.[9]

POLITICAL PARTIES   Candidates receive substantial donations from the national and state committees of the Democratic and Republican Parties. Under the current rules, national parties can give up to $5,000 per election to a House candidate and $42,600 to a Senate candidate. In 2008, the Republican and Democratic Parties raised nearly $2 billion. In competitive races, the parties may provide almost 20 percent of their candidates' total war chests.

POLITICAL ACTION COMMITTEES (PACs)   When interest groups such as labor unions, corporations, trade unions, and ideological issue groups seek to make donations to campaigns, they must do so by establishing **political action committees (PACs)**. PACs are officially recognized fund-raising organizations that are allowed by federal law to participate in federal elections. Under current rules, a PAC can give no more than $5,000 per candidate per election, and $15,000 each year to each of the national party committees.

political action committee (PAC)
Officially registered fund-raising organization that represents interest groups in the political process.

Approximately 4,000 PACs are registered with the FEC. In 2008, the average Senate candidate received $2 million from PACs; the average House candidate received $600,000. On average, PAC contributions accounted for 33 percent of the war chests (campaign funds) of House candidates and 20 percent of the treasuries of Senate candidates. Incumbents, however, tend to benefit the most from PAC money. In 2008, 86 percent of PAC contributions went to incumbents.[10]

Donations from a small number of PACs make up a large proportion of campaign war chests. Five percent of all PACs made 60 percent of the contributions to candidates in recent elections.[11] (To learn more about how PACs allocate campaign contributions, see Figure 12.1.)

MEMBER PACs   In Congress and in state legislatures, well-funded, electorally secure incumbents often contribute campaign money to their party's candidates who are struggling to raise money and/or are in competitive races.[12] This activity began in some state legislatures (notably California), but it is now well-established at the congressional level.[13] Generally, members contribute to other candidates by establishing their own PACs—informally dubbed "leadership" PACs—through which they distribute campaign support to candidates.

Figure 12.1 *How do PACs allocate their campaign contributions?*
Source: Center for Responsive Politics, www.opensecrets.org/lobby, 2008.

| Congressional candidates | Presidential candidates |

| Incumbents | Open seat candidates | Challengers |

| Democrats | Republicans |

In general, members give their contributions to the same candidates who receive the bulk of congressional campaign committee resources. Thus, member contributions at the congressional level have emerged as a major supplement to the campaign resources contributed by the party campaign committees.[14]

PERSONAL SAVINGS   The U.S. Supreme Court ruled in *Buckley* v. *Valeo* (1976) that no limit could be placed on the amount of money candidates can spend from their own families' resources, since such spending is considered a First Amendment right of free speech.[15] For wealthy politicians, this allowance may mean personal spending in the millions.

public funds

Donations from general tax revenues to the campaigns of qualifying presidential candidates.

matching funds

Donations to presidential campaigns whereby every dollar raised from individuals in amounts less than $251 is matched by the federal treasury.

PUBLIC FUNDS   **Public funds** are donations from general tax revenues to the campaigns of qualifying candidates. On the federal level, only presidential candidates receive public funds. Under the FECA (which first established public funding of presidential campaigns), a candidate for president can become eligible to receive public funds during the nomination campaign by raising at least $5,000 in individual contributions of $250 or less in each of twenty states. The candidate can then apply for federal **matching funds,** whereby every dollar raised from individuals in amounts less than $251 is matched by the federal treasury on a dollar-for-dollar basis. Of course, this assumes there is enough money in the Presidential Election Campaign Fund to do so. The fund is accumulated by taxpayers who designate $3 of their taxes for this purpose each year when they send in their federal tax returns. (Only about 20 percent of taxpayers check off the appropriate box, even though participation does not increase their tax burden.) During the 2008 primaries, all of the major candidates except John Edwards opted out of federal matching funds, allowing them to raise considerably more money than the government would have provided.

During the general election campaign, the two major-party presidential nominees can accept an $85 million lump-sum payment from the federal government after the candidate accepts his or her nomination. If the candidate accepts the money, it becomes the sole source for financing the campaign. A candidate may refuse the money and be free from the spending cap the government attaches to it, as Barack Obama did in 2008, subsequently setting a record for the most spent by a candidate for a presidential campaign.

A third-party candidate receives a smaller amount of public funds proportionate to his or her November vote total, if that candidate gains a minimum of 5 percent of the vote. Note that in such a case, the money goes to third-party campaigns only *after* the election is over; no money is given in advance of the general election.

SOFT MONEY GROUPS   Candidates in some races may also receive indirect assistance from groups that raise and spend soft money. In the 2008 election cycle, more than $400 million in soft money contributions were spent targeting races for the presidency and Congress. These funds cannot be spent in coordination with the candidate's campaign, or used to endorse a particular candidate. But, they can and are used to fund issue advocacy, often in the form of campaign advertisements, e-mails, and phone calls. In 2010, soft money contributions to congressional races increased by 73 percent over their 2008 levels.

There are two major types of groups engaged in raising and spending soft money in federal campaigns. The first of these types of groups, **527 political committees,** are tax-exempt organizations created to raise money for political activities such as voter mobilization and issue advocacy. The 527 committees perform many of the same functions as political action committees; the major differentiation between the two lies in the Internal Revenue Service code from which they derive their name. And, in fact, many 527 organizations are affiliated with PACs. During the 2008 election cycle, 527s spent approximately $200 million advocating for candidates. These expenditures favored Democratic candidates by nearly a 3:1 margin. Notable 527s participating in the 2008 election included America Votes and Change to Win on the Democratic side of the aisle, and the College Republican National Committee on the Republican side of the aisle.[16]

The second type of group responsible for raising and spending soft money in recent elections is **501(c) groups.** A 501(c) group is a nonprofit, tax-exempt interest group that can engage in varying levels of political activity, depending on the group. 501(c)3 groups, for example, are not allowed to engage in any political activities, with the exception of voter registration. Other 501(c) groups may take political action as long as it is not their primary purpose. These groups are becoming increasingly important players in American elections. In the 2008 election cycle, 501(c) groups spent a roughly equal amount of money to 527s. Unlike 527s, however, most of these contributions favored Republican candidates. Examples of notable 501(c) groups include the National Rifle Association and the U.S. Chamber of Commerce, both of which lean Republican, and the Planned Parenthood Action Fund, which tends to lean Democratic in its contributions.[17]

527 political committee
Tax-exempt organization created to raise money for political activities such as voter mobilization and issue advocacy; not subject to FEC disclosure rules.

501(c) group
Nonprofit, tax-exempt interest groups that can engage in varying levels of political activity; not subject to FEC disclosure rules.

Reaching Voters

⭐ **12.4 . . . Identify the ways campaigns use the media to reach potential voters.**

The media play a large role in determining what voters actually see and hear about the candidate. Media can take a number of different forms; among these are traditional media, new media, and campaign advertisements.

Traditional media coverage of a political campaign includes content appearing in newspapers and magazines as well as on radio and television. New media coverage includes content that appears on the Internet, in blogs, and on social networking sites. Both traditional and new media can be very difficult for a campaign to control. Campaigns, however, have a great deal of control over the content they include in their campaign advertisements.

Traditional Media

During campaign season, the news media constantly report political news. What they report is largely based on news editors' decisions of what is newsworthy or "fit to print." The press often reports what candidates are doing, such as giving speeches, holding fundraisers, or meeting with party leaders. Reporters may also investigate rumors of a candidate's misdeeds or unflattering personal history, such as run-ins with the law, alleged use of drugs, or alleged sexual improprieties.

Although this free media attention may help candidates increase their name recognition, it may prove frustrating for campaigns, which do not control the content of the coverage. For example, studies have shown that reporters are obsessed with the horserace aspect of politics—who's ahead, who's behind, who's gaining—to the detriment of the substance of the candidates' issues and ideas. Public opinion polls, especially tracking polls, many of them taken by news outlets, dominate coverage on network television in particular, where only a few minutes a night are devoted to politics.[18]

STRATEGIES TO CONTROL MEDIA COVERAGE   Candidates and their media consultants use various strategies in an effort to obtain favorable press coverage. First, campaign staff members often seek to isolate the candidate from the press, thus reducing the chances that reporters will bait a candidate into saying something that might damage his or her cause. Second, the campaign stages media events: activities designed to include brief, clever quotes called sound bites and staged with appealing backdrops so that they will be covered on the television news and in the newspaper. Third, campaign staff and consultants have cultivated a technique termed spin—they put forward the most favorable possible interpretation for their candidate (and the most negative for their opponent) on any circumstance occurring in the campaign. They also work the press to sell their point of view or at least to ensure that it is included in the reporters' stories. Fourth, candidates have found ways to circumvent traditional reporters by appearing on talk shows such as *The Oprah Winfrey Show*, *The O'Reilly Factor*, and *The View*. They also make regular appearances on comedy shows, such as *Saturday Night Live*, *The Late Show*, *The Daily Show*, and *The Colbert Report*.

CANDIDATE DEBATES   The first face-to-face presidential debate in U.S. history did not occur until 1960, and face-to-face debates did not become a regular part of presidential campaigns until the 1980s. However, they are now an established feature of presidential campaigns as well as races for governor, U.S. senator, and many other offices.

Candidates and their staffs recognize the importance of debates as a tool not only for consolidating their voter base but also for correcting misperceptions about the candidate's suitability for office. However, while candidates have complete control over what they say in debates, they do not have control over what the news media will highlight and focus on after the debates. Therefore, even though candidates prepare themselves by rehearsing their responses, they cannot avoid the perils of spontaneity.

How have the rules and format for presidential debates changed since the first televised debates? Presidential debates have come a long way since an ill-at-ease Richard M. Nixon was visually bested by John F. Kennedy in the first set of televised debates. John McCain and Barack Obama's second debate in 2008 was in a town meeting format, where the candidates responded to questions directly posed by audience members.

New Media

Contemporary campaigns have an impressive new array of weapons at their disposal: faster printing technologies, reliable databases, instantaneous Internet publishing and mass e-mail, autodialed pre-recorded messages, video technology, and enhanced telecommunications and teleconferencing. As a result, candidates can gather and disseminate information more quickly and effectively than ever.

The use of new media takes a number of forms. Many candidates use recorded phone messages, or robo-calling, to target narrow constituencies. These messages have been used both to spread negative (and sometimes false) information about an opponent and to raise money and rally supporters.

The most widely used new media tool is, of course, the Internet. The first use of the Internet in national campaigning came in 1992 when the Democratic presidential ticket of Bill Clinton and Al Gore maintained a Web site that stored electronic versions of their biographical summaries, speeches, press releases, and position papers. The Internet remained something of a virtual brochure until the 2000 elections, when candidates began using e-mail and their Web sites as vehicles for fund-raising, recruiting volunteers, and communicating with supporters. By 2006, most campaign Web sites featured downloadable and streaming video and were integrated into the candidate's overall communication and mobilization strategy. In 2008, all of the major candidates running for president and nearly 90 percent of Democratic and Republican congressional candidates maintained a campaign Web site.

ANALYZING VISUALS

Peace Little Girl

In the 1964 election, President Lyndon B. Johnson's campaign produced a television ad that showed a young girl counting the petals she was picking off a daisy. Once she said the number nine, a voice-over started counting down a missile launch that ended in images of a nuclear explosion and a mushroom cloud. The viewer then heard the president's voice saying, "These are the stakes." Examine the still images taken from the ad and then answer the questions.

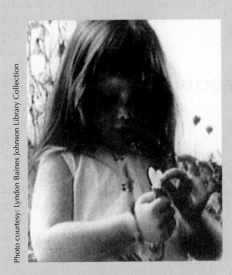

Photo courtesy: Lyndon Baines Johnson Library Collection

Photo courtesy: AP/Wide World Photos

- What was this ad trying to imply?
- Why do you think this ad was considered so shocking and unfair?
- What types of ads would generate similar controversy today? Explain your answer.

Campaign Advertisements

positive ad

Advertising on behalf of a candidate that stresses the candidate's qualifications, family, and issue positions, with no direct reference to the opponent.

negative ad

Advertising on behalf of a candidate that attacks the opponent's character or platform.

contrast ad

Ad that compares the records and proposals of the candidates, with a bias toward the candidate sponsoring the ad.

inoculation ad

Advertising that attempts to counteract an anticipated attack from the opposition before the attack is launched.

Candidates and their media consultants may choose to buy airtime in the form of campaign advertisements. These ads may take a number of different forms. **Positive ads** stress the candidate's qualifications, family, and issue positions with no direct reference to the opponent. Positive ads are usually favored by the incumbent candidate. **Negative ads** attack the opponent's character or platform. And, with the exception of the candidate's brief, legally required statement that he or she approved the ad, a negative ad may not even mention the candidate who is paying for the airing. **Contrast ads** compare the records and proposals of the candidates, with a bias toward the candidate sponsoring the ad. (To learn more about campaign ads see Analyzing Visuals: Peace Little Girl.)

Before the 1980s, well-known incumbents usually ignored negative attacks from their challengers, believing that the proper stance was to be above the fray. But, after some well-publicized defeats of incumbents in the early 1980s in which negative television advertising played a prominent role,[19] incumbents began attacking their challengers in earnest. The new rule of politics became "An attack unanswered is an attack agreed to." In a further attempt to stave off criticisms from challengers, incumbents began anticipating the substance of their opponents' attacks and airing **inoculation ads** early in the campaign to protect themselves in advance from the other side's spots.

Presidential Elections

⭐ **12.5 . . . Describe the electoral procedures used in presidential elections.**

No U.S. election can compare to the presidential contest. This spectacle, held every four years, brings together all the elements of politics and attracts the most ambitious and energetic politicians to the national stage. Voters in a series of state contests that run through the winter and spring of the election year select delegates who will attend each party's national convention. Following the national convention for each party, held in mid- and late summer, there is a final set of fifty separate state elections all held on the Tuesday after the first Monday in November to select the president. This lengthy process exhausts candidates and voters alike, but it allows the diversity of the United States to be displayed in ways a shorter, more homogeneous presidential election process could not.

Primaries and Caucuses

The state party organizations use several types of methods to elect national convention delegates and ultimately select the candidates who will run against each other in the general election:

1. *Winner-take-all primary.* Under this system the candidate who wins the most votes in a state secures all of that state's delegates. While Democrats no longer permit its use because it is viewed as less representative than a proportional system, Republicans generally prefer this process as it enables a candidate to amass a majority of delegates quickly and shortens the divisive primary season.

2. *Proportional representation primary.* Under this system, candidates who secure a threshold percentage of votes are awarded delegates in proportion to the number of popular votes won. Democrats now strongly favor this system and use it in many state primaries, where they award delegates to anyone who wins more than 15 percent in any congressional district. Although proportional representation is probably the fairest way of allocating delegates to candidates, its downfall is that it renders majorities of delegates more difficult to accumulate and thus can

lengthen the presidential nomination contest.

3. *Caucus.* The caucus is the oldest, most party-oriented method of choosing delegates to the national conventions. Traditionally, the caucus was a closed meeting of party activists in each state who selected the party's choice for presidential candidate. Today, caucuses (in Iowa, for example) are more open and attract a wider range of the party's membership. Indeed, new participatory caucuses more closely resemble primary elections than they do the old, exclusive party caucuses.[20]

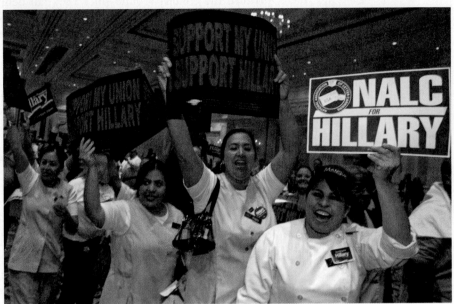

Where are party caucuses held? While voters go to polling places located in buildings such as schools and community centers to vote in primary and general elections, caucuses can be held in living rooms, high school gyms, or even in casinos. Here, union members supporting Senator Hillary Clinton rally for their candidate at a casino before caucuses in Nevada.

Photo courtesy: AP/Wide World Photos

SELECTING A SYSTEM   The mix of preconvention contests has changed over the years, with the most pronounced trend being the shift from caucuses to primary elections. Only seventeen states held presidential primaries in 1968; in 2008, forty states chose this method. In recent years, the vast majority of delegates to each party's national convention have been selected through the primary system.

Many people support the increase in the number of primaries because they believe that they are more democratic than caucuses. Primaries are accessible not only to party activists, but also to most of those registered to vote. Related to this idea, advocates argue that presidential primaries are the best means by which to nominate presidential candidates. Although both primaries and caucuses attract the most ideologically extreme voters in each party, primaries nominate more moderate and appealing candidates—those that primary voters believe can win in the general election. Primaries are also more similar to the general election and thus constitute a rigorous test for the candidates, a chance to display under pressure some of the skills needed to be a successful president.

Critics believe that the qualities tested by the primary system are by no means a complete list of those a president needs to be successful. For instance, skill at handling national and local media representatives is by itself no guarantee of an effective presidency. The exhausting primary schedule may be a better test of a candidate's stamina than of his or her brain power. In addition, critics argue that although primaries may attract more participants than caucuses, this quantity does not substitute for the quality of information held by caucus participants. At a caucus, participants spend several hours learning about politics and the party. They listen to speeches by candidates or their representatives and receive advice from party leaders and elected officials, then cast a well-informed vote.

FRONT-LOADING   The role of primaries and caucuses in the presidential election has been altered by **front-loading,** the tendency of states to choose an early date on the nomination calendar. Seventy percent of all the delegates to both party conventions are now chosen before the end of February. This trend is hardly surprising, given

front-loading
The tendency of states to choose an early date on the nomination calendar.

the added press emphasis on the first contests and the voters' desire to cast their ballots before the competition is decided.

Front-loading has important effects on the nomination process. First, a front-loaded schedule generally benefits the front-runner, since opponents have little time to turn the contest around once they fall behind. Second, front-loading gives an advantage to the candidate who wins the "invisible primary," that is, the one who can raise the bulk of the money *before* the nomination season begins. Once primaries and caucuses begin, there is less opportunity to raise money to finance campaign efforts simultaneously in many states.

However, Internet fund-raising has emerged as a means to soften the advantage of a large campaign fund going into a primary battle, since it allows candidates to raise large sums from many small donors nationwide virtually overnight. All of the major 2008 presidential candidates relied on online donations to finance their campaigns, but the highly compressed schedule still forced even the best-funded candidates to make difficult decisions on how to allocate their financial resources.

Electing a President: The Electoral College

Given the enormous amount of energy, money, and time expended to nominate two major-party presidential contenders, it is difficult to believe that the general election could be more arduous than the nominating contests, but it usually is. The object of the general election campaign is clear: winning a majority of the **Electoral College.** This uniquely American institution consists of representatives of each state who cast the final ballots that actually elect a president. The total number of **electors**—the members of the Electoral College—for each state is equivalent to the number of senators and representatives that state has in the U.S. Congress. The District of Columbia is accorded three electoral votes making 538 the total number of votes cast in the Electoral College. Thus, the magic number for winning the presidency is 270 votes.

Keep in mind that through **reapportionment,** representation in the House of Representatives and consequently in the Electoral College is altered every ten years to reflect population shifts. Reapportionment is simply the reallocation of the number of seats in the House of Representatives that takes place after each decennial census. Projections for the 2010 Census show a sizeable population shift from the Midwest and the Democratic-dominated Northeast to the South and West, where Republicans are much stronger. If Barack Obama runs for reelection and wins the same states in 2012 that he won in 2008, he will win 5 fewer votes. (To learn more about the 2008 Electoral College results, see Figure 12.2.)

HISTORICAL CHALLENGES   The Electoral College was the result of a compromise between those Framers who argued for selection of the president by the Congress and those who favored selection by direct popular election. There are three essentials to understanding the Framers' design of the Electoral College. The system was constructed to: (1) work without political parties; (2) cover both the nominating and electing phases of presidential selection; and, (3) produce a nonpartisan president. Most of the challenges faced by the Electoral College are the result of changes in the practice of elections that have occurred over time. (To learn more about the creation of the Electoral College, see The Living Constitution: Article II, Section 1, Clause 4.)

For example, because the Framers expected partisanship to have little influence, the Electoral College originally was designed to elect the president and vice president from the same pool of candidates; the one who received the most votes would become president and the runner-up would be come vice president. To accommodate this system, each elector was given two votes. Following the development of the first party system, the republic's fourth presidential election soon revealed a flaw in this plan. In 1800, Thomas Jefferson and Aaron Burr were, respectively, the presidential

Electoral College
Representatives of each state who cast the final ballots that actually elect a president.

elector
Member of the Electoral College.

reapportionment
The reallocation of the number of seats in the House of Representatives after each decennial census.

Figure 12.2 *How is voting power apportioned in the Electoral College?*

This map visually represents the respective electoral weights of the fifty states in the 2008 presidential election. For each state, the projected gain or loss of Electoral College votes based on the 2010 Census is indicated in parentheses.

Source: synapse.princeton.edu/~sam/ev_projection_current_map.jpg and www.edssurvey.com/images/File/NR_Appor07wTables.pdf.

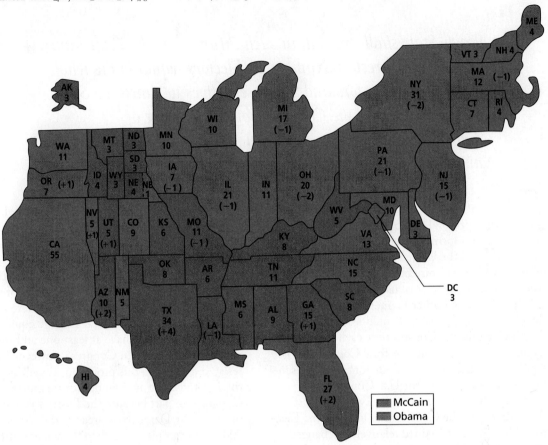

and vice presidential candidates advanced by the Democratic-Republican Party, whose supporters controlled a majority of the Electoral College. Accordingly, each Democratic-Republican elector cast one of his two votes for Jefferson and the other one for Burr. Since there was no way under the constitutional arrangements for electors to earmark their votes separately for president and vice president, the presidential election resulted in a tie between Jefferson and Burr. Even though most understood Jefferson to be the actual choice for president, the Constitution mandated that a tie be decided by the House of Representatives, which was controlled by the Federalists. The controversy was settled in Jefferson's favor, but only after much energy was expended to persuade Federalists not to give Burr the presidency.

The Twelfth Amendment, ratified in 1804 and still the constitutional foundation for presidential elections today, was an attempt to remedy the confusion between the selection of vice presidents and presidents that beset the election of 1800. The amendment provided for separate elections for each office. In the event of a tie or when no candidate received a majority of the total number of electors, the election still went to the House of Representatives; now, however, each state delegation would have one vote to cast for one of the three candidates who had received the greatest number of electoral votes.

The Electoral College modified by the Twelfth Amendment has fared better than the College as originally designed, but it has not been problem free. On three occasions during the nineteenth century, the electoral process resulted in the selection of a president who received fewer votes than his opponent. In 1824, neither John Quincy Adams

The Living Constitution

Each State shall appoint, in such Manner as the Legislature thereof may direct, a Number of Electors, equal to the whole Number of Senators and Representatives to which the State may be entitled in the Congress: but no Senator or Representative, or Person holding an Office of Trust or Profit under the United States, shall be appointed an Elector.

—ARTICLE II, SECTION 1, CLAUSE 2

This clause of the Constitution creates what is called the Electoral College, the representative body of citizens formally responsible for choosing the president of the United States. This body was created as a compromise between some Framers who favored allowing citizens to directly choose their president and other Framers who feared that directly electing a president could lead to tyranny. As stipulated in the Constitution, each state has a number of votes in the Electoral College that is equivalent to the number of senators and representatives that state has in the U.S. Congress.

Since the ratification of the Twelfth Amendment to the Constitution in 1824, the Electoral College has remained relatively unchanged, save for the addition of electors as the size of the House of Representatives and Senate grew. However, one major change in the Electoral College occurred when Congress enacted and the states ratified the Twenty-Third Amendment to the Constitution. This amendment gave the District of Columbia, which had evolved from a dismal swampland to a growing metropolitan area, representation in the Electoral College. The amendment set the number of electors representing the District as equal to the number of electors representing the smallest state, regardless of the District's population. Today, the District has three electors, making it equal with small population states such as Delaware and Wyoming.

This provision could become problematic if the population of the District grows from its present level of 600,000. Then, if the District were to have voting power in the Electoral College equal to its population, it would have at least one additional elector. Republicans in Congress, however, have resisted modifying this provision, as well as giving the District a voting member (or members) of Congress, in part because the District is one of the most heavily Democratic areas of the nation. In 2008, for example, more than 90 percent of the District's residents voted for Barack Obama.

CRITICAL THINKING QUESTIONS

1. Should the Electoral College continue to play a role in the selection of the president? Why or why not?
2. What reforms could be enacted to make the Electoral College a more democratic institution?
3. Should the District of Columbia have representation in the Electoral College equal to its population? Why or why not?

nor Andrew Jackson secured a majority of electoral votes, throwing the election into the House. Although Jackson had more electoral and popular votes than Adams, the House selected the latter as president. In the 1876 contest between Republican Rutherford B. Hayes and Democrat Samuel J. Tilden, no candidate received a majority of electoral votes; the House decided in Hayes's favor even though he had 250,000 fewer popular votes than Tilden. In the election of 1888, President Grover Cleveland secured about 100,000 more popular votes than did Benjamin Harrison, yet Harrison won a majority of the Electoral College vote, and with it the presidency.

No further Electoral College crises have occurred. However, the 2000 presidential election once again brought the Electoral College to the forefront of voters' minds. Throughout the 2000 presidential campaign, many analysts foresaw that the election would likely be the closest since the 1960 race between John F. Kennedy and Richard M. Nixon. Few observers realized, however, that the election would be so close that the winner would not be officially declared for more than five weeks after Election Day. And, no one could have predicted that the Electoral College winner, George W. Bush, would lose the popular vote and become president after the Supreme Court's controversial decision in *Bush* v. *Gore* (2000) stopped a recount of votes cast in Florida. With the margin of the Electoral College results so small (271 for Bush, 267 for Gore), a Gore victory in any number of closely contested states could have given him a majority in the Electoral College.

Congressional Elections

⭐ **12.6** . . . **Explain the incumbency advantage in congressional elections.**

Compared with presidential elections, congressional elections receive scant national attention. Unlike major-party presidential contenders, most candidates for Congress labor in relative obscurity. There are some celebrity nominees for Congress—television stars, sports heroes, and even local TV news anchors. The vast majority of party nominees for Congress, however, are little-known state legislators and local office holders who receive remarkably limited coverage in many states and communities. For them, just establishing name identification in the electorate is the biggest battle.

How was the 1876 presidential election resolved? This cartoon from the 1876 presidential contest between Republican Rutherford B. Hayes and Democrat Samuel J. Tilden describes the frustration of many Americans with interpreting the constitutional procedures for resolving Electoral College disputes. An electoral commission formed by Congress to decide the matter awarded all disputed electors to Hayes, giving him the victory even though he had lost the popular vote by a 51-48 percent margin.

Photo courtesy: The Granger Collection, New York

THE ELECTORAL VOTE.
Now let us look at it from another point of view.

The Incumbency Advantage

The current system enhances the advantages of **incumbency,** or already holding an office. Those people in office tend to remain in office. In a "bad" year such as the Republican wave of 2010, "only" 87 percent of House incumbents won reelection. Senatorial reelection rates can be much more mercurial. In 2006, only 79 percent of senators seeking reelection were victorious. In 2010, 90 percent of incumbents were reelected. To the political novice, these reelection rates might seem surprising, as public trust in government and satisfaction with Congress has remained remarkably low during the very period that reelection rates have been on the rise. To understand the nature of the incumbency advantage it is necessary to explore its primary causes: staff support, visibility, and the "scare-off" effect.

incumbency
Already holding an office.

STAFF SUPPORT   Members of the U.S. House of Representatives are permitted to hire eighteen permanent and four nonpermanent aides to work in their Washington and district offices. Senators typically enjoy far larger staffs, with the actual size determined by the number of people in the state they represent. Both House and Senate members also enjoy the additional benefits provided by the scores of unpaid interns who assist with office duties. Many of the activities of staff members directly or indirectly promote the legislator through constituency services, the wide array of assistance provided by a member of Congress to voters in need. Constituent service may include tracking a lost Social Security check, helping a veteran receive disputed benefits, or finding a summer internship for a college student. Having a responsive constituent service program contributes strongly to incumbency. Research has shown that if a House incumbent's staff helped to solve a problem for a constituent, that constituent rated the incumbent more favorably than constituents who were not assisted by the incumbent,[21] therefore providing the incumbent a great advantage over any challenger.

VISIBILITY   Most incumbents are highly visible in their districts. They have easy access to local media, cut ribbons galore, attend important local funerals, and speak frequently at meetings and community events. Moreover, convenient schedules and generous travel allowances increase the local availability of incumbents. Nearly a fourth of the people in an average congressional district claim to have met their representative, and about half recognize their legislator's name without prompting. This visibility has an electoral payoff, as research shows district attentiveness is at least partly responsible for incumbents' electoral safety.[22]

THE "SCARE-OFF" EFFECT   Research also identifies an indirect advantage of incumbency: the ability of the office holder to fend off challenges from strong opposition candidates, something scholars refer to as the "scare-off" effect.[23] Incumbents have the ability to scare off high-quality challengers because of the institutional advantages of office, such as high name recognition, large war chests, free constituent mailings, staffs attached to legislative offices, and overall experience in running a successful campaign. Potential strong challengers facing this initial uphill battle will often wait until the incumbent retires rather than challenge him or her.[24]

Why Incumbents Lose

While most incumbents win reelection, in every election cycle some members of Congress lose their positions to challengers. There are four major reasons these members lose their reelection bids: redistricting, scandals, presidential coattails, and midterm elections.

REDISTRICTING   At least every ten years, state legislators redraw congressional district lines to reflect population shifts, both in the state and in the nation at large. This very political process may be used to secure incumbency advantage by creating "safe" seats for members of the majority party in the state legislature. But, it can also be used to punish incumbents in the out-of-power party. Some incumbents can be put in the same districts as other incumbents, or other representatives' base of political support can be weakened by adding territory favorable to the opposition party. The number of incumbents who actually lose their reelection bids because of redistricting is lessened by the strategic behavior of redistricted members—who often choose to retire rather than wage an expensive reelection battle.[25] (To learn more about redistricting, see **chapter 6**.)

SCANDALS   Scandals come in many varieties in this age of investigative journalism. The old standby of financial impropriety has been supplemented by other forms of career-ending incidents, such as sexual improprieties. Incumbents implicated in scandals typically do not lose reelections—because they simply choose to retire rather than face defeat.[26] Representative Eric Massa (D–NY), for example, resigned from office in

2010 after accusations of sexual harassment and impropriety with staff members. His seat remained vacant until the November elections, when it was filled by Tom Reed (R–NY).

PRESIDENTIAL COATTAILS The defeat of a congressional incumbent can also occur as a result of presidential coattails. Successful presidential candidates usually carry into office congressional candidates of the same party in the year of their election. The strength of the coattail effect has, however, declined in modern times, as party identification has weakened and the powers and perks of incumbency have grown. Whereas Harry S Truman's party gained seventy-six House seats and nine additional Senate seats in 1948, Barack Obama's party gained only twenty-one House members and eight senators in 2008. (To learn more about presidents' electoral influence, see Table 12.2).

MIDTERM ELECTIONS Elections in the middle of presidential terms, called **midterm elections,** present a threat to incumbents of the president's party. Just as the presidential party usually gains seats in presidential election years, it usually loses seats in off years. The problems and tribulations of governing normally cost a president some popularity, alienate key groups, or cause the public to want to send the president a message of one sort or another. A presidential scandal or economic downturn can underline and expand this circumstance, as the Watergate scandal of 1974 and the recession of 1982 demonstrated. In 2010, the economy once again led to the defeat of incumbents in a midterm election. Democratic incumbents, in particular, lost in record numbers while most Republicans were reelected. All in all, Democrats lost more seats than either party has in an election since 1938.

Most apparent is the tendency of voters to punish the president's party much more severely in the sixth year of an eight-year presidency, a phenomenon associated with retrospective voting. After only two years, voters may still be willing to "give the guy a chance," but after six years, voters are often restless for change.

midterm election
An election that takes place in the middle of a presidential term.

Table 12.2 *How does the president affect congressional elections?*

	Gain (+) or Loss (–) for President's Party[a]				
	Presidential Election Years			**Midterm Election Years**	
President/Year	House	Senate	Year	House	Senate
Truman (D): 1948	+76	+9	1950	−29	−6
Eisenhower (R): 1952	+24	+2	1954	−18	−1
Eisenhower (R): 1956	−2	0	1958	−48	−13
Kennedy (D): 1960	−20	−2	1962	−4	+3
L. Johnson (D): 1964	+38	+2	1966	−47	−4
Nixon (R): 1968	+7	+5	1970	−12	+2
Nixon (R): 1972	+13	−2	*Ford* (R): 1974	−48	−5
Carter (D): 1976	+2	0	1978	−15	−3
Reagan (R): 1980	+33	+12	1982	−26	+1
Reagan (R): 1984	+15	−2	1986	−5	−8
Bush (R): 1988	−3	−1	1990	−9	−1
Clinton (D): 1992	−10	0	1994	−52	−9[b]
Clinton (D): 1996	+10	−2	1998	+5	0
G. W. Bush (R): 2000	−2	−4	2002	+6	+2
G. W. Bush (R): 2004	+3	+4	2006	−30	−6
Obama: 2008	+21	+8	2010	−60[c]	−6

[a] Gains and losses are the difference between the number of seats won by the president's party and the number of seats won by that party in the previous election.

[b] Includes the switch from Democrat to Republican of Alabama U.S. Senator Richard Shelby one day after the election.

[c] As of mid-November 2010, seven House races were still undecided. They are not included in this calculation.

Senate elections are less inclined to follow these off-year patterns than are House elections. The idiosyncratic nature of Senate contests is due to their intermittent scheduling (only one-third of the seats come up for election every two years) and the existence of well-funded, well-known candidates who can sometimes swim against whatever political tide is rising.

TOWARD REFORM: Voter Choice and Turnout

★ **12.7 . . . Assess the effects of several factors that affect voter turnout and voter choice.**

Research on voting behavior seeks primarily to explain two phenomena: Voter choice (that is, what factors lead a person to choose one candidate over another) and voter turnout (what factors contribute to an individual's decision to vote or not vote).

Patterns in Vote Choice

A number of factors affect citizens' choices about which candidate to support. Party affiliation and ideology are at the forefront of these predictors. Other important factors are income and education, race and ethnicity, gender, religion, and political issues. (To learn more about patterns of vote choice, see Figure 12.3.)

Figure 12.3 *How do demographic characteristics affect citizens' vote choice?*
Source: www.cnn.com/ELECTION/2008/results/polls.main/.

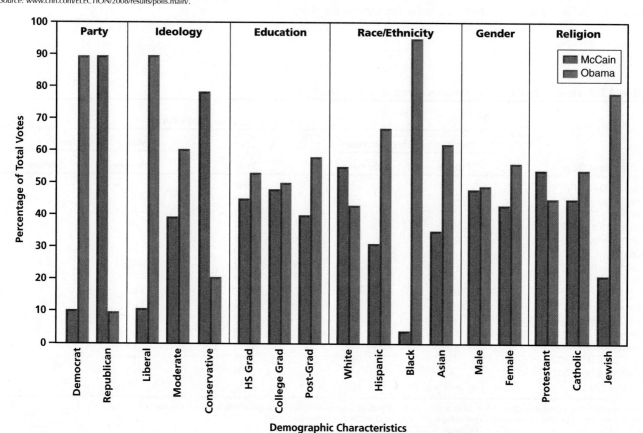

PARTY IDENTIFICATION   Party identification remains the most powerful predictor of vote choice. Stated simply, self-described Democrats tend to vote for Democratic candidates and self-described Republicans tend to vote for Republican candidates. This trend is particularly obvious in less-visible elections, where voters may not know anything about the candidates and need a cue to help them cast their ballot. However, even in presidential elections, there is a high correlation between vote choice and party affiliation. In 2008, for example, 89 percent of self-identified Democrats voted for Senator Barack Obama, and 90 percent of self-identified Republicans voted for Senator John McCain.

IDEOLOGY   Ideology represents one of the most significant divisions in contemporary American politics. Not surprisingly, ideology is very closely related to vote choice. Liberals tend to vote for Democrats, and conservatives tend to vote for Republicans. In 2008, 89 percent of self-described liberals voted for Barack Obama, whereas only 10 percent voted for John McCain. Conservatives, on the other hand, voted for McCain over Obama at a rate of 79 to 20 percent.[27]

INCOME AND EDUCATION   Over the years, income has been a remarkably stable correlate of vote choice. The poor vote more Democratic; the well-to-do vote heavily Republican.[28] The 2008 election was, to some extent, consistent with these trends. Sizeable majorities of those making less than $50,000 annually supported Obama, with 70 percent of those making less than $15,000 annually leading the way. All other income classes were a virtual toss-up, with Obama and McCain each carrying between 46 and 52 percent of the electorate. It can be said, however, that McCain, as the Republican candidate, performed better with voters in middle-class and high-income brackets than he did with poorer voters.

Since income and education are highly correlated—more educated people tend to make more money—it should be no surprise that education follows a somewhat similar pattern. The most educated and the least educated citizens tend to vote Democratic, and those in the middle—for example, with a bachelor's degree—tend to vote Republican.

RACE AND ETHNICITY   Racial and ethnic groups tend to vote in distinct patterns. While whites have shown an increasing tendency to vote Republican, African American voters remain overwhelmingly Democratic in their voting decisions. Despite the best efforts of the Republican Party to garner African American support, this pattern shows no signs of waning. In 2008, Barack Obama's candidacy accelerated this trend, and 95 percent of African Americans voted for him. John McCain received a mere 4 percent of the African American vote.[29]

Hispanics also tend to identify with and vote for Democrats, although not as monolithically as do African Americans. In 2008, for example, Obama received 67 percent of the votes cast by Hispanics; McCain received only 31 percent.

Asian and Pacific Island Americans are more variable in their voting than either the Hispanic or African American communities. It is worth noting the considerable political diversity within this group: Chinese Americans tend to prefer Democratic candidates, but Vietnamese Americans, with strong anti-communist leanings, tend to support Republicans. In the 2008 election, 62 percent of Asian American voters supported Obama and 35 percent of Asian American voters supported McCain.

GENDER   Since 1980, the gender gap, the difference between the voting choices of men and women, has become a staple of American politics. In general, women are more likely to support Democratic candidates and men are more likely to support Republicans. The size of the gender gap varies considerably from election to election, though normally the gender gap is between 5 and 7 percentage points. That is, women support the average Democrat 5 to 7 percent more than men. In 2008, Barack Obama won 56 percent of the female vote, but only 49 percent of the male vote.[30]

RELIGION   Religious groups also have tended to vote in distinct patterns, but some of these traditional differences have declined considerably in recent years. The most cohesive of religious groups has been Jewish voters, a majority of whom have voted for every Democratic presidential candidate since the New Deal realignment. In 2008, 78 percent of Jewish voters supported Senator Barack Obama.

In contrast, Protestants are increasingly Republican in their vote choice. This increase in support owes largely to the rise of social conservatives, as well as the Republican emphasis on personal responsibility.[31] In 2008, 54 percent of Protestants supported Senator John McCain. Republican support is even stronger among evangelical Protestants. Among those voters who self-identified as "born again," 74 percent supported McCain.

Catholic voters are a much more divided group. Historically, Catholic voters tended to identify with the Democratic Party and its support of social justice issues and anti-poverty programs. But, since the 1970s and the rise of the abortion issue, Catholic voters have supported Republican candidates in larger numbers. In the last several presidential elections, the Catholic vote has alternated party support. In 2004, 52 percent of Catholic voters supported Republican President George W. Bush. In 2008, 54 percent of Catholic voters supported Democratic candidate Obama.

ISSUES   In addition to the underlying influences on vote choice discussed above, individual issues can have important effects in any given election year. One of the most important driving forces is the state of the economy.[32] Voters tend to reward the party in government, usually the president's party, during good economic times and punish the party in government during periods of economic downturn. When this occurs, the electorate is exercising **retrospective judgment;** that is, voters are rendering judgment on the party in power based on past performance on particular issues, in this case the economy. At other times, voters might use **prospective judgment;** that is, they vote based on what a candidate pledges to do about an issue if elected.

retrospective judgment
A voter's evaluation of a candidate based on past performance on a particular issue.

prospective judgment
A voter's evaluation of a candidate based on what he or she pledges to do about an issue if elected.

turnout
The proportion of the voting-age public that casts a ballot.

Voter Turnout

Turnout is the proportion of the voting-age public that casts a ballot. In general, all citizens who are age eighteen or older are eligible to vote. States add a number of different regulations to limit the pool of eligible voters, such as restricting felons' participation and requiring voter identification. Voter turnout in the United States is much lower than in other industrialized democracies. Only 40 to 45 percent of the eligible adult population in the United States votes regularly. An additional 25 percent are occasional voters, and 35 percent rarely or never vote. Some of the factors known to influence voter turnout include income and education, race and ethnicity, gender, age, civic engagement, and interest in politics.

INCOME AND EDUCATION   A considerably higher percentage of citizens with annual incomes over $65,000 vote than do citizens with incomes under $35,000. Wealthy citizens are more likely than poor ones to think that the system works for them and that their votes make a difference. In contrast, lower-income citizens often feel alienated from politics, possibly believing that conditions will remain the same no matter who holds office.

As with vote choice, income and education are highly correlated; a higher income is often the result of greater educational attainment. Thus, all other things being equal, college graduates are much more likely to vote than those with less education, and people with advanced degrees are the most likely to vote.

RACE AND ETHNICITY   Despite substantial gains in voting rates among minority groups, especially African Americans, race remains an important factor in voter participation. Whites still tend to vote more regularly than do African Americans, Hispanics, and other minority groups. Several factors help to explain these persistent differences. One reason is the relative income and educational levels of the two racial groups. African Americans tend to be poorer and to have less formal education than whites; as mentioned earlier, both of these factors affect voter turnout. Significantly, though, highly educated and wealthier African Americans are more likely to vote than whites of similar backgrounds.[33] Another explanation focuses on the long-term consequences of the voting barriers that African Americans historically faced in the United States, especially in areas of the Deep South. As discussed in **chapter 5,** in the wake of Reconstruction, the southern states made it extremely difficult for African Americans to register to vote, and only a small percentage of the eligible African American population was registered throughout the South until the 1960s. The Voting Rights Act (VRA) of 1965 helped to change this situation by targeting states that once used literacy or morality tests or poll taxes to exclude minorities from the polls. The act bans any voting device or procedure that interferes with a minority citizen's right to vote, and it requires approval for any changes in voting qualifications or procedures in certain areas where minority registration is not in proportion to the racial composition of the district. It also authorizes the federal government to monitor all elections in areas where discrimination was found to be practiced or where less than 50 percent of the voting-age public was registered to vote in the 1964 election. As a result of the VRA and other civil rights reforms, turnout among African Americans has increased dramatically. (To learn more about the relationship between race and voter turnout, see Figure 12.4).

The Hispanic community in the United States is now slightly larger in size than the African American community; thus, Hispanics have the potential to wield enormous political power. However, turnout among Hispanics is much lower than turnout among whites and African Americans. In 2008, Hispanics comprised almost 13 percent of the U.S. population but only 7.4 percent of those who turned out to vote.

GENDER   With the passage of the Nineteenth Amendment in 1920, women gained the right to vote in the United States. While early polling numbers are not reliable enough to shed light on the voting rate among women in the years immediately following their entry into the voting process, it is generally accepted that in the period following ratification of the Nineteenth Amendment, women voted at a lower rate than men. Recent polls suggest that today women vote at a slightly higher rate than their male counterparts. Since women comprise slightly more than 50 percent of the U.S. population, they now account for a majority of the American electorate.

AGE   A strong correlation exists between age and voter turnout. The Twenty-Sixth Amendment to the Constitution, ratified in 1971, lowered the voting age to eighteen. While this amendment obviously increased the number of eligible voters, it did so by enfranchising the group that is least likely to vote. A much higher percentage of citizens age thirty and older vote than do citizens younger than thirty, although voter turnout decreases over the age of seventy, primarily due to difficulties some older voters have getting to their

Figure 12.4 *How has the racial and ethnic composition of voters changed?*

Source: Pew Research Center, "Dissecting the 2008 Electorate: Most Diverse in U.S. History," April 30, 2009. pewresearch.org/pubs/1209/racial-ethnic-voters-presidential-election.

polling locations. Regrettably, only 70 percent of eligible eighteen- to twenty-nine-year-olds are even registered to vote.[34] The most plausible reason for this is that younger people are more mobile; they have not put down roots in a community. Because voter registration is not automatic, people who relocate have to make an effort to register. As young people marry, have children, and settle down in a community, their likelihood of voting increases.[35]

CIVIC ENGAGEMENT　Individuals who are members of civic organizations, trade and professional organizations, and labor unions are more likely to vote and participate in politics than those who are not members of these or similar types of groups. People who more frequently attend church or other religious services, moreover, also are more likely to vote than people who rarely attend or do not belong to religious institutions.

Many of these organizations emphasize community involvement, which often encourages voting and exposes members to requests from political parties and candidates for support. These groups also encourage participation by providing opportunities for members to develop organizational and communication skills that are relevant for political activity. Union membership is particularly likely to increase voting turnout among people who, on the basis of their education or income, are less likely to vote.[36]

INTEREST IN POLITICS　People who are highly interested in politics constitute only a small minority of the U.S. population. The most politically active Americans—party and issue-group activists—make up less than 5 percent of the country's more than 300 million people. Those who contribute time or money to a party or a candidate during a campaign make up only about 10 percent of the total adult population. Although these percentages appear low, they translate into millions of Americans who are reliable voters and also contribute more than just votes to the system.

Why Don't Americans Turn Out?

There are many reasons why people may choose not to participate in elections. Non-participation may be rooted in something as complicated as an individual's political philosophy, or something as simple as the weather—voter turnout tends to be lower on rainy Election Days. Here, we discuss some of the most common reasons for nonvoting: other commitments, difficulty of registration, difficulty of absentee balloting, the number of elections, voter attitudes, and the weakened influence of political parties.

OTHER COMMITMENTS　According to the U.S. Census Bureau, 17.5 percent of registered nonvoters reported in 2008 that they did not vote because they were too busy or had conflicting work or school schedules. Another 14.9 percent said they did not vote because they were ill, disabled, or had a family emergency. While these reasons account for a large portion of the people surveyed, they also reflect the respondents' desire not to seem uneducated about the candidates and issues or apathetic about the political process. Although some would-be voters are undoubtedly busy, infirm, or otherwise unable to make it to the polls, it is likely that many of these nonvoters are offering an easy excuse and have another reason for failing to vote.

DIFFICULTY OF REGISTRATION　A major reason for lack of participation in the United States remains the relatively low percentage of the adult population that is registered to vote. Requiring citizens to take the initiative to register to vote is an American invention; nearly every other democratic country places the burden of registration on the government rather than on the individual. Thus, the cost (in terms of time and effort) of registering to vote is higher in the United States than it is in other industrialized democracies.

The National Voter Registration Act of 1993, commonly known as the Motor Voter Act, was a significant national attempt to ease the bureaucratic hurdles associated with registering to vote. The law required states to provide the opportunity to register through driver's license agencies, public assistance agencies, and the mail. Researchers estimate that this law has increased voter registration by 5 to 9 percent, and some scholars hypothesize that the law is at least partially responsible for the increases in voter participation experienced in recent elections.

DIFFICULTY OF ABSENTEE VOTING Stringent absentee ballot laws are another factor affecting voter turnout in the United States. Many states, for instance, require citizens to apply in person for absentee ballots, a burdensome requirement given that a person's inability to be present in his or her home state is often the reason for absentee balloting in the first place.

What does an absentee ballot look like? This absentee ballot from the state of Virginia was used during the 2008 presidential election.

Photo courtesy: Saul Loeb/AFP/ Getty Images

NUMBER OF ELECTIONS Another explanation for low voter turnout in the United States is the sheer number and frequency of elections. According to a study by the International Institute for Democracy and Electoral Assistance, the United States typically holds twice as many national elections as other Western democracies, a consequence of the relatively short two-year term of office for members of the House of Representatives.[37] American federalism, with its separate elections at the local, state, and national levels, and its use of primary elections for the selection of candidates, also contributes to the number of elections in which Americans are called on to participate.

VOTER ATTITUDES Voter attitudes also affect the low rates of voter turnout observed in the United States. Some voters are alienated, and others are just plain apathetic, possibly because of a lack of pressing issues in a particular year, satisfaction with the status quo, or uncompetitive elections. Furthermore, many citizens may be turned off by the quality of campaigns in a time when petty issues and personal mudslinging are more prevalent than ever.

WEAKENED INFLUENCE OF POLITICAL PARTIES Political parties today are not as effective as they once were in mobilizing voters, ensuring that they are registered, and getting them to the polls. As we discussed in **chapter 11**, the parties once were grassroots organizations that forged strong party–group links with their supporters. Today, candidate- and issue-centered campaigns and the growth of expansive party bureaucracies have resulted in somewhat more distant parties with which fewer people identify very strongly. While efforts have been made in recent elections to bolster the influence of parties, in particular through sophisticated get-out-the-vote efforts, the parties' modern grassroots activities still pale in comparison to their earlier efforts.

TIMELINE: Recent Developments in Voting

1988   **Early Voting**—Texas is the first state to enact legislation allowing citizens to vote several weeks before Election Day.

1995   **Vote By Mail**— Oregon becomes the first state to hold an election entirely by mail.

2000   **Presidential Election Controversy**—Difficulty counting and certifying votes in Florida draws attention to the need for improvements in voting technology.

1993   **Motor Voter**—The law is intended to facilitate easier voter registration; it requires citizens to be able to register in all public buildings.

Photo courtesy: Tim Boyle/Newsmakers/Getty Images

Ways to Improve Voter Turnout

Reformers have proposed a number of institutional reforms to increase voter turnout in the United States. These include making Election Day a holiday, easing constraints on voter registration, allowing mail and online voting, modernizing the ballot, and strengthening political parties.

MAKE ELECTION DAY A HOLIDAY   Since elections traditionally are held on Tuesdays, the busy workday is an obstacle for many would-be voters. Some reformers have, therefore, proposed that Election Day should be a national holiday. This strategy might backfire, however, if people used the day off to extend vacations or long weekends.

ENABLE EARLY VOTING   In an attempt to make voting more convenient for citizens who may have other commitments on Election Day, thirty-four states (largely in the West, Midwest, and South) currently allow voters to engage in a practice known as early voting. Early voting allows citizens to cast their ballot up to a month before the election—the time frame varies by state—either by mail or at a designated polling location. Critics of early voting, however, charge that the method decreases the importance of the campaign. They also fear that voters who cast early ballots may later come to regret their choices.

PERMIT MAIL AND ONLINE VOTING   Reformers have also proposed several voting methods citizens could do from their own homes. For example, Oregon, Washington, and some California counties vote almost entirely by mail-in ballots. These systems have been credited with increasing voter turnout rates in those states. But, voting by mail has its downside. There are concerns about decreased ballot security and increased potential for fraud with mail-in elections.

2002 **Help America Vote Act**—Federal government enacts legislation designed to help states modernize voting equipment.

2008 **Record Turnout**—Voter turnout in the 2008 presidential election reaches its highest level in more than 40 years.

2006 **Electronic Voting**—The use of electronic voting machines reaches an all-time high; nearly 40 percent of Americans cast ballots using this technology.

2010 **Internet Voting**—Military members and their families living abroad are permitted to use the Internet to cast ballots in the midterm elections.

Some states, including Arizona and Michigan, also use Internet voting to cast ballots in primary elections. In addition, military members and their families from thirty-three states used Internet voting to cast absentee ballots in the 2010 elections.[38] However, Internet voting booths have been slow to catch on with the general public because many voters are suspicious of the security of this method and worry about online hackers and an inability to prevent voter fraud.

MAKE REGISTRATION EASIER Registration laws vary by state, but in most states, people must register prior to Election Day. In the nine states that permit Election Day registration, however, turnout has averaged about 11 percentage points higher in recent elections than in other states, supporting the long-held claim by reformers that voter turnout could be increased if registering to vote were made simpler for citizens.[39]

MODERNIZE THE BALLOT Following the 2000 election, when the outcome of the presidential election in Florida, and by extension the nation, hinged on "hanging chads"—punch-card ballots that had not been fully separated—legislators and other observers called for reforms to modernize the ballot. The federal government even enacted the Help America Vote Act (HAVA) to aid states in upgrading voting equipment.

States and localities have made significant changes in the types of ballots they use as a result of the HAVA. More traditional voting methods such as paper and punch-card ballots (similar to the ballots used in Major League Baseball All-Star balloting) are used in less than 10 percent of jurisdictions today. Most voters use optical-scan sheets (similar to the Scantrons or "bubble sheets" used in many college classes) or electronic voting machines.

Supporters of electronic voting believe that emphasis must be placed on training poll workers, administrators, and voters on how to effectively use the new equipment. Critics believe that the lack of a paper trail leaves electronic machines vulnerable to fraud and worry that the machines could crash during an election. Still other critics cite the expense of the machines. All, however, agree that updating election equipment and ensuring fair elections across the country should be a legislative priority.

STRENGTHEN PARTIES   Reformers have long argued that strengthening the political parties would increase voter turnout, because parties have historically been the organizations in the United States most successful at mobilizing citizens to vote. The challenge is how to go about enacting reforms that strengthen parties. One way, for example, would be to allow political parties to raise and spend greater sums of money during the campaign process. Such a reform, however, raises ethical questions about the role and influence of money in politics. Another potential change would be to enact broader systemic reforms that allow for a multiparty system and facilitate greater party competition. But, these reforms would be very difficult to pass into law.

What Should I Have LEARNED?

Now that you have read this chapter, you should be able to:

★ 12.1 Trace the evolution of political campaigns in the United States, p. 342.

In modern campaigns, there is a predictable pathway toward office that involves nomination and general election campaign strategy. At the nomination phase, it is essential for candidates to secure the support of party identifiers, interest groups, and political activists. In the general election, the candidates must focus on the voters and defining their candidacy in terms acceptable to a majority of voters in the district or state.

★ 12.2 Assess the role of candidates and their staff in the campaign process, p. 343.

The candidate makes appearances, meets voters, raises funds, holds press conferences, gives speeches, and is ultimately responsible for conveying the campaign message and for the success of the campaign. The candidate relies on a campaign manager, professional staff, and political consultants to coordinate the strategy and message of his or her campaign. Volunteer support is also particularly important for mobilizing citizens and getting out the vote.

★ 12.3 Evaluate the ways campaigns raise money, p. 346.

Since the 1970s, campaign financing has been governed by the terms of the Federal Election Campaign Act (FECA). This act was amended in 2002 by the Bipartisan Campaign Reform Act (BCRA). BCRA regulates political advertising and funding from a number of sources from which campaigns raise money, including individuals, political parties, political action committees (PACs), member PACs, personal savings, and public funds. Recently, the Supreme Court has begun to chip away at some of the key tenets of the act. In 2010, the Court in

Citizens United v. *FEC* declared unconstitutional BCRA's ban on electioneering communications made by corporations and unions, likely opening the way for an increase in the power of interest groups and corporations in campaigns and elections.

★ 12.4 Identify the ways campaigns use the media to reach potential voters, p. 351.

Candidates and campaigns rely on three main strategies for reaching voters: traditional media coverage (newspapers, magazines, television, and radio), new media coverage (Internet, blogs, social networking sites), and paid campaign advertisements. Traditional media coverage is the most difficult for candidates to control.

★ 12.5 Describe the electoral procedures used in presidential elections, p. 354.

No U.S. election can compare to the presidential contest held every four years. The parties select presidential candidates through either primary elections or caucuses, with the primary process culminating in each party's national convention, after which the general election campaign begins. The American political system uses indirect electoral representation in the form of the Electoral College.

★ 12.6 Explain the incumbency advantage in congressional elections, p. 359.

In congressional elections, incumbents have a strong advantage over their challengers because of staff support, the visibility they get from being in office, and the "scare-off" effect. Redistricting, scandals, presidential coattails, and midterm elections serve as countervailing forces to the incumbency advantage and are the main sources of turnover in Congress.

⭐ **12.7 Assess the effects of several factors that affect voter turnout and voter choice, p. 363.**

Democrats, liberals, those who are poor or uneducated, African Americans, women, younger Americans, and Jews tend to vote Democratic. Republicans, conservatives, those who are wealthy and moderately educated, whites, men, older Americans, and Protestants tend to vote Republican. Voter turnout is higher, however, among citizens who are white, older, more educated, have higher incomes, belong to civic organizations, and attend religious services more frequently. There are several reasons why Americans do not vote, including other commitments, difficulty registering to vote, difficulty voting by absentee ballot, the number of elections, voter attitudes, and the weakened influence of political parties.

Test Yourself: Campaigns, Elections, and Voting

⭐ **12.1 Trace the evolution of political campaigns in the United States, p. 342.**

One of the primary dangers of the nomination campaign is that
A. candidates can become overly cautious and not talk about issues.
B. many candidates ignore their ideological base.
C. candidates may raise too much money.
D. candidates may attract too much media coverage.
E. candidates can become too extreme.

⭐ **12.2 Assess the role of candidates and their staff in the campaign process, p. 343.**

The head of a political campaign is usually called the
A. campaign consultant.
B. political manager.
C. campaign manager.
D. political strategist.
E. political insider.

⭐ **12.3 Evaluate the ways campaigns raise money, p. 346.**

Most candidates receive a majority of their campaign contributions from
A. individuals.
B. PACs.
C. one of the political parties.
D. a combination of parties and PACs.
E. foreign corporations.

⭐ **12.4 Identify the ways campaigns use the media to reach potential voters, p. 351.**

One of the strategies that campaigns use to control the media is
A. making the candidate more available to the press.
B. staging media events.
C. ignoring negative campaign events.
D. appearing on the major networks' nightly news shows.
E. holding unrehearsed, spontaneous press conferences.

⭐ **12.5 Describe the electoral procedures used in presidential elections, p. 354.**

The most party-centered way of nominating a presidential candidate is
A. proportional primaries.
B. delegates.
C. conventions.
D. winner-take-all primaries.
E. caucuses.

⭐ **12.6 Explain the incumbency advantage in congressional elections, p. 359.**

Which of the following is NOT an explanation for why many incumbents lose reelection?
A. Redistricting
B. Partisanship
C. Scandals
D. Presidential coattails
E. Midterm elections

⭐ **12.7 Assess the effects of several factors that affect voter turnout and voter choice, p. 363.**

The most powerful predictor of vote choice is
A. age.
B. party identification.
C. gender.
D. race.
E. ethnicity.

Essay Questions
1. Why is the candidate so important in the modern campaign?
2. How did *Citizens United* v. *FEC* (2010) change campaign financing in the United States?
3. What are some of the observable patterns in vote choice? How do these patterns affect electoral outcomes?

myp◉liscilab Exercises

Apply what you learned in this chapter on MyPoliSciLab.

◫─Read on **mypoliscilab.com**

eText: Chapter 12

✔●─Study and **Review** on **mypoliscilab.com**

Pre-Test
Post-Test
Chapter Exam
Flashcards

◉─Watch on **mypoliscilab.com**

Video: Candidates Court College Students
Video: Money in the 2008 Presidential Race
Video: Dissecting Party Primaries
Video: State Primary Race
Video: Who are the Super Delegates?

⊕─Explore on **mypoliscilab.com**

Simulation: You Are a Campaign Manager: Lead Obama to Battleground State Victory
Simulation: You Are a Campaign Manager: McCain Navigates Campaign Financing
Simulation: You Are a Media Consultant to a Political Candidate
Simulation: You Are a Campaign Manager: Countdown to 270!
Simulation: You Are Redrawing the Districts in Your State
Simulation: You Are an Informed Voter Helping Your Classmates Decide How to Vote
Comparative: Comparing Political Campaigns
Timeline: Television and Presidential Campaigns
Timeline: Close Calls in Presidential Elections
Visual Literacy: Iowa Caucuses
Visual Literacy: The Electoral College: Campaign Consequences and Mapping the Results
Visual Literacy: Voting Turnout: Who Votes in the United States

Key Terms

campaign consultant, p. 345
campaign manager, p. 345
communications director, p. 345
contrast ad, p. 354
elector, p. 356
Electoral College, p. 356
finance chair, p. 345
501(c) group, p. 351
527 political committee, p. 351
front-loading, p. 355
general election, p. 343

general election campaign, p. 343
get-out-the-vote (GOTV), p. 346
hard money, p. 347
incumbency, p. 359
inoculation ad, p. 354
matching funds, p. 350
midterm election, p. 361
negative ad, p. 354
nomination campaign, p. 342
political action committee (PAC), p. 349
pollster, p. 346

positive ad, p. 354
press secretary, p. 345
primary election, p. 342
prospective judgment, p. 364
public funds, p. 350
reapportionment, p. 356
retrospective judgment, p. 364
soft money, p. 347
turnout, p. 364
voter canvass, p. 346

To Learn More About Campaigns, Elections, and Voting

In the Library

Campbell, Angus, Philip E. Converse, Warren E. Miller, and Donald E. Stokes. *The American Voter*, reprint ed. Chicago: University of Chicago Press, 1980.

Campbell, James E. *The American Campaign: U.S. Presidential Campaigns and the National Vote*, 2nd ed. College Station: Texas A&M University Press, 2008.

Gelman, Andrew. *Red State, Blue State, Rich State, Poor State: Why Americans Vote the Way They Do*, expanded ed. Princeton, NJ: Princeton University Press, 2009.

Green, Donald P., and Alan S. Gerber. *Get Out the Vote: How to Increase Voter Turnout*, 2nd ed. Washington, DC: Brookings Institution, 2008.

Heilemann, John, and Mark Halperin. *Game Change: Obama and the Clintons, McCain and Palin, and the Race of a Lifetime*. New York: Harper, 2010.

Herrnson, Paul S. *Congressional Elections: Campaigning at Home and in Washington*, 5th ed. Washington, DC: CQ Press, 2007.

Jacobson, Gary C. *The Politics of Congressional Elections*, 7th ed. New York: Longman, 2008.

Leighley, Jan E., ed. *The Oxford Handbook of American Elections and Political Behavior.* New York: Oxford University Press, 2010.

Lewis-Beck, Michael S., Helmut Norpoth, William G. Jacoby, and Herbert F. Weisberg. *The American Voter Revisited*. Ann Arbor: University of Michigan Press, 2008.

Sabato, Larry J. *Get in the Booth! A Citizen's Guide to the 2010 Elections.* New York: Longman, 2011.

Skewes, Elizabeth A. *Message Control: How News Is Made on the Presidential Campaign Trail*. Lanham, MD: Rowman and Littlefield, 2007.

Streb, Matthew J. *Rethinking American Electoral Democracy*, 2nd ed. New York: Routledge, 2011.

Trent, Judith S., and Robert V. Friedenberg. *Political Campaign Communication: Principles and Practices*, 6th ed. Westport, CT: Praeger, 2008.

Vavreck, Lynn. *The Message Matters: The Economy and Presidential Campaigns.* Princeton, NJ: Princeton University Press, 2009.

West, M. Darrell. *Air Wars: Television Advertising in Election Campaigns 1952–2008*, 5th ed. Washington, DC: CQ Press, 2009.

On the Web

To learn more about the 2010 U.S. political campaigns, go to *Politico* at **www.politico.com/2010/.**

To learn more about presidential campaign commercials, go to the Living Room Candidate at **www.livingroomcandidate.org.**

To learn more about elections, go to CNN at **www.cnn.com/elections.**

To learn more about voting, go to Project Vote Smart at **www.vote-smart.org.**

13

Social and Economic Policy

After seven years as president, George W. Bush appeared to be presiding over an almost unprecedented economic boom. For fifty-two straight months, the number of jobs available in the United States grew, and unemployment averaged only 5.2 percent. National debt—except for that incurred by the Iraq War—was relatively low, and the gross domestic product was rising. Housing investments, too, were gaining value at tremendous rates.

But, below the surface were some troubling signs. An influx of competitively priced goods led many U.S. companies to relocate factories to nations with lower production costs, such as Mexico, China, India, and Pakistan. These and other relocations had a destabilizing effect on domestic industry. In addition, the economic boom had produced a huge demand for housing, fueled in part by low interest rates. High-risk (subprime) mortgages were

extended to first-time homebuyers and others living beyond their means. And, with economic optimism running high, personal savings rates declined to historic lows, while personal debt rose.

The collusion of these forces soon had negative consequences for even the best of economic indicators. In 2008, approximately 2.6 million people lost their jobs, as large companies downsized and many smaller companies struggled to stay in business. Oil and other commodity prices began to rise rapidly—gasoline prices reached four and even five dollars per gallon in some jurisdictions. These forces combined to push the housing market, the unstable debt markets, and the broader economy—both at home and abroad—into crisis.

Realizing the severity of the economic situation, in February 2008, the Bush

PUTTING AMERICA TO WORK

PROJECT FUNDED BY THE
American Recovery
and
Reinvestment Act

RECOVERY.GOV

STATE OF OHIO
DEPARTMENT OF TRANSPORTATION

The government often takes a prominent role in stimulating the economy. At left, John Maynard Keynes, the father of modern macroeconomic theory, which favors government spending to promote economic growth, speaks at a conference in the 1940s. At right, a sign advertises a road construction project funded by the 2009 American Recovery and Reinvestment Act, an example of Keynesian economics.

administration, along with Congress, announced a $168 billion federal stimulus package to provide Americans with tax rebates and relief intended to help boost consumer demand and reduce economic hardship. But, these efforts were insufficient, and the financial meltdown worsened. The collapse of many financial institutions as a result of the subprime mortgage crisis in September 2008 led Congress to pass the Temporary Assets Relief Program (TARP), an approximately $700 billion bailout of the financial industry.

Although these efforts took great strides to preserve American savings and loan companies, they did little to help average citizens. To address these concerns, in February 2009, President Barack Obama signed the $787 billion American Recovery and Reinvestment Act, designed to cut taxes and create jobs through deficit spending. Among the programs funded by the Recovery Act were road and bridge construction projects, scientific research, and the expansion of Internet access to underserved populations.

Despite these efforts, economic recovery for many individual Americans continues to be slow. By November 2010, unemployment hovered around 10 percent nationally, and the Democratic Party paid the consequences at the ballot box.

Still, it is clear that government has played an important role in helping capitalism recover from its shortcomings.

What Should I Know About . . .

After reading this chapter, you should be able to:

★ **13.1** Trace the stages of the policy-making process, p. 376.

★ **13.2** Describe the evolution of health policy in the United States, p. 382.

★ **13.3** Describe the evolution of income security policy in the United States, p. 387.

★ **13.4** Assess the impact of the budget process on fiscal policy, p. 392.

★ **13.5** Analyze the effect of the Federal Reserve System on monetary policy, p. 394.

★ **13.6** Evaluate the role of public policy in the economic recession and recovery, p. 397.

public policy
An intentional course of action or inaction followed by government in dealing with some problem or matter of concern.

Public policy is an intentional course of action or inaction followed by government in dealing with some problem or matter of concern.[1] Public policies are thus governmental policies; they are authoritative and binding on people. Individuals, groups, and even government agencies that do not comply with policies can be penalized through fines, loss of benefits, or even jail terms. The phrase "course of action" implies that policies develop or unfold over time. They involve more than a legislative decision to enact a law or a presidential decision to issue an executive order. Also important is how the law or executive order is carried out. The impact or meaning of a policy depends on whether it is vigorously enforced, enforced only in some instances, or not enforced at all.

This chapter discusses the policy-making process and examines how it has played out in four domestic and economic policy areas—health care, income security, fiscal policy, and monetary policy. We will thus explore the following topics:

- First, we will examine *the roots of public policy* and *the policy-making process*.

- Second, we will investigate *the evolution of health policy* in the United States, including Medicare, Medicaid, health insurance, and public health.

- Third, we will trace the evolution of *income security policy* from its foundations to today.

- Fourth, we will investigate *fiscal policy,* including its foundations, the impact of globalization, and the budget process.

- Fifth, we will look at the elements of *monetary policy,* including the Federal Reserve System.

- Finally, we will assess the *recession and economic recovery* as it relates to health, income security, fiscal, and monetary policies.

ROOTS OF Public Policy: The Policy-Making Process

⭐ **13.1 . . . Trace the stages of the policy-making process.**

Political scientists and other social scientists have developed many theories and models to explain the formation of public policies. Here, we present a popular model used to describe the policy-making process that views it as a sequence of stages or functional activities. One illustration of such a model is shown in Figure 13.1. This model can be used to analyze any of the issues discussed in this book. Although models such as these can be useful, it is important to remember that they are simplifications of the actual process. Moreover, models for analyzing the policy-making process do not always explain *why* public policies take the specific forms that they do. Nor do models necessarily tell us *who* dominates or controls the formation of public policy.

Policy making typically can be thought of as a process of sequential steps:

1. *Problem recognition.* Identification of an issue that disturbs the people and leads them to call for governmental intervention.

2. *Agenda setting.* Government recognition that a problem is worthy of consideration for governmental intervention.

Figure 13.1 *What are the stages of the public policy process?*
One of the best ways to understand public policy is to examine the process by which policies are made. Although there are many unique characteristics of policy making at the various levels of government, there are commonalities that define the process from which public policies emerge. In the figure, the public policy process is broken down into seven steps. Each step has distinguishing features, but it is important to remember that the steps often merge into one another in a less distinct manner.

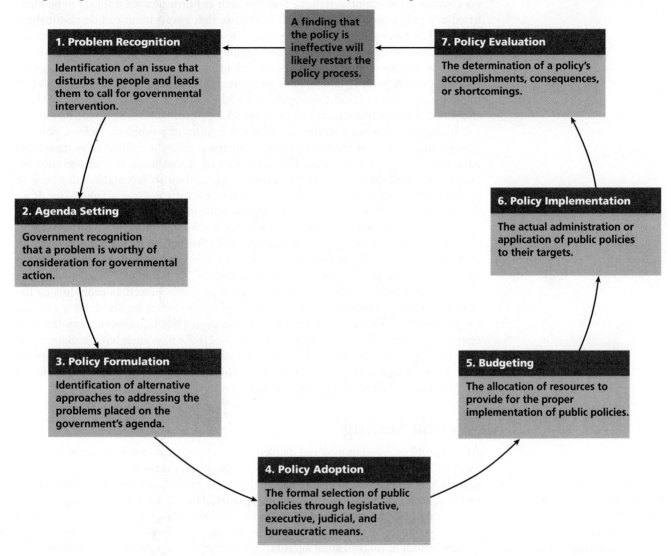

3. *Policy formulation.* Identification of alternative approaches to addressing the problems placed on government's agenda.

4. *Policy adoption.* The formal selection of public policies through legislative, executive, judicial, and bureaucratic means.

5. *Budgeting.* The allocation of resources to provide for the proper implementation of public policies.

6. *Policy implementation.* The actual administration or application of public policies to their targets.

7. *Policy evaluation.* The determination of a policy's accomplishments, consequences, or shortcomings.

With this overview in mind, we examine the various stages of the policy process or cycle.

Problem Recognition and Definition

For a condition to become a problem, there must be some criterion—a standard or value—that leads people to believe that the condition does not have to be accepted and, further, that it is something with which government can deal effectively and appropriately. For example, natural disasters such as hurricanes are unlikely to be identified as a policy problem because there is little that government can do about them directly. The consequences of hurricanes—the human distress and property destruction that they bring—are another matter. Relief from the devastation of natural disasters can be a focus of government action, and agencies such as the Federal Emergency Management Agency (FEMA) have been created to reduce these hardships. When these agencies fail to fulfill their roles, as FEMA did in the wake of Hurricane Katrina in 2005, the public requires answers for why government has not done its job.

Usually there is not a single, agreed-on definition of a problem. Indeed, political struggle often occurs at this stage because how the problem is defined helps determine what sort of action is appropriate. For example, if we define access to transportation for people with disabilities as a transportation problem, then an acceptable solution is to establish other means of transport for disabled citizens, such as a special van service. If we define access to transportation as a civil rights problem, however, then people with disabilities are entitled to equal access to the regular transportation system. The civil rights view triumphed with congressional passage of the Americans with Disabilities Act in 1990, which mandated that local and state governments must make transportation accessible to the elderly and to all people with disabilities.

Note that public policies themselves are frequently viewed as problems or the causes of other problems. Thus, for some people, gun control legislation is a solution to gun violence. To the National Rifle Association (NRA), however, any law that restricts gun ownership is a problem because the NRA views such laws as inappropriately infringing on an individual's constitutional right to keep and bear arms. To social conservatives, legal access to abortion is a problem; for social liberals, laws restricting abortion access fall into the problem category.

Agenda Setting

agenda
A set of issues to be discussed or given attention.

systemic agenda
A discussion agenda; it consists of all public issues that are viewed as requiring governmental attention.

governmental (institutional) agenda
Problems to which public officials feel obliged to devote active and serious attention.

agenda setting
The constant process of forming the list of issues to be addressed by government.

After a problem is recognized and defined as such by a significant segment of society, it must be brought to the attention of public officials and it must secure a place on an **agenda,** or a set of issues to be discussed or given attention. Every political community—national, state, and local—has a **systemic agenda.** The systemic agenda is essentially a discussion agenda; it consists of all issues that are viewed as requiring public attention and as involving matters within the legitimate jurisdiction of governments.[2] A **governmental** or **institutional agenda,** in contrast, is much narrower. It includes only problems to which public officials feel obliged to devote active and serious attention. Not all problems that attract the attention of officials are likely to have been widely discussed by the general public, and not all issues on the systemic agenda end up on the institutional agenda. Issues may move from the systemic agenda to the governmental agenda and vice versa in an almost limitless number of ways. This movement is known as **agenda setting.** Whether because of their influence or skill in developing political support, some people or groups are more successful than others in steering items onto the governmental agenda. Among the most notable—though certainly not the only—agenda-setters are the president, interest groups, and political crises.

Policy Formulation

policy formulation
The crafting of proposed courses of action to resolve public problems.

Policy formulation is the crafting of proposed courses of action to resolve public problems. It has both political and technical components. The political aspect of policy formulation involves determining generally what should be done to address a problem. The technical facet involves correctly stating in specific language what one wants to authorize or accomplish, in order to adequately guide those who must implement policy and to prevent distortion of legislative intent.[3]

Policy formulation may take many forms:

1. *Routine formulation* is the process of altering existing policy proposals or creating new proposals within an issue area the government has previously addressed. For instance, the formulation of policy for veterans' benefits is routine.

2. *Analogous formulation* handles new problems by drawing on experience with similar problems in the past or in other jurisdictions. What has been done in the past to cope with the activities of terrorists? What has been done in other states to deal with child abuse or divorce law reform?

3. *Creative formulation* involves attempts to develop new or unprecedented proposals that represent a departure from existing practices and that will better resolve a problem. For example, plans to develop an anti-missile defense system to shoot down incoming missiles represent a departure from previous defense strategies of mutual destruction.

Policy formulation may be undertaken by various players in the policy process: the president, presidential aides, agency officials, specially appointed task forces and commissions, interest groups, private research organizations (or "think tanks"), and legislators and their staffs. The people engaged in formulation are usually looking ahead toward policy adoption. Particular provisions may be included or excluded from a proposal in an attempt to enhance its likelihood of adoption. To the extent that formulators think in this strategic manner, the formulation and adoption stages of the policy process often overlap. (To learn more about what entities the Framers thought would be responsible for policy formulation, see The Living Constitution: Article I, Section 1.)

Policy Adoption

Policy adoption is the approval of a policy proposal by the people with requisite authority, such as a legislature or chief executive. This approval gives the policy legal force. Because most public policies in the United States result from legislation, policy adoption frequently requires building a series of majority coalitions necessary to secure the enactment of legislation in Congress. To secure the needed votes, a bill may be watered down or modified at any point in the legislative process (see **chapter 6**). Or, the bill may fail to win a majority at one of them and die, at least for the time being.

The tortuous nature of congressional policy adoption has some important consequences. First, complex legislation may require substantial periods of time in order to pass. Second, the legislation passed is often incremental, making only limited or marginal changes in existing policy. Third, legislation is frequently written in general or ambiguous language, as in the Clean Air Act, which provided amorphous instructions to administrators in the Environmental Protection Agency to set air quality standards that would allow for an "adequate margin of safety" to protect the public health. Phrases such as "adequate margin" are highly subjective and open to a wide range of interpretations. Language such as this may provide considerable discretion to the people who implement the law and also leave them in doubt as to its intended purposes.

Budgeting

Most policies require funding in order to be carried out; some policies, such as those providing income security, essentially involve the transfer of money from taxpayers to the government and back to individual beneficiaries. Funding for most policies and agencies is provided through the congressional budget process (discussed later in this chapter). Whether a policy is well funded, poorly funded, or funded at all has a significant effect on its scope, impact, and effectiveness. For example, as a result of limited funding, the Occupational Safety and Health Administration (OSHA) can inspect

policy adoption
The approval of a policy proposal by the people with the requisite authority, such as a legislature.

The Living Constitution

All legislative Powers herein granted shall be vested in a Congress of the United States, which shall consist of a Senate and House of Representatives.

—ARTICLE I, SECTION 1

Article 1, section 1 of the Constitution vests the law-making power in the hands of the legislative branch of government because the Framers believed that Congress, with its large and diverse membership, was a much lesser threat to tyranny than the executive branch. The judicial branch, the Framers felt, was little more than a theoretical necessity and would be the "least dangerous branch."

Today, Congress retains its law-making power and does a great deal of public policy formulation and adoption. But, it is by no means the only source of public policy in the national government. The president, for example, has the power to make public policy by using executive orders. President Barack Obama has used these orders to make policy on subjects such as abortion, foreign policy, energy, and stem cell research.

The bureaucracy is also an important policy-maker. Through a quasi-legislative process known as rule-making, executive branch agencies formulate and implement policies in nearly every imaginable issue area. Rules, in fact, are the largest source of policy decisions made by the national government.

Even the judicial branch, which the Framers thought would be essentially powerless, has evolved into an important source of policy decisions. In recent years the Supreme Court has made policy prescriptions in each of the domestic policy issue areas discussed in this chapter, as well as in criminal justice, civil liberties, and civil rights.

CRITICAL THINKING QUESTIONS

1. Should the legislative branch be the only branch of the national government allowed to make policy decisions? Why or why not?
2. What changes in the last 250 years have led the executive and judicial branches to take larger roles in the policy-making process?
3. Do these interventions in the policy process strengthen or weaken the checks and balances in the system devised by the Framers? Explain your answer.

annually only a small fraction of the workplaces within its jurisdiction. Similarly, the Department of Housing and Urban Development has funds sufficient to provide rent subsidies only to approximately 20 percent of eligible low-income families.

The budgetary process also gives the president and the Congress an opportunity to review the government's many policies and programs, to inquire into their administration, to appraise their value and effectiveness, and to exercise some influence on their conduct. Not all of the government's thousands of programs are fully examined every year. But, over a period of several years, most programs come under scrutiny.

Policy Implementation

policy implementation
The process of carrying out public policy.

Policy implementation is the process of carrying out public policies, most of which are implemented by administrative agencies. Some policies, however, are enforced in other ways. Voluntary compliance by businesses and individuals is one such technique. Examples of this practice include when grocers take out-of-date products off their shelves or when consumers choose not to buy food products after their expiration dates. The courts also get involved in implementation when they are called on to interpret the meaning of legislation, review the legality of agency rules and actions, and determine whether institutions such as prisons and mental hospitals conform to legal and constitutional standards.

Administrative agencies may be authorized to use a number of techniques to implement the public policies within their jurisdictions. These techniques can be categorized as authoritative, incentive, capacity, or hortatory, depending on the behavioral assumptions on which they are based.[4]

1. *Authoritative techniques* for policy implementation rest on the notion that people's actions must be directed or restrained by government in order to prevent or eliminate activities or products that are unsafe, unfair, evil, or immoral. For example, consumer products must meet certain safety regulations, and radio stations can be fined heavily or have their broadcasting licenses revoked if they broadcast obscenities.

2. *Incentive techniques* for policy implementation encourage people to act in their own best interest by offering payoffs or financial inducements to get them to comply with public policies. Such policies may provide tax deductions to encourage charitable giving or the purchase of alternative fuel vehicles such as hybrid automobiles. Farmers also receive subsidies to make their production (or nonproduction) of wheat, cotton, and other goods more profitable. Conversely, sanctions such as high taxes may discourage the purchase and use of such products as tobacco or liquor, and pollution fees may reduce the discharge of pollutants by making this action more costly to businesses.

3. *Capacity techniques* provide people with information, education, training, or resources that enable them to participate in desired activities. The assumption underlying these techniques is that people have the incentive or desire to do what is right but lack the capacity to act accordingly. Job training may enable able-bodied people to find work, and accurate information on interest rates will enable people to protect themselves against interest-rate gouging.

4. *Hortatory techniques* encourage people to comply with policy by appealing to people's "better instincts" in an effort to get them to act in desired ways. In this instance, policy implementers assume that people decide how to act according to their personal values and beliefs. During the Reagan administration, First Lady Nancy Reagan implored young people to "Just say no" to drugs. Hortatory techniques also include the use of highway signs displaying slogans like "Don't Be a Litterbug" and "Don't Mess with Texas" to discourage littering.

Often government will turn to a combination of authoritative, incentive, capacity, and hortatory approaches to reach their goals. For example, public health officials employ all of these tools in their efforts to reduce tobacco use. These techniques include laws prohibiting smoking in public places, taxes on the sales of tobacco products, warning labels on packs of cigarettes, and anti-smoking commercials on television. There is no easy formula that will guarantee successful policy implementation; in practice, many policies only partially achieve their goals.

Policy Evaluation

Practitioners of **policy evaluation** seek to determine whether a course of action is achieving its intended goals. They may also try to determine whether a policy is being fairly or efficiently administered. Policy evaluation may be conducted by a variety of players, including congressional committees, presidential commissions, administrative agencies, the courts, university researchers, private research organizations, and the Government Accountability Office (GAO).

The GAO, created in 1921, conducts hundreds of studies of government agencies and programs each year, either at the request of members of Congress or on its own initiative. The titles of two of its 2010 evaluations convey a notion of the breadth of its work: "Military Readiness: Navy Needs to Reassess its Metrics and Assumptions

policy evaluation
The process of determining whether a course of action is achieving its intended goals.

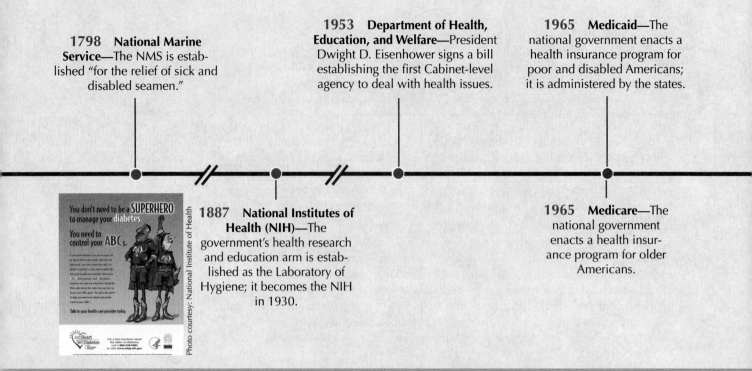

1798   National Marine Service—The NMS is established "for the relief of sick and disabled seamen."

1953   Department of Health, Education, and Welfare—President Dwight D. Eisenhower signs a bill establishing the first Cabinet-level agency to deal with health issues.

1965   Medicaid—The national government enacts a health insurance program for poor and disabled Americans; it is administered by the states.

Photo courtesy: National Institute of Health

1887   National Institutes of Health (NIH)—The government's health research and education arm is established as the Laboratory of Hygiene; it becomes the NIH in 1930.

1965   Medicare—The national government enacts a health insurance program for older Americans.

for Ship Crewing Requirements and Training" and "USDA Crop Disaster Programs: Lessons Learned Can Improve Implementation of New Crop Assistance Program."

Evaluation research and studies can stimulate attempts to modify or terminate policies and thus restart the policy process. Legislators and administrators may formulate and advocate for amendments designed to correct problems or shortcomings in a policy. In 2006, for example, the national legislation establishing the Medicare program was amended to create a prescription drug benefit for senior citizens, known as Medicare Part D. Policies may also be terminated as a result of the evaluation process; for example, through the Airline Deregulation Act of 1978, Congress eliminated the Civil Aeronautics Board and its program of economic regulation of commercial airlines. This action was taken on the assumption that competition in the marketplace would better protect the interests of airline users. Competition indeed reduced the cost of flying on many popular routes.

The demise of programs is relatively rare; more often, a troubled program is modified or allowed to limp along because it provides a popular service. For example, the nation's passenger rail system, Amtrak, remains dependent on government funds. Although its northeastern lines are financially self-sufficient, many of Amtrak's longer distance routes are not able to operate without significant government subsidies. Nevertheless, the more rural routes remain popular with legislators in western states, and thus Amtrak continues to receive government support.[5]

The Evolution of Health Policy

⭐ **13.2** . . . Describe the evolution of health policy in the United States.

Governments in the United States have long been active in the health care field. Beginning in 1798 with the establishment of the National Marine Service (NMS) for "the relief of sick and disabled seamen," the national government has provided health

2006   Medicare Part D—This program creates an optional prescription drug insurance program for senior citizens.

1979   Department of Health and Human Services (HHS)—Under President Jimmy Carter, the Department of Health, Education, and Welfare is split into two Cabinet-level departments, HHS and Education.

2010   Health Insurance Reform—President Barack Obama and the Democratic Congress enact legislation creating a national health insurance program.

care for some segments of the population. Local governments began to establish public health departments in the first half of the nineteenth century, and state health departments followed in the second half. Discoveries related to the causes of diseases and human ailments in the late nineteenth and early twentieth centuries led to significant advances in improving public health. Public sanitation and clean-water programs, pasteurization of milk, immunization programs, and other activities greatly reduced the incidence of infectious and communicable diseases. Public health policies have also been highly effective in reducing the incidence of infectious diseases such as measles, infantile paralysis (poliomyelitis), and smallpox. The increase in American life expectancy from forty-seven in 1900 to over seventy-eight in 2010 is tightly linked to public health programs.

Today, many millions of people receive medical care through the medical branches of the armed forces, the hospitals and medical programs of the Department of Veterans Affairs, and the Indian Health Service. The government estimated that it would spend $78 billion in the 2010 fiscal year for health and human services, the construction and operation of facilities, and the salaries of doctors and other medical personnel.[6]

The national government's involvement in health policy extends to a number of other areas. In the 1960s, the government began funding health programs for senior citizens and the poor, known as Medicare and Medicaid, respectively. And, in 2010, the Democratic Congress passed and President Barack Obama signed into law the Patient Protection and Affordable Care Act, which expanded the federal government's role in the provision of health insurance.

Medicare

Medicare, which was created by Congress and Democratic President Lyndon B. Johnson in 1965, covers persons who are disabled or over age 65. It is administered by the Centers for Medicare and Medicaid Services in the Department of Health and

Medicare
The federal program established during the Lyndon B. Johnson administration that provides medical care to older Americans.

Human Services. Medicare is financed by a payroll tax of 1.45 percent paid by both employees and employers on the total amount of one's wages or salary. In 2014, this tax will increase to 3.8 percent for Americans making more than $200,000 per year. Medicare coverage has four components: Parts A, B, C, and D. Benefits under Part A are granted to all Americans automatically at age sixty-five, when they qualify for Social Security. It covers hospitalization, some skilled nursing care, and home health services.

Part B, which is optional, covers payment for physicians' services, outpatient and diagnostic services, X-rays, and some other items not covered by Part A. Excluded from coverage are eyeglasses, hearing aids, and dentures. This portion of the Medicare program is financed partly by monthly payments from beneficiaries and partly by general tax revenues.

Medicare Part C programs are also known as Medicare Advantage programs. They are administered by private insurance companies and provide coverage that meets or exceeds the coverage of traditional Medicare programs. Medicare Advantage programs may also include additional services for a fee, such as prescription drug coverage and dental and vision insurance.

Medicare Part D is the optional prescription drug benefit that went into effect in 2006. Participants pay a monthly premium of approximately $35; after a $250 annual deductible, 75 percent of their prescription costs are covered. For those whose annual prescription drug costs exceed $5,100, the program pays 95 percent of prescription costs over that amount.

Today, Medicare provides health insurance coverage for more than 45 million Americans. Roughly 20 percent of these enrollees choose Medicare Advantage programs. More than half of Medicare enrollees also choose to take advantage of the Medicare prescription drug benefit.

Medicaid

Medicaid
A government program that subsidizes medical care for the poor.

Medicaid, a government program that subsidizes health insurance for the poor, was enacted in 1965, at the same time as Medicare. It provides health insurance coverage for low-income Americans who meet a set of eligibility requirements. To receive Medicaid benefits, citizens must meet minimum-income thresholds, be disabled, or be pregnant.

Unlike Medicare, which is financed and administered by the national government, Medicaid is a joint venture between national and state governments. The national government provides between 50 and 75 percent of the funding necessary to administer Medicaid programs (depending on state per capita income). This money is given to the states in the form of block grants. States then supplement the national funds with money from their own treasuries. They also are given the latitude to establish eligibility thresholds and the level of benefits available to citizens.

As a result, Medicaid programs vary widely from state to state. Most states provide coverage for all pregnant women and all children less than one year of age. And, in a majority of states, the income requirement is set to provide coverage to citizens with incomes up to 185 percent of the federal poverty line. This is equivalent to an income of about $18,000 for an individual or $37,000 for a family of four. In some states, all low-income residents receive Medicaid assistance, whereas in other states, only one-third of the needy are protected. And, in some states "medically indigent" people—those who do not meet traditional income requirements but have large medical expenses—receive coverage, whereas in other states, these citizens must find their own funding.

In 2009, Medicaid provided coverage for almost 50 million Americans, making it the largest government health insurance program in the United States. This program comes with a substantial price tag: more than $400 billion in national and state funds. Medicaid is also one of the largest and fastest growing portions of state budgets. In recent years, it has accounted for roughly 17 percent of state general expenditures.

Health Insurance

National health insurance was first seriously considered in the 1930s, when Congress was legislating a number of New Deal social programs. But, because of the strong opposition of the American Medical Association (AMA), universal health insurance was not adopted. The AMA and its allies were distrustful of government intervention in their affairs and fearful that regulations would limit their discretion as well as their earnings. In particular, they feared that the intrusion of government into the health care field would limit physician charges, restrict the amount of time approved for specific types of hospital visits, and constrain charges for prescription drugs.

As a result, government health insurance remained on the back burner for many years. It received some consideration during the 1960s, when Congress and the Johnson administration were working to establish Medicare and Medicaid. Health care also received a great deal of attention in the early 1990s, during the first year of President Bill Clinton's term. Clinton established a health care reform task force led by his wife, Hillary, and attempted to compel Congress to adopt legislation creating universal health coverage in the United States. Ultimately, however, these efforts failed. The phrase "socialized medicine" and horror stories about long wait times for medically necessary services in countries with nationalized health care turned public opinion against Clinton and the Democrats.

Clinton's failure at health care reform, as well as the extended period of Republican legislative control that began in 1995, kept national health insurance off the governmental agenda for the next fifteen years. During this time, health care costs and the number of uninsured Americans rose dramatically. By 2008,

---

What did the 2010 health care reform bill do? The Patient Protection and Affordable Care Act extended coverage to more than 45 million uninsured Americans. Although the implementation process has already begun, the full effects of this bill will not be felt until later this decade.

Table 13.1 *What do Americans think about health insurance reform?*

Question	Percentage of Americans Agreeing
Do these changes represent a major change in the direction of the country?	80
Do you support the changes to the health care system that have been enacted by Congress and the Obama administration?	46
Will the overall health care system get better as a result of these changes?	37
Will these changes require everyone to make changes, whether they want to or not?	60
Do you think these changes will increase the federal budget deficit?	65
Is the amount of government involvement in the nation's health care system too much?	49

Source: Washington Post poll, March 23–26, 2010. www.washingtonpost.com.

more than 45 million Americans had no health insurance coverage, and another 20 million were underinsured.

Thus, during the 2008 presidential election, Democratic candidate Barack Obama ran on a platform that promised to bring much-needed reform to the American health insurance system. After taking office, Obama and the Democratic Congress set to work crafting legislation that accomplished their goal. More than a year later—and after a great deal of political wrangling (see **chapter 6**)—on March 23, 2010, President Obama signed into law the Patient Protection and Affordable Care Act.

This legislation marked the first major change in national health policy since the adoption of Medicare and Medicaid in 1965. Its primary purpose was to establish government-run health insurance exchanges to assure that nearly all Americans would have access to health care coverage. These exchanges, which will not be fully implemented until 2014, are financed by a number of taxes and fees, most notably an increase in the Medicare tax for Americans earning more than $200,000 per year. Americans do not have to buy in to these exchanges—they have the option of retaining their private health insurance if they so choose.

The bill also includes a number of other health policy-related provisions. Between now and 2018, for example, the act will expand Medicaid eligibility and subsidize insurance premiums for low-income Americans. It also provides incentives for businesses to offer health insurance—a very costly proposition for many employers. And, importantly, it prevents health insurance companies from denying Americans coverage on the basis of preexisting conditions.

Reaction to the bill has been mixed. Large majorities of Americans believe that the legislation will lead to significant changes in the American health care system. However, only 37 percent of Americans believe that these changes will improve the system. (To learn more about public opinion on health insurance reform, see Table 13.1.)

The legislation has been especially unpopular with state governments. As many as twenty states have already sued or announced that they will sue the national government to block implementation of the policy. These states believe that the act is an infringement on states' reserved powers, which are granted to them under the Tenth Amendment of the U.S. Constitution.

Public Health

Government also plays a major role in managing the growth of both infectious and chronic disease. From AIDS to obesity, public policy makers have attempted to use government power to fight threats to the nation's health. Among the tools employed by government are immunizations, education, advertisements, and regulations. For many contagious diseases such as polio, measles, and chickenpox, the government requires young children to be immunized if they are to be enrolled in day care, preschool, or elementary school. Public health officials also use vaccines in the adult population to manage the spread of diseases such as influenza (the flu). While not requiring citizens to receive flu shots, the government recommends that high-risk groups (infants, senior citizens) receive immunizations and also subsidizes vaccines for low-income populations.

The national government also finances medical research, primarily through the National Institutes of Health (NIH). The National Cancer Institute, the National Heart, Lung, and Blood Institute, the National Institute of Allergy and Infectious Diseases, and the other NIH institutes and centers spend more than $30 billion annually on biomedical research. NIH scientists and scientists at universities, medical schools, and other research facilities receiving NIH research grants conduct the research. Most Americans accept and support extensive government spending on medical research. Congress, in fact, often appropriates more money for medical research than the president recommends.

Income Security Policy

⭐ **13.3** ... **Describe the evolution of income security policy in the United States.**

Income security programs protect people against loss of income because of retirement, disability, unemployment, or death or absence of the family breadwinner. These programs, like the health care issues we have discussed in this chapter, were not a priority for the federal government during much of its first 150 years. However, beginning with the passage of the Social Security Act as a part of the 1930s New Deal, the government began to pay greater attention to this policy area. Today, the federal government administers a range of income security programs. These policies fall into two major areas—non-means-tested programs (in which benefits are provided regardless of income) and means-tested programs (in which benefits are provided to those whose incomes fall below a designated level).

The Foundations of Income Security Policy

With the election of President Franklin D. Roosevelt in 1932, the federal government began to play a more active role in addressing hardships and turmoil that grew out of the Great Depression. An immediate challenge facing the Roosevelt administration was massive unemployment, which was viewed as having a corrosive effect on the economic well-being and moral character of American citizens. In Roosevelt's words, an array of programs to put people back to work would "eliminate the threat that enforced idleness brings to spiritual and moral stability."[7]

A more permanent legacy of the New Deal was the creation of the Social Security program. The intent of Social Security was to go beyond the various "emergency" programs such as the WPA and provide at least a minimum of economic security for all Americans. Passage of the **Social Security Act** in 1935, thus represented the beginning of a permanent welfare state in America and a dedication to the ideal of greater equity. The act consisted of three major components: (1) old-age insurance (what we now call Social Security); (2) public assistance for the needy, aged, blind, and families with dependent children (known as SSI); and, (3) unemployment insurance and compensation. Since that time, the program has been expanded to include a much greater percentage of American workers. It has also become one of the most successful government programs. In the 1930s, poverty rates were highest among the elderly. Today, seniors have the lowest rate of poverty among any age group in the United States.

Social Security Act

A 1935 law that established old age insurance; assistance for the needy, aged, blind, and families with dependent children; and unemployment insurance.

Table 13.2 *How many Americans benefit from income security programs?*

Program Population	Number of Recipients (millions)	Percentage of U.S. Population
Non-Means-Tested		
Social Security (OASDI)	50.5	16.3
Unemployment Insurance	4.6	1.5
Means-Tested		
Supplemental Security Income	7.7	2.5
Temporary Assistance for Needy Families	3.8	1.2
Supplemental Nutrition Assistance Program	39.7	12.8

Sources: Social Security Administration, www.ssa.gov; Department of Health and Human Services, acf.dhhs.gov; Food Research Action Center, www.frac.org; Veterans' Affairs, Bureau of Labor Statistics, www.bls.gov/cps.

Income Security Programs Today

Modern income security programs help a wide variety of citizens to survive in cases of unintentional loss of income. They also help disabled, elderly, and low-income citizens to make ends meet and provide a minimally decent standard of living for themselves and their families. In 2009, the poverty threshold for a four-person family unit was $22,050. (To learn more about the number of Americans who benefit from income security programs, see Table 13.2.)

Many income security programs are **entitlement programs,** government benefits that all citizens meeting eligibility criteria—such as age, income level, or unemployment—are legally "entitled" to receive. Unlike programs such as public housing, military construction, and space exploration, spending for entitlement programs is mandatory and places a substantial ongoing financial burden on the national and state governments.

Income security programs fall into two general categories. Many social insurance programs are **non-means-tested programs** that provide cash assistance to qualified beneficiaries, regardless of income. These social insurance programs operate in a manner somewhat similar to private automobile or life insurance. Contributions are made by or on behalf of the prospective beneficiaries, their employers, or both. When a person becomes eligible for benefits, they are paid as a matter of right, regardless of the person's wealth or unearned income. Among these programs are old age, survivors, and disability insurance (Social Security) and unemployment insurance.

In contrast, **means-tested programs** require that people must have incomes below specified levels to be eligible for benefits. Benefits of means-tested programs may come either as cash or in-kind benefits, such as help with finding employment or child care. Included in the means-tested category are the Supplemental Security Income (SSI) program, Temporary Assistance for Needy Families (TANF), and the Supplemental Nutrition Assistance Program (SNAP, also known as food stamps).

OLD AGE, SURVIVORS, AND DISABILITY INSURANCE As mentioned earlier, the Social Security program is a non-means-tested program that began as old-age insurance, providing benefits only to retired workers. Its coverage was extended to survivors of covered workers in 1939 and to the permanently disabled in 1956. Nearly all employees and most of the self-employed are now covered by Social Security. Americans born before 1938 are eligible to receive full retirement benefits at age sixty-five. The full retirement age gradually rises until it reaches sixty-seven for persons born in 1960 or later. In early 2010, the average monthly Social Security benefit for retired workers was $1,164 with the maximum monthly benefit set at $2,346.

entitlement programs
Government benefits that all citizens meeting eligibility criteria—such as age, income level, or unemployment—are legally "entitled" to receive.

non-means-tested programs
Programs that provide cash assistance to qualified beneficiaries, regardless of income. Among these are Social Security and unemployment insurance.

means-tested programs
Programs that require that beneficiaries have incomes below specified levels to be eligible for benefits. Among these are SSI, TANF, and SNAP.

Social Security is not, as many people believe, a pension program that collects contributions from workers, invests them, and then returns them with interest to beneficiaries. Instead, current workers pay employment taxes that go directly toward providing benefits for retirees. In 2010, for example, a tax of 7.65 percent was levied on the first $106,800 of an employee's wages and placed into the Social Security Trust Fund. An equal tax was levied on employers.

As a result of this system, in recent years, it has become increasingly apparent that the current Social Security system is on a collision course with itself. Americans are living longer and having fewer children. And, beginning in 2010, the Baby Boom generation (roughly speaking, those born in the two decades immediately following World War II) begins to retire. These factors, taken together, skew the number of working Americans per retiree, and lead the Social Security system toward financial insolvency. The trustees of the Social Security Trust Fund have estimated that—barring major policy changes—by 2017, payments to beneficiaries will exceed revenues collected from employees.

A number of proposals have been made to address these shortcomings. Among them are raising the age of eligibility for beneficiaries or increasing the Social Security tax withheld from employees. Both of these proposals have received criticism from citizens—seniors and those who are soon to retire do not want to see their benefits cut or limited, and workers do not want to pay additional taxes.

UNEMPLOYMENT INSURANCE   Unemployment insurance is a non-means-tested program financed by a payroll tax paid by employers. The program benefits full-time employees of companies of four or more people who become unemployed through no fault of their own. Benefits are not paid to unemployed workers who have been fired for personal faults or who quit their jobs, or those who are unwilling to accept suitable employment.

State governments administer unemployment insurance programs. As a result, unemployment programs differ considerably in levels of benefits, length of benefit payment, and eligibility for benefits. For example, in 2009, average weekly benefit payments ranged from less than $200 in Mississippi to almost $500 in Hawaii and Massachusetts. In general, less generous programs exist in southern states, where labor unions are less powerful. Nationwide, only about half of the people who are counted as unemployed at any given time are receiving benefits.

In May 2010, the national unemployment rate stood at 9.7 percent. But, there were considerable differences across the country. In the Dakotas and Nebraska, unemployment rates were slightly less than 5 percent, while levels of unemployment in many southern and western states such as Florida and California were over 10 percent. Unemployment rates also varied considerably across races and by age. For example, levels of unemployment for African American males were nearly twice that of whites, with unemployment rates exceeding 40 percent or greater common among young African American males. (To learn more about variations in unemployment rates, see Figure 13.2.)

SUPPLEMENTAL SECURITY INCOME   The Supplemental Security Income (SSI) program is a means-tested program that began under the Social Security Act as a government benefit for needy elderly or blind citizens. In 1950, Congress extended coverage to needy people who were permanently and totally disabled. Primary funding for SSI is provided by the national government, which prescribes minimum national benefit levels. The states may also choose to supplement national benefits, and forty-eight states take advantage of this option.

To be eligible for SSI, beneficiaries can only have limited income; the lower an individual's income, the higher their SSI payment. SSI beneficiaries may also only have a limited amount of possessions. The total of an individual's

Figure 13.2 *How do state unemployment rates vary?*
In May 2010, the national unemployment rate was 9.7 percent. However, this rate varied tremendously across the country, with the highest levels in the South and West, and the lowest levels in the Midwest.
Source: United States Department of Labor, www.dol.gov.

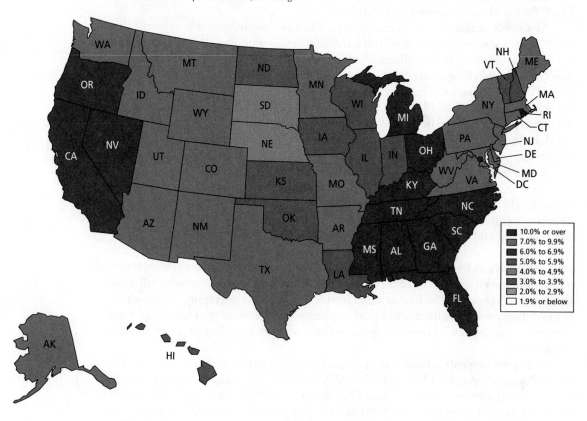

personal resources, including bank accounts, vehicles, and personal property cannot exceed $2,000. In 2010, monthly payments to eligible beneficiaries were about $500 per person.

FAMILY AND CHILD SUPPORT   The Aid to Dependent Children program is a means-tested program that was first established as part of the Social Security Act in 1935. In 1950, it was broadened to include not only dependent children without fathers but also mothers or other adults with whom dependent children were living. At this time, it was retitled the Aid to Families and Dependent Children (AFDC) program. As a result of this change and changes in the American family (including a rise in the birthrate to unwed mothers and a rise in the divorce rate), the family and child support rolls expanded significantly in the latter part of the twentieth century.

By the 1990s, the growth of this program began to attract widespread criticism from many conservatives and moderates, including Democratic President Bill Clinton. Critics pointed to the rising number of recipients and claimed that the AFDC program encouraged promiscuity, out-of-wedlock births, and dependency that resulted in a permanent class of welfare families. To restrict the availability of aid, to ferret out fraud and abuse, and to hold down cost, public officials sought to reform the program.

In what was hailed as the biggest shift in income security policy since the Great Depression, a new family and child support bill, the Personal Responsibility and Work Opportunity Reconciliation Act (PRWORA) of 1996, created the Temporary Assistance for Needy Families (TANF) program to replace AFDC. The most fundamental change enacted in the new law was the switch in funding welfare from an open-ended matching program to a block grant to the states. PRWORA also gave states more flexibility in reforming their welfare programs toward work-oriented goals.

The success of the TANF program has been widely debated. The total number of Americans receiving benefits has fallen. But, there is little evidence that the program has been successful at job training or as a means of reducing economic and social inequality. Despite these potential shortcomings, the act was reauthorized several times during the Bush administration. In 2010, it became the subject of significant political wrangling, and the scope of the program was cut, at least temporarily.

EARNED INCOME TAX CREDIT   The Earned Income Tax Credit (EITC) is a means-tested program created in 1975 at the insistence of Senator Russell Long (D–LA). The intent of the EITC was to enhance the value of working and encourage families to move from welfare to work. Advocates also claimed that the program would enhance spending, which would in turn stimulate the economy. In addition to this stimulus, supporters of the EITC had two other objectives: (1) to increase work incentives among the welfare population; and, (2) to refund indirectly part or all of the Social Security taxes paid by workers with low incomes.[8]

To claim the EITC on tax returns, a person must have earned income during the year. During 2009, an individual's earned income had to be less than $13,440 if there were no qualifying children, $35,463 with one qualifying child, and $43,279 with three or more qualifying children. In recent years, about 23 million families filing federal income tax returns (roughly one tax return in six) claimed the EITC. The success of the national EITC in reducing poverty has led twenty-four states to enact similar state tax credits.[9]

SUPPLEMENTAL NUTRITION ASSISTANCE PROGRAM   The first attempt at this means-tested program (1939–1943), which is more commonly known as food stamps, was primarily an effort to expand domestic markets for farm commodities. Food stamps provided the poor with the ability to purchase more food, thus increasing the demand for American agricultural produce. Attempts to reestablish the program during the Eisenhower administration failed, but in 1961, a $381,000 pilot program began under the Kennedy administration. It was made permanent in 1964 and extended nationwide in 1974.

The method of delivering the food stamp benefit has changed dramatically over time. For much of the program's history, the benefit was administered as actual paper coupons—quite literally, food "stamps"—given to citizens who were eligible for relief. Today, the program is administered entirely using an electronic debt program, much like an ATM card. This change in administration necessitated a formal name change for the program—from food stamps to the Supplemental Nutrition Assistance Program—in 2008. Still, this benefit continues to be an important means of assuring income security. In 2009, more than 40 million Americans received SNAP aid. The average participant received $133 worth of assistance per month. (To learn more about SNAP, see Analyzing Visuals: The Supplemental Nutritional Assistance Program.)

In addition to SNAP, the national government operates several other food programs for the needy. These programs include a special nutritional program for women,

ANALYZING VISUALS

The Supplemental Nutrition Assistance Program

The Supplemental Nutrition Assistance Program (SNAP), more popularly known as the food stamp program, provides benefits to almost 40 million Americans. The average recipient receives $133.13 a month to aid in the purchase of groceries. Citizens may spend these funds at their discretion, subject to minor limitations. Review the purchasing guidelines for SNAP recipients in the state of Alaska (which are typical of most state food stamp programs), and answer the questions.

Food Items That May Be Purchased With Food Stamp Benefits	Food Items That May Not Be Purchased With Food Stamp Benefits
■ Food or food products fit for human consumption ■ Vegetable and herb seeds ■ "Health foods" such as wheat germ, brewer's yeast, and edible seeds ■ Baby formula, diabetic, and diet foods ■ Items used for food preparation and preservation, such as pectin and shortening ■ Snack foods such as candy, chips, gum, and sodas ■ Distilled water and ice, if labeled "For Human Consumption" ■ Meals prepared for the elderly or disabled by authorized agencies	■ Items not meant to be eaten by people, such as laundry starch, pet foods, and decorative dyes ■ Items used for gardening, such as fertilizer and peat moss ■ Health aids such as aspirin and antacids ■ Therapeutic items such as vitamins and minerals ■ Items for food preparation and preservation such as pressure cookers and canning jars ■ Alcoholic beverages and tobacco ■ Nonfoods such as soap, toiletries, paper products, and utensils ■ Prepared hot foods sold in the store and ready to be eaten immediately

Source: Alaska Department of Health and Social Services, www.hss.state.ak.us/dpa/programs/fstamps/howto.html.

■ What differences exist between items that can and cannot be purchased with food stamps?
■ If you were on food stamps, what items might you buy to maximize your budget? What items that you buy today might you not be able to purchase?
■ Would your choices have any nutritional consequences?

infants, and children known as WIC; a school breakfast and lunch program; and an emergency food assistance program.

Fiscal Policy

⭐ **13.4 . . . Assess the impact of the budget process on fiscal policy.**

fiscal policy
The deliberate use of the national government's taxing and spending policies to maintain economic stability.

Fiscal policy is the deliberate use of the national government's taxing and spending policies to maintain economic stability. The president and Congress formulate fiscal policy and conduct it through the federal budget process. The powerful instruments of fiscal policy are budget surpluses and deficits. These are achieved by manipulating the overall or "aggregate" levels of revenue and expenditures.

The Budget

The primary purpose of the national budget is to fund government programs. But, manipulating the budget can also be used as a fiscal policy tool to stabilize the economy and to counteract fluctuations. National budget planning is complex and disjointed, and it begins roughly a year and a half before the beginning of the fiscal year in which it takes effect. The fiscal year begins on October 1 of one calendar year and runs through September 30 of the following calendar year. The fiscal year takes its name from the calendar year in which it ends; thus the time period from October 1, 2011, through September 30, 2012, is designated fiscal year (FY) 2012.

RAISING AND SPENDING MONEY   The national government raises money from a variety of sources, with individual income taxes and social insurance and retirement receipts representing the largest portions of the funds received. Social insurance and retirement receipts include Social Security, hospital insurance, and other taxes; they account for 40.5 percent of total receipts. Income taxes account for the remaining 43.2 percent of total federal government income.[10]

Most government spending is directed toward national defense and human resources. Defense spending consists primarily of maintaining the U.S. armed forces and developing the weapons the military needs; it accounts for 18.8 percent of the budget. Human resources include the spending categories of health, income security, and Social Security. In 2009, the human resources share of total outlays was 61.6 percent. (To learn more about federal receipts and outlays, see Figure 13.3.)

THE CONGRESSIONAL BUDGET PROCESS   The Budget and Accounting Act of 1921 gave the president authority to prepare an annual budget and submit it to Congress for approval. The act also created a staff agency now called the Office of Management and Budget (OMB) to assist the president and handle the details of budget preparation. Although the president sends a budget proposal to Congress in January or February of each year, work on the budget within the executive branch begins nine or ten months earlier. Acting in accordance with presidential decisions on the general structure of the budget, the OMB provides the various departments and agencies with instructions and guidance on presidential priorities to help them in preparing their budget requests. The departments and agencies then proceed to develop their detailed funding requests. The OMB reconciles the discrepancies between presidential and agency preferences, but it should be remembered that the OMB's mission is to defend the presidential budgetary agenda.[11]

To give itself more control over the budget process, Congress enacted the Congressional Budget Act of 1974. The act established a budget process that includes setting overall levels of revenues and expenditures, the size of the budget surplus or deficit, and priorities among different "functional" areas (for example, national defense, transportation, agriculture, foreign aid, and health). It also empowered the House and Senate to establish budget committees to perform these tasks and authorized the

Figure 13.3 *How does the federal government raise and spend money?*

Source: United States Budget, Fiscal Year 2011, www.gpoaccess.gov.

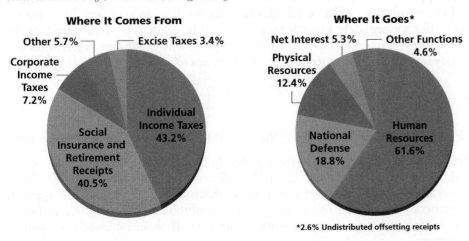

Where It Comes From

Other 5.7%

Excise Taxes 3.4%

Corporate Income Taxes 7.2%

Individual Income Taxes 43.2%

Social Insurance and Retirement Receipts 40.5%

Where It Goes*

Net Interest 5.3%

Other Functions 4.6%

Physical Resources 12.4%

Human Resources 61.6%

National Defense 18.8%

*2.6% Undistributed offsetting receipts

Congressional Budget Office (CBO), a professional staff of technical experts, to assist the budget committees and to provide members of Congress with their own source of budgetary information so they would be more independent of the OMB.

Typically, budget committees hold hearings on the president's proposed budget and set targets for overall revenue and spending and a ceiling for individual categories of spending. Other committees evaluate requests by various agencies. In most years, reconciliation legislation is necessary to ensure that targets are met. Changes in existing tax rates or benefit levels can be proposed in reconciliation bills. The reconciliation procedure also relaxes some of the Senate rules, including the filibuster. It was used in 2010 to enact the health insurance reform bill.

Legislative action on all appropriations bills is supposed to be completed by October 1, the start of the fiscal year. It is rare, however, for Congress to pass all appropriations bills by this date. For programs still unfunded at the start of the fiscal year, Congress can pass a continuing resolution, which authorizes agencies to continue operating on the basis of last year's appropriation until approval of their new budget. This procedure can cause some uncertainty in agency operations. When the president and Congress cannot agree, some programs may be shut down until the terms for a continuing resolution are worked out.

budget deficit
The economic condition that occurs when expenditures exceed revenues.

DEFICITS AND DEBT   Most states are required by constitution or by statute to have a balanced budget—revenues must meet or exceed expenditures—but this is not the norm for the federal government. The federal government rarely spends exactly as much as it raises. Instead, it usually has a budget surplus or deficit. In years when the federal government is under budget, it is said to have a budget surplus—this means that revenues have exceeded expenditures and the government has money left over.

Although the government had surpluses from 1998 to 2001, it is much more common for the federal government to have a **budget deficit,** the economic condition that occurs when expenditures exceed revenues. This is the functional equivalent of the government being "in the red." It may be the result of deficit spending to stimulate the economy, funding of costly policies such as wars or social welfare programs, tax cuts that decrease the amount of money the government receives, or some combination of all of these factors. In recent years, for example, the government has run high deficits as a result of Bush administration tax cuts, the wars in Iraq and Afghanistan, and spending on the bailout and recovery bills. In fiscal year 2010, for example, the federal government was projected to have a budget deficit of $10.6 billion.[12] Although this figure is high in absolute terms, as a percentage of GDP, it remains smaller than the deficits of the 1960s.

In the short term, budget deficits may have positive economic benefits. However, in the long term, running deficits year after year can have negative consequences. The sum of annual budget deficits is known as the national debt; in 2010, this total exceeded $13 trillion. A high national debt such as this can stifle economic growth and cause **inflation,** a rise in the general price levels of an economy. The national debt—like personal debt in the form of credit cards and student loans—must also be paid back with interest. This can be a costly proposition that diverts attention and money from other governmental programs for years to come.

inflation
A rise in the general price levels of an economy.

Monetary Policy

★ **13.5** . . . Analyze the effect of the Federal Reserve System on monetary policy.

monetary policy
A form of government regulation in which the nation's money supply and interest rates are controlled.

The government conducts **monetary policy** by managing the nation's money supply and influencing interest rates. The Federal Reserve System (informally, "the Fed"), especially its Board of Governors, handles much of the day-to-day management of monetary policy. The Fed is given a number of tools to aid its efforts, including the ability to set reserve requirements, control the discount rate, and open market operations.

The Federal Reserve System

Created in 1913 to adjust the money supply to the needs of agriculture, commerce, and industry, the Federal Reserve System comprises the Federal Reserve Board, the Federal Open Market Committee (FOMC), the twelve Federal Reserve Banks in regions throughout the country, and other member banks.[13] Typically, the **Board of Governors** of the Federal Reserve System, a seven-member board that makes most economic decisions regarding interest rates and the supply of money, dominates this process.

The president appoints (subject to Senate confirmation) the seven members of the Board of Governors, who serve fourteen-year, overlapping terms. The president can remove a member for stated causes, but this has never occurred. The president designates one board member to serve as chair for a four-year term, which runs from the midpoint of one presidential term to the midpoint of the next to ensure economic stability during a change of administrations. It also prevents monetary policy from being influenced by political considerations. The current chair, Ben Bernanke, has served since 2006 and was initially appointed by President George W. Bush. He was reappointed by President Barack Obama for a second term beginning in 2010. Prior to this appointment, he served as chair of President George W. Bush's Council of Economic Advisors. (To learn more about recent reforms to the Federal Reserve Board, see Politics Now: Bernanke: A "Big Picture" Reform Approach Needed.)

The Tools of Monetary Policy

The primary monetary policy tools are the setting of reserve requirements for member banks, control of the discount rate, and open market operations. **Reserve requirements** set by the Federal Reserve designate the portion of deposits that member banks must retain as backing for their loans. The reserves determine how much or how little banks can lend to businesses and consumers. For example, if the FRB changed the reserve requirements and allowed banks to keep $10 on hand rather than $15 for every $100 in deposits that it held, it would free up additional money for loans.

The **discount rate** is the rate of interest at which the Federal Reserve Board lends money to member banks. Lowering the discount rate encourages member banks to increase their borrowing from the Fed and extend more loans at lower rates. This expands economic activity, since when rates are lower, more people should be able to qualify for car loans or mortgages. As a consequence of cheaper interest rates, more large durable goods (such as houses and cars) should be produced and sold.

Open market operations are the buying and selling of government securities by the Federal Reserve Bank. The Federal Open Market Committee meets periodically to decide on purchases or sale of government securities to member banks. When member banks buy long-term government bonds,

Board of Governors
In the Federal Reserve System, a seven-member board that makes most economic decisions regarding interest rates and the supply of money.

reserve requirements
Government requirements that a portion of member banks' deposits be retained as backing for their loans.

discount rate
The rate of interest at which the Federal Reserve Board lends money to member banks.

open market operations
The buying and selling of government securities by the Federal Reserve Bank.

THINKING GLOBALLY

Economic Freedom

One way to evaluate how hospitable a country is to business is by looking at the rankings of countries on the Economic Freedom of the World Index prepared by the Economic Freedom Network (www.freetheworld.com). The index weights 42 different factors to assign each country an economic freedom score on a ten-point scale. As the table reveals, Hong Kong has the highest rating for economic freedom, followed by Singapore. Nations with the lowest economic freedom scores include Myanmar and Zimbabwe.

Ranking	Country	Score
1	Hong Kong	8.97
2	Singapore	8.66
6	United States	8.06
19	United Arab Emirates	7.58
39	Spain	7.32
50	Botswana/Kazakhstan	7.12
57	South Africa	7.06
68	Mexico	6.85
82	China	6.54
100	Dominican Republic	6.27
120	Ecuador	5.83
140	Myanmar	3.69
141	Zimbabwe	2.89

Source: Economic Freedom Network, "Economic Freedom of the World: 2009 Annual Report," www.freetheworld.com/2009/reports/world/EFW2009_ch1.pdf.

■ **What factors should be used to define economic freedom around the world?**

■ **What about these rankings is most and least surprising to you? How might you explain these findings?**

■ **China has one of the top five gross domestic products in the world, yet it ranks 82nd in terms of economic freedom—its index score is 6.54. How is it possible to have a large economy while simultaneously lacking a high level of economic freedom?**

POLITICS NOW

Bernanke: A "Big Picture" Reform Approach Needed

June 17, 2010
The Associated Press
www.pressherald.com

By Jeannine Aversa

The Federal Reserve is working to beef up oversight of financial companies to better protect the nation from another financial crisis in the future, Chairman Ben Bernanke said Wednesday.

The Fed chairman's comments come as Congress moves closer to sending President Obama a final legislative package that revamps the nation's financial structure to prevent a replay of the recent financial crisis.

Bernanke welcomed key parts of that package in remarks prepared for delivery to a conference in New York. At the same time, though, Bernanke emphasized that the Fed is moving ahead on its own reforms.

For instance, the Fed is working to strengthen capital requirements for banks so that they'll have bigger and better cushions to protect against any potential losses. And, the Fed is collecting more information on linkages among financial companies to better identify potential channels of financial contagion.

One of the lessons learned from the crisis is that the Fed can't focus solely on the safety and soundness of individual banks, but rather on the health of the financial system as a whole, Bernanke said. The Fed has already moved to examinations that take this broader-picture approach.

"Regulatory agencies must thus supervise financial institutions and critical infrastructures with an eye toward overall financial stability as well as the safety and soundness of each individual institution and system," Bernanke said. . . .

Bernanke embraced provisions contained in both the Senate- and House-passed financial overhaul measures that would create a council of regulators—which includes the Fed—to police for risky practices that could endanger the financial system. Concentrating all such powers within a single agency, he said, could create "regulatory blind spots." . . .

Bernanke also welcomed provisions in the House and Senate bills that would allow for the safe dismantling of a big financial firm, whose failure could put the economy in jeopardy. The mechanism is similar to how the Federal Deposit Insurance Corp. shutters failing banks.

Critical Thinking Questions

1. How do these reforms expand and contract the power of the Federal Reserve Board?
2. Should the government have the power to dismantle failing financial firms? Why or why not?
3. What additional changes need to be made to the government's involvement in the economy in order to forestall another financial crisis?

Who is the chair of the Federal Reserve Board? Fed Chairman Ben Bernanke served as chair of the Council of Economic Advisors before assuming his current role.

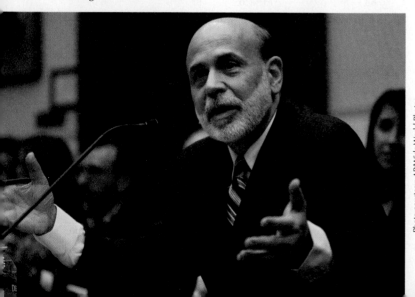

Photo courtesy: AP/Wide World Photos

they make dollar payments to the Fed and reduce the amount of money available for loans. Fed purchases of securities from member banks in essence give the banks an added supply of money. This action increases the availability of loans and should decrease interest rates. Decreases in interest rates stimulate economic activity.

In addition to these formal tools, the FRB can also use "moral suasion" to influence the actions of banks and other members of the financial community by suggestion, exhortation, and informal agreement. Because of its commanding position as a monetary policy maker, the media, economists, and market observers pay attention to verbal signals about economic trends and conditions emitted by the FRB and its chair.

TOWARD REFORM: Recession and Economic Recovery

⭐ **13.6** . . . Evaluate the role of public policy in the economic recession and recovery.

As discussed in the opening vignette, by 2008, it became increasingly clear that the extended period of American **economic stability**—a situation in which there is economic growth, rising national income, high employment, and steadiness in the general level of prices—was quickly coming to an end. Rising unemployment and government expenditures, coupled with a collapsing mortgage industry, created a severe economic downturn. By the end of 2008, this downturn had become a full-blown **recession,** a decline in the economy that occurs as investment sags, production falls off, and unemployment increases.

The national government identified this crisis situation quickly and took a number of actions using fiscal, monetary, and income security policies to attempt to restart economic growth and stimulate the economy. We consider the ways the government used each of these policies in turn.

Health and Income Security Policies

The worsening economic conditions and rising unemployment have put pressure on the national and state governments to expand social welfare programs in the areas of health and income security. Passage of the Patient Protection and Affordable Care Act, for example, constitutes a broad, national intervention into the health care realm. National and state governments also face significant pressure to continue to administer income security programs, even as their rolls grow rapidly. The number of enrollees in the Supplemental Nutrition Assistance Program, for example, has reached record levels. In the state of Michigan, one in every eight residents is enrolled in the program.[14] Economists, furthermore, estimate that there are thousands more Americans who are eligible for the program but have not enrolled.

The most severe consequences of this growth are for state budgets and the national deficit and debt. Recall that states must have balanced budgets—the amount of revenues must be equal to or greater than expenditure levels. Thus, as the rolls for programs such as unemployment insurance and food stamps rise, state costs to administer these programs—and therefore, projected expenditures—rise rapidly. At the same time, however, state revenues in the form of income and sales taxes decline as a result of fewer workers and lower consumer spending. This combination has placed great pressure on state governments. Many states have had to find creative ways to raise revenue or make large budget cuts in other areas in order to make ends meet.

For its part, the federal government has engaged in deficit spending in order to fund these social welfare programs, as well as to help states balance their budgets. The costs of these expenditures will not be fully realized for years, as the nation faces a growing national debt and the threat of economic instability from owing large sums of money to creditors. As the economy recovers, the federal government will also have to deal with questions regarding the financial insolvency of Social Security and other programs, and it will have to address concerns about the rising cost of health care.

A quick review of the increase in health care costs over the past forty years helps to demonstrate the magnitude of the problem. In 1970, Americans spent about $356 per capita on health care costs. But, by 2009, Americans were spending $8,160 per person on health care costs—almost 23 times 1970 levels. These levels far exceed the rate of inflationary growth and are projected to continue to rise to more than $13,000 per capita by 2018.

economic stability
A situation in which there is economic growth, rising national income, high employment, and steadiness in the general level of prices.

recession
A decline in the economy that occurs as investment sags, production falls off, and unemployment increases.

The rising cost of health care is a serious governmental problem for a number of reasons. First, under the Patient Protection and Affordable Care Act of 2010, at least some of these health care costs will be shouldered by or through the government's insurance exchanges when they are fully implemented in 2014. Second, these rising costs coupled with the rising number of beneficiaries and shrinking number of workers are projected to produce budget shortfalls for the Medicare program as soon as 2020.

Fiscal Policy

At the first signs of an economic slowdown in early 2008, the national government acted quickly to stimulate the economy and attempt to reinvigorate consumer spending through the use of fiscal policy. The first of these government actions was to fund a $168 billion stimulus package that included individual tax rebates for most people who had paid taxes for tax year 2007. These payments were designed to encourage lower- and middle-income people to spend money. Most citizens who received a check got $600 if they filed individually, or $1,200 if they filed jointly. There were increasing incentives for dependent children, and decreasing incentives for wealthy Americans. (To learn more about these stimulus payments, see Join the Debate: Do Economic Stimulus Payments Help the Economy?)

But, in late September 2008, it became clear that, despite the government's attempts to stimulate the economy through tax cuts, economic conditions had worsened. The collapse of the subprime mortgage industry had escalated into a full-blown financial crisis necessitating government action. To address this situation, the Bush administration proposed a $700 billion federal bailout package. The plan was intended to reassure the financial markets by allowing the government to buy up the assets that had led to the crisis. This was known as the Troubled Asset Relief Program (TARP) and the monies as TARP funds.

The first version of the bailout plan failed to gather enough votes in the House of Representatives, forcing frenzied rounds of House and Senate negotiation. Efforts were made to make the plan more palatable to politicians up for reelection who were facing constituents overwhelmingly opposed to using taxpayer funds for bailing out Wall Street. President George W. Bush, members of his administration, and congressional leaders sought to present the financial bailout plan as an economic rescue plan. They emphasized the extent to which financial collapse on Wall Street and virtually frozen credit markets would affect the ability of those on Main Street to do business, refinance their homes, or buy a car. As a result of these efforts, Congress passed a modified version of the administration's initial bailout plan known as the Emergency Economic Stabilization Act in October 2008. It provided enhanced oversight of the Treasury Department's use of the $700 billion, an option to use the money to buy equity stakes in faltering banks, some protection to those in danger of losing their homes, and a variety of tax cuts and incentives.

Although the TARP funds helped to stabilize American banks, individuals were still struggling with the economic

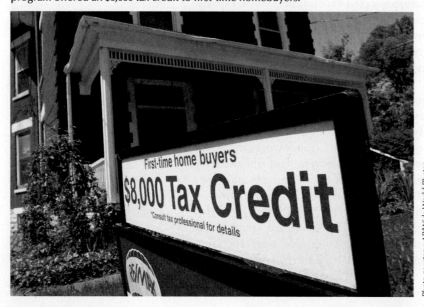

How did the government take action to stimulate the economy in 2009? One program offered an $8,000 tax credit to first-time homebuyers.

Photo courtesy: AP/Wide World Photos

Join the DEBATE | Do Economic Stimulus Payments Help the Economy?

In early 2008, the economy was in decline. Workers were losing their jobs, consumer spending was going down, and families were unable to make mortgage payments and were losing their homes. In an attempt to keep the economy from going into a full-blown recession, the U.S. government agreed to fund a $168 billion stimulus package that included individual tax rebates. Most citizens who received a check got $600 if they filed individually, or $1,200 if they filed jointly.

The political calculus for sending money back to taxpayers seemed clear. Policy makers were signaling to their constituents that they were concerned and doing something to improve the economy generally and the fate of individuals specifically. The economic calculus, however, was less clear. How far would a $600 check go in stimulating growth in jobs and businesses? Would consumers use the money to stimulate the economy by buying new cars or kitchen appliances? Would people save their checks or use them to pay off existing debt instead?

To develop an ARGUMENT FOR economic stimulus payments, think about:

- **The government has a responsibility to prevent economic downturns.** Who would act to prevent recessions and inflation, if not the government? What are the potential consequences of the government taking a "wait and see" approach during a recession?
- **Economic stimulus efforts have the greatest impact on low- and middle-income families, which are hardest hit during a recession.** How do low-and middle-income families benefit from economic stimulus payments? How might these families assist in turning around a troubled economy?
- **Stimulus payments send a powerful message to consumers, businesses, and investors.** How might a stimulus payment help to restore consumer confidence? In what ways do stimulus payments provide corporations with incentives to increase production and forestall layoffs?

To develop an ARGUMENT AGAINST economic stimulus payments, think about:

- **The government should not interfere with market forces.** How does the artificial injection of spending money by the government divert attention from real economic problems? Do stimulus checks only prolong the inevitable?
- **Deficit spending—spending more money than is available—has serious future ramifications.** In what ways is it irresponsible for the government to go into debt that will last for hundreds of years in order to prevent a short recession? What will be the long-term ramifications of this spending?
- **Government cannot control how stimulus payments are used.** Will low- and middle-income families use their stimulus checks to pay for necessities, or for additional purchases that will stimulate the economy? If the money is spent on necessities, how will businesses be helped and jobs generated?

Can economic stimulus payments fuel a troubled economy? Economists disagree on the ability of economic stimulus payments, such as tax rebates, to right an economy on a collision course with itself.

downturn. After he took office in early 2009, one of the first priorities of President Barack Obama was to address this situation by working with Congress to pass an economic stimulus and recovery bill, the American Recovery and Reinvestment Act. This legislation authorized the government to spend more than $787 billion on a variety of tax cuts and public works programs designed to stimulate the economy and to maintain and create jobs in transportation, education, health care, and other industries.

Monetary Policy

Monetary policy is often the preferred way to address an economic crisis, in part because it can be easily implemented and has fewer long-term financial consequences than the deficit spending typified by fiscal policy and the Recovery Act. In early 2008, the Federal Reserve Board responded quickly to the economic slowdown, taking extraordinary action to lower interest rates and engaging in large open-market operations and discount rate reductions to increase liquidity in the markets. In March 2008, the Fed also injected about $200 billion into the U.S. banking system by offering banks low-interest, one-month loans to ease the tightening credit conditions. It later took action to adjust mortgage lending rules and expand the commodities that U.S. markets could borrow against in order to increase the supply of money in the market.

Despite signs of an economic recovery in early 2010, the Fed has continued to keep interest rates low in the hopes of attracting borrowers who will inject money into the market. Projections following the September 2010 meeting of the Fed indicated interest rates would not be raised until early 2011.

Evaluating the Government's Response

Signs of the economic downturn—and the ultimate collapse of the financial institutions—were severe enough that both Republicans and Democrats agreed on the need to act to forestall long-term consequences, both for individuals and the nation at large. It is, however, worth noting that both parties encouraged responses to the economic collapse that were consistent with their political and economic worldviews. Seeing the signs of a downturn in early 2008, for example, President George W. Bush and the Republican Party urged the Fed to take action to increase the supply of money and lower interest rates. The Bush administration also worked with Congress to pass a tax rebate to put more money in citizens' pockets. After taking office in 2009, however, the Democrats, led by President Barack Obama, wasted little time implementing a deficit spending approach through the Recovery Act.

As the economy recovers, economists will debate which of these policy approaches was most effective. Not surprisingly, assessments generally break down on partisan lines. White House economists, for example, credit the Recovery Act for bringing about economic growth and stalling a rise in unemployment in late 2009 and early 2010. Conservative scholars and former Republican governmental officials do not dispute this growth, but they argue that it is the result of monetary policy and decisive bailout actions through the TARP program.[15]

In all likelihood, however, both fiscal and monetary policy, as well as the safety net provided by national and state income security programs, have helped to improve the American economy. It is the government's responsibility to take decisive action in all three areas: fiscal, monetary, and income security policy, to prevent or reduce the impact of future downturns in the business cycle.

What Should I Have LEARNED?

Now that you have read this chapter, you should be able to:

⭐ **13.1 Trace the stages of the policy-making process, p. 376.**

Public policy is an intentional course of action or inaction followed by government in dealing with some problem or matter of concern. A popular model used to describe the policy-making process views it as a sequence of stages that include problem recognition, agenda setting, policy formulation, policy adoption, budgeting, policy implementation, and policy evaluation. Although this model can be useful, it is a simplification of the actual process, and it does not always explain why policies take the forms they do or who controls the formation of public policy.

⭐ **13.2 Describe the evolution of health policy in the United States, p. 382.**

Governments in the United States have a long history of involvement in the health of Americans. Beginning in the 1960s, the government began to fund health programs for senior citizens and the poor, known as Medicare and Medicaid, respectively. And in 2010, after several failed attempts by prior administrations, the Democratic Congress passed and President Barack Obama signed the Patient Protection and Affordable Care Act, expanding the national government's role in providing health insurance. The U.S. government also plays a prominent role in public health through the use of immunizations, education, advertisements, research, and regulations.

⭐ **13.3 Describe the evolution of income security policy in the United States, p. 387.**

Income security programs protect people against loss of income. Income security policy was not a priority for the federal government until the 1930s, when it passed the Social Security Act. Today, the federal government administers a range of income security programs that fall into two major areas: non-means-tested and means-tested programs. Non-means-tested programs are programs that provide cash assistance to qualified beneficiaries regardless of income; they include old age, survivors, and disability insurance, and unemployment insurance. Means-tested programs require that people have incomes below specified levels to be eligible for benefits; they include Supplemental Security Income (SSI), family and child support, the Earned Income Tax Credit (EITC), and the Supplemental Nutrition Assistance Program (food stamps).

⭐ **13.4 Assess the impact of the budget process on fiscal policy, p. 392.**

Fiscal policy is the deliberate use of the national government's taxing and spending policies to maintain economic stability. The federal budget is one of the primary tools of fiscal policy; it can be manipulated to stabilize the economy and to counteract fluctuations in federal revenues. Except for a short period from 1998 to 2001, the federal government has generally run a budget deficit, which can have negative consequences for the economy over the long term.

⭐ **13.5 Analyze the effect of the Federal Reserve System on monetary policy, p. 394.**

Monetary policy is a form of government regulation in which the nation's money supply and interest rates are controlled. The Federal Reserve System ("the Fed") was created in 1913 to adjust the money supply to the needs of agriculture, commerce, and industry. Today, it handles much of the day-to-day management of monetary policy. It has a number of tools to aid its efforts, including the ability to set reserve requirements, or government requirements that a portion of member banks' deposits be retained as backing for their loans; control of the discount rate, or the rate of interest at which the Federal Reserve Board lends money to member banks; and open market operations, which involve the buying and selling of government securities by the Federal Reserve Bank in the securities market.

⭐ **13.6 Evaluate the role of public policy in the economic recession and recovery, p. 397.**

By the end of 2008, the nation was in a full-blown recession, a decline in the economy that occurs as investment sags, production falls off, and unemployment increases. The national government identified the crisis situation quickly and took a number of actions to restart economic growth and stimulate the economy through the use of fiscal, monetary, and income security policy. In terms of fiscal policy, the Bush administration offered tax rebates and proposed a $700 billion federal bailout package for the banking industry known as TARP. When President Barack Obama took office, he worked with Congress to pass the $787 billion American Recovery and Reinvestment Act to help stimulate the economy and to maintain and create new jobs. In terms of monetary policy, the Federal Reserve Board responded to the crisis by cutting interest rates and engaging in open market operations and discount rate reductions. The costs of income security programs during this economic downturn have put a strain on both national and state budgets. One of the most significant issues that policy makers must confront in the area of health policy is the rising cost of care. As citizens live longer, costs increase, placing a burden on individuals, insurance companies, and the federal government.

Test Yourself: Social and Economic Policy

⭐ **13.1 Trace the stages of the policy-making process, p. 376.**

The intentional course of action followed by government in dealing with problems or matters of concern is called
A. policy formulation.
B. social welfare policy.
C. policy administration.
D. public administration.
E. public policy.

⭐ **13.2 Describe the evolution of health policy in the United States, p. 382.**

Medicaid was designed to provide health care
A. for the aged and ill.
B. for the poor.
C. for the working class.
D. for children.
E. for everyone.

⭐ **13.3 Describe the evolution of income security policy in the United States, p. 387.**

Income security programs intended to assist persons whose income falls below a designated level are called
A. security assistance laws.
B. social insurance statutes.
C. means-tested programs.
D. non-means-tested programs.
E. Medicare and Medicaid.

⭐ **13.4 Assess the impact of the budget process on fiscal policy, p. 392.**

When Congress does not complete its appropriations process by the end of the fiscal year, it usually
A. shuts down the government.
B. passes a continuing resolution.

C. sells additional bonds.
D. asks the president for an extension of the fiscal year.
E. increases taxes until the appropriations have been paid in full.

⭐ **13.5 Analyze the effect of the Federal Reserve System on monetary policy, p. 394.**

The portion of a bank's deposits that the bank must retain as backing for its loans is known as the
A. loan requirement.
B. reserve requirement.
C. financial backing proportion.
D. earnest money.
E. fiduciary responsibility.

⭐ **13.6 Evaluate the role of public policy in the economic recession and recovery, p. 397.**

Much of the current economic downturn is attributable to
A. the cost of the war in Iraq.
B. automobile loans.
C. the cost of the No Child Left Behind Act.
D. the cost of presidential campaigns.
E. the subprime mortgage crisis.

Essay Questions

1. What are the seven steps of the policy process? Give specific examples for each step, and discuss why each is important.
2. What is the Patient Protection and Affordable Care Act of 2010, and how did it change health care?
3. What types of non-means-tested income security programs does the government provide?
4. What is the role of Congress in making the federal budget?
5. What is the Federal Reserve System, and how does it regulate U.S. monetary policy?

---

mypoliscilab Exercises

Apply what you learned in this chapter on MyPoliSciLab.

📖—⎡**Read** on **mypoliscilab.com**

  eText: Chapter 13

✓•—⎡**Study** and **Review** on **mypoliscilab.com**

  Pre-Test
  Post-Test
  Chapter Exam
  Flashcards

👁—⎡**Watch** on **mypoliscilab.com**

  Video: Chicago Gun Laws
  Video: Health Care Plan

  Video: The Stimulus Breakdown
  Video: Economic Policy Debate at the G20
  Video: Fed Approves Mortgage Crackdown

⊕—⎡**Explore** on **mypoliscilab.com**

  Simulation: You Are the President and Need to Get a Tax Cut Passed
  Comparative: Comparing Health Systems
  Timeline: The Evolution of Social Welfare Policy
  Visual Literacy: Where the Money Goes
  Visual Literacy: Evaluating Federal Spending And Economic Policy

---

Key Terms

agenda, p. 378
agenda setting, p. 378
Board of Governors, p. 395
budget deficit, p. 394
discount rate, p. 395
economic stability, p. 397
entitlement programs, p. 388
fiscal policy, p. 392
governmental (institutional)
   agenda, p. 378

inflation, p. 394
means-tested programs, p. 388
Medicaid, p. 384
Medicare, p. 383
monetary policy, p. 394
non-means-tested programs,
   p. 388
open market operations,
   p. 395
policy adoption, p. 379

policy evaluation, p. 381
policy formulation, p. 378
policy implementation,
   p. 380
public policy, p. 376
recession, p. 397
reserve requirements,
   p. 395
Social Security Act, p. 387
systemic agenda, p. 378

To Learn More on Social and Economic Policy

In the Library

Dye, Thomas R. *Understanding Public Policy*, 13th ed. New York: Longman, 2010.

Feldstein, Paul. *Health Policy Issues: An Economic Perspective on Health Reform*, 4th ed. Chicago: Health Administration Press, 2007.

Gerston, Larry N. *Public Policy Making: Process and Principles.* Armonk, NY: M.E. Sharpe, 2010.

Hacker, Jacob S. *The Great Risk Shift: The New Economic Insecurity and the Decline of the American Dream.* New York: Oxford University Press, 2008.

Kettl, Donald F. *Deficit Politics: Public Budgeting in Its Institutional and Historical Context*, 2nd ed. New York: Longman, 2010.

Kingdon, John W. *Agendas, Alternatives, and Public Policies*, 2nd ed. New York: Longman, 2002.

Lee, Robert D., Ronald W. Johnson, and Philip G. Joyce. *Public Budgeting Systems*, 8th ed. Boston: Jones and Bartlett, 2007.

Longest, Beaufort B. *Health Policymaking in the United States*, 4th ed. Chicago: Health Administration Press, 2005.

Miller, Roger LeRoy, Daniel K. Benjamin, and Doughlass C. North. *The Economics of Public Issues*, 16th ed. New York: Addison Wesley, 2009.

Oberlander, Jonathan. *The Political Life of Medicare.* Chicago: University of Chicago Press, 2003.

Olson, Laura Katz. *The Politics of Medicaid.* New York: Columbia University Press, 2010.

Page, Benjamin I., and Lawrence R. Jacobs. *Class War: What Americans Really Think About Economic Inequality.* Chicago: University of Chicago Press, 2009.

Schiff, Peter D. *How an Economy Grows and Why It Crashes.* New York: Wiley, 2010.

Sheehan, Frederick. *Panderer to Power: The Untold Story of How Alan Greenspan Enriched Wall Street and Left a Legacy of Recession.* New York: McGraw Hill, 2009.

Washington Post. *Landmark: The Inside Story of America's New Health Care Law and What It Means for All of Us.* New York: Public Affairs, 2010.

On the Web

To learn more about how public policies are prioritized and analyzed, go to the National Center for Policy Analysis Web site at **www.ncpa.org.**

To learn more about public health initiatives and consumer health advisories, go to the National Institutes of Health Web site at **www.nih.gov.**

To learn more about Social Security, go to the Social Security Web site at **www.ssa.gov.**

To learn more about regulation of financial markets, go to the Federal Reserve Board Web site at **www.federalreserve.gov.**

14

Foreign and Defense Policy

From the very outset of his presidency, Barack Obama sought to establish a new foreign policy for the United States. He did so through a series of speeches in which he called for a "new era of engagement" and a "reset" in the United States' relations with other countries.

President Obama first spoke about foreign policy in his February 24, 2009, State of the Union Address. In this speech, he proclaimed that "America cannot meet the threats of this century alone, but the world cannot meet them without America." Later, speaking in Prague, Czech Republic, Obama committed the United States to creating "a world without nuclear weapons" and pledged that his administration would push aggressively for ratification of the Comprehensive Test Ban Treaty and the strengthening of the Nuclear Non-Proliferation Treaty. At the same time he

cautioned his audience that this goal might not be achieved within his lifetime.

President Obama addressed other aspects of American foreign policy when he spoke in Ghana, where he called for a partnership among African countries and the United States. In this speech, many people saw the first outlines of a comprehensive Obama administration foreign policy. He identified four critical policy areas to the United States in the developing world. The first was to support strong and sustainable democratic governments; the second was to provide economic opportunities for all. The third policy area involved taking action to strengthen public health, and the fourth was to resolve conflicts and hold war criminals accountable. In each of these areas, he called for a partnership open to all who were willing to participate.

President Obama spoke in more concrete terms about his foreign policy agenda in two

The president plays a dominant role in the development of foreign and defense policy. At left, President Dwight D. Eisenhower meets with cadets at the U.S. Military Academy at West Point in 1960. At right, President Barack Obama visits West Point in 2009.

subsequent speeches. Speaking at West Point on December 1, 2009, the president announced that he was sending 34,000 additional troops to Afghanistan to "bring this war to a successful conclusion." Citing President Dwight D. Eisenhower as his model, he stressed the importance of balancing means and interests in foreign policy making. Obama also stressed that the United States cannot count on military might alone. Central to American success, he argued, would be drawing on the strength of American values. Many commentators asserted that with this speech, Afghanistan became Obama's war.

In late December 2009, President Obama received the Nobel Peace Prize. The concept of a "just war" was at the center of his acceptance speech. Obama argued that there have been and will be times when force must be used and is morally necessary given the limits of human reason. He continued that in using force it was essential to be clear how war was being conducted and for what reasons and concluded by noting that peace was more than the absence of violence but required the recognition of political, economic, and social rights.

What Should I Know About . . .

After reading this chapter, you should be able to:

★ **14.1** Trace the evolution of U.S. foreign and defense policy, p. 406.

★ **14.2** Explain the developments that led to the rise of the United States as a world power, p. 410.

★ **14.3** Outline the actors that shape foreign and defense policy decision making, p. 415.

★ **14.4** Identify four contemporary foreign and defense policy challenges confronting the United States, p. 421.

★ **14.5** Evaluate the shift in thinking about American power that has occurred in recent decades, p. 430.

Although popular and governmental opinions on the role of the United States in the world have changed dramatically in the last 220 years, many of the fundamental challenges remain the same. Should the United States, for example, isolate itself from other nations or become engaged in international conflicts? When do diplomatic solutions fall short, necessitating warfare? And, how do economic policies at home and abroad affect these relationships?

Evaluating the potential strengths and weaknesses of U.S. foreign policy today starts with acquiring a broad understanding of past foreign and defense policies and the political forces that have shaped them. We must also look closely at the key issues confronting the Obama administration as it attempts to address emerging issues in foreign and defense policy. To explore these issues, we will examine the following:

- First, we will trace *the roots of U.S. foreign and defense policy* in the years before the United States became a world power.

- Second, we will detail U.S. policy before, during, and after the Cold War, examining *the United States as a world power.*

- Third, we will study *foreign and defense policy decision making* and the role of the executive branch, Congress, and other groups in foreign policy making.

- Fourth, we will examine four *contemporary challenges in foreign and defense policy,* including trade, immigration and border security, terrorism, and nuclear weapons.

- Finally, we will evaluate the *rethinking of American power.*

ROOTS OF U.S. Foreign and Defense Policy

⭐ **14.1 . . . Trace the evolution of U.S. foreign and defense policy.**

foreign policy
Area of policy-making that encompasses how one country builds relationships with other countries in order to safeguard its national interest.

defense policy
Area of policy-making that focuses on the strategies that a country uses to protect itself from its enemies.

Foreign and defense policy are two separate areas of policy making. **Foreign policy** relates to how one country (referred to as a state by political scientists) builds relationships with other countries in order to safeguard its national interest. **Defense policy** is comprised of the strategies that a country uses to protect itself from its enemies. However, foreign and defense policy are interrelated. Many problems for which countries use defense policy are better addressed using well-planned foreign policy, and a failure to make good foreign policy can necessitate the use of defense policy.

The historical roots of American foreign and defense policy are found in the period leading up to World War II when the United States emerged as a world power. The importance of these early experiences comes into clearer focus when we consider four distinct periods: the early republic, the United States as an emerging power, World War I, and the interwar period (between World Wars I and II).

Isolationism in the Early Republic

Independence did not change the fundamental foreign policy problem faced by colonial America: steering a safe course between Great Britain and France, the two feuding giants of world politics in the late 1700s. For some of the Framers, the best course of action was in making an alliance with one of these two powers. For other early political leaders, the best course of action was one of neutrality and relative **isolationism,** or a national policy of avoiding participation in foreign affairs. President George Washington articulated the neutrality position most forcefully. In his Farewell Address, he called for a policy that would "steer clear of permanent alliances with any portion of the foreign world."

The dual goals of isolationism and neutrality, however, did not mean that the United States was always able to ignore international conflicts. In the early 1800s, the British naval practice of impressment (stopping ships to seize suspected deserters of the Royal Navy) led Congress to pass the **Embargo Act** in 1807, which prevented U.S. ships from leaving for foreign ports without the approval of the federal government. The Embargo Act was generally unsuccessful. Not only did it fail to change British policy, but it caused economic hardships for U.S. merchants and contributed to the War of 1812 between the United States and Great Britain.

After the 1815 defeat of French leader Napoleon Bonaparte, Europe was at peace for the first time in almost two decades. Europeans celebrated, but the United States feared that European powers would try to expand their control in the Western Hemisphere. To prevent this, President James Monroe issued the **Monroe Doctrine** in 1823. It warned European states that the United States would view "any attempt on their part to extend their system to any portion of this hemisphere as dangerous to our peace and safety." It also promised to continue the American policy of noninterference in the internal concerns of European powers.

isolationism
A national policy of avoiding participation in foreign affairs.

Embargo Act
Legislation passed by Congress in 1807 to prevent U.S. ships from leaving U.S. ports without the approval of the federal government.

Monroe Doctrine
President James Monroe's 1823 pledge that the United States would oppose attempts by European states to extend their political control into the Western Hemisphere.

Growing Power and Influence

Throughout most of the nineteenth century, the United States gained territory, developed economically, and emerged as a world power. This process centered on four areas: trade policy and commerce, continental expansion and manifest destiny, dominance over the Western Hemisphere, and interests in Asia.

TRADE POLICY AND COMMERCE The policy of neutrality articulated in Washington's Farewell Address made free trade a cornerstone of early American foreign policy. Reciprocity and most favored nation status were its guiding principles. Reciprocity meant that the United States government treated foreign traders in the same way that foreign countries treated American traders. Most favored nation status guaranteed that a country's imports into the United States would be given the lowest possible **tariffs**, or taxes on imported goods.

Increased global trade and competition following the end of the Napoleonic Wars led the United States to abandon the policies of reciprocity and most favored nation status. Beginning in 1816, Congress adopted the "American System" of trade protection by adding increasingly higher tariffs, sometimes as high as 100 percent of the value of the goods being imported.[1] High protectionist tariffs remained the American norm well into the twentieth century.

tariffs
Taxes on imported goods.

EXPANSIONISM AND MANIFEST DESTINY During the nineteenth century, the United States acquired immense quantities of land in various ways. It took land from American Indians in wars against the Creek, Seminole, Sioux, Comanche, Apache, and other tribes. It bought territory from the French (the Louisiana Territory), Spanish

TIMELINE: The Development of U.S. Foreign Policy

1796 Washington's Farewell Address—In this speech, Washington calls on the United States to steer clear of permanent alliances.

1823 Monroe Doctrine—This document attempts to limit European interference in the Western Hemisphere.

1904 Roosevelt Corollary—This corollary to the Monroe Doctrine asserts that the United States will police the Western Hemisphere in an attempt to maintain peace and security.

1917 United States Enters World War I—A policy of isolationism makes the United States reluctant to involve itself in this European conflict, but it eventually intervenes out of economic necessity.

Photo courtesy: National Archives Washington DC/The Art Archive

---

(Florida), and Russians (Alaska). It also fought the 1846 Mexican War, acquiring a large expanse of Mexican territory in the American Southwest and California.

manifest destiny
Theory that the United States was divinely mandated to expand across North America to the Pacific Ocean.

Manifest destiny is the summary phrase used to capture the logic behind American continental expansionism. According to this idea, the United States had a divinely mandated obligation to expand across North America to the Pacific and "overspread the continent allotted by Providence for the free development of our multiplying millions."[2] Manifest destiny was viewed as natural and inevitable, far different from the colonial expansion of European states.

DOMINANCE OVER THE WESTERN HEMISPHERE   The twentieth century began with a revision of the Monroe Doctrine. In what came to be known as the **Roosevelt Corollary** to the Monroe Doctrine, President Theodore Roosevelt asserted in 1904 that it was the responsibility of the United States to assure stability in Latin America and the Caribbean. In accordance with this role, the United States would punish wrongdoing and establish order in these nations when their own governments were incapable of doing so.

Roosevelt Corollary
Concept developed by President Theodore Roosevelt early in the twentieth century declaring that it was the responsibility of the United States to assure stability in Latin America and the Caribbean.

Roosevelt was particularly concerned with the Dominican Republic. It was deeply in debt, plagued by growing domestic unrest, and faced the threat of hostile military action by France. Roosevelt blocked French action by taking over customs collection in 1906. Later, the United States sent troops to other states, including Cuba, Haiti, Nicaragua, Panama, and Mexico.

Although these exercises of military power were significant in establishing regional dominance, the signature event of this time period for American foreign policy was the acquisition of the Panama Canal Zone. A treaty in 1900 authorized the construction of a canal that would connect the Atlantic and Pacific Oceans; however, there was debate over where to build the waterway. Two options existed: One route went through Nicaragua; the second route went through Panama, which was then part of Colombia. Roosevelt strongly preferred the Panamanian route. So, when the Colombian government refused

1941 United States Enters World War II—U.S. involvement in World War II begins after the Japanese bomb ships at Pearl Harbor on December 7.

1970 Détente—Signs of outward conflict between the United States and communist nations begin to subside in the 1970s; President Richard M. Nixon symbolizes this thaw with a visit to China.

1947 Cold War Begins—The Cold War between the United States and the Soviet Union defines much of the remainder of the twentieth century.

2001 War on Terrorism—Following the September 11 terrorist attacks on the World Trade Center and the Pentagon, President George W. Bush declares a war on terrorism.

---

to approve the necessary treaty, the Roosevelt administration supported a Panamanian independence movement. When this movement was successful, the U.S. government quickly recognized the independent state and signed an agreement granting the United States the rights to a ten-mile strip of land. Construction of the Panama Canal began in May 1904. It was opened on August 15, 1914.

INTEREST IN ASIA   The 1898 Spanish-American War, fought between the United States and Spain over Spanish policies and presence in Cuba, gave the United States control over the Philippines. As a result, the United States now had a major stake in Asian affairs. The major problems confronting the United States in Asia were the disintegration of China and the rising power of Japan.

In 1898 and 1899, the British approached the United States about joint action to keep China open to all foreign traders. The U.S. government chose not to act in concert with Britain and instead unilaterally issued the Open Door Notes to Russia, Germany, and Great Britain, calling upon them not to discriminate against other investors in their spheres of influence, including China. A major weakness of this strategy was that the Open Door Notes lacked an enforcement mechanism and thus were easily ignored.

In sharp contrast to the unilateral action taken on China, President Theodore Roosevelt sought to contain Japan through a series of international agreements. The most notable of these was the Taft-Katsura Agreement of

How did the Roosevelt Corollary affect American foreign policy? In this political cartoon, President Theodore Roosevelt is shown policing Panama carrying the "big stick" of military intervention proposed by the Roosevelt Corollary.

Photo courtesy: Bettman/CORBIS

1905. This act recognized Japanese preeminence over Korea in return for a Japanese agreement to respect American control over the Philippines and Hawaii.

World War I and the League of Nations

When World War I broke out in Europe in 1914, the United States remained neutral at first. It was a European war, and no U.S. interests were involved. In addition, the United States was largely a nation of European immigrants, and Americans were deeply divided about whom to support. As the war progressed, however, it became increasingly difficult to remain neutral. For example, under Germany's policy of unrestricted submarine warfare, German subs sank U.S. ships carrying cargo to Great Britain and France. Finally, declaring that the United States was fighting "a war to end all wars," in 1917 President Woodrow Wilson led the nation into the conflict. But the United States entered as an "Associated Power" rather than as an "Allied Power" in an attempt to maintain some distance between itself and Europe. Wilson also put forward a statement of American war aims, the Fourteen Points. The Fourteenth Point was the creation of a League of Nations at the conclusion of the war.

collective security
The idea that an attack on one country is an attack on all countries.

At the Paris Peace Conference following the war, Wilson succeeded in getting the League of Nations established. Its guiding principle was **collective security,** the idea that an attack on one country is an attack on all countries. Wilson failed, however, to build support for the League of Nations in the United States. A combination of political partisanship (Wilson, a Democrat, had not included any Republicans in the U.S. delegation to the Paris Peace Conference) and continued isolationist sentiments led to the defeat of the Treaty of Versailles in the Senate. The United States never joined the League.

The Interwar Years

The period between the two world wars saw U.S. foreign policy dominated by two issues: disarmament and isolationism. In 1920, isolationist Senator William Borah offered a resolution inviting Great Britain and Japan to an arms limitation conference. The result was the 1921 Washington Conference, which left a mixed legacy. Although it did not produce lasting security in the Far East or end arms races, it did mark a shift in the global balance of power, because two of the main players represented—the United States and Japan—were from outside Europe.

Support for disarmament also led to the signing of the Kellogg-Briand Pact. In this pact, the United States, Japan, and the great European powers (including Great Britain, France, and Germany) agreed to renounce war "as an instrument of national policy" and to resolve their disputes "by pacific means." This treaty, however, did not stop the United States from taking defensive actions, such as building new naval vessels.

Second, there was a hardening of isolationist sentiment within the United States. This sentiment led Congress to increase tariffs to protect U.S. industry from foreign competition. In 1930, Congress passed the extremely high Smoot-Hawley Tariff Act, and other countries responded by raising their tariffs. The impact that higher tariffs, in conjunction with the Great Depression, had on world trade was dramatic. By 1932, trade dropped to about one-third its former level.[3]

The United States as a World Power

★ 14.2 . . . **Explain the developments that led to the rise of the United States as a world power.**

The status of the United States as a world power was cemented by its entry into and subsequent victory in World War II. Between World War II and the new millennium, American political leaders guided the nation through three distinct periods: the Cold War, détente, and the post–Cold War period. Today, the Obama administration is working to guide the country through the ongoing war on terrorism.

World War II and Its Aftermath

The United States entered World War II with the December 7, 1941, Japanese bombing of Pearl Harbor. The war was fought on two fronts—in Europe and in the Pacific. It concluded in Europe first, in May 1945. It did not end in the Pacific until August or September of that same year, following the United States' decision to drop atomic bombs at Hiroshima and Nagasaki, Japan.

World War II was a watershed in U.S. foreign policy. Prior to the war, isolationist sentiment dominated American thinking on world politics, but after it, internationalism emerged triumphant. Although the United States had rejected membership in the League of Nations, it enthusiastically joined the United Nations (UN). The UN was to be a means by which Big Three allies (the United States, Great Britain, and the Soviet Union) could continue their wartime cooperation and provide for the security of all states.

Believing that protectionist trade policies had led to the rise of dictators and the beginning of World War II, the United States moved to create an additional set of international economic organizations to encourage and manage trade. Collectively they came to be known as the **Bretton Woods System** after Bretton Woods, New Hampshire, where negotiations were held in July 1944. The **International Monetary Fund (IMF)** was created to stabilize international currency transactions. In addition, the International Bank for Reconstruction and Development, also called the **World Bank,** was set up to help the world recover from the destruction of World War II by providing loans for large economic development projects.

Created a little later in 1947 was the **General Agreement on Tariffs and Trade (GATT).** Its mission was to help facilitate international trade negotiations and promote free trade. This process occurred through negotiating "rounds" or multiyear international conferences. GATT ultimately evolved into the World Trade Organization (WTO).

The Cold War and Containment

The Cold War was the defining feature of the international system from the end of World War II in 1945 until the fall of the Berlin Wall in 1989. It was a period of competition, hostility, tension, and occasional moments of cooperation between the Western powers (the United States, Great Britain, and Western Europe) and the communist bloc states (Eastern Europe and the Soviet Union). Although it was frequently intense, the Cold War never escalated into direct and open warfare.

American foreign policy during the Cold War was organized around two key concepts. The first was containment, which held that the "the main element of any United States policy toward the Soviet Union must be that of a long-term, patient but firm and vigilant containment of Russian expansionist tendencies."[4] The second concept was deterrence. During the 1950s and 1960s, the United States and the Soviet Union developed large nuclear arsenals; having stockpiles of weapons of mass destruction on either side of the conflict assured that both sides would prevent one another from actually deploying their arsenals. This created a condition of mutual assured destruction (MAD).

Although the Cold War began in Europe, it quickly became a global conflict. In the 1940s, the conflict spread to the Mediterranean, leading to the Marshall Plan. It also spread to Latin America, especially Cuba, and to Asia. In 1949, for example, Mao Zedong won the Chinese Civil War and aligned China with the Soviet Union, a move that the United States viewed as significantly increasing Soviet power. This action also precipitated the Korean War of the 1950s and the Vietnam War of the 1960s and 1970s.

Bretton Woods System
International financial system devised shortly before the end of World War II that created the World Bank and the International Monetary Fund.

International Monetary Fund (IMF)
International governmental organization created shortly before the end of World War II to stabilize international currency transactions.

World Bank
International governmental organization created shortly before the end of World War II to provide loans for large economic development projects.

General Agreement on Tariffs and Trade (GATT)
Post–World War II economic development program designed to help facilitate international trade negotiations and promote free trade.

Truman Doctrine

U.S. policy initiated in 1947 to provide economic assistance and military aid to countries fighting against communist revolutions or political pressure.

Marshall Plan

European collective recovery program, named after Secretary of State George C. Marshall, that provided extensive American aid to Western Europe after World War II.

North Atlantic Treaty Organization (NATO)

The first peacetime military treaty joined by the United States; NATO is a collective security pact between the United States and Western Europe.

Cuban Missile Crisis

The 1962 confrontation over the deployment of ballistic missiles in Cuba that nearly escalated into war between the United States and the Soviet Union.

THE MARSHALL PLAN   Among the first Cold War trouble spots were Greece and Turkey, both of which came under pressure from communists. In February 1947, Great Britain informed the United States that it could no longer afford to meet its traditional obligations to protect Greece and Turkey. Less than one month later, on March 12, 1947, President Harry S Truman addressed a joint session of Congress and requested economic and military foreign aid for the two countries. The language Truman used as justification was as important as this request for aid. He argued that the United States "must support free peoples who are resisting attempted subjugation by armed minorities or by outside pressure."[5] Known as the **Truman Doctrine,** this policy led the United States to provide economic assistance and military aid to countries fighting against communist revolutions or political pressure.

Three months later, the United States took a major action consistent with this political worldview. Secretary of State George Marshall announced that the United States would help finance Europe's economic recovery. All European states were invited to participate in the drafting of a European collective recovery plan known as the **Marshall Plan.** Importantly, the Soviet Union chose not to participate in this program and prevented Eastern European states from joining as well. This effectively served to divide postwar Europe into two parts.

In 1949, the economic division of Europe was reinforced by its military partition with the establishment of the **North Atlantic Treaty Organization (NATO).** This alliance, the first peacetime military treaty joined by the United States, was a collective security pact between the United States and Western Europe. In retaliation, the Soviet Union organized its Eastern European allies into the Warsaw Pact.

THE COLD WAR IN LATIN AMERICA   Cold War competition between the United States and Soviet Union moved to Latin America in the late 1950s and early 1960s. Fidel Castro, for example, came to power in Cuba in 1959. Following this coup, President Dwight D. Eisenhower approved a plan for sending a small group of Cuban exiles back to Cuba for purposes of conducting a guerrilla warfare campaign against the new leader. This plan evolved into a larger operation, the Bay of Pigs Invasion, authorized by President John F. Kennedy in April 1961. The results were disastrous. Some 1,400 Cuban exiles landed at the Bay of Pigs and quickly were surrounded and defeated by well-equipped and loyal Cuban soldiers.

A little more than a year later, the United States and Soviet Union became locked in a test of wills over the presence of Soviet missiles in Cuba. President Kennedy announced their discovery on national television on October 22, 1962. He also set a deadline for a Soviet response. The crisis ended on October 29 when Soviet Premier Nikita Khrushchev agreed to remove the Soviet missiles.

A positive result of the **Cuban Missile Crisis** was a series of arms control efforts. In 1963, the United States and Soviet Union set up the "hot line" to permit secure and direct communication between the two nations. That same year, the Limited Nuclear Test Ban Treaty (limiting the testing of nuclear weapons) was signed, and in 1968 the Nuclear Non-Proliferation Treaty (preventing the spread of such armaments) was approved.

THE VIETNAM WAR   America's involvement in Vietnam also began in the 1950s. After the end of World War II, France unsuccessfully sought to reestablish its colonial rule over Indochina. President Eisenhower provided the French with financial support but no troops. Militarily defeated, in 1954, France negotiated a withdrawal from Vietnam. The resultant Geneva Peace Accords temporarily divided Vietnam at the 17th parallel, with communist forces in control of the North and democratic forces in control of the South. A unification election scheduled for 1956 was never held, as South Vietnam (with the support of the United States) refused to participate. As a result, North Vietnam began a military campaign to unify the country.

The war became increasingly Americanized in the 1960s under President Lyndon B. Johnson. American forces carried out sustained and massive bombing campaigns against the North, and U.S. ground troops began fighting in the South. The war was a difficult one, fought in unfamiliar terrain with little chance of success. Casualties escalated quickly, and American public opinion began to turn against the war.

In the 1970s, President Richard M. Nixon sought to set the stage for American withdrawal by implementing a policy of Vietnamization, under which the South Vietnamese army would begin to do the bulk of the fighting. To prepare for this turnover, the United States invaded Cambodia to clean out North Vietnamese sanctuaries and increased bombing of North Vietnam. The strategy failed. In spring 1972, North Vietnam attacked the South, forcing Nixon to re-Americanize the war. U.S. forces left South Vietnam in 1973 following the Paris Peace Agreement. South Vietnam fell to communism in April 1975.

Détente and Human Rights

When Richard M. Nixon became president in 1969, he declared it was time to move from "an era of confrontation" to "an era of negotiation" in relations with the Soviet Union.[6] This improvement in U.S.–Soviet relations was called **détente.**[7] At its center was a series of negotiations that sought to use linked rewards and punishments (rather than military power) to contain the Soviet Union.

The greatest success of détente was in the area of arms control, most notably with the signing of the Strategic Arms Limitation Talks (SALT I and SALT II). The greatest failure of détente, however, was an inability to establish agreed-upon rules to govern competition in the developing world, particularly in Africa and the Middle East. Détente also did not extend to Latin America. In Chile, for example, Nixon was forced to use covert action to undermine the government of Salvador Allende and reestablish a strong pro-American regime.

When Jimmy Carter became president in 1977, he changed the emphasis of American foreign policy from the management of the Cold War to the promotion of **human rights,** that is, the protection of people's basic freedoms and needs. The dictators that the United States had relied upon to contain communism were a major target of Carter's policies. Among these was the Shah of Iran. Popular unrest forced the Shah into exile in 1979, but after his ouster, radical Iranians, with the support of Iran's fundamentalist Islamic government, overran the U.S. Embassy in Tehran and held the embassy staff captive. The hostages were not released until the day that Carter left office in 1981.

Republican President Ronald Reagan replaced Carter in the White House. Reagan promised to reestablish American credibility and restore American military strength. The Reagan administration's commitment to ending communism by providing military assistance to anti-communist groups became known as the **Reagan Doctrine.**

détente

The improvement in relations between the United States and the Soviet Union that occurred during the 1970s.

human rights

The protection of people's basic freedoms and needs.

Reagan Doctrine

The Reagan administration's commitment to ending communism by providing military assistance to anti-communist groups.

What was détente? Détente was an improvement in U.S.-Soviet relations that signaled a thaw in the Cold War. One of the most symbolic embodiments of this idea was President Richard M. Nixon's 1972 trip to China, shown here.

Photo courtesy: Ollie Atkins/White House/Time & Life Pictures/Getty Images

The Post–Cold War World

The Cold War effectively ended in 1989 with the fall of communism in the Soviet Union. President George Bush now had to navigate through this new, post–Cold War world. Bush adopted a wait-and-see policy toward the Soviet Union. His administration also responded cautiously to events in China.

The defining moment of the Bush administration's foreign policy, however, was the Persian Gulf War that was brought on by Iraq's invasion of Kuwait in August 1990. Bush responded immediately by freezing all Iraqi and Kuwaiti assets and stopping all trade and financial dealings with Iraq. Bush then turned to the United Nations, who voted to impose economic sanctions and authorized the use of force. Congress did likewise. In January 1991, Operation Desert Storm began with an air campaign against Iraq. Ground forces arrived in February, and soon after, Iraq announced a cease-fire and agreed to a meeting of military commanders to discuss terms for ending the war.

Bush left office in January 1993. The administration of his successor, Bill Clinton, struggled to define a role for the United States in world affairs. Eventually, the Clinton administration settled on the concept of **enlargement,** or actively promoting the expansion of democracy and free markets throughout the world. There are two main types of enlargement: economic and democratic.

Economic enlargement was easier to accomplish. Clinton secured Senate approval for the North American Free Trade Agreement (NAFTA), an agreement promoting free movement of goods and services among Canada, Mexico, and the United States. He followed up this success by obtaining Senate approval for permanent most favored nation status for China and completing negotiations leading to the establishment of the World Trade Organization. Democratic enlargement proved more difficult. In practice, democratic enlargement was driven off the foreign policy agenda by the need to deal with conflict in failed states, such as Somalia, Yugoslavia, and Haiti.

enlargement
Policy implemented during the Clinton administration in which the United States would actively promote the expansion of democracy and free markets throughout the world.

How did the September 11 terrorist attacks affect American politics? The south tower of the World Trade Center collapsed September 11, 2001, after it was struck by a hijacked airplane. The north tower, also struck by a hijacked plane, collapsed shortly after. The attacks caused enormous loss of life and resulted in the beginning of an ongoing war on terrorism.

Photo courtesy: Thomas Nillson/Getty Images

The War on Terrorism

At first, the George W. Bush administration largely distanced itself from Clinton's legacy of enlargement. The administration rejected the international global warming treaty known as the Kyoto Protocol, withdrew from the Anti-Ballistic Missile Treaty, and refused to participate in the formation of the International Criminal Court. But, political events soon intervened. The terrorist attacks of September 11, 2001, ushered in a new era in American foreign policy.

SEPTEMBER 11 AND THE WAR IN AFGHANISTAN On September 11, 2001, nineteen members of the al-Qaeda terrorist organization headed by Osama bin Laden hijacked four U.S. commercial airliners and crashed two of them into the World Trade Center in New York City and

POLITICS**NOW**

| WORLD | NATION | LOCAL | POLITICS | OPINION | HEALTH & SCIENCE | ARTS | SPORTS | LEISURE |

Islamist Websites: McChrystal Fired Because Afghan War Is Lost

By CNN Wire Staff

June 25, 2010
CNN
www.cnn.com

The recent change in commanders in Afghanistan is proof the U.S and its allies have lost the war, statements posted on two Islamist websites said Thursday.

Taliban spokesman Qari Mohammad Yousif Ahmadi said in one statement President Barack Obama wanted to save face by firing Gen. Stanley McChrystal and bringing in Gen. David Petraeus. McChrystal was relieved of duty—although he technically resigned—Wednesday after he and his staff made comments in a *Rolling Stone* magazine article that appear to mock top civilian officials, including the vice president.

"History is evident of more powerful and experienced generals than General McChrystal and empires mightier than the United States of America being surrendered and bowed down before the Afghans," Ahmadi said, according to the website statement.

Ahmadi said McChrystal's strategy of increasing the number of troops in Afghanistan had been futile and led to the change in commanders. The Taliban spokesman said the change in command is useless because Petraeus, the new Afghan commander, is weak.

"Indeed, he has got no (more) special qualities than General McChrystal had," Ahmadi said in his statement.

In another statement, a group calling itself the Islamic Emirate of Afghanistan said Petraeus is mentally worn out because of the lengthy war, which began in October 2001.

"Nine years of military actions, different strategies and back-breaking monetary and life damages at the hands of mujahedeen have left the crusaders totally in distress," the statement said.

Last week, when Petraeus briefly fainted at a Senate Armed Services Committee meeting, dehydration was cited as the cause. But the website said it was a sign that Petraeus knows the war in Afghanistan is lost.

"General Petraeus, being witness to the incidents in Afghanistan is the only person who realizes the gravity of (the) situation and described this situation well by falling unconscious," the Islamic Emirate of Afghanistan said.

"Through this action he gave the answer to many questions to which the members of committee were eager to listen. They should learn from this answer by General Petraeus and start working for the well being of their masses."

Ahmadi, in his statement, said Petraeus has "left a big question mark on his physical and mental health."

Critical Thinking Questions

1. Why does President Obama have the power to hire and fire military commanders? Should he have this power? Why or why not?
2. How do Islamic groups' accounts of McChrystal's firing differ from those of U.S. news sources?
3. What lessons does this story teach us about American foreign policy in general? How does it illustrate the difficulties in dealing with foreign states and individuals?

---

one into the Pentagon outside Washington, D.C. The fourth plane crashed into an open field in Somerset County, Pennsylvania. More than 3,000 people lost their lives that day.

The administration declared a global **war on terrorism** to weed out terrorist operatives throughout the world. It demanded that the Taliban-led government of Afghanistan expel Osama bin Laden and al-Qaeda and sever its ties with international terrorist groups. When this did not occur, the United States began aerial strikes against terrorist facilities and Taliban military targets inside Afghanistan on October 7, 2001. On the ground, the United States relied heavily on support from troops provided by the Northern Alliance, a coalition that opposed the Taliban. The Taliban

war on terrorism

An international action, initiated by President George W. Bush after the 9/11 attacks, to weed out terrorist operatives throughout the world.

proved no match for this combination of air and ground power and its last stronghold fell on December 16. Osama bin Laden, however, was not captured. (To learn more about the war in Afghanistan, see Politics Now: Islamist Websites: McChrystal Fired Because Afghan War Is Lost.)

THE WAR IN IRAQ A broader foreign policy agenda emerged in President Bush's 2002 State of the Union Address. In this speech, Bush identified Iraq, North Korea, and Iran as an "axis of evil" that threatened American security interests. A movement toward war with Iraq soon developed. Following a series of authorization negotiations with Congress, Operation Iraqi Freedom began on March 19, 2003, with a decapitation strike aimed at targets in Baghdad. On April 9, Baghdad fell, and one month later, Bush declared the "mission accomplished."

Clearly, the Bush administration did not plan for a long or contested occupation of Iraq, but the reality on the ground soon challenged this vision. American casualties began to rise, and in September 2004, U.S. casualties reached 1,000. By mid-2008, more than 4,000 U.S. military personnel and Department of Defense civilians had died in Iraq, and 30,000 had been reported wounded. The Obama administration announced an end to formal combat operations in 2010, with combat forces scheduled to leave Iraq by 2011. However, violence in the region continues.

Foreign and Defense Policy Decision Making

⭐ **14.3** . . . Outline the actors that shape foreign and defense policy decision making.

The basic structure of foreign and defense policy decision making is laid out in the Constitution. The executive branch is the most powerful branch of government in the formulation and implementation of U.S. foreign and defense policy. Congress also influences and shapes policy through oversight, treaties, appointments, appropriations, and the War Powers Act. In addition, interest groups such as the military-industrial complex also play an important role.

The Constitution

When the Framers of the U.S. Constitution met in Philadelphia in 1789, they wanted a stronger national government to keep the United States out of European affairs and to keep Europe out of American affairs. As a result, the power to formulate and implement foreign policy was given to the national government rather than the states. In addition, many foreign and military powers not enumerated in the Constitution were accorded to the national government. (To learn more about these powers, see The Living Constitution: Article I, Section 8.)

The Framers of the Constitution divided national authority for foreign and military policy functions between the president and Congress. The Framers named the president commander in chief of the armed forces but gave Congress power to fund the army and navy and to declare war. The president has authority to negotiate and sign treaties, but those agreements only take effect after the Senate ratifies them by a two-thirds majority. Similarly, the president appoints ambassadors and other key foreign and military affairs officials, but the Senate must give its advice and consent to nominees.

The Living Constitution

To provide for calling forth the Militia to execute the Laws of the Union, suppress Insurrections and repel Invasions;
To provide for organizing, arming, and disciplining, the Militia, and for governing such Part of them as may be employed in the Service of the United States . . .

—ARTICLE I, SECTION 8

A fundamental weakness of the Articles of Confederation was that it did not grant the national government adequate means for national defense. This defect hampered the Revolutionary War effort. These clauses of the Constitution consequently give the federal government the authority to call up the state militias in times of national emergency or distress. The clauses address the understanding that military training, proficiency, and organization should be uniform across state and national forces so as to ensure effectiveness and efficiency in military operations.

Despite the fact that the militia clauses passed the convention, many Anti-Federalists were concerned that the federal government would call together the state militias for unjust ends. They believed that state governments should control their militias in order to prevent any deceit on the part of the federal government. To this end, the states were given authority to name militia officers and train their forces. During the War of 1812—to the consternation of President James Madison—two state governments withheld their militias from the national government. The Supreme Court has since held that, except for constitutional prohibitions, the Congress has "unlimited" authority over the state militias. And, the National Defense Act of 1916 mandated the use of the term "National Guard" and gave the president the authority to mobilize the National Guard during times of national emergency or war.

Throughout U.S. history, the National Guard has proven effective and essential in defending the United States. The National Guard, for example, plays a significant role in American efforts in Iraq and Afghanistan. The militia clauses ensure the unity, effectiveness, and strength of the United States military not only during wartime, but also during other national emergencies.

CRITICAL THINKING QUESTIONS

1. According to the Constitution, the president is the commander in chief of the armed forces. But, Congress has the power to organize the military, fund it, and call it to duty. How does this division of authority work in practice?
2. Should individual states retain the right to withhold National Guard troops if the state government does not approve of the way that the president intends to use them?
3. Should states continue to maintain separate National Guards, or should all troops be integrated into the national military? Defend your argument.

The Executive Branch

The executive branch is the central place for creating and implementing U.S. foreign and defense policy; within the executive branch, the president is the most important individual. Among executive departments, the Department of State is primarily responsible for foreign, diplomatic activity and the Department of Defense for military policy.

Other executive agencies, such as the National Security Council, the Joint Chiefs of Staff, and the Central Intelligence Agency provide additional resources for the president. The Department of Homeland Security also has a role to play in foreign and defense policy making.

THE PRESIDENT   The president is preeminent in foreign and defense policy. Presidents have greater access to and control over information than any other government official or agency, and the president alone can act with little fear that his actions will be countermanded. As such, we tend to discuss U.S. foreign policy in terms of presidential action.

Presidents have also come to increasingly rely on organizations and individuals located within the White House to help them make foreign policy. The most notable of these organizations is the National Security Council (NSC), led by the national security advisor. The NSC brings together key foreign policy actors from the Departments of State and Defense, intelligence officials, military leaders, and presidential advisors. The organization's primary goal is to advise and assist the president on foreign and defense policy, particularly in crisis situations when speed in decision making is essential. Originally the national security advisor was a neutral voice in the decision-making process, but over time, this appointee has become a powerful voice, independent of the president, in policy making.

Department of State

Chief executive branch department responsible for formulation and implementation of U.S. foreign policy.

Department of Defense

Chief executive branch department responsible for formulation and implementation of U.S. defense and military policy.

Joint Chiefs of Staff

Military advisory body that includes the Army chief of staff, the Air Force chief of staff, the chief of naval operations, and the Marine commandant.

THE DEPARTMENTS OF STATE, DEFENSE, AND HOMELAND SECURITY

According to tradition, the **Department of State** is the chief executive branch department responsible for formulation and implementation of U.S. foreign policy. The State Department serves as a linkage between foreign governments and U.S. policy makers and as a source of advice on how to deal with problems. Today the State Department's position of prominence has been challenged from many directions. Within the White House, the national security advisor may hold competing views. And, the complexity of foreign policy problems has given increased importance to the views of the Departments of Defense, Treasury, and Commerce.

The **Department of Defense** is the chief executive branch department responsible for formulation and implementation of U.S. military policy. It came into existence after World War II, when the War Department and the Navy Department were combined into a central clearinghouse for military affairs. The voice of the Department of Defense in policy making is greatest in questions involving the use of military force.

Speaking to the president with one voice, however, has not always been easy. Numerous lines of disagreement exist. Among the most prominent are disagreements between professional military officers and civilians working in the Secretary of Defense's office and between the separate branches of the armed services (Army, Navy, Coast Guard, Air Force, Marines) over missions, weapons, and priorities. To overcome these differences in outlook, the president relies on the **Joint Chiefs of Staff,** the military advisory body that includes the Army chief of staff, the Air Force chief of staff, the chief of naval operations, and the Marine commandant.

Who are the Joint Chiefs of Staff? The Joint Chiefs of Staff are the heads of all of the branches of the U.S. military. Here, these officials meet with President Barack Obama and other advisors in the White House Situation Room.

Photo courtesy: Official White House Photo by Pete Souza

The **Department of Homeland Security,** the Cabinet department created after the 9/11 terrorist attacks to coordinate domestic security efforts, straddles the line between foreign and domestic policy making. The department brought together twenty-two existing agencies, approximately thirty newly created agencies or offices, and 180,000 employees under a single secretary. Among its key units are Transportation Security Administration (TSA), the organization responsible for aviation security; the Federal Emergency Management Agency (FEMA), the primary federal disaster relief organization; Customs and Border Protection; the Coast Guard; the Secret Service; and immigration services and enforcement.

Department of Homeland Security

Cabinet department created after the 9/11 terrorist attacks to coordinate domestic security efforts.

THE INTELLIGENCE COMMUNITY   The intelligence community is a term used to describe the agencies of the U.S. government that are involved in the collection and analysis of information, counterintelligence (the protection of U.S. intelligence), and covert action. The head of the intelligence community is the Director of National Intelligence (DNI).

Beyond the CIA, other key members of the intelligence community include the Bureau of Intelligence and Research in the Department of State, the Defense Intelligence Agency, the military service intelligence agencies, the National Security Agency in the Department of Defense, the Federal Bureau of Investigation, and the Department of Homeland Security. Coordinating these units has always been a problem. Budgetary control has proven to be illusive, because a large percentage of the intelligence community's budget goes to the Department of Defense and is not under the direct control of the DNI. Differences of opinion on important issues such as Soviet military strength during the Cold War and Iraq's possession of weapons of mass destruction in the early twenty-first century often translate into long-standing appropriations conflicts. In addition, conflict over covert action is a growing problem. At one time, the CIA had a monopoly over this policy area, but now the Department of Defense also plays an active role.

Congress

The U.S. Constitution gave Congress fewer responsibilities in foreign and defense policy than the president; nevertheless, the legislative branch plays a significant role in the policy process. Most commentators would agree that Congress is the second most important actor in shaping American foreign and defense policy.[8] Congress influences foreign and defense policy through its congressional leadership, oversight, approval of treaties and appointments, appropriations, and the War Powers Act.

OVERSIGHT   The most common method of congressional oversight is holding hearings monitoring agency activities, as well as the content and conduct of U.S. policy. Another method of conducting congressional oversight is by establishing reporting requirements. The Department of State, for example, is required to submit annual evaluations of other nations' human rights practices, religious freedoms, anti-drug and narcotics efforts, their stance on human trafficking, and nuclear proliferation activities. The president must also notify Congress "in a timely fashion" of CIA covert actions. In addition to these methods, Congress routinely carries out committee hearings monitoring agency activities, as well as the content and conduct of U.S. foreign policy.

TREATIES AND EXECUTIVE AGREEMENTS   The Constitution gives the Senate explicit power to approve treaties, but the Senate has rejected treaties only twenty times in U.S. history.[9] The most famous of these unapproved treaties is the Treaty of Versailles, which established the League of Nations.

Presidents can avoid the treaty process by using executive agreements, which unlike treaties do not require Senate approval. Prior to 1972, the president did not have to inform Congress of the text of these accords. Although many executive agreements deal with routine foreign policy matters, a great many also involve major military commitments on the part of the United States.

APPOINTMENTS   Although the Constitution gives the president the power to appoint ambassadors and others involved in foreign and defense policy, it gives the Senate the responsibility to provide advice and consent on these appointments. The Senate has not exercised this power in any systematic fashion. It has given its approval to nominees with little expertise largely on the basis of their party affiliation and contributions to presidential campaign funds. It has also rejected otherwise qualified nominees because of objections to the president's foreign policies.

Presidents have long circumvented congressional approval by using and creating new positions not subject to Senate confirmation. Most recent presidents have created policy "czars" to coordinate the administration's foreign policy in specific areas. President Obama, for example, has established czars for the Middle East peace process, border security with Mexico, and the war in Afghanistan.

APPROPRIATIONS   Congress also shapes foreign and defense policy through its power to appropriate funds, and it influences when and where the United States fights through its control of the budget. Although the power to go to war is shared by the executive and legislative branches of government, the power to appropriate funds belongs to the legislature alone. (To learn more about U.S. defense spending, see Figure 14.1.)

Figure 14.1 *How has defense spending changed over time?*
Defense spending was at its highest absolute levels during World War II. Today, as a result of the wars in Iraq and Afghanistan, it continues to stand at relatively high levels, about $644 billion constant dollars in 2010.

Source: Mackenzie Eaglen, "U.S. Defense Spending: The Mismatch Between Plans and Resources," *The Heritage Foundation* (June 7, 2010): www.heritage.org.

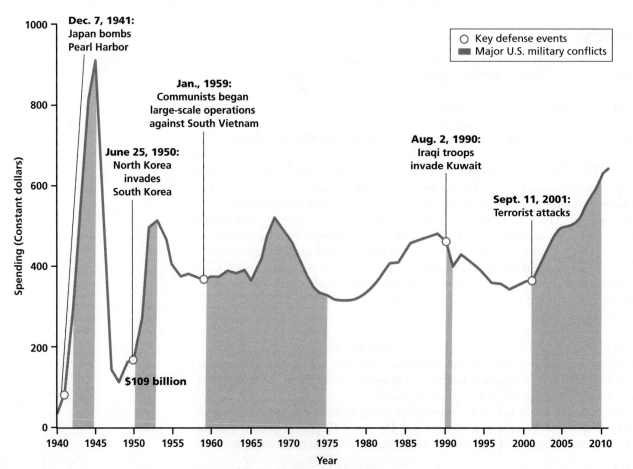

One of the problems Congress faces in using its budgetary powers to set the foreign policy agenda is that after the president publicly commits the United States to a high profile course of action, it is hard for Congress to stop effort on that initiative. After President George W. Bush committed troops to Iraq, for example, several legislators made attempts in 2007 and 2008 to curtail funding for operations in Iraq. All failed to generate sufficient support, and many generated substantial criticism for their perceived lack of support for American troops.

THE WAR POWERS ACT   Frustrated with its inability to influence policy on Vietnam, a war that deeply divided the nation, Congress passed the **War Powers Act** in 1973 to try to prevent future interventions overseas without specific congressional approval. Under the act, the president is required to consult with Congress before deploying American troops into hostile situations. Under certain conditions, the president is required to report to Congress within forty-eight hours of the deployment. A presidential report can trigger a sixty-day clock that requires congressional approval for any continued military involvement past the sixty-day window. If Congress does not give explicit approval within sixty days, the president then has thirty days to withdraw the troops. Under the act, the president can respond to an emergency such as rescuing endangered Americans but cannot engage in a prolonged struggle without congressional approval.

The War Powers Act has not been an effective restraint on presidential military adventurism. No president has recognized its constitutionality, nor has any president felt obligated to inform Congress of military action.

War Powers Act
Passed by Congress in 1973; the president is limited in the deployment of troops overseas to a sixty-day period in peacetime (which can be extended for an extra thirty days to permit withdrawal) unless Congress explicitly gives its approval for a longer period.

Interest Groups

Four types of interest groups are especially active in trying to influence foreign and defense policy decisions. Business groups are the first type of interest group that lobbies heavily on foreign policy issues. Particularly controversial is the lobbying carried out by defense industries, often in cooperation with the military. These groups are often identified as the **military-industrial complex,** a term coined by President Dwight D. Eisenhower.

Ethnic interest groups are a second type of interest group that is heavily involved in foreign policy decision making. The two groups that are generally the most influential are the American-Israel Public Affairs Committee (AIPAC) and the Cuban-American National Foundation (CANF).

Foreign governments and companies are a third type of organized interest lobbying in this area. The most common concerns of foreign governments are acquiring foreign aid and preventing hostile legislation from being passed. Foreign companies also actively lobby to gain access to the American market and improve the terms under which their investments in the United States are made.

Ideological-public interest groups are the final type of interest group active in foreign policy lobbying. This broad category consists of think tanks such as the Brookings Institute and the Heritage Foundation, nongovernmental organizations such as Amnesty International, and religious organizations. Opinions on major foreign policy issues such as isolationism versus interventionism often vary widely based on political ideology.

military-industrial complex
The alliance formed by the U.S. armed forces and defense industries.

Contemporary Challenges in Foreign and Defense Policy

★ **14.4 . . . Identify four contemporary foreign and defense policy challenges confronting the United States.**

The Obama administration faces a series of foreign and defense policy challenges. In this section we highlight four of the most pressing concerns: trade, border security and immigration, terrorism, and the spread of nuclear weapons. For each, we present an overview of basic concepts, a survey of policy options, and an in-depth case study.

Trade

Countries adopt one of three basic approaches in constructing their international trade policy: protectionism, strategic trade, and free trade. First, countries may engage in **protectionism.** In this trade policy, a country takes steps to close off its markets to foreign goods. It may also provide domestic producers with subsidies to help them compete against foreign imports.

protectionism

A trade policy wherein a country closes off its markets to foreign goods.

Second, countries may embrace a **strategic trade policy.** Under such a trade policy, governments identify key industries that they want to see grow. They then provide those industries with economic support through tax breaks, low interest loans, and other benefits. In the United States, computers, aerospace, and biotechnology are sectors that have often been singled out for support. The driving force behind modern American strategic trade policy is China. It is now the second largest market for new cars.

strategic trade policy

A trade policy wherein governments identify key industries that they wish to see grow and enact policies to support this economic enlargement.

Finally, countries may choose a **free trade system.** The hallmark of such a system is limited government interference in international trade. Goods and services cross borders based on supply and demand and according to the principle of comparative advantage, in which countries sell goods they can produce most efficiently and buy from countries what they cannot. Creating and supporting a free trade system has been a major goal of U.S. trade policy since World War II.

free trade system

A system of international trade with limited government interference.

MAKING TRADE POLICY   Three broad policy options exist for the United States under a free trade approach. The first is to emphasize bilateral trade, or trade between two nations. Although it is no longer the most popular option, such trade has a rich history in the United States and continues to be used on a limited basis today.

In an attempt to adapt to globalization and incorporate a greater number of trading partners, presidents have increasingly turned to regional trade agreements. Such agreements involve more than two but as few as three states. This was the case with the 1993 **North American Free Trade Agreement (NAFTA),** which unites the economies of Mexico, Canada, and the United States. NAFTA created the world's largest regional free trade area with a market of some 439 million people and $16.2 trillion in goods and services produced annually.

North American Free Trade Agreement (NAFTA)

Agreement that promotes free movement of goods and services among Canada, Mexico, and the United States.

Most modern trade agreements are concluded under a global free trade system. The best known (but not necessarily most successful) example of this system is the **World Trade Organization (WTO),** an international organization created in 1995 to supervise and open international trade. Like its predecessor, the General Agreement on Tariffs and Trade, the WTO reaches agreements through negotiating rounds.

World Trade Organization (WTO)

An international organization created in 1995 to supervise and open international trade.

THE CASE OF CHINA   From 1949 to 1979, China and the United States existed in virtual economic isolation from one another. A far different picture exists today. China and the United States are major bilateral trading partners and powerful voices in the WTO. They also are competitors in potential Asian regional trading systems.

The bilateral trade relationship between the United States and China has grown dramatically over the past three decades. In 1980, the year after the first U.S.-China bilateral trade agreement was signed, total trade was valued at $5 billion. By 2009, it was valued at $366 billion. This has made China the United States' second largest trading partner, the single largest source of imports in the United States, and its third largest export market.

Two issues have been of particular concern to American policy makers judging the impact of Chinese imports on the U.S. economy. The first is the loss of jobs that appears to be the result of the surge in Chinese imports. The second major issue involves health and safety problems associated with Chinese imports.

Still, China joined the WTO in 2001 (with American support). As a condition of its membership, China agreed to undertake a series of reforms. Among them were pledges to reduce tariffs on agricultural and industrial products, limit agricultural subsidies, open its banking system to foreign banks, permit full trading rights to foreign firms, and respect intellectual property rights. China's failure to fully meet these conditions has been a repeated source of conflict with the United States and others. In early 2010, the United States had eight WTO complaints pending against China. For its part, China had four cases pending against the United States. China, for example, has protested a September 2009 decision by the Obama administration to place additional tariffs (taxes) on tires imported from China.

Regional trade issues with China are an emerging concern for the United States. A significant movement in the direction of an Asian regional trade block occurred in January 2010 when a Free Trade Area was created between China and the Association of South East Asian (ASEAN) states. Japan and India also have such agreements with ASEAN. The economic potential of an Asian trading block is great and has significant consequences for the American economy.

Immigration and Border Security

The immigration issue is a growing concern in American foreign and domestic policy. In 2008, for example, more than one million individuals became naturalized citizens, and thousands of others immigrated to the United States. Mexico, India, and the Philippines were the most frequent birthplaces of these new Americans.

The Formation of the European Union

Today, the European Union (EU) is a political, legal, economic, military, and monetary union of twenty-seven countries. Its members include traditional powers such as the United Kingdom and France, as well as emerging nations such as Hungary and Estonia. But, it was not always such a diverse alliance.

The roots of the EU lie in a multilateral trade agreement formed following World War II. In 1951, the "inner six"—Belgium, France, Luxembourg, Italy, the Netherlands, and West Germany—joined together to form the European Coal and Steel Community. Member states of the community agreed to create a common market for coal and steel, in the hopes of creating postwar economic growth. Members also hoped that such an alliance would help to forestall further war on the European continent.

- Has the European Coal and Steel Community (and later, the EU) been successful in achieving its goal of economic growth for Europe?

- Which modern trade alliances, if any, do you envision undergoing a similar evolution? Should more alliances follow this pattern?

- Should the United States apply to join the European Union? Why or why not?

Four distinctions are helpful to keep in mind in considering migration flows. The first deals with the primary factors that influence an individual's decision to cross an international border. These factors are identified as being either a "push" or a "pull." Push factors such as political instability and poverty drive people to leave their home country or place of residence. In contrast, pull factors such as the availability of jobs, political freedoms, and the presence of an existing ethnic community attract individuals to a specific location.

A second distinction is between voluntary and forced migration. Voluntary migrants make a free and independent decision to move; often they are pursuing work or family goals. Forced migrants, in contrast, often feel they have no choice but to move. This may be as a result of a natural disaster, economic depression, military conflict, or government policy.

A third distinction is between legal and illegal migration. This distinction is at the heart of much of the immigration debate in the United States. Legal immigrants are documented immigrants that come to the United States with proper approval and disclosure. Illegal immigrants, in contrast, come without documentation or government knowledge.

The final distinction is the special status of refugees. International law defines a refugee as an individual who has left their country and cannot return due to a "well-founded fear of being persecuted for reasons of race, religion, nationality, membership of a particular social group, or political opinion." It is up to the country in which the refugee is seeking asylum to determine if these conditions apply. Once identified as refugees, individuals cannot be sent back to their homeland without their consent.

MAKING IMMIGRATION POLICY   The presence of large numbers of immigrants can be a source of international and domestic tension. Countries have three broadly defined options to choose from in responding to an influx of immigrants or refugees. The first option is to create an open-door policy that welcomes virtually all immigrants.

The second option is to set restrictive quotas or outright restrictions on who may enter a country. This can be accomplished in a number of ways. In the United States, the open door first began to close in the late nineteenth century in response to public protests about the number of Asian immigrants to the United States. The 1882 Immigration Act, for example, established a 50-cent "head tax" on immigrants.

The third option is to attempt to blockade a country's borders. Current U.S. policy with regard to entry by sea, for example, is defined as "wet foot/dry foot." If an individual can reach U.S. shores, they are eligible to request refugee or immigrant status. If they are intercepted on the sea, where the Coast Guard has a large patrol, they are returned home. (To learn more about the debate over immigration policy, see Join the Debate: Should the United States Adopt an Open Borders Policy?)

THE CASE OF MEXICO   The U.S.-Mexico border is 1,969 miles long. It is the world's most frequently crossed border. Some 250 million people cross it legally every year, with another 500,000 illegal crossings taking place. It is also deadly. From 1998 to 2004, 1,954 migrants died trying to cross the border.

Mexican immigration into the United States is not new. The earliest Mexican immigrants to the United States came in the late nineteenth century to build railroads across the southwest and for workers to harvest crops. The same motivation drove later Mexican immigration. The Mexican Contract Labor Program, better known as the Bracero Program, operated from 1942 to 1964. Researchers estimate that between 1943 and 1946, about 75,000 Mexicans entered the United States each year. From 1947 to 1954, the average annual migration was almost 150,000. In the last ten years of the Bracero Program, the average annual number of migrant worker contracts recorded was 333,000.[10]

The September 11 terrorist attacks dramatically altered citizens' views on immigration in the United States. Citizens repeatedly reaffirmed their belief in the need for a border fence and dramatic increases in the number of Border Patrol agents. Though additional patrolmen were hired almost immediately after the attacks, little progress was made on the fence until 2006, when President George W. Bush signed the Secure Fence Act. This legislation called for the creation of a double-reinforced fence along 700 miles of the U.S.-Mexico border where illegal drug trafficking and immigration were most common.

The "fence" is actually made up of several different barrier projects. In some locations, it is a physical structure. In others, it is a virtual fence made up of mobile towers, radar, cameras, and vehicles retrofitted with laptops, satellite phones, or handheld devices. At the time of President Barack Obama's inauguration in January 2009, more than 580 miles of fence had been completed.

In more recent years, concern over terrorists crossing the U.S.-Mexico border has been overtaken by a concern for mounting drug-related violence. To address Mexican drug trafficking, the Bush administration began the Merida Initiative, a $1.4 billion aid program for Mexico and Central American countries to fight drug cartels. Commentators have noted two complicating factors that may severely limit the success of this program. The first is the continuing demand for drugs in the United States. Second, weapons purchased in the United States and taken across the border fuel much of the violence. Firearms dealers in Houston alone have sold over $350,000 worth of weapons that have ended up in the hands of Mexican gangs. Opposition to changing gun laws in the United States makes it unlikely that this source of weapons will disappear.

Join the DEBATE | Should the United States Adopt an Open Borders Policy?

The borders of modern countries can be classified in one of two major ways: open and closed. Regions with open borders, such as the European Union and the American states, allow relatively easy entry and exit from one country (or state) to another. In contrast, countries and regions with closed borders restrict the movement and entry of noncitizens.

In recent years, there has been a vocal movement to close the U.S. border and take steps to assure that it is sealed as tightly as possible, particularly along the southern border with Mexico. But, some people argue that the government should not intervene in such border control issues, and instead should open the borders and allow the labor market to dictate the flow of immigrants into the country. Should the United States adopt an open borders policy? Or, are there legitimate policy concerns that necessitate tighter regulations on American immigration and border security?

To develop an ARGUMENT FOR open borders, think about how:

■ **The free market is best equipped to regulate the flow of laborers from one country to another.** Should supply and demand dictate immigration and emigration from one country to another? How could government intervention limit economic growth?

■ **Open borders promote cultural diversity.** How do greater numbers of immigrants provide Americans with exposure to new beliefs and ideas? How does this diversity of opinion benefit democratic deliberation?

■ **Policing borders is economically inefficient.** How much money does the national government spend on border security each year? Could this money be better spent on other programs?

To develop an ARGUMENT AGAINST open borders, think about how:

■ **Opening the borders could stunt economic growth and prosperity.** How might too many immigrants actually weaken economic growth? Should government have the ultimate authority in regulating the national economy?

■ **American political culture must be protected.** How might immigrants alter American values and beliefs? Why might these changes weaken the polity?

■ **Policing borders is necessary to control drug trafficking and other illegal activity.** How might reducing border security lead to increases in drug and other crimes? If the national government does not regulate this activity, what dangers does it pose to society?

Should the United States adopt an open borders policy? At least with respect to Mexico, Americans have attempted to close the border in recent years, going so far as to build a physical fence in many areas.

Terrorism

Terrorism is violence for purposes of political intimidation. Governments may engage in terrorism, but so too can nongovernmental organizations. Terrorism is used to protect the environment, stop abortions, preserve racial supremacy, defeat imperialism, and enrich drug traffickers.

Terrorism also is not a new phenomenon, and may last for generations. The first wave of modern terrorism, for example, advanced an anti-government agenda and began in Russia in the early twentieth century. It was set in motion by the political and economic reforms of the czars. Disappointment with these policies led to a series of assassinations through Europe, including the assassination of Archduke Ferdinand that helped spark World War I.

The second wave of modern terrorism began in the 1920s and ended in the 1960s. Defining themselves as freedom fighters, colonial terrorists sought to obtain independence from European powers. Prominent examples of countries with factions of freedom fighters include Ireland, Israel, Cyprus, and Algeria. Hit-and-run tactics in urban areas and guerrilla warfare in rural areas became defining features of this second wave of terrorism.

The third wave of modern terrorism contained elements of each of the two preceding waves. The Vietnam War set it in motion. One part of this wave was comprised of Marxist groups such as the Weather Underground in the United States, which directed its terrorism at capitalist institutions. The second part of this wave of terrorists was made up of groups seeking self-determination for ethnic minority groups. Prominent examples included the Palestine Liberation Organization and the Irish Republican Army. This wave lost much of its energy in the 1980s as the anti-capitalist revolutions failed to occur and separatist groups met military defeat.

The defining features of the current wave of terrorism are twofold. First, it is based in religion, especially Islam. Its initial energy was drawn from three events in 1979: the start of a new Muslim century, the ouster of the shah in Iran, and the Soviet invasion of Afghanistan. The United States is a special target of this religious wave of terrorism. The common goal shared by Islamic terrorist groups has been to drive the United States out of the Middle East and to return this region to Muslim rule.

Even before 9/11, this wave of terrorist activity had produced a steady flow of attacks on the United States. Marine barracks were attacked in Lebanon in 1983, the World Trade Center was struck in 1993, American embassies in Kenya and Tanzania were attacked in 1998, and the *USS Cole* was attacked in 2000. Notably, while earlier waves of terrorism focused on assassinating key individuals or the symbolic killing of relatively small numbers of individuals, these more recent attacks resulted in large numbers of casualties.

MAKING COUNTERTERRORISM POLICY   American policy makers have four policy instruments to choose from in designing a strategy to combat terrorism. The first policy tool is diplomacy. The essence of the diplomatic challenge in fighting terrorism is to get other states to assist the United States in combating terrorism. This requires cooperation not only in defeating terrorists beyond their borders but also in taking on terrorist groups and their sympathizers within their own countries.

A second policy tool is military power. The critical question is how a country best fights a war against terrorism. Modern state warfare is essentially a series of discrete and separate steps that build on one another and culminate in destroying the opponent's "center of gravity." Terrorists, in contrast, fight cumulative wars. No single military action lays the foundation for the next, and military undertakings need not occur in a given sequence. Terrorism attacks the enemy through a series of largely independent and episodic strikes that, when added together, have an effect that is far greater than the sum of the individual military actions.

Policy makers may also use economic power to defeat terrorism. Economic power can be used to defeat terrorism in two different ways. First, it can be used to coerce states to stop supporting terrorists through the imposition of economic sanctions. The goal of sanctions is to affect a hostile government's decision-making process by imposing economic hardship on the country. The second use of economic power in a war against terrorism is to provide foreign aid to alleviate the social, economic, and political conditions that may give rise to terrorism. As intuitively appealing as it is to use foreign aid to combat terrorism, much uncertainty exists about the link between poverty and terrorism.

Finally, policy makers may use covert or undercover action to combat terrorism. Skeptics question the cost effectiveness of covert action that is designed to neutralize specific individuals or groups. Before he resigned, Director of Central Intelligence George Tenet noted that even if the United States had found and killed Osama bin Laden earlier, it probably would not have stopped the September 11 terrorist attacks.

THE CASE OF AL-QAEDA   Al-Qaeda is a militant Islamic terrorist group founded in Pakistan in the late 1980s. Its initial purpose was to conduct a *jihad*, or holy war, in the name of the Islamic religion. The United States was not initially a major target of the group, which was formed in part to oppose Soviet occupation of Afghanistan. But, following the Persian Gulf War, its leader, Osama bin Laden, returned to his homeland of Saudi Arabia. When that country was threatened by Iraqi President Saddam Hussein, bin Laden offered his forces to Saudi King Fahd. His offer was turned down, and instead King Fahd allowed U.S. troops into Saudi Arabia. Bin Laden vehemently objected to this intrusion of foreign troops. His outspoken opposition to the American presence led to U.S. enmity and bin Laden's exile to Sudan. From there, he fled back to Afghanistan, where he directed the September 11, 2001, terrorist attacks.

Prior to declaring war on terrorism after 9/11, the United States responded with military force against terrorists three times and made several efforts to capture Osama bin Laden. The earliest reported covert action program to capture bin Laden involved the recruitment of a team of Afghan tribal members in the mid-1990s. The last effort before 9/11 involved the recruitment of a guerrilla commander in 1999. In between these two episodes, the Central Intelligence Agency contacted and recruited at least three proxy forces from Pakistan, Uzbekistan, and Afghanistan to try to capture or kill bin Laden.

Following 9/11, the United States moved from covert action and limited strikes to large-scale military action in the war on terrorism. On September 20, 2001, President George W. Bush issued an ultimatum to the Taliban government of Afghanistan to turn over Osama bin Laden and close all terrorist camps operating in that country. The Taliban rejected this demand, and on October 7, the United States and Great Britain began Operation Enduring Freedom. In early November, the Taliban fled Kabul, and in December, the United Nations set up an International Security Assistance Force to help a new Afghan government establish its authority.

Who is the leader of al-Qaeda? Osama bin Laden, seen here in an Afghani bunker, is the leader of the al-Qaeda organization.

Photo courtesy: AP/Wide World Photos

Nuclear Weapons

Two questions provide the starting point for thinking about how to control nuclear weapons. The first question is, why do countries go nuclear? No single reason exists, but three motivations are particularly common. The first involves defense. Countries seek to have nuclear weapons so that they do not have to depend on other nations for help.

The second reason for going nuclear involves the pursuit of international prestige. Nuclear weapons bring prestige because of the central role military power plays in world politics. Possessing nuclear weapons elevates a country into a small select group of states whose power dwarfs all others.

Domestic politics are a third motivating factor behind countries' efforts to acquire nuclear weapons. Pressure to "go nuclear" may come from the military seeking to add to its power, scientists seeking to demonstrate their knowledge and qualifications, political parties seeking electoral victory and running on a strong defense platform, or individual leaders seeking to realize political power for themselves or their country.

A second major question is, how inevitable is the proliferation or spread of nuclear weapons? The historical record suggests that that extreme fear of these weapons is unnecessary. As evidenced by Germany, Japan, and other industrialized countries, having access to technologies associated with weapons of mass destruction does not compel countries to seek or use these weapons. More recently, Libya, South Africa, Ukraine, Belarus, and Kazakhstan have all turned away from the possession or pursuit of nuclear weapons.

MAKING ARMS PROLIFERATION POLICY   Efforts to deal with nuclear weapons and the means of delivering them have taken numerous forms. Several strategies traditionally have been used to limit arms proliferation: disarmament, arms control, defense, and counterproliferation.

Disarmament takes the very existence of weapons as the cause for conflict and hopes to secure peace through eliminating the means of conflict. The first nuclear disarmament proposal to command global attention was the Baruch Plan. Presented by the United States at the United Nations in 1946, it sought to place all aspects of nuclear energy production and use under international control. The Soviet Union, as a permanent member of the UN Security Council, rejected the Baruch Plan, and it was not implemented.

A second strategy is arms control. It takes the existence of conflict between countries as a given in world politics and seeks to find ways of reducing the danger that those conflicts will become deadly. Reducing the numbers and types of weapons at the disposal of policy makers is one approach.

The first major breakthrough in arms control of nuclear weapons came after the Cuban Missile Crisis. A "hot line" was set up between Washington and Moscow, allowing the leaders in the United States and the Soviet Union to communicate directly in a crisis.

A third strategy is denial. The goal of denial is to prevent would-be nuclear states from gaining access to the technology they need to make or deliver nuclear weapons. Denial has become more difficult in a globalized world, though many nations continue to pursue this goal. The key international groups working on arms denial are the Nuclear Suppliers Group and the Missile Technology Control Regime.

A fourth strategy is defense; this strategy is gaining popularity today. Essentially, this goal encourages the creation of a system to block or intercept attacks from other countries. Surprise missile tests by Iran and North Korea in 1998 provided new political backing for the creation of a missile defense system. In December 2002, President George W. Bush acted on this plan, ordering the initial deployment of long-range missile interceptors in Alaska and California.

A final strategy that is embraced by many countries today is counterproliferation. It involves the use of preemptive military action against a country or terrorist group. Counterproliferation begins with the assumption that certain terrorist groups and some states cannot be deterred because they have given evidence of responding irrationally to threats of military force or other forms of coercion. The most frequently cited example is Israel's 1981 raid on Iraq's Osiraq nuclear reactor. One of the major challenges to counterproliferation is its effectiveness. Critics argue that attempts at preemptive action will not forestall the driving force behind an attack, and may actually make the situation worse by altering public opinion in the attacked state.

THE CASE OF NORTH KOREA   Except for periods of direct military conflict—such as the Korean War in 1950 and crises such as when North Korea seized the American spy ship the *USS Pueblo* in 1968 and held its crew captive—direct U.S. diplomatic contacts with North Korea have been all but absent. The United States, however, has worked through its allies (including South Korea) and international organizations to attempt to prevent North Korea from developing and using nuclear technology. Limitations on the development of such weaponry were a condition of the peace agreement signed to end the Korean War.

The United States also maintains an active surveillance program that monitors the activities of the North Korean government. In 1993, for example, the Central Intelligence Agency believed that there was a fifty-fifty chance that North Korea had developed nuclear technology. The Defense Intelligence Agency declared it already had a working nuclear weapon. The United States demonstrated its disapproval of this arms program in two ways. It asked the United Nations to impose sanctions on North Korea, and it sent Patriot missiles to South Korea as a defense mechanism.

Ultimately, this conflict was resolved a year later, when North and South Korea reached a new agreement on denuclearizing the Korean peninsula, the Agreed Framework. The Agreed Framework included an agreement by North Korea to freeze its existing nuclear program and allow external monitoring by the International Atomic Energy Association (IAEA), a promise by the United States to supply it with oil and other fuels, and an agreement by both sides to move to full normalization of political and economic relations.

Implementation of the agreement was troubled from the start. Oil was slow to be delivered, U.S. economic sanctions were not effectively removed, and most importantly, full diplomatic relations were never established, largely because the United States objected to what it saw as continued North Korean nuclear activity. In 1998, for example, the United States identified an underground site it suspected of being involved in nuclear activities and North Korea tested a ballistic missile.

By the end of 2002, relations between the United States and North Korea had deteriorated sharply. Fuel imports to North Korea were suspended, and North Korea terminated its freeze on the plutonium-based nuclear facility. In early 2003, it expelled IAEA inspectors and withdrew from the international Nuclear Non-Proliferation Treaty. The Agreed Framework was now held to be null and void by both sides.

Movement beyond this point has been slow and halting. In 2003, the United States proposed multilateral talks with North Korea on its nuclear program. North Korea initially refused, asserting that this was a bilateral matter. But, under pressure from China, North Korea agreed to multilateral talks between those three states. Later, the talks were expanded and became known as the Six Party Talks when South Korea, Japan, and Russia joined the United States, North Korea, and China. As these negotiations dragged on, North Korea continued with its nuclear program. In October 2003, it announced that it had tested a nuclear weapon. The United Nations responded by imposing economic sanctions on the transfer of military and technological materials and luxury goods to North Korea and freezing North Korean assets that were not being used to meet basic needs.

In 2007, the Six Party Talks finally led to a bilateral agreement between North Korea and the United States. But, relations again turned sour when North Korea tested a rocket in April 2009. In response, the United States tightened economic sanctions, which North Korea labeled a "declaration of war." Then, in November 2010, North Korea fired shells at a South Korean island setting off one of the most serious skirmishes between North and South Korea in decades. The United States joined other nations in condemning the attack, ensuring continued tensions between the United States and North Korea for the foreseeable future.

TOWARD REFORM: Rethinking American Power

★ **14.5 . . . Evaluate the shift in thinking about American power that has occurred in recent decades.**

The United States emerged from the Cold War as the world's dominant power. With no major challengers, it was able to act unilaterally. Allies were welcome but not essential. Today, the United States remains a dominant power in world politics, but its margin of error appears to be reduced, and the costs of unilateral action are higher. The lengthy wars in Iraq and Afghanistan and a struggling global economy are major reasons for these barriers.

Not surprisingly, the result of this decline in global power is renewed interest in multilateral foreign policy initiatives. The best allies for the United States, however, are unclear. To some observers, China is both the primary challenger to the United States and its most logical partner. This is reflected in calls for an alliance to manage the international economy. Other scholars call for a "League of Democracies." In the view of these individuals, the United States should partner with other democracies to counter countries that sponsor or harbor terrorists. Still a third view argues against standing alliances with any set of states. These people favor forming temporary alliances to counter particular challenges as they arise.

Deciding whether to act alone or with others is only part of the decision that needs to be made about how to use American power. Just as important is the question of what type of power to use. The major choice is between hard power and soft power. Hard power is the power to coerce, or to make another country do what the United States wants. It is most frequently seen as being rooted in defense policy and military strength, but economic strength can also be used as hard power. Soft power is the ability to persuade; it is most commonly seen in foreign policy making. It attracts other countries to the United States in a positive and voluntary fashion. American political, economic, and legal ideas and values as well as its scientific and technological research are seen as crucial elements of the United States' soft power. Many assert that while its hard power has declined of late the United States' soft power remains unchallenged in world politics.

Complicating the use of hard or soft power is uncertainty about the American public's support for foreign policy initiatives. The bipartisan consensus on the need to contain communism during the Cold War has long vanished, and no new consensus has emerged. Instead, portions of the American public are deeply divided over how to proceed, while others have become largely apathetic.

It can also be difficult to get citizens to devote attention to foreign policy issues. This is known as the "guns" and "butter" theory. Generally speaking, most citizens are more interested in domestic policy issues ("butter") because they have a greater impact on their everyday lives. It is only in case of emergency or times of crisis that citizens express significant concern over foreign policy issues ("guns"). This complicates foreign policy making, and can make it difficult for foreign policy issues to occupy space on the policy agenda. (To learn more about public opinion on domestic and foreign policy, see Analyzing Visuals: The Most Important Problem, 1947–2009.)

ANALYZING VISUALS

The Most Important Problem, 1947–2009

Public support can be essential to carrying out U.S. foreign policy goals. However, especially in times of peace or domestic crisis, it can be difficult to get Americans to devote attention to international policy issues. In order to gauge citizens' support for foreign and domestic policy concerns, pollsters generally ask citizens a question such as, "What do you think is the most important problem facing the country today?" Review the trend in these results from 1947 to 2009, and then answer the questions.

Source: Harold W. Stanley and Richard G. Niemi, eds., *Vital Statistics on American Politics, 2007–2008* (Washington, D.C.: CQ Press, 2008). Reprinted by permission. Updated by authors.

■ How has interest in domestic and foreign policy issues changed over time?

■ At what times do Americans generally place priority on domestic policy issues? Foreign policy issues?

■ Which domestic and foreign policy issues do you think most affect citizens' policy priorities? Why?

What Should I Have LEARNED?

Now that you have read this chapter, you should be able to:

⭐ **14.1 Trace the evolution of U.S. foreign and defense policy, p. 406.**

U.S. foreign and defense policy has evolved. Foreign and defense policy played a minor role in American politics for most of the nation's first century. As U.S. economic interests expanded, the United States intervened more and more overseas, especially in Latin America and Asia. After a delayed entry into World War I, America retreated into isolation.

⭐ **14.2 Explain the developments that led to the rise of the United States as a world power, p. 410.**

The United States' status as a world power was cemented by its entry into, and subsequent victory, in World War II.

Since that time, America has experienced several distinct periods, including the Cold War, détente, and the post–Cold War period. After World War II, foreign and defense policy often dominated the American political agenda, with a focus on internationalism rather than isolationism. American foreign policy during the Cold War was organized around containment and deterrence. The period of détente sought to use linked rewards and punishments rather than military power to contain the Soviet Union. The post–Cold War period was ushered in by the fall of communism in the Soviet Union and featured policies of enlargement to promote the expansion of democracy and free markets throughout the world. The September 11, 2001, terrorist attacks marshaled in a new era of engagement in American foreign policy, as the United States pursued a war on terrorism both at home and overseas in Iraq and Afghanistan.

⭐ 14.3 Outline the actors that shape foreign and defense policy decision making, p. 415.

The basic structure of foreign and defense policy decision making is laid out in the Constitution. The executive branch of government dominates foreign and defense policy. The president is preeminent, with the Departments of State, Defense, and Homeland Security also playing important roles. Congress also influences and shapes policy through oversight, treaties, appointments, appropriations, and the War Powers Act. Four types of interest groups are also especially active in trying to influence foreign and defense policy decisions; these groups include the military-industrial complex, ethnic interest groups, foreign governments and companies, and ideological-public interest groups.

⭐ 14.4 Identify four contemporary foreign and defense policy challenges confronting the United States, p. 421.

The United States faces four major challenges in foreign and defense policy during the twenty-first century. They are trade, border security and immigration, terrorism, and controlling the spread of nuclear weapons. In terms of trade, China presents the United States with the biggest challenge because of the loss of jobs associated with a surge in Chinese imports, and the health and safety

problems associated with Chinese imports. In terms of immigration and border security, Mexico presents the greatest challenge. Approximately 500,000 people illegally cross the Mexico border each year; these illegal crossings are increasingly associated with drug-related and gang violence. The biggest challenge related to terrorism comes from al-Qaeda, the perpetrators of the September 11, 2001, terrorist attacks. Al-Qaeda's highly decentralized network of terrorist cells makes it difficult to achieve victory in the traditional sense. Finally, one significant challenge related to nuclear weapons comes from North Korea. This country has allegedly tested nuclear weapons and refuses to submit to inspections or to respond to sanctions.

⭐ 14.5 Evaluate the shift in thinking about American power that has occurred in recent decades, p. 430.

The United States emerged from the Cold War as the world's dominant power, and it was able to act unilaterally. Allies were welcome but not essential. Today, although the United States remains a dominant power, the costs of unilateral action are higher, and there has been a renewed interest in multilateral foreign policy initiatives. Many people assert that although the United States' hard power—its ability to coerce other countries into doing what it wants—has declined, its soft power, the power to persuade other countries, has increased and remains unchallenged in world politics.

Test Yourself: Foreign and Defense Policy

⭐ 14.1 Trace the evolution of U.S. foreign and defense policy, p. 406.

In his 1796 Farewell Address, George Washington suggested that the United States
  A. make peace treaties with France.
  B. avoid international trade.
  C. avoid permanent alliances.
  D. depend heavily on Europe for trade.
  E. make peace treaties with England.

⭐ 14.2 Explain the developments that led to the rise of the United States as a world power, p. 410.

The strategy of opposing Soviet expansion with military forces, economic assistance, and political influence was known as
  A. containment.
  B. alliance theory.
  C. balance of power.
  D. preventionism.
  E. isolationism.

⭐ 14.3 Outline the actors that shape foreign and defense policy decision making, p. 415.

The Framers intended to
  A. endow the states with foreign policy powers.
  B. divide foreign policy powers between the Congress and the president.
  C. give all foreign policy powers to the president.
  D. give the states and federal government equal foreign policy powers.
  E. give the Supreme Court the power to declare war.

⭐ 14.4 Identify four contemporary foreign and defense policy challenges confronting the United States, p. 421.

Which of the following is NOT a major foreign policy challenge facing the United States?
  A. Immigration
  B. Nuclear weapons
  C. Trade
  D. Health care
  E. Terrorism

★ **14.5 Evaluate the shift in thinking about American power that has occurred in recent decades, p. 430.**

The power to coerce, or to make another country do what the United States wants, is known as
  A. manipulation.
  B. enlargement.
  C. multilateralism.
  D. hard power.
  E. the Powell Doctrine.

Essay Questions

  1. What were the Monroe Doctrine and the Roosevelt Corollary, and how did they define early American foreign policy?

  2. How did the Cold War define U.S. foreign policy for much of the twentieth century?
  3. What is the military-industrial complex, and how does it influence U.S. foreign policy?
  4. Why is Mexican immigration a major foreign policy issue in the United States today?
  5. Should the United States pursue bilateral or multilateral foreign policy? Defend your answer.

---

mypolicilab Exercises

Apply what you learned in this chapter on MyPoliSciLab.

📖 **Read** on **mypolscilab.com**

  eText: Chapter 14

✔ **Study** and **Review** on **mypolscilab.com**

  Pre-Test
  Post-Test
  Chapter Exam
  Flashcards

👁 **Watch** on **mypolscilab.com**

  Video: NYC's Subway Surveillance System
  Video: Sanctions on Iran
  Video: Three Vivid Years—But Progress?

⊕ **Explore** on **mypolscilab.com**

  Simulation: You Are President John F. Kennedy
  Simulation: You Are the Newly Appointed Ambassador to the Country of Dalmatia
  Simulation: You Are the President of the United States
  Comparative: Comparing Foreign and Security Policy
  Timeline: The Evolution of Foreign Policy
  Visual Literacy: Evaluating Defense Spending

Key Terms

Bretton Woods System, p. 411
collective security, p. 410
Cuban Missile Crisis, p. 412
defense policy, p. 406
Department of Defense, p. 418
Department of Homeland Security, p. 419
Department of State, p. 418
détente, p. 413
Embargo Act, p. 407
enlargement, p. 414
foreign policy, p. 406
free trade system, p. 422

General Agreement on Tariffs and Trade (GATT), p. 411
human rights, p. 413
International Monetary Fund (IMF), p. 411
isolationism, p. 407
Joint Chiefs of Staff, p. 418
manifest destiny, p. 408
Marshall Plan, p. 412
military-industrial complex, p. 421
Monroe Doctrine, p. 407
North American Free Trade Agreement (NAFTA), p. 422

North Atlantic Treaty Organization (NATO), p. 412
protectionism, p. 422
Reagan Doctrine, p. 413
Roosevelt Corollary, p. 408
strategic trade policy, p. 422
tariffs, p. 407
Truman Doctrine, p. 412
war on terrorism, p. 415
War Powers Act, p. 421
World Bank, p. 411
World Trade Organization (WTO), p. 422

To Learn More on Foreign and Defense Policy

In the Library

Allison, Graham F., and Philip Zelikow. *Essence of Decision: Explaining the Cuban Missile Crisis,* 2nd ed. New York: Pearson, 1999.

Axelrod, Alan. *American Treaties and Alliances.* Washington, DC: CQ Press, 2000.

Bacevich, Andrew. *Washington Rules: America's Path to Permanent War.* New York: Metropolitan Books, 2010.

Byman, Daniel, and Matthew C. Waxman. *The Dynamics of Coercion: American Foreign Policy and the Limits of Military Might.* New York: Cambridge University Press, 2002.

Ervin, Clark Kent. *Open Target: Where America Is Vulnerable to Attack.* New York: Palgrave Macmillan, 2006.

Goldstein, Joshua S., and Jon C. Pevehouse. *International Relations,* 9th ed. New York: Longman, 2009.

Hook, Steven W. *U.S. Foreign Policy: The Paradox of World Power,* 3rd ed. Washington, DC: CQ Press, 2010.

Howard, Russell D., James J. F. Forest, and Joanne Moore. *Homeland Security and Terrorism: Readings and Interpretations.* New York: McGraw-Hill, 2006.

Hunt, Michael H. *Ideology and U.S. Foreign Policy.* New Haven, CT: Yale University Press, 2009.

Kagan, Robert. *Dangerous Nation: America's Foreign Policy from Its Earliest Days to the Dawn of the Twentieth Century.* New York: Vintage, 2007.

Kaufman, Joyce P. *A Concise History of U.S. Foreign Policy,* 2nd ed. Lanham, MD: Rowman and Littlefield, 2010.

Kennan, George F. *American Diplomacy, 1900–1950.* Chicago: University of Chicago Press, 1951.

Lowenthal, Mark M. *Intelligence: From Secrets to Policy,* 4th ed. Washington, DC: CQ Press, 2008.

McCormick, James M. *American Foreign Policy and Process,* 5th ed. New York: Wadsworth, 2009.

Nye, Joseph S., Jr. *The Paradox of American Power: Why the World's Only Superpower Can't Go It Alone.* New York: Oxford University Press, 2002.

On the Web

To learn more about the reach and worldwide involvement of the United Nations, go to **www.unsystem.org.**

To learn more about the Department of Defense and U.S. military operations around the globe, go to **www.defenselink.mil.**

To learn more about the State Department, go to **www.state.gov.**

To learn more about the CIA and the larger intelligence community, go to **www.cia.gov.**

The Declaration of Independence

In Congress, July 4, 1776
The Unanimous Declaration of the Thirteen United States of America

When in the Course of human events it becomes necessary for one people to dissolve the political bands which have connected them with another, and to assume, among the powers of the earth, the separate and equal station to which the Laws of Nature and of Nature's God entitle them, a decent respect to the opinions of mankind requires that they should declare the causes which impel them to the separation.

We hold these truths to be self-evident, that all men are created equal, that they are endowed by their Creator with certain unalienable Rights, that among these are Life, Liberty and the pursuit of Happiness. That to secure these rights, Governments are instituted among Men, deriving their just powers from the consent of the governed. That whenever any Form of Government becomes destructive of these ends, it is the Right of the People to alter or to abolish it, and to institute new Government, laying its foundation on such principles and organizing its powers in such form, as to them shall seem most likely to effect their Safety and Happiness. Prudence, indeed, will dictate that Governments long established should not be changed for light and transient causes; and accordingly all experience hath shewn that mankind are more disposed to suffer, while evils are sufferable, than to right themselves by abolishing the forms to which they are accustomed. But when a long train of abuses and usurpations, pursuing invariably the same Object evinces a design to reduce them under absolute Despotism, it is their right, it is their duty, to throw off such Government, and to provide new Guards for their future security. —Such has been the patient sufferance of these Colonies; and such is now the necessity which constrains them to alter their former Systems of Government. The history of the present King of Great Britain is a history of repeated injuries and usurpations, all having in direct object the establishment of an absolute Tyranny over these States. To prove this, let Facts be submitted to a candid world.

He has refused his Assent to Laws, the most wholesome and necessary for the public good.

He has forbidden his Governors to pass Laws of immediate and pressing importance, unless suspended in their operation till his Assent should be obtained; and when so suspended, he has utterly neglected to attend to them.

He has refused to pass other Laws for the accommodation of large districts of people, unless those people would relinquish the right of Representation in the Legislature, a right inestimable to them and formidable to tyrants only.

He has called together legislative bodies at places unusual, uncomfortable, and distant from the depository of their Public Records, for the sole purpose of fatiguing them into compliance with his measures.

He has dissolved Representative Houses repeatedly, for opposing with manly firmness his invasions on the rights of the people.

He has refused for a long time, after such dissolutions, to cause others to be elected; whereby the Legislative Powers, incapable of Annihilation, have returned to the People at large for their exercise, the State remaining in the mean time exposed to all the dangers of invasion from without, and convulsions within.

He has endeavored to prevent the population of these States; for that purpose obstructing the Laws of Naturalization of Foreigners; refusing to pass others to encourage their migration hither, and raising the conditions of new Appropriations of Lands.

He has obstructed the Administration of Justice, by refusing his Assent to Laws for establishing Judiciary powers.

He has made Judges dependent on his Will alone, for the tenure of their offices, and the amount and payment of their salaries.

He has erected a multitude of New Offices, and sent hither swarms of Officers to harass our people, and eat out their substance.

He has kept among us, in times of peace, Standing Armies without the Consent of our legislatures.

He has affected to render the Military independent of and superior to the Civil power.

He has combined with others to subject us to a jurisdiction foreign to our constitution, and unacknowledged by our laws, giving his Assent to their Acts of pretended Legislation:

For quartering large bodies of armed troops among us:

For protecting them, by a mock Trial, from punishment for any Murders which they should commit on the Inhabitants of these States:

For cutting off our Trade with all parts of the world:

For imposing Taxes on us without our Consent:

For depriving us in many cases, of the benefits of Trial by Jury:

For transporting us beyond Seas to be tried for pretended offences:

For abolishing the free System of English Laws in a neighboring Province, establishing therein an Arbitrary government, and enlarging its Boundaries so as to render it at once an example and fit instrument for introducing the same absolute rule into these Colonies:

For taking away our Charters, abolishing our most valuable Laws, and altering fundamentally the Forms of our Governments:

For suspending our own Legislatures, and declaring themselves invested with power to legislate for us in all cases whatsoever.

He has abdicated Government here, by declaring us out of his Protection and waging War against us.

He has plundered our seas, ravaged our Coasts, burnt out towns, and destroyed the lives of our people.

He is at this time transporting large Armies of foreign Mercenaries to compleat the works of death, desolation and tyranny, already begun with circumstances of Cruelty and perfidy scarcely paralleled in the most barbarous ages, and totally unworthy the Head of a civilized nation.

He has constrained our fellow Citizens taken Captive on the high Seas to bear Arms against their Country, to become the executioners of their friends and Brethren, or to fall themselves by their Hands.

He has excited domestic insurrections amongst us, and has endeavored to bring on the inhabitants of our frontiers, the merciless Indian Savages, whose known rule of warfare, is an undistinguished destruction of all ages, sexes and conditions.

In every stage of these Oppressions We have Petitioned for Redress in the most humble terms: Our repeated Petitions have been answered only by repeated injury: A Prince, whose character is thus marked by every act which may define a Tyrant, is unfit to be the ruler of a free people.

Nor have We been wanting in attention to our British brethren. We have warned them from time to time of attempts by their legislature to extend an unwarrantable jurisdiction over us. We have reminded them of the circumstances of our emigration and settlement here. We have appealed to their native justice and magnanimity; and we have conjured them by the ties of our common kindred to disavow these usurpations, which would inevitably interrupt our connections and correspondence. They too have been deaf to the voice of justice and consanguinity. We must, therefore, acquiesce in the necessity, which denounces our Separation, and hold them, as we hold the rest of mankind, Enemies in War, in Peace Friends.

We, therefore, the Representatives of the United States of America, in General Congress, Assembled, appealing to the Supreme Judge of the world for the rectitude of our intentions, do, in the Name, and by Authority of the good People of these Colonies, solemnly publish and declare, That these United Colonies are, and of Right ought to be Free and Independent States; that they are Absolved from all Allegiance to the British Crown, and that all political connection between them and the State of Great Britain, is and ought to be totally dissolved: and that as Free and Independent States, they have full power to levy War, conclude Peace, contract Alliances, establish Commerce, and to do all other Acts and Things which Independent States may of right do. And for the support of this Declaration, with a firm reliance on the protection of Divine Providence, we mutually pledge to each other our Lives, our Fortunes and our sacred Honor.

JOHN HANCOCK

NEW HAMPSHIRE
Josiah Bartlett
William Whipple
Matthew Thornton

MASSACHUSETTS
Samuel Adams
John Adams
Robert Treat Paine
Elbridge Gerry

RHODE ISLAND AND PROVIDENCE PLANTATIONS
Stephen Hopkins
William Ellery

CONNECTICUT
Roger Sherman
Samuel Huntington
William Williams
Oliver Wolcott

NEW YORK
William Floyd
Philip Livingston
Francis Lewis
Lewis Morris

NEW JERSEY
Richard Stockton
John Witherspoon
Francis Hopkinson
John Hart
Abraham Clark

PENNSYLVANIA
Robert Morris
Benjamin Rush
Benjamin Franklin
John Morton
George Clymer
James Smith
George Taylor
James Wilson
George Ross

DELAWARE
Caesar Rodney
George Read
Thomas McKean

MARYLAND
Samuel Chase
William Paca

Thomas Stone
Charles Carroll

VIRGINIA
George Wythe
Richard Henry Lee
Thomas Jefferson
Benjamin Harrison
Thomas Nelson, Jr.
Francis Lightfoot Lee
Carter Braxton

NORTH CAROLINA
William Hooper
Joseph Hewes
John Penn

SOUTH CAROLINA
Edward Rutledge
Thomas Heyward, Jr.
Thomas Lynch, Jr.
Arthur Middleton

GEORGIA
Button Gwinnett
Lyman Hall
George Walton

The Federalist Papers

The Federalist Papers, essays initially released alone and serially by proponents of the U.S. Constitution, provide us with firsthand views of the Framers' intentions. John Jay, James Madison, and Alexander Hamilton were engaged in the writing of the Constitution, and they used *The Federalist Papers* to help persuade citizens to support ratification of that document. Jay was later named the first chief justice of the Supreme Court of the United States, Madison served as the nation's fourth president, and Hamilton (prevented from seeking the presidency by his birth in the British West Indies) was the first secretary of the treasury. Annotated below are three of the most often read and cited of the essays.

Federalist No. 10
November 22, 1787
James Madison
To the People of the State of New York:

Controlling factions, or groups of like-minded citizens united in a common interest adverse to the interests of the community, was a major concern of the Framers. In *Federalist No. 10*, James Madison argues that one of the best ways to check the power of faction is to create a republican form of government.

Among the numerous advantages promised by a well constructed Union, none deserves to be more accurately developed than its tendency to break and control the violence of faction. The friend of popular governments, never finds himself so much alarmed for their character and fate, as when he contemplates their propensity to this dangerous vice.

● Madison notes the Framers' concern with the role of factions, which he believes are one of the greatest threats to popular government. This fear is likely derived from concerns of the Framers (many of whom were political elites) about the political power of the masses. Uprisings such as Shays's Rebellion underscored this fear. ●

He will not fail therefore to set a due value on any plan which, without violating the principles to which he is attached, provides a proper cure for it. The instability, injustice and confusion introduced into the public councils, have in truth been the mortal diseases under which popular governments have every where perished; as they continue to be the favorite and fruitful topics from which the adversaries to liberty derive their most specious. The valuable improvements made by the American Constitutions on the popular models, both ancient and modern, cannot certainly be too much admired; but it would be an unwarrantable partiality, to contend that they have as effectually obviated the danger on this side as was wished and expected.

● Here, Madison anticipates citizens' concerns about the new government's ability to address problems suffered by other countries. Perhaps as a result, the U.S. Constitution has become one the most enduring of written constitutions. ●

Complaints are every where heard from our most considerate and virtuous citizens, equally the friends of public and private faith, and of public and personal liberty, that our governments are too unstable; that the public good is disregarded in the conflicts of rival parties; and that measures are too often decided, not according to the rules of justice, and the rights of the minor party, but by the superior force of an interested and over-bearing majority. However anxiously we may wish that these complaints had no foundation, the evidence of known facts will not permit us to deny that they are in some degree true. It will be found indeed, on a candid review of our situation, that some of the distresses under which we labor, have been erroneously charged on the operation of our governments; but it will be found, at the same time, that other causes will not alone account for many of our heaviest misfortunes; and particularly, for that prevailing and increasing distrust of public engagements, and alarm for private rights, which are echoed from one end of the continent to the other. These must be chiefly, if not wholly, effects of the unsteadiness and injustice, with which a factious spirit has tainted our public administrations.

● Here, Madison acknowledges the weaknesses of government under the Articles of Confederation. Among these are a lack of concern for the public good, a disregard for the rights of the minority, and the failure to preserve citizens' personal liberties. Concerns about individual rights are the cornerstone of much of Enlightenment philosophy; both Thomas Hobbes and John Locke discussed the rights individuals would have to give up to government in exchange for security and protection. The ideas of Locke, in particular, informed the Declaration of Independence. ●

By a faction I understand a number of citizens, whether amounting to a majority or minority of the whole, who are united and actuated by some common impulse of passion, or of interest, adverse to the rights of other citizens, or to the permanent and aggregate interests of the community.

● For the first time, Madison outlines his idea of a faction: a group of citizens united in an interest that negatively affects the interests of the community. He voices his belief that such factions must be guarded against by government—an idea that motivated the Framers throughout their work on the Constitution as they balanced the interests of competing groups such as large and small states, slave and nonslave states, and northern and southern states. ●

There are two methods of curing the mischiefs of faction: the one, by removing its causes; the other, by controlling its effects.

● For a government to succeed, it must either remove the causes of faction or find a way to control or mediate disparate views, however strongly held. ●

There are again two methods of removing the causes of faction: the one by destroying the liberty which is essential to its existence; the other, by giving to every citizen the same opinions, the same passions, and the same interests.

● Madison specifies two ways to remove the *causes* of faction: destroying the liberty necessary for factions to survive, and creating a citizenry united by common opinion. As we will see, Madison finds both of these options unsatisfactory. Thus, later in the essay, he discusses methods of controlling the *effects* of faction, among which are the creation of the new government. ●

It could never be more truly said than of the first remedy, that it is worse than the disease. Liberty is to faction, what air is to fire, an aliment without which it instantly expires. But it could not be a less folly to abolish liberty, which is essential to political life, because it nourishes faction, than it would be to wish the annihilation of air, which is essential to animal life, because it imparts to fire its destructive agency.

● Here, Madison begins to discuss why it is impossible to control the causes of faction. He takes pains to note that curtailing citizens' liberties is out of the question. This was an issue of particular concern to Anti-Federalists, who later insisted on the addition of a Bill of Rights to the Constitution. ●

The second expedient is as impracticable, as the first would be unwise. As long as the reason of man continues fallible, and he is at liberty to exercise it, different opinions will be formed. As long as the connection subsists between his reason and his self-love, his opinions and his passions will have a reciprocal influence on each other; and the former will be objects to which the latter will attach themselves. The diversity in the faculties of men from which the rights of property originate, is not less an insuperable obstacle to a uniformity of interests. The protection of these faculties is the first object of Government. From the protection of different and unequal faculties of acquiring property, the possession of different degrees and kinds of property immediately results: and from the influence of these on the sentiments and views of the respective proprietors, ensues a division of the society into different interests and parties.

The latent causes of faction are thus sown in the nature of man; and we see them everywhere brought into different degrees of activity, according to the different circumstances of civil society.

A zeal for different opinions concerning religion, concerning Government and many other points, as well of speculation as of practice; an attachment to different leaders ambitiously contending for pre-eminence and power; or to persons of other descriptions whose fortunes have been interesting to the human passions, have in turn divided mankind into parties, inflamed them with mutual animosity, and rendered them much more disposed to vex and oppress each other, than to cooperate for their common good. So strong is this propensity of mankind to fall into mutual animosities, that where no substantial occasion presents itself, the most frivolous and fanciful distinctions have been sufficient to kindle their unfriendly passions, and excite their most violent conflicts. But the most common and durable source of factions, has been the various and unequal distribution of property. Those who hold, and those who are without property, have ever formed distinct interests in society. Those who are creditors, and those who are debtors, fall under a like discrimination. A landed interest, a manufacturing interest, a mercantile interest, a monied interest, with many lesser interests, grow up of necessity in civilized nations, and divide them into different classes, actuated by different sentiments and views. The regulation of these various and interfering interests forms the principal task of modern Legislation, and involves the spirit of party and faction in the necessary and ordinary operations of Government.

No man is allowed to be a judge in his own cause, because his interest would certainly bias his judgment, and, not improbably, corrupt his integrity. With equal, nay with greater reason, a body of men, are unfit to be both judges and parties, at the same time; yet, what are many of the most important acts of legislation, but so many judicial determinations, not indeed concerning the rights of single persons, but concerning the rights of large bodies of citizens, and what are the different classes of legislators, but advocates and parties to the causes which they determine? Is a law proposed concerning private debts? It is a question to which the creditors are parties on one side, and the debtors on the other. Justice ought to hold the balance between them. Yet the parties are and must be themselves the judges; and the most numerous party, or, in other words, the most powerful faction, must be expected to prevail. Shall domestic manufactures be encouraged, and in what degree, by restrictions on foreign manufactures? are questions which would be differently decided by the landed and the manufacturing classes; and probably by neither, with a sole regard to justice and the public good. The apportionment of taxes on the various descriptions of property, is an act which seems to require the most exact impartiality; yet, there is perhaps no legislative act in which greater opportunity and temptation are given to a predominant party, to trample on the rules of justice. Every shilling with which they over-burden the inferior number, is a shilling saved to their own pockets.

It is in vain to say, that enlightened statesmen will be able to adjust these clashing interests, and render them all subservient to the public good. Enlightened statesmen will not always be at the helm. Nor, in many cases, can such an adjustment be made at all, without taking into view indirect and remote considerations, which will rarely prevail over the immediate interest which one party may find in disregarding the rights of another, or the good of the whole.

● In these paragraphs, Madison discusses why expecting citizens to share the same opinions is also an impracticable solution to controlling the causes of factions. He notes people's natural and inherent divisions, many of which are rooted in the division of property. These differences are necessary to the survival of society, and it is the role of government to mediate between these competing interests. ●

The inference to which we are brought, is, that the *causes* of faction cannot be removed; and that relief is only to be sought in the means of controlling its *effects*.

● Here, Madison transitions from trying to remove the causes of faction to considering mechanisms that can control the effects of faction. ●

If a faction consists of less than a majority, relief is supplied by the republican principle, which enables the majority to defeat its sinister views by regular vote. It may clog the administration, it may convulse the society, but it will be unable to execute and mask its violence under the forms of the Constitution. When a majority is included in a faction, the form of popular government on the other hand enables it to sacrifice to its ruling passion or interest, both the public good and the rights of other citizens. To secure the public good, and private rights, against the danger of such a faction, and at the same time to preserve the spirit and the form of popular government, is then the great object to which our enquiries are directed. Let me add that it is the great desideratum, by which alone this form of government can be rescued from the opprobrium under which it has so long labored, and be recommended to the esteem and adoption of mankind.

● In this paragraph, Madison introduces how to secure public goods and private rights from the "danger of faction." He concludes that there is little concern about the danger of faction when such a group is made up of less than a majority (a minority) of citizens. However, preventing majority factions from trampling the rights of minorities is a much more challenging proposition. ●

By what means is this object attainable? Evidently by one of two only. Either the existence of the same passion or interest in a majority at the same time, must be prevented; or the majority, having such co-existent passion or interest, must be rendered, by their number and local situation, unable to concert and carry into effect schemes of oppression. If the impulse and the opportunity be suffered to coincide, we well know that neither moral nor religious motives can be relied on as an adequate control. They are not found to be such on the injustice and violence of individuals, and lose their efficacy in proportion to the number combined together; that is, in proportion as their efficacy becomes needful.

● Madison argues that faction can be controlled in only two ways: eliminating the existence of a majority, or preventing majorities from carrying out acts of oppression. He notes that neither moral nor religious motives control the will of the majority. Thus, another remedy is necessary. ●

From this view of the subject, it may be concluded, that a pure Democracy, by which I mean, a Society, consisting of a small number of citizens, who assemble and administer the Government in person, can admit of no cure for the mischiefs of faction. A common passion or interest will, in almost every case, be felt by a majority of the whole; a communication and concert results from the form of Government itself; and there is nothing to check the inducements to sacrifice the weaker party, or an obnoxious individual. Hence it is, that such Democracies have ever been spectacles of turbulence and contention; have ever been found

incompatible with personal security, or the rights of property; and have in general been as short in their lives, as they have been violent in their deaths. Theoretic politicians, who have patronized this species of Government, have erroneously supposed, that by reducing mankind to a perfect equality in their political rights, they would, at the same time, be perfectly equalized and assimilated in their possessions, their opinions, and their passions.

● Madison begins to explore governmental solutions to the mischief of faction. He notes that "pure" or direct democracy cannot control factions. In such a system, Madison explains, it is almost impossible to prevent a majority of citizens from coming together to oppress the minority; this is especially true because no mechanism exists to check the power of the majority. ●

A republic, by which I mean a government in which the scheme of representation takes place, opens a different prospect, and promises the cure for which we are seeking. Let us examine the points in which it varies from pure democracy, and we shall comprehend both the nature of the cure and the efficacy which it must derive from the union.

● Continuing to explore governmental solutions to faction, Madison notes that republican government, such as that created under the Constitution, provides the cure to alleviate the problems of faction. ●

The two great points of difference, between a democracy and a republic, are, first, the delegation of the government, in the latter, to a small number of citizens, elected by the rest; secondly, the greater number of citizens, and greater sphere of country, over which the latter may be extended.

The effect of the first difference is, on the one hand, to refine and enlarge the public views, by passing them through the medium of a chosen body of citizens, whose wisdom may best discern the true interest of their country, and whose patriotism and love of justice, will be least likely to sacrifice it to temporary or partial considerations. Under such a regulation, it may well happen, that the public voice, pronounced by the representatives of the people, will be more consonant to the public good, than if pronounced by the people themselves, convened for the purpose. On the other hand the effect may be inverted. Men of factious tempers, of local prejudices, or of sinister designs, may by intrigue, by corruption, or by other means, first obtain the suffrages, and then betray the interest of the people. The question resulting is, whether small or extensive republics are most favorable to the election of proper guardians of the public weal, and it is clearly decided in favor of the latter by two obvious considerations.

● Here, Madison further delineates the important differences between a pure democracy and a republic (representative democracy). First, he argues that a republic is superior because it delegates authority from the masses to their elected representatives. This allows government to filter public opinion, placing the long-term public good above citizens' short-term and individual interests. He acknowledges that some elected officials may be affected by "corruption" or "intrigue," but he notes that the size of the republic—explored in the following paragraphs—helps to limit these concerns. ●

In the first place, it is to be remarked that, however small the republic may be, the representatives must be raised to a certain number, in order to guard against the cabals of a few; and that however large it may be, they must be limited to a certain number, in order to guard against the confusion of a multitude. Hence, the number of representatives in the two cases not being in proportion to that of the constituents, and being proportionally greatest in the small republic, it follows, that if the proportion of fit characters be not less in the large than in the small republic, the former will present a greater option, and consequently a greater probability of a fit choice.

In the next place, as each Representative will be chosen by a greater number of citizens in the large than in the small Republic, it will be more difficult for unworthy candidates to practise with success the vicious arts, by which elections are too often carried; and the suffrages of the people being more free, will be more likely to center on men who possess the most attractive merit, and the most diffusive and established characters.

● Madison argues that the second reason a republic is superior to a democracy is that a republic can be extended over a much larger class of citizens than a democracy. He notes that an effective government must strike a balance between the number of the governed and the number of their representatives, or governors. In identifying the correct number of representatives, Madison argues that it is necessary to guarantee a number large enough to guard against the corrupt few, but not so many that there will be collective action problems. He admits that striking this balance is easier in a large republic than a small one. A larger republic also makes corruption less likely and enlightened representatives more likely. ●

It must be confessed, that in this, as in most other cases, there is a mean, on both sides of which inconveniences will be found to lie. By enlarging too much the number of electors, you render the representatives too little acquainted with all their local circumstances and lesser interests; as by reducing it too much, you render him unduly attached to these, and too little fit to comprehend and pursue great and national objects. The Federal Constitution forms a happy combination in this respect; the great and aggregate interests being referred to the national, the local and particular, to the state legislatures.

● Madison notes that the unique federal system created by the Framers—which divided power between the state and national governments—provides an especially good structure for a republican government. ●

The other point of difference is, the greater number of citizens and extent of territory which may be brought within the compass of Republican, than of Democratic Government; and it is this circumstance principally which renders factious combinations less to be dreaded in the former, than in the latter. The smaller the society, the fewer probably will be the distinct parties and interests composing it; the fewer the distinct parties and interests, the more frequently will a majority be found of the same party; and the smaller the number of individuals composing a majority, and the smaller the compass within which they are placed, the more easily will they concert and execute their plans of oppression. Extend the sphere, and you take in a greater variety of parties and interests; you make it less probable that a majority of the whole will have a common motive to invade the rights of other citizens; or if such a common motive exists, it will be more difficult for all who feel it to discover their own strength, and to act in unison with each other. Besides other impediments, it may be remarked, that where

there is a consciousness of unjust or dishonorable purposes, communication is always checked by distrust, in proportion to the number whose concurrence is necessary.

● Madison continues his defense of the value of a large republic. He reiterates that in a smaller society, citizens' opinions are more likely to be homogenous, and oppression more probable. However, larger societies have greater diversity. In such societies, it is more difficult for a faction to invade the rights of other citizens in an unjust way. ●

Hence it clearly appears, that the same advantage, which a Republic has over a Democracy, in controlling the effects of faction, is enjoyed by a large over a small Republic—is enjoyed by the Union over the States composing it. Does this advantage consist in the substitution of Representatives, whose enlightened views and virtuous sentiments render them superior to local prejudices, and to schemes of injustice? It will not be denied, that the Representation of the Union will be most likely to possess these requisite endowments. Does it consist in the greater security afforded by a greater variety of parties, against the event of any one party being able to outnumber and oppress the rest? In an equal degree does the increased variety of parties, comprised within the Union, increase this security? Does it, in fine, consist in the greater obstacles opposed to the concert and accomplishment of the secret wishes of an unjust and interested majority? Here, again, the extent of the Union gives it the most palpable advantage.

The influence of factious leaders may kindle a flame within their particular States, but will be unable to spread a general conflagration through the other States: a religious sect, may degenerate into a political faction in a part of the Confederacy but the variety of sects dispersed over the entire face of it, must secure the national Councils against any danger from that source: a rage for paper money, for an abolition of debts, for an equal division of property, or for any other improper or wicked project, will be less apt to pervade the whole body of the Union, than a particular member of it; in the same proportion as such a malady is more likely to taint a particular county or district, than an entire State.

● Madison states that the very size of the union, with its thirteen states with different cultures and traditions, makes the federal system created by the Constitution what Benjamin Franklin called "our last best choice." He argues that, under the federal system, while factions may rise in individual states, they will be less likely to overtake the entire union. ●

In the extent and proper structure of the Union, therefore, we behold a Republican remedy for the diseases most incident to Republican Government. And according to the degree of pleasure and pride, we feel in being Republicans, ought to be our zeal in cherishing the spirit, and supporting the character of Federalists.

● Proudly calling supporters of the new Constitution Federalists, Madison concludes that the document creates a republican form of government workable for the ages. This form of government, in his estimation, is the best possible way to control the effects of faction, or "the diseases most incident to Republican Government." ●

PUBLIUS

Federalist No. 51

February 6, 1788
James Madison
To the People of the State of New York:

Federalist No. 51 is one of the most widely cited of all *The Federalist Papers*. In it, James Madison carefully explains how the structure of the new government helps to protect citizens' individual liberties. He contends that the Constitution contains two main protections: a system of checks and balances, and a federal system of government that divides power between state and national governments. Perhaps the most famous line of this paper is "Ambition must be made to counteract ambition."

To what expedient then shall we finally resort for maintaining in practice the necessary partition of power among the several departments, as laid down in the Constitution? The only answer that can be given is, that as all these exterior provisions are found to be inadequate, the defect must be supplied, by so contriving the interior structure of the government, as that its several constituent parts may, by their mutual relations, be the means of keeping each other in their proper places. Without presuming to undertake a full development of this important idea, I will hazard a few general observations, which may perhaps place it in a clearer light, and enable us to form a more correct judgment of the principles and structure of the government planned by the convention.

● Here, Madison summarizes the central theme of this essay: exploring how the Constitution creates a system of checks and balances that prevents any faction of individuals from becoming too powerful. In the following paragraphs, Madison begins a lengthy discussion of this mechanism. ●

In order to lay a due foundation for that separate and distinct exercise of the different powers of government, which to a certain extent, is admitted on all hands to be essential to the preservation of liberty, it is evident that each department should have a will of its own; and consequently should be so constituted, that the members of each should have as little agency as possible in the appointment of the members of the others. Were this principle rigorously adhered to, it would require that all the appointments for the supreme executive, legislative, and judiciary magistracies, should be drawn from the same fountain of authority, the people, through channels, having no communication whatever with one another. Perhaps such a plan of constructing the several departments would be less difficult in practice than it may in contemplation appear.

● The first necessary step is to devise a system where each institution has its own unique power. This is the system of separation of powers. To preserve this system, Madison notes that in an ideal world, officials in each branch should have very little ability to influence the selection of officials serving in any other branch; officials should all be selected by the people. ●

Some difficulties however, and some additional expense, would attend the execution of it. Some deviations therefore from the principle must be admitted. In the constitution of the judiciary department in particular, it might be inexpedient to insist rigorously on the principle; first, because peculiar qualifications being essential in the members, the primary consideration ought to be to select that mode of choice, which best secures these qualifications; secondly, because the permanent tenure by which the appointments are held in that department, must soon destroy all sense of dependence on the authority conferring them.

● In this section, Madison points out the difficulties with allowing the people to directly select their leaders. For example, members of the federal judiciary must have unique qualifications and are appointed for life. The general public might not be able to make the most appropriate decisions about who should fill these positions.

Notably, the Framers appear to have had little faith in the people's ability to choose their leaders in other branches of government as well. A number of provisions of the Constitution, such as the selection of senators by state legislators and the use of the Electoral College, reveal the Framers' fears of mob rule. ●

It is equally evident that the members of each department should be as little dependent as possible on those of the others, for the emoluments annexed to their offices. Were the executive magistrate, or the judges, not independent of the legislature in this particular, their independence in every other would be merely nominal.

But the great security against a gradual concentration of the several powers in the same department, consists in giving to those who administer each department, the necessary constitutional means, and personal motives, to resist encroachments of the others. The provision for defense must in this, as in all other cases, be made commensurate to the danger of attack. Ambition must be made to counteract ambition.

● Here, Madison stresses that there must be constitutional protections in place to ensure that those working within one branch of the government will be able to act independently of the other branches. In the most famous phrase of *Federalist No 51*, Madison declares, "Ambition must be made to counteract ambition." This forms the theoretical foundation for a system of checks and balances. ●

The interest of the man must be connected with the constitutional right of the place. It may be a reflection on human nature, that such devices should be necessary to control the abuses of government. But what is government itself but the greatest of all reflections on human nature? If men were angels, no government would be necessary. If angels were to govern men, neither external nor internal controls on government would be necessary. In framing a government which is to be administered by men over men, the great difficulty lies in this: you must first enable the government to control the governed; and in the next place, oblige it to control itself. A dependence on the people is no doubt the primary control on the government; but experience has taught mankind the necessity of auxiliary precautions.

● Madison argues that, if people behaved in an ideal way, government and all the controls that it provides would be unnecessary. However, as theorists such as Thomas Hobbes argued, people in their natural state cannot be trusted. History is replete with examples of tyranny present in other forms of government. Thus, a government must be fashioned that can control the people as well as itself. ●

This policy of supplying by opposite and rival interests, the defect of better motives, might be traced through the whole system of human affairs, private as well as public. We see it particularly displayed in all the subordinate distributions of power; where the constant aim is to divide and arrange the several offices in such a manner as that each may be a check on the other; that the private interest of every individual, may be a sentinel over the public rights. These inventions of prudence cannot be less requisite in the distribution of the supreme powers of the state.

But it is not possible to give to each department an equal power of self defense. In republican government the legislative authority, necessarily, predominates. The remedy for this inconveniency is, to divide the legislature into different branches; and to render them by different modes of election, and different principles of action, as little connected with each other, as the nature of their common functions, and their common dependence on the society, will admit. It may even be necessary to guard against dangerous encroachments by still further precautions. As the weight of the legislative authority requires that it should be thus divided, the weakness of the executive may require, on the other hand, that it should be fortified. An absolute negative, on the legislature, appears at first view to be the natural defense with which the executive magistrate should be armed. But perhaps it would be neither altogether safe, nor alone sufficient. On ordinary occasions, it might not be exerted with the requisite firmness; and on extraordinary occasions, it might be prefidiously abused.

May not this defect of an absolute negative be supplied, by some qualified connection between this weaker department, and the weaker branch of the stronger department, by which the latter may be led to support the constitutional rights of the former, without being too much detached from the rights of its own department? If the principles on which these observations are founded be just, as I persuade myself they are, and they be applied as a criterion, to the several state constitutions, and to the federal constitution, it will be found, that if the latter does not perfectly correspond with them, the former are infinitely less able to bear such a test.

● Here, Madison begins to discuss the separation of powers between the three branches of the national government. He argues that it is not practicable to give these branches equal power; the legislature will always dominate. The best way to limit the tyranny of this branch, Madison argues, is to divide the power of the legislature into two—to create a bicameral legislature.

In contrast, he contends that the power of the executive branch may not be sufficient to check the power of Congress. Thus, the Framers empower the executive with "an absolute negative on the legislature," exemplified by the power to veto acts of Congress. ●

There are moreover two considerations particularly applicable to the federal system of America, which place that system in a very interesting point of view.

● Below, Madison identifies the strengths of the federal system as a solution to potential ills inherent in the republic. ●

First. In a single republic, all the power surrendered by the people, is submitted to the administration of a single government; and usurpations are guarded against by a division of the government into distinct and separate departments. In the compound republic of America, the power surrendered by the people, is first divided between two distinct governments, and then the portion allotted to each, subdivided among distinct and separate departments. Hence a double security arises to the rights of the people. The different governments will control each other; at the same time that each will be controlled by itself.

● Madison introduces the notion of a compound (federal) republic. Unlike a unitary system where the people offer up all power to a single government, in a compound republic such as the one created by the Constitution, power is divided in many ways. First, power is split between the states and the national government. Second, within the national government, there exists the "double security" of three branches of government, each with checks and balances on the others. ●

Second. It is of great importance in a republic, not only to guard the society against the oppression of its rulers; but to guard one part of the society against the injustice of the other part. Different interests necessarily exist in different classes of citizens.

● Here, Madison discusses the second purpose of the republic: to protect the citizens from themselves. Specifically, he argues that it is necessary to devise a government that protects the rights and interests of one faction from those of another faction. ●

If a majority be united by a common interest, the rights of the minority will be insecure. There are but two methods of providing against this evil: the one by creating a will in the community independent of the majority, that is, of the society itself; the other by comprehending in the society so many separate descriptions of citizens, as will render an unjust combination of a majority of the whole, very improbable, if not impracticable. The first method prevails in all governments possessing an hereditary or self appointed authority. This at best is but a precarious security; because a power independent of the society may as well espouse the unjust views of the major, as the rightful interests, of the minor party, and may possibly be turned against both parties. The second method will be exemplified in the federal republic of the United States. While all authority in it will be derived from and dependent on the society, the society itself will be broken into so many parts, interests and classes of citizens, that the rights of individuals or of the minority, will be in little danger from interested combinations of the majority. In a free government, the security for civil rights must be the same as for religious rights. It consists in the one case in the multiplicity of interests, and in the other, in the multiplicity of sects. The degree of security in both cases will depend on the number of interests and sects; and this may be presumed to depend on the extent of country and number of people comprehended under the same government.

• Madison notes that there are two ways to protect the rights of citizens in the face of a united minority. First, a social movement or movements may arise in opposition to the will of the majority. This system, he notes, is used in monarchies, but with little success. The second option—and the option used in the new federal republic—is the division of society into so many interests and classes that it is difficult for the majority to trample the wishes of the minority. •

This view of the subject must particularly recommend a proper federal system to all the sincere and considerate friends of republican government. Since it shows that in exact proportion as the territory of the union may be formed into more circumscribed confederacies or states, oppressive combinations of a majority will be facilitated, the best security under the republican form, for the rights of every class of citizens, will be diminished; and consequently, the stability and independence of some member of the government, the only other security, must be proportionally increased. Justice is the end of government. It is the end of civil society.

It ever has been, and ever will be pursued, until it be obtained, or until liberty be lost in the pursuit. In a society under the forms of which the stronger faction can readily unite and oppress the weaker, anarchy may as truly be said to reign, as in a state of nature where the weaker individual is not secured against the violence of the stronger; and as in the latter state even the stronger individuals are prompted by the uncertainty of their condition, to submit to a government which may protect the weak as well as themselves; so, in the former state, will the more powerful factions or parties be gradually induced by a like motive, to wish for a government which will protect all parties, the weaker as well as the more powerful. It can be little doubted, that if the state of Rhode Island

was separated from the confederacy, and left to itself, the insecurity of rights under the popular form of government within such narrow limits, would be displayed by such reiterated oppressions of factious majorities, that some power altogether independent of the people would soon be called for by the voice of the very factions whose misrule had proved the necessity of it. In the extended republic of the United States, and among the great variety of interests, parties and sects which it embraces, a coalition of a majority of the whole society could seldom take place on any other principles than those of justice and the general good; and there being thus less danger to a minor from the will of the major party, there must be less pretext also, to provide for the security of the former, by introducing into the government a will not dependent on the latter; or in other words, a will independent of the society itself. It is no less certain than it is important, notwithstanding the contrary opinions which have been entertained, that the larger the society, provided it lie within a practicable sphere, the more duly capable it will be of self government. And happily for the *republican cause*, the practicable sphere may be carried to a very great extent, by a judicious modification and mixture of the *federal principle*.

• In the conclusion to this essay, Madison reiterates the advantages of the federal system of government proposed under the Constitution: forming a union between the various states will strengthen protection of citizens' individual liberties, increase security, and promote justice. •

PUBLIUS

Federalist No. 78
May 28, 1788
Alexander Hamilton
To the People of the State of New York:

Federalist No. 78 is the first of six *Federalist Papers* that discuss the judicial branch. Alexander Hamilton's analysis focuses on several points. Among these are the method of judicial selection, tenure in office, and the scope of judicial authority. This piece is perhaps best known for its defense of lifetime terms for judges, as well as its declaration that the judiciary would be the "least dangerous branch."

We proceed now to an examination of the judiciary department of the proposed government.

In unfolding the defects of the existing Confederation, the utility and necessity of a federal judicature have been clearly pointed out. It is the less necessary to recapitulate the considerations there

urged, as the propriety of the institution in the abstract is not disputed; the only questions which have been raised being relative to the manner of constituting it, and to its extent. To these points, therefore, our observations shall be confined.

• Government under the Articles of Confederation lacked a federal judiciary. The Framers found this system unworkable, and, theoretically, at least, believed in the necessity of a federal judiciary under the new Constitution. They had, however, given little thought to the form and structure of this new institution of government. ●

The manner of constituting it seems to embrace these several objects: 1st. The mode of appointing the judges. 2d. The tenure by which they are to hold their places. 3d. The partition of the judiciary authority between different courts, and their relations to each other.

First. As to the mode of appointing the judges; this is the same with that of appointing the officers of the Union in general, and has been so fully discussed in the two last numbers, that nothing can be said here which would not be useless repetition.

● Hamilton spends little time discussing the method of judicial selection. He notes that the authors of *The Federalist Papers* had already discussed in great detail the appointing power of the executive branch (who were chosen in the same way). ●

Second. As to the tenure by which the judges are to hold their places: this chiefly concerns their duration in office; the provisions for their support; the precautions for their responsibility.

● This paper instead will focus on judicial term length and compensation, as well as judges' role within the political system. ●

According to the plan of the convention, all judges who may be appointed by the United States are to hold their offices *during good behavior*; which is conformable to the most approved of the State constitutions and among the rest, to that of this State. Its propriety having been drawn into question by the adversaries of that plan, is no light symptom of the rage for objection, which disorders their imaginations and judgments. The standard of good behavior for the continuance in office of the judicial magistracy, is certainly one of the most valuable of the modern improvements in the practice of government. In a monarchy it is an excellent barrier to the despotism of the prince; in a republic it is a no less excellent barrier to the encroachments and oppressions of the representative body. And it is the best expedient which can be devised in any government, to secure a steady, upright, and impartial administration of the laws.

● Hamilton argues that judges should serve only as long as they exhibit good behavior. The application of such a standard helps to guard against tyranny and despotism, which the Framers feared from their experiences under the British crown. ●

Whoever attentively considers the different departments of power must perceive, that, in a government in which they are separated from each other, the judiciary, from the nature of its functions, will always be the least dangerous to the political rights of the Constitution; because it will be least in a capacity to annoy or injure them. The Executive not only dispenses the honors, but holds the sword of the community. The legislature not only commands the purse, but prescribes the rules by which the duties and rights of every citizen are to be regulated. The judiciary, on the contrary, has no influence over either the sword or the purse; no direction either of the strength or of the wealth of the society; and can take no active resolution whatever. It may truly be said to have neither *force* nor *will*, but merely judgment; and must ultimately depend upon the aid of the executive arm even for the efficacy of its judgments.

● This is perhaps the most famous paragraph of Hamilton's treatise. Here, he argues that the judiciary will be the "least dangerous branch." The legislature has "the purse," or the power to raise and spend revenues. The executive has "the sword," or the ability to carry out the laws of the nation. The judiciary, however, has "neither force

nor will, but merely judgment." Furthermore, even after a federal court has reached a decision on a case, Hamilton argues, it is dependent on the executive branch to carry out its will. ●

This simple view of the matter suggests several important consequences. It proves incontestably, that the judiciary is beyond comparison the weakest of the three departments of power[1]; that it can never attack with success either of the other two; and that all possible care is requisite to enable it to defend itself against their attacks. It equally proves, that though individual oppression may now and then proceed from the courts of justice, the general liberty of the people can never be endangered from that quarter; I mean so long as the judiciary remains truly distinct from both the legislature and the Executive. For I agree, that "there is no liberty, if the power of judging be not separated from the legislative and executive powers."[2] And it proves, in the last place, that as liberty can have nothing to fear from the judiciary alone, but would have every thing to fear from its union with either of the other departments; that as all the effects of such a union must ensue from a dependence of the former on the latter, notwithstanding a nominal and apparent separation; that as, from the natural feebleness of the judiciary, it is in continual jeopardy of being overpowered, awed, or influenced by its co-ordinate branches; and that as nothing can contribute so much to its firmness and independence as permanency in office, this quality may therefore be justly regarded as an indispensable ingredient in its constitution, and, in a great measure, as the citadel of the public justice and the public security.

● As a result of its limited power, Hamilton argues, the judiciary poses little threat to citizens' liberties. ●

The complete independence of the courts of justice is peculiarly essential in a limited Constitution. By a limited Constitution, I understand one which contains certain specified exceptions to the legislative authority; such, for instance, as that it shall pass no bills of attainder, no ex-post-facto laws, and the like. Limitations of this kind can be preserved in practice no other way than through the medium of courts of justice, whose duty it must be to declare all acts contrary to the manifest tenor of the Constitution void. Without this, all the reservations of particular rights or privileges would amount to nothing.

Some perplexity respecting the rights of the courts to pronounce legislative acts void, because contrary to the Constitution, has arisen from an imagination that the doctrine would imply a superiority of the judiciary to the legislative power. It is urged that the authority which can declare the acts of another void, must necessarily be superior to the one whose acts may be declared void. As this doctrine is of great importance in all the American constitutions, a brief discussion of the ground on which it rests cannot be unacceptable.

There is no position which depends on clearer principles, than that every act of a delegated authority, contrary to the tenor of the commission under which it is exercised, is void. No legislative act, therefore, contrary to the Constitution, can be valid. To deny this, would be to affirm, that the deputy is greater than his principal; that the servant is above his master; that the representatives of the people are superior to the people themselves; that men acting by virtue of powers, may do not only what their powers do not authorize, but what they forbid.

If it be said that the legislative body are themselves the constitutional judges of their own powers, and that the construction they put upon them is conclusive upon the other departments, it may be answered, that this cannot be the natural presumption, where it is not to be collected from any particular provisions in the Constitution. It is not otherwise to be supposed, that the Constitution could intend to enable the representatives of the people to substitute their *will* to that of their constituents. It is far more rational to suppose, that the courts were designed to be an intermediate body between the people and the legislature, in order, among other things, to keep the latter within the limits assigned to their authority. The interpretation of the laws is the proper and peculiar province of the courts. A constitution is, in fact, and must be regarded by the judges, as a fundamental law. It therefore belongs to them to ascertain its meaning, as well as the meaning of any particular act proceeding from the legislative body. If there should happen to be an irreconcilable variance between the two, that which has the superior obligation and validity ought, of course, to be preferred; or, in other words, the Constitution ought to be preferred to the statute, the intention of the people to the intention of their agents.

Nor does this conclusion by any means suppose a superiority of the judicial to the legislative power. It only supposes that the power of the people is superior to both; and that where the will of the legislature, declared in its statutes, stands in opposition to that of the people, declared in the Constitution, the judges ought to be governed by the latter rather than the former. They ought to regulate their decisions by the fundamental laws, rather than by those which are not fundamental.

This exercise of judicial discretion, in determining between two contradictory laws, is exemplified in a familiar instance. It not uncommonly happens, that there are two statutes existing at one time, clashing in whole or in part with each other, and neither of them containing any repealing clause or expression. In such a case, it is the province of the courts to liquidate and fix their meaning and operation. So far as they can, by any fair construction, be reconciled to each other, reason and law conspire to dictate that this should be done; where this is impracticable, it becomes a matter of necessity to give effect to one, in exclusion of the other. The rule which has obtained in the courts for determining their relative validity is, that the last in order of time shall be preferred to the first. But this is a mere rule of construction, not derived from any positive law, but from the nature and reason of the thing. It is a rule not enjoined upon the courts by legislative provision, but adopted by themselves, as consonant to truth and propriety, for the direction of their conduct as interpreters of the law. They thought it reasonable, that between the interfering acts of an *equal* authority, that which was the last indication of its will should have the preference.

But in regard to the interfering acts of a superior and subordinate authority, of an original and derivative power, the nature and reason of the thing indicate the converse of that rule as proper to be followed. They teach us that the prior act of a superior ought to be preferred to the subsequent act of an inferior and subordinate authority; and that accordingly, whenever a particular statute contravenes the Constitution, it will be the duty of the judicial tribunals to adhere to the latter and disregard the former.

● **Hamilton argues that the courts must remain independent of the authority of the legislative and executive branches. This independence is particularly important because the courts must be able to declare legislative acts void when they conflict with the Constitution, the superior law of the land. Many scholars point to this**

text as an early defense of the Supreme Court's power of judicial review, although it is not explicitly stated in the Constitution. ●

It can be of no weight to say that the courts, on the pretense of a repugnancy, may substitute their own pleasure to the constitutional intentions of the legislature. This might as well happen in the case of two contradictory statutes; or it might as well happen in every adjudication upon any single statute. The courts must declare the sense of the law; and if they should be disposed to exercise *will* instead of *judgment*, the consequence would equally be the substitution of their pleasure to that of the legislative body. The observation, if it prove any thing, would prove that there ought to be no judges distinct from that body.

If, then, the courts of justice are to be considered as the bulwarks of a limited Constitution against legislative encroachments, this consideration will afford a strong argument for the permanent tenure of judicial offices, since nothing will contribute so much as this to that independent spirit in the judges which must be essential to the faithful performance of so arduous a duty.

This independence of the judges is equally requisite to guard the Constitution and the rights of individuals from the effects of those ill humors, which the arts of designing men, or the influence of particular conjunctures, sometimes disseminate among the people themselves, and which, though they speedily give place to better information, and more deliberate reflection, have a tendency, in the meantime, to occasion dangerous innovations in the government, and serious oppressions of the minor party in the community. Though I trust the friends of the proposed Constitution will never concur with its enemies,[3] in questioning that fundamental principle of republican government, which admits the right of the people to alter or abolish the established Constitution, whenever they find it inconsistent with their happiness, yet it is not to be inferred from this principle, that the representatives of the people, whenever a momentary inclination happens to lay hold of a majority of their constituents, incompatible with the provisions in the existing Constitution, would, on that account, be justifiable in a violation of those provisions; or that the courts would be under a greater obligation to connive at infractions in this shape, than when they had proceeded wholly from the cabals of the representative body. Until the people have, by some solemn and authoritative act, annulled or changed the established form, it is binding upon themselves collectively, as well as individually; and no presumption, or even knowledge, of their sentiments, can warrant their representatives in a departure from it, prior to such an act. But it is easy to see, that it would require an uncommon portion of fortitude in the judges to do their duty as faithful guardians of the Constitution, where legislative invasions of it had been instigated by the major voice of the community.

But it is not with a view to infractions of the Constitution only, that the independence of the judges may be an essential safeguard against the effects of occasional ill humors in the society. These sometimes extend no farther than to the injury of the private rights of particular classes of citizens, by unjust and partial laws. Here also the firmness of the judicial magistracy is of vast importance in mitigating the severity and confining the operation of such laws. It not only serves to moderate the immediate mischiefs of those which may have been passed, but it operates as a check upon the legislative body in passing them; who, perceiving that obstacles to the success of iniquitous intention are to be expected from the scruples of the courts, are in a manner compelled, by the very motives of the injustice they meditate, to qualify their attempts. This is a circumstance calculated to have more influence upon the character of our governments, than but few may be aware of. The benefits of the integrity and moderation of the judiciary have already been felt in more States than one; and though they may have displeased those whose sinister expectations they may have disappointed, they must have commanded the esteem and applause of all the virtuous and disinterested. Considerate men, of every description, ought to prize whatever will tend to beget or fortify that temper in the courts: as no man can be sure that he may not be to-morrow the victim of a spirit of injustice, by which he may be a gainer to-day. And every man must now feel, that the inevitable tendency of such a spirit is to sap the foundations of public and private confidence, and to introduce in its stead universal distrust and distress.

That inflexible and uniform adherence to the rights of the Constitution, and of individuals, which we perceive to be indispensable in the courts of justice, can certainly not be expected from judges who hold their offices by a temporary commission. Periodical appointments, however regulated, or by whomsoever made, would, in some way or other, be fatal to their necessary independence. If the power of making them was committed either to the Executive or legislature, there would be danger of an improper complaisance to the branch which possessed it; if to both, there would be an unwillingness to hazard the displeasure of either; if to the people, or to persons chosen by them for the special purpose, there would be too great a disposition to consult popularity, to justify a reliance that nothing would be consulted but the Constitution and the laws.

● Hamilton argues that the judiciary's role as defender of the Constitution makes it absolutely necessary that judges serve life terms. Serving for life allows judges to put the law above all other considerations and to take positions that they might be less willing to take if they were beholden to citizens for reappointment or reelection. ●

There is yet a further and a weightier reason for the permanency of the judicial offices, which is deducible from the nature of the qualifications they require. It has been frequently remarked, with great propriety, that a voluminous code of laws is one of the inconveniences necessarily connected with the advantages of a free government. To avoid an arbitrary discretion in the courts, it is indispensable that they should be bound down by strict rules and precedents, which serve to define and point out their duty in every particular case that comes before them; and it will readily be conceived from the variety of controversies which grow out of the folly and wickedness of mankind, that the records of those precedents must unavoidably swell to a very considerable bulk, and must demand long and laborious study to acquire a competent knowledge of them. Hence it is, that there can be but few men in the society who will have sufficient skill in the laws to qualify them for the stations of judges. And making the proper deductions for the ordinary depravity of human nature, the number must be still smaller of those who unite the requisite integrity with the requisite knowledge. These considerations apprise us, that the government can have no great option between fit character; and that a temporary duration in office, which would naturally discourage such characters from quitting a lucrative line of practice to accept a seat on the bench, would have a tendency to throw the administration of justice into hands less able, and less well qualified, to conduct it with utility and dignity. In the present circumstances of this country, and in those in which it is likely to be for a long time to come, the disadvantages on this score would be greater than they may at first sight appear; but it must be confessed, that they are far inferior to those which present themselves under the other aspects of the subject.

● Another argument for life tenure of judges is the complexity of the laws. There are a limited number of citizens who are qualified for this position, and without life tenure, these people would be reluctant to serve on the bench. This was particularly true in the earliest days of the judiciary, when the courts lacked prestige and required a great deal of travel around the country, largely on horseback. Providing job security was one way the Framers thought they could compensate for these shortcomings. ●

Upon the whole, there can be no room to doubt that the convention acted wisely in copying from the models of those constitutions which have established *good behavior* as the tenure of their judicial offices, in point of duration; and that so far from being blamable on this account, their plan would have been inexcusably defective, if it had wanted this important feature of good government. The experience of Great Britain affords an illustrious comment on the excellence of the institution.

PUBLIUS

---

1. The celebrated Montesquieu, speaking of them, says: "Of the three powers above mentioned, the judiciary is next to nothing."—"Spirit of Laws," vol. 1, page 186.
2. Idem, page 181.
3. Vide "Protest of the Minority of the Convention of Pennsylvania," Martin's Speech, etc.

Presidents, Congresses, and Chief Justices: 1789–2010

Term	President and Vice President	Party of President	Congress	Majority Party		Chief Justice of the United States
				House	Senate	
1789–1797	**George Washington** John Adams	None	1st 2nd 3rd 4th	(N/A) (N/A) (N/A) (N/A)	(N/A) (N/A) (N/A) (N/A)	John Jay (1789–1795) John Rutledge (1795) Oliver Ellsworth (1796–1800)
1797–1801	**John Adams** Thomas Jefferson	Federalist	5th 6th	(N/A) Fed	(N/A) Fed	Oliver Ellsworth (1796–1800) John Marshall (1801–1835)
1801–1809	**Thomas Jefferson** Aaron Burr (1801–1805) George Clinton (1805–1809)	Democratic-Republican	7th 8th 9th 10th	Dem-Rep Dem-Rep Dem-Rep Dem-Rep	Dem-Rep Dem-Rep Dem-Rep Dem-Rep	John Marshall (1801–1835)
1809–1817	**James Madison** George Clinton (1809–1812)[a] Elbridge Gerry (1813–1814)[a]	Democratic-Republican	11th 12th 13th 14th	Dem-Rep Dem-Rep Dem-Rep Dem-Rep	Dem-Rep Dem-Rep Dem-Rep Dem-Rep	John Marshall (1801–1835)
1817–1825	**James Monroe** Daniel D. Tompkins	Democratic-Republican	15th 16th 17th 18th	Dem-Rep Dem-Rep Dem-Rep Dem-Rep	Dem-Rep Dem-Rep Dem-Rep Dem-Rep	John Marshall (1801–1835)
1825–1829	**John Quincy Adams** John C. Calhoun	National-Republican	19th 20th	Nat'l Rep Dem	Nat'l Rep Dem	John Marshall (1801–1835)
1829–1837	**Andrew Jackson** John C. Calhoun (1829–1832)[c] Martin Van Buren (1833–1837)	Democratic	21st 22nd 23rd 24th	Dem Dem Dem Dem	Dem Dem Dem Dem	John Marshall (1801–1835) Roger B. Taney (1836–1864)
1837–1841	**Martin Van Buren** Richard M. Johnson	Democratic	25th 26th	Dem Dem	Dem Dem	Roger B. Taney (1836–1864)
1841	**William H. Harrison**[a] John Tyler (1841)	Whig				Roger B. Taney (1836–1864)
1841–1845	**John Tyler** (VP vacant)	Whig	27th 28th	Whig Dem	Whig Whig	Roger B. Taney (1836–1864)
1845–1849	**James K. Polk** George M. Dallas	Democratic	29th 30th	Dem Whig	Dem Dem	Roger B. Taney (1836–1864)
1849–1850	**Zachary Taylor**[a] Millard Fillmore	Whig	31st	Dem	Dem	Roger B. Taney (1836–1864)
1850–1853	**Millard Fillmore** (VP vacant)	Whig	32nd	Dem	Dem	Roger B. Taney (1836–1864)

Term	President and Vice President	Party of President	Congress	Majority Party		Chief Justice of the United States
				House	Senate	
1853–1857	**Franklin Pierce** William R. D. King (1853)[a]	Democratic	33rd 34th	Dem Rep	Dem Dem	Roger B. Taney (1836–1864)
1857–1861	**James Buchanan** John C. Breckinridge	Democratic	35th 36th	Dem Rep	Dem Dem	Roger B. Taney (1836–1864)
1861–1865	**Abraham Lincoln**[a] Hannibal Hamlin (1861–1865) Andrew Johnson (1865)	Republican	37th 38th	Rep Rep	Rep Rep	Roger B. Taney (1836–1864) Salmon P. Chase (1864–1873)
1865–1869	**Andrew Johnson** (VP vacant)	Republican	39th 40th	Union Rep	Union Rep	Salmon P. Chase (1864–1873)
1869–1877	**Ulysses S. Grant** Schuyler Colfax (1869–1873) Henry Wilson (1873–1875)[a]	Republican	41st 42nd 43rd 44th	Rep Rep Rep Dem	Rep Rep Rep Rep	Salmon P. Chase (1864–1873) Morrison R. Waite (1874–1888)
1877–1881	**Rutherford B. Hayes** William A. Wheeler	Republican	45th 46th	Dem Dem	Rep Dem	Morrison R. Waite (1874–1888)
1881	**James A. Garfield**[a] Chester A. Arthur	Republican	47th	Rep	Rep	Morrison R. Waite (1874–1888)
1881–1885	**Chester A. Arthur** (VP vacant)	Republican	48th	Dem	Rep	Morrison R. Waite (1874–1888)
1885–1889	**Grover Cleveland** Thomas A. Hendricks (1885)[a]	Democratic	49th 50th	Dem Dem	Rep Rep	Morrison R. Waite (1874–1888) Melville W. Fuller (1888–1910)
1889–1893	**Benjamin Harrison** Levi P. Morton	Republican	51st 52nd	Rep Dem	Rep Rep	Melville W. Fuller (1888–1910)
1893–1897	**Grover Cleveland** Adlai E. Stevenson	Democratic	53rd 54th	Dem Rep	Dem Rep	Melville W. Fuller (1888–1910)
1897–1901	**William McKinley**[a] Garret A. Hobart (1897–1899)[a] Theodore Roosevelt (1901)	Republican	55th 56th	Rep Rep	Rep Rep	Melville W. Fuller (1888–1910)
1901–1909	**Theodore Roosevelt** (VP vacant, 1901–1905) Charles W. Fairbanks (1905–1909)	Republican	57th 58th 59th 60th	Rep Rep Rep Rep	Rep Rep Rep Rep	Melville W. Fuller (1888–1910)
1909–1913	**William Howard Taft** James S. Sherman (1909–1912)[a]	Republican	61st 62nd	Rep Dem	Rep Rep	Melville W. Fuller (1888–1910) Edward D. White (1910–1921)
1913–1921	**Woodrow Wilson** Thomas R. Marshall	Democratic	63rd 64th 65th 66th	Dem Dem Dem Rep	Dem Dem Dem Rep	Edward D. White (1910–1921)
1921–1923	**Warren G. Harding**[a] Calvin Coolidge	Republican	67th	Rep	Rep	William Howard Taft (1921–1930)
1923–1929	**Calvin Coolidge** (VP vacant, 1923–1925) Charles G. Dawes (1925–1929)	Republican	68th 69th 70th	Rep Rep Rep	Rep Rep Rep	William Howard Taft (1921–1930)
1929–1933	**Herbert Hoover** Charles Curtis	Republican	71st 72nd	Rep Dem	Rep Rep	William Howard Taft (1921–1930) Charles Evans Hughes (1930–1941)

Term	President and Vice President	Party of President	Congress	Majority Party		Chief Justice of the United States
				House	Senate	
1933–1945	**Franklin D. Roosevelt**[a] John Nance Garner (1933–1941) Henry A. Wallace (1941–1945) Harry S Truman (1945)	Democratic	73rd 74th 75th 76th 77th 78th	Dem Dem Dem Dem Dem Dem	Dem Dem Dem Dem Dem Dem	Charles Evans Hughes (1930–1941) Harlan F. Stone (1941–1946)
1945–1953	**Harry S Truman** (VP vacant, 1945–1949) Alben W. Barkley (1949–1953)	Democratic	79th 80th 81st 82nd	Dem Rep Dem Dem	Dem Rep Dem Dem	Harlan F. Stone (1941–1946) Frederick M. Vinson (1946–1953)
1953–1961	**Dwight D. Eisenhower** Richard M. Nixon	Republican	83rd 84th 85th 86th	Rep Dem Dem Dem	Rep Dem Dem Dem	Frederick M. Vinson (1946–1953) Earl Warren (1953–1969)
1961–1963	**John F. Kennedy**[a] Lyndon B. Johnson (1961–1963)	Democratic	87th	Dem	Dem	Earl Warren (1953–1969)
1963–1969	**Lyndon B. Johnson** (VP vacant, 1963–1965) Hubert H. Humphrey (1965–1969)	Democratic	88th 89th 90th	Dem Dem Dem	Dem Dem Dem	Earl Warren (1953–1969)
1969–1974	**Richard M. Nixon**[b] Spiro Agnew (1969–1973)[c] Gerald R. Ford (1973–1974)[d]	Republican	91st 92nd	Dem Dem	Dem Dem	Earl Warren (1953–1969) Warren E. Burger (1969–1986)
1974–1977	**Gerald R. Ford** Nelson A. Rockefeller[d]	Republican	93rd 94th	Dem Dem	Dem Dem	Warren E. Burger (1969–1986)
1977–1981	**Jimmy Carter** Walter Mondale	Democratic	95th 96th	Dem Dem	Dem Dem	Warren E. Burger (1969–1986)
1981–1989	**Ronald Reagan** George Bush	Republican	97th 98th 99th 100th	Dem Dem Dem Dem	Rep Rep Rep Dem	Warren E. Burger (1969–1986) William H. Rehnquist (1986–2005)
1989–1993	**George Bush** Dan Quayle	Republican	101st 102nd	Dem Dem	Dem Dem	William H. Rehnquist (1986–2005)
1993–2001	**Bill Clinton** Al Gore	Democratic	103rd 104th 105th 106th	Dem Rep Rep Rep	Dem Rep Rep Rep	William H. Rehnquist (1986–2005)
2001–2009	**George W. Bush** Dick Cheney	Republican	107th 108th 109th 110th	Rep Rep Rep Dem	Dem Rep Rep Dem	William H. Rehnquist (1986–2005) John G. Roberts Jr. (2005–)
2009–2013	**Barack Obama** Joe Biden	Democratic	111th 112th	Dem Rep	Dem Dem	John G. Roberts Jr. (2005–)

[a]Died in office.
[b]Resigned from the presidency.
[c]Resigned from the vice presidency.
[d]Appointed vice president.

SELECTED SUPREME COURT CASES

- *Abington School District* v. *Schempp* (1963): The Court ruled that state-mandated Bible reading or recitation of the Lord's Prayer in public schools was unconstitutional.
- *Ashcroft* v. *Free Speech Coalition* (2002): The Court ruled that the Child Online Protection Act of 1998 was unconstitutional because it was too vague in its reliance on "community standards" to define what is harmful to minors.
- *Atkins* v. *Virginia* (2002): Execution of the mentally retarded is prohibited by the Eighth Amendment's cruel and unusual punishment clause.
- *Baker* v. *Carr* (1962): Watershed case establishing the principle of one person, one vote, which requires that each legislative district within a state have the same number of eligible voters so that representation is equitably based on population.
- *Barron* v. *Baltimore* (1833): Decision that limited the application of the Bill of Rights to the actions of Congress alone.
- *Baze* v. *Rees* (2008): The Supreme Court upheld the use of executions by "lethal injection."
- *Benton* v. *Maryland* (1969): Incorporated the Fifth Amendment's double jeopardy clause.
- *Boerne* v. *Flores* (1997): The Court ruled that Congress could not force the Religious Freedom Restoration Act upon the state governments.
- *Boumediene* v. *Bush* (2008): The Supreme Court ruled unconstitutional the provision of the Military Commissions Act of 2006 stripping the federal courts of their jurisdiction to hear *habeas corpus* petitions from detainees at a U.S. military prison at Guantanamo Bay, Cuba.
- *Bowers* v. *Hardwick* (1986): Unsuccessful attempt to challenge Georgia's sodomy law. The case was overturned by *Lawrence* v. *Texas* in 2003.
- *Brandenburg* v. *Ohio* (1969): The Court fashioned the direct incitement test for deciding whether certain kinds of speech could be regulated by the government. This test holds that advocacy of illegal action is protected by the First Amendment unless imminent action is intended and likely to occur.
- *Brown* v. *Board of Education* (1954): Supreme Court decision holding that school segregation is inherently unconstitutional because it violates the Fourteenth Amendment's guarantee of equal protection; marked the end of legal segregation in the United States.
- *Brown* v. *Board of Education II* (1955): Follow-up to *Brown* v. *Board of Education*, this case laid out the process for school desegregation and established the concept of dismantling segregationist systems "with all deliberate speed."
- *Buckley* v. *Valeo* (1976): The Court ruled that money spent by an individual or political committee in support or opposition of a candidate (but independent of the candidate's campaign) was a form of symbolic speech, and therefore could not be limited under the First Amendment.
- *Bush* v. *Gore* (2000): Case that effectively decided the 2000 election for George W. Bush; ruled that counting of disputed ballots in Florida must stop.
- *Cantwell* v. *Connecticut* (1940): The Supreme Court incorporated the freedom of religion, ruling that the freedom to believe is absolute, but the freedom to act is subject to the regulation of society.
- *Caperton* v. *A.T. Massey Coal Co.* (2009): Case dealing with when a jurist must recuse him or herself from a case; the Court ruled that receiving campaign contributions from a litigant should render a justice ineligible to hear a case.
- *Chaplinsky* v. *New Hampshire* (1942): Established the Supreme Court's rationale for distinguishing between protected and unprotected speech.
- *Chicago, B&Q R.R. Co.* v. *Chicago* (1897): Incorporated the Fifth Amendment's just compensation clause.
- *Chisholm* v. *Georgia* (1793): The Court interpreted its jurisdiction under Article III, section 2, of the Constitution to include the right to hear suits brought by a citizen of one state against another state.
- *Christian Legal Society* v. *Martinez* (2010): The Court ruled a university could deny recognition and therefore funding to a student group that limited its membership to only a small segment of the student population.
- *Citizens United* v. *FEC* (2010): The Court ruled that limits on corporate campaign spending amounted to prohibitions on free speech.
- *Civil Rights Cases* (1883): Name attached to five cases brought under the Civil Rights Act of 1875. In 1883, the Supreme Court decided that discrimination in a variety of public accommodations, including theaters, hotels, and railroads, could not be prohibited by the act because such discrimination was private discrimination and not state discrimination.
- *Clinton* v. *City of New York* (1998): The Court ruled that the line-item veto was unconstitutional because it gave powers to the president denied him by the U.S. Constitution.
- *Coker* v. *Georgia* (1977): The Court ruled that the death penalty could not be applied to a crime that did not involve killing or attempted killing.
- *Coleman* v. *Miller* (1939): The Supreme Court ruled that amendments could remain indefinitely before the public unless Congress had set a specific time limit on the ratification process.
- *Cooper* v. *Aaron* (1958): Case wherein the Court broke with tradition and issued a unanimous decision against the Little Rock School Board, ruling that the district's evasive schemes to avoid the *Brown II* decision were illegal.

- *Craig* v. *Boren* (1976): The Court ruled that keeping drunk drivers off the roads may be an important governmental objective, but allowing women aged eighteen to twenty-one to drink alcoholic beverages while prohibiting men of the same age from drinking is not substantially related to that goal.

- *D.C.* v. *Heller* (2008): The Supreme Court ruled that D.C.'s ban on handgun ownership was unconstitutional.

- *DeJonge* v. *Oregon* (1937): Incorporated the First Amendment's right to freedom of assembly.

- *Dred Scott* v. *Sandford* (1857): Concluded that the U.S. Congress lacked the constitutional authority to bar slavery in the territories; this decision narrowed the scope of national power while it enhanced that of the states. This case marked the first time since *Marbury* v. *Madison* that the Supreme Court found an act of Congress unconstitutional.

- *Duncan* v. *Louisiana* (1968): Incorporated the Sixth Amendment's trial by jury clause.

- *Eisenstadt* v. *Baird* (1972): The Court extended the right to privacy to include unmarried individuals' access to birth control.

- *Engel* v. *Vitale* (1962): The Court ruled that the recitation in public classrooms of a nondenominational prayer was unconstitutional and a violation of the establishment clause.

- *Energy Reserves Group* v. *Kansas Power & Light* (1983): The Court ruled that the contract clause does not prohibit the state from "impairing" contracts if a regulation is intended to address a "broad and general social or economic problem."

- *Furman* v. *Georgia* (1972): The Supreme Court used this case to end capital punishment, at least in the short run. (The case was overturned by *Gregg* v. *Georgia* in 1976.)

- *Gibbons* v. *Ogden* (1824): The Court upheld broad congressional power over interstate commerce.

- *Gideon* v. *Wainwright* (1963): The Court granted indigents the right to counsel in felony cases.

- *Gitlow* v. *New York* (1925): Incorporated the free speech clause of the First Amendment, ruling that the states were not completely free to limit forms of political expression.

- *Gonzales* v. *Carhart* (2007): The Court ruled that the Partial-Birth Abortion Ban Act was constitutional; this was a dramatic reversal of *Stenberg* v. *Carhart* (2000).

- *Granholm* v. *Heald* (2005): The Court ruled that states could not ban out-of-state wineries from shipping directly to consumers, citing the Twenty-First Amendment.

- *Gratz* v. *Bollinger* (2003): The Court struck down the University of Michigan's undergraduate point system, which gave minority applicants twenty automatic points simply because they were minorities.

- *Gravel* v. *U.S.* (1972): The Supreme Court held that the speech or debate clause does not immunize members of Congress or their aides from criminal inquiry, if their activities are part of the legislative process. A alleged or proven illegal actions do not create immunity.

- *Gregg* v. *Georgia* (1976): Overturning *Furman* v. *Georgia*, the case ruled that Georgia's rewritten death penalty statute is constitutional.

- *Griswold* v. *Connecticut* (1965): Supreme Court case that established the Constitution's implied right to privacy.

- *Grutter* v. *Bollinger* (2003): The Court voted to uphold the constitutionality of the University of Michigan Law School's affirmative action policy, which gave preference to minority students.

- *Hamdan* v. *Rumsfeld* (2006): The Court ruled that detainees in the war on terrorism were entitled to the protections of the Geneva Convention and the procedural rights of the Uniform Code of Military Justice, since Congress had not approved of President George W. Bush's system of military tribunals. Congress passed the Military Commissions Act in 2006 to address the Court's ruling in *Hamdan*.

- *Harper* v. *Board of Elections* (1966): The Supreme Court rejected a constitutional challenge to the Voting Rights Act of 1965.

- *Hernandez* v. *Texas* (1954): The Supreme Court struck down discrimination based on ethnicity and class in a landmark decision for Hispanic rights groups.

- *Home Building and Loan Association* v. *Blaisdell* (1934): The Court ruled that a Depression-era law passed by the Minnesota legislature forgiving mortgage payments by homeowners to banks did not violate the contract clause.

- *House* v. *Bell* (2006): A Tennessee death-row inmate who had otherwise exhausted his federal appeals was provided an exception due to the availability of DNA evidence suggesting his innocence; the case recognized the potential exculpatory power of DNA evidence.

- *INS* v. *Chadha* (1983): The Court ruled that the legislative veto as it was used in many circumstances was unconstitutional because it violated both the bicameralism principles of Article I, section 1, and the presentment clause of Article I, section 7, clause 3.

- *Katzenbach* v. *Morgan* (1966): The Supreme Court held that Congress could enact laws establishing rights beyond what the Court said the Constitution required, as long as such laws were designed to establish a remedial constitutional right or protect citizens from a potential constitutional violation.

- *Kelo* v. *New London* (2004): The Court ruled that government could take private property and then sell it to private developers so long as that property was slated for economic development that would benefit the surrounding community.

- *Kimel et al.* v. *Florida Board of Regents* (2000): The Supreme Court ruled that states are immune from suits by individuals alleging age discrimination in state government employment.

- *Klopfer* v. *North Carolina* (1967): Incorporated the Sixth Amendment's right to a speedy trial.

- *Korematsu* v. *U.S.* (1944): In this case, the Court ruled that the internment of Japanese and other ethnic Americans during World War II was constitutional.

- *Lawrence* v. *Texas* (2003): The Court reversed its 1986 ruling in *Bowers* v. *Hardwick* by finding a Texas statute that banned sodomy to be unconstitutional.

- *Ledbetter* v. *Goodyear Tire & Rubber Company* (2007): In a 5–4 decision, the Court ruled that women could not seek redress of grievances for discrimination that had occurred over a period of years under the provisions of the Equal Pay Act. This decision was overturned by the Lily Ledbetter Fair Pay Act of 2009, the first bill signed into law by President Barack Obama.

- *Lemon* v. *Kurtzman* (1971): The Court determined that direct government assistance to religious schools is unconstitutional. In the majority opinion, the Court created what has become known as the *Lemon* test for deciding if a law is in violation of the establishment clause.

- *LULAC* v. *Perry* (2006): The Court ruled that part of the 2004 Texas redistricting plan violated the Voting Rights Act of 1965 because it deprived Hispanic citizens of the right to elect a representative of their choosing.

- *Luther* v. *Borden* (1849): The Court ruled that U.S. Constitution can not identify opposing intra-state governments; the meaning of a republican government was a "political question" not subject to judicial review.

- *Malloy* v. *Hogan* (1964): Incorporated the Fifth Amendment's self-incrimination clause.

- *Mapp* v. *Ohio* (1961): Incorporated a portion of the Fourth Amendment by establishing that illegally obtained evidence cannot be used at trial.

- *Marbury* v. *Madison* (1803): Case in which the Court first asserted the power of judicial review in finding that a congressional statute extending the Court's original jurisdiction was unconstitutional.

- *Martin* v. *Hunter's Lessee* (1816): The Court's power of judicial review in regard to state law was clarified in this case.

- *McCleskey* v. *Zant* (1991): On this appeal of *McCleskey* v. *Kemp* (1987), the Court produced new standards designed to make it much more difficult for death-row inmates to file repeated appeals.

- *McConnell* v. *FEC* (2003): The Court ruled that generally speaking, the Bipartisan Campaign Finance Reform Act of 2002 did not violate the First Amendment.

- *McCulloch* v. *Maryland* (1819): The Court upheld the power of the national government and denied the right of a state to tax a national bank. The Court's broad interpretation of the necessary and proper clause paved the way for later rulings upholding expansive federal powers.

- *McDonald* v. *Chicago* (2010): The Supreme Court held that a Chicago ban on handguns and regulations on rifles and shotguns was unconstitutional; this decision also incorporated the Second Amendment.

- *Minor* v. *Happersett* (1875): The Supreme Court examined the privileges and immunities clause of the Fourteenth Amendment, ruling that voting was not a privilege of citizenship.

- *Miranda* v. *Arizona* (1966): The Fifth Amendment requires that individuals arrested for a crime must be advised of their right to remain silent and to have counsel present.

- *Muller* v. *Oregon* (1908): Case that ruled Oregon's law barring women from working more than ten hours a day was constitutional; also attempted to define women's unique status as mothers to justify their differential treatment.

- *Near* v. *Minnesota* (1931): By ruling that a state law violated the freedom of the press, the Supreme Court incorporated the free press provision of the First Amendment.

- *Nebraska Press Association* v. *Stuart* (1976): Prior restraint case; the Court ruled that a trial judge could not prohibit the publication or broadcast of information about a murder trial.

- *Nevada Department of Human Resources* v. *Hibbs* (2003): The Court upheld the ability of state employees to sue the state for violating the Family and Medical Leave Act.

- *New York* v. *U.S.* (1992): The Court struck down a key provision of a federal environmental law, revisiting the New Deal assumptions that underlay its modern interpretation of the Tenth Amendment.

- *New York Times Co.* v. *Sullivan* (1964): The Supreme Court ruled that simply publishing a defamatory falsehood is not enough to justify a libel judgment. "Actual malice" must be proved to support a finding of libel against a public figure.

- *New York Times Co.* v. *U.S.* (1971): Also called the Pentagon Papers case; the Supreme Court ruled that any attempt by the government to prevent expression carried "a heavy presumption" against its constitutionality.

- *Nixon* v. *U.S.* (1993): The Supreme Court ruled that government officials who are the subject of impeachment proceedings may not challenge them in court.

- *In re Oliver* (1948): Incorporated the Sixth Amendment's right to a public trial.

- *Oregon* v. *Mitchell* (1970): The Supreme Court ruled that Congress had no authority to establish the voting age in state and local elections. Congress responded by drafting the Twenty-Sixth Amendment, which was quickly ratified by the states.

- *Palko* v. *Connecticut* (1937): Set the Court's rationale of selective incorporation, a judicial doctrine whereby most but not all of the protections found in the Bill of Rights are made applicable to the states via the Fourteenth Amendment.

- *Parker* v. *Gladden* (1966): Incorporated the Sixth Amendment's right to an impartial trial.

- *Planned Parenthood of Southeastern Pennsylvania* v. *Casey* (1992): This case was an unsuccessful attempt to challenge Pennsylvania's restrictive abortion regulations.

- *Plessy* v. *Ferguson* (1896): *Plessy* challenged a Louisiana statute requiring that railroads provide separate accommodations for blacks and whites. The Court found that separate but equal accommodations did not violate the equal protection clause of the Fourteenth Amendment.

- *Pointer* v. *Texas* (1965): Incorporated the Sixth Amendment's right of defendants to confront witnesses.

- *Pollock* v. *Farmers' Loan & Trust Co.* (1895): The Court struck down the Income Tax Act of 1894 as unconstitutional.

- *Powell* v. *McCormack* (1969): The Supreme Court ruled that the House's authority to expel a member was limited to those already in office.

- *R.A.V.* v. *City of St. Paul* (1992): The Court concluded that St. Paul, Minnesota's Bias-Motivated Crime Ordinance violated the First Amendment because it regulated speech based on the content of the speech.

- *Reed* v. *Reed* (1971): Turned the tide in terms of constitutional litigation, ruling that the equal protection clause of the Fourteenth Amendment prohibited unreasonable classifications based on sex.

- *Regents of the University of California* v. *Bakke* (1978): A sharply divided Court concluded that the university's rejection of Bakke as a student was illegal because the use of strict affirmative action quotas was inappropriate.

- *Reynolds* v. *Sims* (1964): The Court decided that every person should have an equally weighted vote in electing governmental representatives.

- *Richmond Newspapers* v. *Virginia* (1980): The Court ruled that the right to attend criminal trials was implicit in the guarantees of the First Amendment.

- *Robinson* v. *California* (1962): Incorporated the Eighth Amendment's right to freedom from cruel and unusual punishment.

- *Roe* v. *Wade* (1973): The Supreme Court found that a woman's right to an abortion was protected by the right to privacy that could be implied from specific guarantees found in the Bill of Rights and the Fourteenth Amendment.

- *Romer* v. *Evans* (1996): The first time the Supreme Court ruled any legislative, executive, or judicial action at any state or local level designed to bar discrimination based on sexual preference was unconstitutional.

- *Roper* v. *Simmons* (2005): Execution of minors violates the Eighth Amendment's prohibition on cruel and unusual punishment.

- *Roth* v. *U.S.* (1957): The Court held that in order to be obscene, material must be "utterly without redeeming social value."

- *San Antonio Independent School District* v. *Rodriguez* (1973): Case in which the Supreme Court upheld the constitutionality of a Texas school financing law based on property taxes.

- *Schenck* v. *U.S.* (1919): Case in which the Supreme Court interpreted the First Amendment to allow Congress to restrict speech that is "of such a nature as to create a clear and present danger that will bring about the substantive evils that Congress has a right to prevent."

- *Seminole Tribe* v. *Florida* (1996): Congress cannot impose a duty on states forcing them to negotiate with Indian tribes; the state's sovereign immunity protects it from a congressional directive about how to do business.

- *Solem* v. *Helm* (1983): The Court developed a "proportionality" standard that required punishments, even simple incarceration, to bear a rational relationship to the offense.

- *South Carolina* v. *Dole* (1984): The Supreme Court ruled that Congress may require the states to set a certain age for the consumption of alcohol in return for participation in a federal program without violating the Twenty-First Amendment.

- *Stenberg* v. *Carhart* (2000): The Court ruled that a Nebraska "partial birth" abortion statute was unconstitutionally vague and unenforceable, calling into question the laws of twenty-nine other states.

- *Stromberg* v. *California* (1931): The Court overturned the conviction of a director of a Communist youth camp under a state statute prohibiting the display of a red flag.

- *Swann* v. *Charlotte-Mecklenberg Board of Education* (1971): The Supreme Court ruled that all vestiges of *de jure* discrimination must be eliminated at once.

- *Tennessee* v. *Lane* (2004): Upheld application of the Americans with Disabilities Act to state courthouses.

- *Texas* v. *Johnson* (1989): The Court overturned the conviction of a Texas man found guilty of setting fire to an American flag.

- *Tinker* v. *Des Moines Independent School District* (1969): The Court upheld students' rights to express themselves by wearing black armbands symbolizing protest of the Vietnam War.

- *U.S.* v. *Darby Lumber Co.* (1941): The Supreme Court ruled that the Tenth Amendment states a truism about the relationship between the boundaries of national and state power—that the states retain those powers not specifically set out in the Constitution as belonging to the national government.

- *U.S.* v. *Lopez* (1995): The Court invalidated a section of the Gun Free School Zones Act, ruling that regulating guns did not fall within the scope of the commerce clause, and therefore was not within the powers of the federal government. Only states have the authority to ban guns in school zones.

- *U.S.* v. *Miller* (1939): The first time the Supreme Court addressed the constitutionality of the Second Amendment; ruled that the amendment was only intended to protect a citizen's right to own ordinary militia weapons.

- *U.S.* v. *Morrison* (2000): The Court ruled that portions of the Violence Against Women Act were unconstitutional because Congress had overstepped its boundaries under the commerce clause.

- *U.S.* v. *Nixon* (1974): In a case involving President Richard M. Nixon's refusal to turn over tape recordings of his conversations, the Court ruled that executive privilege does not grant the president an absolute right to secure all presidential documents.

- *U.S.* v. *Printz* (1997): The Court cited the Tenth Amendment to strike down an important section of the Brady Bill, a federal law that required states to conduct background checks on prospective gun buyers.

- *U.S.* v. *Salerno* (1987): The Court ruled that a judge has the power to deny a criminal defendant bail as a "preventative measure."

- *U.S. Term Limits* v. *Thornton* (1995): The Supreme Court ruled that states do not have the authority to enact term limits for federal elected officials.

- *Washington* v. *Texas* (1967): Incorporated the Sixth Amendment's right to a compulsory trial.

- *Webster* v. *Reproductive Health Services* (1989): In upholding several restrictive abortion regulations, the Court opened the door for state governments to enact new restrictions on abortion.

- *Weeks* v. *U.S.* (1914): Case wherein the Supreme Court adopted the exclusionary rule, which bars the use of illegally obtained evidence at trial.

- *Weems* v. *U.S.* (1910): The Court concluded that any punishment considered "excessive" would violate the cruel and unusual punishment clause.

- *Wisconsin* v. *Yoder* (1972): The Court ruled that Amish children could not be placed in compulsory education after the eighth grade; doing so would violate the First Amendment guarantee of freedom of religion.

- *Wolf* v. *Colorado* (1949): The Court ruled that illegally obtained evidence did not necessarily have to be eliminated from use during trial.

- *Yick Wo* v. *Hopkins* (1886): The Supreme Court ruled that a San Francisco ban on cleaners operating in wooden buildings (two-thirds of which were owned by persons of Chinese ancestry) violated the Fourteenth Amendment in its application.

- *Youngstown Sheet & Tube Co.* v. *Sawyer* (1952): The Court invalidated President Harry S Truman's seizure of the nation's steel mills.

A

administrative adjudication: A quasi-judicial process in which a bureaucratic agency settles disputes between two parties in a manner similar to the way courts resolve disputes.

administrative discretion: The ability of bureaucrats to make choices concerning the best way to implement congressional or executive intentions.

affirmative action: Policies designed to give special attention or compensatory treatment to members of a previously disadvantaged group.

agenda: A set of issues to be discussed or given attention.

agenda setting: The constant process of forming the list of issues to be addressed by government.

American dream: An American ideal of a happy, successful life, which often includes wealth, a house, a better life for one's children, and for some, the ability to grow up to be president.

amicus curiae: "Friend of the court"; *amici* may file briefs or even appear to argue their interests orally before the court.

Anti-Federalists: Those who favored strong state governments and a weak national government; opposed the ratification of the U.S. Constitution.

appellate court: Court that generally reviews only findings of law made by lower courts.

appellate jurisdiction: The power vested in particular courts to review and/or revise the decision of a lower court.

apportionment: The process of allotting congressional seats to each state following the decennial census according to their proportion of the population.

Articles of Confederation: The compact among the thirteen original colonies that created a loose league of friendship, with the national government drawing its powers from the states.

B

Barron v. Baltimore (1833): The Supreme Court ruled that the due process clause of the Fifth Amendment did not apply to the actions of states. This decision limited the Bill of Rights to the actions of Congress alone.

bicameral legislature: A two-house legislature.

bill: A proposed law.

bill of attainder: A law declaring an act illegal without a judicial trial.

Bill of Rights: The first ten amendments to the U.S. Constitution, which largely guarantee specific rights and liberties.

Black Codes: Laws denying most legal rights to newly freed slaves; passed by southern states following the Civil War.

block grant: A large grant given to a state by the federal government with only general spending guidelines.

Board of Governors: In the Federal Reserve System, a seven-member board that makes most economic decisions regarding interest rates and the supply of money.

Bretton Woods System: International financial system devised shortly before the end of World War II that created the World Bank and the International Monetary Fund.

brief: A document containing the legal written arguments in a case filed with a court by a party prior to a hearing or trial.

Brown v. Board of Education (1954): U.S. Supreme Court decision holding that school segregation is inherently unconstitutional because it violates the Fourteenth Amendment's guarantee of equal protection.

budget deficit: The economic condition that occurs when expenditures exceed revenues.

bureaucracy: The thousands of federal government agencies and institutions that implement and administer federal laws and programs.

C

Cabinet: The formal body of presidential advisers who head the fifteen executive departments. Presidents often add others to this body of formal advisers.

campaign consultant: A private-sector professional who sells to a candidate the technologies, services, and strategies required to get that candidate elected.

campaign manager: The individual who travels with the candidate and coordinates the campaign.

candidate-centered politics: Politics that focuses on the candidates, their particular issues, and character rather than party affiliation.

categorical grant: Grant that allocates federal funds to states for a specific purpose.

checks and balances: A constitutionally mandated structure that gives each of the three branches of government some degree of oversight and control over the actions of the others.

citizen journalists: Ordinary individuals who collect, report, and analyze news content.

civic virtue: The tendency to form small-scale associations for the public good.

civil law: Codes of behavior related to the conduct and relationships between individuals or groups.

civil liberties: The personal guarantees and freedoms that the federal government cannot abridge by law, constitution, or judicial interpretation.

civil rights: The government-protected rights of individuals against arbitrary or discriminatory treatment by governments or individuals.

Civil Rights Act of 1964: Wide-ranging legislation passed by Congress to outlaw segregation in public facilities and discrimination in employment, education, and voting; created the Equal Employment Opportunity Commission.

Civil Rights Cases (1883): Name attached to five cases brought under the Civil Rights Act of 1875. In 1883, the Supreme Court decided that discrimination in a variety of public accommodations, including theaters, hotels, and railroads, could not be prohibited by the act because such discrimination was private discrimination and not state discrimination.

civil service system: The merit system by which many federal bureaucrats are selected.

clear and present danger test: Test articulated by the Supreme Court in *Schenck v. U.S.* (1919) to draw the line between protected and unprotected speech; the Court looks to see "whether the words used" could "create a clear and present danger that they will bring about substantive evils" that Congress seeks "to prevent."

cloture: Mechanism requiring sixty senators to vote to cut off debate.

collective good: Something of value that cannot be withheld from a nonmember of a group, for example, a tax write-off or a better environment.

collective security: The idea that an attack on one country is an attack on all countries.

Committees of Correspondence: Organizations in each of the American colonies created to keep colonists abreast of developments with the British; served as powerful molders of public opinion against the British.

communications director: The person who develops the overall media strategy for the candidate.

concurrent powers: Powers shared by the national and state governments.

conference committee: Special joint committee created to reconcile differences in bills passed by the House and Senate.

Congressional Budget Act of 1974: Act that established the congressional budget process by laying out a plan for congressional action on the annual budget resolution, appropriations, reconciliation, and any other revenue bills.

congressional review: A process whereby Congress can nullify agency regulations by a joint resolution of legislative disapproval.

conservative: One who believes that a government is best that governs least and that big government can only infringe on individual, personal, and economic rights.

constitution: A document establishing the structure, functions, and limitations of a government.

constitutional courts: Federal courts specifically created by the U.S. Constitution or by Congress pursuant to its authority in Article III.

content regulations: Limitations on the substance of the mass media.

contrast ad: Ad that compares the records and proposals of the candidates, with a bias toward the candidate sponsoring the ad.

cooperative federalism: The intertwined relationship between the national, state, and local governments that began with the New Deal.

criminal law: Codes of behavior related to the protection of property and individual safety.

critical election: An election that signals a party realignment through voter polarization around new issues and personalities.

Cuban Missile Crisis: The 1962 confrontation over the deployment of ballistic missiles in Cuba that nearly escalated into war between the United States and the Soviet Union.

D

dealignment: A general decline in party identification and loyalty in the electorate.

Declaration of Independence: Document drafted by Thomas Jefferson in 1776 that proclaimed the right of the American colonies to separate from Great Britain.

deep background: Information provided to a journalist that will not be attributed to any source.

defense policy: Area of policy-making that focuses on the strategies that a country uses to protect itself from its enemies.

delegate: Role played by an elected representative who votes the way his or her constituents would want him or her to, regardless of his or her own opinions.

democracy: A system of government that gives power to the people, whether directly or through elected representatives.

Department of Defense: Chief executive branch department responsible for formulation and implementation of U.S. defense and military policy.

Department of Homeland Security: Cabinet department created after the 9/11 terrorist attacks to coordinate domestic security efforts.

Department of State: Chief executive branch department responsible for formulation and implementation of U.S. foreign policy.

departments: Major administrative units with responsibility for a broad area of government operations. Departmental status usually indicates a permanent national interest in a particular governmental function, such as defense, commerce, or agriculture.

détente: The improvement in relations between the United States and the Soviet Union that occurred during the 1970s.

direct democracy: A system of government in which members of the polity meet to discuss all policy decisions and then agree to abide by majority rule.

direct incitement test: Test articulated by the Supreme Court in *Brandenburg* v. *Ohio* (1969) that holds that advocacy of illegal action is protected by the First Amendment unless imminent lawless action is intended and likely to occur.

discharge petition: Petition that gives a majority of the House of Representatives the authority to bring an issue to the floor in the face of committee inaction.

discount rate: The rate of interest at which the Federal Reserve Board lends money to member banks.

disturbance theory: The theory that interest groups form as a result of changes in the political system.

double jeopardy clause: Part of the Fifth Amendment that protects individuals from being tried twice for the same offense in the same jurisdiction.

***Dred Scott* v. *Sandford* (1857):** The Supreme Court concluded that the U.S. Congress lacked the constitutional authority to bar slavery in the territories. This decision narrowed the scope of national power, while it enhanced that of the states.

dual federalism: The belief that having separate and equally powerful levels of government is the best arrangement.

due process clause: Clause contained in the Fifth and Fourteenth Amendments. Over the years, it has been construed to guarantee to individuals a variety of rights ranging from economic liberty to criminal procedural rights to protection from arbitrary governmental action.

E

earmark: Funds that an appropriations bill designates for specific projects within a state or congressional district.

economic stability: A situation in which there is economic growth, rising national income, high employment, and steadiness in the general level of prices.

Eighth Amendment: Part of the Bill of Rights that states: "Excessive bail shall not be required, nor excessive fines imposed, nor cruel and unusual punishments inflicted."

elector: Member of the Electoral College.

Electoral College: Representatives of each state who cast the final ballots that actually elect a president.

Embargo Act: Legislation passed by Congress in 1807 to prevent U.S. ships from leaving U.S. ports without the approval of the federal government.

enlargement: Policy implemented during the Clinton administration in which the United States would actively promote the expansion of democracy and free markets throughout the world.

entitlement programs: Government benefits that all citizens meeting eligibility criteria—such as age, income level, or unemployment—are legally "entitled" to receive.

enumerated powers: Seventeen specific powers granted to Congress under Article I, section 8, of the Constitution.

Equal Pay Act of 1963: Legislation that requires employers to pay men and women equal pay for equal work.

equal protection clause: Section of the Fourteenth Amendment that guarantees that all citizens receive "equal protection of the laws."

Equal Rights Amendment: Proposed amendment to the Constitution that states "Equality of rights under the law shall not be denied or abridged by the United States or any state on account of sex."

equal time rule: The rule that requires broadcast stations to sell air time equally to all candidates in a political campaign if they choose to sell it to any.

establishment clause: The first clause of the First Amendment; it directs the national government not to sanction an official religion.

exclusionary rule: Judicially created rule that prohibits police from using illegally seized evidence at trial.

executive agreements: Formal international agreements entered into by the president that do not require the advice and consent of the U.S. Senate.

Executive Office of the President (EOP): A mini-bureaucracy created in 1939 to help the president oversee the executive branch bureaucracy.

executive order: Rule or regulation issued by the president that has the effect of law. All executive orders must be published in the *Federal Register*.

executive privilege: An implied presidential power that allows the president to refuse to disclose information regarding confidential conversations or national security to Congress or the judiciary.

***ex post facto* law:** Law that makes an act punishable as a crime even if the action was legal at the time it was committed.

exit polls: Polls conducted as voters leave selected polling places on Election Day.

extradition clause: Part of Article IV of the Constitution that requires states to extradite, or return, criminals to states where they have been convicted or are to stand trial.

F

Federal Employees Political Activities Act of 1993: The 1993 liberalization of the Hatch Act. Federal employees are now allowed to run for office in nonpartisan elections and to contribute money to campaigns in partisan elections.

federal system: System of government where the national government and state governments share power, derive all authority from the people.

Federalists: Those who favored a stronger national government and supported the proposed U.S. Constitution; later became the first U.S. political party.

The Federalist Papers: A series of eighty-five political essays written by Alexander Hamilton, James Madison, and John Jay in support of ratification of the U.S. Constitution.

Fifteenth Amendment: One of the three Civil War Amendments; specifically enfranchised newly freed male slaves.

Fifth Amendment: Part of the Bill of Rights that imposes a number of restrictions on the federal government with respect to the rights of persons suspected of committing a crime. It provides for indictment by a grand jury and protection against self-incrimination, and prevents the national government from denying a person life, liberty, or property without the due process of law. It also prevents the national government from taking property without just compensation.

fighting words: Words that, "by their very utterance inflict injury or tend to incite an immediate breach of peace." Fighting words are not subject to the restrictions of the First Amendment.

filibuster: A formal way of halting Senate action on a bill by means of long speeches or unlimited debate.

finance chair: The individual who coordinates the financial business of the campaign.

First Amendment: Part of the Bill of Rights that imposes a number of restrictions on the federal government with respect to civil liberties, including freedom of religion, speech, press, assembly, and petition.

First Continental Congress: Meeting held in Philadelphia from September 5 to October 26, 1774, in which fifty-six delegates (from every colony except Georgia) adopted a resolution in opposition to the Coercive Acts.

fiscal policy: The deliberate use of the national government's taxing and spending policies to maintain economic stability.

501(c) group: Nonprofit, tax-exempt interest groups that can engage in varying levels of political activity; not subject to FEC disclosure rules.

527 political committee: Tax-exempt organization created to raise money for political activities such as voter mobilization and issue advocacy; not subject to FEC disclosure rules.

foreign policy: Area of policy-making that encompasses how one country builds relationships with other countries in order to safeguard its national interest.

Fourteenth Amendment: One of the three Civil War Amendments; guarantees equal protection and due process of the law to all U.S. citizens.

Fourth Amendment: Part of the Bill of Rights that reads: "The right of the people to be secure in their persons, houses, papers, and effects, against unreasonable searches and seizures, shall not be violated, and no Warrants shall issue, but upon probable cause, supported by Oath or affirmation, and particularly describing the place to be searched, and the persons or things to be seized."

framing: The process by which a news organization defines a political issue and consequently affects opinion about the issue.

free exercise clause: The second clause of the First Amendment; it prohibits the U.S. government from interfering with a citizen's right to practice his or her religion.

free rider problem: Potential members fail to join a group because they can get the benefit, or collective good, sought by the group without contributing the effort.

free trade system: A system of international trade with limited government interference.

front-loading: The tendency of states to choose an early date on the nomination calendar.

full faith and credit clause: Section of Article IV of the Constitution that ensures judicial decrees and contracts made in one state will be binding and enforceable in any other state.

fundamental freedoms: Those rights defined by the Court to be essential to order, liberty, and justice and therefore entitled to the highest standard of review.

G

General Agreement on Tariffs and Trade (GATT): Post–World War II economic development program designed to help facilitate international trade negotiations and promote free trade.

general election: Election in which voters decide which candidates will actually fill elective public offices.

general election campaign: Phase of a political campaign aimed at winning election to office.

gerrymandering: The drawing of congressional districts to produce a particular electoral outcome without regard to the shape of the district.

get-out-the-vote (GOTV): A push at the end of a political campaign to encourage supporters to go to the polls.

***Gibbons v. Ogden* (1824):** The Supreme Court upheld broad congressional power to regulate interstate commerce. The Court's broad interpretation of the Constitution's commerce clause paved the way for later rulings upholding expansive federal powers.

government: The formal vehicle through which policies are made and affairs of state are conducted.

government corporations: Businesses established by Congress to perform functions that could be provided by private businesses.

governmental (institutional) agenda: Problems to which public officials feel obliged to devote active and serious attention.

grandfather clause: Voter qualification provision in many southern states that allowed only those whose grandfathers had voted before Reconstruction to vote unless they passed a wealth or literacy test.

Great Compromise: The final decision of the Constitutional Convention to create a two-house legislature with the lower house elected by the people and with powers divided between the two houses. It also made national law supreme.

H

hard money: Campaign contributions that are regulated and limited by the Federal Election Commission.

Hatch Act: The 1939 act to prohibit civil servants from taking activist roles in partisan campaigns. This act prohibited federal employees from making political contributions, working for a particular party, or campaigning for a particular candidate.

hold: A tactic by which a senator asks to be informed before a particular bill or nomination is brought to the floor. This request signals leadership that a member may have objections to the bill (or nomination) and should be consulted before further action is taken.

Honest Leadership and Open Government Act of 2007: Lobbying reform banning gifts to members of Congress and their staffs, toughening disclosure requirements, and increasing time limits on moving from the federal government to the private sector.

human rights: The protection of people's basic freedoms and needs.

I

impeachment: The power delegated to the House of Representatives in the Constitution to charge the president, vice president, or other "civil officers," including federal judges, with "Treason, Bribery, or other high Crimes and Misdemeanors." This is the first step in the constitutional process of removing such government officials from office.

implementation: The process by which a law or policy is put into operation.

implied powers: Powers derived from the enumerated powers and the necessary and proper clause. These powers are not stated specifically but are considered to be reasonably implied through the exercise of delegated powers.

incorporation doctrine: An interpretation of the Constitution that holds that the due process clause of the Fourteenth Amendment requires that state and local governments also guarantee those rights.

incumbency: Already holding an office.

independent executive agencies: Governmental units that closely resemble a Cabinet department but have narrower areas of responsibility, and perform services rather than regulatory functions.

independent regulatory commission: An entity created by Congress outside a major executive department.

indirect democracy: A system of government that gives citizens the opportunity to vote for representatives who work on their behalf.

inflation: A rise in the general price levels of an economy.

inherent powers: Powers that belong to the president because they can be inferred from the Constitution.

inoculation ad: Advertising that attempts to counteract an anticipated attack from the opposition before the attack is launched.

interagency councils: Working groups created to facilitate coordination of policy making and implementation across a host of governmental agencies.

interest group: An organized group that tries to influence public policy.

International Monetary Fund (IMF): International governmental organization created shortly before the end of World War II to stabilize international currency transactions.

interstate compacts: Contracts between states that carry the force of law; generally now used as a tool to address multistate policy concerns.

iron triangles: The relatively stable relationships and patterns of interaction that occur among agencies, interest groups, and congressional committees or subcommittees.

isolationism: A national policy of avoiding participation in foreign affairs.

issue networks: The loose and informal relationships that exist among a large number of actors who work in broad policy areas.

J

Jim Crow laws: Laws enacted by southern states that required segregation in public schools, theaters, hotels, and other public accommodations.

Joint Chiefs of Staff: Military advisory body that includes the Army chief of staff, the Air Force chief of staff, the chief of naval operations, and the Marine commandant.

joint committee: Standing committee that includes members from both houses of Congress to conduct investigations or special studies.

judicial activism: A philosophy of judicial decision making that posits judges should use their power broadly to further justice.

judicial implementation: How and whether judicial decisions are translated into actual public policies affecting more than the immediate parties to a lawsuit.

judicial restraint: A philosophy of judicial decision making that posits courts should allow the decisions of other branches of government to stand, even when they offend a judge's own principles.

judicial review: Power of the courts to review acts of other branches of government and the states.

Judiciary Act of 1789: Legislative act that established the basic three-tiered structure of the federal court system.

jurisdiction: Authority vested in a particular court to hear and decide the issues in a particular case.

L

legislative courts: Courts established by Congress for specialized purposes, such as the Court of Appeals for Veterans Claims.

Lemon test: Three-part test created by the Supreme Court for examining the constitutionality of religious establishment issues.

libel: Written statement that defames a person's character.

liberal: One who favors governmental involvement in the economy and in the provision of social services and who takes an activist role in protecting the rights of women, the elderly, minorities, and the environment.

libertarian: One who believes in limited government and no governmental interference in personal liberties.

lobbying: The activities of a group or organization that seek to persuade political leaders to support the group's position.

lobbyist: Interest group representative who seeks to influence legislation that will benefit his or her organization or client through political and/or financial persuasion.

logrolling: Vote trading; voting to support a colleague's bill in return for a promise of future support.

M

majority leader: The head of the party with the second highest number of elected representatives in the House of Representatives or the Senate.

majority party: The political party in each house of Congress with the second most members.

majority rule: The central premise of direct democracy in which only policies that collectively garner the support of a majority of voters will be made into law.

manifest destiny: Theory that the United States was divinely mandated to expand across North America to the Pacific Ocean.

***Marbury v. Madison* (1803):** Case in which the Supreme Court first asserted the power of judicial review by finding that the congressional statute extending the Court's original jurisdiction was unconstitutional.

margin of error: A measure of the accuracy of a public opinion poll.

markup: A session in which committee members offer changes to a bill before it goes to the floor.

Marshall Plan: European collective recovery program, named after Secretary of State George C. Marshall, that provided extensive American aid to Western Europe after World War II.

mass media: The entire array of organizations through which information is collected and disseminated to the general public.

matching funds: Donations to presidential campaigns whereby every dollar raised from individuals in amounts less than $251 is matched by the federal treasury.

Mayflower Compact: Document written by the Pilgrims while at sea enumerating the scope of their government and its expectations of citizens.

***McCulloch v. Maryland* (1819):** The Supreme Court upheld the power of the national government and denied the right of a state to tax the federal bank using the Constitution's supremacy clause. The Court's broad interpretation of the necessary and proper clause paved the way for later rulings upholding expansive federal powers.

means-tested programs: Programs that require that beneficiaries have incomes below specified levels to be eligible for benefits. Among these are SSI, TANF, and SNAP.

media effects: The influence of news sources on public opinion.

Medicaid: A government program that subsidizes medical care for the poor.

Medicare: The federal program established during the Lyndon B. Johnson administration that provides medical care to older Americans.

mercantilism: An economic theory designed to increase a nation's wealth through the development of commercial industry and a favorable balance of trade.

merit system: A system of employment based on qualifications, test scores, and ability, rather than party loyalty.

midterm election: An election that takes place in the middle of a presidential term.

military-industrial complex: The alliance formed by the U.S. armed forces and defense industries.

minority leader: The head of the party with the second highest number of elected representatives in the House of Representatives or the Senate.

minority party: The political party in each house of Congress with the second most members.

***Miranda* rights:** Statements that must be made by the police informing a suspect of his or her constitutional rights protected by the Fifth Amendment, including the right to an attorney provided by the court if the suspect cannot afford one.

***Miranda v. Arizona* (1966):** A landmark Supreme Court ruling that held the Fifth Amendment requires that individuals arrested for a crime must be advised of their right to remain silent and to have counsel present.

moderate: A person who takes a relatively centrist or middle-of-the-road view on most political issues.

monarchy: A form of government in which power is vested in hereditary kings and queens who govern in the interests of all.

monetary policy: A form of government regulation in which the nation's money supply and interest rates are controlled.

Monroe Doctrine: President James Monroe's 1823 pledge that the United States would oppose attempts by European states to extend their political control into the Western Hemisphere.

muckraking: A form of journalism, in vogue in the early twentieth century, devoted to exposing misconduct by government, business, and individual politicians.

N

narrowcasting: Targeting media programming at specific populations within society.

national convention: A party meeting held in the presidential election year for the purposes of nominating a presidential and vice presidential ticket and adopting a platform.

national party platform: A statement of the general and specific philosophy and policy goals of a political party, usually promulgated at the national convention.

natural law: A doctrine that society should be governed by certain ethical principles that are part of nature and, as such, can be understood by reason.

necessary and proper clause: The final paragraph of Article I, section 8, of the Constitution, which gives Congress the authority to pass all laws "necessary and proper" to carry out the enumerated powers specified in the Constitution; also called the elastic clause.

negative ad: Advertising on behalf of a candidate that attacks the opponent's character or platform.

New Deal: The name given to the program of "Relief, Recovery, Reform" begun by President Franklin D. Roosevelt in 1933 to bring the United States out of the Great Depression.

New Federalism: Federal–state relationship proposed by Reagan administration during the 1980s; hallmark is returning administrative powers to the state governments.

New Jersey Plan: A framework for the Constitution proposed by a group of small states. Its key points were a one-house legislature with one vote for each state, a Congress with the ability to raise revenue, and a Supreme Court with members appointed for life.

New York Times Co. v. Sullivan (1964): The Supreme Court concluded that "actual malice" must be proved to support a finding of libel against a public figure.

news media: Media providing the public with new information about subjects of public interest.

Nineteenth Amendment: Amendment to the Constitution that guaranteed women the right to vote.

Ninth Amendment: Part of the Bill of Rights that makes it clear that rights not enumerated in the Constitution or Bill of Rights does not mean that others do not exist.

nomination campaign: Phase of a political campaign aimed at winning a primary election.

non-means-tested programs: Programs that provide cash assistance to qualified beneficiaries, regardless of income. Among these are Social Security and unemployment insurance.

North American Free Trade Agreement (NAFTA): Agreement that promotes free movement of goods and services among Canada, Mexico, and the United States.

North Atlantic Treaty Organization (NATO): The first peacetime military treaty joined by the United States; NATO is a collective security pact between the United States and Western Europe.

nullification: The purported right of a state to declare void a federal law.

O

Office of Management and Budget (OMB): The office that prepares the president's annual budget proposal, reviews the budget and programs of the executive departments, supplies economic forecasts, and conducts detailed analyses of proposed bills and agency rules.

off the record: Information provided to a journalist that will not be released to the public.

oligarchy: A form of government in which the right to participate is conditioned on the possession of wealth, social status, military position, or achievement.

on background: Information provided to a journalist that will not be attributed to a named source.

on the record: Information provided to a journalist that can be released and attributed by name to the source.

open market operations: The buying and selling of government securities by the Federal Reserve Bank.

original jurisdiction: The jurisdiction of courts that hear a case first, usually in a trial. These courts determine the facts of a case.

P

pardon: An executive grant providing restoration of all rights and privileges of citizenship to a specific individual charged or convicted of a crime.

party caucus or conference: A formal gathering of all party members.

party identification: A citizen's personal affinity for a political party, usually expressed by a tendency to vote for the candidates of that party.

party realignment: Dramatic shifts in partisan preferences that drastically alter the political landscape.

patron: A person who finances a group or individual activity.

patronage: Jobs, grants, or other special favors that are given as rewards to friends and political allies for their support.

Pendleton Act: Reform measure that established the principle of federal employment on the basis of open, competitive exams and created the Civil Service Commission.

personal liberty: A key characteristic of U.S. democracy. Initially meaning freedom *from* governmental interference, today it includes demands for freedom *to* engage in a variety of practices without governmental interference or discrimination.

***Plessy v. Ferguson* (1896):** Supreme Court case that challenged a Louisiana statute requiring that railroads provide separate accommodations for blacks and whites. The Court found that separate but equal accommodations did not violate the equal protection clause of the Fourteenth Amendment.

pluralist theory: The theory that political power is distributed among a wide array of diverse and competing interest groups.

pocket veto: If Congress adjourns during the ten days the president has to consider a bill passed by both houses of Congress, the bill is considered vetoed without the president's signature.

policy adoption: The approval of a policy proposal by the people with the requisite authority, such as a legislature.

policy evaluation: The process of determining whether a course of action is achieving its intended goals.

policy formulation: The crafting of proposed courses of action to resolve public problems.

policy implementation: The process of carrying out public policy.

political action committee (PAC): Officially registered fund-raising organization that represents interest groups in the political process.

political culture: Commonly shared attitudes, beliefs, and core values about how government should operate.

political equality: The principle that all citizens are the same in the eyes of the law.

political ideology: The coherent set of values and beliefs about the purpose and scope of government held by groups and individuals.

political machine: A party organization that recruits voter loyalty with tangible incentives and is characterized by a high degree of control over member activity.

political party: A group of office holders, candidates, activists, and voters who identify with a group label and seek to elect to public office individuals who run under that label.

political socialization: The process through which individuals acquire their political beliefs and values.

politico: Role played by an elected representative who acts as a trustee or as a delegate, depending on the issue.

politics: The study of who gets what, when, and how—or how policy decisions are made.

pollster: A campaign consultant who conducts public opinion surveys.

poll tax: A tax levied in many southern states and localities that had to be paid before an eligible voter could cast a ballot.

popular consent: The principle that governments must draw their powers from the consent of the governed.

popular sovereignty: The notion that the ultimate authority in society rests with the people.

population ecology theory: The theory that the formation of political organizations is conditional on the resources allocated to a given issue area.

pork: Legislation that allows representatives to bring money and jobs to their districts in the form of public works programs, military bases, or other programs.

positive ad: Advertising on behalf of a candidate that stresses the candidate's qualifications, family, and issue positions, with no direct reference to the opponent.

precedent: A prior judicial decision that serves as a rule for settling subsequent cases of a similar nature.

preemption: A concept that allows the national government to override state or local actions in certain areas.

president pro tempore: The official chair of the Senate; usually the most senior member of the majority party.

press briefing: A relatively restricted session between a press secretary or aide and the press.

press conference: An unrestricted session between an elected official and the press.

press release: A document offering an official comment or position.

press secretary: The individual charged with interacting and communicating with journalists on a daily basis.

primary election: Election in which voters decide which of the candidates will represent the party in the general election.

prior restraint: Constitutional doctrine that prevents the government from prohibiting speech or publication before the fact; generally held to be in violation of the First Amendment.

privileges and immunities clause: Part of Article IV of the Constitution guaranteeing that the citizens of each state are afforded the same rights as citizens of all other states.

progressive federalism: Movement that gives state officials significant leeway in acting on issues normally considered national in scope, such as the environment and consumer protection.

prospective judgment: A voter's evaluation of a candidate based on what he or she pledges to do about an issue if elected.

protectionism: A trade policy wherein a country closes off its markets to foreign goods.

public funds: Donations from general tax revenues to the campaigns of qualifying presidential candidates.

public opinion: What the public thinks about a particular issue or set of issues at any point in time.

public opinion polls: Interviews or surveys with samples of citizens that are used to estimate the feelings and beliefs of the entire population.

public policy: An intentional course of action or inaction followed by government in dealing with some problem or matter of concern.

push polls: Polls taken for the purpose of providing information on an opponent that would lead respondents to vote against that candidate.

R

random sampling: A method of poll selection that gives each person in a group the same chance of being selected.

Reagan Doctrine: The Reagan administration's commitment to ending communism by providing military assistance to anti-communist groups.

reapportionment: The reallocation of the number of seats in the House of Representatives after each decennial census.

recession: A decline in the economy that occurs as investment sags, production falls off, and unemployment increases.

reconciliation: A procedure that allows consideration of controversial issues affecting the budget by limiting debate to twenty hours, thereby ending threat of a filibuster.

redistricting: The process of redrawing of congressional districts to reflect increases or decreases in seats allotted to the states, as well as population shifts within a state.

regulations: Rules that govern the operation of all government programs that have the force of law.

republic: A government rooted in the consent of the governed; a representative or indirect democracy.

reserve requirements: Government requirements that a portion of member banks' deposits be retained as backing for their loans.

reserved (or police) powers: Powers reserved to the states by the Tenth Amendment that lie at the foundation of a state's right to legislate for the public health and welfare of its citizens.

retrospective judgment: A voter's evaluation of a candidate based on past performance on a particular issue.

right to privacy: The right to be left alone; a judicially created principle encompassing a variety of individual actions protected by the penumbras or shadows cast by several constitutional amendments, including the First, Third, Fourth, Ninth, and Fourteenth Amendments.

Roe v. Wade (1973): The Supreme Court found that a woman's right to an abortion was protected by the right to privacy that could be implied from specific guarantees found in the Bill of Rights applied to the states through the Fourteenth Amendment.

Roosevelt Corollary: Concept developed by President Theodore Roosevelt early in the twentieth century declaring that it was the responsibility of the United States to assure stability in Latin America and the Caribbean.

rule making: A quasi-legislative process that results in regulations that have the characteristics of a legislative act.

Rule of Four: At least four justices of the Supreme Court must vote to consider a case before it can be heard.

S

sample: A subset of the whole population selected to be questioned for the purposes of prediction or gauging opinion.

Second Continental Congress: Meeting that convened in Philadelphia on May 10, 1775, at which it was decided that an army should be raised and George Washington of Virginia was named commander in chief.

secular realignment: The gradual rearrangement of party coalitions, based more on demographic shifts than on shocks to the political system.

select (or special) committee: Temporary committee appointed for a specific purpose.

selective incorporation: A judicial doctrine whereby most but not all of the protections found in the Bill of Rights are made applicable to the states via the Fourteenth Amendment.

senatorial courtesy: A process by which presidents, when selecting district court judges, defer to the senators in whose state the vacancy occurs.

senatorial courtesy: Process by which presidents generally defer selection of district court judges to the choice of senators of their own party who represent the state where the vacancy occurs.

seniority: Time of continuous service on a committee.

separation of powers: A way of dividing the power of government among the legislative, executive, and judicial branches, each staffed separately, with equality and independence of each branch ensured by the Constitution.

Seventeenth Amendment: Amendment to the U.S. Constitution that made senators directly elected by the people; removed their selection from state legislatures.

Sixteenth Amendment: Amendment to the U.S. Constitution that authorized Congress to enact a national income tax.

Sixth Amendment: Part of the Bill of Rights that sets out the basic requirements of procedural due process for federal courts to follow in criminal trials. These include speedy and public trials, impartial juries, trials in the state where crime was committed, notice of the charges, the right to confront and obtain favorable witnesses, and the right to counsel.

slander: Untrue spoken statements that defame the character of a person.

social capital: Cooperative relationships that facilitate the resolution of collective problems.

social conservative: One who believes that traditional moral teachings should be supported and furthered by the government.

social contract: An agreement between the people and their government signifying their consent to be governed.

social contract theory: The belief that people are free and equal by natural right, and that this in turn requires that all people give their consent to be governed; espoused by John Locke and influential in the writing of the Declaration of Independence.

Social Security Act: A 1935 law that established old age insurance; assistance for the needy, aged, blind, and families with dependent children; and unemployment insurance.

soft money: Campaign contributions that are not regulated or limited by the Federal Election Commission.

solicitor general: The fourth-ranking member of the Department of Justice; responsible for handling nearly all appeals on behalf of the U.S. government to the Supreme Court.

Speaker of the House: The only officer of the House of Representatives specifically mentioned in the Constitution; the chamber's most powerful position; traditionally a member of the majority party

spoils system: The firing of public-office holders of a defeated political party to replace them with loyalists of the newly elected party.

Stamp Act Congress: Meeting of representatives of nine of the thirteen colonies held in New York City in 1765, during which representatives drafted a document to send to the king listing how their rights had been violated.

standing committee: Committee to which proposed bills are referred; continues from one Congress to the next.

stare decisis : In court rulings, a reliance on past decisions or precedents to formulate decisions in new cases.

strategic trade policy: A trade policy wherein governments identify key industries that they wish to see grow and enact policies to support this economic enlargement.

stratified sampling: A variation of random sampling; the population is divided into subgroups and weighted based on demographic characteristics of the national population.

straw poll: Unscientific survey used to gauge public opinion on a variety of issues and policies.

strict constructionist: An approach to constitutional interpretation that emphasizes interpreting the Constitution as it was written and intended by the Framers.

strict scrutiny: A heightened standard of review used by the Supreme Court to determine the constitutional validity of a challenged practice.

substantive due process: Judicial interpretation of the Fifth and Fourteenth Amendments' due process clauses that protects citizens from arbitrary or unjust state or federal laws.

suffrage movement: The drive for voting rights for women that took place in the United States from 1890 to 1920.

supremacy clause: Portion of Article VI of the U.S. Constitution mandating that national law is supreme to (that is, supersedes) all other laws passed by the states or by any other subdivision of government.

suspect classification: Category or class, such as race, that triggers the highest standard of scrutiny from the Supreme Court.

symbolic speech: Symbols, signs, and other methods of expression generally also considered to be protected by the First Amendment.

systemic agenda: A discussion agenda; it consists of all public issues that are viewed as requiring governmental attention.

T

tariffs: Taxes on imported goods.

Tenth Amendment: The final part of the Bill of Rights that defines the basic principle of American federalism in stating that the powers not delegated to the national government are reserved to the states or to the people.

Thirteenth Amendment: One of the three Civil War Amendments; specifically bans slavery in the United States.

Three-Fifths Compromise: Agreement reached at the Constitutional Convention stipulating that each slave was to be counted as three-fifths of a person for purposes of determining population for representation in the U.S. House of Representatives.

Title IX: Provision of the Education Amendments of 1972 that bars educational institutions receiving federal funds from discriminating against female students.

totalitarianism: A form of government in which power resides in a leader who rules according to self-interest and without regard for individual rights and liberties.

tracking polls: Continuous surveys that enable a campaign or news organization to chart a candidate's daily rise or fall in support.

trade association: A group that represents a specific industry.

transactions theory: The theory that public policies are the result of narrowly defined exchanges among political actors.

trial court: Court of original jurisdiction where cases begin.

Truman Doctrine: U.S. policy initiated in 1947 to provide economic assistance and military aid to countries fighting against communist revolutions or political pressure.

trustee: Role played by an elected representative who listens to constituents' opinions and then uses his or her best judgment to make a final decision.

turnout: The proportion of the voting-age public that casts a ballot.

Twenty-Fifth Amendment: Adopted in 1967 to establish procedures for filling vacancies in the office of president and vice president as well as providing for procedures to deal with the disability of a president.

Twenty-Second Amendment: Adopted in 1951; prevents a president from serving more than two terms, or more than ten years if he came to office via the death, resignation, or impeachment of his predecessor.

U

***U.S. v. Nixon* (1974):** Supreme Court ruling on power of the president, finding that there is no absolute constitutional executive privilege allowing a president to refuse to comply with a court order to produce information needed in a criminal trial.

unfunded mandates: National laws that direct state or local governments to comply with federal rules or regulations (such as clean air or water standards) but contain little or no federal funding to defray the cost of meeting these requirements.

unitary system: System of government where the local and regional governments derive all authority from a strong national government.

V

veto: Formal constitutional authority of the president to reject bills passed by both houses of the legislative body, thus preventing the bill from becoming law without further congressional activity.

veto power: The formal, constitutional authority of the president to reject bills passed by both houses of Congress, thus preventing them from becoming law without further congressional action.

Virginia Plan: The first general plan for the Constitution offered in Philadelphia. Its key points were a bicameral legislature, and an executive and a judiciary chosen by the national legislature.

voter canvass: The process by which a campaign reaches individual voters, either by door-to-door solicitation or by telephone.

W

war on terrorism: An international action, initiated by President George W. Bush after the 9/11 attacks, to weed out terrorist operatives throughout the world.

War Powers Act: Passed by Congress in 1973; the president is limited in the deployment of troops overseas to a sixty-day period in peacetime (which can be extended for an extra thirty days to permit withdrawal) unless Congress explicitly gives its approval for a longer period.

whip: Party leader who keeps close contact with all members of his or her party, takes vote counts on key legislation, prepares summaries of bills, and acts as a communications link within a party.

World Bank: International governmental organization created shortly before the end of World War II to provide loans for large economic development projects.

World Trade Organization (WTO): An international organization created in 1995 to supervise and open international trade.

writ of *certiorari*: A request for the Supreme Court to order up the records from a lower court to review the case.

writs of *habeas corpus*: Court orders in which a judge requires authorities to prove that a prisoner is being held lawfully and that allow the prisoner to be freed if the judge is not persuaded by the government's case. *Habeas corpus* rights imply that prisoners have a right to know what charges are being made against them.

Y

yellow journalism: A form of newspaper publishing in vogue in the late nineteenth century that featured pictures, comics, color, and sensationalized news coverage.

Chapter 1

1. John Hammond, *Leah and Rachael, or the Two Fruitful Sisters, Virginia and Maryland; their Present Condition Impartially Stated and Related* (London: Force Tracts, 1656).

2. Thomas Hobbes, *Leviathan*, ed. Richard Tuck (New York: Cambridge University Press, 1996).

3. John Locke, *Two Treaties of Government*, ed. Peter Lasleti (New York: Cambridge University Press, 1988).

4. Jack C. Plano and Milton Greenberg. *The American Political Dictionary*, 6th ed. (New York: Holt, Rinehart and Winston, 1982).

5. Albert B. Saye, et al., *Principles of American Government*, 5th ed. (Englewood Cliffs, NJ: Prentice Hall, 1966), 5.

6. Pew Forum on Religion and Public Life, "Growing Number of Americans Say Islam Encourages Violence" (July 24, 2003).

7. Susan A. MacManus, *Young v. Old. Generational Combat in the 21st Century* (Boulder, CO: Westview, 1995), 3.

8. Dennis Cauchon, "Who Will Take Care of an Older Population?" *USA Today* (October 25, 2005): 1–2B.

9. James B. Gimpel and Kimberly A. Karnes, "The Rural Side of the Urban-Rural Gap," *PS: Political Science and Politics* (July 2006): 467–72.

10. CNN Exit Polls, www.cnn.com/election/2008/results/polls.

11. Gallup Poll, June 11–14, 2007.

12. This discussion draws heavily from Terence Ball and Richard Dagger, *Political Ideologies and the Democratic Ideal*, 5th ed. (New York: Longman, 2004), 2.

13. Isaiah Berlin, *The Crooked Timber of Humanity: Chapters in the History of Ideas* (New York: Vintage, 1992), 1.

14. Jack C. Plano and Milton Greenberg, *The American Political Dictionary*, 9th ed. (Fort Worth, TX: Harcourt Brace, 1993), 16.

15. Philip E. Converse, "The Nature of Belief Systems in Mass Publics," in David E. Apter, ed., *Ideology and Discontent* (New York: Free Press, 1964), 206–21.

16. Research 2000 Poll, February 22–25, 2010.

Chapter 2

1. See Richard B. Bernstein with Jerome Agel, *Amending America* (New York: New York Times Books, 1993), 138–40.

2. *Oregon* v. *Mitchell*, 400 U.S. 112 (1970).

3. Bernstein with Agel, *Amending America*, 139.

4. For an account of the early development of the colonies, see D. W. Meining, *The Shaping of America*, vol. 1: *Atlantic America, 1492–1800* (New Haven, CT: Yale University Press, 1986).

5. For an excellent chronology of the events leading up to the writing of the Declaration of Independence and the colonists' break with Great Britain, see Calvin D. Lonton, ed., *The Bicentennial Almanac* (Nashville, TN: Thomas Nelson, 1975).

6. See Garry Wills, *Inventing America: Jefferson's Declaration of Independence* (New York: Random House, 1978). Wills argues that the Declaration was signed solely to secure foreign aid for the ongoing war effort.

7. For more about the Articles of Confederation, see Merrill Jensen, *The Articles of Confederation* (Madison: University of Wisconsin Press, 1940).

8. Charles A. Beard, *An Economic Interpretation of the Constitution of the United States,* reissue ed. (Mineola, NY: Dover, 2004).

9. John Patrick Diggins, "Power and Authority in American History: The Case of Charles A. Beard and His Critics," *American Historical Review* 86 (October 1981): 701–30; and Robert Brown, *Charles Beard and the Constitution: A Critical Analysis of "An Economic Interpretation of the Constitution"* (Princeton, NJ: Princeton University Press, 1956).

10. Jackson Turner Main, *The Anti-Federalists: Critics of the Constitution, 1781–1788* (Chapel Hill: University of North Carolina, 2004).

11. Gordon S. Wood, *The Creation of the American Republic, 1776–1787,* reissue ed. (New York: Knopf, 1983).

12. For more on the political nature of compromise at the convention, see Calvin C. Jillson. *Constitution Making: Conflict and Consensus in the Federal Constitution of 1787* (New York: Agathon, 1988).

13. Bernard Bailyn, *The Ideological Origins of the American Revolution* (Cambridge, MA: Belknap Press, 1967).

14. Federal Republicans favored a republican or representative form of government (do not confuse this term with the modern Republican Party, which came into being in 1854; see **chapter 12**). Ultimately, the word *federal* referred to the form of government embodied in the new Constitution, and *confederation* referred to a "league of states," as under the Articles, and later was applied in the "Confederacy" of 1861–1865 that governed the southern states.

15. See Ralph Ketcham, ed., *The Anti-Federalist Papers and the Constitutional Debates* (New York: New American Library, 1986).

16. See Herbert J. Storing, *What the Anti-Federalists Were For* (Chicago: University of Chicago Press, 1981), for a fuller discussion of Anti-Federalist views.

17. David E. Kyvig, *Repealing National Prohibition* (Chicago: University of Chicago Press, 1978).

18. See Jane J. Mansbridge, *Why We Lost the ERA* (Chicago: University of Chicago Press, 1986).

19. *Marbury* v. *Madison*, 5 U.S. 137 (1803).

20. See, for example, the speech by Attorney General Edwin Meese III before the American Bar Association, July 9, 1985, Washington, DC. See also Antonin Scalia and Amy Gutman, eds., *A Matter of Interpretation: Federal Courts and the Law* (Princeton, NJ: Princeton University Press, 1998).

21. See, for example, the speech by Associate Justice William J. Brennan Jr. at Georgetown University Text and Teaching Symposium, October 10, 1985, Washington, DC.

22. Bruce Ackerman, *We the People: Foundations* (Cambridge, MA: Belknap Press, 1991).

Chapter 3

1. Randal C. Archibold, "Arizona Enacts Stringent Law on Immigration," *New York Times* (April 23, 2010): A1.

2. Archibold, "Arizona Enacts Stringent Law."

3. Archibold, "Arizona Enacts Stringent Law."

4. John Mountjoy, "Interstate Cooperation: Interstate Compacts Make a Comeback," *Council of State Governments,* www.csg.org.

5. *McCulloch* v. *Maryland,* 17 U.S. 316 (1819).

6. For more on *McCulloch,* see Richard E. Ellis, *Aggressive Nationalism: McCulloch v. Maryland and the Foundation of Federal Authority in the Young Republic* (New York: Oxford University Press, 2008).

7. *Gibbons* v. *Ogden,* 22 U.S. 1 (1824).

8. For more on *Gibbons,* see Thomas H. Cox, Gibbons *v.* Ogden: *Law and Society in the Early Republic* (Athens: Ohio University Press, 2010).

9. *Barron* v. *Baltimore,* 32 U.S. 243 (1833)

10. For more on *Barron,* see Brendan J. Doherty, "Interpreting the Bill of Rights and the Nature of Federalism: *Barron* v. *City of Baltimore,*" *Journal of Supreme Court History* 32 (2007): 211–28.

11. *Dred Scott* v. *Sandford,* 60 U.S. 393 (1857).

12. Daniel J. Elazar, *The American Partnership* (Chicago: University of Chicago Press, 1962).

13. *Pensacola Telegraph* v. *Western Union,* 96 U.S. 1 (1877).

14. *U.S.* v. *E. C. Knight,* 156 U.S. 1 (1895).

15. *Pollock* v. *Farmers Loan and Trust,* 157 U.S. 429 (1895); and *Springer* v. *U.S.,* 102 U.S. 586 (1881).

16. Jeff Shesol, *Supreme Power: Franklin Roosevelt vs. the Supreme Court* (New York: W.W. Norton, 2010).

17. *NLRB* v. *Jones and Laughlin Steel Co.,* 301 U.S. 1 (1937).

18. *U.S.* v. *Darby Lumber Co.,* 312 U.S. 100 (1941).

19. *Wickard* v. *Filburn,* 317 U.S. 111 (1942).

20. Morton Grodzins, "Centralization and Decentralization in the American Federal System," in Robert A. Goldwin, ed., *A Nation of States* (Chicago: Rand McNally, 1963), 3–4.

21. Alice M. Rivlin, *Reviving the American Dream* (Washington, DC: Brookings Institution, 1992), 98.

22. Richard P. Nathan, et al., *Reagan and the States* (Princeton, NJ: Princeton University Press, 1987), 4.

23. Gene Healy and Timothy Lynch, "Power Surge: The Constitutional Record of George W. Bush," (Washington, DC: Cato Institute, 2006): 20.

24. Linda Greenhouse, "The Rehnquist Court and Its Imperiled States' Rights Legacy," *New York Times* (June 12, 2005): A3.

25. *U.S.* v. *Lopez,* 514 U.S. 549 (1995).

26. *U.S.* v. *Morrison,* 529 U.S. 598 (2000).

27. Paul E. Peterson, *The Price of Federalism* (Washington, DC: Brookings Institution Press, 1995).

28. Jonathan Strong, "Congressional Research Service Memo Raises Fresh Constitutional Concerns about Obamacare." *Daily Caller* (May 2, 2010): www.dailycaller.com.

29. William J. Kovacs, quoted in John Schwartz, "Obama Seems to Be Open to a Broader Role for States." *New York Times* (January 30, 2009): A16.

Chapter 4

1. Paul Duggan, "Lawyer Who Wiped Out D.C. Ban Says It's About Liberties, Not Guns," *Washington Post* (March 18, 2007): A1.

2. *D.C.* v. *Heller,* 554 U.S. 290 (2008).

3. *McDonald* v. *City of Chicago,* 561 U.S. (2010).

4. The absence of a bill of rights led Mason to refuse to sign the proposed Constitution, noting that he "would sooner chop off his right hand than put it to the Constitution as it now stands." Quoted in Eric Black, *Our Constitution: The Myth That Binds Us* (Boulder, CO: Westview, 1988), 75.

5. Quoted in Jack N. Rakove, "Madison Won Passage of the Bill of Rights but Remained a Skeptic," *Public Affairs Report* (March 1991): 6.

6. *Barron* v. *Baltimore,* 32 U.S. 243 (1833).

7. *Allgeyer* v. *Louisiana,* 165 U.S. 578 (1897).

8. *Gitlow* v. *New York,* 268 U.S. 652 (1925).

9. *Near* v. *Minnesota,* 283 U.S. 697 (1931). For more about *Near,* see Fred W. Friendly, *Minnesota Rag: The Dramatic Story of the Landmark Case That Gave New Meaning to Freedom of the Press* (New York: Random House, 1981).

10. *Palko* v. *Connecticut,* 302 U.S. 319 (1937).

11. *Zobrest* v. *Catalina Foothills School District,* 506 U.S. 813 (1992).

12. *Engel* v. *Vitale,* 370 U.S. 421 (1962).

13. *Abington School District* v. *Schempp,* 374 U.S. 203 (1963).

14. *Lemon* v. *Kurtzman,* 403 U.S. 602 (1971).

15. *Widmar* v. *Vincent,* 454 U.S. 263 (1981).

16. *Rosenberger* v. *University of Virginia,* 515 U.S. 819 (1995).

17. *Mitchell* v. *Helms,* 530 U.S. 793 (2000).

18. *Zelman* v. *Simmons-Harris,* 536 U.S. 639 (2002).

19. *Lee* v. *Weisman,* 505 U.S. 577 (1992).

20. *McCreary County* v. *ACLU of Kentucky,* 545 U.S. 844 (2005).

21. *Salazar* v. *Buono* 559 U.S. ___ (2010).

22. *Employment Division, Dept. of Human Resources of Oregon* v. *Smith,* 494 U.S. 872 (1990).

23. *Boerne* v. *Flores,* 521 U.S. 507 (1997).

24. *Gonzales* v. *O Centro Espirita Beneficente União do Vegetal,* 546 U.S. 418 (2006).

25. David M. O'Brien, *Constitutional Law and Politics,* vol. 2: *Civil Rights and Civil Liberties* (New York: Norton, 1991), 345.

26. See Frederick Siebert, *The Rights and Privileges of the Press* (New York: Appleton-Century, 1934), 886, 931–40.

27. *Schenck* v. *U.S.,* 249 U.S. 47 (1919).

28. *Brandenburg* v. *Ohio,* 395 U.S. 444 (1969).

29. *New York Times Co.* v. *U.S.,* 403 U.S. 713 (1971).

30. *Nebraska Press Association* v. *Stuart,* 427 U.S. 539 (1976).

31. *Abrams* v. *U.S.,* 250 U.S. 616 (1919).

32. *Stromberg* v. *California,* 283 U.S. 359 (1931).

33. *Tinker* v. *Des Moines Independent Community School District,* 393 U.S. 503 (1969).

34. *Morse* v. *Frederick,* 551 U.S. 393 (2007).

35. *R.A.V.* v. *City of St. Paul,* 505 U.S. 377 (1992).

36. *Virginia* v. *Black,* 538 U.S. 343 (2003).

37. *Chaplinsky* v. *New Hampshire,* 315 U.S. 568 (1942).

38. *New York Times Co.* v. *Sullivan,* 376 U.S. 254 (1964).

39. *Chaplinsky* v. *New Hampshire,* 315 U.S. 568 (1942).

40. *Miller* v. *California,* 413 U.S. 15 (1973).

41. *Barnes* v. *Glen Theater,* 501 U.S. 560 (1991).

42. *Reno* v. *American Civil Liberties Union,* 521 U.S. 844 (1997); David G. Savage, "Ban on 'Virtual' Child Porn Is Upset by Court," *Los Angeles Times* (April 17, 2002): A1; and *Ashcroft* v. *American Civil Liberties Union,* 542 U.S. 656 (2004).

43. *U.S.* v. *Williams,* 553 U.S. 285 (2008).

44. *DeJonge* v. *Oregon,* 229 U.S. 353 (1937).

45. *Barron* v. *Baltimore,* 32 U.S. 243 (1833).

46. *Dred Scott* v. *Sandford,* 60 U.S. 393 (1857).

47. *U.S.* v. *Miller,* 307 U.S. 174 (1939).

48. *D.C.* v. *Heller,* 554 U.S. 290 (2008).

49. *Heller* v. *District of Columbia,* civil action 08-1289 (2010).

50. *McDonald* v. *City of Chicago,* 561 U.S. ___ (2010).

51. *U.S.* v. *Sokolov,* 490 U.S. 1 (1989).

52. *Georgia* v. *Randolph,* 547 U.S. 103 (2006).

53. *Hester* v. *U.S.*, 265 U.S. 57 (1924).

54. *Johnson* v. *U.S.*, 333 U.S. 10 (1948).

55. *Michigan* v. *Tyler*, 436 U.S. 499 (1978).

56. *Carroll* v. *U.S.*, 267 U.S. 132 (1925).

57. *U.S.* v. *Arvizu*, 534 U.S. 266 (2002).

58. *South Dakota* v. *Neville*, 459 U.S. 553 (1983).

59. *Skinner* v. *Railway Labor Executives' Association*, 489 U.S. 602 (1989).

60. *Vernonia School District* v. *Acton*, 515 U.S. 646 (1995).

61. *Board of Education of Independent School District No. 92 of Pottawatomie County* v. *Earls*, 536 U.S. 822 (2002).

62. *Counselman* v. *Hitchcock*, 142 U.S. 547 (1892).

63. *Brown* v. *Mississippi*, 297 U.S. 278 (1936).

64. *Miranda* v. *Arizona*, 384 U.S. 436 (1966).

65. *Rhode Island* v. *Innis*, 446 U.S. 291 (1980).

66. *Arizona* v. *Fulminante*, 499 U.S. 279 (1991).

67. *Weeks* v. *U.S.*, 232 U.S. 383 (1914).

68. *Mapp* v. *Ohio*, 367 U.S. 643 (1961).

69. *Stone* v. *Powell*, 428 U.S. 465 (1976).

70. *Powell* v. *Alabama*, 287 U.S. 45 (1932).

71. *Johnson* v. *Zerbst*, 304 U.S. 458 (1938).

72. *Gideon* v. *Wainwright*, 372 U.S. 335 (1963).

73. *Argersinger* v. *Hamlin*, 407 U.S. 25 (1972).

74. *Rothgery* v. *Gillespie County*, 554 U.S. 191 (2008).

75. *Rompilla* v. *Beard*, 545 U.S. 374 (2005).

76. *Hernandez* v. *Texas*, 347 U.S. 475 (1954).

77. *Batson* v. *Kentucky*, 476 U.S. 79 (1986).

78. *J.E.B.* v. *Alabama*, 511 U.S. 127 (1994).

79. *Maryland* v. *Craig*, 497 U.S. 836 (1990).

80. See Michael Meltsner, *Cruel and Unusual: The Supreme Court and Capital Punishment* (New York: Random House, 1973).

81. *Furman* v. *Georgia*, 408 U.S. 238 (1972).

82. *Gregg* v. *Georgia*, 428 U.S. 153 (1976).

83. *Baze* v. *Rees*, 553 U.S. 35 (2008).

84. *Atkins* v. *Virginia*, 536 U.S. 304 (2002); and *Roper* v. *Simmons*, 543 U.S. 551 (2005).

85. *House* v. *Bell*, 547 U.S. 518 (2006).

86. *District Attorney's Office for the Third Judicial District* v. *Osborne*, 557 U.S. ___ (2009).

87. *Olmstead* v. *U.S.*, 277 U.S. 438 (1928).

88. *Griswold* v. *Connecticut*, 381 U.S. 481 (1965).

89. *Eisenstadt* v. *Baird*, 410 U.S. 113 (1972).

90. *Roe* v. *Wade*, 410 U.S. 113 (1973).

91. *Webster* v. *Reproductive Health Services*, 492 U.S. 490 (1989).

92. *Planned Parenthood of Southeastern Pennsylvania* v. *Casey*, 502 U.S. 1056 (1992).

93. *Stenberg* v. *Carhart*, 530 U.S. 914 (2000).

94. Alison Young, "States Seek New Ways to Restrict New Abortions," *USA Today* (April 26, 2010): 1A.

95. *Bowers* v. *Hardwick*, 478 U.S. 186 (1986); and *Lawrence* v. *Texas*, 539 U.S. 558 (2003).

96. Jennifer Levin, "Alternative Reality About Public, War," *Associated Press* (May 29, 2007).

97. "Surveillance Under the USA Patriot Act," American Civil Liberties Union, April 3, 2003.

98. *Rasul* v. *Bush*, 542 U.S. 466 (2004).

99. *Boumediene* v. *Bush*, 553 U.S. 723 (2008).

100. *Hamdan* v. *Rumsfeld*, 548 U.S. 557 (2006).

101. Shane Scott, et al., "Secret U.S. Endorsement of Severe Interrogations," *New York Times* (October 7, 2007): A1.

102. Jennifer Loven and Devlin Barrett, "CIA Officials Won't Be Prosecuted for Waterboarding, Obama Admin Says," *Huffington Post* (April 16, 2009), www.huffingtonpost.com.

Chapter 5

1. Dan Eggen, "Civil Rights Focus Shift Roils Staff at Justice," *Washington Post* (December 13, 2005): A1; and Adam Zagorin, "Why Were These U.S. Attorneys Fired?" *Time* (March 7, 2007).

2. *Civil Rights Cases*, 109 U.S. 3 (1883).

3. *Plessy* v. *Ferguson*, 163 U.S. 537 (1896).

4. *Williams* v. *Mississippi*, 170 U.S. 213 (1898); and *Cummins* v. *Richmond County Board of Education*, 175 U.S. 528 (1899).

5. *Missouri* ex rel. *Gaines* v. *Canada*, 305 U.S. 337 (1938).

6. *Sweatt* v. *Painter*, 339 U.S. 629 (1950); and *McLaurin* v. *Oklahoma*, 339 U.S. 637 (1950).

7. *Brown* v. *Board of Education*, 347 U.S. 483 (1954).

8. But see Gerald Rosenberg, *The Hollow Hope: Can Courts Bring About Social Change?* (Chicago: University of Chicago Press, 1991).

9. Quoted in Williams, *Eyes on the Prize*, 10.

10. *Brown* v. *Board of Education II*, 349 U.S. 294 (1955).

11. Quoted in Williams, *Eyes on the Prize*, 37.

12. *Cooper* v. *Aaron*, 358 U.S. 1 (1958).

13. Jo Freeman, *The Politics of Women's Liberation* (New York: Longman, 1975), 57.

14. *Reed* v. *Reed*, 404 U.S. 71 (1971).

15. *Craig* v. *Boren*, 429 U.S. 190 (1976).

16. *Mississippi University for Women* v. *Hogan*, 458 U.S. 718 (1982).

17. *Craig* v. *Boren*, 429 U.S. 190 (1976).

18. *Orr* v. *Orr*, 440 U.S. 268 (1979).

19. *J.E.B.* v. *Alabama* ex rel. *TB*, 440 U.S. 268 (1979).

20. *U.S.* v. *Virginia*, 518 U.S. 515 (1996).

21. *Rostker* v. *Goldberg*, 453 U.S. 57 (1981).

22. *Michael M.* v. *Superior Court of Sonoma County*, 450 U.S. 464 (1981).

23. *Nguyen* v. *INS*, 533 U.S. 53 (2001).

24. *Rostker* v. *Goldberg*, 453 U.S. 57 (1981).

25. *U.S.* v. *Virginia*, 518 U.S. 515 (1996).

26. *Ledbetter* v. *Goodyear Tire and Rubber Co.*, 550 U.S. 618 (2007).

27. *Meritor Savings Bank* v. *Vinson*, 477 U.S. 57 (1986).

28. *Oncale* v. *Sundowner Offshore Services, Inc.*, 523 U.S. 75 (1998).

29. *Hishon* v. *King & Spalding*, 467 U.S. 69 (1984).

30. *Johnson* v. *Transportation Agency*, 480 U.S. 616 (1987).

31. Joyce Gelb and Marian Lief Palley, *Women and Public Policies* (Charlottesville: University of Virginia Press, 1996).

32. *Davis* v. *Monroe County Board of Education*, 526 U.S. 629 (1999).

33. *Jackson* v. *Birmingham Board of Education*, 544 U.S. 167 (2005).

34. *Hernandez* v. *Texas*, 347 U.S. 475 (1954).

35. *White* v. *Register*, 412 U.S. 755 (1973).

36. *San Antonio Independent School District* v. *Rodriguez*, 411 U.S. 1 (1973).

37. *Edgewood Independent School District* v. *Kirby*, 777 SW 2d 391 (1989).

38. "MALDEF Pleased with Settlement of California Public Schools Inequity Case, *Williams* v. *California*," August 13, 2004: www.maldef.com.

39. *LULAC* v. *Perry*, 548 U.S. 399 (2006).

40. Dee Brown, *Bury My Heart at Wounded Knee* (New York: Holt, Rinehart and Winston, 1971).

41. Roger Daniels, *Asian America: Chinese and Japanese in the United States Since 1850* (Seattle: University of Washington Press, 1988).

42. *Yick Wo* v. *Hopkins*, 118 U.S. 356 (1886).

43. *Ozawa* v. *U.S.*, 260 U.S. 178 (1922).

44. *Korematsu* v. *U.S.*, 323 U.S. 214 (1944).

45. Diane Helene Miller, *Freedom to Differ: The Shaping of the Gay and Lesbian Struggle for Civil Rights* (New York: New York University Press, 1998).

46. Sarah Brewer, et al., "Sex and the Supreme Court: Gays, Lesbians, and Justice," in Craig A. Rimmerman, et al., eds., *The Politics of Gay Rights* (Chicago: University of Chicago Press, 2000).

47. Evan Gerstmann, *The Constitutional Underclass: Gays, Lesbians, and the Failure of Class-Based Equal Protection* (Chicago: University of Chicago Press, 1999).

48. *Romer* v. *Evans*, 517 U.S. 620 (1996).

49. *Lawrence* v. *Texas*, 539 U.S. 558 (2003).

50. Joan Biskupic, "Court's Opinion on Gay Rights Reflects Trends," *USA Today* (July 18, 2003): 2A.

51. David Pfeiffer, "Overview of the Disability Movement: History, Legislative Record and Political Implications," *Policy Studies Journal* (Winter 1993): 724–42; and "Understanding Disability Policy," *Policy Studies Journal* (Spring 1996): 157–74.

52. Joan Biskupic, "Supreme Court Limits Meaning of Disability," *Washington Post* (June 23, 1999): A1.

53. *Sutton* v. *United Air Lines, Inc.*, 527 U.S. 471 (1999).

54. *Tennessee* v. *Lane*, 541 U.S. 509 (2004).

55. American Association of People with Disabilities, www.aapd-dc.org.

56. *Regents of the University of California* v. *Bakke*, 438 U.S. 265 (1978).

57. *United Steelworkers of America* v. *Weber*, 443 U.S. 193 (1979).

58. *Johnson* v. *Santa Clara County*, 480 U.S. 616 (1987).

59. Ruth Marcus, "Hill Coalition Aims to Counter Court in Job Bias," *Washington Post* (February 8, 1990): A10.

60. *Grutter* v. *Bollinger*, 539 U.S. 306 (2003).

61. *Gratz* v. *Bollinger*, 539 U.S. 306 (2003).

Chapter 6

1. "House Passes Historic Healthcare Overhaul," *Los Angeles Times* (May 22, 2010): www.latimes.com; and "Our View on Balancing the Budget: One Lonely Plan in Congress Highlights Tough Choices," *USA Today* (September 6, 2010): www.usatoday.com.

2. Brandice Canes-Wrone, David W. Brady, and John Cogan, "Out of Step, Out of and Office; Electoral Accountability and House Members' Voting," American Political Science Review, (2002) 96(1): 127–40.

3. Richard F. Fenno Jr., "U.S. House Members in Their Constituencies: An Exploration," *American Political Science Review* 71 (September 1977): 883–917.

4. Richard F. Fenno Jr., *Home Style: House Members in Their Districts* (New York: Longman, 2009), 32; and Judy Schneider and Michael L. Koempel, *Congressional Deskbook 2005–2007: 109th Congress* (Alexandria, VA: Capital Net, 2005).

5. Hedrick Smith, *The Power Game* (New York: Ballantine Books, 1989), 108.

6. Jennifer E. Manning, "Membership of the 111th Congress: A Profile," *Congressional Research Service Report for Congress* (July 19, 2009): www.openers.com.

7. "Congress Has Wealth to Weather Economic Downturn," (March 13, 2008): www.opensecrets.org.

8. Gary W. Cox and Jonathan N. Katz, "Why Did the Incumbency Advantage in U.S. House Elections Grow?" *American Journal of Political Science* 40 (May 1996): 478–97; Kenneth N. Bickers and Robert M. Stein, "The Electoral Dynamics of the Federal Pork Barrel," *American Journal of Political Science* 40 (November 1996): 1300–26; "2010 Overview: Incumbent Advantage," www.opensecrets.org; and Scott Ashworth and Ethan Bueno de Mesquita, "Electoral Selection, Strategic Challenger Entry, and the Incumbency Advantage." *Journal of Politics* 70 (October 2008): 1006–1025.

9. Marjorie Randon Hershey, "Congressional Elections," in Gerald M. Pomper, et al., *The Election of 1992: Reports and Interpretations* (Chatham, NJ: Chatham House, 1993), 159.

10. Quinn Bowman and Chris Amico, "Congress Loses Hundreds of Years of Experience," *PBS News Hour* (November 5, 2010): www.pbs.org/newshour.

11. "How to Rig an Election," *Economist* (April 25, 2002).

12. In *Davis* v. *Bandemer*, 478 U.S. 109 (1986), the Court found that gerrymandering was not a political question but was unable to determine a standard by which to judge constitutionality.

13. *Wesberry* v. *Sanders*, 376 U.S. 1 (1964).

14. *Reynolds* v. *Sims*, 377 U.S. 533 (1964).

15. *Thornburg* v. *Gingles*, 478 U.S. 30 (1986).

16. *Shaw* v. *Reno*, 509 U.S. 630 (1993).

17. *LULAC* v. *Perry*, 548 U.S. 399 (2006).

18. "What Is the Democratic Caucus?" www.dcaucusweb.house.gov.

19. David R. Mayhew, "Supermajority Rule in the U.S. Senate," *PS: Political Science and Politics* 36 (January 2003): 31–36.

20. Barbara Sinclair, "The Struggle over Representation and Law-making in Congress: Leadership Reforms in the 1990s," in James A. Thurber and Roger H. Davidson, eds., *Remaking Congress: Change and Stability in the 1990s* (Washington, DC: CQ Press, 1995), 105.

21. Woodrow Wilson, *Congressional Government: A Study in American Politics* (Cambridge, MA: Riverside Press, 1885).

22. Roger H. Davidson, "Congressional Committees in the New Reform Era: From Combat to the Contract," in Thurber and Davidson, *Remaking Congress*, 28.

23. Christopher Deering and Steven S. Smith, *Committees in Congress*, 3rd ed. (Washington, DC: CQ Press, 1997).

24. Wilson, *Congressional Government*.

25. Kenneth A. Shepsle, *The Giant Jigsaw Puzzle: Democratic Committee Assignments in the Modern House* (Chicago: University of Chicago Press, 1978).

26. *Wall Street Journal* (April 13, 1973): 10.

27. "The Mysteries of the Congressional Review Act." *Harvard Law Review* 122 (June 2009): 2163–2183.

28. Quoted in Stewart M. Powell, "Lee Fight Signals Tougher Battles Ahead on Nomination," *Commercial Appeal* (December 21, 1997): A15.

29. Warren E. Miller and Donald Stokes, "Constituency Influence in Congress," *American Political Science Review* 57 (March 1963): 45–57.

30. Barbara S. Romzck and Jennifer A. Utter, "Congressional Legislative Staff: Political Professionals or Clerks?" *American Journal of Political Science* 41 (October 1997): 1251–79; and Michael T. Heaney, "Brokering Health Policy: Coalitions, Parties, and Interest Group Influence," *Journal of Health Politics, Policy, and Law* 31 (October 2006): 887–944.

31. Russell A. Miller, "Lords of Democracy: The Judicialization of 'Pure Politics' in the United States and Germany," *Washington and Lee Law Review* 61 (2004): 587.

Chapter 7

1. "Two Hundred Years of Presidential Funerals," *Washington Post* (June 10, 2004): C14.

2. Gail Russell Chaddock, "The Rise of Mourning in America," *Christian Science Monitor* (June 11, 2004): 1.

3. Richard E. Neustadt, *Presidential Power and the Modern Presidency* (New York: Free Press, 1991).

4. Winston Solberg, *The Federal Convention and the Formation of the Union of the American States* (Indianapolis, IN: Bobbs-Merrill, 1958), 235.

5. Benjamin I. Page and Mark P. Petracca, *The American Presidency* (New York: McGraw-Hill, 1983), 262.

6. Jim Lobe, "Bush 'Unsigns' War Crimes Treaty," AlterNet, (May 6, 2002) www.alternet.org. See also Lincoln P. Bloomfield Jr., "The U.S. Government and the International Criminal Court," Remarks to the Parliamentarians for Global Action, Consultative Assembly of Parliamentarians for the International Criminal Court and the Rule of Laws, address delivered at the United Nations, New York, September 12, 2003.

7. *Public Papers of the Presidents* (1963), 889.

8. Quoted in Neustadt, *Presidential Power*, 9.

9. Quoted in Page and Petracca, *The American Presidency*, 57.

10. Samuel Kernell, *Going Public: New Strategies of Presidential Leadership*, 4th ed. (Washington, DC: CQ Press, 2006), 3.

11. Jeffrey Cohen, "Presidential Rhetoric and the Public Agenda," *American Journal of Political Science* 39 (February 1995): 87–107.

12. Neustadt, *Presidential Power*, 1–10.

13. George Reedy, *The Twilight of the Presidency* (New York: New American Library 1971), 38–39.

14. Kernell, *Going Public*.

15. See Louis Fisher, *Constitutional Conflicts Between Congress and the President*, 7th ed. (Lawrence: University Press of Kansas, 2007).

16. Franklin D. Roosevelt, Press Conference, July 23, 1937.

17. See Cary Covington, et al., "A 'Presidency-Augmented' Model of Presidential Success on House Roll Call Votes," *American Journal of Political Science* 39 (November 1995): 1001–24; and Wayne P. Steger, "Presidential Policy Initiation and the Politics of Agenda Control," *Congress & the Presidency*, 24 (Spring 1997): 102–14.

18. Quoted in Thomas E. Cronin, *The State of the Presidency*, 2nd ed. (Boston: Little, Brown, 1980), 169.

19. *Youngstown Sheet and Tube v. Sawyer*, 343 U.S. 579 (1952).

20. Charlie Savage, "Are Signing Statements Constitutional?" *Boston Globe* (April 30, 2006).

21. Josh Gerstein, "Obama: Ignore Signing Statements," *Politico* (March 9, 2009).

22. Charlie Savage, "Obama Takes New Route to Opposing Parts of Laws," *New York Times* (January 9, 2010): A1.

Chapter 8

1. Gallup Poll, July 10–12, 2009.

2. Harold D. Lasswell, *Politics: Who Gets What, When and How* (New York: McGraw-Hill, 1938).

3. David Osborne and Ted Gaebler, *Reinventing Government* (Reading, MA: Addison-Wesley, 1992), 20–21.

4. Office of Personnel Management, *The Fact Book*, www.opm.gov/feddata/factbook/2007/factbook2007.pdf.

5. Barbara Slavin, "State Department Having Staffing Trouble," *USA Today* (December 2005): 10A.

6. Cam Simpson and Christopher Conkey, "U.S. News: Obama Aims to Use Fewer Contractors," *Wall Street Journal* (February 28, 2009): www.wsj.com.

7. "A Century of Government Growth," *Washington Post* (January 3, 2000): A17. On the difficulty of counting the exact number of government agencies, see David Nachmias and David H. Rosenbloom, *Bureaucratic Government: U.S.A.* (New York: St. Martin's Press, 1980).

8. The classic work on regulatory commissions is Marver Bernstein, *Regulating Business by Independent Commission* (Princeton, NJ: Princeton University Press, 1955).

9. H. H. Gerth and C. Wright Mills, *From Max Weber* (New York: Oxford University Press, 1958).

10. Michael Lipsky, *Street-Level Bureaucracy: Dilemmas of the Individual in Public Services* (New York: Russell Sage Foundation, 1980).

11. Cornelius M. Kerwin, *Rulemaking: How Government Agencies Write Law and Make Policy*, 2nd ed. (Washington, DC: CQ Press, 1999), xv.

12. George A. Krause, "Presidential Use of Executive Orders, 1953–1994," *American Politics Quarterly* 25 (October 1997): 458–81.

13. Irene Murphy, *Public Policy on the Status of Women* (Lexington, MA: Lexington Books, 1974).

14. Rosemary O'Leary, *Environmental Change: Federal Courts and the EPA* (Philadelphia: Temple University Press, 1993).

15. Wendy Hansen, et al., "Specialized Courts, Bureaucratic Agencies, and the Politics of U.S. Trade Policy," *American Journal of Political Science* 39 (August 1995): 529–57.

Chapter 9

1. Adam Liptak, "Court Under Roberts is Most Conservative in Decades," *New York Times* (July 25, 2010): A1.

2. Julius Goebel Jr., *History of the Supreme Court of the United States, vol. 1: Antecedents and Beginnings to 1801* (New York: Macmillan, 1971), 206.

3. *Marbury v. Madison*, 5 U.S. 137 (1803); and *Martin v. Hunter's Lessee*, 14 U.S. 304 (1816).

4. *Fletcher v. Peck*, 10 U.S. 87 (1810); *Martin v. Hunter's Lessee*, 14 U.S. 304 (1816); and *Cohens v. Virginia*, 19 U.S. 264 (1821).

5. *McCulloch v. Maryland*, 17 U.S. 316 (1819).

6. *Marbury v. Madison*, 5 U.S. 137 (1803).

7. *Marbury v. Madison*, 5 U.S. 137 (1803).

8. This discussion draws heavily on Jack C. Plano and Milton Greenberg, *The American Political Dictionary*, 10th ed. (Fort Worth, TX: Harcourt Brace, 1996), 247.

9. David W. Neubauer, *Judicial Process: Law, Courts, and Politics* (Pacific Grove, CA: Brooks/Cole, 1991), 57.

10. Cases involving citizens from different states can be filed in state or federal court.

11. Sheldon Goldman and Elliot E. Slotnick, "Clinton's First Term Judiciary: Many Bridges to Cross," *Judicature* (May/June 1997): 254–55.

12. Quoted in Lawrence Baum, *The Supreme Court*, 3rd ed. (Washington, DC: CQ Press, 1989), 108.

13. See Barbara A. Perry, *A Representative Supreme Court? The Impact of Race, Religion, and Gender on Appointments* (New York: Greenwood, 1991). Clarence Thomas was raised a Catholic but attended an Episcopalian church at the time of his appointment, having been

barred from Catholic sacraments because of his remarriage. He again, however, is attending Roman Catholic services.

14. John Brigham, *The Cult of the Court* (Philadelphia: Temple University Press, 1987).

15. Stephen L. Wasby, *The Supreme Court in the Federal Judicial System*, 4th ed. (Chicago: Nelson-Hall, 1988), 194.

16. Wasby, *The Supreme Court in the Federal Judicial System*, 199. Much of this change occurred as the result of an increase in state criminal cases, of which nearly 100 percent concerned constitutional questions.

17. Paul Wahlbeck, et al., "Ghostwriters on the Court?: A Stylistic Analysis of U.S. Supreme Court Opinion Drafts," *American Politics Research*, 30 (March 2002): 166–92. Wahlbeck, et al. note that "between 1969 and 1972—the period during which the justices each became entitled to a third law clerk . . . the number of opinions increased by about 50 percent and the number of words tripled."

18. Richard A. Posner, *The Federal Courts: Crisis and Reform* (Cambridge, MA: Harvard University Press, 1985), 114.

19. Todd C. Peppers, *Courtiers of the Marble Palace: The Rise and Influence of the Supreme Court Law Clerk* (Palo Alto, CA: Stanford University Press, 2006).

20. Edward Lazarus, *Closed Chambers: The First Eyewitness Account of the Epic Struggles Inside the Supreme Court* (New York: Times Books, 1998).

21. "Retired Chief Justice Warren Attacks Freund Study Group's Composition and Proposal," *American Bar Association Journal* 59 (July 1973): 728.

22. Kathleen Werdegar, "The Solicitor General and Administrative Due Process," *George Washington Law Review* (1967–1968): 482.

23. Rebecca Mae Salokar, *The Solicitor General: The Politics of Law* (Philadelphia: Temple University Press, 1992), 3.

24. See, for example, Lawrence Baum, *The Supreme Court*, 4th ed. (Washington, DC: CQ Press, 1992), 106.

25. Richard C. Cortner, *The Supreme Court and Civil Liberties* (Palo Alto, CA: Mayfield, 1975), vi.

26. Gregory A. Caldeira and John R. Wright, "*Amicus Curiae* Before the Supreme Court: Who Participates, When and How Much?" *Journal of Politics* 52 (August 1990): 803.

27. Donald L. Horowitz, *The Courts and Social Policy* (Washington, DC: Brookings Institution, 1977), 538.

28. *Webster* v. *Reproductive Health Services*, 492 U.S. 490 (1989).

29. See, for example, Tracey E. George and Lee Epstein, "On the Nature of Supreme Court Decision Making," *American Political Science Review*, 86 (1992): 323–37; Melinda Gann Hall and Paul Brace, "Justices' Responses to Case Facts: An Interactive Model," *American Politics Quarterly* (April 1996): 237–61; Lawrence Baum, *The Puzzle of Judicial Behavior* (Ann Arbor: University of Michigan Press, 1997); Gregory N. Flemming, et al., "An Integrated Model of Privacy Decision Making in State Supreme Courts," *American Politics Quarterly* 26 (January 1998): 35–58; Richard L. Pacelle Jr., et al., "Keepers of the Covenant or Platonic Guardians?: Decision Making on the U.S. Supreme Court," *American Politics Research* (September 2007): 694–725; and David E. Klein and Gregory Mitchell, *The Psychology of Judicial Decision Making* (New York: Cambridge University Press, 2010).

30. Jeffrey A. Segal and Harold J. Spaeth, *The Supreme Court and the Attitudinal Model Revisited* (New York: Cambridge University Press, 2002).

31. See C. Neal Tate and Roger Handberg, "Time Binding and Theory Building in Personal Attribute Models of Supreme Court Voting Behavior, 1916–1988," *American Political Science Review*, 35 (1991): 460–80; and Donald R. Songer and Sue Davis, "The Impact of Party and Region on Voting Decisions in the U.S. Courts of Appeals, 1955–86," *Western Political Quarterly* 43 (1990): 830–44.

32. H.W. Perry, *Deciding to Decide: Agenda Setting in the United States Supreme Court* (Cambridge, MA: Harvard University Press, 1991); and Gregory A. Caldeira, et al., "Strategic Voting and Gatekeeping in the Supreme Court," *Journal of Law, Economics, and Organization* 15 (1999): 549–72.

33. Forrest Maltzman and Paul J. Walhbeck, "May It Please the Chief?: Opinion Assignments in the Rehnquist Court," *American Journal of Political Science* 40 (1996): 421–43.

34. James F. Spriggs, et al., "Bargaining on the U.S. Supreme Court: Justices' Responses to Majority Opinion Drafts," *Journal of Politics* 61 (1999): 485–506.

35. Kevin T. McGuire and James A. Stimson, "The Least Dangerous Branch Revisited: New Evidence on Supreme Court Responsiveness to Public Preferences," *Journal of Politics* 66 (2004): 1018–35.

36. Charles M. Cameron, et al., "Strategic Auditing in a Political Hierarchy: An Informational Model of the Supreme Court's *Certiorari* Decisions," *American Political Science Review*, 94 (2000): 101–16.

37. Pablo T. Spiller and Rafael Gely, "Congressional Control or Judicial Independence: The Determinants of U.S. Supreme Court Labor-Relations Decisions, 1949–1988," *RAND Journal of Economics* 23 (1992): 463–92.

38. Timothy R. Johnson and Andrew D. Martin, "The Public's Conditional Response to Supreme Court Decisions," *American Political Science Review*, 92 (June 1998): 299–309.

39. *Korematsu* v. *U.S.*, 323 U.S. 214 (1944).

40. *Youngstown Sheet & Tube Co.* v. *Sawyer*, 343 U.S. 579 (1952). The Supreme Court ruled that President Truman's seizure and operation of U.S. steel mills in the face of a strike threat were unconstitutional, because the Constitution implied no such broad executive power. See Alan Westin, *Anatomy of a Constitutional Law Case* (New York: Macmillan, 1958); and Maeva Marcus, *Truman and the Steel Seizure Case* (New York: Columbia University Press, 1977).

41. *U.S.* v. *Nixon*, 418 U.S. 683 (1974).

42. Gallup Poll, August 31–September 2, 2009.

43. Alixandra B. Yanus, "Neither Force nor Will: A Theory of Judicial Power," doctoral dissertation, University of North Carolina, 2010.

44. *Boumediene* v. *Bush*, 553 U.S. 723 (2008).

45. "Supreme Court Cases Overruled by Subsequent Decision," www .gpoaccess.gov/constitution/pdf/con041.pdf.

46. Kevin T. McGuire, "Public Schools, Religious Establishments, and the U.S. Supreme Court: An Examination of Policy Compliance," *American Politics Research*, 37 (2009): 50–74.

47. *Reynolds* v. *Sims*, 377 U.S. 533 (1964).

48. *Mississippi University for Women* v. *Hogan*, 458 U.S. 718 (1982).

Chapter 10

1. Alan M. Winkler, "Public Opinion," in Jack Greene, ed., *The Encyclopedia of American Political History* (New York: Charles Scribner's Sons, 1988).

2. *Literary Digest* 125 (November 14, 1936): 1.

3. Robert S. Erikson, et al., *American Public Opinion: Its Origin, Contents, and Impact* (New York: Wiley, 1980), 28.

4. Francis J. Connolly and Charley Manning, "What 'Push Polling' Is and What It Isn't," *Boston Globe* (August 16, 2001): A21.

5. Richard Dawson and Kenneth Prewitt, *Political Socialization*, 2nd ed. (Boston: Little, Brown, 1977), 33.

6. Margaret Trevor, "Political Socialization, Party Identification, and the Gender Gap," *Public Opinion Quarterly* 63 (Spring 1999): 62–89.

7. Edward S. Greenberg, "The Political Socialization of Black Children," in Edward S. Greenberg, ed., *Political Socialization* (New York: Atherton, 1970), 131.

8. Joseph Carroll, "Iraq Support Split Along Racial Lines" in Alec M. Gallup and Frank Newport, eds. *The Gallup Poll* (Lanham, MO: Rowman and Likefield, 2006), 369.

9. Elaine S. Povich, "Courting Hispanics: Group's Votes Could Shift House Control," *Newsday* (April 21, 2002): A4.

10. Susan A. MacManus, *Young v. Old: Generational Combat in the 21st Century* (Boulder, CO: Westview, 1995).

11. Robert D. Hess and Judith V. Tomey, *The Development of Political Attitudes in Children* (Piscataway, NJ: Transaction Publishers, 2006), 43–44.

12. James Simon and Bruce D. Merrill, "Political Socialization in the Classroom Revisited: The Kids Voting Program," *Social Science Journal* 35 (1998): 29–42.

13. Harris Interactive, Inc., "Internet Users Now Spending an Average of 13 Hours a Week Online," (December 23, 2009): www .harrisinteractive.com.

14. Pew Project for Excellence in Journalism, 2008.

15. Barbara Kellerman, "Bottom's Up: Why Followers Matter," *Washington Post* blog (February 6, 2009): views-washingtonpost.com.

16. National Geographic-Roper Public Affairs Poll, December 17, 2005–January 20, 2006, www.nationalgeographic.com.

17. See Mitchell Stephens, *A History of News: From the Drum to the Satellite* (New York: Viking, 1989).

18. See Shelley Ross, *Fall from Grace* (New York: Ballantine, 1988), chapter 12.

19. Richard L. Rubin, *Press, Party, and Presidency* (New York: Norton, 1981), 38–39.

20. Stephen Bates, *If No News, Send Rumors* (New York: St. Martin's, 1989), 185.

21. See Doris A. Graber, *Mass Media and American Politics*, 3rd ed. (Washington, DC: CQ Press, 1989), 12; and Thomas C. Leonard, *The Power of the Press: The Birth of American Political Reporting* (New York: Oxford University Press, 1986), chapter 7.

22. Annenberg National Election Study, 2004, www. annenbergpublicpolicycenter.org.

23. Robert J. Klotz, The *Politics of Internet Communication* (Lanham, MD: Rowman and Littlefield, 2004).

24. Cass R. Sunstein, *Republic.com 2.0* (Princeton, NJ: Princeton University Press, 2007); and Anthony G. Wilhelm, *Digital Nation* (Cambridge, MA: MIT Press, 2004).

25. Pew Research Center for the People and the Press, "Maturing Internet News Audience—Broader Than Deep: Online Papers Modestly Boost Newspaper Readership," July 30, 2006, www .pewresearch.org.

26. Sunstein, *Republic.com 2.0*.

27. Donald L. Jorand and Benjamin I. Page, "Shaping Foreign Policy Opinions: The Role of TV News," *Journal of Conflict Resolution* 36 (June 1992): 227–41.

28. *New York Times Co.* v. *U.S.*, 403 U.S. 713 (1971).

29. Project for Excellence in Journalism, "Capitol Hill Reporters Update," www.journalism.org.

30. John R. Hibbing and Elizabeth Theiss-Morse, *Congress as Public Enemy: Political Attitudes Toward American Political Institutions* (New York: Cambridge University Press, 1995).

31. Karen Aho, "Broadcasters Want Access, But Will They Deliver Serious Coverage?" *Columbia Journalism Review* 5 (September/ October 2003), www.cjr.org.

32. Tony Mauro, "A Gun Case in Need of Some Explaining: But Because of Our Reclusive Court, Today's Argument Is All We'll Get," *USA Today* (March 2, 2010): www.usatoday.com.

33. Benjamin I. Page, et al., "What Moves Public Opinion?" *American Political Science Review* 81 (March 1987): 23–44.

34. Shanto Iyengar and Donald R. Kinder, *News That Matters*, reprint ed. (Chicago: University of Chicago Press, 1989).

35. American Society of Newspaper Editors, *The Changing Face of the Newsroom* (Washington, DC: ASNE, 1989), 33; William Schneider and I. A. Lewis, "Views on the News," *Public Opinion* 8 (August/ September 1985): 6–11, 58–59; and S. Robert Lichter, et al., *The Media Elite* (Bethesda, MD: Adler and Adler, 1986).

36. Eric Alterman, *What Liberal Media? The Truth About Bias and the News* (New York: Basic Books, 2003).

37. Pew Research Center for the People and the Press, "Press Accuracy Rating Hits Two Decade Long," www.people-press.org.

38. Pew Research Center for the People and the Press, "News Media's Improved Image Proves Short-Lived," August 4, 2002, www.pewresearch.org.

39. Project for Excellence in Journalism, "State of the News Media 2010," www.stateofthemedia.org.

40. Pew Research Center for the People and the Press, "Strong Support for Watching Role, Despite Public Criticism of News Media," www.pewresearch.org.

Chapter 11

1. Graham Wilson, *Interest Groups in the United States* (New York: Oxford University Press, 1981), 4.

2. V. O. Key, *Politics, Parties, and Pressure Groups* (New York, Crowell, 1942), 23.

3. John H. Aldrich, *Why Parties? The Origin and Transformation of Party Politics in America* (Chicago: University of Chicago Press, 1995).

4. By contrast, Great Britain did not develop truly national, broad-based parties until the 1870s.

5. See *Historical Statistics of the United States: Colonial Times to 1970*, part 2, series Y-27-28 (Washington, DC: Government Printing Office, 1975), based on unpublished data prepared by Walter Dean Burnham. See also Harold W. Stanley and Richard G. Niemi, *Vital Statistics on American Politics 2009–2009* (Washington, DC: CQ Press, 2009), for contemporary turnout figures.

6. On the subject of party realignment, see Walter Dean Burnham, *Critical Elections and the Mainsprings of American Politics* (New York: Norton, 1970); Kristi Andersen, *The Creation of a Democratic Majority* (Chicago: University of Chicago Press, 1979); and John R. Petrocik, "Realignment: New Party Coalitions and the Nationalization of the South," *Journal of Politics* 49 (May 1987): 347–75.

7. See, for example, V. O. Key Jr., "A Theory of Critical Elections," *Journal of Politics* 17 (February 1955): 3–18.

8. For a discussion of secular realignment in the South, see Jeffrey M. Stonecash, "Class and Party: Secular Realignment and the Survival of Democrats Outside the South," *Political Research Quarterly* 53:4 (2000): 731–52.

9. Morris P. Fiorina, "Parties and Partisanship: A 40-Year Retrospective," *Political Behavior* 24 (2002): 93–115.

10. Bruce E. Keith, et al., *The Myth of the Independent Voter* (Berkeley: University of California Press, 1992).

11. E. E. Schattschneider, *Party Government* (New York: Farrar and Rinehart, 1942).

12. John Green and Paul S. Herrnson, eds., *Responsible Partisanship: The Evolution of American Political Parties Since the 1950s* (Lawrence: University Press of Kansas, 2003).

13. See David E. Price, *Bringing Back the Parties* (Washington, DC: CQ Press, 1984), 284–8.

14. Congressional Quarterly Vote Studies, www.innovation.cq.com.

15. Earl Black and Merle Black, *The Rise of Southern Republicans* (Cambridge, MA: Harvard University Press, 2002).

16. William H. Flanigan and Nancy H. Zingale, *Political Behavior of the American Electorate*, 12th ed. (Washington, DC: CQ Press, 2010).

17. Flanigan and Zingale, *Political Behavior of the American Electorate*.

18. The Pew Forum on Religion and Public Life, "U.S. Religious Landscape Survey," (February 2008).

19. Flanigan and Zingale, *Political Behavior of the American Electorate*.

20. Robert D. Putnam, "Bowling Alone: America's Declining Social Capital," *Journal of Democracy* 6 (1995): 650–65; and Putnam, *Bowling Alone: The Collapse and Revival of American Community* (New York: Simon and Schuster, 2000).

21. Everett Carll Ladd, quoted in Richard Morin, "Who Says We're Not Joiners," *Washington Post* (May 2, 1999): B5.

22. John Brehm and Wendy Rahn, "Individual-Level Evidence for the Causes and Consequences of Social Capital," *American Journal of Political Science* 41 (July 1997): 999.

23. Mark Schneider, et al., "Institutional Arrangements and the Creation of Social Capital: The Effects of Public School Choice," *American Political Science Review* 91 (March 1997): 82–93.

24. Nicholas Lemann, "Kicking in Groups," *Atlantic Monthly* (April 1996), NEXIS.

25. David B. Truman, *The Governmental Process: Political Interests and Public Opinion* (New York: Knopf, 1951), ch. 16.

26. Mancur Olson, *The Logic of Collective Action* (Cambridge, MA: Harvard University Press, 1965).

27. E. E. Schattschneider, *The Semisovereign People* (New York: Holt Rinehart, and Winston, 1960), 35.

28. David Lowery and Virginia Gray, "The Population Ecology of Gucci Gulch or the Natural Regulation of Interest Group Numbers in the American States," *American Journal of Political Science* 39 (February 1995): 1–29.

29. Walker, *Mobilizing Interest Groups in America*.

30. Olson, *The Logic of Collective Action*.

31. Lee Epstein, *Conservatives in Court* (Knoxville: University of Tennessee Press, 1985).

32. Jack L. Walker, "The Origins and Maintenance of Interest Groups in America," *American Political Science Review* 77 (June 1983): 390–406.

33. Peter Steinfels, "Moral Majority to Dissolve: Says Mission Accomplished," *New York Times* (June 12, 1989): A14.

34. Some political scientists speak of "iron rectangles," reflecting the growing importance of a fourth party, the courts, in the lobbying process.

35. Clement E. Vose, "Litigation as a Form of Pressure Group Activity," *Annals* 319 (September 1958): 20–31.

36. Paul M. Collins Jr., *Friends of the Supreme Court* (New York: Oxford University Press, 2008).

37. Robert A. Goldberg, *Grassroots Resistance: Social Movements in Twentieth Century America* (Belmont, CA: Wadsworth, 1991).

38. Richard Simons, "Bush Signs Bill to Tighten Lobbying Rules," *Los Angeles Times* (September 15, 2007): A13.

Chapter 12

1. See "Candidates and Nominations," in Paul S. Herrnson, *Congressional Elections: Campaigning at Home and in Washington*, 4th ed. (Washington, DC: CQ Press, 2004), 35–68.

2. Dennis W. Johnson, *No Place for Amateurs: How Political Consultants Are Reshaping American Democracy* (New York: Routledge, 2001).

3. See www.opensecrets.org.

4. *McConnell* v. *FEC*, 540 U.S. 93 (2003).

5. *FEC* v. *Wisconsin Right to Life, Inc.*, 551 U.S. 449 (2007).

6. *Davis* v. *FEC*, 554 U.S. 729 (2008).

7. *Citizens United* v. *FEC*, 558 U.S. 50 (2010).

8. Herrnson, *Congressional Elections*, 133.

9. Center for Responsive Politics, www.opensecrets.org/pres08/sourceall.php?cycle=2008.

10. Center for Responsive Politics, www.opensecrets.org/bigpicture/wherefrom.php?cycle=2008.

11. See www.opensecrets.org.

12. Amy Keller, "Helping Each Other Out: Members Dip into Campaign Funds for Fellow Candidates," *Roll Call* (June 15, 1998): 1.

13. For member contribution activity at the state level, see Jay K. Dow, "Campaign Contributions and Intercandidate Transfers in the California Assembly," *Social Science Quarterly* 75 (1994): 867–80. For member contribution activity at the congressional level, see Bruce A. Larson, "Ambition and Money in the U.S. House of Representatives: Analyzing Campaign Contributions from Incumbents' Leadership PACs and Reelection Committees" (Ph.D. dissertation, University of Virginia, 1998). For a briefer account, see Paul S. Herrnson, "Money and Motives: Spending in House Elections," in Lawrence C. Dodd and Bruce I. Oppenheimer, eds., *Congress Reconsidered*, 6th ed. (Washington, DC: CQ Press, 1997).

14. Larson, "Ambition and Money in the U.S. House of Representatives."

15. *Buckley* v. *Valeo*, 424 U.S. 1 (1976).

16. Campaign Finance Institute, "501(c) Groups Emerge as Big Players Alongside 527s." www.cfinst.org. Information also drawn from www.opensecrets.org/527s/types.php.

17. Campaign Finance Institute, "501(c) Groups Emerge." Information also drawn from www.opensecrets.org/527s/types.php.

18. Girish Gulati, et al., "News Coverage of Political Campaigns," in Lynda Kaid, ed., *The Handbook of Political Communication Research* (New York: Lawrence Erlbaum, 2004).

19. Five liberal Democratic U.S. senators, including George McGovern of South Dakota, were defeated in this way in 1980, for example.

20. Elaine Ciulla Kamarck and Kenneth M. Goldstein, "The Rules Matter: Post-Reform Presidential Nominating Politics," in L. Sandy Maisel, ed., *The Parties Respond: Changes in American Parties and Campaigns* (Boulder, CO: Westview, 1994), 174.

21. George Serra, "What's in It for Me?: The Impact of Congressional Casework on Incumbent Evaluation," *American Politics Quarterly* 22 (1994): 403–20.

22. Glenn R. Parker and Suzanne L. Parker, "Correlates and Effects of Attention to District by U.S. House Members," *Legislative Studies Quarterly* 10 (May 1985): 223–42.

23. Jamie L. Carson, "Strategy, Selection, and Candidate Competition in U.S. House and Senate Elections," *Journal of Politics* 67 (2005): 1–28.

24. Gary W. Cox and Jonathan N. Katz, "Why Did the Incumbency Advantage in U.S. House Elections Grow?" *American Journal of Political Science* 40 (May 1996): 478–97.

25. Sunhil Ahuja, et al., "Modern Congressional Election Theory Meets the 1992 House Elections," *Political Research Quarterly* 47 (1994): 909–21; and Paul S. Herrnson, *Congressional Elections*.

26. Gary C. Jacobson and Michael A. Dimock, "Checking Out: The Effects of Bank Overdrafts on the 1992 House Elections," *American Journal of Political Science* 38 (1994): 601–24; and Herrnson, *Congressional Elections*.

27. CNN, 2008 election results, www.cnn.com/ELECTION/2008/.

28. Warren E. Miller and J. Merrill Shanks, *The New American Voter* (Cambridge, MA: Harvard University Press, 1996), 270.

29. CNN, 2008 election results, www.cnn.com/ELECTION/2008/.

30. CNN, 2008 election results, www.cnn.com/ELECTION/2008/.

31. John C. Green, *The Faith Factor: How Religion Influences American Elections* (Westport, CT: Praeger, 2007).

32. Michael S. Lewis-Beck and Mary Stegmaier, "Economic Determinants of Electoral Outcomes," *Annual Review of Political Science* 3 (2000): 183–219.

33. Thomas M. Guterbock and Bruce London, "Race, Political Orientation, and Participation: An Empirical Test of Four Competing Theories," *American Sociological Review* 48 (1983): 439–53.

34. Karlo Bakkios Marcelo, et al., "Young Voter Registration and Turnout Trends," www.civicyouth.org. Estimates of young voter registration vary widely, in large part because they are often based on polling numbers, and these numbers are subject to overreporting as well as difficulties in reaching and surveying this demographic group.

35. See, for example, Laura Stoker and M. Kent Jennings, "Life-Cycle Transitions and Political Participation: The Case of Marriage," *American Political Science Review* 89 (1995): 421–36; and Paul R. Abramson, et al., *Change and Continuity in the 1996 Elections* (Washington, DC: CQ Press, 1998).

36. Sidney Verba, et al., *Voice and Equality: Civic Voluntarism in American Politics* (New York: Belknap, 1996). Data on relationship between religious service attendance and voting were calculated by the authors with data obtained from the Pew Research Center's study *Political Landscape More Favorable to Democrats: Trends in Political Values and Core Attitudes, 1987–2007*, March 22, 2007.

37. International Institute for Democracy and Electoral Assistance, "Global Database," www.idea.int/vt/survey/voter_turnout_pop2.cfm.

38. Ian Urbina, "States Move to Allow Overseas and Military Voters to Cast Ballots by Internet," *New York Times* (May 7, 2010).

39. "Voters Win with Election Day Registration," A Demos Policy Brief, Winter 2008, www.demos.org. For a summary of voter registration laws and requirements for all states, see www.usgovinfo .about.com/blvrbystate.htm.

Chapter 13

1. This discussion draws on James E. Anderson, *Public Policymaking: An Introduction*, 2nd ed. (Boston: Houghton Mifflin, 1994), 5.

2. Roger W. Cobb and Charles D. Elder, *Participation in American Politics: The Dynamics of Agenda-Building*, 2nd ed. (Baltimore, MD: Johns Hopkins University Press, 1983), 85.

3. Charles O. Jones, *An Introduction to the Study of Public Policy*, 3rd ed. (Monterey, CA: Brooks/Cole, 1984), 87–89.

4. This discussion draws on Anne Schneider and Helen Ingram, "Behavioral Assumptions of Policy Tools," *Journal of Politics* 52 (May 1990): 510–29.

5. Government Accountability Office, "Amtrak Management: Systematic Problems Require Actions to Improve Efficiency, Effectiveness, and Accountability," GAO-06-145, April 2005, www.gao.gov.

6. "Fiscal Year 2006: Mid-Session Review Budget of the U.S. Government," July 13, 2005, www.whitehouse.gov/omb/budget/ fy2006/pdf/06msr.pdf.

7. Ronald Edsforth, *The New Deal: America's Response to the Great Depression* (Boston: Blackwell, 2000), 137.

8. Colin Campbell and William Pierce, *The Earned Income Tax Credit* (Washington, DC: American Enterprise Institute, 1980).

9. Center on Budget and Policy Priorities, *The Earned Income Tax Credit: Boosting Employment, Aiding the Working Poor*, www.cbpp.org.

10. Congressional Budget Office, "Revenues, Outlays, Deficits, Surpluses, and Debt Held by the Public, 1968 to 2007," cbo.gov/ budget/data/historical.xls.

11. This discussion on budgeting draws on James E. Anderson, *Public Policymaking: An Introduction*, 2nd ed. (Boston: Houghton Mifflin, 1994), ch. 5.

12. Budget of the United States Government, 2011 Fiscal Year, www .gpoaccess.gov/usbudget/fy11/pdf/hist.pdf.

13. About 38 percent of the nation's commercial banks are members of the Federal Reserve System. See www.richmondfed.org.

14. Erik Eckholm, "As Jobs Vanish and Prices Rise, Food Stamp Use Nears Record." *New York Times* (March 31, 2008): A1.

15. Edmund L. Andrews, "Economists See Limited Boost from Stimulus," *New York Times* (August 6, 2009): www.nytimes.com.

Chapter 14

1. Alfred E. Eckes Jr., *Opening America's Market: U.S. Foreign Trade Policy Since 1776* (Chapel Hill: University of North Carolina Press, 1995).

2. John L. O'Sullivan, writing in 1845, quoted in Julius W. Pratt, "The Ideology of American Expansion," in Avery Craven, ed., *Essays in Honor of William E. Dodd* (Chicago: University of Chicago Press, 1935), 343–4.

3. Charles P. Kindleberger, *The World in Depression, 1929–1939* (Berkeley: University of California Press, 1986).

4. Mr. X., "The Sources of Soviet Conduct," *Foreign Affairs* (July 1947): 566–82. Mr. X. was later revealed to be U.S. ambassador and diplomat George Kennan.

5. Harry S Truman, Speech to Congress, April 12, 1947.

6. Richard M. Nixon, Inaugural Address, January 20, 1969, Public Papers of the Presidents of the United States (Washington, DC: Government Printing Office).

7. Michael Froman, *The Development of the Idea of Détente* (New York: St. Martin's, 1982).

8. James M. Lindsay, "Congress, Foreign Policy, and the New Institutionalism," *International Studies Quarterly* 38 (June 1994): 281–304.

9. *Congress A to Z*, 4th ed. (Washington, DC: CQ Press, 2003).

10. Glenn Hastedt, *Encyclopedia of American Foreign Policy* (New York: Facts on File Library of American History, 2004).

Gender. *See also* Women
 discrimination based on, 141, 147–151
 and Fourteenth Amendment violations,
  149–150
 and juror selection, 120–121
 and party identification, 323t, 324
 as political socialization agent, 286,
  286t
 and vote choice, 324, 362f, 363–364
Gender gap, 324, 363–364
General Accounting Office. *See*
 Government Accountability Office
 (GAO)
General Agreement on Tariffs and Trade
 (GATT), 411, 422
General election campaigns, 343
General elections, 343. *See also specific
 elections*
General Motors (GM), 329
General Social Survey, 283
General welfare, 13
Geneva Convention, 128
George III, king of England, 29, 30, 308
Germany, 55, 409, 423
Gerrymandering, 173, 173f. *See also*
 Redistricting
Get out the vote (GOTV), 320–321, 333,
 346, 370
Gibbons v. *Ogden* (1824), 88, 452
Gibbs, Robert, 301f, 302
G.I. Bill, 227
Gideon, Clarence Earl, 120
Gideon v. *Wainwright* (1963), 68, 109t,
 120, 452
Gingrich, Newt, 96, 96f
Ginsburg, Ruth Bader
 on abortion, 127
 background of, 150
 and full faith and credit clause, 86
 profile of, 259t
 on sex discrimination, 151
Gitlow, Benjamin, 108
Gitlow v. *New York* (1455), 452
Gitlow v. *New York* (1925), 66, 108, 109t,
 112, 452
Glassner, Barry, 19
Globalization, 240
Goddard, Terry, 156
Godspeed (ship), 2
Going public, 215
Golden Age, 312–313
Gold Rush, 13, 137
Gompers, Samuel, 329
Gonzales, Alberto, 130, 134
Gonzales v. *Carhart* (2007), 72, 126–127,
 244–245, 452
Gore, Al, 218f
 election of 1992, 353
 election of 2000, 60, 359, 365f
Government Accountability Office
 (GAO), 193, 381–382
Governmental agendas, 378
Government corporations, 233

Government, overview of, 82–83, 82f. *See
 also* National government; State
 governments
Grandfather clauses, 140
Granholm v. *Heald* (2005), 76, 452
Grant, Ulysses S., 72, 76
Grants, block, 96
Grants-in-aid, categorical, 95
Grassroots activities, 331, 346
Gratz v. *Bollinger* (2003), 162, 452
Gravel v. *U.S.* (1972), 55, 452
Gray, Horace, 265
Great Britain
 in Afghanistan war, 427
 bicameral legislative model, 169
 constitution of, 44
 English Bill of Rights (1689), 68–69
 events leading to Revolutionary War
  with, 28–29
 and French and Indian War, 27
 judicial review in, 249
 monarchs in, 6, 26, 29, 30, 308
 origins of party whips, 176
 religious persecution in, 6
 and Roosevelt Corollary, 409
 taxation of colonies by, 27
 unitary system in, 32, 82–83
 unitary system of, 84
 and War of 1812, 407
 and World War II, 411
Great Compromise, 35–36, 168
Great Depression, 92, 314, 410. *See also*
 New Deal
Great Society, 95, 227
Green Party, 316
Gregg v. *Georgia* (1976), 121, 452
Griswold, Estelle, 124f
Griswold v. *Connecticut* (1965), 66, 69, 72,
 123, 127, 452
Grutter v. *Bollinger* (2003), 162, 452
Guantanamo detainees, 128–130, 271
Gulf oil spill (2010), 98, 239f
Gun control
 and drug trafficking, 424
 interest groups opposing, 330
 and judicial nominations, 262
 legislation addressing, 116
 Supreme Court on, 97, 104–105,
  115–116
Gun rights. *See* Second Amendment
Guns and butter theory, 430

Habeas corpus. See Writ of *habeas corpus*
Haiti, 408, 414
Hamdan v. *Rumsfeld* (2006), 61, 452
Hamilton, Alexander
 on Bill of Rights, 107
 on Electoral College, 36
 and *Federalist Papers,* 43, 59, 69, 204
 on judiciary, 62, 246, 247, 250
 and national bank, 69–70
 and ratification of Constitution, 44
 on role of national government, 33

Hannity, Sean, 293
Hard money, 347
Hard power, 430
Harding, Warren G., 184
Harlan, John Marshall, 113, 140
Harper v. *Board of Elections* (1966), 77, 452
Harris Interactive, 281–282
Harrison, Benjamin, 60, 358
Harrison, William H., 78, 202
Hastings, Alcee, 54
Hatch, Orrin, 41
Hatch Act (1939), 233
Hate speech, 113–114
Hawaii, 13, 94, 410
Hayes, Rutherford B., 358
Health care reform. *See* Patient
 Protection and Affordable Care Act
 (2010)
Health insurance companies, 386
Health policy
 background of, 382–383
 Medicaid, 384
 medical research, 387
 Medicare, 16, 287, 382, 383–384
 national health insurance, 94, 383,
  385–386
 per capita health care costs, 397–398
 public expenditures for, 383
 public health, 386–387
 timeline of, 382–383
Hearst, William Randolph, 291
Heller, Dick, 104–105
Help America Vote Act (2002), 369
Henry, Patrick, 27
Heritage Foundation, 421
Hernandez v. *Texas* (1954), 152, 452
Hispanic Americans. *See also specific
 groups*
 civil rights issues for, 152–153
 in Congress, 171f, 172
 and Democratic Party, 324
 discrimination against, 152–153
 and immigration, 152
 as judges/justices, 259
 in jury pools, 120
 political ideology of, 286
 population trends of, 14, 14f
 and Supreme Court, 152–153
 voting trends of, 363, 365
Hobbes, Thomas, 7–9
Hold, defined, 183
Holland. *See* Netherlands
Home Building and Loan Assn. v. *Blaisdell*
 (1934), 59, 452
Home Rule Charters, 186
Homeland security. *See* Department of
 Homeland Security
Homosexuals. *See* Gays and lesbians
Honest Leadership and Open
 Government Act (2007), 335
Hong Kong, 395
Hoover, Herbert, 92
House v. *Bell* (2006), 123, 452

Chapter 1

1.1 C   1.2 A   1.3 C   1.4 C   1.5 D   1.6 D   1.7 B

Chapter 2

2.1 C   2.2 D   2.3 A   2.4 E   2.5 B   2.6 D

Chapter 3

3.1 D   2.2 C   3.3 C   3.4 A   3.5 E   3.6 C

Chapter 4

4.1 D   4.2 C   4.3 A   4.4 C   4.5 D   4.6 C   4.7 A

Chapter 5

5.1 B   5.2 D   5.3 D   5.4 C   5.5 A   5.6 C

Chapter 6

6.1 A   6.2 E   6.3 A   6.4 C   6.5 B   6.6 D

Chapter 7

7.1 C   7.2 D   7.3 B   7.4 D   7.5 C   7.6 D

Chapter 8

8.1 A   8.2 B   8.3 B   8.4 D

Chapter 9

9.1 C   9.2 D   9.3 B   9.4 E   9.5 B   9.6 D   9.7 A

Chapter 10

10.1 C   10.2 A   10.3 B   10.4 E   10.5 C   10.6 A   10.7 D

Chapter 11

11.1 D   11.2 E   11.3 A   11.4 A   11.5 A   11.6 C   11.7 C

Chapter 12

12.1 E   12.2 C   12.3 A   12.4 B   12.5 E   12.6 B   12.7 B

Chapter 13

13.1 E   13.2 B   13.3 C   13.4 B   13.5 B   13.6 E

Chapter 14

14.1 C   14.2 A   14.3 B   14.4 D   14.5 D

TIMELINE: Selected Events in American Government and Politics

1952 **National Election Studies (NES)**—Researchers at the University of Michigan begin conducting surveys every four years to measure political attitudes and behaviors of the American electorate.

1971 **FECA Legitimizes PACs**—The Federal Election Campaign Act establishes a formal role for political action committees in the electoral process and creates rules for financial disclosure.

1939 *Grapes of Wrath* **Published**—John Steinbeck's novel draws attention to the plight of migrant farm workers.

1965 *Griswold v. Connecticut*—The Supreme Court explains the right to privacy and uses it to strike down a Connecticut statute prohibiting married couples' access to birth control.

1973 **Repeal of Termination Act**—Marks the establishment of a policy to encourage self-governance by Indian nations.

1941 **U.S. Enters World War II**—U.S. involvement in World War II begins after the Japanese bomb ships at Pearl Harbor on December 7.

1964 **Civil Rights Act**—The Civil Rights Act outlaws discrimination in public places; it is one of the earliest of President Lyndon B. Johnson's Great Society initiatives, which also included Medicare, Medicaid, and the Voting Rights Act of 1965.

1972 **Watergate Break In**—A break-in at the Watergate Hotel launches an investigation into President Richard M. Nixon that results in his eventual resignation from office.

1932 **The New Deal**—President Franklin D. Roosevelt (FDR) ushers in a new era marked by a growing federal bureaucracy and an active role for the president in the legislative process.

1980 **Cable News Network**—Founded by media mogul Ted Turner, CNN makes national and international events available instantaneously around the globe.

2010 **Health Care Reform**—President Barack Obama and the Democratic Congress enact legislation creating a national health insurance program.

1994 **Devolution Revolution**—Republicans, led by then House Minority Whip Newt Gingrich, introduce a "Contract with America," in which they pledge to scale back the federal government.

1993 **Motor Voter Law**—The law is intended to facilitate easier voter registration; it requires citizens to be able to register in all public buildings.

2002 **Creation of the Department of Homeland Security**—Following the September 11, 2001 terrorist attacks, the nation identifies a need for greater coordination of domestic security activities.

2007 **First Woman Speaker of the House**—Representative Nancy Pelosi is sworn in as the first woman Speaker of the House.

1992 **Tracking Polls Introduced**—These daily moving-average polls allow candidates to monitor short-term trends in public opinion.

2003 **_Lawrence_ v. _Texas_**—In overruling _Bowers_ v. _Hardwick_ (1986), the Supreme Court, for the first time, concludes that the right to privacy applies to homosexuals.

2008 **Record Voter Turnout**—Voter turnout in the 2008 presidential election—in which Barack Obama is elected president—reaches its highest level in more than 40 years.